UNLOCKING THE
NEW
TESTAMENT

A SIDE-BY-SIDE COMMENTARY

RICHARD J. ALLEN

Covenant Communications, Inc.

Cover image: *Behold the Man* © Simon Dewey Courtesy of Altus Fine Art. For print information, visit www.altusfineart.com.
Cover and book design © 2010 by Covenant Communications, Inc.

Published by Covenant Communications, Inc.
American Fork, Utah

Printed in Canada
First Printing: October 2010

16 15 14 13 12 11 10   10 9 8 7 6 5 4 3 2 1
ISBN-13 978-1-60861-119-5

INTRODUCTION

The record of the Savior's mortal ministry of mercy and Atonement is sacred evidence of the scope and power of His infinite love and redemption. This priceless chronicle reinforces and strengthens our personal commitment to truly honor our covenants.

The greatest story ever told did not emerge without roots or context. It was the fulfillment of a divine plan originating in the premortal realm before the foundations of the world. "Here am I, send me" (Abr. 3:27) were the words that inaugurated the mission of salvation for all mankind.

From the moment that God the Father approved and activated this holy commission for His First Begotten, "full of grace and truth" (John 1:14), to bring about the eternal plan of happiness, the pathway toward the ultimate triumph of light over darkness, good over evil, life over death, was established with irreversible momentum and infinite power. The Beloved Son of God was to become the "author of eternal salvation unto all them that obey Him" (Heb. 5:9). He was to ensure the perpetuity of life beyond death. He was to be "the life and the light of the world" (Alma 38:9; D&C 10:70; 11:28). That is the message of the New Testament.

With the voice of prophecy, Isaiah declared, "For unto us a child is born, unto us a son is given" (Isa. 9:6). This child, born of Mary in the stable, was Jehovah of the Old Testament, signifying "the Unchangeable One," "the Eternal I Am." He was the Son of God—the only Begotten Son of God in the flesh. This little child born beneath the light of a new star was the Messiah or (in the Greek formulation) the Christ, meaning, the "Anointed"—the one divinely commissioned, authorized, and foreordained to complete the mission of the Atonement.

This little child, who "grew, and waxed strong in spirit, filled with wisdom," having the "grace of God . . . upon him" (Luke 2:40), was the Great Creator, the Word of God, the Giver of Life, the Light of the World. This young child grew into manhood and immersed Himself in the ministry of salvation. He was Emmanuel (or Immanuel), "God among us," with a mortal mission of divine sanctification as the Messenger of the Covenant who condescended to come among us as the Good Shepherd, fearing neither betrayal nor death. This Son of God, "full of grace and truth" (2 Ne. 2:6; D&C 66:12; 93:11; Moses 1:6, 32; 5:7; 6:52; 7:11) was Jesus, "God is help," even the Redeemer, the one chosen to bring about the infinite sacrifice and Atonement on behalf of mankind—the Lamb of God, the Bread of Life.

Passing through the Crucifixion and Resurrection, according to the will of the Father, He became the Life of the World, even the great King, Judge, Mediator, Advocate, and Bridegroom—the same who is to come again in glory to inaugurate the millennial reign and serve as our Law Giver, the Prince of Peace, and the Covenant Father of all who will believe on Him and overcome in faith and righteousness.

The New Testament tells this story of salvation and hope through the mouths of personal witnesses who labored with Jesus in the ministry, suffered with Him as He wrought the infinite Atonement, gloried with Him in the Resurrection, obeyed His commandment to take the message of the gospel unto all the world (Matt. 28:19–20), and in many cases sealed their testimony with their lives.

The New Testament means, in effect, the "new covenant," or the covenant between God and His children that binds them to Him with sacred promises to be fulfilled on the basis of everlasting principles and powers inherent in His design to "bring to pass the immortality and eternal life of man" (Moses 1:39). This covenant or testament was ordained of God and foretold by His prophets:

"Behold, the days come, saith the Lord, that I will make a new covenant with the house of Israel, and with the house of Judah:

"Not according to the covenant that I made with their fathers in the day that I took them by the hand to bring them out of the land of Egypt; which my covenant they brake, although I was an husband unto them, saith the Lord:

"But this shall be the covenant that I will make with the house of Israel; After those days, saith the Lord, I will put my law in their inward parts, and write it in their hearts; and will be their God, and they shall be my people" (Jer. 31:31–33).

Can we write the message of the New Testament in our hearts and become the "children of the prophets" and the "children of the covenant" (3 Ne. 20:25–26)? Can we follow in the footsteps of the Savior and become, as He commanded, "even as I am" (3 Ne. 27:27)? The answer given by the New Testament and confirmed by the resurrected Savior to the ancient American Saints is a resounding "Yes"—if we will but honor our covenants and mold our daily lives in the spirit of meekness and righteousness after the patterns set by our Lord and Master.

This work attempts to present the patterns, principles, and precepts of salvation that are formulated in the New Testament as the record given of Christ's ministry of hope and life, confirmed by all the holy scriptures. We are told that "the government shall be upon his shoulder: and his name shall be called Wonderful, Counsellor, The mighty God, The everlasting Father, The Prince of Peace" (Isa. 9:6). We are assured "that there shall be no other name given nor any other way nor means whereby salvation can come unto the children of men, only in and through the name of Christ, the Lord Omnipotent" (Mosiah 3:17). In that spirit, the author hopes that this volume will help the reader to understand and apply the scriptures prayerfully and invite the Spirit to confirm these truths and sustain every noble effort to come unto Christ and follow in His footsteps.

You are encouraged to "liken the scriptures" unto yourselves, as Nephi counseled, "that ye may have hope" (1 Ne. 19:23, 24).

Appreciation is expressed for the undeviating support of the staff members of Covenant Communications and their devoted interest in this project. Special thanks go to my wife, Carol Lynn Allen, for her support and encouragement.

HOW TO USE THIS BOOK

The left column on each page contains the actual text of the New Testament without chapter headings or footnotes. The page numbers are structured with a slash so that the number after the slash corresponds to the exact page number in the New Testament, making this book ideal for classroom use.

The right column on each page contains commentary that corresponds with the New Testament text to its left.

Boxes that provide background information on people found in the New Testament are taken from *New Testament Who's Who* (American Fork, UT: Covenant Communications, 2010), also written by Richard Allen.

CITATIONS USED IN THIS BOOK

Asay, Carlos E., *Family Pecan Trees: Planting a Legacy of Faith at Home* (Salt Lake City: Deseret Book Company, 1992).

Benson, Ezra Taft, *Come unto Christ* (Salt Lake City: Deseret Book Company, 1983).

_____, *God, Family, Country: Our Three Great Loyalties* (Salt Lake City: Deseret Book Company, 1974).

_____, *The Teachings of Ezra Taft Benson* (Salt Lake City: Bookcraft, Inc., 1988).

Berrett, William E. and Alma P. Burton, *Readings in LDS Church History* (Salt Lake City: Deseret Book Company, 1967).

Brewster, Hoyt W., Jr., *Behold, I Come Quickly: The Last Days and Beyond* (Salt Lake City: Deseret Book Company, 1994).

Brown, Hugh B., *Continuing the Quest* (Salt Lake City: Deseret Book Company, 1961).

Clarke, Adam, *Clarke's Commentary: Matthew to Revelation* (1810–1826).

Condie, Spencer J., *In Perfect Balance* (Salt Lake City: Bookcraft, Inc., 1993).

Coogan, Michael D., ed., *The New Oxford Annotated Bible* (New York: Oxford University Press, Inc., 2001).

Cook, Gene R., *Receiving Answers to Our Prayers* (Salt Lake City: Deseret Book Company, 1996).

Draper, Richard D., *The Lord of the Gospels: The 1990 Sperry Symposium on the New Testament*, Bruce A. Van Orden and Brent L. Top, eds. (Salt Lake City: Deseret Book Company, 1990).

Featherstone, Vaughn J., *The Incomparable Christ: Our Master and Model* (Salt Lake City: Deseret Book Company, 1995).

Freeman, James M., *Manners and Customs of the Bible* (New Kensington, PA: Whitaker House Publishers, 1996).

Grant, Heber J., *Gospel Standards,* comp. G. Homer Durham, (Salt Lake City: Deseret Book Company, 1981).

Harris, Victor W., Susan Easton Black, and Mark Ogletree, eds., *We Believe in Christ* (Orem, UT: Granite Publishing and Distributing, 2001).

Hendriksen, William, *Survey of the Bible: A Treasury of Bible*

Information (Grand Rapids, MI: BakerBooks, 1995).

Hinckley, Gordon B., *Be Thou an Example* (Salt Lake City: Deseret Book Company, 1981).

_____, *Faith: The Essence of True Religion* (Salt Lake City: Deseret Book Company, 1989).

_____, *Standing for Something: 10 Neglected Virtues that Will Heal Our Hearts and Homes* (New York: Random House, Inc., 2001).

_____, *Teachings of Gordon B. Hinckley* (Salt Lake City: Deseret Book Company, 1997).

History of the Church.

Hunter, Howard W., *That We Might Have Joy* (Salt Lake City: Deseret Book Company, 1994).

_____, *The Teachings of Howard W. Hunter*, Clyde J. Williams, ed. (Salt Lake City: Deseret Book Company, 1997).

Jackson, Kent P. and Robert L. Millet, *Studies in Scripture, Volume 5: The Gospels* (Salt Lake City: Deseret Book Company, 1986).

José Luis González-Balado, comp., *Mother Theresa: In My Own Words* (New York: Random House, 1997).

Josephus, Flavius, *The Complete Works of Flavius Josephus.*

Journal of Discourses.

Kapp, Ardeth Greene, *I Walk By Faith* (Salt Lake City: Deseret Book Company, 1987).

Kimball, Spencer W., *Faith Precedes the Miracle* (Salt Lake City: Deseret Book Company, 1972).

_____, *President Kimball Speaks Out* (Salt Lake City: Deseret Book Company, 1981).

_____, *The Miracle of Forgiveness* (Salt Lake City: Bookcraft, Inc., 1969).

_____, *The Teachings of Spencer W. Kimball*, Edward L. Kimball, ed. Salt Lake City: Bookcraft, Inc., 1982).

Lee, Harold B., *Decisions for Successful Living* (Salt Lake City: Deseret Book Company, 1973).

_____, *The Teachings of Harold B. Lee*, Clyde J. Williams, ed. (Salt Lake City: Bookcraft, Inc., 1996).

Lewis, C.S., *Mere Christianity* (San Francisco, CA: HarperSanFrancisco, 1952).

Ludlow, Daniel H., *A Companion to Your Study of the Book of Mormon* (Salt Lake City: Deseret Book Company, 1976).

_____, *A Companion to Your Study of the New Testament: The Four Gospels,* 2 vols. (Salt Lake City: Deseret Book Company, 1978).

_____, ed., *The Encyclopedia of Mormonism* (New York: Macmillan Publishing Company, 1992).

Lund, Gerald N., *Jesus Christ, Key to the Plan of Salvation* (Salt Lake City: Deseret Book Company, 1991).

_____, *New Testament Symposium* (Salt Lake City: Deseret Book Company).

_____, *Selected Writings of Gerald N. Lund: Gospel Scholar Series* (Salt Lake City: Deseret Book Company, 1999).

Mackie, George M., *Bible Manners and Customs* (Uhrichsville, OH: Barbour Publishing, Inc., 1994).

Madsen, Truman G., *Joseph Smith the Prophet* (Salt Lake City: Bookcraft, Inc., 1993).

Matthews, Robert J., *Behold the Messiah* (Salt Lake City: Bookcraft, Inc., 1994).

Maxwell, Neal A., *All These Things Shall Give Thee Experience* (Salt Lake City: Deseret Book Company, 1979).

_____, *If Thou Endure It Well* (Salt Lake City: Bookcraft, Inc., 1996).

_____, *Men and Women of Christ* (Salt Lake City: Bookcraft, Inc., 1991).

_____, *Notwithstanding My Weakness* (Salt Lake City: Deseret Book Company, 1981).

_____, *One More Strain of Praise* (Salt Lake City: Deseret Book Company, 1999).

McConkie, Bruce R., *Doctrinal New Testament Commentary,* 3 vols. (Salt Lake City: Bookcraft, Inc., 1973).

_____, *Doctrines of the Restoration: Sermons and Writings of Bruce R. McConkie.*

_____, *Mormon Doctrine* (Salt Lake City: Bookcraft, Inc., 1966).

_____, *The Millennial Messiah* (Salt Lake City: Deseret Book Company, 1982).

_____, *The Mortal Messiah,* 4 vols. (Salt Lake City: Deseret Book Company, 1979–1981).

_____, *The Promised Messiah* (Salt Lake City: Deseret Book Company, 1978).

McConkie, Joseph Fielding and Donald W. Parry, *A Guide to Scriptural Symbols* (Salt Lake City: Bookcraft, Inc., 1990).

McConkie, Oscar W., Jr., *Angels* (Salt Lake City: Deseret Book Company, 1975).

Millet, Robert L., *Alive in Christ: The Miracle of Spiritual Rebirth* (Salt Lake City: Deseret Book Company, 1997).

_____, *An Eye Single to the Glory of God: Reflections on the Cost of Discipleship* (Salt Lake City: Deseret Book

Company, 1991).

Nelson, Russell M., *Perfection Pending and Other Favorite Discourses* (Salt Lake City: Deseret Book Company, 1998).

_____, *The Power Within Us* (Salt Lake City: Deseret Book Company, 1988).

Newell, Lloyd D., *The Divine Connection: Understanding Your Inherent Worth* (Salt Lake City: Deseret Book Company, 1992).

Newquist, Jerreld L., ed., *Gospel Truth: Discourses and Writings of President George Q. Cannon* (Salt Lake City: Deseret Book Company, 1987).

Packer, Boyd K., *Teach Ye Diligently* (Salt Lake City: Deseret Book Company, 1975).

Parry, Donald W., Jay A. Parry, and Tina M. Peterson, *Understanding Isaiah* (Salt Lake City: Deseret Book Company, 1998).

Petersen, Mark E., *Abraham: Friend of God* (Salt Lake City: Deseret Book Company, 1979).

Porter, Bruce D., *The King of Kings* (Salt Lake City: Deseret Book Company, 2000).

Pratt, Parley P., *Autobiography of Parley Parker Pratt* (Salt Lake City: Deseret Book Company, 1938).

_____, *Key to the Science of Theology* (Salt Lake City: Deseret Book Company, 1855).

Rihbani, Abraham Mitrie, *The Syrian Christ* (Boston: Houghton Mifflin, 1916).

Roberts, B. H., *Seventy's Course in Theology*, 5 vols. (Salt Lake City: Deseret Book Company, 1912).

Robinson, Stephen E., *Are Mormons Christians?* (Salt Lake City: Bookcraft, Inc., 1991).

_____, *Believing Christ: The Parable of the Bicycle and Other Good News* (Salt Lake City: Deseret Book Company, 1992).

Romney, Marion G., *Learning for the Eternities*, comp. George J. Romney, (Salt Lake City: Deseret Book Company, 1977).

Sill, Sterling W., *The Law of the Harvest* (Salt Lake City: Bookcraft, Inc., 1963).

Smith, George Albert, *Sharing the Gospel with Others* (Salt Lake City: Deseret Book Company, 1948).

_____, *The Teachings of George Albert Smith*, Robert and Susan McIntosh, eds. (Salt Lake City: Bookcraft, Inc., 1996).

Smith, Hyrum M. and Janne M. Sjodahl, *Doctrine and Covenants Commentary* (Salt Lake City: Deseret Book Company, 1923).

Smith, Joseph Fielding, *Answers to Gospel Questions*, comp. Joseph Fielding Smith, Jr., 5 vols. (Salt Lake City: Deseret Book Company).

_____, *Church History and Modern Revelation*, 4 vols. (Salt Lake City: Deseret Book Company, 1947–1950).

_____, *Doctrines of Salvation*, comp. Bruce R. McConkie, 3 vols. (Salt Lake City: Bookcraft, Inc., 1954–1956).

Smith, Joseph, *Discourses of the Prophet Joseph Smith*.

_____, *Lectures on Faith*.

_____, *Teachings of the Prophet Joseph Smith*, sel. Joseph Fielding Smith (Salt Lake City: Deseret Book Company, 1976).

Snow, Lorenzo, *The Teachings of Lorenzo Snow*, comp. Clyde J. Williams (Salt Lake City: Bookcraft, Inc., 1984).

Talmage, James E., *Jesus the Christ* (Salt Lake City: Deseret Book Company, 1983).

_____, *The Parables of James E. Talmage*, comp. Albert L. Zobell, Jr. (Salt Lake City: Deseret Book Company, 1973).

_____, *The Vitality of Mormonism* (Salt Lake City: Deseret Book Company, 1919).

Taylor, John, *The Gospel Kingdom: Selections from the Writings and Discourses of John Taylor*, G. Homer Durham, ed. (Salt Lake City: Deseret Book Company, 1943).

The Redeemer: Reflections on the Life and Teachings of Jesus Christ.

Vos, Howard F., *Nelson's New Illustrated Bible Manners and Customs: How the People of the Bible Really Lived* (Nashville, TN: Thomas Nelson Publishers, 1999).

Wells, Robert E., *The Mount and the Master* (Salt Lake City: Deseret Book Company, 1991).

Whitney, Orson F., *Life of Heber C. Kimball* (Salt Lake City: Stevens and Wallis, 1945).

Widtsoe, John A., *Evidences and Reconciliations* (Salt Lake City: Deseret Book Company, 1943).

_____, *Gospel Doctrine: Selections from the Sermons and Writings of Joseph F. Smith* (Salt Lake City: Deseret Book Company, 1919).

_____, *Man and the Dragon and Other Essays* (Salt Lake City: Bookcraft, Inc., 1947).

Wight, Fred H., *Manners and Customs of Bible Lands* (Chicago: Moody Bible Institute, 1953).

Woodruff, Wilford, *The Discourses of Wilford Woodruff*, G. Homer Durham, ed. (Salt Lake City: Bookcraft, Inc., 1946).

Young, Brigham, *Discourses of Brigham Young*, John Widtsoe, ed. (Salt Lake City: Shadow Mountain, 1954).

THE GOSPEL ACCORDING TO
ST. MATTHEW

1. The book of the generation of Jesus Christ, the son of David, the son of Abraham.

2. Abraham begat Isaac; and Isaac begat Jacob; and Jacob begat Judas and his brethren;

3. And Judas begat Phares and Zara of Thamar; and Phares begat Esrom; and Esrom begat Aram;

4. And Aram begat Aminadab; and Aminadab begat Naasson; and Naasson begat Salmon;

5. And Salmon begat Booz of Rachab; and Booz begat Obed of Ruth; and Obed begat Jesse;

6. And Jesse begat David the king; and David the king begat Solomon of her that had been the wife of Urias;

7. And Solomon begat Roboam; and Roboam begat Abia; and Abia begat Asa;

8. And Asa begat Josaphat; and Josaphat begat Joram; and Joram begat Ozias;

9. And Ozias begat Joatham; and Joatham begat Achaz; and Achaz begat Ezekias;

10. And Ezekias begat Manasses; and Manasses begat Amon; and Amon begat Josias;

11. And Josias begat Jechonias and his brethren, about the time they were carried away to Babylon:

12. And after they were brought to Babylon, Jechonias begat Salathiel; and Salathiel begat Zorobabel;

13. And Zorobabel begat Abiud; and Abiud begat Eliakim; and Eliakim begat Azor;

14. And Azor begat Sadoc; and Sadoc begat Achim; and Achim begat Eliud;

15. And Eliud begat Eleazar; and Eleazar begat Matthan; and Matthan begat Jacob;

16. And Jacob begat Joseph the husband of Mary, of whom was born Jesus, who is called Christ.

17. So all the generations from Abraham to David are fourteen generations; and from David until the carrying away into Babylon are fourteen generations; and from the carrying away into Babylon unto Christ are fourteen generations.

18. ¶ Now the birth of Jesus Christ was on this wise: When as his mother Mary was espoused to

Matt. 1:1–17—Matthew was addressing his Gospel to a people who needed to understand that Jesus of Nazareth was, in very fact, the king of Israel. As a student of Jewish history and culture, Matthew was very careful to outline the ancestry of Jesus so that He could be established as a descendant of Abraham and of David.

Luke, too, outlines the genealogy of the Savior (see Luke 3:23–38), but there are some interesting differences in the two genealogies. One is that Matthew's genealogy demonstrates the royal lineage; Luke's genealogy is a personal pedigree that does not concern itself with descendency through the throne.

Another interesting difference is that Matthew specifically mentions five women: Tamar, Rahab, Ruth, Bathsheba, and Mary, the mother of Jesus. Robert L. Millet (see *A Symposium on the New Testament*, 138–139) suggests three possible reasons why the four women other than Mary were mentioned by Matthew: 1) each was known as a sinner, and the Savior came to save all of us from sin; 2) each had a union with her partner that seemed "scandalous" but played a unique role in continuing the sacred lineage of the Savior; and 3) each was considered a "foreigner," which emphasizes that the Savior was physically related to the Gentiles.

"Luke's record is regarded . . . as the pedigree of Mary, while Matthew's is accepted as that of Joseph" (Talmage, *Jesus the Christ*, 81).

Matt. 1:18—Mary, the mother of our Lord Jesus Christ, was a paragon of virtue, obedience, and rectitude. Similarly, righteous mothers through all generations of time have set the standard for enduring sacrifice and love, fulfilling their eternal commission to bring into the world the sons and daughters of God. As such, they participate in the work and glory of God "to bring to pass the immortality and eternal life of man" (Moses 1:39) and merit our everlasting gratitude and honor.

Joseph, before they came together, she was found with child of the Holy Ghost.

19. Then Joseph her husband, being a just man, and not willing to make her a publick example, was minded to put her away privily.

20. But while he thought on these things, behold, the angel of the Lord appeared unto him in a dream, saying, Joseph, thou son of David, fear not to take unto thee Mary thy wife: for that which is conceived in her is of the Holy Ghost.

21. And she shall bring forth a son, and thou shalt call his name JESUS: for he shall save his people from their sins.

22. Now all this was done, that it might be fulfilled which was spoken of the Lord by the prophet, saying,

23. Behold, a virgin shall be with child, and shall bring forth a son, and they shall call his name Emmanuel, which being interpreted is, God with us.

24. Then Joseph being raised from sleep did as the angel of the Lord had bidden him, and took unto him his wife:

25. And knew her not till she had brought forth her firstborn son: and he called his name JESUS.

CHAPTER 2

1. Now when Jesus was born in Bethlehem of Judæa in the days of Herod the king, behold, there came wise men from the east to Jerusalem,

2. Saying, Where is he that is born King of the Jews? for we have seen his star in the east, and are come to worship him.

3. When Herod the king had heard these things, he was troubled, and all Jerusalem with him.

4. And when he had gathered all the chief priests and scribes of the people together, he demanded of them where Christ should be born.

5. And they said unto him, In Bethlehem of Judæa: for thus it is written by the prophet,

6. And thou Bethlehem, in the land of Juda, art not the least among the princes of Juda: for out of thee shall come a Governor, that shall rule my people Israel.

7. Then Herod, when he had privily called the wise men, inquired of them diligently what time the star appeared.

8. And he sent them to Bethlehem, and said, Go and search diligently for the young child; and when ye have found him, bring me word again, that I may come and worship him also.

9. When they had heard the king, they departed; and, lo, the star, which they saw in the east, went be-

Matt. 1:21, 25—The Savior's name, which had been given by the angel to both Mary and Joseph, was one that was well known and fairly common in Israel: the Aramaic *Yeshuëa,* meaning "the Lord is Salvation" or "savior." The Greek translation of the name is *Jesus,* and the Hebrew translation is *Yoshu'a* or *Joshua.* Because the Aramaic forms of *Jesus* and *he will save* are almost identical, the text of verse 21 is saying, in other words, "You shall call his name 'savior,' because he will save" (see *The New Oxford Annotated Bible,* 1172).

All the prophets throughout the millennia before His birth who spoke of Jesus gave promise of His saving grace; see, for example, Isa. 12:2–3 and Isa. 45:17.

Jesus' very name, then, taught a profound lesson about His role in the work of His Father.

Matt. 2:1–12—While our traditional Christmas celebrations include three wise men, we do not know how many wise men actually came from the East to visit the Savior. There may have been as few as two or as many as an entire congregation. We do know that, according to Elder Bruce R. McConkie, they had been promised by the Lord that they would not die until they had seen and worshipped Christ (see *The Mortal Messiah,* 1:358). Some believe that the wise men were Jews who lived in the East; others believe that they came from Persia, because the Greek word translated to "wise men" is *Magoi,* a Persian word (in English, *Magi).*

Matt. 2:2—The "star" that shone in the heavens at the Savior's birth was prophesied by Samuel the Lamanite (see Hel. 14:2–6), who wrote that "great lights" would appear in the heaven and that "a new star" would arise that would cause the skies to remain light for an entire night.

Matt. 2:3, 7–8—As we know, Herod was "troubled" by the prospect that a "new king" had been born, one that posed a direct threat to him.

fore them, till it came and stood over where the young child was.

10. When they saw the star, they rejoiced with exceeding great joy.

11. ¶ And when they were come into the house, they saw the young child with Mary his mother, and fell down, and worshipped him: and when they had opened their treasures, they presented unto him gifts; gold, and frankincense, and myrrh.

12. And being warned of God in a dream that they should not return to Herod, they departed into their own country another way.

13. And when they were departed, behold, the angel of the Lord appeareth to Joseph in a dream, saying, Arise, and take the young child and his mother, and flee into Egypt, and be thou there until I bring thee word: for Herod will seek the young child to destroy him.

14. When he arose, he took the young child and his mother by night, and departed into Egypt:

15. And was there until the death of Herod: that it might be fulfilled which was spoken of the Lord by the prophet, saying, Out of Egypt have I called my son.

16. ¶ Then Herod, when he saw that he was mocked of the wise men, was exceeding wroth, and sent forth, and slew all the children that were in Bethlehem, and in all the coasts thereof, from two years old and under, according to the time which he had diligently inquired of the wise men.

17. Then was fulfilled that which was spoken by Jeremy the prophet, saying,

18. In Rama was there a voice heard, lamentation, and weeping, and great mourning, Rachel weeping for her children, and would not be comforted, because they are not.

19. ¶ But when Herod was dead, behold, an angel of the Lord appeareth in a dream to Joseph in Egypt,

20. Saying, Arise, and take the young child and his mother, and go into the land of Israel: for they are dead which sought the young child's life.

21. And he arose, and took the young child and his mother, and came into the land of Israel.

22. But when he heard that Archelaus did reign in Judæa in the room of his father Herod, he was afraid to go thither: notwithstanding, being warned of God in a dream, he turned aside into the parts of Galilee:

23. And he came and dwelt in a city called Nazareth: that it might be fulfilled which was spoken by the prophets, He shall be called a Nazarene.

CHAPTER 3

1. In those days came John the Baptist, preaching in the wilderness of Judæa,

2. And saying, Repent ye: for the kingdom of heaven is at hand.

3. For this is he that was spoken of by the prophet Esaias, saying, The voice of one crying in the wilderness, Prepare ye the way of the Lord, make his paths straight.

Matt. 2:11—Note that the wise men visited a house, not a stable, and that they came to see a "young child," not a newborn babe. Scholars believe that the wise men may have arrived as many as two years after Jesus was born.

Matt. 2:11—It was customary in the East, where the wise men traveled from, to present gifts whenever they asked to see or speak with a monarch or prince.

Matt. 2:16–18—At the time of Herod's edict to destroy all children aged two and under, John the Baptist was six months older than Jesus, and would have fallen under the edict. By angelic direction, Joseph and Mary took Jesus and fled to Egypt. Following Zacharias's direction, Elisabeth took John into the mountains, where she hid him and fed him on locusts and honey.

Matt. 2:22—In Herod's will, he divided his kingdom among his three sons; Archelaus was given Judea. He ruled with the same kind of cruelty as his father; on the first Passover of his reign, he ordered 3,000 Jews to be massacred. His brother Antipas was more humane, and the Holy family settled in his province of Galilee, where they could enjoy relative safety.

Matt. 2:23—Never mentioned in the rest of the Bible, Nazareth was a small village with an estimated population of 200 in Galilee. It was sometimes referred to as "the White City" because many of the homes in the village were constructed of white stone. Nazareth was also called "Flowery" because of all the beautiful flowers that dotted the valley and its surrounding hills.

Matt. 3:1–6—John's important role was *forerunner of the Savior*. In ancient times, forerunners ran ahead of the king's chariot, clearing the way of any obstacles or debris and loudly proclaiming the coming of the king. All four of the Gospels illustrate John as a proclaimer of the Savior, one who went ahead (a forerunner) and prepared the way; John came to "bear witness" (John 1:6–7) of the Savior and to overthrow the apostasy that existed among the Jews.

We know that he baptized many before he baptized Jesus, who described His cousin as a "burning and shining light" (John 5:35) whose testimony would stand in judgment against those who refused to believe and obey what He taught.

4. And the same John had his raiment of camel's hair, and a leathern girdle about his loins; and his meat was locusts and wild honey.

5. Then went out to him Jerusalem, and all Judæa, and all the region round about Jordan,

6. And were baptized of him in Jordan, confessing their sins.

7. ¶ But when he saw many of the Pharisees and Sadducees come to his baptism, he said unto them, O generation of vipers, who hath warned you to flee from the wrath to come?

8. Bring forth therefore fruits meet for repentance:

9. And think not to say within yourselves, We have Abraham to our father: for I say unto you, that God is able of these stones to raise up children unto Abraham.

10. And now also the axe is laid unto the root of the trees: therefore every tree which bringeth not forth good fruit is hewn down, and cast into the fire.

11. I indeed baptize you with water unto repentance: but he that cometh after me is mightier than I, whose shoes I am not worthy to bear: he shall baptize you with the Holy Ghost, and with fire:

12. Whose fan is in his hand, and he will throughly purge his floor, and gather his wheat into the garner; but he will burn up the chaff with unquenchable fire.

13. ¶ Then cometh Jesus from Galilee to Jordan unto John, to be baptized of him.

14. But John forbad him, saying, I have need to be baptized of thee, and comest thou to me?

15. And Jesus answering said unto him, Suffer it to be so now: for thus it becometh us to fulfil all righteousness. Then he suffered him.

16. And Jesus, when he was baptized, went up straightway out of the water: and, lo, the heavens were opened unto him, and he saw the Spirit of God descending like a dove, and lighting upon him:

17. And lo a voice from heaven, saying, This is my beloved Son, in whom I am well pleased.

CHAPTER 4

1. Then was Jesus led up of the Spirit into the wilderness to be tempted of the devil.

2. And when he had fasted forty

Matt. 3:4—In our day, locusts are still eaten by the Beduoins in the Middle East; the insects are salted, dried, and eaten with butter or wild honey. Even today, only the poorest eat them. The fact that John subsisted on a diet of locusts tells us something of the extreme poverty in which he was raised (see James M. Freeman, *Manners and Customs of the Bible,* 333).

Matt. 3:9—"Judaism held that the posterity of Abraham had an assured place in the kingdom of the expected Messiah, and that no proselyte from among the Gentiles could possibly attain the rank and distinction of which the 'children' were sure. John's forceful assertion that God could raise up, from the stones on the river bank, children to Abraham, meant to those who heard that even the lowest of the human family might be preferred before themselves unless they repented and reformed" (Talmage, *Jesus the Christ,* 115).

Matt. 3:15—To "fulfill all righteousness" means that one keeps every commandment, receives every ordinance, and does everything necessary to attain eternal life. The Savior "fulfilled all righteousness" through His baptism in four ways: 1) He humbled Himself; 2) He covenanted to obey the Father's commandments; 3) He fulfilled the requirement (baptism) for entering the celestial kingdom; and 4) He set the example for all of us to follow (see 2 Ne. 31:4–11).

Matt. 3:16—"[John the Baptist] had the privilege of beholding the Holy Ghost descend in the form of a dove, or rather in the *sign* of the dove, in witness of that administration. The sign of the dove was instituted before the creation of the world, a witness for the Holy Ghost, and the devil cannot come in the sign of a dove. The Holy Ghost is a personage, and is in the form of a personage. It does not confine itself to the *form* of the dove, but in *sign* of the dove. The Holy Ghost cannot be transformed into a dove; but the sign of a dove was given to John to signify the truth of the deed, as the dove is an emblem or token of truth and innocence" (*Teachings of the Prophet Joseph Smith,* 275–276).

days and forty nights, he was afterward an hungred.

3. And when the tempter came to him, he said, If thou be the Son of God, command that these stones be made bread.

4. But he answered and said, It is written, Man shall not live by bread alone, but by every word that proceedeth out of the mouth of God.

5. Then the devil taketh him up into the holy city, and setteth him on a pinnacle of the temple,

6. And saith unto him, If thou be the Son of God, cast thyself down: for it is written, He shall give his angels charge concerning thee: and in their hands they shall bear thee up, lest at any time thou dash thy foot against a stone.

7. Jesus said unto him, It is written again, Thou shalt not tempt the Lord thy God.

8. Again, the devil taketh him up into an exceeding high mountain, and sheweth him all the kingdoms of the world, and the glory of them;

9. And saith unto him, All these things will I give thee, if thou wilt fall down and worship me.

10. Then saith Jesus unto him, Get thee hence, Satan: for it is written, Thou shalt worship the Lord thy God, and him only shalt thou serve.

11. Then the devil leaveth him, and, behold, angels came and ministered unto him.

12. ¶ Now when Jesus had heard that John was cast into prison, he departed into Galilee;

13. And leaving Nazareth, he came and dwelt in Capernaum, which is upon the sea coast, in the borders of Zabulon and Nephthalim:

14. That it might be fulfilled which was spoken by Esaias the prophet, saying,

15. The land of Zabulon, and the land of Nephthalim, by the way of the sea, beyond Jordan, Galilee of the Gentiles;

16. The people which sat in darkness saw great light; and to them which sat in the region and shadow of death light is sprung up.

17. ¶ From that time Jesus began to preach, and to say, Repent: for the kingdom of heaven is at hand.

18. ¶ And Jesus, walking by the sea of Galilee, saw two brethren, Simon called Peter, and Andrew his brother, casting a net into the sea: for they were fishers.

19. And he saith unto them, Follow me, and I will make you fishers of men.

Matt. 4:1–11 — The Apostle Paul wrote of the Savior, "For we have not an high priest which cannot be touched with the feeling of our infirmities; but was in all points tempted like as we are, yet without sin" (Heb. 4:15). In this account, the Savior is tempted in three ways: He is asked by the adversary to turn stones into bread (thereby easing the hunger of a forty-day fast), to hurl himself from the pinnacle of the temple (thereby demonstrating His power), and to worship Satan, who promised to give Him all the kingdoms of the world. President David O. McKay pointed out that nearly all the temptations we suffer will fall into one of those three categories: 1) a temptation of the appetite, 2) a temptation of pride or vanity, or 3) a desire for the riches of the world (see *Improvement Era*, Nov. 1965, 961).

Matt. 4:1–11 — The Joseph Smith Translation of these passages clarifies that Satan did *not* lead Jesus to the places in which He faced temptation. The Prophet makes it clear that Jesus went to the wilderness to be with His Father; after that, the Spirit, not the adversary, took Him to the pinnacle of the temple and to the high mountain. Only then did Satan approach Him; Satan never directed or led Him.

Matt. 4:10 — "The importance of not accommodating temptation in the least degree is underlined by the Savior's example. . . . He could have opened the door and flirted with danger by saying, 'All right, Satan, I'll listen to your proposition. I need not succumb, I need not yield, I need not accept—but I'll listen.'

"Christ did not so rationalize. He positively and promptly closed the discussion, and commanded: 'Get thee hence, Satan,' meaning, likely, 'Get out of my sight—get out of my presence—I will not listen—I will have nothing to do with you.' . . . This is our proper pattern, if we would prevent sin rather than be faced with the much more difficult task of curing it" (Spencer W. Kimball, *The Miracle of Forgiveness*, 216).

Matt. 4:17 — Jesus opened His ministry with a message to believe and repent, the key that Elder Bruce R. McConkie says "opens the door to an understanding of all of Jesus' teachings" (*The Mortal Messiah*, 2:7).

20. And they straightway left their nets, and followed him.

21. And going on from thence, he saw other two brethren, James the son of Zebedee, and John his brother, in a ship with Zebedee their father, mending their nets; and he called them.

22. And they immediately left the ship and their father, and followed him.

23. ¶ And Jesus went about all Galilee, teaching in their synagogues, and preaching the gospel of the kingdom, and healing all manner of sickness and all manner of disease among the people.

24. And his fame went throughout all Syria: and they brought unto him all sick people that were taken with divers diseases and torments, and those which were possessed with devils, and those which were lunatick, and those that had the palsy; and he healed them.

25. And there followed him great multitudes of people from Galilee, and from Decapolis, and from Jerusalem, and from Judæa, and from beyond Jordan.

CHAPTER 5

1. And seeing the multitudes, he went up into a mountain: and when he was set, his disciples came unto him:

2. And he opened his mouth, and taught them, saying,

3. Blessed are the poor in spirit: for theirs is the kingdom of heaven.

4. Blessed are they that mourn: for they shall be comforted.

5. Blessed are the meek: for they shall inherit the earth.

6. Blessed are they which do hunger and thirst after righteousness: for they shall be filled.

7. Blessed are the merciful: for they shall obtain mercy.

8. Blessed are the pure in heart: for they shall see God.

9. Blessed are the peacemakers: for they shall be called the children of God.

10. Blessed are they which are persecuted for righteousness' sake: for theirs is the kingdom of heaven.

11. Blessed are ye, when men shall revile you, and persecute you, and shall say all manner of evil against you falsely, for my sake.

12. Rejoice, and be exceeding glad: for great is your reward in

Matt. 4:20—The word *straightway* means to follow a straight path (in this case, following the Savior) boldly, immediately, and without hesitation. It is a word that calls for action and personal commitment, and sets the tone for our own attitude toward the gospel.

Matt. 5:1–12—Each of the Beatitudes begins with the word *blessed,* translated from the Greek *makarios,* which means "privileged to receive divine favor." Another possible translation could be "oh, the happiness of," signifying a state of well-being. Appearing as it does at the beginning of each Beatitude, it brings with it a promise of ways we can attain well-being and a state of joy that resides deep in the soul.

Matt. 5:3—"Poor in spirit" indicates an awareness of our dependence on the Savior. The Book of Mormon adds great clarity to this verse by specifying "Blessed are the poor in spirit who come unto me" (3 Ne. 12:3). Being poor in spirit alone is not a virtue, but can become so if it leads to the humility that then enables us to repent, be baptized, and make and keep sacred covenants.

Matt. 5:5—*Meekness* is a state of voluntary humility; it connotes one who is strong, God-fearing, courageous, slow to anger, humble, teachable, and willing to listen for the Spirit to guide his or her life. The Lord has guaranteed that His grace is sufficient for the meek (see Ether 12:26).

Matt. 5:6—President Harold B. Lee counseled that any who have been extremely hungry or thirsty, to a point of distress, "may begin to understand how the Master meant we should hunger and thirst after righteousness" (*Decisions for Successful Living,* 58).

Matt. 5:7—"Mercy is of the very essence of the gospel of Jesus Christ. The degree to which each of us is able to extend it becomes an expression of the reality of our discipleship under Him who is our Lord and Master" (Gordon B. Hinckley, *Ensign,* May 1990, 69).

Matt. 5:8—Purity of heart is reflected in our behavior, our thoughts, our intentions, and our noblest affections toward God. We can't be made pure and perfect on our own, but with the help of Christ we can be made pure and perfect. What are your thoughts concerning this sacred process of purification and perfection through the grace and power of the Lord?

heaven: for so persecuted they the prophets which were before you.

13. ¶ Ye are the salt of the earth: but if the salt have lost his savour, wherewith shall it be salted? it is thenceforth good for nothing, but to be cast out, and to be trodden under foot of men.

14. Ye are the light of the world. A city that is set on an hill cannot be hid.

15. Neither do men light a candle, and put it under a bushel, but on a candlestick; and it giveth light unto all that are in the house.

16. Let your light so shine before men, that they may see your good works, and glorify your Father which is in heaven.

17. ¶ Think not that I am come to destroy the law, or the prophets: I am not come to destroy, but to fulfil.

18. For verily I say unto you, Till heaven and earth pass, one jot or one tittle shall in no wise pass from the law, till all be fulfilled.

19. Whosoever therefore shall break one of these least commandments, and shall teach men so, he shall be called the least in the kingdom of heaven: but whosoever shall do and teach them, the same shall be called great in the kingdom of heaven.

20. For I say unto you, That except your righteousness shall exceed the righteousness of the scribes and Pharisees, ye shall in no case enter into the kingdom of heaven.

21. ¶ Ye have heard that it was said by them of old time, Thou shalt not kill; and whosoever shall kill shall be in danger of the judgment:

22. But I say unto you, That whosoever is angry with his brother without a cause shall be in danger of the judgment: and whosoever shall say to his brother, Raca, shall be in danger of the council: but whosoever shall say, Thou fool, shall be in danger of hell fire.

23. Therefore if thou bring thy gift to the altar, and there rememberest that thy brother hath ought against thee;

24. Leave there thy gift before the altar, and go thy way; first be reconciled to thy brother, and then come and offer thy gift.

25. Agree with thine adversary quickly, whiles thou art in the way with him; lest at any time the adversary deliver thee to the judge, and the judge deliver thee to the officer, and thou be cast into prison.

26. Verily I say unto thee, Thou shalt by no means come out thence, till thou hast paid the uttermost farthing.

27. ¶ Ye have heard that it was said by them of old time, Thou shalt not commit adultery:

28. But I say unto you, That who-

Matt. 5:8—Elder Bruce R. McConkie promised that we have the privilege of seeing the face of God while we are yet in mortality (see *Ensign,* Nov. 1977, 34). "Never cease striving till you have seen God face to face. Strengthen your faith; cast off your doubts, your sins, and all your unbelief, and nothing can prevent you from coming to God" (Parley P. Pratt, *Autobiography of Parley Parker Pratt,* 123).

Matt. 5:13—Salt was important in ancient Israel, not only for flavoring food, but as part of religious offerings. The salt referred to here was likely bituminous salt from the Dead Sea, which was used to neutralize the smell of burning flesh from sacrifices in the temple. If that salt became spoiled by exposure and was no longer useful for its original purpose, it was tossed along the walks to keep people from slipping in wet weather—and, therefore, was literally "trodden under foot of men."

Matt. 5:14–16—"The missionary servants of The Church of Jesus Christ today are sent forth, not to assail or ridicule the beliefs of men, but to set before the world a superior light, by which the smoky dimness of the flickering flames of man-made creeds shall be apparent. The work of the Church is constructive, not destructive" (James E. Talmage, *The Parables of James E. Talmage,* 6).

Matt. 5:18—The word *jot* refers to the *yodh,* the smallest letter in the Hebrew alphabet (comparable to the dot on an i). The word *tittle* refers to the horn-like points on a Hebrew letter (comparable to crossing a t).

Matt. 5:22—"It takes a lifetime to build a character; the scandal-monger can destroy it almost overnight" (John A. Widtsoe, *Man and the Dragon,* 247).

Matt. 5:23–26—Each of us has been or will be wronged; it is our responsibility to banish hatred from our hearts, get rid of evil thoughts toward another, and do everything in our power to reconcile with one another without involving civil or Church courts, wherever possible (see Joseph F. Smith, *Gospel Doctrine: Selections from the Sermons and Writings of Joseph F. Smith,* 257).

Matt. 5:27—Adultery is described as "cheating," and "cheating it is, for it robs virtue, it robs loyalty, it robs sacred promises, it robs self-respect, it robs truth" (Gordon B. Hinckley, *Teachings of Gordon B. Hinckley,* 5).

soever looketh on a woman to lust after her hath committed adultery with her already in his heart.

29. And if thy right eye offend thee, pluck it out, and cast it from thee: for it is profitable for thee that one of thy members should perish, and not that thy whole body should be cast into hell.

30. And if thy right hand offend thee, cut if off, and cast it from thee: for it is profitable for thee that one of thy members should perish, and not that thy whole body should be cast into hell.

31. It hath been said, Whosoever shall put away his wife, let him give her a writing of divorcement:

32. But I say unto you, That whosoever shall put away his wife, saving for the cause of fornication, causeth her to commit adultery: and whosoever shall marry her that is divorced committeth adultery.

33. ¶ Again, ye have heard that it hath been said by them of old time, Thou shalt not forswear thyself, but shalt perform unto the Lord thine oaths:

34. But I say unto you, Swear not at all; neither by heaven; for it is God's throne:

35. Nor by the earth; for it is his footstool: neither by Jerusalem; for it is the city of the great King.

36. Neither shalt thou swear by thy head, because thou canst not make one hair white or black.

37. But let your communication be, Yea, yea; Nay, nay: for whatsoever is more than these cometh of evil.

38. ¶ Ye have heard that it hath been said, An eye for an eye, and a tooth for a tooth:

39. But I say unto you, That ye resist not evil: but whosoever shall smite thee on thy right cheek, turn to him the other also.

40. And if any man will sue thee at the law, and take away thy coat, let him have thy cloke also.

41. And whosoever shall compel thee to go a mile, go with him twain.

42. Give to him that asketh thee, and from him that would borrow of thee turn not thou away.

43. ¶ Ye have heard that it hath been said, Thou shalt love thy neighbour, and hate thine enemy.

44. But I say unto you, Love your enemies, bless them that curse you, do good to them that hate you, and pray for them which despitefully use you, and persecute you;

45. That ye may be the children of your Father which is in heaven: for he maketh his sun to rise on the evil and on the good, and sendeth rain on the just and on the unjust.

Matt. 5:29–30 — The acts described in these verses — plucking out an eye, cutting off a hand — seem at first glance to be exaggerated acts that would never actually be done. These are known as *figures of speech* that, while not taken literally, demonstrate unusually firm resolve. Such figures of speech are common in writing from the era of the Bible.

Matt. 5:31–32 — The term *putting away of a wife* as used by Jesus was not the same as a legal divorce. Before Christ, a man could divorce ("put away") his wife for any reason simply by saying the words; at that point, she was entitled only to whatever was on her person (clothing and jewelry, which was one reason why women in Old Testament times adorned themselves with abundant coins and jewelry). Later, the law of Moses specified that a husband had to give his wife a written bill of divorcement (see Deut. 24:1). At that time, adultery did not have any bearing on divorce; a man who committed adultery was considered only to have invaded the rights of another man, and a woman guilty of adultery was put to death. With His ministry, the Savior made adultery the only acceptable cause for divorce (see Fred H. Wight, *Manners and Customs of Bible Lands,* 125).

Matt. 5:33–37 — Oaths were extremely common under the law of Moses, and a statement that was not an oath was generally ignored. The Pharisees taught that there were two kinds of oaths: if the name of God was in an oath, its violation amounted to perjury. If the name of God was not part of the oath, it was considered only a slight offense (see James M. Freeman, *Manners and Customs of the Bible,* 338).

Matt. 5:40–42 — "These instructions were directed primarily to the apostles. . . . In their ministry it would be better to suffer material loss or personal indignity and imposition at the hands of wicked oppressors, than to bring about an impairment of efficiency and a hindrance in work through resistance and contention" (Talmage, *Jesus the Christ,* 219).

Matt. 5:41 — Some reason that we have been asked to go the second mile because that's where the Lord put all the blessings (see Hartmon Rector, Jr., *Ensign,* May 1979, 30).

Matt 5:43–47 — Elder Bruce R. McConkie counseled that the way to perfect the soul is to love one's enemies and to bless those that curse us (see *The Mortal Messiah,* 2:142).

46. For if ye love them which love you, what reward have ye? do not even the publicans the same?

47. And if ye salute your brethren only, what do ye more than others? do not even the publicans so?

48. Be ye therefore perfect, even as your Father which is in heaven is perfect.

CHAPTER 6

1. Take heed that ye do not your alms before men, to be seen of them: otherwise ye have no reward of your Father which is in heaven.

2. Therefore when thou doest thine alms, do not sound a trumpet before thee, as the hypocrites do in the synagogues and in the streets, that they may have glory of men. Verily I say unto you, They have their reward.

3. But when thou doest alms, let not thy left hand know what thy right hand doeth:

4. That thine alms may be in secret: and thy Father which seeth in secret himself shall reward thee openly.

5. ¶ And when thou prayest, thou shalt not be as the hypocrites are: for they love to pray standing in the synagogues and in the corners of the streets, that they may be seen of men. Verily I say unto you, They have their reward.

6. But thou, when thou prayest, enter into thy closet, and when thou hast shut thy door, pray to thy Father which is in secret; and thy Father which seeth in secret shall reward thee openly.

7. But when ye pray, use not vain repetitions, as the heathen do: for they think that they shall be heard for their much speaking.

8. Be not ye therefore like unto them: for your Father knoweth what things ye have need of, before ye ask him.

9. After this manner therefore pray ye: Our Father which art in heaven, Hallowed be thy name.

10. Thy kingdom come. Thy will be done in earth, as it is in heaven.

11. Give us this day our daily bread.

12. And forgive us our debts, as we forgive our debtors.

Matt. 5:48—This scripture, said Elder Mark E. Petersen, allows us to "see ourselves in an entirely new light—not as the descendants of ape-like creatures living an aimless existence, but as the descendants of Almighty God, with the possibility of becoming like him!" (Conference Report, Oct. 1968, 100). President Gordon B. Hinckley counseled that attaining perfection is a lifelong process that will be fraught with error and that will take much effort, but "He will help us. He will bless us. He will comfort and sustain us. He will help us do more, and be more, than we can ever accomplish or be on our own" (*Standing for Something,* 178).

Matt. 6:1–4—*Alms,* a word that comes from the Greek word meaning "acts of religious devotion," also appears in the Book of Mormon (see 3 Ne. 13:1–4) and the Doctrine and Covenants (see D&C 88:2; 112:1). *Giving alms* is an act of donating to the poor.

Matt. 6:7—The counsel given here by the Savior was in direct contrast to the teaching of many of the rabbis of the time, who maintained that oft-repeated prayers with their repetitions had certain efficacy, even when the repetitions lacked meaning.

An example of this occurred later in the New Testament when the Apostle Paul heard an angry mob repeat the same phrase for a period of two hours (see Acts 19:34). It also occurred when Elijah challenged the worshipers of Baal; in answer to his challenge, they called on their god "from morning even unto noon, saying, O Baal, hear us" (1 Kgs. 18:26).

Matt. 6:11—The phrase *eating bread* in the Bible is roughly the same as "eating a meal." In the East, an estimated three-fourths of the population live almost entirely on bread or other products made chiefly of wheat or barley flour. A prayer to provide one with "daily bread," then, would be tantamount to asking for provision of the food that sustains and nourishes.

Matt. 6:12—"Some injuries are so hurtful and deep that they cannot be healed without help from a higher power and hope for perfect justice and restitution in the next life. . . . [The Savior] understands our pain and will walk with us even in our darkest hours" (James E. Faust, *Ensign,* Nov. 2001, 20).

13. And lead us not into temptation, but deliver us from evil: For thine is the kingdom, and the power, and the glory, for ever. Amen.

14. For if ye forgive men their trespasses, your heavenly Father will also forgive you:

15. But if ye forgive not men their trespasses, neither will your Father forgive your trespasses.

16. ¶ Moreover when ye fast, be not, as the hypocrites, of a sad countenance: for they disfigure their faces, that they may appear unto men to fast. Verily I say unto you, They have their reward.

17. But thou, when thou fastest, anoint thine head, and wash thy face;

18. That thou appear not unto men to fast, but unto thy Father which is in secret: and thy Father, which seeth in secret, shall reward thee openly.

19. ¶ Lay not up for yourselves treasures upon earth, where moth and rust doth corrupt, and where thieves break through and steal:

20. But lay up for yourselves treasures in heaven, where neither moth nor rust doth corrupt, and where thieves do not break through nor steal:

21. For where your treasure is, there will your heart be also.

22. The light of the body is the eye: if therefore thine eye be single, thy whole body shall be full of light.

23. But if thine eye be evil, thy whole body shall be full of darkness. If therefore the light that is in thee be darkness, how great is that darkness!

24. ¶ No man can serve two masters: for either he will hate the one, and love the other; or else he will hold to the one, and despise the other. Ye cannot serve God and mammon.

25. Therefore I say unto you, Take no thought for your life, what ye shall eat, or what ye shall drink; nor yet for your body, what ye shall put on. Is not the life more than meat, and the body than raiment?

26. Behold the fowls of the air: for they sow not, neither do they reap, nor gather into barns; yet your heavenly Father feedeth them. Are ye not much better than they?

27. Which of you by taking thought can add one cubit unto his stature?

28. And why take ye thought for raiment? Consider the lilies of the field, how they grow; they toil not, neither do they spin:

29. And yet I say unto you, That even Solomon in all his glory was not arrayed like one of these.

30. Wherefore, if God so clothe the grass of the field, which to day is, and to morrow is cast into the oven, shall he not much more clothe you, O ye of little faith?

31. Therefore take no thought, saying, What shall we eat? or, What

Matt. 6:13—The wording of this verse suggests erroneously that the Lord would influence us to do evil unless we specifically asked Him not to. The Joseph Smith Translation provides clarity by stating, "And suffer us not to be led into temptation" (JST, Matt. 6:14). The motive is rather that we ask the Lord's help in strengthening us so we can resist evil and temptation.

Matt. 6:16–18—We fast not to gain the honors of the world, but to show devotion to God and to plead that the blessings of heaven will flow to our families as well as those who need special help. Fasting is an act of rejoicing that should be motivated by our love of the Savior.

Matt. 6:19–20—"Treasures on earth" are those temporal evidences of wealth that can erode, be stolen, or otherwise be damaged by temporal elements. "Treasures in heaven" refer to the attributes of godliness—truth, faith, mercy, knowledge, justice—that endure eternally.

Matt. 6:22—The phrase *if therefore thine eye be single* refers to having our eye (or mind, or soul) single to the glory of God, setting ourselves solidly on the path to righteousness and working to build the kingdom of God. It should be our primary motive.

Matt. 6:24—In referring to "two masters," President George Albert Smith wrote, "There is a line of demarkation, well defined, between the Lord's territory and the devil's. If you will stay on the Lord's side of the line you will be under his influence and will have no desire to do wrong; but if you cross to the devil's side of the line one inch, you are in the tempter's power, and if he is successful, you will not be able to think or even reason properly, because you will have lost the spirit of the Lord" (*Sharing the Gospel with Others*, 42).

Matt. 6:25–34—In this passage, the word *merimnesete*—meaning to be anxious about something, and loosely translated as "take no thought for"—is used six times. The Lord is inviting us, in other words, to give up our anxiety over the elements of our life over which we have no control but that we believe affect our well-being. He is telling us that those uncontrollable elements of our lives will take care of themselves, one thing at a time—that we should focus on current problems, and not become unduly anxious about the problems of tomorrow (see Kent P. Jackson and Robert L. Millet, eds., *Studies in Scripture, Vol. 5: The Gospels*, 245–246).

shall we drink? or, Wherewithal shall we be clothed?

32. (For after all these things do the Gentiles seek:) for your heavenly Father knoweth that ye have need of all these things.

33. But seek ye first the kingdom of God, and his righteousness; and all these things shall be added unto you.

34. Take therefore no thought for the morrow: for the morrow shall take thought for the things of itself. Sufficient unto the day is the evil thereof.

CHAPTER 7

1. Judge not, that ye be not judged.

2. For with what judgment ye judge, ye shall be judged: and with what measure ye mete, it shall be measured to you again.

3. And why beholdest thou the mote that is in thy brother's eye, but considerest not the beam that is in thine own eye?

4. Or how wilt thou say to thy brother, Let me pull out the mote out of thine eye; and, behold, a beam is in thine own eye?

5. Thou hypocrite, first cast out the beam out of thine own eye; and then shalt thou see clearly to cast out the mote out of thy brother's eye.

6. ¶ Give not that which is holy unto the dogs, neither cast ye your pearls before swine, lest they trample them under their feet, and turn again and rend you.

7. ¶ Ask, and it shall be given you; seek, and ye shall find; knock, and it shall be opened unto you:

8. For every one that asketh receiveth; and he that seeketh findeth; and to him that knocketh it shall be opened.

9. Or what man is there of you, whom if his son ask bread, will he give him a stone?

10. Or if he ask a fish, will he give him a serpent?

11. If ye then, being evil, know how to give good gifts unto your children, how much more shall your Father which is in heaven give good things to them that ask him?

12. Therefore all things whatso-

Matt. 6:33—The Lord was teaching the principle of priorities with respect to seeking wealth. As we seek to live the law of consecration, we can ask ourselves, *Will what I do bless lives, bring others closer to God and Christ, and build up the kingdom of God?* These are the things a consecrated life can do. In our complex world, there are many overlapping priorities that compete for our attention. What are our thoughts about cultivating harmony and peace by setting priorities based on sacrificing for the Lord and His children?

Matt. 6:34—In this verse, the Greek word *kakia* is translated as "evil." It might be more appropriate to consider it as "problems" or "troubles," rendering this verse, "Sufficient unto the day are the problems thereof."

Matt. 7:1–5—These verses are often misinterpreted as an edict that we should not judge either our fellow men or principles of right and wrong. Such is not true; we are actually commanded to do both those things. What these verses warn is that we are to use wise and righteous judgment so that we will be judged the same way (see Bruce R. McConkie, *Doctrinal New Testament Commentary,* 1:245).

Elder Dallin H. Oaks also cautioned that there is a difference between "final judgments"—declaring that a person has forfeited all right or possibility to be useful in serving the Lord, which we are forbidden to do—and "intermediate judgments," which allow us to determine our own behavior. Intermediate judgments, which are righteous, always allow for the role of the Atonement in bringing about change in the lives of others who seek it and use its healing power (see *Ensign,* Aug. 1999, 7, 9).

Matt. 7:6–12—While sin thrusts itself upon us unbidden, enticing us and tempting us without effort on our part, all good things—all "mysteries" and all wisdom—require effort on our part. There are certain things we must do if we want to learn the mysteries of the kingdom: we must ponder, study, pray, and act upon those things we learn. Above all, we must become humble, pleading with the Lord to be particularly sensitive to the promptings of His Spirit. When we have done all those things, we will receive revelation through the Holy Ghost (see Spencer W. Kimball, *The Teachings of Spencer W. Kimball,* 63).

Matt. 7:9—The loaves of bread used during the Savior's time bore striking resemblance to the flat round stones common in that area.

ever ye would that men should do to you, do ye even so to them: for this is the law and the prophets.

13. ¶ Enter ye in at the strait gate: for wide is the gate, and broad is the way, that leadeth to destruction, and many there be which go in thereat:

14. Because strait is the gate, and narrow is the way, which leadeth unto life, and few there be that find it.

15. ¶ Beware of false prophets, which come to you in sheep's clothing, but inwardly they are ravening wolves.

16. Ye shall know them by their fruits. Do men gather grapes of thorns, or figs of thistles?

17. Even so every good tree bringeth forth good fruit; but a corrupt tree bringeth forth evil fruit.

18. A good tree cannot bring forth evil fruit, neither can a corrupt tree bring forth good fruit.

19. Every tree that bringeth not forth good fruit is hewn down, and cast into the fire.

20. Wherefore by their fruits ye shall know them.

21. ¶ Not every one that saith unto me, Lord, Lord, shall enter into the kingdom of heaven; but he that doeth the will of my Father which is in heaven.

22. Many will say to me in that day, Lord, Lord, have we not prophesied in thy name? and in thy name have cast out devils? and in thy name done many wonderful works?

23. And then will I profess unto them, I never knew you: depart from me, ye that work iniquity.

24. ¶ Therefore whosoever heareth these sayings of mine, and doeth them, I will liken him unto a wise man, which built his house upon a rock:

25. And the rain descended, and the floods came, and the winds blew, and beat upon that house; and it fell not: for it was founded upon a rock.

26. And every one that heareth these sayings of mine, and doeth them not, shall be likened unto a foolish man, which built his house upon the sand:

27. And the rain descended, and

Matt. 7:12—During the Savior's time, the scriptures (our Old Testament) were divided into three major sections. The *Law* referred to here was the Torah, or the five books of Moses (Genesis, Exodus, Leviticus, Numbers, and Deuteronomy). The *Prophets* referred to here were the writings of various prophets (such as Isaiah and Ezekiel). This verse, then, points out that the counsel to treat others as you would have them treat you is given in both sections of scripture. (The third section, not referred to in this verse, was The *Writings,* comprised of the historical and poetic books of the Old Testament.)

Matt. 7:13–14—The "strait" gate is the one proven to lead to eternal life, and the scriptures not only advise us to enter therein, but also teach us how to find that gate.

Matt. 7:21—Some "are so thoughtless as to have the idea that they will decide for themselves, contrary to the Lord's advice, what they will do and yet expect to receive an inheritance in the Celestial Kingdom, but they are doomed to disappointment" (George Albert Smith, Conference Report, Oct. 1943, 46).

the floods came, and the winds blew, and beat upon that house; and it fell: and great was the fall of it.

28. And it came to pass, when Jesus had ended these sayings, the people were astonished at his doctrine:

29. For he taught them as one having authority, and not as the scribes.

CHAPTER 8

1. When he was come down from the mountain, great multitudes followed him.

2. And, behold, there came a leper and worshipped him, saying, Lord, if thou wilt, thou canst make me clean.

3. And Jesus put forth his hand, and touched him, saying, I will; be thou clean. And immediately his leprosy was cleansed.

4. And Jesus saith unto him, See thou tell no man; but go thy way, shew thyself to the priest, and offer the gift that Moses commanded, for a testimony unto them.

5. ¶ And when Jesus was entered into Capernaum, there came unto him a centurion, beseeching him,

6. And saying, Lord, my servant lieth at home sick of the palsy, grievously tormented.

7. And Jesus saith unto him, I will come and heal him.

8. The centurion answered and said, Lord, I am not worthy that thou shouldest come under my roof: but speak the word only, and my servant shall be healed.

9. For I am a man under authority, having soldiers under me: and I say to this man, Go, and he goeth; and to another, Come, and he cometh; and to my servant, Do this, and he doeth it.

10. When Jesus heard it, he marvelled, and said to them that followed, Verily I say unto you, I have not found so great faith, no, not in Israel.

11. And I say unto you, That many shall come from the east and west, and shall sit down with Abraham, and Isaac, and Jacob, in the kingdom of heaven.

12. But the children of the kingdom shall be cast out into outer darkness: there shall be weeping and gnashing of teeth.

13. And Jesus said unto the centurion, Go thy way; and as thou hast believed, so be it done unto thee. And his servant was healed in the selfsame hour.

14. ¶ And when Jesus was come into Peter's house, he saw his wife's mother laid, and sick of a fever.

15. And he touched her hand, and the fever left her: and she arose, and ministered unto them.

16. ¶ When the even was come, they brought unto him many that were possessed with devils: and he cast out the spirits with his word, and healed all that were sick:

Matt. 7:29—Anciently, scribes were simply officers who did writing of various kinds. But following the Babylonian captivity of the Jews, scribes were tasked not only with writing, but also with interpreting the law, keeping the oral tradition, lecturing, and commenting on various aspects of the law. By the time of Christ, the people had become dependent for their knowledge of scripture on the scribes, especially since many of them were unable to understand or read the language in which the scriptures were written (see James M. Freeman, *Manners and Customs of the Bible*, 341–42).

Matt. 8:2–4—"True leprosy, as known in modern times, is an affliction characterized by the appearance of nodules in the eyebrows, the cheeks, the nose, and the lobes of the ears, also in the hands and feet, where the disease eats into the joints, causing the falling off of fingers and toes. If nodules do not appear, their place is taken by spots of blanched or discolored skin (Macular leprosy). Both forms are based upon a functional degeneration of the nerves of the skin. Its cause was discovered by Hansen in 1871 to be a specific bacillus. Defective diet, however, seems to serve as a favorable condition for the culture of the bacillus. Leprosy was one of the few abnormal conditions of the body which the Levitical law declared unclean. Elaborate provision was therefore made for testing its existence and for the purification of those who were cured of it" (Talmage, *Jesus the Christ*, 186).

Matt. 8:4—Why was the leper asked to keep his healing a secret? Elder Bruce R. McConkie gave two possible reasons: First, by Levitical law, the leper had to go to a priest and be declared clean through specific ceremonial requirements, something that might have been difficult had the priests known that Jesus was involved in the healing. Second, the Savior likely wanted to avoid even greater persecution against Himself and His work (see *Doctrinal New Testament Commentary*, 1:174).

17. That it might be fulfilled which was spoken by Esaias the prophet, saying, Himself took our infirmities, and bare our sicknesses.

18. ¶ Now when Jesus saw great multitudes about him, he gave commandment to depart unto the other side.

19. And a certain scribe came, and said unto him, Master, I will follow thee whithersoever thou goest.

20. And Jesus saith unto him, The foxes have holes, and the birds of the air have nests; but the Son of man hath not where to lay his head.

21. And another of his disciples said unto him, Lord, suffer me first to go and bury my father.

22. But Jesus said unto him, Follow me; and let the dead bury their dead.

23. ¶ And when he was entered into a ship, his disciples followed him.

24. And, behold, there arose a great tempest in the sea, insomuch that the ship was covered with the waves: but he was asleep.

25. And his disciples came to him, and awoke him, saying, Lord, save us: we perish.

26. And he saith unto them, Why are ye fearful, O ye of little faith? Then he arose, and rebuked the winds and the sea; and there was a great calm.

27. But the men marvelled, saying, What manner of man is this, that even the winds and the sea obey him!

28. ¶ And when he was come to the other side into the country of the Gergesenes, there met him two possessed with devils, coming out of the tombs, exceeding fierce, so that no man might pass by that way.

29. And, behold, they cried out, saying, What have we to do with thee, Jesus, thou Son of God? art thou come hither to torment us before the time?

30. And there was a good way off from them an herd of many swine feeding.

31. So the devils besought him, saying, If thou cast us out, suffer us to go away into the herd of swine.

32. And he said unto them, Go. And when they were come out, they went into the herd of swine: and, behold, the whole herd of swine ran violently down a steep place into the sea, and perished in the waters.

33. And they that kept them fled, and went their ways into the city, and told every thing, and what was befallen to the possessed of the devils.

34. And, behold, the whole city came out to meet Jesus: and when they saw him, they besought him that he would depart out of their coasts.

CHAPTER 9

1. And he entered into a ship, and passed over, and came into his own city.

2. And, behold, they brought to him a man sick of the palsy, lying on a bed: and Jesus seeing their faith said unto the sick of the palsy; Son, be of good cheer; thy sins be forgiven thee.

3. And, behold, certain of the scribes said within themselves, This man blasphemeth.

4. And Jesus knowing their thoughts said, Wherefore think ye evil in your hearts?

Matt. 8:24–38 — Joseph Smith explained, "The great principle of happiness consists in having a body. The Devil has no body, and herein is his punishment. He is pleased when he can obtain the tabernacle of [a] man, and when cast out by the Savior, he asked to go into the herd of swine, showing that he would prefer a swine's body to having none. All beings who have bodies have power over those who have not. The Devil has no power over us, only as we permit him; the moment we revolt at anything which comes from God, the Devil takes power."

Christ calming the storm

5. For whether is easier, to say, Thy sins be forgiven thee; or to say, Arise, and walk?

6. But that ye may know that the Son of man hath power on earth to forgive sins, (then saith he to the sick of the palsy,) Arise, take up thy bed, and go unto thine house.

7. And he arose, and departed to his house.

8. But when the multitudes saw it, they marvelled, and glorified God, which had given such power unto men.

9. ¶ And as Jesus passed forth from thence, he saw a man, named Matthew, sitting at the receipt of custom: and he saith unto him, Follow me. And he arose, and followed him.

10. ¶ And it came to pass, as Jesus sat at meat in the house, behold, many publicans and sinners came and sat down with him and his disciples.

11. And when the Pharisees saw it, they said unto his disciples, Why eateth your Master with publicans and sinners?

12. But when Jesus heard that, he said unto them, They that be whole need not a physician, but they that are sick.

13. But go ye and learn what that meaneth, I will have mercy, and not sacrifice: for I am not come to call the righteous, but sinners to repentance.

14. ¶ Then came to him the disciples of John, saying, Why do we and the Pharisees fast oft, but thy disciples fast not?

15. And Jesus said unto them, Can the children of the bride-chamber mourn, as long as the bridegroom is with them? but the days will come, when the bridegroom shall be taken from them, and then shall they fast.

16. No man putteth a piece of new cloth unto an old garment, for that which is put in to fill it up taketh from the garment, and the rent is made worse.

17. Neither do men put new wine into old bottles: else the bottles break, and the wine runneth out, and the bottles perish: but they put new wine into new bottles, and both are preserved.

18. ¶ While he spake these things unto them, behold, there came a certain ruler, and worshipped him, saying, My daughter is even now dead: but come and lay thy hand upon her, and she shall live.

19. And Jesus arose, and followed him, and so did his disciples.

20. ¶ And, behold, a woman, which was diseased with an issue of blood twelve years, came behind him, and touched the hem of his garment:

21. For she said within herself, If I may but touch his garment, I shall be whole.

22. But Jesus turned him about, and when he saw her, he said, Daughter, be of good comfort; thy faith hath made thee whole. And the woman was made whole from that hour.

23. And when Jesus came into the ruler's house, and saw the minstrels and the people making a noise,

24. He said unto them, Give place: for the maid is not dead, but sleepeth. And they laughed him to scorn.

Matt. 9:2–8—We know that the paralytic who was healed had complied with the law of forgiveness, or else the Savior would not have declared that his sins were forgiven. The Savior always conformed to His own laws (see Bruce R. McConkie, *Doctrinal New Testament Commentary*, 1:178).

Matt. 9:9–13—When Jesus told the Pharisees that He came to call the sinners—not the righteous—to repentance, He was pointing out that the Pharisees had become blind to their own sins (see Robert J. Matthews, *A Bible! A Bible!*, 226-227). The Savior's declaration reminds us that we are all sick and in need of what He came to offer.

Matt. 9:15—*Children of the bride-chamber* are the friends and acquaintances who participated in the wedding party. The word *child* is a form of speech that shows the relationship between a person and some characteristic that person possesses.

Matt. 9:16–17—The Joseph Smith Translation adds to this account an important passage that demonstrates His rejection of the Pharisees' baptism and His declaration that all old covenants were now superseded by the new and everlasting covenant that He provided:

Then said the Pharisees unto him, Why will ye not receive us with our baptism, seeing we keep the whole law?

But Jesus said unto them, Ye keep not the law. If ye had kept the law, ye would have received me, for I am he who gave the law.

I receive not you with your baptism, because it profiteth you nothing.

For when that which is new is come, the old is ready to be put away (JST, Matt. 9:17–22).

Matt. 9:17—"Bottles" at the time of Christ were made of animal skins. When new, the skins expanded with the fermentation of the wine; when old, they became dried and brittle. Any fermentation of the wine then caused the skins to burst, or "break."

Matt. 9:23–26—Not only does this story bear witness of the Savior's incredible power as the giver of life, but it helps us understand His compassion in going Himself to a humble home to perform a miracle—demonstrating His love for the individual and His commitment to each of His sheep.

25. But when the people were put forth, he went in, and took her by the hand, and the maid arose.

26. And the fame hereof went abroad into all that land.

27. ¶ And when Jesus departed thence, two blind men followed him, crying, and saying, Thou Son of David, have mercy on us.

28. And when he was come into the house, the blind men came to him: and Jesus saith unto them, Believe ye that I am able to do this? They said unto him, Yea, Lord.

29. Then touched he their eyes, saying, According to your faith be it unto you.

30. And their eyes were opened; and Jesus straitly charged them, saying, See that no man know it.

31. But they, when they were departed, spread abroad his fame in all that country.

32. ¶ As they went out, behold, they brought to him a dumb man possessed with a devil.

33. And when the devil was cast out, the dumb spake: and the multitudes marvelled, saying, It was never so seen in Israel.

34. But the Pharisees said, He casteth out devils through the prince of the devils.

35. And Jesus went about all the cities and villages, teaching in their synagogues, and preaching the gospel of the kingdom, and healing every sickness and every disease among the people.

36. ¶ But when he saw the multitudes, he was moved with compassion on them, because they fainted, and were scattered abroad, as sheep having no shepherd.

37. Then saith he unto his disciples, The harvest truly is plenteous, but the labourers are few;

38. Pray ye therefore the Lord of the harvest, that he will send forth labourers into his harvest.

CHAPTER 10

1. And when he had called unto him his twelve disciples, he gave them power against unclean spirits, to cast them out, and to heal all manner of sickness and all manner of disease.

2. Now the names of the twelve apostles are these; The first, Simon, who is called Peter, and Andrew his brother; James the son of Zebedee, and John his brother;

3. Philip, and Bartholomew; Thomas, and Matthew the publican; James the son of Alphæus, and Lebbæus, whose surname was Thaddæus;

4. Simon the Canaanite, and Judas Iscariot, who also betrayed him.

5. These twelve Jesus sent forth, and commanded them, saying, Go not into the way of the Gentiles, and into any city of the Samaritans enter ye not:

Christ healing the blind

Matt. 10:2–4 — The New Testament provides four separate lists of the Apostles called by Jesus: one each in Matthew, Mark, Luke, and Acts. Interestingly, none of the lists is identical to another. Each lists Peter first, and the three that mention Judas Iscariot (all but the list in Acts, since he had already died by the time that list was made) list him last. Other than that, the order in which the Apostles are listed varies.

Apostles — then and now — are called to be "special witnesses of the name of Christ in all the world" (D&C 107:23). The word *Apostle* means "one who is sent forth." To prepare Himself for calling His Apostles, the Savior spent the night on a mountain, praying and communing with His Father. The next day, He called His disciples, and chose twelve from among them to be His Apostles. These He not only sent forth to preach the gospel of the kingdom and to proclaim that salvation comes only by Christ, but He also gave them power to cast out devils and heal sicknesses (see Mark 3:15). He also gave them the sealing power (see Matt. 18:18).

Matt. 10:5 — The mortal ministry of Jesus seems to have been confined to the house of Israel. Once the apostolic dispensation was ushered in following the Savior's Resurrection, the field of labor was broadened to include the entire world (see Acts 10).

6. But go rather to the lost sheep of the house of Israel.

7. And as ye go, preach, saying, The kingdom of heaven is at hand.

8. Heal the sick, cleanse the lepers, raise the dead, cast out devils: freely ye have received, freely give.

9. Provide neither gold, nor silver, nor brass in your purses,

10. Nor scrip for your journey, neither two coats, neither shoes, nor yet staves: for the workman is worthy of his meat.

11. And into whatsoever city or town ye shall enter, inquire who in it is worthy; and there abide till ye go thence.

12. And when ye come into an house, salute it.

13. And if the house be worthy, let your peace come upon it: but if it be not worthy, let your peace return to you.

14. And whosoever shall not receive you, nor hear your words, when ye depart out of that house or city, shake off the dust of your feet.

15. Verily I say unto you, It shall be more tolerable for the land of Sodom and Gomorrha in the day of judgment, than for that city.

16. ¶ Behold, I send you forth as sheep in the midst of wolves: be ye therefore wise as serpents, and harmless as doves.

17. But beware of men: for they will deliver you up to the councils, and they will scourge you in their synagogues;

18. And ye shall be brought before governors and kings for my sake, for a testimony against them and the Gentiles.

19. But when they deliver you up, take no thought how or what ye shall speak: for it shall be given you in that same hour what ye shall speak.

20. For it is not ye that speak, but the Spirit of your Father which speaketh in you.

21. And the brother shall deliver up the brother to death, and the father the child: and the children shall rise up against their parents, and cause them to be put to death.

22. And ye shall be hated of all men for my name's sake: but he that endureth to the end shall be saved.

23. But when they persecute you in this city, flee ye into another: for verily I say unto you, Ye shall not have gone over the cities of Israel, till the Son of man be come.

24. The disciple is not above his master, nor the servant above his lord.

25. It is enough for the disciple that he be as his master, and the servant as his lord. If they have called the master of the house Beelzebub, how much more shall they call them of his household?

26. Fear them not therefore: for

Matt. 10:14 — According to the scribes, the dust of heathen lands had the power to defile; during the time of the Savior, it was forbidden to carry so much as a plant or herb from a heathen land in case any dust might cling to it. This injunction of the Savior basically says that areas where people rejected the message of the gospel were to be considered impure, profane, or heathen — and, therefore, the dust of that area should be removed from the feet so it wouldn't defile those in areas that had accepted the gospel.

Matt. 10:16–18 — Ironically, the Savior's message was one of peace and love, yet those who taught that message inspired wrath and hatred to the point of persecution. These verses, as well as Matt. 10:21–25, were likely offered by the Savior so His Apostles would know what they were to face and how to respond to the persecution.

Matt. 10:19–20 — This promise is extended to all who prepare, study, and take the message of God to the world, including parents who teach their children: we will be inspired what to say as we teach and defend the truth.

Matt. 10:22 — "There are times when we feel that we can't endure — that we can't face what's ahead of us; . . . that we can't carry the heavy load. There is more built-in strength in all of us than we sometimes suppose. And what we once said we couldn't do or couldn't live with or couldn't carry, we find ourselves somehow doing and enduring . . . and we find strength and endurance and hidden resources within ourselves" (Richard L. Evans, *Improvement Era,* Oct. 1970, 32).

there is nothing covered, that shall not be revealed; and hid, that shall not be known.

27. What I tell you in darkness, that speak ye in light: and what ye hear in the ear, that preach ye upon the housetops.

28. And fear not them which kill the body, but are not able to kill the soul: but rather fear him which is able to destroy both soul and body in hell.

29. Are not two sparrows sold for a farthing? and one of them shall not fall on the ground without your Father.

30. But the very hairs of your head are all numbered.

31. Fear ye not therefore, ye are of more value than many sparrows.

32. Whosoever therefore shall confess me before men, him will I confess also before my Father which is in heaven.

33. But whosoever shall deny me before men, him will I also deny before my Father which is in heaven.

34. Think not that I am come to send peace on earth: I came not to send peace, but a sword.

35. For I am come to set a man at variance against his father, and the daughter against her mother, and the daughter in law against her mother in law.

36. And a man's foes shall be they of his own household.

37. He that loveth father or mother more than me is not worthy of me: and he that loveth son or daughter more than me is not worthy of me.

38. And he that taketh not his cross, and followeth after me, is not worthy of me.

39. He that findeth his life shall lose it: and he that loseth his life for my sake shall find it.

40. ¶ He that receiveth you receiveth me, and he that receiveth me receiveth him that sent me.

41. He that receiveth a prophet in the name of a prophet shall receive a prophet's reward; and he that receiveth a righteous man in the name of a righteous man shall receive a righteous man's reward.

42. And whosoever shall give to drink unto one of these little ones a cup of cold water only in the name of a disciple, verily I say unto you, he shall in no wise lose his reward.

CHAPTER 11

1. And it came to pass, when Jesus had made an end of commanding his twelve disciples, he departed thence to teach and to preach in their cities.

Matt. 10:34—This scripture has been erroneously interpreted to mean that God approves of so-called "holy wars" in which His purposes are brought to pass through violence and force. Such is not the case. In this verse, the Savior acknowledges that the peace He brings will be transitory until He comes as Prince of Peace in His millennial reign. In the meantime, the "sword" of persecution—sometimes from family members—is wielded against those who accept the gospel of Jesus Christ (see Bruce R. McConkie, *Doctrinal New Testament Commentary,* 1:335).

Matt. 10:35–37—Clearly the Savior taught that we love and honor our parents and other family members. But these verses warn that we may sometimes be forced to choose between pleasing the Lord and pleasing a family member or other loved one, and that we must give the Lord our fullest allegiance. We are not justified in preserving family peace and unity at the expense of forsaking the gospel.

Matt. 10:38—To "take up our cross" means to put down our sins, repent, and forgive others, thereby applying the Atonement in our lives. Robert L. Millet taught, "In some ways, the call to discipleship is also a call to suffer. It is a call to bear with the trials of this life and particularly the indifference or rejection of those who despise the way of holiness" (*An Eye Single to the Glory of God: Reflections on the Cost of Discipleship,* 40).

Matt. 10:40—The words of the living prophet always take precedence over those of the past. When we accept the Lord, we accept without reservation the prophets and Apostles who bear witness of Him. How is accepting and following the prophets of God the same thing as following the Father and the Son?

Matt. 10:41—When we accept the prophet and obey his counsels, we receive what he receives: eternal life and exaltation in the celestial kingdom.

2. Now when John had heard in the prison the works of Christ, he sent two of his disciples,

3. And said unto him, Art thou he that should come, or do we look for another?

4. Jesus answered and said unto them, Go and shew John again those things which ye do hear and see:

5. The blind receive their sight, and the lame walk, the lepers are cleansed, and the deaf hear, the dead are raised up, and the poor have the gospel preached to them.

6. And blessed is he, whosoever shall not be offended in me.

7. ¶ And as they departed, Jesus began to say unto the multitudes concerning John, What went ye out into the wilderness to see? A reed shaken with the wind?

8. But what went ye out for to see? A man clothed in soft raiment? behold, they that wear soft clothing are in kings' houses.

9. But what went ye out for to see? A prophet? yea, I say unto you, and more than a prophet.

10. For this is he, of whom it is written, Behold, I send my messenger before thy face, which shall prepare thy way before thee.

11. Verily I say unto you, Among them that are born of women there hath not risen a greater than John the Baptist: notwithstanding he that is least in the kingdom of heaven is greater than he.

12. And from the days of John the Baptist until now the kingdom of heaven suffereth violence, and the violent take it by force.

13. For all the prophets and the law prophesied until John.

14. And if ye will receive it, this is Elias, which was for to come.

15. He that hath ears to hear, let him hear.

16. ¶ But whereunto shall I liken this generation? It is like unto children sitting in the markets, and calling unto their fellows,

17. And saying, We have piped unto you, and ye have not danced; we have mourned unto you, and ye have not lamented.

18. For John came neither eating nor drinking, and they say, He hath a devil.

19. The Son of man came eating and drinking, and they say, Behold a man gluttonous, and a winebibber, a friend of publicans and sinners. But wisdom is justified of her children.

20. ¶ Then began he to upbraid the cities wherein most of his mighty works were done, because they repented not:

21. Woe unto thee, Chorazin! woe unto thee, Bethsaida! for if the mighty works, which were done in you, had been done in Tyre and Sidon, they would have repented long ago in sackcloth and ashes.

22. But I say unto you, It shall be more tolerable for Tyre and Sidon at the day of judgment, than for you.

23. And thou, Capernaum, which art exalted unto heaven, shalt be brought down to hell: for if the mighty works, which have been done in thee, had been done in

Matt. 11:2–3—One of the most difficult aspects of John's ministry was persuading his followers that they should follow not him, but Jesus. For months after Jesus was baptized, there were those who still stubbornly clung to John in the belief that He was the promised Messiah. John's sending forth of the two disciples was to convince *them,* not him, that Jesus was the Christ.

Matt. 11:11—"How is it that John was considered one of the greatest prophets? . . .

"First. He was entrusted with a divine mission of preparing the way before the face of the Lord. Whoever had such a trust committed to him before or since? No man.

"Secondly. He was entrusted with the important mission, and it was required at his hands, to baptize the Son of Man. . . .

"Thirdly. John, at that time, was the only legal administrator in the affairs of the kingdom there was then on the earth, and holding the keys of power. The Jews had to obey his instructions or be damned" (Joseph Smith, *Teachings of the Prophet Joseph Smith,* 275–76).

Matt. 11:16–17—Even today, children in Palestine keep up the tradition of imitating adults at weddings and funerals, dancing and pretending to play pipes and other musical instruments. These verses refer to those stubborn children who, despite the happiness around them, refuse to participate—and represent those of us who refuse to accept the invitation extended to us.

Matt. 11:19—In the Old Testament, "son of man" almost always means "human" or "mortal." In each occurrence of the phrase in the New Testament, it refers to Jesus Christ.

Matt. 11:23–24—The Savior loved Capernaum; it was where He delivered two of His greatest discourses, performed most of the miracles of His mortal ministry, and labored for two of the three years of that ministry. When the inhabitants of Capernaum refused to repent, the Savior pronounced this prophecy. The city has gone from a thriving 15,000 inhabitants in Jesus' time to a desolate place of nothing more than ruins today.

Sodom, it would have remained until this day.

24. But I say unto you, That it shall be more tolerable for the land of Sodom in the day of judgment, than for thee.

25. ¶ At that time Jesus answered and said, I thank thee, O Father, Lord of heaven and earth, because thou hast hid these things from the wise and prudent, and hast revealed them unto babes.

26. Even so, Father: for so it seemed good in thy sight.

27. All things are delivered unto me of my Father: and no man knoweth the Son, but the Father; neither knoweth any man the Father, save the Son, and he to whomsoever the Son will reveal him.

28. ¶ Come unto me, all ye that labour and are heavy laden, and I will give you rest.

29. Take my yoke upon you, and learn of me; for I am meek and lowly in heart: and ye shall find rest unto your souls.

30. For my yoke is easy, and my burden is light.

CHAPTER 12

1. At that time Jesus went on the sabbath day through the corn; and his disciples were an hungred, and began to pluck the ears of corn, and to eat.

2. But when the Pharisees saw it, they said unto him, Behold, thy disciples do that which is not lawful to do upon the sabbath day.

3. But he said unto them, Have ye not read what David did, when he was an hungred, and they that were with him;

4. How he entered into the house of God, and did eat the shewbread, which was not lawful for him to eat, neither for them which were with him, but only for the priests?

5. Or have ye not read in the law, how that on the sabbath days the priests in the temple profane the sabbath, and are blameless?

6. But I say unto you, That in this place is one greater than the temple.

7. But if ye had known what this meaneth, I will have mercy, and not sacrifice, ye would not have condemned the guiltless.

8. For the Son of man is Lord even of the sabbath day.

9. And when he was departed thence, he went into their synagogue:

10. ¶ And, behold, there was a man which had his hand withered. And they asked him, saying, Is it lawful to heal on the sabbath days? that they might accuse him.

11. And he said unto them, What

Matt. 11:28—There are three meanings of *rest*: 1) relief during mortality, 2) the perfected rest of paradise after we die, and 3) the immortal glory of rising to live forever with the Lord (see Bruce R. McConkie, *The Promised Messiah,* 318).

Matt. 11:28–30—In the Savior's time, a *yoke* was used by farmers who tilled the fields; it joined two animals together, allowing their combined strength to take some of the burden from the first animal and enabling the pair of animals to more easily bear the heavy burden of the plow. In like manner, when we yoke ourselves to the Savior, we are allowing Him to take from us some of the heavy burdens we face in mortality.

Matt. 11:29—"When you choose to follow Christ, you choose to be changed" (Ezra Taft Benson, *Ensign,* Nov. 1985, 5).

Matt. 12:1–2—The Pharisees did not object to Jesus and His disciples plucking a handful of corn in a field; such was freely allowed, and such remains customary today in the Middle East. People were allowed to take just enough corn to satisfy their hunger, but not enough to sell to others. What the Pharisees objected to in this case was that the corn was plucked on the Sabbath.

Matt. 12:8—President David O. McKay reminded us that among the other reasons for Sabbath observance (such as embracing rest as a way to help the body), there is one important reason that outweighs all others: "Keeping holy the Sabbath Day is a law of God, resounding through the ages from Mt. Sinai. You cannot transgress the law of God without circumscribing your spirit" (Conference Report, Oct. 1956, 90).

Matt. 12:9–15—As Elder Russell M. Nelson reminds us, our behavior on the Sabbath tells the Lord volumes about our regard for Him and our feelings about the covenants under which we have been placed. If we are honest and true in keeping the Sabbath holy and in using that day to focus on the Lord and His works, we give a personal sign that He is of primary importance in our lives. When we fail to do so, we give a personal sign of the opposite: that our devotions are not upon Him (see *The Power Within Us,* 126–127).

man shall there be among you, that shall have one sheep, and if it fall into a pit on the sabbath day, will he not lay hold on it, and lift it out?

12. How much then is a man better than a sheep? Wherefore it is lawful to do well on the sabbath days.

13. Then saith he to the man, Stretch forth thine hand. And he stretched it forth; and it was restored whole, like as the other.

14. ¶ Then the Pharisees went out, and held a council against him, how they might destroy him.

15. But when Jesus knew it, he withdrew himself from thence: and great multitudes followed him, and he healed them all;

16. And charged them that they should not make him known:

17. That it might be fulfilled which was spoken by Esaias the prophet, saying,

18. Behold my servant, whom I have chosen; my beloved, in whom my soul is well pleased: I will put my spirit upon him, and he shall shew judgment to the Gentiles.

19. He shall not strive, nor cry; neither shall any man hear his voice in the streets.

20. A bruised reed shall he not break, and smoking flax shall he not quench, till he send forth judgment unto victory.

21. And in his name shall the Gentiles trust.

22. ¶ Then was brought unto him one possessed with a devil, blind, and dumb: and he healed him, insomuch that the blind and dumb both spake and saw.

23. And all the people were amazed, and said, Is not this the son of David?

24. But when the Pharisees heard it, they said, This fellow doth not cast out devils, but by Beelzebub the prince of the devils.

25. And Jesus knew their thoughts, and said unto them, Every kingdom divided against itself is brought to desolation; and every city or house divided against itself shall not stand:

26. And if Satan cast out Satan, he is divided against himself; how shall then his kingdom stand?

27. And if I by Beelzebub cast out devils, by whom do your children cast them out? therefore they shall be your judges.

28. But if I cast out devils by the Spirit of God, then the kingdom of God is come unto you.

29. Or else how can one enter into a strong man's house, and spoil his goods, except he first bind the strong man? and then he will spoil his house.

30. He that is not with me is against me; and he that gathereth not with me scattereth abroad.

31. ¶ Wherefore I say unto you, All manner of sin and blasphemy shall be forgiven unto men: but the blasphemy against the Holy Ghost shall not be forgiven unto men.

32. And whosoever speaketh a word against the Son of man, it shall be forgiven him: but whosoever speaketh against the Holy Ghost, it shall not be forgiven him, neither in

Matt. 12:15–21 — The prophecy by Esias (Isaiah) that the Messiah would bring salvation to the Gentiles was beginning to be fulfilled here. Among the "multitudes" referred to in verse 15 were people from Sidon and Tyre, from areas beyond Jordan, and from Idumea (see Mark 3:7–12), all areas that were inhabited at least partially by non-Israelites, or Gentiles.

Matt. 12:22–30 — This testimony, echoed by the other Gospel writers, is that Jesus has power over devils and unclean spirits. His kingdom includes all the spirits ever created by God the Father, including those who are evil, and will eventually triumph over evil (see Kent P. Jackson and Robert L. Millet, eds., *Studies in Scripture, Vol. 5: The Gospels*, 220–21).

Matt. 12:30 — The Savior's specific reference was to the scribes and Pharisees who in their disobedience fought against the Savior and tried to persuade people against Him. The same injunction applies to us today: if we are not for Him, not sharing His teachings and obeying His commandments, we become at best indifferent and at worst opposed. Either way, we are "against Him."

Matt. 12:31–32 — Elder Bruce R. McConkie explained the meaning of *blasphemy against the Holy Ghost:* it is "falsely denying Christ after receiving a perfect revelation of him from the Holy Ghost" (*Mormon Doctrine*, 86). In order to sin against the Holy Ghost, we must receive the gospel, receive absolute knowledge of the divinity of Jesus Christ through the Holy Ghost, and then deny that knowledge, thereby putting the Savior to open shame — an act that Elder McConkie equates to "crucifying unto oneself the Son of God afresh" and "commit[ting] murder by assenting unto the Lord's death" (*Doctrinal New Testament Commentary,* 1:273–74). President Spencer W. Kimball clarified that blasphemy against the Holy Ghost requires "such knowledge that it is manifestly impossible for the rank and file to commit such a sin" (*Teachings of Spencer W. Kimball,* 23).

this world, neither in the world to come.

33. Either make the tree good, and his fruit good; or else make the tree corrupt, and his fruit corrupt: for the tree is known by his fruit.

34. O generation of vipers, how can ye, being evil, speak good things? for out of the abundance of the heart the mouth speaketh.

35. A good man out of the good treasure of the heart bringeth forth good things: and an evil man out of the evil treasure bringeth forth evil things.

36. But I say unto you, That every idle word that men shall speak, they shall give account thereof in the day of judgment.

37. For by thy words thou shalt be justified, and by thy words thou shalt be condemned.

38. ¶ Then certain of the scribes and of the Pharisees answered, saying, Master, we would see a sign from thee.

39. But he answered and said unto them, An evil and adulterous generation seeketh after a sign; and there shall no sign be given to it, but the sign of the prophet Jonas:

40. For as Jonas was three days and three nights in the whale's belly; so shall the Son of man be three days and three nights in the heart of the earth.

41. The men of Nineveh shall rise in judgment with this generation, and shall condemn it: because they repented at the preaching of Jonas; and, behold, a greater than Jonas is here.

42. The queen of the south shall rise up in the judgment with this generation, and shall condemn it: for she came from the uttermost parts of the earth to hear the wisdom of Solomon; and, behold, a greater than Solomon is here.

43. When the unclean spirit is gone out of a man, he walketh through dry places, seeking rest, and findeth none.

44. Then he saith, I will return into my house from whence I came out; and when he is come, he findeth it empty, swept, and garnished.

45. Then goeth he, and taketh with himself seven other spirits more wicked than himself, and they enter in and dwell there: and the last state of that man is worse than the first. Even so shall it be also unto this wicked generation.

46. ¶ While he yet talked to the people, behold, his mother and his brethren stood without, desiring to speak with him.

47. Then one said unto him, Behold, thy mother and thy brethren stand without, desiring to speak with thee.

48. But he answered and said unto him that told him, Who is my mother? and who are my brethren?

49. And he stretched forth his hand toward his disciples, and said, Behold my mother and my brethren!

50. For whosoever shall do the will of my Father which is in heaven, the same is my brother, and sister, and mother.

Matt. 12:36 — We see around us many examples of men being unfairly judged, examples of injustices occurring for a variety of reasons. We can rest assured that in the final judgment, God will judge fairly and righteously, and no one will be punished for something for which he is not guilty (see Spencer W. Kimball, *The Teachings of Spencer W. Kimball*, 47).

Matt. 12:38–39 — There are two problems with "signs." First, and probably most important, is that faith never follows signs; on the contrary, signs, when they are given, follow faith, and are given to those who believe and who have obeyed the will of God. Second, signs are sought by those who don't want to give up their sins unless they are *forced* to; those who are righteous give up their sins because they love the Lord, not because a sign has convinced them to do so. Instead of seeking signs, we should seek gifts of the Spirit through faith, study, prayer, practice, and devotion to righteousness.

Matt. 12:46–50 — The covenant of baptism into The Church of Jesus Christ of Latter-day Saints is a covenant of adoption into the Lord's family. When we are baptized, we become in mortality His brothers, sisters, mothers, and children in a "special and restricted sense" (Bruce R. McConkie, *Doctrinal New Testament Commentary*, 1:280).

CHAPTER 13

1. The same day went Jesus out of the house, and sat by the sea side.

2. And great multitudes were gathered together unto him, so that he went into a ship, and sat; and the whole multitude stood on the shore.

3. And he spake many things unto them in parables, saying, Behold, a sower went forth to sow;

4. And when he sowed, some seeds fell by the way side, and the fowls came and devoured them up:

5. Some fell upon stony places, where they had not much earth: and forthwith they sprung up, because they had no deepness of earth:

6. And when the sun was up, they were scorched; and because they had no root, they withered away.

7. And some fell among thorns; and the thorns sprung up, and choked them:

8. But other fell into good ground, and brought forth fruit, some an hundredfold, some sixtyfold, some thirtyfold.

9. Who hath ears to hear, let him hear.

10. And the disciples came, and said unto him, Why speakest thou unto them in parables?

11. He answered and said unto them, Because it is given unto you to know the mysteries of the kingdom of heaven, but to them it is not given.

12. For whosoever hath, to him shall be given, and he shall have more abundance: but whosoever hath not, from him shall be taken away even that he hath.

13. Therefore speak I to them in parables: because they seeing see not; and hearing they hear not, neither do they understand.

14. And in them is fulfilled the prophecy of Esaias, which saith, By hearing ye shall hear, and shall not understand; and seeing ye shall see, and shall not perceive:

15. For this people's heart is waxed gross, and their ears are dull of hearing, and their eyes they have closed; lest at any time they should see with their eyes, and hear with their ears, and should understand with their heart, and should be converted, and I should heal them.

16. But blessed are your eyes, for they see: and your ears, for they hear.

17. For verily I say unto you, That many prophets and righteous men have desired to see those things which ye see, and have not seen them; and to hear those things which ye hear, and have not heard them.

18. ¶ Hear ye therefore the parable of the sower.

19. When any one heareth the word of the kingdom, and understandeth it not, then cometh the wicked one, and catcheth away that which was sown in his heart. This is he which received seed by the way side.

Matt. 13:1–3, 10–11—Jesus rarely used parables when speaking to His disciples, but often used them when speaking to the multitudes: He wanted His disciples to understand, but did *not* want the multitudes to understand until they were ready. He also used parables in areas where opposition was strongest against Him.

The word *parable* means "comparison" or "setting side-by-side"; while simple words or phrases can be used to compare, Jesus generally used longer stories or examples as parables when teaching the multitudes. He often used exaggeration to achieve the contrast He needed, and used other forms of speech—such as similes and metaphors—to draw comparisons or to transfer characteristics from one thing to another or from an object to a person.

Every single element of a parable is not intended to portray meaning. Instead, we should look to the overall message of the parable to find the meaning the Lord intended.

Matt. 13:3–8—Elder Bruce R. McConkie sees the parable of the sower as a parable of four kinds of soil: 1) the soil by the wayside represents those whose hearts are hardened and in whose hearts the word cannot even sprout; 2) the soil in stony places represents those who believe but who do not endure to the end; 3) the soil where thorns grow represent those who hear and receive the word of God but who continue to allow the influence of the things of the world; and 4) the good soil represents those who receive the word with an honest heart, keep the commandments, and endure to the end (see *The Mortal Messiah*, 2:249–53).

Matt. 13:9—"You who are spiritually-minded . . . understand that the power that has given you physical sensation is the power of the same God that gives you understanding of the truth. The latter power is inward" (Brigham Young, *Discourses of Brigham Young*, 421).

20. But he that received the seed into stony places, the same is he that heareth the word, and anon with joy receiveth it;

21. Yet hath he not root in himself, but dureth for a while: for when tribulation or persecution ariseth because of the word, by and by he is offended.

22. He also that received seed among the thorns is he that heareth the word; and the care of this world, and the deceitfulness of riches, choke the word, and he becometh unfruitful.

23. But he that received seed into the good ground is he that heareth the word, and understandeth it; which also beareth fruit, and bringeth forth, some an hundredfold, some sixty, some thirty.

24. ¶ Another parable put he forth unto them, saying, The kingdom of heaven is likened unto a man which sowed good seed in his field:

25. But while men slept, his enemy came and sowed tares among the wheat, and went his way.

26. But when the blade was sprung up, and brought forth fruit, then appeared the tares also.

27. So the servants of the householder came and said unto him, Sir, didst not thou sow good seed in thy field? from whence then hath it tares?

28. He said unto them, An enemy hath done this. The servants said unto him, Wilt thou then that we go and gather them up?

29. But he said, Nay; lest while ye gather up the tares, ye root up also the wheat with them.

30. Let both grow together until the harvest: and in the time of harvest I will say to the reapers, Gather ye together first the tares, and bind them in bundles to burn them: but gather the wheat into my barn.

31. ¶ Another parable put he forth unto them, saying, The kingdom of heaven is like to a grain of mustard seed, which a man took, and sowed in his field:

32. Which indeed is the least of all seeds: but when it is grown, it is the greatest among herbs, and becometh a tree, so that the birds of the air come and lodge in the branches thereof.

33. ¶ Another parable spake he unto them; The kingdom of heaven is like unto leaven, which a woman took, and hid in three measures of meal, till the whole was leavened.

34. All these things spake Jesus unto the multitude in parables; and without a parable spake he not unto them:

35. That it might be fulfilled which was spoken by the prophet, saying, I will open my mouth in parables; I will utter things which have been kept secret from the foundation of the world.

36. Then Jesus sent the multitude away, and went into the house: and his disciples came unto him, saying, Declare unto us the parable of the tares of the field.

37. He answered and said unto them, He that soweth the good seed is the Son of man;

38. The field is the world; the good seed are the children of the king-

Matt. 13:21—We need to drive our roots deep in the gospel and allow them to grow and thrive in fertile soil. This we do by seeking continual revelation, serving with eager dedication, accepting others for their unique strengths, and welcoming opportunities to do new and meaningful things in the kingdom.

Matt. 13:24–30—Tares are poisonous weeds that look so much like wheat that they can't be distinguished until they are fully grown. Tares are often compared to the darnel weed, a type of bearded rye grass that grows today in Palestine. It's unwise to try to weed out the tares when they are young; doing so would involve the unavoidable weeding out of the wheat as well.

Joseph Smith indicated that the Savior is waiting to weed out the tares (the wicked) until the harvest—the end of the world—so the wheat (the righteous) will not inadvertently be plucked out and the Church will not be destroyed.

Matt. 13:25—A similar custom is still taking place in India today. If one man wants to harm another, he waits until his enemy has finished working in the fields and has gone to sleep. He then steals quietly into his enemy's field and spreads the seed of a troublesome weed, which chokes out the growth of the good crops and often takes years to eradicate.

Matt. 13:31–32—The mustard seed, while not literally the "least of all seeds," is used by the Savior in parable to denote the smallest possible or least possible thing. The mature mustard plant, while certainly not the "greatest" among herbs, is used by the Savior to denote the largest or strongest thing. Joseph Smith wrote, "The kingdom of heaven is like unto a mustard seed. Behold, then is not this the kingdom of heaven that is raising its head in the last days in the majesty of its God, even the Church of the Latter-day Saints, like an impenetrable, immovable rock in the midst of the mighty deep, exposed to the storms and tempests of Satan, but has, thus far, remained steadfast" (*History of the Church*, 2:268).

Matt. 13:33—In addition to applying to the growth of faith in the hearts of all men, the parable of the leaven also represents the rise of the latter-day Church. Joseph Smith said that "the Church of the Latter-day Saints has taken its rise from a little leaven that was put into three witnesses. Behold, how much this is like the parable! It is fast leavening the lump, and will soon leaven the whole" (*Teachings of the Prophet Joseph Smith*, 100).

dom; but the tares are the children of the wicked one;

39. The enemy that sowed them is the devil; the harvest is the end of the world; and the reapers are the angels.

40. As therefore the tares are gathered and burned in the fire; so shall it be in the end of this world.

41. The Son of man shall send forth his angels, and they shall gather out of his kingdom all things that offend, and them which do iniquity;

42. And shall cast them into a furnace of fire: there shall be wailing and gnashing of teeth.

43. Then shall the righteous shine forth as the sun in the kingdom of their Father. Who hath ears to hear, let him hear.

44. ¶ Again, the kingdom of heaven is like unto treasure hid in a field; the which when a man hath found, he hideth, and for joy thereof goeth and selleth all that he hath, and buyeth that field.

45. ¶ Again, the kingdom of heaven is like unto a merchant man, seeking goodly pearls:

46. Who, when he had found one pearl of great price, went and sold all that he had, and bought it.

47. ¶ Again, the kingdom of heaven is like unto a net, that was cast into the sea, and gathered of every kind:

48. Which, when it was full, they drew to shore, and sat down, and gathered the good into vessels, but cast the bad away.

49. So shall it be at the end of the world: the angels shall come forth, and sever the wicked from among the just,

50. And shall cast them into the furnace of fire: there shall be wailing and gnashing of teeth.

51. Jesus saith unto them, Have ye understood all these things? They say unto him, Yea, Lord.

52. Then said he unto them, Therefore every scribe which is instructed unto the kingdom of heaven is like unto a man that is an householder, which bringeth forth out of his treasure things new and old.

53. ¶ And it came to pass, that when Jesus had finished these parables, he departed thence.

54. And when he was come into his own country, he taught them in their synagogue, insomuch that they were astonished, and said, Whence hath this man this wisdom, and these mighty works?

55. Is not this the carpenter's son? is not his mother called Mary? and his brethren, James, and Joses, and Simon, and Judas?

56. And his sisters, are they not all with us? Whence then hath this man all these things?

57. And they were offended in him. But Jesus said unto them, A prophet is not without honour, save in his own country, and in his own house.

58. And he did not many mighty works there because of their unbelief.

Matt. 13:41–43 — A year after the Church was organized, the Lord said the time would speedily come when peace would be taken from the earth (see D&C 1:35). President Joseph Fielding Smith said, "That time has come. *Peace has departed from the world. The devil has power over his own dominion. . . .* I think this should be *a time of warning,* not only to the Latter-day Saints, but to all the world" (*Doctrines of Salvation,* 3:48–49).

Matt. 13:44 — It has been customary in the East for millennia for people to keep their own money in their possession; to this day, they become very creative in finding places to hide their money, jewelry, and other valuables. While closets are often used, as well as secret vaults under the house, valuables are often buried in the field in places known to no one but the owner. Sadly, people often die without sharing such locations even with family members, and the individual's wealth may never be discovered.

Matt. 13:47–53 — Among those who join the Church are a great diversity of individuals, people who join the Church for a wide variety of reasons and who demonstrate a broad diversity of honor and integrity in following the commandments after they have joined. Those who come into the fold for the wrong reasons or who fail to follow the Savior after joining the Church will be cast away. All of us who have been caught in the gospel net have the power to become exalted, but we must work out our salvation "with fear and trembling" before the Lord (Philip. 2:12) instead of merely relying on our baptism to save us (see Bruce R. McConkie, *The Mortal Messiah,* 2:266–67).

Matt. 13:55–56 — We know that Jesus had both brothers and sisters. While the sisters are not named, we are given the names of at least some of His brothers in verse 55. According to many, the James referred to in this verse is likely the writer of the Epistle of James.

CHAPTER 14

1. At that time Herod the tetrarch heard of the fame of Jesus,

2. And said unto his servants, This is John the Baptist; he is risen from the dead; and therefore mighty works do shew forth themselves in him.

3. ¶ For Herod had laid hold on John, and bound him, and put him in prison for Herodias' sake, his brother Philip's wife.

4. For John said unto him, It is not lawful for thee to have her.

5. And when he would have put him to death, he feared the multitude, because they counted him as a prophet.

6. But when Herod's birthday was kept, the daughter of Herodias danced before them, and pleased Herod.

7. Whereupon he promised with an oath to give her whatsoever she would ask.

8. And she, being before instructed of her mother, said, Give me here John Baptist's head in a charger.

9. And the king was sorry: nevertheless for the oath's sake, and them which sat with him at meat, he commanded it to be given her.

10. And he sent, and beheaded John in the prison.

11. And his head was brought in a charger, and given to the damsel: and she brought it to her mother.

12. And his disciples came, and took up the body, and buried it, and went and told Jesus.

13. ¶ When Jesus heard of it, he departed thence by ship into a desert place apart: and when the people had heard thereof, they followed him on foot out of the cities.

14. And Jesus went forth, and saw a great multitude, and was moved with compassion toward them, and he healed their sick.

15. ¶ And when it was evening, his disciples came to him, saying, This is a desert place, and the time is now past; send the multitude away, that they may go into the villages, and buy themselves victuals.

16. But Jesus said unto them, They need not depart; give ye them to eat.

17. And they say unto him, We have here but five loaves, and two fishes.

18. He said, Bring them hither to me.

19. And he commanded the multitude to sit down on the grass, and took the five loaves, and the two fishes, and looking up to heaven, he blessed, and brake, and gave the loaves to his disciples, and the disciples to the multitude.

20. And they did all eat, and were filled: and they took up of the fragments that remained twelve baskets full.

21. And they that had eaten were about five thousand men, beside women and children.

22. ¶ And straightway Jesus constrained his disciples to get into a ship, and to go before him unto the other side, while he sent the multitudes away.

23. And when he had sent the multitudes away, he went up into a mountain apart to pray: and when the evening was come, he was there alone.

24. But the ship was now in the midst of the sea, tossed with waves: for the wind was contrary.

25. And in the fourth watch of the night Jesus went unto them, walking on the sea.

26. And when the disciples saw him

Salome

walking on the sea, they were troubled, saying, It is a spirit; and they cried out for fear.

27. But straightway Jesus spake unto them, saying, Be of good cheer; it is I; be not afraid.

28. And Peter answered him and said, Lord, if it be thou, bid me come unto thee on the water.

29. And he said, Come. And when Peter was come down out of the ship, he walked on the water, to go to Jesus.

30. But when he saw the wind boisterous, he was afraid; and beginning to sink, he cried, saying, Lord, save me.

31. And immediately Jesus stretched forth his hand, and caught him, and said unto him, O thou of little faith, wherefore didst thou doubt?

32. And when they were come into the ship, the wind ceased.

33. Then they that were in the ship came and worshipped him, saying, Of a truth thou art the Son of God.

34. ¶ And when they were gone over, they came into the land of Gennesaret.

35. And when the men of that place had knowledge of him, they sent out into all that country round about, and brought unto him all that were diseased;

36. And besought him that they might only touch the hem of his garment: and as many as touched were made perfectly whole.

CHAPTER 15

1. Then came to Jesus scribes and Pharisees, which were of Jerusalem, saying,

2. Why do thy disciples transgress the tradition of the elders? for they wash not their hands when they eat bread.

3. But he answered and said unto them, Why do ye also transgress the commandment of God by your tradition?

4. For God commanded, saying, Honour thy father and mother: and, He that curseth father or mother, let him die the death.

5. But ye say, Whosoever shall say to his father or his mother, It is a gift, by whatsoever thou mightest be profited by me;

6. And honour not his father or his mother, he shall be free. Thus have ye made the commandment of God of none effect by your tradition.

7. Ye hypocrites, well did Esaias prophesy of you, saying,

8. This people draweth nigh unto me with their mouth, and honoureth me with their lips; but their heart is far from me.

9. But in vain they do worship me, teaching for doctrines the commandments of men.

10. ¶ And he called the multitude, and said unto them, Hear, and understand:

11. Not that which goeth into the mouth defileth a man; but that which cometh out of the mouth, this defileth a man.

12. Then came his disciples, and said unto him, Knowest thou that the Pharisees were offended, after they heard this saying?

13. But he answered and said, Every plant, which my heavenly

Matt. 14:29–33 — It is instructive to note that Peter successfully walked on the water to meet Jesus until he started looking at what was happening around him (the wind was becoming "boisterous"). At that point, he started to sink in the water. How like Peter we are! How often do we pay more attention to the things that are going on around us — videos, music, television, sports, our careers, the need to please others — than we do to the Savior and His teachings?

Matt. 15:1–20 — Developing purity of soul and cleanliness of mind requires us to follow Jesus' example in consistently giving no heed to temptation and in allowing virtue to "garnish [our] thoughts unceasingly" (see Neal A. Maxwell, *One More Strain of Praise,* 66).

Matt. 15:11 — "Stay out of the gutter in your conversation. Foul talk defiles the man who speaks it" (Gordon B. Hinckley, *Teachings of Gordon B. Hinckley,* 496).

Father hath not planted, shall be rooted up.

14. Let them alone: they be blind leaders of the blind. And if the blind lead the blind, both shall fall into the ditch.

15. Then answered Peter and said unto him, Declare unto us this parable.

16. And Jesus said, Are ye also yet without understanding?

17. Do not ye yet understand, that whatsoever entereth in at the mouth goeth into the belly, and is cast out into the draught?

18. But those things which proceed out of the mouth come forth from the heart; and they defile the man.

19. For out of the heart proceed evil thoughts, murders, adulteries, fornications, thefts, false witness, blasphemies:

20. These are the things which defile a man: but to eat with unwashen hands defileth not a man.

21. ¶ Then Jesus went thence, and departed into the coasts of Tyre and Sidon.

22. And, behold, a woman of Canaan came out of the same coasts, and cried unto him, saying, Have mercy on me, O Lord, thou Son of David; my daughter is grievously vexed with a devil.

23. But he answered her not a word. And his disciples came and besought him, saying, Send her away; for she crieth after us.

24. But he answered and said, I am not sent but unto the lost sheep of the house of Israel.

25. Then came she and worshipped him, saying, Lord, help me.

26. But he answered and said, It is not meet to take the children's bread, and to cast it to dogs.

27. And she said, Truth, Lord: yet the dogs eat of the crumbs which fall from their masters' table.

28. Then Jesus answered and said unto her, O woman, great is thy faith: be it unto thee even as thou wilt. And her daughter was made whole from that very hour.

29. And Jesus departed from thence, and came nigh unto the sea of Galilee; and went up into a mountain, and sat down there.

30. And great multitudes came unto him, having with them those that were lame, blind, dumb, maimed, and many others, and cast them down at Jesus' feet; and he healed them:

31. Insomuch that the multitude wondered, when they saw the dumb to speak, the maimed to be whole, the lame to walk, and the blind to see: and they glorified the God of Israel.

32. ¶ Then Jesus called his disciples unto him, and said, I have compassion on the multitude, because they continue with me now three days, and have nothing to eat: and I will not send them away fasting, lest they faint in the way.

33. And his disciples say unto him, Whence should we have so much bread in the wilderness, as to fill so great a multitude?

34. And Jesus saith unto them, How many loaves have ye? And they said, Seven, and a few little fishes.

35. And he commanded the multitude to sit down on the ground.

36. And he took the seven loaves and the fishes, and gave thanks, and brake them, and gave to his disciples, and the disciples to the multitude.

37. And they did all eat, and were

Matt. 15:21–28 — Traditionally, it was the Jews who were entitled to the healing power; those who were Gentiles, who had not been baptized and placed under covenant, were healed only under conditions of unusual faith or devotion. In this example, the Savior delayed granting the woman's desire because she was a Gentile—but once He had determined her great faith, He bestowed the desired healing both as a reward to her and as a lesson to His disciples about the blessings that follow great faith and persistent prayer, even on behalf of those not of the chosen lineage of Israel (see Bruce R. McConkie, *Doctrinal New Testament Commentary*).

Christ feeding the multitudes

filled: and they took up of the broken meat that was left seven baskets full.

38. And they that did eat were four thousand men, beside women and children.

39. And he sent away the multitude, and took ship, and came into the coasts of Magdala.

CHAPTER 16

1. The Pharisees also with the Sadducees came, and tempting desired him that he would shew them a sign from heaven.

2. He answered and said unto them, When it is evening, ye say, It will be fair weather: for the sky is red.

3. And in the morning, It will be foul weather to day: for the sky is red and lowring. O ye hypocrites, ye can discern the face of the sky; but can ye not discern the signs of the times?

4. A wicked and adulterous generation seeketh after a sign; and there shall no sign be given unto it, but the sign of the prophet Jonas. And he left them, and departed.

5. And when his disciples were come to the other side, they had forgotten to take bread.

6. ¶ Then Jesus said unto them, Take heed and beware of the leaven of the Pharisees and of the Sadducees.

7. And they reasoned among themselves, saying, It is because we have taken no bread.

8. Which when Jesus perceived, he said unto them, O ye of little faith, why reason ye among yourselves, because ye have brought no bread?

9. Do ye not yet understand, neither remember the five loaves of the five thousand, and how many baskets ye took up?

10. Neither the seven loaves of the four thousand, and how many baskets ye took up?

11. How is it that ye do not understand that I spake it not to you concerning bread, that ye should beware of the leaven of the Pharisees and of the Sadducees?

12. Then understood they how that he bade them not beware of the leaven of bread, but of the doctrine of the Pharisees and of the Sadducees.

13. ¶ When Jesus came into the coasts of Cæsarea Philippi, he asked his disciples, saying, Whom do men say that I the Son of man am?

14. And they said, Some say that thou art John the Baptist: some, Elias; and others, Jeremias, or one of the prophets.

15. He saith unto them, But whom say ye that I am?

16. And Simon Peter answered and said, Thou art the Christ, the Son of the living God.

17. And Jesus answered and said unto him, Blessed art thou, Simon Barhona: for flesh and blood hath not revealed it unto thee, but my Father which is in heaven.

18. And I say also unto thee, That

Matt. 16:16–17—We can come to know that Jesus is the Christ in the same way Peter did—by revelation. It is the only way. It is central to the gospel plan that we receive a witness by the power of the Holy Ghost that Jesus is the Christ. This comes as we study, pray, and live His doctrine, knowing that He was indeed sent from God the Father to be the Savior of the world (see John 7:17–18). What has been your experience in gaining truth in this manner?

Matt. 16:17—Of the experience of revelation, President Lorenzo Snow wrote the following:

"Some two or three weeks after being baptized, one day while engaged in my studies, I began to reflect upon the fact that I had not obtained a knowledge of the truth of the work. . . .

"I had no sooner opened my lips in an effort to pray, than I heard a sound, just above my head, like the rustling of silken robes, and immediately the Spirit of God descended upon me, completely enveloping my whole person, filling me, from the crown of my head to the soles of my feet, and O, the joy and happiness I felt! No language can describe the almost instantaneous transition from a dense cloud of mental and spiritual darkness into a refulgence of light and knowledge, as it was at that time imparted to my understanding. I then received a perfect knowledge that God lives, that Jesus Christ is the Son of God, and of the restoration of the holy priesthood and the fullness of the Gospel. It was a complete baptism—a tangible immersion in the heavenly principle or element, the Holy Ghost; and even more real and physical in its effects upon every part of my system than the immersion by water. . . .

"I cannot tell how long I remained in the full flow of the blissful enjoyment and divine enlightenment, but it was several minutes before the celestial element which filled and surrounded me began gradually to withdraw. . . . That night, as I retired to rest, the same wonderful manifestations were repeated, and continued to be for several successive nights" (quoted in William E. Berrett and Alma P. Burton, *Readings in LDS Church History,* 1:89–90).

thou art Peter, and upon this rock I will build my church; and the gates of hell shall not prevail against it.

19. And I will give unto thee the keys of the kingdom of heaven: and whatsoever thou shalt bind on earth shall be bound in heaven: and whatsoever thou shalt loose on earth shall be loosed in heaven.

20. Then charged he his disciples that they should tell no man that he was Jesus the Christ.

21. ¶ From that time forth began Jesus to shew unto his disciples, how that he must go unto Jerusalem, and suffer many things of the elders and chief priests and scribes, and be killed, and be raised again the third day.

22. Then Peter took him, and began to rebuke him, saying, Be it far from thee, Lord: this shall not be unto thee.

23. But he turned, and said unto Peter, Get thee behind me, Satan: thou art an offence unto me: for thou savourest not the things that be of God, but those that be of men.

24. ¶ Then said Jesus unto his disciples, If any man will come after me, let him deny himself, and take up his cross, and follow me.

25. For whosoever will save his life shall lose it: and whosoever will lose his life for my sake shall find it.

26. For what is a man profited, if he shall gain the whole world, and lose his own soul? or what shall a man give in exchange for his soul?

27. For the Son of man shall come in the glory of his Father with his angels; and then he shall reward every man according to his works.

28. Verily I say unto you, There be some standing here, which shall not taste of death, till they see the Son of man coming in his kingdom.

CHAPTER 17

1. And after six days Jesus taketh Peter, James, and John his brother, and bringeth them up into an high mountain apart,

2. And was transfigured before them: and his face did shine as the sun, and his raiment was white as the light.

Notes: _____

_____

_____

_____

_____

_____

_____

_____

_____

_____

_____

_____

_____

_____

_____

_____

Matt. 16:27–28 — "We can draw the conclusion that there is to be a day when all will be judged of their works, and rewarded according to the same; that those who have kept the faith will be crowned with a crown of righteousness; be clothed in white raiment; be admitted to the marriage feast; be free from every affliction, and reign with Christ on the earth, where, according to the ancient promise, they will partake of the fruit of the vine new in the glorious kingdom with Him" (Joseph Smith, *Discourses of the Prophet Joseph Smith*, 82–83).

3. And, behold, there appeared unto them Moses and Elias talking with him.

4. Then answered Peter, and said unto Jesus, Lord, it is good for us to be here: if thou wilt, let us make here three tabernacles; one for thee, and one for Moses, and one for Elias.

5. While he yet spake, behold, a bright cloud overshadowed them: and behold a voice out of the cloud, which said, This is my beloved Son, in whom I am well pleased; hear ye him.

6. And when the disciples heard it, they fell on their face, and were sore afraid.

7. And Jesus came and touched them, and said, Arise, and be not afraid.

8. And when they had lifted up their eyes, they saw no man, save Jesus only.

9. And as they came down from the mountain, Jesus charged them, saying, Tell the vision to no man, until the Son of man be risen again from the dead.

10. And his disciples asked him, saying, Why then say the scribes that Elias must first come?

11. And Jesus answered and said unto them, Elias truly shall first come, and restore all things.

12. But I say unto you, That Elias is come already, and they knew him not, but have done unto him whatsoever they listed. Likewise shall also the Son of man suffer of them.

13. Then the disciples understood that he spake unto them of John the Baptist.

14. ¶ And when they were come to the multitude, there came to him a certain man, kneeling down to him, and saying,

15. Lord, have mercy on my son: for he is lunatick, and sore vexed: for ofttimes he falleth into the fire, and oft into the water.

16. And I brought him to thy disciples, and they could not cure him.

17. Then Jesus answered and said, O faithless and perverse generation, how long shall I be with you? how long shall I suffer you? bring him hither to me.

18. And Jesus rebuked the devil; and he departed out of him: and the child was cured from that very hour.

19. Then came the disciples to Jesus apart, and said, Why could not we cast him out?

20. And Jesus said unto them, Because of your unbelief: for verily I say unto you, If ye have faith as a grain of mustard seed, ye shall say unto this mountain, Remove hence to yonder place; and it shall remove; and nothing shall be impossible unto you.

21. Howbeit this kind goeth not out but by prayer and fasting.

22. ¶ And while they abode in Galilee, Jesus said unto them, The Son of man shall be betrayed into the hands of men:

23. And they shall kill him, and the third day he shall be raised again. And they were exceeding sorry.

24. ¶ And when they were come to Capernaum, they that received tribute money came to Peter, and said, Doth not your master pay tribute?

Matt. 17:1–9—*Transfiguration* involves a special change in both appearance and being from a lower to a higher state. Following transfiguration, which happened to a number of prophets throughout time, a person is in a most exalted and glorious state.

While we don't have all the details of what happened on the Mount of Transfiguration when Jesus and His three Apostles went up to "a high mountain apart," we do know that Jesus was strengthened and prepared for the trials that were ahead of Him. We know that the Apostles saw in vision the transfiguration of the earth as well as the death and Resurrection of the Savior; they also received special insights and blessings.

We know that Moses and Elijah—translated beings who had not tasted death—appeared and with Jesus gave the keys of the kingdom to Peter, James, and John. And we know that God the Father was present on the mountain; while His form was hidden by a cloud, the three Apostles heard His voice (see Bruce R. McConkie, *Doctrinal New Testament Commentary,* 1:400–402; *Teachings of the Prophet Joseph Smith,* 158; and Bruce R. McConkie, *Mormon Doctrine,* 718–719).

Matt. 17:10–11—"'Elias' is a title of office; every restorer, forerunner, or one sent of God to prepare the way for greater developments in the gospel plan, is an Elias. The appellative 'Elias' is in fact both a personal name and a title" (James E. Talmage, *Jesus the Christ,* 375). *Elias* is also used to designate a person who restores something of particular importance. Some have suggested that it is a composite of men who hold the title of *Elias* rather than a single individual. Others have suggested that prophets who hold the title of *Elias* include Adam, Noah, Elijah, Jesus Christ, John the Baptist, Peter, James, John the Revelator, and Joseph Smith. *Elias* also appears in the New Testament as the Greek translation of the Hebrew name *Elijah.*

Matt. 17:20—"If a man has not faith enough to do one thing, he may have faith to do another: if he cannot remove a mountain, he may heal the sick" (Joseph Smith, *History of the Church,* 5:355).

Matt. 17:22–23—Though Jesus repeatedly taught of His death and Resurrection, his disciples did not comprehend the concept of resurrection. They knew that Jesus would go to Jerusalem and die, but they didn't seem to understand what would happen after that (see Richard D. Draper, *The Lord of the Gospels: The 1990 Sperry Symposium on the New Testament,* 43).

25. He saith, Yes. And when he was come into the house, Jesus prevented him, saying, What thinkest thou, Simon? of whom do the kings of the earth take custom or tribute? of their own children, or of strangers?

26. Peter saith unto him, Of strangers. Jesus saith unto him, Then are the children free.

27. Notwithstanding, lest we should offend them, go thou to the sea, and cast an hook, and take up the fish that first cometh up; and when thou hast opened his mouth, thou shalt find a piece of money: that take, and give unto them for me and thee.

CHAPTER 18

1. At the same time came the disciples unto Jesus, saying, Who is the greatest in the kingdom of heaven?

2. And Jesus called a little child unto him, and set him in the midst of them,

3. And said, Verily I say unto you, Except ye be converted, and become as little children, ye shall not enter into the kingdom of heaven.

4. Whosoever therefore shall humble himself as this little child, the same is greatest in the kingdom of heaven.

5. And whoso shall receive one such little child in my name receiveth me.

6. But whoso shall offend one of these little ones which believe in me, it were better for him that a millstone were hanged about his neck, and that he were drowned in the depth of the sea.

7. ¶ Woe unto the world because of offences! for it must needs be that offences come; but woe to that man by whom the offence cometh!

8. Wherefore if thy hand or thy foot offend thee, cut them off, and cast them from thee: it is better for thee to enter into life halt or maimed, rather than having two hands or two feet to be cast into everlasting fire.

9. And if thine eye offend thee, pluck it out, and cast it from thee: it is better for thee to enter into life with one eye, rather than having two eyes to be cast into hell fire.

10. Take heed that ye despise not one of these little ones; for I say unto you, That in heaven their angels do always behold the face of my Father which is in heaven.

11. For the Son of man is come to save that which was lost.

12. How think ye? if a man have an hundred sheep, and one of them be gone astray, doth he not leave the ninety and nine, and goeth into the mountains, and seeketh that which is gone astray?

13. And if so be that he find it, verily I say unto you, he rejoiceth more of that sheep, than of the ninety and nine which went not astray.

14. Even so it is not the will of your Father which is in heaven, that one of these little ones should perish.

Matt. 18:1–6—"Christ would not have had His chosen representatives become childish; far from it, they had to be men of courage, fortitude, and force; but He would have them become childlike. The distinction is important. Those who belong to Christ must become like little children in obedience, truthfulness, trustfulness, purity, humility, and faith. The child is an artless, natural, trusting believer; the childish one is careless, foolish, and neglectful. . . . Whosoever shall offend, that is cause to stumble or go astray, one such child of Christ, incurs guilt so great that it would have been better for him had he met death even by violence before he had so sinned" (James E. Talmage, *Jesus the Christ,* 359).

Matt. 18:3—Conversion, taught President Gordon B. Hinckley, is not "a matter of the head only. It is a matter of the heart" (*Stand a Little Taller,* 58).

Matt. 18:6–10—Above and beyond the harming of an innocent child, this injunction from the Savior applies to those who seek to destroy the faith of any person, who seek to cause any person to lose his grip on the iron rod, or who seek to lead any person away from the word of God (see Harold B. Lee, Conference Report, Apr. 1971, 92).

Matt. 18:11–14—"The hundred sheep represent one hundred Sadducees and Pharisees . . . [the one represents] one poor publican, which the Pharisees and Sadducees despised. . . . There is joy in the presence of the angels of God over one sinner that repenteth, more than over ninety-and-nine just persons that are so [professedly] righteous; they will be damned anyhow; you cannot save them" (Joseph Smith, *History of the Church,* 5:262).

Matt. 18:12–14—As President Gordon B. Hinckley put it, the ninety and nine "will go along pretty well," but it is "the one that we need to help. . . . They are worth saving and bringing back" (*Teachings of Gordon B. Hinckley,* 539).

15. ¶ Moreover if thy brother shall trespass against thee, go and tell him his fault between thee and him alone: if he shall hear thee, thou hast gained thy brother.

16. But if he will not hear thee, then take with thee one or two more, that in the mouth of two or three witnesses every word may be established.

17. And if he shall neglect to hear them, tell it unto the church: but if he neglect to hear the church, let him be unto thee as an heathen man and a publican.

18. Verily I say unto you, Whatsoever ye shall bind on earth shall be bound in heaven: and whatsoever ye shall loose on earth shall be loosed in heaven.

19. Again I say unto you, That if two of you shall agree on earth as touching any thing that they shall ask, it shall be done for them of my Father which is in heaven.

20. For where two or three are gathered together in my name, there am I in the midst of them.

21. ¶ Then came Peter to him, and said, Lord, how oft shall my brother sin against me, and I forgive him? till seven times?

22. Jesus saith unto him, I say not unto thee, Until seven times: but, Until seventy times seven.

23. ¶ Therefore is the kingdom of heaven likened unto a certain king, which would take account of his servants.

24. And when he had begun to reckon, one was brought unto him, which owed him ten thousand talents.

25. But forasmuch as he had not to pay, his lord commanded him to be sold, and his wife, and children, and all that he had, and payment to be made.

26. The servant therefore fell down, and worshipped him, saying, Lord, have patience with me, and I will pay thee all.

27. Then the lord of that servant was moved with compassion, and loosed him, and forgave him the debt.

28. But the same servant went out, and found one of his fellowservants, which owed him an hundred pence: and he laid hands on him, and took him by the throat, saying, Pay me that thou owest.

29. And his fellowservant fell down at his feet, and besought him, saying, Have patience with me, and I will pay thee all.

30. And he would not: but went and cast him into prison, till he should pay the debt.

31. So when his fellowservants saw what was done, they were very sorry, and came and told unto their lord all that was done.

32. Then his lord, after that he had called him, said unto him, O thou wicked servant, I forgave thee all that debt, because thou desiredst me:

33. Shouldest not thou also have had compassion on thy fellowservant, even as I had pity on thee?

34. And his lord was wroth, and delivered him to the tormentors, till he should pay all that was due unto him.

35. So likewise shall my heavenly

Matt. 18:18—The keys of the kingdom are the power, right, and authority to preside over the affairs of the Church; these keys include the sealing power, which is the power to bind and seal on earth in the Lord's name with His authority. That which is bound on earth in the proper way and by the proper authority will then be ratified in heaven (see Bruce R. McConkie, *Doctrinal New Testament Commentary,* 1:389). These keys were bestowed upon Peter in his day, were restored to the Prophet Joseph Smith in this dispensation, and are held by the prophets and Apostles on the earth today, who can perform ordinances that are valid in the eternities.

"Now the great and grand secret of the whole matter, and the *summum bonum* of the whole subject that is lying before us, consists in obtaining the powers of the Holy Priesthood. . . . This, therefore, is the sealing and binding power, and, in one sense of the word, the keys of the kingdom, which consist in the key of knowledge" (*Joseph Smith's Commentary on the Bible,* 100).

Matt. 18:23–34—The message of the parable of the unmerciful servant is that we, who expect God to forgive us completely of even the greatest sins, may be unwilling to forgive others of comparatively small offenses. A talent was the equivalent of 6,000 pence, so 10,000 talents equaled 600,000 pence. Carrying this through to its conclusion, the unmerciful servant was forgiven 600,000 units, but was unwilling to forgive someone else of even one (see Spencer W. Kimball, *Faith Precedes the Miracle,* 192).

Matt. 18:34—A *tormentor* was a jailer who was allowed to beat and torture the debtor until the creditor was paid. Debtors were, at the very least, supplied the smallest amount of food—barely enough to sustain life—and beaten with a fifteen-pound chain. Some of the demonstration was intended to make the debtor's friends so sympathetic that they would pay the debt on their friend's behalf to secure his freedom (see James M. Freeman, *Manners and Customs of the Bible,* 355).

Father do also unto you, if ye from your hearts forgive not every one his brother their trespasses.

CHAPTER 19

1. And it came to pass, that when Jesus had finished these sayings, he departed from Galilee, and came into the coasts of Judæa beyond Jordan;

2. And great multitudes followed him; and he healed them there.

3. ¶ The Pharisees also came unto him, tempting him, and saying unto him, Is it lawful for a man to put away his wife for every cause?

4. And he answered and said unto them, Have ye not read, that he which made them at the beginning made them male and female,

5. And said, For this cause shall a man leave father and mother, and shall cleave to his wife: and they twain shall be one flesh?

6. Wherefore they are no more twain, but one flesh. What therefore God hath joined together, let not man put asunder.

7. They say unto him, Why did Moses then command to give a writing of divorcement, and to put her away?

8. He saith unto them, Moses because of the hardness of your hearts suffered you to put away your wives: but from the beginning it was not so.

9. And I say unto you, Whosoever shall put away his wife, except it be for fornication, and shall marry another, committeth adultery: and whoso marrieth her which is put away doth commit adultery.

10. ¶ His disciples say unto him, If the case of the man be so with his wife, it is not good to marry.

11. But he said unto them, All men cannot receive this saying, save they to whom it is given.

12. For there are some eunuchs, which were so born from their mother's womb: and there are some eunuchs, which were made eunuchs of men: and there be eunuchs, which have made themselves eunuchs for the kingdom of heaven's sake. He that is able to receive it, let him receive it.

13. ¶ Then were there brought unto him little children, that he should put his hands on them, and pray: and the disciples rebuked them.

14. But Jesus said, Suffer little children, and forbid them not, to come unto me: for of such is the kingdom of heaven.

15. And he laid his hands on them, and departed thence.

16. ¶ And, behold, one came and said unto him, Good Master, what good thing shall I do, that I may have eternal life?

17. And he said unto him, Why callest thou me good? there is none good but one, that is, God: but if thou wilt enter into life, keep the commandments.

18. He saith unto him, Which? Jesus said, Thou shalt do no murder, Thou shalt not commit adultery, Thou shalt not steal, Thou shalt not bear false witness,

Matt. 19:1–2—*Putting away a wife* was not the same as divorcing a wife; it was a Mosaic custom that did not involve judicial investigation or action by an established court (see James E. Talmage, *Jesus the Christ,* 474). The act of "putting away a wife" that Jesus spoke against caused such a woman and any subsequent husband to commit adultery, since she had not been granted a legal divorce.

Matt. 19:13–15—According to Elder Bruce R. McConkie, little children "are alive in Christ and shall have eternal life. For them the family unit will continue, and the fulness of exaltation is theirs. No blessing shall be withheld. They shall rise in immortal glory, grow to full maturity, and live forever in the highest heaven of the celestial kingdom" (*Ensign,* Apr. 1977, 3). Elder McConkie clarified:

• A child is an adult in a newly born body.

• We are adults before we are born into mortality, and we are adults after our death.

• All children are pure and innocent at birth because of the Atonement.

• Joseph Smith taught that children will inherit the celestial kingdom.

• Children who die before the age of accountability will marry and live in family units.

• Children who die before the age of accountability will not be tested or tempted in paradise or during the millennium.

• The same conditions apply to those who are mentally deficient, regardless of their age, for they are as little children.

Joseph Smith taught, "The Lord takes many away, even in infancy, that they may escape the envy of man, and the sorrows and evils of this present world; they were too pure, too lovely, to live on earth" (*Teachings of the Prophet Joseph Smith,* 197).

19. Honour thy father and thy mother: and, Thou shalt love thy neighbour as thyself.

20. The young man saith unto him, All these things have I kept from my youth up: what lack I yet?

21. Jesus said unto him, If thou wilt be perfect, go and sell that thou hast, and give to the poor, and thou shalt have treasure in heaven: and come and follow me.

22. But when the young man heard that saying, he went away sorrowful: for he had great possessions.

23. ¶ Then said Jesus unto his disciples, Verily I say unto you, That a rich man shall hardly enter into the kingdom of heaven.

24. And again I say unto you, It is easier for a camel to go through the eye of a needle, than for a rich man to enter into the kingdom of God.

25. When his disciples heard it, they were exceedingly amazed, saying, Who then can be saved?

26. But Jesus beheld them, and said unto them, With men this is impossible; but with God all things are possible.

27. ¶ Then answered Peter and said unto him, Behold, we have forsaken all, and followed thee; what shall we have therefore?

28. And Jesus said unto them, Verily I say unto you, That ye which have followed me, in the regeneration when the Son of man shall sit in the throne of his glory, ye also shall sit upon twelve thrones, judging the twelve tribes of Israel.

29. And every one that hath forsaken houses, or brethren, or sisters, or father, or mother, or wife, or children, or lands, for my name's sake, shall receive an hundredfold, and shall inherit everlasting life.

30. But many that are first shall be last; and the last shall be first.

CHAPTER 20

1. For the kingdom of heaven is like unto a man that is an householder, which went out early in the morning to hire labourers into his vineyard.

2. And when he had agreed with the labourers for a penny a day, he sent them into his vineyard.

3. And he went out about the third hour, and saw others standing idle in the marketplace,

4. And said unto them; Go ye also into the vineyard, and whatsoever is right I will give you. And they went their way.

5. Again he went out about the sixth and ninth hour, and did likewise.

6. And about the eleventh hour he went out, and found others standing idle, and saith unto them, Why stand ye here all the day idle?

7. They say unto him, Because no man hath hired us. He saith unto them, Go ye also into the vineyard; and whatsoever is right, that shall ye receive.

8. So when even was come, the lord

Matt. 19:24—Throughout His parables and other teachings, the Savior often used hyperbole (exaggeration) to make a point. Such is likely the case here. Many biblical scholars believe that the Savior was referring to a small gate in the city wall known as "the eye of the needle"; in order to pass through the gate, the camel had to be on its knees, and all its goods had to be unloaded. In other words, it was difficult, but not entirely impossible, for a camel to go through the eye of a needle. The message here seems to be that worldly riches make it more difficult, but certainly not impossible, to keep the perspectives that contribute to exaltation.

Matt. 19:27–29—"Let us here observe, that a religion that does not require the sacrifice of all things never has power sufficient to produce the faith necessary unto life and salvation. . . . When a man has offered in sacrifice all that he has for the truth's sake, not even withholding his life, and believing before God that he has been called to make this sacrifice because he seeks to do his will, he does know, most assuredly, that God does and will accept his sacrifice and offering, and that he has not, nor will not seek his face in vain. Under these circumstances, then, he can obtain the faith necessary for him to lay hold on eternal life" (Joseph Smith, *Lectures on Faith,* 69).

Matt. 19:28—According to Elder Bruce R. McConkie, the Twelve will judge the righteous (those resurrected in the first resurrection); the Savior alone will judge the wicked (those who come forth in the second resurrection) (see *Doctrinal New Testament Commentary,* 3:577).

Matt. 19:30—There is not a pay scale in the celestial kingdom. The poorest and lowliest servant and the most accomplished Apostle both receive all that the Father has if each has met the requirement.

of the vineyard saith unto his steward, Call the labourers, and give them their hire, beginning from the last unto the first.

9. And when they came that were hired about the eleventh hour, they received every man a penny.

10. But when the first came, they supposed that they should have received more; and they likewise received every man a penny.

11. And when they had received it, they murmured against the goodman of the house,

12. Saying, These last have wrought but one hour, and thou hast made them equal unto us, which have borne the burden and heat of the day.

13. But he answered one of them, and said, Friend, I do thee no wrong: didst not thou agree with me for a penny?

14. Take that thine is, and go thy way: I will give unto this last, even as unto thee.

15. Is it not lawful for me to do what I will with mine own? Is thine eye evil, because I am good?

16. So the last shall be first, and the first last: for many be called, but few chosen.

17. ¶ And Jesus going up to Jerusalem took the twelve disciples apart in the way, and said unto them,

18. Behold, we go up to Jerusalem; and the Son of man shall be betrayed unto the chief priests and unto the scribes, and they shall condemn him to death,

19. And shall deliver him to the Gentiles to mock, and to scourge, and to crucify him: and the third day he shall rise again.

20. Then came to him the mother of Zebedee's children with her sons, worshipping him, and desiring a certain thing of him.

21. And he said unto her, What wilt thou? She saith unto him, Grant that these my two sons may sit, the one on thy right hand, and the other on the left, in thy kingdom.

22. But Jesus answered and said, Ye know not what ye ask. Are ye able to drink of the cup that I shall drink of, and to be baptized with the baptism that I am baptized with? They say unto him, We are able.

23. And he saith unto them, Ye shall drink indeed of my cup, and be baptized with the baptism that I am baptized with: but to sit on my right hand, and on my left, is not mine to give, but it shall be given to them for whom it is prepared of my Father.

24. And when the ten heard it, they were moved with indignation against the two brethren.

25. But Jesus called them unto him, and said, Ye know that the princes of the Gentiles exercise dominion over them, and they that are great exercise authority upon them.

26. But it shall not be so among you: but whosoever will be great among you, let him be your minister;

27. And whosoever will be chief among you, let him be your servant:

28. Even as the Son of man came not to be ministered unto, but to minister, and to give his life a ransom for many.

29. And as they departed from Jericho, a great multitude followed him.

30. ¶ And, behold, two blind men

Notes: _____

Matt. 20:20–28—Service is not something we merely endure in the hope of gaining salvation. The celestial kingdom consists of service—and our salvation is intertwined with the salvation of others, making service the path that leads to eternal life.

sitting by the way side, when they heard that Jesus passed by, cried out, saying, Have mercy on us, O Lord, thou Son of David.

31. And the multitude rebuked them, because they should hold their peace: but they cried the more, saying, Have mercy on us, O Lord, thou Son of David.

32. And Jesus stood still, and called them, and said, What will ye that I shall do unto you?

33. They say unto him, Lord, that our eyes may be opened.

34. So Jesus had compassion on them, and touched their eyes: and immediately their eyes received sight, and they followed him.

CHAPTER 21

1. And when they drew nigh unto Jerusalem, and were come to Bethphage, unto the mount of Olives, then sent Jesus two disciples,

2. Saying unto them, Go into the village over against you, and straightway ye shall find an ass tied, and a colt with her: loose them, and bring them unto me.

3. And if any man say ought unto you, ye shall say, The Lord hath need of them; and straightway he will send them.

4. All this was done, that it might be fulfilled which was spoken by the prophet, saying,

5. Tell ye the daughter of Sion, Behold, thy King cometh unto thee, meek, and sitting upon an ass, and a colt the foal of an ass.

6. And the disciples went, and did as Jesus commanded them,

7. And brought the ass, and the colt, and put on them their clothes, and they set him thereon.

8. And a very great multitude spread their garments in the way; others cut down branches from the trees, and strawed them in the way.

9. And the multitudes that went before, and that followed, cried, saying, Hosanna to the Son of David: Blessed is he that cometh in the name of the Lord; Hosanna in the highest.

10. And when he was come into Jerusalem, all the city was moved, saying, Who is this?

11. And the multitude said, This is Jesus the prophet of Nazareth of Galilee.

12. ¶ And Jesus went into the temple of God, and cast out all them that sold and bought in the temple, and overthrew the tables of the moneychangers, and the seats of them that sold doves,

13. And said unto them, It is written, My house shall be called the house of prayer; but ye have made it a den of thieves.

14. And the blind and the lame came to him in the temple; and he healed them.

15. And when the chief priests and scribes saw the wonderful things that he did, and the children crying in the temple, and saying, Hosanna to the Son of David; they were sore displeased,

16. And said unto him, Hearest thou what these say? And Jesus saith unto them, Yea; have ye never read, Out of the mouth of babes and sucklings thou hast perfected praise?

17. ¶ And he left them, and went out of the city into Bethany; and he lodged there.

18. Now in the morning as he returned into the city, he hungered.

Matt. 20:29–34 — We are told that the blind who were healed, receiving their sight, "followed him" (verse 34). When we "follow Him," keeping His commandments and obeying His precepts, we receive our spiritual sight, sight that will bring us eternal life.

Matt. 21:2–7 — In His triumphal entry to Jerusalem, the Savior rode a white ass or colt. White animals were reserved for princes, judges, prophets, or other people of privilege and high standing; by entering the city on a white animal, Jesus verified that He was its king.

Matt. 21:8 — Anciently, people traditionally waved palm branches to welcome kings or revered visitors. It was also tradition that flowers, branches, carpets, and garments were strewn on the ground as a sign of great honor and respect for conquerors and royalty. The *garments* in this verse refer to large outer mantles, somewhat like cloaks or coats (see James M. Freeman, *Manners and Customs of the Bible,* 358–59).

Matt. 21:9 — The word *hosanna* is a Greek form of the Hebrew expression for "Save us now" (see James E. Talmage, *Jesus the Christ,* 486). According to Truman G. Madsen, combining this word with the waving of palm branches had two meanings: first, it was a plea for redemption; second, it was a plea that Jesus accept the invitation to visit Jerusalem and its temple (see *Joseph Smith the Prophet,* 75).

Matt. 21:12–17 — Elder Bruce R. McConkie taught that "righteous anger" is an attribute of God, whose anger is "everlastingly kindled" against the wicked (*Mormon Doctrine,* 37). "The incident of Christ's forcible clearing of the temple is a contradiction of the traditional conception of Him as of One so gentle and unassertive in demeanor as to appear unmanly. Gentle He was, and patient under affliction, merciful and long-suffering in dealing with contrite sinners, yet stern and inflexible in the presence of hypocrisy, and unsparing in His denunciation of persistent evil-doers. . . . He, who often wept with compassion, at other times evinced in word and action the righteous anger of a God" (James E. Talmage, *Jesus the Christ,* 148).

19. And when he saw a fig tree in the way, he came to it, and found nothing thereon, but leaves only, and said unto it, Let no fruit grow on thee henceforward for ever. And presently the fig tree withered away.

20. And when the disciples saw it, they marvelled, saying, How soon is the fig tree withered away!

21. Jesus answered and said unto them, Verily I say unto you, If ye have faith, and doubt not, ye shall not only do this which is done to the fig tree, but also if ye shall say unto this mountain, Be thou removed, and be thou cast into the sea; it shall be done.

22. And all things, whatsoever ye shall ask in prayer, believing, ye shall receive.

23. ¶ And when he was come into the temple, the chief priests and the elders of the people came unto him as he was teaching, and said, By what authority doest thou these things? and who gave thee this authority?

24. And Jesus answered and said unto them, I also will ask you one thing, which if ye tell me, I in like wise will tell you by what authority I do these things.

25. The baptism of John, whence was it? from heaven, or of men? And they reasoned with themselves, saying, If we shall say, From heaven; he will say unto us, Why did ye not then believe him?

26. But if we shall say, Of men; we fear the people; for all hold John as a prophet.

27. And they answered Jesus, and said, We cannot tell. And he said unto them, Neither tell I you by what authority I do these things.

28. ¶ But what think ye? A certain man had two sons; and he came to the first, and said, Son, go work to day in my vineyard.

29. He answered and said, I will not: but afterward he repented, and went.

30. And he came to the second, and said likewise. And he answered and said, I go, sir: and went not.

31. Whether of them twain did the will of his father? They say unto him, The first. Jesus saith unto them, Verily I say unto you, That the publicans and the harlots go into the kingdom of God before you.

32. For John came unto you in the way of righteousness, and ye believed him not: but the publicans and the harlots believed him: and ye, when ye had seen it, repented not afterward, that ye might believe him.

33. ¶ Hear another parable: There was a certain householder, which planted a vineyard, and hedged it round about, and digged a winepress in it, and built a tower, and let it out to husbandmen, and went into a far country:

34. And when the time of the fruit drew near, he sent his servants to the husbandmen, that they might receive the fruits of it.

Matt. 21:18–22—The fig tree is still very common in Palestine, and its fruit is well known and esteemed. There are three basic kinds of fig trees in the East: 1) the early fig, which ripens at the end of June; 2) the summer fig, which ripens in August; and 3) the winter fig, which ripens after the leaves have fallen from the tree and whose fruit is larger and darker; it is often not harvested until spring. In all cases, the fruit begins to develop before the leaves, so it would stand to reason that a fig tree with leaves would also have fruit. In this case, there was no fruit (see James E. Talmage, *Jesus the Christ,* 501). By cursing the barren fig tree, Jesus:

• demonstrated that He had the power to destroy.

• showed that He had control over all things.

• showed the fate of the nation that had rejected Him: "The leafy, fruitless tree was a symbol of Judaism, which loudly proclaimed itself as the only true religion of the age, and condescendingly invited all the world to come and partake of its rich ripe fruit; when in truth it was but an unnatural growth of leaves, with no fruit of the season" (James E. Talmage, *Jesus the Christ,* 142).

Matt. 21:23–27—From the beginning to our day, it is essential that any who teach or administer do so with the proper authority; in order to be binding in heaven, our actions on earth need to be performed by one who has authority to speak and act for the Father.

Matt. 21:28–32—The chief priests, scribes, Pharisees, and elders were like the second son; when told to labor in the vineyard, he said he would, but did not. As a result, the vineyard was overgrown, and whatever poor fruit matured was left to fall on the ground and rot. The publicans and sinners on whom the first group vented their contempt were like the first son; after initially ignoring the Father's call, they repented and went to work, trying with all their might to make amends for the time they had lost and for their arrogant attitude in initially refusing the call (see James E. Talmage, *Jesus the Christ,* 494).

35. And the husbandmen took his servants, and beat one, and killed another, and stoned another.

36. Again, he sent other servants more than the first: and they did unto them likewise.

37. But last of all he sent unto them his son, saying, They will reverence my son.

38. But when the husbandmen saw the son, they said among themselves, This is the heir; come, let us kill him, and let us seize on his inheritance.

39. And they caught him, and cast him out of the vineyard, and slew him.

40. When the lord therefore of the vineyard cometh, what will he do unto those husbandmen?

41. They say unto him, He will miserably destroy those wicked men, and will let out his vineyard unto other husbandmen, which shall render him the fruits in their seasons.

42. Jesus saith unto them, Did ye never read in the scriptures, The stone which the builders rejected, the same is become the head of the corner: this is the Lord's doing, and it is marvellous in our eyes?

43. Therefore say I unto you, The kingdom of God shall be taken from you, and given to a nation bringing forth the fruits thereof.

44. And whosoever shall fall on this stone shall be broken: but on whomsoever it shall fall, it will grind him to powder.

45. And when the chief priests and Pharisees had heard his parables, they perceived that he spake of them.

46. But when they sought to lay hands on him, they feared the multitude, because they took him for a prophet.

CHAPTER 22

1. And Jesus answered and spake unto them again by parables, and said,

2. The kingdom of heaven is like unto a certain king, which made a marriage for his son,

3. And sent forth his servants to call them that were bidden to the wedding: and they would not come.

4. Again, he sent forth other servants, saying, Tell them which are bidden, Behold, I have prepared my dinner: my oxen and my fatlings are killed, and all things are ready: come unto the marriage.

5. But they made light of it, and went their ways, one to his farm, another to his merchandise:

6. And the remnant took his servants, and entreated them spitefully, and slew them.

7. But when the king heard thereof, he was wroth: and he sent forth his armies, and destroyed those murderers, and burned up their city.

8. Then saith he to his servants, The wedding is ready, but they which were bidden were not worthy.

9. Go ye therefore into the highways, and as many as ye shall find, bid to the marriage.

10. So those servants went out into the highways, and gathered together all as many as they found,

Matt. 21:33–46—The parable of the wicked husbandmen (symbolized by the corrupt priests, elders, scribes, and Pharisees of the Savior's day) represents Heavenly Father's dealings with men from the days of Adam through the Second Coming.

Notes: _____

_____

_____

_____

_____

_____

_____

_____

_____

_____

_____

_____

_____

_____

_____

_____

_____

Matt. 22:1–14—The parable of the marriage of the king's son teaches that we will not be qualified to enter the celestial kingdom unless we have been cleansed of all worldly filth and have taken upon ourselves the name of Christ, represented in the parable by the garment (see Mark E. Petersen, *Abraham: Friend of God*, 112).

both bad and good: and the wedding was furnished with guests.

11. ¶ And when the king came in to see the guests, he saw there a man which had not on a wedding garment:

12. And he saith unto him, Friend, how camest thou in hither not having a wedding garment? And he was speechless.

13. Then said the king to the servants, Bind him hand and foot, and take him away, and cast him into outer darkness; there shall be weeping and gnashing of teeth.

14. For many are called, but few are chosen.

15. ¶ Then went the Pharisees, and took counsel how they might entangle him in his talk.

16. And they sent out unto him their disciples with the Herodians, saying, Master, we know that thou art true, and teachest the way of God in truth, neither carest thou for any man: for thou regardest not the person of men.

17. Tell us therefore, What thinkest thou? Is it lawful to give tribute unto Cæsar, or not?

18. But Jesus perceived their wickedness, and said, Why tempt ye me, ye hypocrites?

19. Shew me the tribute money. And they brought unto him a penny.

20. And he saith unto them, Whose is this image and superscription?

21. They say unto him, Cæsar's. Then saith he unto them, Render therefore unto Cæsar the things which are Cæsar's; and unto God the things that are God's.

22. When they had heard these words, they marvelled, and left him, and went their way.

23. ¶ The same day came to him the Sadducees, which say that there is no resurrection, and asked him,

24. Saying, Master, Moses said, If a man die, having no children, his brother shall marry his wife, and raise up seed unto his brother.

25. Now there were with us seven brethren: and the first, when he had married a wife, deceased, and, having no issue, left his wife unto his brother:

26. Likewise the second also, and the third, unto the seventh.

27. And last of all the woman died also.

28. Therefore in the resurrection whose wife shall she be of the seven? for they all had her.

29. Jesus answered and said unto them, Ye do err, not knowing the scriptures, nor the power of God.

30. For in the resurrection they neither marry, nor are given in marriage, but are as the angels of God in heaven.

31. But as touching the resurrection of the dead, have ye not read that which was spoken unto you by God, saying,

32. I am the God of Abraham, and the God of Isaac, and the God of Jacob? God is not the God of the dead, but of the living.

33. And when the multitude heard this, they were astonished at his doctrine.

34. ¶ But when the Pharisees had heard that he had put the Sadducees to silence, they were gathered together.

Matt. 22:15–22 — "Every human being is stamped with the image and superscription of God, however blurred and indistinct the line may have become through the corrosion or attrition of sin; and as unto Caesar should be rendered the coins upon which his effigy appeared, so unto God should be given the souls that bear His image. Render unto the world the stamped pieces that are made legally current by the insignia of worldly powers, and give unto God and His service, yourselves—the divine mintage of His eternal realm" (James E. Talmage, *Jesus the Christ*, 506).

Matt. 22:17 — This was a loaded question. Had the Savior answered that it was not lawful to pay taxes to Caesar, he would have been guilty of treason, and could have been put to death. If he had answered the opposite—that it was lawful to pay taxes to Caesar—he would have stirred up the anger of the Jews, who were burdened by heavy taxation after being conquered by the Romans. Neither answer was safe, so the Savior answered by asking His tempters His own question (see Boyd K. Packer, *Teach Ye Diligently*, 66–68).

Notes: _____

_____

_____

_____

_____

_____

_____

_____

_____

_____

_____

_____

_____

_____

_____

_____

_____

_____

35. Then one of them, which was a lawyer, asked him a question, tempting him, and saying,
36. Master, which is the great commandment in the law?
37. Jesus said unto him, Thou shalt love the Lord thy God with all thy heart, and with all thy soul, and with all thy mind.
38. This is the first and great commandment.
39. And the second is like unto it, Thou shalt love thy neighbour as thyself.
40. On these two commandments hang all the law and the prophets.
41. ¶ While the Pharisees were gathered together, Jesus asked them,
42. Saying, What think ye of Christ? whose son is he? They say unto him, The Son of David.
43. He saith unto them, How then doth David in spirit call him Lord, saying,
44. The Lord said unto my Lord, Sit thou on my right hand, till I make thine enemies thy footstool?
45. If David then call him Lord, how is he his son?
46. And no man was able to answer him a word, neither durst any man from that day forth ask him any more questions.

CHAPTER 23

1. Then spake Jesus to the multitude, and to his disciples,
2. Saying, The scribes and the Pharisees sit in Moses' seat:
3. All therefore whatsoever they bid you observe, that observe and do; but do not ye after their works: for they say, and do not.
4. For they bind heavy burdens and grievous to be borne, and lay them on men's shoulders; but they themselves will not move them with one of their fingers.
5. But all their works they do for to be seen of men: they make broad their phylacteries, and enlarge the borders of their garments,
6. And love the uppermost rooms at feasts, and the chief seats in the synagogues,
7. And greetings in the markets, and to be called of men, Rabbi, Rabbi.
8. But be not ye called Rabbi: for one is your Master, even Christ; and all ye are brethren.
9. And call no man your father upon the earth: for one is your Father, which is in heaven.
10. Neither be ye called masters: for one is your Master, even Christ.
11. But he that is greatest among you shall be your servant.
12. And whosoever shall exalt himself shall be abased; and he that shall humble himself shall be exalted.

Matt. 22:37–40 — "The gospel teaches us to love our neighbor as ourselves, and if we will do that, we will not be distressed, we will not have our feelings wounded, part of us will not be well-to-do while others are living in poverty. If we love our neighbor as ourselves, we will all do our full part, and our Heavenly Father has promised us blessings in return" (George Albert Smith, *The Teachings of George Albert Smith*, 135).

"All that has been revealed for the salvation of man from the beginning to our own time is circumscribed, included in, and a part of these two great laws. If we love the Lord with all the heart, with all the soul, and with all the mind, and our neighbors as ourselves, then there is nothing more to be desired. Then we will be in harmony with the total of sacred law" (Joseph Fielding Smith, Conference Report, Apr. 1943, 12).

Matt. 22:42 — The Pharisees responded as they did because Mary, the mother of Jesus, was a direct descendant of King David.

According to President David O. McKay, this question is "the most vital, the most far reaching query in this unsettled, distracted world. . . . What you sincerely in your heart think of Christ will determine what you are" (Conference Report, Apr. 1951, 93).

Matt. 23:11 — Jesus was teaching the people and His disciples to follow a pathway diverging from the course of the hypocritical scribes and Pharisees who were obsessed with station and the honors of men. Leadership is all about service. The term *servant leader* is really the operant mode in leadership. One cannot lead or influence others unless he or she is perceived as one who serves and cares about those who are led. Think of the Church leaders whom you have come to admire in your lifetime. What qualities stand out to you in their service?

Matt. 23:12 — Without humility there is no growth. Humility is the beginning virtue of exaltation. Humility is that quality that brings into our hearts a love of our fellowmen and a feeling of connectedness to all mankind. Humility causes us to relate to God in prayerful gratitude and love because we realize that we are His children, and we acknowledge our dependence on Him.

13. ¶ But woe unto you, scribes and Pharisees, hypocrites! for ye shut up the kingdom of heaven against men: for ye neither go in yourselves, neither suffer ye them that are entering to go in.

14. Woe unto you, scribes and Pharisees, hypocrites! for ye devour widows' houses, and for a pretence make long prayer: therefore ye shall receive the greater damnation.

15. Woe unto you, scribes and Pharisees, hypocrites! for ye compass sea and land to make one proselyte, and when he is made, ye make him twofold more the child of hell than yourselves.

16. Woe unto you, ye blind guides, which say, Whosoever shall swear by the temple, it is nothing; but whosoever shall swear by the gold of the temple, he is a debtor!

17. Ye fools and blind: for whether is greater, the gold, or the temple that sanctifieth the gold?

18. And, Whosoever shall swear by the altar, it is nothing; but whosoever sweareth by the gift that is upon it, he is guilty.

19. Ye fools and blind: for whether is greater, the gift, or the altar that sanctifieth the gift?

20. Whoso therefore shall swear by the altar, sweareth by it, and by all things thereon.

21. And whoso shall swear by the temple, sweareth by it, and by him that dwelleth therein.

22. And he that shall swear by heaven, sweareth by the throne of God, and by him that sitteth thereon.

23. Woe unto you, scribes and Pharisees, hypocrites! for ye pay tithe of mint and anise and cummin, and have omitted the weightier matters of the law, judgment, mercy, and faith: these ought ye to have done, and not to leave the other undone.

24. Ye blind guides, which strain at a gnat, and swallow a camel.

25. Woe unto you, scribes and Pharisees, hypocrites! for ye make clean the outside of the cup and of the platter, but within they are full of extortion and excess.

26. Thou blind Pharisee, cleanse first that which is within the cup and platter, that the outside of them may be clean also.

27. Woe unto you, scribes and Pharisees, hypocrites! for ye are like unto whited sepulchres, which indeed appear beautiful outward, but are within full of dead men's bones, and of all uncleanness.

28. Even so ye also outwardly appear righteous unto men, but within ye are full of hypocrisy and iniquity.

29. Woe unto you, scribes and Pharisees, hypocrites! because ye build the tombs of the prophets, and garnish the sepulchres of the righteous,

30. And say, If we had been in the days of our fathers, we would not have been partakers with them in the blood of the prophets.

31. Wherefore ye be witnesses unto yourselves, that ye are the children of them which killed the prophets.

32. Fill ye up then the measure of your fathers.

Matt. 23:13–39—We aren't certain of the exact origin of the term *Pharisee*, but it is likely that it derived from the Hebrew word *parash*, which means something very similar to the concept of "separatist." With their strict observance of the law of Moses, they actually did consider themselves to be set apart from the rest of the Jews.

The Pharisees believed that men were accountable for their actions, but that God predestined some things. They also believed in angels and demons, which set them apart from the Sadducees.

Usually scholars and preachers rather than priests, they accepted both the written and oral laws and were mildly anti-Roman in their political beliefs. The Pharisees were the only Jewish sect to survive the Jewish revolt against Rome shortly after Jesus was crucified; modern-day Judaism descended from the Pharisees (see Kent P. Jackson and Robert L. Millet, eds., *Studies in Scripture, Vol. 5: The Gospels,* 22–24).

Matt. 23:24—"There is so much to learn about the great eternal verities which shape our destiny that it seems a shame to turn our attention everlastingly to the minutiae and insignificant things. . . . There is such a thing as getting so tied up with little fly specks on the great canvas which depicts the whole plan of salvation that we lose sight of what the life and the light and the glory of eternal reward are all about" (Bruce R. McConkie, *Doctrines of the Restoration,* 232).

Matt. 23:25—The word *hypocrite* describes a person who pretends to have beliefs or principles that he does not have, or who pretends to be what he isn't; it is especially descriptive of one who pretends to be religious or virtuous when, in fact, he is not.

Matt. 23:29–33—As President Boyd K. Packer pointed out, people who will not sustain and uphold their bishop or their stake president will not sustain and uphold the prophet and president of the Church (see *Brigham Young University Speeches of the Year,* March 23, 1965, 5). The Lord's servants are His representatives in the priesthood offices in the ward, stake, and general Church organization—something we should keep in mind "when we are tempted to disregard our presiding authorities, bishops, quorum and stake presidents, etc." (Marion G. Romney, Conference Report, Oct. 1960, 73).

33. Ye serpents, ye generation of vipers, how can ye escape the damnation of hell?

34. ¶ Wherefore, behold, I send unto you prophets, and wise men, and scribes: and some of them ye shall kill and crucify; and some of them shall ye scourge in your synagogues, and persecute them from city to city:

35. That upon you may come all the righteous blood shed upon the earth, from the blood of righteous Abel unto the blood of Zacharias son of Barachias, whom ye slew between the temple and the altar.

36. Verily I say unto you, All these things shall come upon this generation.

37. O Jerusalem, Jerusalem, thou that killest the prophets, and stonest them which are sent unto thee, how often would I have gathered thy children together, even as a hen gathereth her chickens under her wings, and ye would not!

38. Behold, your house is left unto you desolate.

39. For I say unto you, Ye shall not see me henceforth, till ye shall say, Blessed is he that cometh in the name of the Lord.

CHAPTER 24

1. And Jesus went out, and departed from the temple: and his disciples came to him for to shew him the buildings of the temple.

2. And Jesus said unto them, See ye not all these things? verily I say unto you, There shall not be left here one stone upon another, that shall not be thrown down.

3. ¶ And as he sat upon the mount of Olives, the disciples came unto him privately, saying, Tell us, when shall these things be? and what shall be the sign of thy coming, and of the end of the world?

4. And Jesus answered and said unto them, Take heed that no man deceive you.

5. For many shall come in my name, saying, I am Christ; and shall deceive many.

6. And ye shall hear of wars and rumours of wars: see that ye be not troubled: for all these things must come to pass, but the end is not yet.

7. For nation shall rise against nation, and kingdom against kingdom: and there shall be famines, and pestilences, and earthquakes, in divers places.

8. All these are the beginning of sorrows.

Matt. 23:34–36—In commenting on the failure of the Jews to save their ancestors and for slaying Zacharias, Joseph Smith said, "Hence as they possessed greater privileges than any other generation, not only pertaining to themselves, but to their dead, their sin was greater, as they not only neglected their own salvation but that of their progenitors, and hence their blood was required at their hands" (*History of the Church*, 4:599).

Matt. 24—This discourse, which the Savior gave on the Mount of Olives, is known as the Olivet Discourse, and is one of the most complete discussions of the Second Coming that was ever given by Jesus Himself.

Matt. 24:1—By choosing the destruction of the temple as His illustration, the Savior aptly taught that a seemingly solid, stable nation would be overthrown, even if it did not at the time seem possible. To the disciples who looked at the temple, it was no wonder that they marveled at the idea that it could be destroyed. A single stone was nine feet broad, seven and a half feet high, and sixty-seven and a half feet long. The pillars that supported the porches were crafted from a single stone and were more than thirty-seven feet high. But, as we know, the mighty temple was eventually destroyed and its stones scattered, just as the nation was destroyed and scattered (see Bruce R. McConkie, *Doctrinal New Testament Commentary*, 1:637).

Matt. 24:6–8—"The wars and desolations of our day will make the hostilities of the past seem like feeble skirmishes among childish combatants" (Bruce R. McConkie, *The Mortal Messiah*, 3:441).

Matt. 24:7—General Omar Bradley stated, "With the monstrous weapons man already has, humanity is in danger of being trapped in this world by its moral adolescence. Our knowledge of science has clearly outstripped our capacity to control it. (We have too many men of science; too few men of God.) We have grasped the mystery of the atom and rejected the Sermon on the Mount. Man is stumbling blindly through a spiritual darkness while toying with the precarious secrets of life and death. The world has achieved brilliance without wisdom, power without conscience. Ours is a world of nuclear giants and ethical infants. We know more about war than we know about peace; more about killing than we know about living" (quoted in Hugh B. Brown, *Continuing the Quest*, 254–55).

9. Then shall they deliver you up to be afflicted, and shall kill you: and ye shall be hated of all nations for my name's sake.

10. And then shall many be offended, and shall betray one another, and shall hate one another.

11. And many false prophets shall rise, and shall deceive many.

12. And because iniquity shall abound, the love of many shall wax cold.

13. But he that shall endure unto the end, the same shall be saved.

14. And this gospel of the kingdom shall be preached in all the world for a witness unto all nations; and then shall the end come.

15. When ye therefore shall see the abomination of desolation, spoken of by Daniel the prophet, stand in the holy place, (whoso readeth, let him understand:)

16. Then let them which be in Judæa flee into the mountains:

17. Let him which is on the housetop not come down to take any thing out of his house:

18. Neither let him which is in the field return back to take his clothes.

19. And woe unto them that are with child, and to them that give suck in those days!

20. But pray ye that your flight be not in the winter, neither on the sabbath day:

21. For then shall be great tribulation, such as was not since the beginning of the world to this time, no, nor ever shall be.

22. And except those days should be shortened, there should no flesh be saved: but for the elect's sake those days shall be shortened.

23. Then if any man shall say unto you, Lo, here is Christ, or there; believe it not.

24. For there shall arise false Christs, and false prophets, and shall shew great signs and wonders; insomuch that, if it were possible, they shall deceive the very elect.

25. Behold, I have told you before.

26. Wherefore if they shall say unto you, Behold, he is in the desert; go not forth: behold, he is in the secret chambers; believe it not.

27. For as the lightning cometh out of the east, and shineth even unto the west; so shall also the coming of the Son of man be.

28. For wheresoever the carcase is, there will the eagles be gathered together.

29. ¶ Immediately after the tribulation of those days shall the sun be darkened, and the moon shall not give her light, and the stars shall fall from heaven, and the powers of the heavens shall be shaken:

30. And then shall appear the sign of the Son of man in heaven: and then shall all the tribes of the earth mourn, and they shall see the Son

Matt. 24:12—"A diet of violence or pornography dulls the senses, and future exposures need to be rougher and more extreme. Soon the person is desensitized and is unable to react in a sensitive, caring, responsible manner, especially to those in his own home and family" (Marvin J. Ashton, *Ensign*, Nov. 1977, 71).

Matt. 24:13—The "burning that destroys every corruptible thing is the same burning that cleanses the righteous. Evil and sin and dross will be burned out of their souls because they qualify to abide the day, even though all their works have not been as those of Enoch and Elijah. If only perfect people were saved, there would be only one saved soul—the Lord Jesus" (Bruce R. McConkie, *The Millennial Messiah*, 544).

Matt. 24:23–27—"Among the requirements that God has laid upon us is to pay heed to His living prophets, [something that] will be particularly hard in ours, the final dispensation. . . . The reasons for the hardness of this doctrine are quite simple: First, these are the winding-up times when there will be a dramatic convergence of the growth of the Church and an intensification of evil in the world—all of which will make for some real wrenching. Second, the degree of deceit will be so great that even the very elect will be almost deceived (Matt. 24:24). Third, the tribulations will be such that, as the Savior said, they will exceed the tribulations of any other time" (Neal A. Maxwell, *All These Things Shall Give Thee Experience*, 101–102).

Matt. 24:29—The Joseph Smith Translation makes clear that the signs listed in this verse will occur after the abomination of desolation sweeps Jerusalem for the *second time*—in other words, at almost the very hour of the Second Coming. The original siege of Jerusalem—in which the Roman legions slaughtered 1.1 million Jews, destroyed the temple, and flattened the city—was simply a prelude. In the final destruction, the entire world will be at war, and every modern weapon will be used, but Jerusalem will be the center of the conflict (see Bruce R. McConkie, *Doctrinal New Testament Commentary*, 1:659, 678).

of man coming in the clouds of heaven with power and great glory.

31. And he shall send his angels with a great sound of a trumpet, and they shall gather together his elect from the four winds, from one end of heaven to the other.

32. Now learn a parable of the fig tree; When his branch is yet tender, and putteth forth leaves, ye know that summer is nigh:

33. So likewise ye, when ye shall see all these things, know that it is near, even at the doors.

34. Verily I say unto you, This generation shall not pass, till all these things be fulfilled.

35. Heaven and earth shall pass away, but my words shall not pass away.

36. ¶ But of that day and hour knoweth no man, no, not the angels of heaven, but my Father only.

37. But as the days of Noe were, so shall also the coming of the Son of man be.

38. For as in the days that were before the flood they were eating and drinking, marrying and giving in marriage, until the day that Noe entered into the ark,

39. And knew not until the flood came, and took them all away; so shall also the coming of the Son of man be.

40. Then shall two be in the field; the one shall be taken, and the other left.

41. Two women shall be grinding at the mill; the one shall be taken, and the other left.

42. ¶ Watch therefore: for ye know not what hour your Lord doth come.

43. But know this, that if the goodman of the house had known in what watch the thief would come, he would have watched, and would not have suffered his house to be broken up.

44. Therefore be ye also ready: for in such an hour as ye think not the Son of man cometh.

45. Who then is a faithful and wise servant, whom his lord hath made ruler over his household, to give them meat in due season?

46. Blessed is that servant, whom his lord when he cometh shall find so doing.

47. Verily I say unto you, That he shall make him ruler over all his goods.

48. But and if that evil servant shall say in his heart, My lord delayeth his coming;

49. And shall begin to smite his fellowservants, and to eat and drink with the drunken;

50. The lord of that servant shall come in a day when he looketh not for him, and in an hour that he is not aware of,

51. And shall cut him asunder, and appoint him his portion with the hypocrites: there shall be weeping and gnashing of teeth.

Matt. 24:30–31 — "Then will appear one grand sign of the Son of Man in heaven. But what will the world do? They will say it is a planet, a comet, etc. But the Son of Man will come as the sign of the coming of the Son of Man, which will be as the light of the morning cometh out of the east" (Joseph Smith; see D&C 88:93).

Matt. 24:32–33 — The "summer" Jesus talked about is "now upon us." We need to take care that we continue to nourish our individual testimony so that it will not be withered and scorched at the coming events (see Neal A. Maxwell, *All These Things Shall Give Thee Experience*, 123).

Matt. 24:36 — The Joseph Smith Translation of Mark 13:32 makes clear that Jesus — who knows all things — knows the exact time of His return (see Bruce R. McConkie, *Doctrinal New Testament Commentary*, 1:667). The important thing we gain from His answer is that there will be many signs, yet His coming will come when many least expect it (see Kent P. Jackson and Robert L. Millet, eds., *Studies in Scripture, Vol. 5: The Gospels*, 398).

Matt. 24:37 — Our day is similar to that of Noah. Many believe that the heavens are sealed and that revelation has ceased. Many do not believe in God, and many are unprepared. And, as Elder Sterling W. Sill observed, "even though the combined sins of Sodom, Babylon, and ancient Rome all glare at us from our own newspaper headlines, yet we are far from changing our ways" (*Improvement Era*, June 1966, 503).

Matt. 24:40–41 — When the earth is transfigured (see D&C 63:20–21), those who will remain on it will be those who are living at the least a law that will allow them to inherit the terrestrial kingdom. When the earth becomes a celestial sphere, only those who will inherit the celestial kingdom will be allowed to remain on it.

Matt. 24:42–51 — "For those who truly love the Lord, the 'when' of the Second Coming really does not matter. They are not faithful simply because He may come in judgment any minute; they keep the commandments because they love the truth and want to do what is right" ("Not Even the Angels Know Time of the Second Coming," *Church News*, Feb. 11, 1989).

CHAPTER 25

1. Then shall the kingdom of heaven be likened unto ten virgins, which took their lamps, and went forth to meet the bridegroom.
2. And five of them were wise, and five were foolish.
3. They that were foolish took their lamps, and took no oil with them:
4. But the wise took oil in their vessels with their lamps.
5. While the bridegroom tarried, they all slumbered and slept.
6. And at midnight there was a cry made, Behold, the bridegroom cometh; go ye out to meet him.
7. Then all those virgins arose, and trimmed their lamps.
8. And the foolish said unto the wise, Give us of your oil; for our lamps are gone out.
9. But the wise answered, saying, Not so; lest there be not enough for us and you: but go ye rather to them that sell, and buy for yourselves.
10. And while they went to buy, the bridegroom came; and they that were ready went in with him to the marriage: and the door was shut.
11. Afterward came also the other virgins, saying, Lord, Lord, open to us.
12. But he answered and said, Verily I say unto you, I know you not.
13. Watch therefore, for ye know neither the day nor the hour wherein the Son of man cometh.
14. ¶ For the kingdom of heaven is as a man travelling into a far country, who called his own servants, and delivered unto them his goods.
15. And unto one he gave five talents, to another two, and to another one; to every man according to his several ability; and straightway took his journey.
16. Then he that had received the five talents went and traded with the same, and made them other five talents.
17. And likewise he that had received two, he also gained other two.
18. But he that had received one went and digged in the earth, and hid his lord's money.
19. After a long time the lord of those servants cometh, and reckoneth with them.
20. And so he that had received five talents came and brought other five talents, saying, Lord, thou deliveredst unto me five talents: behold, I have gained beside them five talents more.
21. His lord said unto him, Well done, thou good and faithful servant: thou hast been faithful over a few things, I will make thee ruler over many things: enter thou into the joy of thy lord.
22. He also that had received two talents came and said, Lord, thou deliveredst unto me two talents: behold, I have gained two other talents beside them.
23. His lord said unto him, Well done, good and faithful servant; thou hast been faithful over a few things, I will make thee ruler over many things: enter thou into the joy of thy lord.
24. Then he which had received the one talent came and said, Lord, I knew thee that thou art an hard man, reaping where thou hast not sown, and gathering where thou hast not strawed:
25. And I was afraid, and went

Matt. 25:1–13 — "The parable of the ten virgins is intended to represent the second coming of the Son of man, the coming of the Bridegroom to meet the bride, the Church, the Lamb's wife, in the last days; and I expect that the Savior was about right when he said, in reference to the members of the church, that five of them were wise and five were foolish; for when the Lord of heaven comes in power and great glory to reward every man according to the deeds done in the body, if he finds one-half of those professing to be members of his Church prepared for salvation, it will be as many as can be expected, judging by the course that many are pursuing" (Wilford Woodruff, *Journal of Discourses*, 18:110).

Matt. 25:3–4 — The oil represents the Holy Ghost. Those who are prepared, then, are those whose lives are filled with the Holy Ghost (see Joseph Fielding McConkie and Donald W. Parry, *A Guide to Scriptural Symbols*, 88).

Matt. 25:8–9 — "This Church has before it many close places through which it will have to pass before the work of God is crowned with victory. . . . The difficulties will be of such a character that the man or woman who does not possess this personal knowledge or witness will fall. . . . The time will come when no man nor woman will be able to endure on borrowed light. Each will have to be guided by the light within himself" (Orson F. Whitney, *Life of Heber C. Kimball*, 449–450).

Matt. 25:21 — In the Savior's parable of the talents, the Lord made clear that each individual receives an appropriate endowment of talents and gifts. It's not the quantity of talents that counts, but the results—how they are applied in order to magnify the results. We catch a glimpse of the grand feelings of satisfaction we will experience if we can endure to the end in valor and righteousness, having served in faith and devotion, and at last be welcomed by the Lord and Master with acceptance and rejoicing.

Ultimately, the Savior will welcome the good and faithful home again with confirming and acceptance and blessings of greater joy. In smaller but still significant measure, we can lift up and encourage others along the highways and byways of life by frequently recognizing their good desires and efforts and by praising them with sincerity and genuine respect for their service in Zion. How have you been able to bless the lives of others by recognizing the ways in which they have been a "good and faithful servant"?

and hid thy talent in the earth: lo, there thou hast that is thine.

26. His lord answered and said unto him, Thou wicked and slothful servant, thou knewest that I reap where I sowed not, and gather where I have not strawed:

27. Thou oughtest therefore to have put my money to the exchangers, and then at my coming I should have received mine own with usury.

28. Take therefore the talent from him, and give it unto him which hath ten talents.

29. For unto every one that hath shall be given, and he shall have abundance: but from him that hath not shall be taken away even that which he hath.

30. And cast ye the unprofitable servant into outer darkness: there shall be weeping and gnashing of teeth.

31. ¶ When the Son of man shall come in his glory, and all the holy angels with him, then shall he sit upon the throne of his glory:

32. And before him shall be gathered all nations: and he shall separate them one from another, as a shepherd divideth his sheep from the goats:

33. And he shall set the sheep on his right hand, but the goats on the left.

34. Then shall the King say unto them on his right hand, Come, ye blessed of my Father, inherit the kingdom prepared for you from the foundation of the world:

35. For I was an hungred, and ye gave me meat: I was thirsty, and ye gave me drink: I was a stranger, and ye took me in:

36. Naked, and ye clothed me: I was sick, and ye visited me: I was in prison, and ye came unto me.

37. Then shall the righteous answer him, saying, Lord, when saw we thee an hungred, and fed thee? or thirsty, and gave thee drink?

38. When saw we thee a stranger, and took thee in? or naked, and clothed thee?

39. Or when saw we thee sick, or in prison, and came unto thee?

40. And the King shall answer and say unto them, Verily I say unto you, Inasmuch as ye have done it unto one of the least of these my brethren, ye have done it unto me.

41. Then shall he say also unto them on the left hand, Depart from me, ye cursed, into everlasting fire, prepared for the devil and his angels:

42. For I was an hungred, and ye gave me no meat: I was thirsty, and ye gave me no drink:

43. I was a stranger, and ye took me not in: naked, and ye clothed me not: sick, and in prison, and ye visited me not.

44. Then shall they also answer him, saying, Lord, when saw we thee an hungred, or athirst, or a stranger, or naked, or sick, or in prison, and did not minister unto thee?

45. Then shall he answer them, saying, Verily I say unto you, Inas-

Matt. 25:14–30—"Without a strict observance of all [God's] divine requirements, you may at last be found wanting. And if so, you will admit that your lot will be cast among the unprofitable servants. We beseech you therefore, brethren, to improve upon all things committed to your charge, that you lose not your reward" (Joseph Smith, *Joseph Smith's Commentary on the Bible,* 113–14).

Matt. 25:32–33—During the day, while in the pasture, sheep and goats are allowed to mingle, but because they do not graze well together, they must be separated in the evening. The goats prefer the young leaves of trees, while the sheep prefer grass; the goats are happy to eat during the hottest part of the day, while the sheep look for a shady spot in which to lie down. There are other important differences between them as well. Goats are more playful, bolder, more vigorous, more apt to climb to dangerous places, and more difficult to control. So while they—like the righteous and the wicked—may be together for a time, there will come a point when they will be separated (see Fred H. Wight, *Manners and Customs of Bible Lands,* 166–67, and James M. Freeman, *Manners and Customs of the Bible,* 379).

Matt. 25:40—In the Savior's parable of the sheep and the goats, we learn that our service to God's children is truly our service to God. When we serve one of the "least," we serve one of the greatest, for *all* of God's children—even the most marginal and forgotten—are majestic sons and daughters of the Almighty, worthy in every respect of our attention and love. To remember them and serve them is to remember and serve the Lord. In His ministry, the Savior went out of His way to serve the downtrodden, the rejected, those despised of the leading classes.

"Jesus comes to meet us. To welcome him, let us go to him.

"He comes to us in the hungry, the naked, the lonely, the alcoholic, the drug addict, the prostitute, the street beggars.

"He may come to you or me in a father who is alone, in a mother, in a brother, or in a sister.

"If we reject them, if we do not go out to meet them, we reject Jesus himself" (*Mother Teresa: In My Own Words,* 29).

much as ye did it not to one of the least of these, ye did it not to me.

46. And these shall go away into everlasting punishment: but the righteous into life eternal.

CHAPTER 26

1. And it came to pass, when Jesus had finished all these sayings, he said unto his disciples,

2. Ye know that after two days is the feast of the passover, and the Son of man is betrayed to be crucified.

3. Then assembled together the chief priests, and the scribes, and the elders of the people, unto the palace of the high priest, who was called Caiaphas,

4. And consulted that they might take Jesus by subtilty, and kill him.

5. But they said, Not on the feast day, lest there be an uproar among the people.

6. ¶ Now when Jesus was in Bethany, in the house of Simon the leper,

7. There came unto him a woman having an alabaster box of very precious ointment, and poured it on his head, as he sat at meat.

8. But when his disciples saw it, they had indignation, saying, To what purpose is this waste?

9. For this ointment might have been sold for much, and given to the poor.

10. When Jesus understood it, he said unto them, Why trouble ye the woman? for she hath wrought a good work upon me.

11. For ye have the poor always with you; but me ye have not always.

12. For in that she hath poured this ointment on my body, she did it for my burial.

13. Verily I say unto you, Wheresoever this gospel shall be preached in the whole world, there shall also this, that this woman hath done, be told for a memorial of her.

14. ¶ Then one of the twelve, called Judas Iscariot, went unto the chief priests,

15. And said unto them, What will ye give me, and I will deliver him unto you? And they covenanted with him for thirty pieces of silver.

16. And from that time he sought opportunity to betray him.

17. ¶ Now the first day of the feast of unleavened bread the disciples came to Jesus, saying unto him, Where wilt thou that we prepare for thee to eat the passover?

18. And he said, Go into the city to such a man, and say unto him, The Master saith, My time is at hand; I will keep the passover at thy house with my disciples.

19. And the disciples did as Jesus had appointed them; and they made ready the passover.

20. Now when the even was come, he sat down with the twelve.

21. And as they did eat, he said, Verily I say unto you, that one of you shall betray me.

22. And they were exceeding sorrowful, and began every one of them to say unto him, Lord, is it I?

23. And he answered and said, He

Matt. 26:7—The word *sat* would be more accurately expressed as *reclined,* because it was the custom of the day for guests at a meal to recline on a bed covered with cushions or pillows. Guests leaned on the elbow of one arm and reached for food with the other hand (see James M. Freeman, *Manners and Customs of the Bible,* 383).

Matt. 26:7, 9—During the times of Jesus, oil was common and was very inexpensive. Ointment, on the other hand, was difficult to obtain and was usually very expensive.

Matt. 26:15—Thirty pieces of silver, "of many times greater purchasing power with the Jews in that day than now with us, was the price fixed by the law as that of a slave" (James E. Talmage, *Jesus the Christ,* 548).

Matt. 26:17–20—John intimates that the last supper "occurred before the Feast of the Passover (John 13:1, 2). . . . John also specifies that the day of the crucifixion was 'the preparation of the passover' (19:14), and that the next day, which was Saturday, the Sabbath, 'was an high day' (verse 31), that is a Sabbath rendered doubly sacred because of its being also a feast day" (James E. Talmage, *Jesus the Christ,* 572).

The most important religious act of the year was the offering of the Passover lamb. The lamb was subjected to intense examination; it had to be a first-year male, and had to be completely free of any blemish. It had to be killed on the fourteenth of the month without a single bone being broken, and it had to be roasted with fire. It was eaten by the entire family in great haste, and any leftovers were burned in the fire instead of being saved for the next day (see Fred H. Wight, *Manners and Customs of Bible Lands,* 164).

that dippeth his hand with me in the dish, the same shall betray me.

24. The Son of man goeth as it is written of him: but woe unto that man by whom the Son of man is betrayed! it had been good for that man if he had not been born.

25. Then Judas, which betrayed him, answered and said, Master, is it I? He said unto him, Thou hast said.

26. ¶ And as they were eating, Jesus took bread, and blessed it, and brake it, and gave it to the disciples, and said, Take, eat; this is my body.

27. And he took the cup, and gave thanks, and gave it to them, saying, Drink ye all of it;

28. For this is my blood of the new testament, which is shed for many for the remission of sins.

29. But I say unto you, I will not drink henceforth of this fruit of the vine, until that day when I drink it new with you in my Father's kingdom.

30. And when they had sung an hymn, they went out into the mount of Olives.

31. Then saith Jesus unto them, All ye shall be offended because of me this night: for it is written, I will smite the shepherd, and the sheep of the flock shall be scattered abroad.

32. But after I am risen again, I will go before you into Galilee.

33. Peter answered and said unto him, Though all men shall be offended because of thee, yet will I never be offended.

34. Jesus said unto him, Verily I say unto thee, That this night, before the cock crow, thou shalt deny me thrice.

35. Peter said unto him, Though I should die with thee, yet will I not deny thee. Likewise also said all the disciples.

36. ¶ Then cometh Jesus with them unto a place called Gethsemane, and saith unto the disciples, Sit ye here, while I go and pray yonder.

37. And he took with him Peter and the two sons of Zebedee, and began to be sorrowful and very heavy.

38. Then saith he unto them, My soul is exceeding sorrowful, even unto death: tarry ye here, and watch with me.

39. And he went a little further, and fell on his face, and prayed, saying, O my Father, if it be possible, let this cup pass from me: nevertheless not as I will, but as thou wilt.

40. And he cometh unto the disciples, and findeth them asleep, and

Matt. 26:21–25 — Some have theorized that because Judas associated with the Savior, his betrayal caused him to become a son of perdition. President Joseph F. Smith disagreed with that assumption: "To my mind it strongly appears that not one of the disciples possessed sufficient light, knowledge nor wisdom, at the time of the crucifixion, for either exaltation or condemnation. . . . But not knowing that Judas did commit the unpardonable sin; nor that he was a 'son of perdition without hope' who will die the second death, nor what knowledge he possessed by which he was able to commit so great a sin, I prefer, until I know better, to take the merciful view that he may be numbered among those for whom the blessed Master prayed, 'Father, forgive them; for they know not what they do'" (*Gospel Doctrine*, 5th ed., 433–35).

Matt. 26:26–28 — The Savior instituted the sacrament among His disciples just before His experience in Gethsemane and Golgotha. This "new testament" or "new covenant" was established by the Savior that we might remember Him and apply the Atonement in our lives through repentance and by following gospel principles. Since this scripture was given before His atoning sacrifice, and He had not yet been "broken," He blessed the bread first and then broke it. When the resurrected Lord visited the Saints on the American continent, He broke the bread first—because He had already accomplished His atoning sacrifice—and then He blessed it (see 3 Ne. 18:3).

"Who is there among us that does not wound his spirit by word, thought, or deed, from Sabbath to Sabbath? We do things for which we are sorry, and desire to be forgiven, or we have erred against someone and given injury. If there is a feeling in our hearts that we are sorry for what we have done; if there is a feeling in our souls that we would like to be forgiven, then the method to obtain forgiveness is not through rebaptism . . . but it is to repent of our sins, to go to those against whom we have sinned or transgressed and obtain their forgiveness, and then repair to the sacrament table where, if we have sincerely repented and put ourselves in proper condition, we shall be forgiven, and spiritual healing will come to our souls" (Melvin J. Ballard, *Improvement Era*, 22:1026).

Matt. 26:31–35 — "An indication of the strength of our testimonies is the degree to which we demonstrate our loyalty to the Savior and our loyalty to the principles which He taught" (Spencer J. Condie, *In Perfect Balance*, 193).

saith unto Peter, What, could ye not watch with me one hour?

41. Watch and pray, that ye enter not into temptation: the spirit indeed is willing, but the flesh is weak.

42. He went away again the second time, and prayed, saying, O my Father, if this cup may not pass away from me, except I drink it, thy will be done.

43. And he came and found them asleep again: for their eyes were heavy.

44. And he left them, and went away again, and prayed the third time, saying the same words.

45. Then cometh he to his disciples, and saith unto them, Sleep on now, and take your rest: behold, the hour is at hand, and the Son of man is betrayed into the hands of sinners.

46. Rise, let us be going: behold, he is at hand that doth betray me.

47. ¶ And while he yet spake, lo, Judas, one of the twelve, came, and with him a great multitude with swords and staves, from the chief priests and elders of the people.

48. Now he that betrayed him gave them a sign, saying, Whomsoever I shall kiss, that same is he: hold him fast.

49. And forthwith he came to Jesus, and said, Hail, master; and kissed him.

50. And Jesus said unto him, Friend, wherefore art thou come? Then came they, and laid hands on Jesus, and took him.

51. And, behold, one of them which were with Jesus stretched out his hand, and drew his sword, and struck a servant of the high priest's, and smote off his ear.

52. Then said Jesus unto him, Put up again thy sword into his place: for all they that take the sword shall perish with the sword.

53. Thinkest thou that I cannot now pray to my Father, and he shall presently give me more than twelve legions of angels?

54. But how then shall the scriptures be fulfilled, that thus it must be?

55. In that same hour said Jesus to the multitudes, Are ye come out as against a thief with swords and staves for to take me? I sat daily with you teaching in the temple, and ye laid no hold on me.

56. But all this was done, that the scriptures of the prophets might be fulfilled. Then all the disciples forsook him, and fled.

57. ¶ And they that had laid hold on Jesus led him away to Caiaphas the high priest, where the scribes and the elders were assembled.

58. But Peter followed him afar off unto the high priest's palace, and went in, and sat with the servants, to see the end.

59. Now the chief priests, and elders, and all the council, sought false witness against Jesus, to put him to death;

60. But found none: yea, though many false witnesses came, yet found they none. At the last came two false witnesses,

61. And said, This fellow said, I am able to destroy the temple of God, and to build it in three days.

62. And the high priest arose, and said unto him, Answerest thou nothing? what is it which these witness against thee?

63. But Jesus held his peace. And the high priest answered and said

Matt. 26:36–46—"Christ's agony in the garden is unfathomable by the finite mind, both as to intensity and cause. The thought that He suffered through fear of death is untenable. Death to Him was preliminary to resurrection and triumphal return to the Father from whom He had come, and to a state of glory even beyond what He had before possessed; and, moreover, it was within His power to lay down His life voluntarily. He struggled and groaned under a burden such as no other being who had lived on earth might even conceive as possible. It was not physical pain, nor mental anguish alone, that caused Him to suffer such torture as to produce an extrusion of blood from every pore; but a spiritual agony of soul such as only God was capable of experiencing. No other man, however great his powers of physical or mental endurance, could have suffered so; for his human organism would have succumbed, and syncope would have produced unconsciousness and welcome oblivion. In that hour of anguish Christ met and overcame all the horrors that Satan, 'the prince of this world,' could inflict. . . .

"In some manner, actual and terribly real though to man incomprehensible, the Savior took upon Himself the burden of the sins of mankind from Adam to the end of the world. . . .

"The further tragedy of the night, and the cruel inflictions that awaited Him on the morrow, to culminate in the frightful tortures of the cross, could not exceed the bitter anguish through which He had successfully passed" (James E. Talmage, *Jesus the Christ,* 568).

Matt. 26:48—A kiss was the most "traitorous token" that could have been chosen for the betrayal. For millennia—certainly among the Jews of the day, and even among the prophets of old—a kiss was a token of love and fellowship of pure religion (see Bruce R. McConkie, *Doctrinal New Testament Commentary,* 1:781).

Matt. 26:57–68—Much of what Jesus went through during His trial, in the presence of the Sanhedrin, occurred illegally during the night. Because trials were forbidden by law at night, the same group reconvened in the morning to go through the ritual of a formal trial then (see Bruce R. McConkie, *Doctrinal New Testament Commentary,* 1:175–76). The Sanhedrin consisted of seventy-one ordained scholars, including Levites, priests, scribes, Pharisees, Sadducees, and some people of other political persuasion.

unto him, I adjure thee by the living God, that thou tell us whether thou be the Christ, the Son of God.

64. Jesus saith unto him, Thou hast said: nevertheless I say unto you, Hereafter shall ye see the Son of man sitting on the right hand of power, and coming in the clouds of heaven.

65. Then the high priest rent his clothes, saying, He hath spoken blasphemy; what further need have we of witnesses? behold, now ye have heard his blasphemy.

66. What think ye? They answered and said, He is guilty of death.

67. Then did they spit in his face, and buffeted him; and others smote him with the palms of their hands,

68. Saying, Prophesy unto us, thou Christ, Who is he that smote thee?

69. ¶ Now Peter sat without in the palace: and a damsel came unto him, saying, Thou also wast with Jesus of Galilee.

70. But he denied before them all, saying, I know not what thou sayest.

71. And when he was gone out into the porch, another maid saw him, and said unto them that were there, This fellow was also with Jesus of Nazareth.

72. And again he denied with an oath, I do not know the man.

73. And after a while came unto him they that stood by, and said to Peter, Surely thou also art one of them; for thy speech betrayeth thee.

74. Then began he to curse and to swear, saying, I know not the man. And immediately the cock crew.

75. And Peter remembered the word of Jesus, which said unto him, Before the cock crow, thou shalt deny me thrice. And he went out, and wept bitterly.

CHAPTER 27

1. When the morning was come, all the chief priests and elders of the people took counsel against Jesus to put him to death:

2. And when they had bound him, they led him away, and delivered him to Pontius Pilate the governor.

3. ¶ Then Judas, which had betrayed him, when he saw that he was condemned, repented himself, and brought again the thirty pieces of silver to the chief priests and elders,

4. Saying, I have sinned in that I have betrayed the innocent blood. And they said, What is that to us? see thou to that.

5. And he cast down the pieces of silver in the temple, and departed, and went and hanged himself.

6. And the chief priests took the silver pieces, and said, It is not lawful for to put them into the treasury, because it is the price of blood.

7. And they took counsel, and bought with them the potter's field, to bury strangers in.

8. Wherefore that field was called, The field of blood, unto this day.

9. Then was fulfilled that which was spoken by Jeremy the prophet,

Matt. 26:67—During the time of the Savior, spitting in the face was considered the most grievous insult possible and the utmost contempt that could be expressed. *Buffeted* means that those present struck the Savior with their fists; normally, men who quarreled struck each other with open palms instead (see James M. Freeman, *Manners and Customs of the Bible,* 389).

Matt. 26:69–75—Peter "proved himself unequal for the trial; but afterwards he gained power. . . . And if we could read in detail the life of Abraham, or the lives of other great and holy men, we would doubtless find that their efforts to be righteous were not always crowned with success. Hence we should not be discouraged if we should be overcome in a weak moment; but, on the contrary, straightway repent of the error or the wrong we may have committed, and as far as possible repair it, and then seek to God for renewed strength to go on and do better" (Lorenzo Snow, *Journal of Discourses,* 20:190).

Matt. 27:1—Even though "the chief priests and elders" were supposedly the spiritual leaders of Judaism, they violated the law in a dozen ways in their treatment of Jesus. Some of the violations included:

• Every trial was to be held during daylight hours.

• Every trial was to be held in a room of the temple.

• A trial could not be held the day before the Sabbath.

• No person could be convicted on the basis of his own testimony.

• If two witnesses disagreed, the accused was to be acquitted.

• If the judges were unanimous in their conviction, the accused was to be acquitted (since it meant he had no advocate in the court).

• A prisoner could not be convicted and executed on the same day.

All of these laws, and others, were violated in the case of Jesus (see Gerald N. Lund, *New Testament Symposium,* 1984, 27).

Matt. 27:3–10—"There is an apparent discrepancy between the account of Judas Iscariot's death given by Matthew (27:3–10) and that in Acts (1:16–20). According to the first, Judas hanged himself; the second states that he fell headlong, 'and all his bowels gushed out.' If both records be accurate, the wretched man probably hanged himself, and afterward fell, possibly through the breaking of the cord or branch to which it was attached" (James E. Talmage, *Jesus the Christ,* 602).

saying, And they took the thirty pieces of silver, the price of him that was valued, whom they of the children of Israel did value;

10. And gave them for the potter's field, as the Lord appointed me.

11. And Jesus stood before the governor: and the governor asked him, saying, Art thou the King of the Jews? And Jesus said unto him, Thou sayest.

12. And when he was accused of the chief priests and elders, he answered nothing.

13. Then said Pilate unto him, Hearest thou not how many things they witness against thee?

14. And he answered him to never a word; insomuch that the governor marvelled greatly.

15. Now at that feast the governor was wont to release unto the people a prisoner, whom they would.

16. And they had then a notable prisoner, called Barabbas.

17. Therefore when they were gathered together, Pilate said unto them, Whom will ye that I release unto you? Barabbas, or Jesus which is called Christ?

18. For he knew that for envy they had delivered him.

19. ¶ When he was set down on the judgment seat, his wife sent unto him, saying, Have thou nothing to do with that just man: for I have suffered many things this day in a dream because of him.

20. But the chief priests and elders persuaded the multitude that they should ask Barabbas, and destroy Jesus.

21. The governor answered and said unto them, Whether of the twain will ye that I release unto you? They said, Barabbas.

22. Pilate saith unto them, What shall I do then with Jesus which is called Christ? They all say unto him, Let him be crucified.

23. And the governor said, Why, what evil hath he done? But they cried out the more, saying, Let him be crucified.

24. ¶ When Pilate saw that he could prevail nothing, but that rather a tumult was made, he took water, and washed his hands before the multitude, saying, I am innocent of the blood of this just person: see ye to it.

25. Then answered all the people, and said, His blood be on us, and on our children.

26. ¶ Then released he Barabbas unto them: and when he had scourged Jesus, he delivered him to be crucified.

27. Then the soldiers of the governor took Jesus into the common hall, and gathered unto him the whole band of soldiers.

28. And they stripped him, and put on him a scarlet robe.

29. ¶ And when they had platted a crown of thorns, they put it upon his head, and a reed in his right hand: and they bowed the knee before him, and mocked him, saying, Hail, King of the Jews!

30. And they spit upon him, and took the reed, and smote him on the head.

31. And after that they had mocked him, they took the robe off from him, and put his own raiment on him, and led him away to crucify him.

32. And as they came out, they

Matt. 27:11–14 — The Sanhedrin "led Jesus, bound, to the judgment hall of Pontius Pilate; but with strict scrupulosity they refrained from entering the hall lest they become defiled; for the judgment chamber was part of the house of a Gentile, and somewhere therein might be leavened bread, even to be near which would render them ceremonially unclean. Let every one designate for himself the character of men afraid of the mere proximity of leaven, while thirsting for innocent blood!" (James E. Talmage, *Jesus the Christ*, 632).

Matt. 27:15 — It was Jewish custom to punish criminals during the major feasts, since there would be many more people on hand to witness the punishment than there would normally have been. Many scholars believe that the privilege of demanding the release of a prisoner was given in instructions to Pilate, since normally the governor could not do such a thing; only the emperor could pardon a condemned criminal (see James M. Freeman, *Manners and Customs of the Bible*, 391).

Matt. 27:24 — "Pilate knew what was right but lacked the moral courage to do it. He was afraid of the Jews, and more afraid of hostile influence at Rome. He was afraid of his conscience, but more afraid of losing his official position" (James E. Talmage, *Jesus the Christ*, 601).

Matt. 27:25 — The Jews cried that the Savior's blood be upon them. Almost in answer, "some thirty years later, and on that very spot, was judgment pronounced against some of the best in Jerusalem; and among the 3,600 victims of the governor's fury, of whom not a few were scourged and crucified right over against the Pretorium, were many of the noblest of the citizens of Jerusalem. . . . A few years more, and hundreds of crosses bore Jewish mangled bodies within sight of Jerusalem. And still have these wanderers seemed to bear, from century to century, and from land to land, that burden of blood; and still does it seem to weigh 'on us and our children'" (James E. Talmage, *Jesus the Christ*, 600).

Matt. 27:24–38 — "Death by crucifixion was at once the most lingering and most painful of all forms of execution. The victim lived in ever increasing torture. . . . The spikes so cruelly driven through hands and feet penetrated and crushed sensitive nerves and quivering tendons, yet inflicted no moral wound. The welcome relief of death came through the exhaustion caused by intense and unremitting pain" (James E. Talmage, *Jesus the Christ*, 607).

found a man of Cyrene, Simon by name: him they compelled to bear his cross.

33. And when they were come unto a place called Golgotha, that is to say, a place of a skull,

34. ¶ They gave him vinegar to drink mingled with gall: and when he had tasted thereof, he would not drink.

35. And they crucified him, and parted his garments, casting lots: that it might be fulfilled which was spoken by the prophet, They parted my garments among them, and upon my vesture did they cast lots.

36. And sitting down they watched him there;

37. And set up over his head his accusation written, THIS IS JESUS THE KING OF THE JEWS.

38. Then were there two thieves crucified with him, one on the right hand, and another on the left.

39. ¶ And they that passed by reviled him, wagging their heads,

40. And saying, Thou that destroyest the temple, and buildest it in three days, save thyself. If thou be the Son of God, come down from the cross.

41. Likewise also the chief priests mocking him, with the scribes and elders, said,

42. He saved others; himself he cannot save. If he be the King of Israel, let him now come down from the cross, and we will believe him.

43. He trusted in God; let him deliver him now, if he will have him: for he said, I am the Son of God.

44. The thieves also, which were crucified with him, cast the same in his teeth.

45. Now from the sixth hour there was darkness over all the land unto the ninth hour.

46. And about the ninth hour Jesus cried with a loud voice, saying, Eli, Eli, lama sabachthani? that is to say, My God, my God, why hast thou forsaken me?

47. Some of them that stood there, when they heard that, said, This man calleth for Elias.

48. And straightway one of them ran, and took a spunge, and filled it with vinegar, and put it on a reed, and gave him to drink.

49. The rest said, Let be, let us see whether Elias will come to save him.

50. ¶ Jesus, when he had cried again with a loud voice, yielded up the ghost.

51. And, behold, the veil of the temple was rent in twain from the top to the bottom; and the earth did quake, and the rocks rent;

52. And the graves were opened; and many bodies of the saints which slept arose,

53. And came out of the graves after his resurrection, and went into the holy city, and appeared unto many.

54. Now when the centurion, and they that were with him, watching Jesus, saw the earthquake, and those things that were done, they feared greatly, saying, Truly this was the Son of God.

55. And many women were there beholding afar off, which followed

Matt. 27:34—The gall that was offered to Jesus contained a substance that would help deaden His pain. As Elder Bruce R. McConkie taught, "Jesus tasted but did not drink; he chose to suffer and die with a clear mind and his senses unimpaired" (*Doctrinal New Testament Commentary,* 1:817).

Matt. 27:46—"It seems, that in addition to the fearful suffering incident to crucifixion, the agony of Gethsemane had recurred, intensified beyond human power to endure. In that bitterest hour the dying Christ was alone, alone in most terrible reality. That the supreme sacrifice of the Son might be consummated in all its fulness, the Father seems to have withdrawn the support of His immediate Presence, leaving to the Savior of men the glory of complete victory over the forces of sin and death" (James E. Talmage, *Jesus the Christ,* 612).

Matt. 27:49—This reference to Elias was a mocking one. According to Jewish tradition, Elias (Elijah) had often appeared to save those who were in great danger (see Bruce R. McConkie, *Doctrinal New Testament Commentary,* 1:828).

Matt. 27:52–53—According to Elder Bruce R. McConkie, all those who were resurrected with Christ—as well as all who have since been resurrected—came forth with celestial bodies and have an inheritance in the celestial kingdom (see D&C 88:96–102) (see *Mormon Doctrine,* 639).

Matt. 27:54—The centurion and soldiers had witnessed the crucifixion from beginning to end. They, along with a number of Galilean witnesses, recognized too late that the man they had crucified truly was the Son of God.

Jesus from Galilee, ministering unto him:

56. Among which was Mary Magdalene, and Mary the mother of James and Joses, and the mother of Zebedee's children.

57. When the even was come, there came a rich man of Arimathæa, named Joseph, who also himself was Jesus' disciple:

58. He went to Pilate, and begged the body of Jesus. Then Pilate commanded the body to be delivered.

59. And when Joseph had taken the body, he wrapped it in a clean linen cloth,

60. And laid it in his own new tomb, which he had hewn out in the rock: and he rolled a great stone to the door of the sepulchre, and departed.

61. And there was Mary Magdalene, and the other Mary, sitting over against the sepulchre.

62. ¶ Now the next day, that followed the day of the preparation, the chief priests and Pharisees came together unto Pilate,

63. Saying, Sir, we remember that that deceiver said, while he was yet alive, After three days I will rise again.

64. Command therefore that the sepulchre be made sure until the third day, lest his disciples come by night, and steal him away, and say unto the people, He is risen from the dead: so the last error shall be worse than the first.

65. Pilate said unto them, Ye have a watch: go your way, make it as sure as ye can.

66. So they went, and made the sepulchre sure, sealing the stone, and setting a watch.

CHAPTER 28

1. In the end of the sabbath, as it began to dawn toward the first day of the week, came Mary Magdalene and the other Mary to see the sepulchre.

2. And, behold, there was a great earthquake: for the angel of the Lord descended from heaven, and came and rolled back the stone from the door, and sat upon it.

3. His countenance was like lightning, and his raiment white as snow:

4. And for fear of him the keepers did shake, and became as dead men.

5. And the angel answered and said unto the women, Fear not ye: for I know that ye seek Jesus, which was crucified.

6. He is not here: for he is risen, as he said. Come, see the place where the Lord lay.

7. And go quickly, and tell his disciples that he is risen from the dead; and, behold, he goeth before you into Galilee; there shall ye see him: lo, I have told you.

8. And they departed quickly from the sepulchre with fear and great joy; and did run to bring his disciples word.

9. ¶ And as they went to tell his disciples, behold, Jesus met them, saying, All hail. And they came and held him by the feet, and worshipped him.

10. Then said Jesus unto them, Be not afraid: go tell my brethren that they go into Galilee, and there shall they see me.

Matt. 27:56—"Mary Magdalene became one of the closest friends Christ had among women; her devotion to Him as her Healer and as the One whom she adored as the Christ, was unswerving; she stood close by the cross while other women tarried afar off in the time of His mortal agony; she was among the first at the sepulchre on the resurrection morning, and was the first mortal to look upon and recognize a resurrected Being—the Lord whom she had loved with all the fervor of spiritual adoration. To say that this woman, chosen from among women as deserving of such distinctive honors, was once a fallen creature, her soul seared by the heat of unhallowed lust, is to contribute to the perpetuating of an error for which there is no excuse" (James E. Talmage, *Jesus the Christ*, 247).

Matt. 27:64—By placing guards at the sepulchre, the Pharisees actually put the Resurrection beyond doubt, making it impossible to claim that the disciples had taken Christ's body. In doing so, "they closed their own mouths in a vain attempt to destroy the effects of his resurrection from the dead upon the minds of the people and upon the history of the world" (Joseph F. Smith, *Gospel Doctrine: Selections from the Sermons and Writings of Joseph F. Smith*, 464).

Matt. 28:6—"The open tomb itself testified of the Risen Lord; its solid rocks wept for joy, and all eternity joined the great Hallelujah chorus: He is risen; he is risen; Christ the Lord is risen today!" (Bruce R. McConkie, *The Mortal Messiah*, 4:261).

11. ¶ Now when they were going, behold, some of the watch came into the city, and shewed unto the chief priests all the things that were done.

12. And when they were assembled with the elders, and had taken counsel, they gave large money unto the soldiers,

13. Saying, Say ye, His disciples came by night, and stole him away while we slept.

14. And if this come to the governor's ears, we will persuade him, and secure you.

15. So they took the money, and did as they were taught: and this saying is commonly reported among the Jews until this day.

16. ¶ Then the eleven disciples went away into Galilee, into a mountain where Jesus had appointed them.

17. And when they saw him, they worshipped him: but some doubted.

18. And Jesus came and spake unto them, saying, All power is given unto me in heaven and in earth.

19. ¶ Go ye therefore, and teach all nations, baptizing them in the name of the Father, and of the Son, and of the Holy Ghost:

20. Teaching them to observe all things whatsoever I have commanded you: and, lo, I am with you alway, even unto the end of the world. Amen.

THE GOSPEL ACCORDING TO

ST. MARK

CHAPTER 1

1. The beginning of the gospel of Jesus Christ, the Son of God;

2. As it is written in the prophets, Behold, I send my messenger before thy face, which shall prepare thy way before thee.

3. The voice of one crying in the wilderness, Prepare ye the way of the Lord, make his paths straight.

4. John did baptize in the wilderness, and preach the baptism of

Matt. 28:16–20 — We know almost nothing about the Savior's glorious appearance on the mountain in Galilee, but according to Elder Bruce R. McConkie, it is clear that it was planned and prearranged, and can be compared to His ministry among the Nephites (see *The Promised Messiah,* 281).

Christ leaving the tomb

repentance for the remission of sins.

5. And there went out unto him all the land of Judæa, and they of Jerusalem, and were all baptized of him in the river of Jordan, confessing their sins.

6. And John was clothed with camel's hair, and with a girdle of a skin about his loins; and he did eat locusts and wild honey;

7. And preached, saying, There cometh one mightier than I after me, the latchet of whose shoes I am not worthy to stoop down and unloose.

8. I indeed have baptized you with water: but he shall baptize you with the Holy Ghost.

9. And it came to pass in those days, that Jesus came from Nazareth of Galilee, and was baptized of John in Jordan.

10. And straightway coming up out of the water, he saw the heavens opened, and the Spirit like a dove descending upon him:

11. And there came a voice from heaven, saying, Thou art my beloved Son, in whom I am well pleased.

12. And immediately the Spirit driveth him into the wilderness.

13. And he was there in the wilderness forty days, tempted of Satan; and was with the wild beasts; and the angels ministered unto him.

14. Now after that John was put in prison, Jesus came into Galilee, preaching the gospel of the kingdom of God,

15. And saying, The time is fulfilled, and the kingdom of God is at hand: repent ye, and believe the gospel.

16. Now as he walked by the sea of Galilee, he saw Simon and Andrew his brother casting a net into the sea: for they were fishers.

17. And Jesus said unto them, Come ye after me, and I will make you to become fishers of men.

18. And straightway they forsook their nets, and followed him.

19. And when he had gone a little further thence, he saw James the son of Zebedee, and John his brother, who also were in the ship mending their nets.

20. And straightway he called them: and they left their father Zebedee in the ship with the hired servants, and went after him.

21. And they went into Capernaum; and straightway on the sabbath day he entered into the synagogue, and taught.

22. And they were astonished at his doctrine: for he taught them as one that had authority, and not as the scribes.

23. And there was in their synagogue a man with an unclean spirit; and he cried out,

24. Saying, Let us alone; what have we to do with thee, thou Jesus of Nazareth? art thou come to destroy us? I know thee who thou art, the Holy One of God.

25. And Jesus rebuked him, saying, Hold thy peace, and come out of him.

John the Baptist

Mark 1:21–28—"Demon possession" as referred to in the scriptures is not the same as other afflictions, nor is it to be confused with mental illness of any kind, including dissociation or multiple personality disorder. It consists of an "independent, foreign personality which is always evil and always operative. This foreign personality has entered and has gained mastery over the individual. When the demon is cast out, he may choose another person or even an animal as his next place of residence" (William Hendriksen, *Survey of the Bible: A Treasury of Bible Information,* 4th ed., 151).

26. And when the unclean spirit had torn him, and cried with a loud voice, he came out of him.

27. And they were all amazed, insomuch that they questioned among themselves, saying, What thing is this? what new doctrine is this? for with authority commandeth he even the unclean spirits, and they do obey him.

28. And immediately his fame spread abroad throughout all the region round about Galilee.

29. And forthwith, when they were come out of the synagogue, they entered into the house of Simon and Andrew, with James and John.

30. But Simon's wife's mother lay sick of a fever, and anon they tell him of her.

31. And he came and took her by the hand, and lifted her up; and immediately the fever left her, and she ministered unto them.

32. And at even, when the sun did set, they brought unto him all that were diseased, and them that were possessed with devils.

33. And all the city was gathered together at the door.

34. And he healed many that were sick of divers diseases, and cast out many devils; and suffered not the devils to speak, because they knew him.

35. And in the morning, rising up a great while before day, he went out, and departed into a solitary place, and there prayed.

36. And Simon and they that were with him followed after him.

37. And when they had found him, they said unto him, All men seek for thee.

38. And he said unto them, Let us go into the next towns, that I may preach there also: for therefore came I forth.

39. And he preached in their synagogues throughout all Galilee, and cast out devils.

40. And there came a leper to him, beseeching him, and kneeling down to him, and saying unto him, If thou wilt, thou canst make me clean.

41. And Jesus, moved with compassion, put forth his hand, and touched him, and saith unto him, I will; be thou clean.

42. And as soon as he had spoken, immediately the leprosy departed from him, and he was cleansed.

43. And he straitly charged him, and forthwith sent him away;

44. And saith unto him, See thou say nothing to any man: but go thy way, shew thyself to the priest, and offer for thy cleansing those things which Moses commanded, for a testimony unto them.

45. But he went out, and began to publish it much, and to blaze abroad the matter, insomuch that Jesus could no more openly enter into the city, but was without in desert places: and they came to him from every quarter.

CHAPTER 2

1. And again he entered into Capernaum, after some days; and it was noised that he was in the house.

2. And straightway many were gathered together, insomuch that there was no room to receive them, no, not so much as about the door: and he preached the word unto them.

3. And they come unto him, bringing one sick of the palsy, which was borne of four.

Notes:

4. And when they could not come nigh unto him for the press, they uncovered the roof where he was: and when they had broken it up, they let down the bed wherein the sick of the palsy lay.

5. When Jesus saw their faith, he said unto the sick of the palsy, Son, thy sins be forgiven thee.

6. But there were certain of the scribes sitting there, and reasoning in their hearts,

7. Why doth this man thus speak blasphemies? who can forgive sins but God only?

8. And immediately when Jesus perceived in his spirit that they so reasoned within themselves, he said unto them, Why reason ye these things in your hearts?

9. Whether is it easier to say to the sick of the palsy, Thy sins be forgiven thee; or to say, Arise, and take up thy bed, and walk?

10. But that ye may know that the Son of man hath power on earth to forgive sins, (he saith to the sick of the palsy,)

11. I say unto thee, Arise, and take up thy bed, and go thy way into thine house.

12. And immediately he arose, took up the bed, and went forth before them all; insomuch that they were all amazed, and glorified God, saying, We never saw it on this fashion.

13. And he went forth again by the sea side; and all the multitude resorted unto him, and he taught them.

14. And as he passed by, he saw Levi the son of Alphæus sitting at the receipt of custom, and said unto him, Follow me. And he arose and followed him.

15. And it came to pass, that, as Jesus sat at meat in his house, many publicans and sinners sat also together with Jesus and his disciples: for there were many, and they followed him.

16. And when the scribes and Pharisees saw him eat with publicans and sinners, they said unto his disciples, How is it that he eateth and drinketh with publicans and sinners?

17. When Jesus heard it, he saith unto them, They that are whole have no need of the physician, but they that are sick: I came not to call the righteous, but sinners to repentance.

18. And the disciples of John and of the Pharisees used to fast: and they come and say unto him, Why do the disciples of John and of the Pharisees fast, but thy disciples fast not?

19. And Jesus said unto them, Can the children of the bridechamber fast, while the bridegroom is with them? as long as they have the bridegroom with them, they cannot fast.

20. But the days will come, when the bridegroom shall be taken away from them, and then shall they fast in those days.

21. No man also seweth a piece of new cloth on an old garment: else the new piece that filled it up taketh away from the old, and the rent is made worse.

22. And no man putteth new wine into old bottles: else the new wine doth burst the bottles, and the wine is spilled, and the bottles will be marred: but new wine must be put into new bottles.

23. And it came to pass, that he went through the corn fields on the sabbath day; and his disciples began, as they went, to pluck the ears of corn.

24. And the Pharisees said unto him, Behold, why do they on the sabbath day that which is not lawful?

25. And he said unto them, Have ye never read what David did,

The life and teachings of Jesus

when he had need, and was an hungred, he, and they that were with him?

26. How he went into the house of God in the days of Abiathar the high priest, and did eat the shewbread, which is not lawful to eat but for the priests, and gave also to them which were with him?

27. And he said unto them, The sabbath was made for man, and not man for the sabbath:

28. Therefore the Son of man is Lord also of the sabbath.

CHAPTER 3

1. And he entered again into the synagogue; and there was a man there which had a withered hand.

2. And they watched him, whether he would heal him on the sabbath day; that they might accuse him.

3. And he saith unto the man which had the withered hand, Stand forth.

4. And he saith unto them, Is it lawful to do good on the sabbath days, or to do evil? to save life, or to kill? But they held their peace.

5. And when he had looked round about on them with anger, being grieved for the hardness of their hearts, he saith unto the man, Stretch forth thine hand. And he stretched it out: and his hand was restored whole as the other.

6. And the Pharisees went forth, and straightway took counsel with the Herodians against him, how they might destroy him.

7. But Jesus withdrew himself with his disciples to the sea: and a great multitude from Galilee followed him, and from Judæa,

8. And from Jerusalem, and from Idumæa, and from beyond Jordan; and they about Tyre and Sidon, a great multitude, when they had heard what great things he did, came unto him.

9. And he spake to his disciples, that a small ship should wait on him because of the multitude, lest they should throng him.

10. For he had healed many; insomuch that they pressed upon him for to touch him, as many as had plagues.

11. And unclean spirits, when they saw him, fell down before him, and cried, saying, Thou art the Son of God.

12. And he straitly charged them that they should not make him known.

13. And he goeth up into a mountain, and calleth unto him whom he would: and they came unto him.

14. And he ordained twelve, that they should be with him, and that he might send them forth to preach,

15. And to have power to heal sicknesses, and to cast out devils:

16. And Simon he surnamed Peter;

17. And James the son of Zebedee, and John the brother of James; and he surnamed them Boanerges, which is, The sons of thunder:

18. And Andrew, and Philip, and Bartholomew, and Matthew, and Thomas, and James the son of Alphæus, and Thaddæus, and Simon the Canaanite,

Mark 2:27—When the Pharisees observed the Lord's disciples picking ears of corn (heads of grain) in the fields on the Sabbath, they were offended. The Lord reminded them that David, when hungered, was offered hallowed bread by the high priest of the Lord, something that was appropriate but not according to the letter of the law. When this happened, David and his followers were fleeing the murderous plots of King Saul and needed help.

The Savior shed light on the genuine spirit of the Sabbath. Too many times the Sabbath day is viewed as a day of "do nots" rather than an opportunity to do many things that are holy and uplifting: worship, pay homage to our Heavenly Father and Savior, rest from our daily labors, be filled with the words of truth, bless our brothers and sisters, and be with family. How can you help others remove the Sabbath day from a context of restrictions and prohibitions and place it into a context of doing good, creating joy, and blessing lives?

The Twelve Apostles

19. And Judas Iscariot, which also betrayed him: and they went into an house.

20. And the multitude cometh together again, so that they could not so much as eat bread.

21. And when his friends heard of it, they went out to lay hold on him: for they said, He is beside himself.

22. ¶ And the scribes which came down from Jerusalem said, He hath Beelzebub, and by the prince of the devils casteth he out devils.

23. And he called them unto him, and said unto them in parables, How can Satan cast out Satan?

24. And if a kingdom be divided against itself, that kingdom cannot stand.

25. And if a house be divided against itself, that house cannot stand.

26. And if Satan rise up against himself, and be divided, he cannot stand, but hath an end.

27. No man can enter into a strong man's house, and spoil his goods, except he will first bind the strong man; and then he will spoil his house.

28. Verily I say unto you, All sins shall be forgiven unto the sons of men, and blasphemies wherewith soever they shall blaspheme:

29. But he that shall blaspheme against the Holy Ghost hath never forgiveness, but is in danger of eternal damnation:

30. Because they said, He hath an unclean spirit.

31. ¶ There came then his brethren and his mother, and, standing without, sent unto him, calling him.

32. And the multitude sat about him, and they said unto him, Behold, thy mother and thy brethren without seek for thee.

33. And he answered them, saying, Who is my mother, or my brethren?

34. And he looked round about on them which sat about him, and said, Behold my mother and my brethren!

35. For whosoever shall do the will of God, the same is my brother, and my sister, and mother.

CHAPTER 4

1. And he began again to teach by the sea side: and there was gathered unto him a great multitude, so that he entered into a ship, and sat in the sea; and the whole multitude was by the sea on the land.

2. And he taught them many things by parables, and said unto them in his doctrine,

3. Hearken; Behold, there went out a sower to sow:

4. And it came to pass, as he sowed, some fell by the way side, and the fowls of the air came and devoured it up.

5. And some fell on stony ground, where it had not much earth; and immediately it sprang up, because it had no depth of earth:

6. But when the sun was up, it was scorched; and because it had no root, it withered away.

7. And some fell among thorns, and the thorns grew up, and choked it, and it yielded no fruit.

8. And other fell on good ground, and did yield fruit that sprang up and increased; and brought forth, some thirty, and some sixty, and some an hundred.

9. And he said unto them, He that hath ears to hear, let him hear.

Notes: _____

_____

_____

_____

_____

_____

_____

_____

_____

_____

_____

_____

_____

_____

_____

_____

_____

_____

Mark 4:9—"It is recorded that some have eyes to see, and see not; ears to hear, and hear not; hearts have they, but they understand not. You who are spiritually-minded, who have the visions of your minds opened . . . understand that the power that has given you physical sensation is the power of the same God that gives you understanding of the truth. The latter power is inward. My inward eyes see, my inward hands handle, my inward taste tastes of the word of God" (Brigham Young, *Discourses of Brigham Young,* John A. Widtsoe, ed., 421).

10. And when he was alone, they that were about him with the twelve asked of him the parable.

11. And he said unto them, Unto you it is given to know the mystery of the kingdom of God: but unto them that are without, all these things are done in parables:

12. That seeing they may see, and not perceive; and hearing they may hear, and not understand; lest at any time they should be converted, and their sins should be forgiven them.

13. And he said unto them, Know ye not this parable? and how then will ye know all parables?

14. ¶ The sower soweth the word.

15. And these are they by the way side, where the word is sown; but when they have heard, Satan cometh immediately, and taketh away the word that was sown in their hearts.

16. And these are they likewise which are sown on stony ground; who, when they have heard the word, immediately receive it with gladness;

17. And have no root in themselves, and so endure but for a time: afterward, when affliction or persecution ariseth for the word's sake, immediately they are offended.

18. And these are they which are sown among thorns; such as hear the word,

19. And the cares of this world, and the deceitfulness of riches, and the lusts of other things entering in, choke the word, and it becometh unfruitful.

20. And these are they which are sown on good ground; such as hear the word, and receive it, and bring forth fruit, some thirtyfold, some sixty, and some an hundred.

21. ¶ And he said unto them, Is a candle brought to be put under a bushel, or under a bed? and not to be set on a candlestick?

22. For there is nothing hid, which shall not be manifested; neither was any thing kept secret, but that it should come abroad.

23. If any man have ears to hear, let him hear.

24. And he said unto them, Take heed what ye hear: with what measure ye mete, it shall be measured to you: and unto you that hear shall more be given.

25. For he that hath, to him shall be given: and he that hath not, from him shall be taken even that which he hath.

26. ¶ And he said, So is the kingdom of God, as if a man should cast seed into the ground;

27. And should sleep, and rise night and day, and the seed should spring and grow up, he knoweth not how.

28. For the earth bringeth forth fruit of herself; first the blade, then the ear, after that the full corn in the ear.

29. But when the fruit is brought forth, immediately he putteth in the sickle, because the harvest is come.

30. ¶ And he said, Whereunto shall we liken the kingdom of God? or with what comparison shall we compare it?

31. It is like a grain of mustard seed, which, when it is sown in the earth, is less than all the seeds that be in the earth:

32. But when it is sown, it groweth

Parable of the sower

Mark 4:26–29 — The parable of the seed growing by itself reminds us that certain things need to be done if we want a seed to grow: we need to cultivate the soil, plant the seed, water it, fertilize it, and give it every other opportunity to grow. But nothing we do can actually create that growth. The seed grows only by the power of God. Likewise, as we make efforts to share the gospel, we need to create all the optimum conditions — but realize and solidly understand that the seed we have planted grows in the heart of the recipient only by the power of God and through the influence of the Holy Ghost (see Bruce R. McConkie, *Doctrinal New Testament Commentary*, 1:292).

Mark 4:30–32 — In this parable, the Savior predicted both the inconspicuous beginning and the tremendous growth of His Church in these latter days. He declared with his comparison to the mustard seed that the Church would eventually become a great tree that would provide refuge for many among its powerful branches (see Ezra Taft Benson, *Come Unto Christ*, 80).

up, and becometh greater than all herbs, and shooteth out great branches; so that the fowls of the air may lodge under the shadow of it.

33. And with many such parables spake he the word unto them, as they were able to hear it.

34. But without a parable spake he not unto them: and when they were alone, he expounded all things to his disciples.

35. And the same day, when the even was come, he saith unto them, Let us pass over unto the other side.

36. And when they had sent away the multitude, they took him even as he was in the ship. And there were also with him other little ships.

37. And there arose a great storm of wind, and the waves beat into the ship, so that it was now full.

38. And he was in the hinder part of the ship, asleep on a pillow: and they awake him, and say unto him, Master, carest thou not that we perish?

39. And he arose, and rebuked the wind, and said unto the sea, Peace, be still. And the wind ceased, and there was a great calm.

40. And he said unto them, Why are ye so fearful? how is it that ye have no faith?

41. And they feared exceedingly, and said one to another, What manner of man is this, that even the wind and the sea obey him?

CHAPTER 5

1. And they came over unto the other side of the sea, into the country of the Gadarenes.

2. And when he was come out of the ship, immediately there met him out of the tombs a man with an unclean spirit,

3. Who had his dwelling among the tombs; and no man could bind him, no, not with chains:

4. Because that he had been often bound with fetters and chains, and the chains had been plucked asunder by him, and the fetters broken in pieces: neither could any man tame him.

5. And always, night and day, he was in the mountains, and in the tombs, crying, and cutting himself with stones.

6. But when he saw Jesus afar off, he ran and worshipped him,

7. And cried with a loud voice, and said, What have I to do with thee, Jesus, thou Son of the most high God? I adjure thee by God, that thou torment me not.

8. For he said unto him, Come out of the man, thou unclean spirit.

9. And he asked him, What is thy name? And he answered, saying, My name is Legion: for we are many.

10. And he besought him much that he would not send them away out of the country.

11. Now there was there nigh unto the mountains a great herd of swine feeding.

12. And all the devils besought him, saying, Send us into the swine, that we may enter into them.

13. And forthwith Jesus gave them leave. And the unclean spirits went out, and entered into the swine: and the herd ran violently down a steep place into the sea, (they were about two thousand;) and were choked in the sea.

14. And they that fed the swine fled, and told it in the city, and in the country. And they went out to see what it was that was done.

15. And they come to Jesus, and see him that was possessed with the

Matt. 4:35–41 — All of us have adversity in our lives, including the Savior. His "ship" was tossed and buffeted most of His life, and He was certainly not spared pain and grief and suffering. For all of us, it is the same: some adversities will cause mere anxiety, while other may strain our faith and nearly destroy us. The Savior's injunction to peace reminds us that we must have faith for the journey—the *entire* experience—and not just for the times of calm. Regardless of how fiercely the tempest was raging that night in the ship, the Savior brought peace; He can do the same for us today (see Howard W. Hunter, *Ensign,* Nov. 1984, 34–35).

Mark 5:1–20 — Devils, demons, and evil spirits are those beings who aligned with Lucifer in the war of rebellion during our pre-mortal existence. They—one-third of our Father's spirit children—were cast down to earth but were forever denied physical bodies. As a result, they seek to inhabit the bodies of other people. Jesus taught His disciples that they had the power to cast out evil spirits, a power that is still available today through the power of the priesthood (see D&C 107:3) (see Oscar W. McConkie, Jr., *Angels,* 69).

Mark 5:9 — The word *legion* suggests that "a great host of spirits had taken up unlawful tenancy in the body of one man. Literally, a legion in the Roman army amounted to some six thousand men; figuratively, a legion is an indefinitely large number. The number here was so great as to cause some two thousand swine to careen crazily down a steep slope and drown themselves in the sea" (Bruce R. McConkie, *Doctrinal New Testament Commentary,* 1:312).

devil, and had the legion, sitting, and clothed, and in his right mind: and they were afraid.

16. And they that saw it told them how it befell to him that was possessed with the devil, and also concerning the swine.

17. And they began to pray him to depart out of their coasts.

18. And when he was come into the ship, he that had been possessed with the devil prayed him that he might be with him.

19. Howbeit Jesus suffered him not, but saith unto him, Go home to thy friends, and tell them how great things the Lord hath done for thee, and hath had compassion on thee.

20. And he departed, and began to publish in Decapolis how great things Jesus had done for him: and all men did marvel.

21. And when Jesus was passed over again by ship unto the other side, much people gathered unto him: and he was nigh unto the sea.

22. And, behold, there cometh one of the rulers of the synagogue, Jairus by name; and when he saw him, he fell at his feet,

23. And besought him greatly, saying, My little daughter lieth at the point of death: I pray thee, come and lay thy hands on her, that she may be healed; and she shall live.

24. And Jesus went with him; and much people followed him, and thronged him.

25. And a certain woman, which had an issue of blood twelve years,

26. And had suffered many things of many physicians, and had spent all that she had, and was nothing bettered, but rather grew worse,

27. When she had heard of Jesus, came in the press behind, and touched his garment.

28. For she said, If I may touch but his clothes, I shall be whole.

29. And straightway the fountain of her blood was dried up; and she felt in her body that she was healed of that plague.

30. And Jesus, immediately knowing in himself that virtue had gone out of him, turned him about in the press, and said, Who touched my clothes?

31. And his disciples said unto him, Thou seest the multitude thronging thee, and sayest thou, Who touched me?

32. And he looked round about to see her that had done this thing.

33. But the woman fearing and trembling, knowing what was done in her, came and fell down before him, and told him all the truth.

34. And he said unto her, Daughter, thy faith hath made thee whole; go in peace, and be whole of thy plague.

35. While he yet spake, there came from the ruler of the synagogue's house certain which said, Thy daughter is dead: why troublest thou the Master any further?

36. As soon as Jesus heard the word that was spoken, he saith unto the ruler of the synagogue, Be not afraid, only believe.

37. And he suffered no man to follow him, save Peter, and James, and John the brother of James.

38. And he cometh to the house of the ruler of the synagogue, and seeth the tumult, and them that wept and wailed greatly.

39. And when he was come in, he saith unto them, Why make ye this ado, and weep? the damsel is not dead, but sleepeth.

40. And they laughed him to scorn. But when he had put them all out, he taketh the father and the mother of the damsel, and them that were with him, and entereth in where the damsel was lying.

41. And he took the damsel by the hand, and said unto her, Talitha

Daughter of Jairus

Mark 5:36—"The problem with most of us is that we are afraid to stand up for what we believe, to be witnesses for what is true and right. We want to do the right thing, but we are troubled by fears. So we sit back, and the world drifts about us, and society increasingly adopts attitudes and standards of behavior that most of us do not approve of" (Gordon B. Hinckley, *Standing for Something,* 168).

cumi; which is, being interpreted, Damsel, I say unto thee, arise.

42. And straightway the damsel arose, and walked; for she was of the age of twelve years. And they were astonished with a great astonishment.

43. And he charged them straitly that no man should know it; and commanded that something should be given her to eat.

CHAPTER 6

1. And he went out from thence, and came into his own country; and his disciples follow him.

2. And when the sabbath day was come, he began to teach in the synagogue: and many hearing him were astonished, saying, From whence hath this man these things? and what wisdom is this which is given unto him, that even such mighty works are wrought by his hands?

3. Is not this the carpenter, the son of Mary, the brother of James, and Joses, and of Juda, and Simon? and are not his sisters here with us? And they were offended at him.

4. But Jesus said unto them, A prophet is not without honour, but in his own country, and among his own kin, and in his own house.

5. And he could there do no mighty work, save that he laid his hands upon a few sick folk, and healed them.

6. And he marvelled because of their unbelief. And he went round about the villages, teaching.

7. ¶ And he called unto him the twelve, and began to send them forth by two and two; and gave them power over unclean spirits;

8. And commanded them that they should take nothing for their journey, save a staff only; no scrip, no bread, no money in their purse:

9. But be shod with sandals; and not put on two coats.

10. And he said unto them, In what place soever ye enter into an house, there abide till ye depart from that place.

11. And whosoever shall not receive you, nor hear you, when ye depart thence, shake off the dust under your feet for a testimony against them. Verily I say unto you, It shall be more tolerable for Sodom and Gomorrha in the day of judgment, than for that city.

12. And they went out, and preached that men should repent.

13. And they cast out many devils, and anointed with oil many that were sick, and healed them.

14. And king Herod heard of him; (for his name was spread abroad:) and he said, That John the Baptist was risen from the dead, and therefore mighty works do shew forth themselves in him.

15. Others said, That it is Elias. And others said, That it is a prophet, or as one of the prophets.

16. But when Herod heard thereof, he said, It is John, whom I beheaded: he is risen from the dead.

17. For Herod himself had sent forth and laid hold upon John, and bound him in prison for Herodias' sake, his brother Philip's wife: for he had married her.

18. For John had said unto Herod, It is not lawful for thee to have thy brother's wife.

19. Therefore Herodias had a quarrel

Notes: _____

_____

_____

_____

_____

_____

_____

_____

_____

_____

_____

_____

_____

_____

_____

_____

_____

_____

Mark 6:6–13 — When Jesus gave His twelve disciples power and authority to preach the gospel, there were certain restrictions. They were not to preach to all men; they were sent to the House of Israel, but not to the Gentiles. Each man was to hear the gospel in his own time and season. They were given specific direction, too, on *what* they were to preach: the gospel of the kingdom, with emphasis that salvation comes only through the Savior Jesus Christ (see Bruce R. McConkie, *The Mortal Messiah,* 2:309–10).

Mark 6:13 — This verse reveals something about healing that is not discussed anywhere else in the four Gospels: the Apostles anointed the sick *with oil*. There is only one other place in the entire New Testament where anointing the sick with oil is mentioned, and that is in James 5:14–16.

against him, and would have killed him; but she could not:

20. For Herod feared John, knowing that he was a just man and an holy, and observed him; and when he heard him, he did many things, and heard him gladly.

21. And when a convenient day was come, that Herod on his birthday made a supper to his lords, high captains, and chief estates of Galilee;

22. And when the daughter of the said Herodias came in, and danced, and pleased Herod and them that sat with him, the king said unto the damsel, Ask of me whatsoever thou wilt, and I will give it thee.

23. And he sware unto her, Whatsoever thou shalt ask of me, I will give it thee, unto the half of my kingdom.

24. And she went forth, and said unto her mother, What shall I ask? And she said, The head of John the Baptist.

25. And she came in straightway with haste unto the king, and asked, saying, I will that thou give me by and by in a charger the head of John the Baptist.

26. And the king was exceeding sorry; yet for his oath's sake, and for their sakes which sat with him, he would not reject her.

27. And immediately the king sent an executioner, and commanded his head to be brought: and he went and beheaded him in the prison,

28. And brought his head in a charger, and gave it to the damsel: and the damsel gave it to her mother.

29. And when his disciples heard of it, they came and took up his corpse, and laid it in a tomb.

30. And the apostles gathered themselves together unto Jesus, and told him all things, both what they had done, and what they had taught.

31. And he said unto them, Come ye yourselves apart into a desert place, and rest a while: for there were many coming and going, and they had no leisure so much as to eat.

32. And they departed into a desert place by ship privately.

33. And the people saw them departing, and many knew him, and ran afoot thither out of all cities, and outwent them, and came together unto him.

34. And Jesus, when he came out, saw much people, and was moved with compassion toward them, because they were as sheep not having a shepherd: and he began to teach them many things.

35. And when the day was now far spent, his disciples came unto him, and said, This is a desert place, and now the time is far passed:

36. Send them away, that they may go into the country round about, and into the villages, and buy themselves bread: for they have nothing to eat.

37. He answered and said unto them, Give ye them to eat. And they say unto him, Shall we go and buy two hundred pennyworth of bread, and give them to eat?

38. He saith unto them, How many loaves have ye? go and see. And when they knew, they say, Five, and two fishes.

39. And he commanded them to

Mark 6:31—In this account, the crowds who were "coming and going" were so great that the Savior and His disciples did not even have time to eat. Notice what the Savior did next, as mentioned in verse 32: He took His disciples away by ship, where they could escape the press of the crowds and get some rest and renewal. Striking a healthy and proper balance in our lives is one of our most important obligations. As Elder Neal A. Maxwell put it, "When our pace exceeds our strength and means, the result is prostration instead of sustained dedication" (*Notwithstanding My Weakness*, 7).

Mark 6:36–46—Some, skeptical of the Savior's miraculous feeding of the five thousand, have attempted to dismiss it as something less. Some claim that the multitude actually ate lunches that they brought with them. Others have claimed that the Savior hypnotized the crowd, thereby convincing them that they were full. Such an explanation, of course, has no way of dismissing the fragments of the loaves and fishes, which after the crowd was fed filled twelve baskets. This was a miracle: "The Creator of the universe, out of five loaves and two fishes, made food that fed them all" (J. Reuben Clark, Jr., *Behold the Lamb of God*, 20).

make all sit down by companies upon the green grass.

40. And they sat down in ranks, by hundreds, and by fifties.

41. And when he had taken the five loaves and the two fishes, he looked up to heaven, and blessed, and brake the loaves, and gave them to his disciples to set before them; and the two fishes divided he among them all.

42. And they did all eat, and were filled.

43. And they took up twelve baskets full of the fragments, and of the fishes.

44. And they that did eat of the loaves were about five thousand men.

45. And straightway he constrained his disciples to get into the ship, and to go to the other side before unto Bethsaida, while he sent away the people.

46. And when he had sent them away, he departed into a mountain to pray.

47. And when even was come, the ship was in the midst of the sea, and he alone on the land.

48. And he saw them toiling in rowing; for the wind was contrary unto them: and about the fourth watch of the night he cometh unto them, walking upon the sea, and would have passed by them.

49. But when they saw him walking upon the sea, they supposed it had been a spirit, and cried out:

50. For they all saw him, and were troubled. And immediately he talked with them, and saith unto them, Be of good cheer: it is I; be not afraid.

51. And he went up unto them into the ship; and the wind ceased: and they were sore amazed in themselves beyond measure, and wondered.

52. For they considered not the miracle of the loaves: for their heart was hardened.

53. And when they had passed over, they came into the land of Gennesaret, and drew to the shore.

54. And when they were come out of the ship, straightway they knew him,

55. And ran through that whole region round about, and began to carry about in beds those that were sick, where they heard he was.

56. And whithersoever he entered, into villages, or cities, or country, they laid the sick in the streets, and besought him that they might touch if it were but the border of his garment: and as many as touched him were made whole.

CHAPTER 7

1. Then came together unto him the Pharisees, and certain of the scribes, which came from Jerusalem.

2. And when they saw some of his disciples eat bread with defiled, that is to say, with unwashen, hands, they found fault.

3. For the Pharisees, and all the Jews, except they wash their hands oft, eat not, holding the tradition of the elders.

4. And when they come from the market, except they wash, they eat not. And many other things there be, which they have received to hold, as the washing of cups, and pots, brasen vessels, and of tables.

5. Then the Pharisees and scribes asked him, Why walk not thy disciples according to the tradition of the elders, but eat bread with unwashen hands?

6. He answered and said unto them, Well hath Esaias prophesied of you hypocrites, as it is written, This

Mark 6:56—In several places in the New Testament, we read accounts of people who were healed simply by touching the border or hem of the Savior's garment. A major reason, of course, had to do with their faith to be healed. A reason why they sought the border or hem in particular may have been because of a divine commandment that garments have a certain color of border so that all Israel would "look upon it, and remember all the commandments of the Lord, and do them" (Num. 15:41). Because of such a command, the people may have considered the border or hem to be "holy."

Mark 7:1–13—The Pharisees had great influence during the time of Jesus, and much of that influence was due to their control over what was called the "oral law." They claimed that Moses on Sinai received the law in two parts: the *written law*, which was contained on the tablets and preserved in the five books of Moses (Genesis, Exodus, Leviticus, Numbers, and Deuteronomy); and the *oral law*, which was given by the Lord orally to Moses and which was then preserved through the generations by the Pharisees and their predecessors (sometimes also called "the tradition of the Fathers"). Whenever they were unable to find answers in the scriptures, the Pharisees resorted to "oral law," adapting to whatever situation in which they found themselves. Since they were the only ones who "knew" this oral law, no one was able to challenge them or call into question the innovations they created from such law (see Kent P. Jackson and Robert L. Millet, eds., *Studies in Scripture, Vol. 5: The Gospels*, 22–23).

people honoureth me with their lips, but their heart is far from me.

7. Howbeit in vain do they worship me, teaching for doctrines the commandments of men.

8. For laying aside the commandment of God, ye hold the tradition of men, as the washing of pots and cups: and many other such like things ye do.

9. And he said unto them, Full well ye reject the commandment of God, that ye may keep your own tradition.

10. For Moses said, Honour thy father and thy mother; and, Whoso curseth father or mother, let him die the death:

11. But ye say, If a man shall say to his father or mother, It is Corban, that is to say, a gift, by whatsoever thou mightest be profited by me; he shall be free.

12. And ye suffer him no more to do ought for his father or his mother;

13. Making the word of God of none effect through your tradition, which ye have delivered: and many such like things do ye.

14. ¶ And when he had called all the people unto him, he said unto them, Hearken unto me every one of you, and understand:

15. There is nothing from without a man, that entering into him can defile him: but the things which come out of him, those are they that defile the man.

16. If any man have ears to hear, let him hear.

17. And when he was entered into the house from the people, his disciples asked him concerning the parable.

18. And he saith unto them, Are ye so without understanding also? Do ye not perceive, that whatsoever thing from without entereth into the man, it cannot defile him;

19. Because it entereth not into his heart, but into the belly, and goeth out into the draught, purging all meats?

20. And he said, That which cometh out of the man, that defileth the man.

21. For from within, out of the heart of men, proceed evil thoughts, adulteries, fornications, murders,

22. Thefts, covetousness, wickedness, deceit, lasciviousness, an evil eye, blasphemy, pride, foolishness:

23. All these evil things come from within, and defile the man.

24. ¶ And from thence he arose, and went into the borders of Tyre and Sidon, and entered into an house, and would have no man know it: but he could not be hid.

25. For a certain woman, whose young daughter had an unclean spirit, heard of him, and came and fell at his feet:

26. The woman was a Greek, a Syrophenician by nation; and she besought him that he would cast forth the devil out of her daughter.

27. But Jesus said unto her, Let the children first be filled: for it is not meet to take the children's bread, and to cast it unto the dogs.

28. And she answered and said unto him, Yes, Lord: yet the dogs under the table eat of the children's crumbs.

Mark 7:1–23—Here is provided a strong reminder that it is not what's on the outside that counts, but what is on the inside. The things which "come out" of man—things like impurity, covetousness, deceit, pride, foolishness, wickedness, lasciviousness, and an evil eye (see verses 21–23)—are what corrupt, not the things "from without" (see verse 15).

Notes:

29. And he said unto her, For this saying go thy way; the devil is gone out of thy daughter.

30. And when she was come to her house, she found the devil gone out, and her daughter laid upon the bed.

31. ¶ And again, departing from the coasts of Tyre and Sidon, he came unto the sea of Galilee, through the midst of the coasts of Decapolis.

32. And they bring unto him one that was deaf, and had an impediment in his speech; and they beseech him to put his hand upon him.

33. And he took him aside from the multitude, and put his fingers into his ears, and he spit, and touched his tongue;

34. And looking up to heaven, he sighed, and saith unto him, Ephphatha, that is, Be opened.

35. And straightway his ears were opened, and the string of his tongue was loosed, and he spake plain.

36. And he charged them that they should tell no man: but the more he charged them, so much the more a great deal they published it;

37. And were beyond measure astonished, saying, He hath done all things well: he maketh both the deaf to hear, and the dumb to speak.

CHAPTER 8

1. In those days the multitude being very great, and having nothing to eat, Jesus called his disciples unto him, and saith unto them,

2. I have compassion on the multitude, because they have now been with me three days, and have nothing to eat:

3. And if I send them away fasting to their own houses, they will faint by the way: for divers of them came from far.

4. And his disciples answered him, From whence can a man satisfy these men with bread here in the wilderness?

5. And he asked them, How many loaves have ye? And they said, Seven.

6. And he commanded the people to sit down on the ground: and he took the seven loaves, and gave thanks, and brake, and gave to his disciples to set before them; and they did set them before the people.

7. And they had a few small fishes: and he blessed, and commanded to set them also before them.

8. So they did eat, and were filled: and they took up of the broken meat that was left seven baskets.

9. And they that had eaten were about four thousand: and he sent them away.

10. ¶ And straightway he entered into a ship with his disciples, and came into the parts of Dalmanutha.

11. And the Pharisees came forth, and began to question with him, seeking of him a sign from heaven, tempting him.

12. And he sighed deeply in his spirit, and saith, Why doth this generation seek after a sign? verily I say unto you, There shall no sign be given unto this generation.

13. And he left them, and entering into the ship again departed to the other side.

14. ¶ Now the disciples had forgotten to take bread, neither had they in the ship with them more than one loaf.

15. And he charged them, saying, Take heed, beware of the leaven of the Pharisees, and of the leaven of Herod.

16. And they reasoned among themselves, saying, It is because we have no bread.

17. And when Jesus knew it, he saith

Jesus feeding the five thousand

unto them, Why reason ye, because ye have no bread? perceive ye not yet, neither understand? have ye your heart yet hardened?

18. Having eyes, see ye not? and having ears, hear ye not? and do ye not remember?

19. When I brake the five loaves among five thousand, how many baskets full of fragments took ye up? They say unto him, Twelve.

20. And when the seven among four thousand, how many baskets full of fragments took ye up? And they said, Seven.

21. And he said unto them, How is it that ye do not understand?

22. ¶ And he cometh to Bethsaida; and they bring a blind man unto him, and besought him to touch him.

23. And he took the blind man by the hand, and led him out of the town; and when he had spit on his eyes, and put his hands upon him, he asked him if he saw ought.

24. And he looked up, and said, I see men as trees, walking.

25. After that he put his hands again upon his eyes, and made him look up: and he was restored, and saw every man clearly.

26. And he sent him away to his house, saying, Neither go into the town, nor tell it to any in the town.

27. ¶ And Jesus went out, and his disciples, into the towns of Cæsarea Philippi: and by the way he asked his disciples, saying unto them, Whom do men say that I am?

28. And they answered, John the Baptist: but some say, Elias; and others, One of the prophets.

29. And he saith unto them, But whom say ye that I am? And Peter answereth and saith unto him, Thou art the Christ.

30. And he charged them that they should tell no man of him.

31. And he began to teach them, that the Son of man must suffer many things, and be rejected of the elders, and of the chief priests, and scribes, and be killed, and after three days rise again.

32. And he spake that saying openly. And Peter took him, and began to rebuke him.

33. But when he had turned about and looked on his disciples, he rebuked Peter, saying, Get thee behind me, Satan: for thou savourest not the things that be of God, but the things that be of men.

34. ¶ And when he had called the people unto him with his disciples also, he said unto them, Whosoever will come after me, let him deny himself, and take up his cross, and follow me.

35. For whosoever will save his life shall lose it; but whosoever shall lose his life for my sake and the gospel's, the same shall save it.

36. For what shall it profit a man, if he shall gain the whole world, and lose his own soul?

37. Or what shall a man give in exchange for his soul?

38. Whosoever therefore shall be ashamed of me and of my words in this adulterous and sinful generation; of him also shall the Son of man be ashamed, when he cometh in the glory of his Father with the holy angels.

Notes: _____

_____

_____

_____

_____

_____

_____

_____

_____

_____

_____

_____

_____

_____

_____

_____

_____

Mark 8:35—"To the millions of the humble and honest in heart who are discouraged, weary, grief-stricken, despairing, and who would see Jesus, and who, seeing him, would know him, we repeat the words spoken by Jesus to this generation: '. . . every soul who forsaketh his sins and cometh unto me, and calleth on my name, and obeyeth my voice, and keepeth my commandments, shall see my face and know that I am'" (J. Reuben Clark, Jr., *Behold the Lamb of God,* 233).

Mark 8:36—"When your mind is on the things of the world, you lose the Spirit of the Lord in your work" (Gordon B. Hinckley, *Stand a Little Taller,* 340).

Mark 8:38—"The inhabitants of the earth will be rewarded according to their works. Some will receive the exaltation in the kingdom of God to become gods themselves and have blessings of eternal increase. Some will be assigned to the terrestrial kingdom to remain separately and singly forever, and some will be cast into 'outer darkness, where there is weeping and wailing, and gnashing of teeth'" (Joseph Fielding Smith, *Answers to Gospel Questions,* 5:8).

CHAPTER 9

1. And he said unto them, Verily I say unto you, That there be some of them that stand here, which shall not taste of death, till they have seen the kingdom of God come with power.

2. ¶ And after six days Jesus taketh with him Peter, and James, and John, and leadeth them up into an high mountain apart by themselves: and he was transfigured before them.

3. And his raiment became shining, exceeding white as snow; so as no fuller on earth can white them.

4. And there appeared unto them Elias with Moses: and they were talking with Jesus.

5. And Peter answered and said to Jesus, Master, it is good for us to be here: and let us make three tabernacles; one for thee, and one for Moses, and one for Elias.

6. For he wist not what to say; for they were sore afraid.

7. And there was a cloud that overshadowed them: and a voice came out of the cloud, saying, This is my beloved Son: hear him.

8. And suddenly, when they had looked round about, they saw no man any more, save Jesus only with themselves.

9. And as they came down from the mountain, he charged them that they should tell no man what things they had seen, till the Son of man were risen from the dead.

10. And they kept that saying with themselves, questioning one with another what the rising from the dead should mean.

11. ¶ And they asked him, saying, Why say the scribes that Elias must first come?

12. And he answered and told them, Elias verily cometh first, and restoreth all things; and how it is written of the Son of man, that he must suffer many things, and be set at nought.

13. But I say unto you, That Elias is indeed come, and they have done unto him whatsoever they listed, as it is written of him.

14. ¶ And when he came to his disciples, he saw a great multitude about them, and the scribes questioning with them.

15. And straightway all the people, when they beheld him, were greatly amazed, and running to him saluted him.

16. And he asked the scribes, What question ye with them?

17. And one of the multitude answered and said, Master, I have brought unto thee my son, which hath a dumb spirit;

18. And wheresoever he taketh him, he teareth him: and he foameth, and gnasheth with his teeth, and pineth away: and I spake to thy disciples that they should cast him out; and they could not.

19. He answereth him, and saith, O faithless generation, how long shall I be with you? how long shall I suffer you? bring him unto me.

20. And they brought him unto

Mark 9:2–10—While they were on the Mount of Transfiguration, it seems that Peter, James, and John received their own endowments (see *Doctrines of Salvation*, 2:165). It seems also that they received the more sure word of prophecy and that they were sealed up to eternal life (see 2 Pet. 1:16–19 and D&C 131:5).

Jesus transfigured on the Mount of Transfiguration

Notes: _____

_____

_____

_____

_____

_____

_____

_____

_____

_____

_____

_____

_____

_____

_____

him: and when he saw him, straightway the spirit tare him; and he fell on the ground, and wallowed foaming.

21. And he asked his father, How long is it ago since this came unto him? And he said, Of a child.

22. And ofttimes it hath cast him into the fire, and into the waters, to destroy him: but if thou canst do any thing, have compassion on us, and help us.

23. Jesus said unto him, If thou canst believe, all things are possible to him that believeth.

24. And straightway the father of the child cried out, and said with tears, Lord, I believe; help thou mine unbelief.

25. When Jesus saw that the people came running together, he rebuked the foul spirit, saying unto him, Thou dumb and deaf spirit, I charge thee, come out of him, and enter no more into him.

26. And the spirit cried, and rent him sore, and came out of him: and he was as one dead; insomuch that many said, He is dead.

27. But Jesus took him by the hand, and lifted him up; and he arose.

28. And when he was come into the house, his disciples asked him privately, Why could not we cast him out?

29. And he said unto them, This kind can come forth by nothing, but by prayer and fasting.

30. ¶ And they departed thence, and passed through Galilee; and he would not that any man should know it.

31. For he taught his disciples, and said unto them, The Son of man is delivered into the hands of men, and they shall kill him; and after that he is killed, he shall rise the third day.

32. But they understood not that saying, and were afraid to ask him.

33. ¶ And he came to Capernaum: and being in the house he asked them, What was it that ye disputed among yourselves by the way?

34. But they held their peace: for by the way they had disputed among themselves, who should be the greatest.

35. And he sat down, and called the twelve, and saith unto them, If any man desire to be first, the same shall be last of all, and servant of all.

36. And he took a child, and set him in the midst of them: and when he had taken him in his arms, he said unto them,

37. Whosoever shall receive one of such children in my name, receiveth me: and whosoever shall receive me, receiveth not me, but him that sent me.

38. ¶ And John answered him, saying, Master, we saw one casting out devils in thy name, and he followeth not us: and we forbad him, because he followeth not us.

39. But Jesus said, Forbid him not: for there is no man which shall do a miracle in my name, that can lightly speak evil of me.

40. For he that is not against us is on our part.

41. For whosoever shall give you a cup of water to drink in my name,

Mark 9:24—In our most desperate hours, many of us may have cried to the Lord to help our unbelief. We pave the way for that assistance from the Lord by choosing to obey the commandments cheerfully and without murmuring, doing those things that the Lord asks of us with exactness and without questioning. If we do, the Lord helps us, and our faith becomes "powerful, vibrant, and unshakable" (L. Whitney Clayton, *Ensign,* Nov. 2001, 29).

Mark 9:33–37—The Savior teaches here that He expects us to become as little children—to *receive* for ourselves the qualities that make little children so precious to Him. Some of those qualities include honesty, innocence, trust, faith, frankness, and an appreciation for the simple things of life (see Richard L. Evans, *Ensign,* March 1971, 17).

Notes: _____

_____

_____

_____

_____

_____

_____

_____

_____

_____

_____

_____

_____

_____

_____

_____

_____

_____

_____

_____

because ye belong to Christ, verily I say unto you, he shall not lose his reward.

42. And whosoever shall offend one of these little ones that believe in me, it is better for him that a millstone were hanged about his neck, and he were cast into the sea.

43. And if thy hand offend thee, cut it off: it is better for thee to enter into life maimed, than having two hands to go into hell, into the fire that never shall be quenched:

44. Where their worm dieth not, and the fire is not quenched.

45. And if thy foot offend thee, cut it off: it is better for thee to enter halt into life, than having two feet to be cast into hell, into the fire that never shall be quenched:

46. Where their worm dieth not, and the fire is not quenched.

47. And if thine eye offend thee, pluck it out: it is better for thee to enter into the kingdom of God with one eye, than having two eyes to be cast into hell fire:

48. Where their worm dieth not, and the fire is not quenched.

49. For every one shall be salted with fire, and every sacrifice shall be salted with salt.

50. Salt is good: but if the salt have lost his saltness, wherewith will ye season it? Have salt in yourselves, and have peace one with another.

CHAPTER 10

1. And he arose from thence, and cometh into the coasts of Judæa by the farther side of Jordan: and the people resort unto him again; and, as he was wont, he taught them again.

2. ¶ And the Pharisees came to him, and asked him, Is it lawful for a man to put away his wife? tempting him.

3. And he answered and said unto them, What did Moses command you?

4. And they said, Moses suffered to write a bill of divorcement, and to put her away.

5. And Jesus answered and said unto them, For the hardness of your heart he wrote you this precept.

6. But from the beginning of the creation God made them male and female.

7. For this cause shall a man leave his father and mother, and cleave to his wife;

8. And they twain shall be one flesh: so then they are no more twain, but one flesh.

9. What therefore God hath joined together, let not man put asunder.

10. And in the house his disciples asked him again of the same matter.

11. And he saith unto them, Whosoever shall put away his wife, and marry another, committeth adultery against her.

12. And if a woman shall put away her husband, and be married to another, she committeth adultery.

13. ¶ And they brought young children to him, that he should touch them: and his disciples rebuked those that brought them.

14. But when Jesus saw it, he was much displeased, and said unto them, Suffer the little children to come unto me, and forbid them not: for of such is the kingdom of God.

15. Verily I say unto you, Whosoever shall not receive the kingdom of God as a little child, he shall not enter therein.

16. And he took them up in his arms, put his hands upon them,

Mark 9:41—"How commendable and weighted with blessings is the help and hospitality rendered by the saints to others of their number who are serving on the Lord's errand" (Bruce R. McConkie, *Doctrinal New Testament Commentary,* 3:414).

Mark 9:42–50—We often read this passage of scripture and focus on the sin of offending, of destroying the faith of an individual or leading him away from the word of God. Our attention should also be focused on what President Spencer W. Kimball called "the great objective of all our work": to "build character and increase faith in the lives of those whom we serve." As he pointed out, that service, as well as the offense and destruction, applies just as much to adults who believe and trust in God as it does to small children (see *The Teachings of Spencer W. Kimball,* 79).

Mark 10:11–12—To "put away" under the law of Moses was the equivalent of simply "leaving" a spouse today without going through the official process of divorce. Without a legal divorce, a man or woman who married someone else did, indeed, commit adultery because the original marriage was still in force.

While adultery is a very serious offense, it can be forgiven in most cases if there is heartfelt and complete repentance followed by complete adherence to the Lord's laws. However, after a person has advanced in righteousness and light to a point of having his or her calling and election made sure, "If a man commit adultery, he cannot receive the celestial kingdom of God. Even if he is saved in any kingdom, it cannot be the celestial kingdom" (Joseph Smith, *History of the Church,* 6:81).

Mark 10:13–16—"Truly [the doctrine of little children being saved] is one of the sweetest and most soul-satisfying doctrines of the gospel! . . . Joseph Smith's statements, as recorded in the Book of Mormon and latter-day revelation, came as a refreshing breeze of pure truth: *little children shall be saved*" (Bruce R. McConkie, *Ensign,* Apr. 1977, 7).

and blessed them.

17. ¶ And when he was gone forth into the way, there came one running, and kneeled to him, and asked him, Good Master, what shall I do that I may inherit eternal life?

18. And Jesus said unto him, Why callest thou me good? there is none good but one, that is, God.

19. Thou knowest the commandments, Do not commit adultery, Do not kill, Do not steal, Do not bear false witness, Defraud not, Honour thy father and mother.

20. And he answered and said unto him, Master, all these have I observed from my youth.

21. Then Jesus beholding him loved him, and said unto him, One thing thou lackest: go thy way, sell whatsoever thou hast, and give to the poor, and thou shalt have treasure in heaven: and come, take up the cross, and follow me.

22. And he was sad at that saying, and went away grieved: for he had great possessions.

23. ¶ And Jesus looked round about, and saith unto his disciples, How hardly shall they that have riches enter into the kingdom of God!

24. And the disciples were astonished at his words. But Jesus answereth again, and saith unto them, Children, how hard is it for them that trust in riches to enter into the kingdom of God!

25. It is easier for a camel to go through the eye of a needle, than for a rich man to enter into the kingdom of God.

26. And they were astonished out of measure, saying among themselves, Who then can be saved?

27. And Jesus looking upon them saith, With men it is impossible, but not with God: for with God all things are possible.

28. ¶ Then Peter began to say unto him, Lo, we have left all, and have followed thee.

29. And Jesus answered and said, Verily I say unto you, There is no man that hath left house, or brethren, or sisters, or father, or mother, or wife, or children, or lands, for my sake, and the gospel's,

30. But he shall receive an hundredfold now in this time, houses, and brethren, and sisters, and mothers, and children, and lands, with persecutions; and in the world to come eternal life.

31. But many that are first shall be last; and the last first.

32. ¶ And they were in the way going up to Jerusalem; and Jesus went before them: and they were amazed; and as they followed, they were afraid. And he took again the twelve, and began to tell them what things should happen unto him,

33. Saying, Behold, we go up to Jerusalem; and the Son of man shall be delivered unto the chief priests, and unto the scribes; and they shall condemn him to death, and shall deliver him to the Gentiles:

34. And they shall mock him, and shall scourge him, and shall spit

Notes: _____

_____
_____
_____
_____
_____
_____
_____
_____
_____
_____
_____
_____
_____
_____
_____
_____
_____
_____

Mark 10:28–31 — President Harold B. Lee bore witness that the only way to claim kinship to the Savior is to be "willing to sacrifice all he possesses in the world, not even withholding his own life if it were necessary" (Conference Report, Oct. 1965, 131).

Mark 10:32–34 — Breaking the bonds of death in the Resurrection was the fourth and final requirement for the Savior to become the Redeemer. The other three were 1) taking upon Himself mortality, 2) taking upon Himself the sins of all mankind through His suffering in Gethsemane, and 3) giving His life on the cross (see Marion G. Romney, *Ensign,* May 1982, 6).

upon him, and shall kill him: and the third day he shall rise again.

35. ¶ And James and John, the sons of Zebedee, come unto him, saying, Master, we would that thou shouldest do for us whatsoever we shall desire.

36. And he said unto them, What would ye that I should do for you?

37. They said unto him, Grant unto us that we may sit, one on thy right hand, and the other on thy left hand, in thy glory.

38. But Jesus said unto them, Ye know not what ye ask: can ye drink of the cup that I drink of? and be baptized with the baptism that I am baptized with?

39. And they said unto him, We can. And Jesus said unto them, Ye shall indeed drink of the cup that I drink of; and with the baptism that I am baptized withal shall ye be baptized:

40. But to sit on my right hand and on my left hand is not mine to give; but it shall be given to them for whom it is prepared.

41. And when the ten heard it, they began to be much displeased with James and John.

42. But Jesus called them to him, and saith unto them, Ye know that they which are accounted to rule over the Gentiles exercise lordship over them; and their great ones exercise authority upon them.

43. But so shall it not be among you: but whosoever will be great among you, shall be your minister:

44. And whosoever of you will be the chiefest, shall be servant of all.

45. For even the Son of man came not to be ministered unto, but to minister, and to give his life a ransom for many.

46. ¶ And they came to Jericho: and as he went out of Jericho with his disciples and a great number of people, blind Bartimæus, the son of Timæus, sat by the highway side begging.

47. And when he heard that it was Jesus of Nazareth, he began to cry out, and say, Jesus, thou Son of David, have mercy on me.

48. And many charged him that he should hold his peace: but he cried the more a great deal, Thou Son of David, have mercy on me.

49. And Jesus stood still, and commanded him to be called. And they call the blind man, saying unto him, Be of good comfort, rise; he calleth thee.

50. And he, casting away his garment, rose, and came to Jesus.

51. And Jesus answered and said unto him, What wilt thou that I should do unto thee? The blind man said unto him, Lord, that I might receive my sight.

52. And Jesus said unto him, Go thy way; thy faith hath made thee whole. And immediately he received his sight, and followed Jesus in the way.

CHAPTER 11

1. And when they came nigh to Jerusalem, unto Bethphage and Bethany, at the mount of Olives, he sendeth forth two of his disciples,

2. And saith unto them, Go your way into the village over against you: and as soon as ye be entered into it, ye shall find a colt tied, whereon never man sat; loose him, and bring him.

3. And if any man say unto you, Why do ye this? say ye that the Lord hath need of him; and straightway he will send him hither.

4. And they went their way, and found the colt tied by the door with-

Mark 10:35–45 — We will have arrived at a glorious day when we find ourselves rendering service naturally, as a result of the purity of our hearts, instead of viewing service as something we must merely endure and perform (see Marion G. Romney, *Ensign,* June 1984, 6).

Mark 10:46–52 — As He encountered the blind Bartimaeus, the Savior knew not only of this man's worthiness and simple faith, but of his suffering. As a result, the Savior granted the desired blessing immediately. Imagine the joy of being able to see for the first time — and of the first sight being that of Jesus Christ! (see Vaughn J. Featherstone, *The Incomparable Christ: Our Master and Model,* 75).

Notes: _____

_____

_____

_____

_____

_____

_____

_____

_____

_____

_____

_____

_____

_____

_____

_____

_____

_____

out in a place where two ways met; and they loose him.

5. And certain of them that stood there said unto them, What do ye, loosing the colt?

6. And they said unto them even as Jesus had commanded: and they let them go.

7. And they brought the colt to Jesus, and cast their garments on him; and he sat upon him.

8. And many spread their garments in the way: and others cut down branches off the trees, and strawed them in the way.

9. And they that went before, and they that followed, cried, saying, Hosanna; Blessed is he that cometh in the name of the Lord:

10. Blessed be the kingdom of our father David, that cometh in the name of the Lord: Hosanna in the highest.

11. And Jesus entered into Jerusalem, and into the temple: and when he had looked round about upon all things, and now the eventide was come, he went out unto Bethany with the twelve.

12. ¶ And on the morrow, when they were come from Bethany, he was hungry:

13. And seeing a fig tree afar off having leaves, he came, if haply he might find any thing thereon: and when he came to it, he found nothing but leaves; for the time of figs was not yet.

14. And Jesus answered and said unto it, No man eat fruit of thee hereafter for ever. And his disciples heard it.

15. ¶ And they come to Jerusalem: and Jesus went into the temple, and began to cast out them that sold and bought in the temple, and overthrew the tables of the moneychangers, and the seats of them that sold doves;

16. And would not suffer that any man should carry any vessel through the temple.

17. And he taught, saying unto them, Is it not written, My house shall be called of all nations the house of prayer? but ye have made it a den of thieves.

18. And the scribes and chief priests heard it, and sought how they might destroy him: for they feared him, because all the people was astonished at his doctrine.

19. And when even was come, he went out of the city.

20. ¶ And in the morning, as they passed by, they saw the fig tree dried up from the roots.

21. And Peter calling to remembrance saith unto him, Master, behold, the fig tree which thou cursedst is withered away.

22. And Jesus answering saith unto them, Have faith in God.

23. For verily I say unto you, That whosoever shall say unto this mountain, Be thou removed, and be thou cast into the sea; and shall not doubt in his heart, but shall believe that those things which he saith shall come to pass; he shall have whatsoever he saith.

24. Therefore I say unto you, What things soever ye desire, when ye pray, believe that ye receive them, and ye shall have them.

25. And when ye stand praying, forgive, if ye have ought against any: that your Father also which is in heaven may forgive you your trespasses.

26. But if ye do not forgive, neither will your Father which is in heaven forgive your trespasses.

27. ¶ And they come again to Jerusalem: and as he was walking in the temple, there come to him the chief priests, and the scribes, and the elders,

Mark 11:1–10 — The triumphal entry of Jesus into Jerusalem was in a very real way a prelude to the "greater day of triumph only a few days distant. Before His crucifixion, He had spoken of His personal triumph over worldly things. . . . But there was yet that *greater day* of *victory* when He triumphed over death and opened the way to a universal resurrection" (Harold B. Lee, Conference Report, April 1955, 20).

Notes: _____

_____

_____

_____

_____

_____

_____

_____

_____

_____

_____

_____

_____

_____

_____

_____

_____

Mark 11:20–21 — "What a loss to the individual and to humanity if the vine does not grow, the tree does not bear fruit, the soul does not expand through service! One must live, not merely exist; he must do, not merely be; he must grow, not just stagnate" (Spencer W. Kimball, *President Kimball Speaks Out*, 44).

28. And say unto him, By what authority doest thou these things? and who gave thee this authority to do these things?

29. And Jesus answered and said unto them, I will also ask of you one question, and answer me, and I will tell you by what authority I do these things.

30. The baptism of John, was it from heaven, or of men? answer me.

31. And they reasoned with themselves, saying, If we shall say, From heaven; he will say, Why then did ye not believe him?

32. But if we shall say, Of men; they feared the people: for all men counted John, that he was a prophet indeed.

33. And they answered and said unto Jesus, We cannot tell. And Jesus answering saith unto them, Neither do I tell you by what authority I do these things.

CHAPTER 12

1. And he began to speak unto them by parables. A certain man planted a vineyard, and set an hedge about it, and digged a place for the winefat, and built a tower, and let it out to husbandmen, and went into a far country.

2. And at the season he sent to the husbandmen a servant, that he might receive from the husbandmen of the fruit of the vineyard.

3. And they caught him, and beat him, and sent him away empty.

4. And again he sent unto them another servant; and at him they cast stones, and wounded him in the head, and sent him away shamefully handled.

5. And again he sent another; and him they killed, and many others; beating some, and killing some.

6. Having yet therefore one son, his wellbeloved, he sent him also last unto them, saying, They will reverence my son.

7. But those husbandmen said among themselves, This is the heir; come, let us kill him, and the inheritance shall be ours.

8. And they took him, and killed him, and cast him out of the vineyard.

9. What shall therefore the lord of the vineyard do? he will come and destroy the husbandmen, and will give the vineyard unto others.

10. And have ye not read this scripture; The stone which the builders rejected is become the head of the corner:

11. This was the Lord's doing, and it is marvellous in our eyes?

12. And they sought to lay hold on him, but feared the people: for they knew that he had spoken the parable against them: and they left him, and went their way.

13. ¶ And they send unto him certain of the Pharisees and of the Herodians, to catch him in his words.

14. And when they were come, they say unto him, Master, we know that thou art true, and carest for no man: for thou regardest not the person of men, but teachest the way of God in truth: Is it lawful to give tribute to Cæsar, or not?

15. Shall we give, or shall we not give? But he, knowing their hypocrisy, said unto them, Why tempt ye me? bring me a penny, that I may see it.

16. And they brought it. And he saith unto them, Whose is this image and superscription? And they said unto him, Cæsar's.

17. And Jesus answering said unto them, Render to Cæsar the things that are Cæsar's, and to God the things that are God's. And they marvelled at him.

Mark 11:27–33 — Jesus "is the Father by divine investiture of authority, meaning that the Father–Elohim has placed his name upon the Son, has given him his own power and authority, and has authorized him to speak in the first person as though he were the original or primal Father. . . . His words and acts were and are those of the Father! . . . They are so perfectly united in all things that, in like circumstances, they think the same thoughts, speak the same words, and do the same acts" (Bruce R. McConkie, *The Promised Messiah*, 63–64).

Notes: _____

_____

_____

_____

_____

_____

_____

_____

_____

_____

_____

_____

_____

_____

_____

_____

_____

_____

_____

_____

_____

_____

_____

_____

18. ¶ Then come unto him the Sadducees, which say there is no resurrection; and they asked him, saying,

19. Master, Moses wrote unto us, If a man's brother die, and leave his wife behind him, and leave no children, that his brother should take his wife, and raise up seed unto his brother.

20. Now there were seven brethren: and the first took a wife, and dying left no seed.

21. And the second took her, and died, neither left he any seed: and the third likewise.

22. And the seven had her, and left no seed: last of all the woman died also.

23. In the resurrection therefore, when they shall rise, whose wife shall she be of them? for the seven had her to wife.

24. And Jesus answering said unto them, Do ye not therefore err, because ye know not the scriptures, neither the power of God?

25. For when they shall rise from the dead, they neither marry, nor are given in marriage; but are as the angels which are in heaven.

26. And as touching the dead, that they rise: have ye not read in the book of Moses, how in the bush God spake unto him, saying, I am the God of Abraham, and the God of Isaac, and the God of Jacob?

27. He is not the God of the dead, but the God of the living: ye therefore do greatly err.

28. ¶ And one of the scribes came, and having heard them reasoning together, and perceiving that he had answered them well, asked him, Which is the first commandment of all?

29. And Jesus answered him, The first of all the commandments is, Hear, O Israel; The Lord our God is one Lord:

30. And thou shalt love the Lord thy God with all thy heart, and with all thy soul, and with all thy mind, and with all thy strength: this is the first commandment.

31. And the second is like, namely this, Thou shalt love thy neighbour as thyself. There is none other commandment greater than these.

32. And the scribe said unto him, Well, Master, thou hast said the truth: for there is one God; and there is none other but he:

33. And to love him with all the heart, and with all the understanding, and with all the soul, and with all the strength, and to love his neighbour as himself, is more than all whole burnt offerings and sacrifices.

34. And when Jesus saw that he answered discreetly, he said unto him, Thou art not far from the kingdom of God. And no man after that durst ask him any question.

35. ¶ And Jesus answered and said, while he taught in the temple, How say the scribes that Christ is the Son of David?

36. For David himself said by the Holy Ghost, The Lord said to my Lord, Sit thou on my right hand, till I make thine enemies thy footstool.

37. David therefore himself calleth him Lord; and whence is he then his son? And the common people heard him gladly.

38. ¶ And he said unto them in his doctrine, Beware of the scribes, which love to go in long clothing, and love salutations in the marketplaces,

Mark 12:18—The Sadducees—most of whom were priests—were a small group of very wealthy and influential aristocrats who controlled the Jerusalem temple as well as the members of the sect. The temple itself generated a substantial amount of money, and those funds were controlled by the Sadducees. The high priest of the Sadducees was also the head of the Sanhedrin, the governing council of the Jews, so the Sadducees also had a great deal of prominence in the government. They cooperated with the Romans in exchange for a continuation of their various privileges, something that angered many Jews. Unlike the Pharisees, the Sadducees did not accept the "oral law," or "traditions of the Fathers," and believed that only the Torah was valid. They believed in free agency, but did *not* believe in angels, demons, resurrection of the dead, or the continued existence of the spirit following death.

Because they were generally resented by the Jews, they did not have any moral influence over the people as a whole. In AD 66 the Jews revolted, killing most of the Sadducees as traitors. Those who were not killed lost their wealth, their base of power, and their function in Jewish society (see Kent P. Jackson and Robert L. Millet, eds., *Studies in Scripture, Vol. 5: The Gospels,* 24–25).

Mark 12:18–27—Because the Sadducees did not believe in resurrection of the dead or the continued existence of the spirit following death, they did not believe in any sort of marriage after death. As a result, this is the only answer the Savior could have given them.

Mark 12:38–40—The Pharisees, priests, and rabbis loved their blindness, demonstrated by the fact that their acts were evil and that they would not acknowledge either their evil acts or their ignorance. They were determined to destroy the Savior; if one plot failed, they had another waiting. Theirs was "unrepentant malice" toward Him. In these verses, as Elder Bruce R. McConkie so aptly put it, turning to "His disciples, but in the audience of all the people, He rolled over their guilty heads, with crash on crash of moral anger, the thunder of His utter condemnation" (*The Mortal Messiah,* 3:390).

39. And the chief seats in the synagogues, and the uppermost rooms at feasts:

40. Which devour widows' houses, and for a pretence make long prayers: these shall receive greater damnation.

41. ¶ And Jesus sat over against the treasury, and beheld how the people cast money into the treasury: and many that were rich cast in much.

42. And there came a certain poor widow, and she threw in two mites, which make a farthing.

43. And he called unto him his disciples, and saith unto them, Verily I say unto you, That this poor widow hath cast more in, than all they which have cast into the treasury:

44. For all they did cast in of their abundance; but she of her want did cast in all that she had, even all her living.

CHAPTER 13

1. And as he went out of the temple, one of his disciples saith unto him, Master, see what manner of stones and what buildings are here!

2. And Jesus answering said unto him, Seest thou these great buildings? there shall not be left one stone upon another, that shall not be thrown down.

3. And as he sat upon the mount of Olives over against the temple, Peter and James and John and Andrew asked him privately,

4. Tell us, when shall these things be? and what shall be the sign when all these things shall be fulfilled?

5. And Jesus answering them began to say, Take heed lest any man deceive you:

6. For many shall come in my name, saying, I am Christ; and shall deceive many.

7. And when ye shall hear of wars and rumours of wars, be ye not troubled: for such things must needs be; but the end shall not be yet.

8. For nation shall rise against nation, and kingdom against kingdom: and there shall be earthquakes in divers places, and there shall be famines and troubles: these are the beginnings of sorrows.

9. ¶ But take heed to yourselves: for they shall deliver you up to councils; and in the synagogues ye shall be beaten: and ye shall be brought before rulers and kings for my sake, for a testimony against them.

10. And the gospel must first be published among all nations.

11. But when they shall lead you, and deliver you up, take no thought beforehand what ye shall speak, neither do ye premeditate: but whatsoever shall be given you in that hour, that speak ye: for it is not ye that speak, but the Holy Ghost.

12. Now the brother shall betray the brother to death, and the father the son; and children shall rise up against their parents, and shall cause them to be put to death.

13. And ye shall be hated of all men for my name's sake: but he that shall endure unto the end, the same shall be saved.

14. ¶ But when ye shall see the abomination of desolation, spoken of by Daniel the prophet, standing where it ought not, (let him that readeth understand,) then let them that be in Judæa flee to the mountains:

Mark 12:34–37 — "In their apostate darkness, these Jews were unable to envision the reality that their promised Messiah would be born both as the Son of David and the Son of the Highest" (Bruce R. McConkie, *Mormon Doctrine*, 741).

Mark 12:42–44 — "On the books of the heavenly accountants that widow's contribution was entered as a munificent gift, surpassing in worth the largess of kings" (James E. Talmage, *Jesus the Christ*, 520).

Mark 13:1–2 — Just hearing about the events of the Second Coming, which "were still centuries away troubled them. It is not surprising that we who live in the day when those signs are being fulfilled should also be troubled. But the Lord specifically commanded his disciples, 'Be not troubled' (D&C 45:35)" (Gerald N. Lund, *Selected Writings of Gerald N. Lund: Gospel Scholar Series*, 325–26).

Mark 13:3–6 — "It suffices for us to know that the saints in that day — in the dispensation of death, in the era of martyrdom — became followers of the lowly Nazarene, only to have their blood mingled with the blood of all the martyrs of the past, that together that great river of blood might cry unto the Lord of Hosts till he, in his own good time, chose to avenge it" (Bruce R. McConkie, *The Mortal Messiah*, 3:427–29).

Mark 13:10 — The charge to take the gospel to all nations is, in President Gordon B. Hinckley's estimation, the greatest challenge given to any organization in the world. "That challenge, I am confident, will be met by the growing generation and by generations yet to come. To our youth I say . . . great is your responsibility, tremendous is your opportunity" (*Teachings of Gordon B. Hinckley*, 292).

15. And let him that is on the housetop not go down into the house, neither enter therein, to take any thing out of his house:

16. And let him that is in the field not turn back again for to take up his garment.

17. But woe to them that are with child, and to them that give suck in those days!

18. And pray ye that your flight be not in the winter.

19. For in those days shall be affliction, such as was not from the beginning of the creation which God created unto this time, neither shall be.

20. And except that the Lord had shortened those days, no flesh should be saved: but for the elect's sake, whom he hath chosen, he hath shortened the days.

21. And then if any man shall say to you, Lo, here is Christ; or, lo, he is there; believe him not:

22. For false Christs and false prophets shall rise, and shall shew signs and wonders, to seduce, if it were possible, even the elect.

23. But take ye heed: behold, I have foretold you all things.

24. ¶ But in those days, after that tribulation, the sun shall be darkened, and the moon shall not give her light,

25. And the stars of heaven shall fall, and the powers that are in heaven shall be shaken.

26. And then shall they see the Son of man coming in the clouds with great power and glory.

27. And then shall he send his angels, and shall gather together his elect from the four winds, from the uttermost part of the earth to the uttermost part of heaven.

28. Now learn a parable of the fig tree; When her branch is yet tender, and putteth forth leaves, ye know that summer is near:

29. So ye in like manner, when ye shall see these things come to pass, know that it is nigh, even at the doors.

30. Verily I say unto you, that this generation shall not pass, till all these things be done.

31. Heaven and earth shall pass away: but my words shall not pass away.

32. ¶ But of that day and that hour knoweth no man, no, not the angels which are in heaven, neither the Son, but the Father.

33. Take ye heed, watch and pray: for ye know not when the time is.

34. For the Son of man is as a man taking a far journey, who left his house, and gave authority to his servants, and to every man his work, and commanded the porter to watch.

35. Watch ye therefore: for ye know not when the master of the house cometh, at even, or at midnight, or at the cockcrowing, or in the morning:

36. Lest coming suddenly he find you sleeping.

37. And what I say unto you I say unto all, Watch.

CHAPTER 14

1. After two days was the feast of the passover, and of unleavened bread: and the chief priests and the scribes sought how they might take him by craft, and put him to death.

2. But they said, Not on the feast day, lest there be an uproar of the people.

Mark 13:21–23—One of the commandments we have been given is to obey the living prophet, sometimes expressed as "following the Brethren." That specifically means we are to follow the counsel of the First Presidency and the Quorum of the Twelve. There are several reasons why this is particularly difficult for some, especially in this, the last dispensation:

First, because this is the winding-up scene of the earth, there will be unprecedented growth of the Church, but there will also be unprecedented evil. The two will collide as never before, which might provide real difficulty for many.

Second, we know that there will also be unprecedented levels of deceit. As a result, Matthew wrote, even the very elect will "almost be deceived" (Matt. 24:24).

Finally, the tribulations that will afflict us during this winding-up scene will be greater than those of any other time (see D&C 43:28; 45:67–68). It is tribulation that causes many to waver or fail in their faith (see Neal A. Maxwell, *All These Things Shall Give Thee Experience*, 101–102).

Mark 13:25—The great physical changes that will take place when the Lord comes for the second time will cause the earth to reel to and fro, which will certainly make it appear as though the stars are being hurled throughout the heavens, or "falling" (see Bruce R. McConkie, *Doctrinal New Testament Commentary*, 1:678).

Mark 13:28–29—Elder Neal A. Maxwell counseled that our responsibility is to be balanced: to heed the signs and watch for their fulfillment without overreacting, but to avoid the "dulled heedlessness" of those in the days of Noah (see *If Thou Endure It Well*, 12).

Mark 13:32—The phrase "neither the Son" was stated during the Savior's mortal probation, and it is very reasonable to think that at that time, He may not have known the exact time of the Second Coming. But after He was resurrected and had assumed His place at the right hand of the Father, such timing was revealed to Him (see Hoyt W. Brewster, Jr., *Behold, I Come Quickly: The Last Days and Beyond*, 18).

Mark 14:1–2—As Elder Bruce R. McConkie pointed out, it was the very ones who should have been teaching the people to follow the Messiah—the chief priests and scribes—who plotted His death (see *Doctrinal New Testament Commentary*, 1:696).

3. ¶ And being in Bethany in the house of Simon the leper, as he sat at meat, there came a woman having an alabaster box of ointment of spikenard very precious; and she brake the box, and poured it on his head.

4. And there were some that had indignation within themselves, and said, Why was this waste of the ointment made?

5. For it might have been sold for more than three hundred pence, and have been given to the poor. And they murmured against her.

6. And Jesus said, Let her alone; why trouble ye her? she hath wrought a good work on me.

7. For ye have the poor with you always, and whensoever ye will ye may do them good: but me ye have not always.

8. She hath done what she could: she is come aforehand to anoint my body to the burying.

9. Verily I say unto you, Wheresoever this gospel shall be preached throughout the whole world, this also that she hath done shall be spoken of for a memorial of her.

10. ¶ And Judas Iscariot, one of the twelve, went unto the chief priests, to betray him unto them.

11. And when they heard it, they were glad, and promised to give him money. And he sought how he might conveniently betray him.

12. ¶ And the first day of unleavened bread, when they killed the passover, his disciples said unto him, Where wilt thou that we go and prepare that thou mayest eat the passover?

13. And he sendeth forth two of his disciples, and saith unto them, Go ye into the city, and there shall meet you a man bearing a pitcher of water: follow him.

14. And wheresoever he shall go in, say ye to the goodman of the house, The Master saith, Where is the guestchamber, where I shall eat the passover with my disciples?

15. And he will shew you a large upper room furnished and prepared: there make ready for us.

16. And his disciples went forth, and came into the city, and found as he had said unto them: and they made ready the passover.

17. And in the evening he cometh with the twelve.

18. And as they sat and did eat, Jesus said, Verily I say unto you, One of you which eateth with me shall betray me.

19. And they began to be sorrowful, and to say unto him one by one, Is it I? and another said, Is it I?

20. And he answered and said unto them, It is one of the twelve, that dippeth with me in the dish.

21. The Son of man indeed goeth, as it is written of him: but woe to that man by whom the Son of man is betrayed! good were it for that man if he had never been born.

22. ¶ And as they did eat, Jesus took bread, and blessed, and brake it, and gave to them, and said, Take, eat: this is my body.

23. And he took the cup, and when he had given thanks, he gave it to them: and they all drank of it.

24. And he said unto them, This is my blood of the new testament, which is shed for many.

25. Verily I say unto you, I will drink no more of the fruit of the vine, until that day that I drink it new in the kingdom of God.

26. ¶ And when they had sung an hymn, they went out into the mount of Olives.

27. And Jesus saith unto them, All ye shall be offended because of me

Mark 14:3–9 — The woman with the alabaster box in these verses was not Mary Magdalene, nor was it Mary of Bethany — both of whom were considered to be righteous women of good character. Instead, she was a sinner, likely a woman who was considered unvirtuous (see Bruce R. McConkie, *Doctrinal New Testament Commentary,* 1:265).

Mark 14:10–11 — "Satan can have no power over human souls unless it is given to him by them. People are subject to him only when they hearken to his enticements. In other words, Judas was an evil traitor because of personal wickedness, because he preferred to live after the manner of the world, because he 'loved Satan more than God.' He truly had become 'carnal, sensual, and devilish' by choice" (Bruce R. McConkie, *The Mortal Messiah,* 4:15).

Notes: _____

_____

_____

_____

_____

_____

_____

_____

_____

_____

_____

_____

_____

Mark 14:22–25 — "Every act of our lives *can* become a sacramental experience when we take upon us his name. Then, when our performance falls short in spite of our striving for perfection, we will find ourselves eagerly and anxiously, and with a deeper sense of gratitude than ever before, drawn to the Sabbath day and the sacramental altar" (Ardeth Greene Kapp, *I Walk By Faith,* 12).

this night: for it is written, I will smite the shepherd, and the sheep shall be scattered.

28. But after that I am risen, I will go before you into Galilee.

29. But Peter said unto him, Although all shall be offended, yet will not I.

30. And Jesus saith unto him, Verily I say unto thee, That this day, even in this night, before the cock crow twice, thou shalt deny me thrice.

31. But he spake the more vehemently, If I should die with thee, I will not deny thee in any wise. Likewise also said they all.

32. And they came to a place which was named Gethsemane: and he saith to his disciples, Sit ye here, while I shall pray.

33. And he taketh with him Peter and James and John, and began to be sore amazed, and to be very heavy;

34. And saith unto them, My soul is exceeding sorrowful unto death: tarry ye here, and watch.

35. And he went forward a little, and fell on the ground, and prayed that, if it were possible, the hour might pass from him.

36. And he said, Abba, Father, all things are possible unto thee; take away this cup from me: nevertheless not what I will, but what thou wilt.

37. And he cometh, and findeth them sleeping, and saith unto Peter, Simon, sleepest thou? couldest not thou watch one hour?

38. Watch ye and pray, lest ye enter into temptation. The spirit truly is ready, but the flesh is weak.

39. And again he went away, and prayed, and spake the same words.

40. And when he returned, he found them asleep again, (for their eyes were heavy,) neither wist they what to answer him.

41. And he cometh the third time, and saith unto them, Sleep on now, and take your rest: it is enough, the hour is come; behold, the Son of man is betrayed into the hands of sinners.

42. Rise up, let us go; lo, he that betrayeth me is at hand.

43. ¶ And immediately, while he yet spake, cometh Judas, one of the twelve, and with him a great multitude with swords and staves, from the chief priests and the scribes and the elders.

44. And he that betrayed him had given them a token, saying, Whomsoever I shall kiss, that same is he; take him, and lead him away safely.

45. And as soon as he was come, he goeth straightway to him, and saith, Master, master; and kissed him.

46. ¶ And they laid their hands on him, and took him.

47. And one of them that stood by drew a sword, and smote a servant of the high priest, and cut off his ear.

48. And Jesus answered and said unto them, Are ye come out, as against a thief, with swords and with staves to take me?

49. I was daily with you in the temple teaching, and ye took me not: but the scriptures must be fulfilled.

50. And they all forsook him, and fled.

51. And there followed him a certain young man, having a linen cloth cast about his naked body; and the young men laid hold on him:

52. And he left the linen cloth, and fled from them naked.

53. ¶ And they led Jesus away to the high priest: and with him were assembled all the chief priests and the elders and the scribes.

54. And Peter followed him afar off, even into the palace of the high priest: and he sat with the servants, and warmed himself at the fire.

55. And the chief priests and all the

Mark 14:27–31—"Peter was determined to follow Christ wherever he went, even to the laying down of his own life (John 13:36–37). It is true that he later denied the Savior, as Christ had prophesied: but after the Holy Ghost came upon Peter, he did lay down his life for Christ" (Monte S. Nyman, *Great Are the Words of Isaiah*, 49–50).

Mark 14:32—Knowing the origin of the word *Gethsemane* can help us more fully appreciate what occurred there. *Gethsemane* comes from the Hebrew words *Geth [Gath]*, meaning "press," and *semane [shemen]*, meaning "oil"—and therefore means "the press of oil." The word has reference to huge stone presses that were used to squeeze the oil from olives or the juice from grapes; such presses would have been found in Gethsemane, which was a grove of olive trees. In like manner, the Savior was "pressed" in that garden by the weight of the sins of all mankind until His blood flowed from His skin (see Stephen E. Robinson, *Believing Christ: The Parable of the Bicycle and Other Good News*, 119).

Mark 14:36—Doing the Father's will implies doing all that He commands, without reservation (see Franklin D. Richards, Conference Report, Apr. 1969, 20).

Jesus betrayed in the garden

council sought for witness against Jesus to put him to death; and found none.

56. For many bare false witness against him, but their witness agreed not together.

57. And there arose certain, and bare false witness against him, saying,

58. We heard him say, I will destroy this temple that is made with hands, and within three days I will build another made without hands.

59. But neither so did their witness agree together.

60. And the high priest stood up in the midst, and asked Jesus, saying, Answerest thou nothing? what is it which these witness against thee?

61. But he held his peace, and answered nothing. Again the high priest asked him, and said unto him, Art thou the Christ, the Son of the Blessed?

62. And Jesus said, I am: and ye shall see the Son of man sitting on the right hand of power, and coming in the clouds of heaven.

63. Then the high priest rent his clothes, and saith, What need we any further witnesses?

64. Ye have heard the blasphemy: what think ye? And they all condemned him to be guilty of death.

65. And some began to spit on him, and to cover his face, and to buffet him, and to say unto him, Prophesy: and the servants did strike him with the palms of their hands.

66. ¶ And as Peter was beneath in the palace, there cometh one of the maids of the high priest:

67. And when she saw Peter warming himself, she looked upon him, and said, And thou also wast with Jesus of Nazareth.

68. But he denied, saying, I know not, neither understand I what thou sayest. And he went out into the porch; and the cock crew.

69. And a maid saw him again, and began to say to them that stood by, This is one of them.

70. And he denied it again. And a little after, they that stood by said again to Peter, Surely thou art one of them: for thou art a Galilæan, and thy speech agreeth thereto.

71. But he began to curse and to swear, saying, I know not this man of whom ye speak.

72. And the second time the cock crew. And Peter called to mind the word that Jesus said unto him, Before the cock crow twice, thou shalt deny me thrice. And when he thought thereon, he wept.

CHAPTER 15

1. And straightway in the morning the chief priests held a consultation with the elders and scribes and the whole council, and bound Jesus, and carried him away, and delivered him to Pilate.

2. And Pilate asked him, Art thou the King of the Jews? And he answering said unto him, Thou sayest it.

3. And the chief priests accused him of many things: but he answered nothing.

4. And Pilate asked him again, saying, Answerest thou nothing? behold how many things they witness against thee.

5. But Jesus yet answered nothing; so that Pilate marvelled.

6. Now at that feast he released unto them one prisoner, whomsoever they desired.

Notes: _____
_____
_____
_____
_____
_____
_____
_____
_____
_____
_____
_____
_____
_____
_____
_____
_____
_____
_____

Mark 14:66–72—"I personally believe this was the beginning of the conversion of Peter. Up to this time Peter had never questioned his own ability to cleave to truth. . . . Perhaps, as so many of us, he lacked humility. As a result of this experience, however, he *learned* humility. There is no question of his remorse, for he wept bitterly at his own weakness. I feel, however, that a great change began to work in Peter, beginning with this knowledge of his own weakness" (Theodore M. Burton, "Convince or Convert?" *Brigham Young University Speeches of the Year,* Oct. 6, 1964, 3–4).

Mark 15:2–5—"No ruler—however supreme and autocratic; however subject to the political pressures and passions of the populace; however prejudiced toward a race and a people—no ruler knowingly and willfully sends an innocent man to death unless prior sins have seared his conscience, tied his hands, and buried his instinct to deal justly. Through all his length of days, Pilate had been and then was an evil man, inured to blood and hardened against violence" (Bruce R. McConkie, *The Mortal Messiah,* 4:171).

7. And there was one named Barabbas, which lay bound with them that had made insurrection with him, who had committed murder in the insurrection.

8. And the multitude crying aloud began to desire him to do as he had ever done unto them.

9. But Pilate answered them, saying, Will ye that I release unto you the King of the Jews?

10. For he knew that the chief priests had delivered him for envy.

11. But the chief priests moved the people, that he should rather release Barabbas unto them.

12. And Pilate answered and said again unto them, What will ye then that I shall do unto him whom ye call the King of the Jews?

13. And they cried out again, Crucify him.

14. Then Pilate said unto them, Why, what evil hath he done? And they cried out the more exceedingly, Crucify him.

15. ¶ And so Pilate, willing to content the people, released Barabbas unto them, and delivered Jesus, when he had scourged him, to be crucified.

16. And the soldiers led him away into the hall, called Prætorium; and they call together the whole band.

17. And they clothed him with purple, and platted a crown of thorns, and put it about his head,

18. And began to salute him, Hail, King of the Jews!

19. And they smote him on the head with a reed, and did spit upon him, and bowing their knees worshipped him.

20. And when they had mocked him, they took off the purple from him, and put his own clothes on him, and led him out to crucify him.

21. And they compel one Simon a Cyrenian, who passed by, coming out of the country, the father of Alexander and Rufus, to bear his cross.

22. And they bring him unto the place Golgotha, which is, being interpreted, The place of a skull.

23. And they gave him to drink wine mingled with myrrh: but he received it not.

24. And when they had crucified him, they parted his garments, casting lots upon them, what every man should take.

25. And it was the third hour, and they crucified him.

26. And the superscription of his accusation was written over, THE KING OF THE JEWS.

27. And with him they crucify two thieves; the one on his right hand, and the other on his left.

28. And the scripture was fulfilled, which saith, And he was numbered with the transgressors.

29. And they that passed by railed on him, wagging their heads, and saying, Ah, thou that destroyest the temple, and buildest it in three days,

30. Save thyself, and come down from the cross.

31. Likewise also the chief priests mocking said among themselves with the scribes, He saved others; himself he cannot save.

32. Let Christ the King of Israel descend now from the cross, that we may see and believe. And they that were crucified with him reviled him.

33. And when the sixth hour was come, there was darkness over the whole land until the ninth hour.

34. And at the ninth hour Jesus cried with a loud voice, saying, Eloi, Eloi, lama sabachthani? which is, being interpreted, My God, my God, why hast thou forsaken me?

35. And some of them that stood by, when they heard it, said, Behold, he calleth Elias.

Mark 15:15–28 — Crucifixion "was unanimously considered the most horrible form of death. Among the Romans also the degradation was a part of the infliction, and the punishment if applied to freemen was only used in the case of the vilest criminals. . . . The criminal carried his own cross, or at any rate a part of it. . . . The place of execution was outside the city, often in some public road or other conspicuous place. Arrived at the place of execution, the sufferer was stripped naked, the dress being the perquisite of the soldiers. The cross was then driven into the ground, so that the feet of the condemned were a foot or two above the earth, and he was lifted upon it; or else stretched upon it on the ground and then he was lifted up with it. It was the custom to station soldiers to watch the cross, so as to prevent the removal of the sufferer while yet alive. This was necessary from the lingering character of the death, which sometimes did not supervene even for three days, and was at last the result of gradual benumbing and starvation. . . . In most cases the body was suffered to rot on the cross by the action of sun and rain, or to be devoured by birds and beasts" (James E. Talmage, *Jesus the Christ*, 618).

36. And one ran and filled a spunge full of vinegar, and put it on a reed, and gave him to drink, saying, Let alone; let us see whether Elias will come to take him down.

37. And Jesus cried with a loud voice, and gave up the ghost.

38. And the veil of the temple was rent in twain from the top to the bottom.

39. And when the centurion, which stood over against him, saw that he so cried out, and gave up the ghost, he said, Truly this man was the Son of God.

40. There were also women looking on afar off: among whom was Mary Magdalene, and Mary the mother of James the less and of Joses, and Salome;

41. (Who also, when he was in Galilee, followed him, and ministered unto him;) and many other women which came up with him unto Jerusalem.

42. ¶ And now when the even was come, because it was the preparation, that is, the day before the sabbath,

43. Joseph of Arimathæa, and honourable counsellor, which also waited for the kingdom of God, came, and went in boldly unto Pilate, and craved the body of Jesus.

44. And Pilate marvelled if he were already dead: and calling unto him the centurion, he asked him whether he had been any while dead.

45. And when he knew it of the centurion, he gave the body to Joseph.

46. And he bought fine linen, and took him down, and wrapped him in the linen, and laid him in a sepulchre which was hewn out of a rock, and rolled a stone unto the door of the sepulchre.

47. And Mary Magdalene and Mary the mother of Joses beheld where he was laid.

CHAPTER 16

1. And when the sabbath was past, Mary Magdalene, and Mary the mother of James, and Salome, had bought sweet spices, that they might come and anoint him.

2. And very early in the morning the first day of the week, they came unto the sepulchre at the rising of the sun.

3. And they said among themselves, Who shall roll us away the stone from the door of the sepulchre?

4. And when they looked, they saw that the stone was rolled away: for it was very great.

5. And entering into the sepulchre, they saw a young man sitting on the right side, clothed in a long white garment; and they were affrighted.

6. And he saith unto them, Be not affrighted: Ye seek Jesus of Nazareth, which was crucified: he is risen; he is not here: behold the place where they laid him.

7. But go your way, tell his disciples and Peter that he goeth before you into Galilee: there shall ye see him, as he said unto you.

8. And they went out quickly, and fled from the sepulchre; for they trembled and were amazed: neither said they any thing to any man; for they were afraid.

9. ¶ Now when Jesus was risen early the first day of the week, he appeared first to Mary Magdalene, out of whom he had cast seven devils.

10. And she went and told them that had been with him, as they mourned and wept.

11. And they, when they had heard

Mark 15:33–38 — The Savior made seven utterances while hanging on the cross, utterances that mark the end of His mortal ministry:

• He asked the Father to forgive those who crucified Him (see Luke 23:34).

• He told one of the thieves crucified with Him that he would be that day in paradise (see Luke 23:43).

• He addressed Mary and John the Beloved regarding their relationship to each other (see John 19:26–27).

• He cried out to the Father, "My God, my God, why hast thou forsaken me?" (Mark 15:34).

• He said He was thirsty (see John 19:28).

• He proclaimed the end had come by saying, "It is finished" (John 19:30).

• He cried in a loud voice, "Father, into thy hands I commend my spirit" (Luke 23:46).

Mark 15:43 — Joseph of Arimathæa was a disciple of Jesus, but out of fear had not made his discipleship public.

Mark 16:1–8 — "Because Jesus came forth from the grave on the first day of the week, to commemorate that day and to keep in remembrance the glorious reality of the resurrection, the ancient apostles, as guided by the Spirit, changed the Sabbath to Sunday" (Bruce R. McConkie, *Doctrinal New Testament Commentary,* 1:841).

Mark 16:6 — "The resurrection of Jesus Christ is the most stupendous miracle of all time. . . . Nearness to the event gives increased value to the evidence given by the apostles. A deeper value of their testimony lies in the fact that with Jesus' death the apostles were stricken with discouragement and gloom. . . . They were left alone, and they seemed confused and helpless. . . . What, then, was it that suddenly changed these disciples to confident, fearless, heroic preachers of the gospel of Jesus Christ? It was the revelation that Christ had risen from the grave" (David O. McKay, Conference Report, Apr. 1966, 56–57).

Mark 16:9–11 — This indicates that during the time Jesus' body and spirit were separated, He was in paradise, preaching the gospel to those from the days of Noah who had been swept away in the flood (see Joseph L. Wirthlin, Conference Report, Apr. 1945, 69).

that he was alive, and had been seen of her, believed not.

12. ¶ After that he appeared in another form unto two of them, as they walked, and went into the country.

13. And they went and told it unto the residue: neither believed they them.

14. ¶ Afterward he appeared unto the eleven as they sat at meat, and upbraided them with their unbelief and hardness of heart, because they believed not them which had seen him after he was risen.

15. And he said unto them, Go ye into all the world, and preach the gospel to every creature.

16. He that believeth and is baptized shall be saved; but he that believeth not shall be damned.

17. And these signs shall follow them that believe; In my name shall they cast out devils; they shall speak with new tongues;

18. They shall take up serpents; and if they drink any deadly thing, it shall not hurt them; they shall lay hands on the sick, and they shall recover.

19. ¶ So then after the Lord had spoken unto them, he was received up into heaven, and sat on the right hand of God.

20. And they went forth, and preached every where, the Lord working with them, and confirming the word with signs following. Amen.

THE GOSPEL ACCORDING TO

ST. LUKE

CHAPTER 1

1. Forasmuch as many have taken in hand to set forth in order a declaration of those things which are most surely believed among us,

2. Even as they delivered them unto us, which from the beginning were eyewitnesses, and ministers of the word;

3. It seemed good to me also, having

Mark 16:12–13 — When Jesus appeared to the disciples on the road to Emmaus, they did not recognize Him, because He looked, talked, acted, and seemed like any ordinary preacher. What a marvelous way for the Savior to teach that a resurrected being retains the same qualities and features as a mortal man! (see Bruce R. McConkie, *Doctrinal New Testament Commentary,* 1:850).

Mark 16:14 — By eating and drinking with His Apostles, the Savior demonstrated clearly the material nature of His resurrected body (see Bruce R. McConkie, *Doctrinal New Testament Commentary,* 3:136).

This verse also gives us insight into the nature of God the Father. "The logic is not difficult: Jesus is God; Jesus has a body of flesh and bones; there, God, in the person of the resurrected Son, has a body of flesh and bones. . . . God must be understood to have a tangible body" (Stephen E. Robinson, *Are Mormons Christians?,* 81–82).

Mark 16:19–20 — "The Lord's ascension was accomplished. It was as truly a literal departure of a material being as His resurrection had been an actual return of His spirit to His own physical body. Now the disciples began to comprehend more fully that He had truly 'overcome the world'" (Ezra Taft Benson, *The Teachings of Ezra Taft Benson,* 17).

Luke 1:1–4 — The method of Luke's writing was to gather the oral testimony of eyewitness accounts, combining his own interviews (including an interview of the Savior's mother) with Matthew's account and other written accounts. His goal was to create a narrative that would convince the Gentiles that Jesus was the Son of God.

had perfect understanding of all things from the very first, to write unto thee in order, most excellent Theophilus,

4. That thou mightest know the certainty of those things, wherein thou hast been instructed.

5. ¶ There was in the days of Herod, the king of Judæa, a certain priest named Zacharias, of the course of Abia: and his wife was of the daughters of Aaron, and her name was Elisabeth.

6. And they were both righteous before God, walking in all the commandments and ordinances of the Lord blameless.

7. And they had no child, because that Elisabeth was barren, and they both were now well stricken in years.

8. And it came to pass, that while he executed the priest's office before God in the order of his course,

9. According to the custom of the priest's office, his lot was to burn incense when he went into the temple of the Lord.

10. And the whole multitude of the people were praying without at the time of incense.

11. And there appeared unto him an angel of the Lord standing on the right side of the altar of incense.

12. And when Zacharias saw him, he was troubled, and fear fell upon him.

13. But the angel said unto him, Fear not, Zacharias: for thy prayer is heard; and thy wife Elisabeth shall bear thee a son, and thou shalt call his name John.

14. And thou shalt have joy and gladness; and many shall rejoice at his birth.

15. For he shall be great in the sight of the Lord, and shall drink neither wine nor strong drink; and he shall be filled with the Holy Ghost, even from his mother's womb.

16. And many of the children of Israel shall he turn to the Lord their God.

17. And he shall go before him in the spirit and power of Elias, to turn the hearts of the fathers to the children, and the disobedient to the wisdom of the just; to make ready a people prepared for the Lord.

18. And Zacharias said unto the angel, Whereby shall I know this? for I am an old man, and my wife well stricken in years.

19. And the angel answering said unto him, I am Gabriel, that stand in the presence of God; and am sent to speak unto thee, and to shew thee these glad tidings.

20. And, behold, thou shalt be dumb, and not able to speak, until the day that these things shall be performed, because thou believest not my words, which shall be fulfilled in their season.

21. And the people waited for Zacharias, and marvelled that he tarried so long in the temple.

22. And when he came out, he could not speak unto them: and they perceived that he had seen a vision in the temple: for he beckoned unto them, and remained speechless.

23. And it came to pass, that, as soon as the days of his ministration

Luke 1:3 — Theophilus, a name meaning "friend of God," was likely used here by Luke as a literary device, signifying that he was writing to those who feared God (see Kent P. Jackson and Robert L. Millet, eds., *Studies in Scripture, Vol. 5: The Gospels,* 90).

Luke 1:17 — *Elias* is a name or term used to designate any prophet who performs a preparatory work. Joseph Smith stated, "The spirit of Elias is to prepare the way for a greater revelation of God. [It] is the Priesthood of Elias, or the Priesthood that Aaron was ordained unto. And when God sends a man into the world to prepare for a greater work, holding the keys of the power of Elias, it was called the doctrine of Elias, even from the early ages of the world" (*Teachings of the Prophet Joseph Smith,* 335).

Luke 1:19 — Gabriel is Noah. According to the Prophet Joseph Smith, "he stands next in authority to Adam in the Priesthood; he was called of God to this office, and was the father of all living in this day, and to him was given the dominion. These men held keys first on earth, and then in heaven" (*Teachings of the Prophet Joseph Smith,* 157).

were accomplished, he departed to his own house.

24. And after those days his wife Elisabeth conceived, and hid herself five months, saying,

25. Thus hath the Lord dealt with me in the days wherein he looked on me, to take away my reproach among men.

26. And in the sixth month the angel Gabriel was sent from God unto a city of Galilee, named Nazareth,

27. To a virgin espoused to a man whose name was Joseph, of the house of David; and the virgin's name was Mary.

28. And the angel came in unto her, and said, Hail, thou that art highly favoured, the Lord is with thee: blessed art thou among women.

29. And when she saw him, she was troubled at his saying, and cast in her mind what manner of salutation this should be.

30. And the angel said unto her, Fear not, Mary: for thou hast found favour with God.

31. And, behold, thou shalt conceive in thy womb, and bring forth a son, and shalt call his name JESUS.

32. He shall be great, and shall be called the Son of the Highest: and the Lord God shall give unto him the throne of his father David:

33. And he shall reign over the house of Jacob for ever; and of his kingdom there shall be no end.

34. Then said Mary unto the angel, How shall this be, seeing I know not a man?

35. And the angel answered and said unto her, The Holy Ghost shall come upon thee, and the power of the Highest shall overshadow thee: therefore also that holy thing which shall be born of thee shall be called the Son of God.

36. And, behold, thy cousin Elisabeth, she hath also conceived a son in her old age: and this is the sixth month with her, who was called barren.

37. For with God nothing shall be impossible.

38. And Mary said, Behold the handmaid of the Lord; be it unto me according to thy word. And the angel departed from her.

39. And Mary arose in those days, and went into the hill country with haste, into a city of Juda;

40. And entered into the house of Zacharias, and saluted Elisabeth.

41. And it came to pass, that, when Elisabeth heard the salutation of Mary, the babe leaped in her womb; and Elisabeth was filled with the Holy Ghost:

42. And she spake out with a loud voice, and said, Blessed art thou among women, and blessed is the fruit of thy womb.

43. And whence is this to me, that the mother of my Lord should come to me?

44. For, lo, as soon as the voice of thy salutation sounded in mine ears, the babe leaped in my womb for joy.

45. And blessed is she that believed: for there shall be a performance of those things which were told her from the Lord.

46. And Mary said, My soul doth magnify the Lord,

47. And my spirit hath rejoiced in God my Saviour.

Luke 1:27—Girls were usually betrothed (espoused) at the age of twelve, though it was sometimes earlier; boys were usually a little older. The betrothal was in essence an engagement, and involved a ceremony in the presence of witnesses during which the man presented a gift to the woman. Though the actual marriage generally didn't take place for about a year after the betrothal ceremony, after the betrothal ceremony the woman was called a wife; she could be divorced, could be put to death for adultery, and would become a widow if the man to whom she was betrothed died. Among all classes of people, betrothals were commonly between relatives, both because daughters were kept secluded (and therefore didn't have an opportunity to meet many men) and because of the desire to keep dowries and inheritances within the family. The marriage of first or second cousins was common, as was the marriage of an uncle to a niece (see Howard F. Vos, *Nelson's New Illustrated Bible Manners and Customs: How the People of the Bible Really Lived,* 488–89).

Luke 1:34–35—"That Child to be born of Mary was begotten of Elohim, the Eternal Father, not in violation of natural law but in accordance with a higher manifestation thereof; and, the offspring from that association of supreme sanctity, celestial Sireship, and pure though mortal maternity, was of right to be called the 'Son of the Highest.' In His nature would be combined the powers of Godhood with the capacity and possibilities of mortality; and this through the ordinary operation of the fundamental law of heredity, declared of God, demonstrated by science, and admitted by philosophy, that living beings shall propagate—after their kind. The Child Jesus was to inherit the physical, mental, and spiritual traits, tendencies, and powers that characterized His parents—one immortal and glorified—God, the other human—woman" (James E. Talmage, *Jesus the Christ,* 77).

48. For he hath regarded the low estate of his handmaiden: for, behold, from henceforth all generations shall call me blessed.

49. For he that is mighty hath done to me great things; and holy is his name.

50. And his mercy is on them that fear him from generation to generation.

51. He hath shewed strength with his arm; he hath scattered the proud in the imagination of their hearts.

52. He hath put down the mighty from their seats, and exalted them of low degree.

53. He hath filled the hungry with good things; and the rich he hath sent empty away.

54. He hath holpen his servant Israel, in remembrance of his mercy;

55. As he spake to our fathers, to Abraham, and to his seed for ever.

56. And Mary abode with her about three months, and returned to her own house.

57. Now Elisabeth's full time came that she should be delivered; and she brought forth a son.

58. And her neighbours and her cousins heard how the Lord had shewed great mercy upon her; and they rejoiced with her.

59. And it came to pass, that on the eighth day they came to circumcise the child; and they called him Zacharias, after the name of his father.

60. And his mother answered and said, Not so; but he shall be called John.

61. And they said unto her, There is none of thy kindred that is called by this name.

62. And they made signs to his father, how he would have him called.

63. And he asked for a writing table, and wrote, saying, His name is John. And they marvelled all.

64. And his mouth was opened immediately, and his tongue loosed, and he spake, and praised God.

65. And fear came on all that dwelt round about them: and all these sayings were noised abroad throughout all the hill country of Judæa.

66. And all they that heard them laid them up in their hearts, saying, What manner of child shall this be! And the hand of the Lord was with him.

67. And his father Zacharias was filled with the Holy Ghost, and prophesied, saying,

68. Blessed be the Lord God of Israel; for he hath visited and redeemed his people,

69. And hath raised up an horn of salvation for us in the house of his servant David;

70. As he spake by the mouth of his holy prophets, which have been since the world began:

71. That we should be saved from our enemies, and from the hand of all that hate us;

72. To perform the mercy promised to our fathers, and to remember his holy covenant;

73. The oath which he sware to our father Abraham,

74. That he would grant unto us, that we being delivered out of the hand of our enemies might serve him without fear,

75. In holiness and righteousness before him, all the days of our life.

76. And thou, child, shalt be called the prophet of the Highest: for thou

Luke 1:46–56 — Within these verses are two beautiful psalms that not only reflect feelings of gratitude, but remind us of principles and doctrines by which we should live. One is the psalm of Mary, adopted by many churches and known by the Latin name *Magnificat,* as she responded to Elizabeth's inspired greeting. The other is the psalm of Zacharias, adopted by many by the Latin name *Benedictus,* a song of praise about the birth and naming of his son, John the Baptist.

The birth of John the Baptist

shalt go before the face of the Lord to prepare his ways;

77. To give knowledge of salvation unto his people by the remission of their sins,

78. Through the tender mercy of our God; whereby the dayspring from on high hath visited us,

79. To give light to them that sit in darkness and in the shadow of death, to guide our feet into the way of peace.

80. And the child grew, and waxed strong in spirit, and was in the deserts till the day of his shewing unto Israel.

CHAPTER 2

1. And it came to pass in those days, that there went out a decree from Cæsar Augustus, that all the world should be taxed.

2. (And this taxing was first made when Cyrenius was governor of Syria.)

3. And all went to be taxed, every one into his own city.

4. And Joseph also went up from Galilee, out of the city of Nazareth, into Judaea, unto the city of David, which is called Bethlehem; (because he was of the house and lineage of David:)

5. To be taxed with Mary his espoused wife, being great with child.

6. And so it was, that, while they were there, the days were accomplished that she should be delivered.

7. And she brought forth her firstborn son, and wrapped him in swaddling clothes, and laid him in a manger; because there was no room for them in the inn.

8. And there were in the same country shepherds abiding in the field, keeping watch over their flock by night.

9. And, lo, the angel of the Lord came upon them, and the glory of the Lord shone round about them: and they were sore afraid.

10. And the angel said unto them, Fear not: for, behold, I bring you good tidings of great joy, which shall be to all people.

11. For unto you is born this day in the city of David a Saviour, which is Christ the Lord.

12. And this shall be a sign unto you; Ye shall find the babe wrapped in swaddling clothes, lying in a manger.

13. And suddenly there was with the angel a multitude of the heavenly host praising God, and saying,

14. Glory to God in the highest, and on earth peace, good will toward men.

15. And it came to pass, as the angels were gone away from them into heaven, the shepherds said one to another, Let us now go even unto Bethlehem, and see this thing which is come to pass, which the Lord hath made known unto us.

16. And they came with haste, and found Mary, and Joseph, and the babe lying in a manger.

17. And when they had seen it, they made known abroad the saying which was told them concerning this child.

Luke 2:1–5—"The taxing herein referred to may properly be understood as an enrollment, or a registration, whereby a census of Roman subjects would be secured. . . . Had the census been taken by the usual Roman method, each person would have been enrolled at the town of his residence; but the Jewish custom, for which the Roman law had respect, necessitated registration at the cities or towns claimed by the respective families as their ancestral homes" (James E. Talmage, *Jesus the Christ,* 86).

Luke 2:5—At this time, Mary was no longer simply espoused (engaged) to Joseph. An angel had instructed him to marry her, and he had done so to protect her. At this time, then, the legal marriage had taken place (see Bruce R. McConkie, *Doctrinal New Testament Commentary,* 91).

Luke 2:7—The inns of the New Testament were not like Western inns of today. An "inn" was generally like a guest room in a home, and hospitality was considered to be a religious duty. With so many people in town for the celebration of Passover, there were simply no guest rooms left, and Mary and Joseph had to settle for the best accommodation available, which was in a stable; these stables were commonly at the rear of homes or buildings (see Fred H. Wight, *Manners and Customs of Bible Lands,* 272).

Luke 2:11—A *savior* is one who saves. Jesus is the Savior because He saved us from both physical death (through the Resurrection) and spiritual death (through the Atonement).

Luke 2:12—Swaddling clothes were strips of cotton or linen bandages that were wrapped tightly around newborn babies after the baby was washed and rubbed with salt. The swaddling clothes kept the infant's arms tightly at its sides and its legs tightly bound together; the band also wrapped under the chin and around the forehead. Infants from wealthy families were wrapped in more costly apparel, such as fine white shawls (see Fred H. Wight, *Manners and Customs of Bible Lands,* 108–109).

Luke 2:16—There is some dispute about whether the "manger" was a manger or a stall, and whether it might have been in the stable or in a nearby cave (see James M. Freeman, *Bible Manners and Customs of the Bible,* 405–406).

18. And all they that heard it wondered at those things which were told them by the shepherds.

19. But Mary kept all these things, and pondered them in her heart.

20. And the shepherds returned, glorifying and praising God for all the things that they had heard and seen, as it was told unto them.

21. And when eight days were accomplished for the circumcising of the child, his name was called JESUS, which was so named of the angel before he was conceived in the womb.

22. And when the days of her purification according to the law of Moses were accomplished, they brought him to Jerusalem, to present him to the Lord;

23. (As it is written in the law of the Lord, Every male that openeth the womb shall be called holy to the Lord;)

24. And to offer a sacrifice according to that which is said in the law of the Lord, A pair of turtledoves, or two young pigeons.

25. And, behold, there was a man in Jerusalem, whose name was Simeon; and the same man was just and devout, waiting for the consolation of Israel: and the Holy Ghost was upon him.

26. And it was revealed unto him by the Holy Ghost, that he should not see death, before he had seen the Lord's Christ.

27. And he came by the Spirit into the temple: and when the parents brought in the child Jesus, to do for him after the custom of the law,

28. Then took he him up in his arms, and blessed God, and said,

29. Lord, now lettest thou thy servant depart in peace, according to thy word:

30. For mine eyes have seen thy salvation,

31. Which thou hast prepared before the face of all people;

32. A light to lighten the Gentiles, and the glory of thy people Israel.

33. And Joseph and his mother marvelled at those things which were spoken of him.

34. And Simeon blessed them, and said unto Mary his mother, Behold, this child is set for the fall and rising again of many in Israel; and for a sign which shall be spoken against;

35. (Yea, a sword shall pierce through thy own soul also,) that the thoughts of many hearts may be revealed.

36. And there was one Anna, a prophetess, the daughter of Phanuel, of the tribe of Aser: she was of a great age, and had lived with an husband seven years from her virginity;

37. And she was a widow of about fourscore and four years, which departed not from the temple, but served God with fastings and prayers night and day.

38. And she coming in that instant gave thanks likewise unto the Lord, and spake of him to all them that looked for redemption in Jerusalem.

39. And when they had performed all things according to the law of the Lord, they returned into Galilee, to their own city Nazareth.

40. And the child grew, and waxed strong in spirit, filled with wisdom: and the grace of God was upon him.

41. Now his parents went to Jerusalem every year at the feast of the passover.

42. And when he was twelve years old, they went up to Jerusalem after the custom of the feast.

Luke 2:20—"The shepherds to whom the angels appeared were the keepers of the temple flocks, a conjecture based on an ancient Jewish tradition that the Messiah would be revealed from *Migdal Eder*, 'the tower of the flock.' . . . this could mean none other than the special flocks consecrated to the temple. If this is so, then lambs born years later into those same flocks may have been among those offered in the temple at the time of Christ's Passover sacrifice on the cross" (Bruce D. Porter, *The King of Kings*, 23).

Luke 2:21—Jewish boys were circumcised when eight days old in a ceremony involving both the rabbi or priest and the father. During the ceremony, which was first given to Abraham (see Gen. 17:9–14), the child was given a name; afterward, the family celebrated with a meal. Circumcision was a sign that the family kept the Abrahamic covenant (see Fred H. Wight, *Manners and Customs of Bible Lands*, 109).

Luke 2:22–24—After giving birth, women in Israel remained in seclusion; the period was forty days after the birth of a boy, eighty days after the birth of a girl. At the end of the period of seclusion, the woman brought to the priest a lamb for a burnt offering and either a young pigeon or turtledove for a sin offering. A woman of lesser economic status was allowed to bring just the fowl. The fact that Mary and Joseph brought only birds is a testament to the modest circumstances of the couple (see Bruce R. McConkie, *Doctrinal New Testament Commentary*, 1:99).

Luke 2:25—*The consolation of Israel* is the Messiah, who would come to bring comfort and solace.

Luke 2:35—The "sword" in this reference is figurative only.

Luke 2:40—"He came among men to experience all the natural conditions of mortality; . . . His boyhood was actual boyhood, His development was as necessary and as real as that of all children. . . . The Child grew, and with growth there came to Him expansion of mind, development of faculties, and progression in power and understanding. . . . Our knowledge of Jewish life in that age justifies the inference that the Boy was well taught in the law and the scriptures, for such was the rule. He garnered knowledge by study, and gained wisdom by prayer, thought, and effort" (James E. Talmage, *Jesus the Christ*, 105–106).

43. And when they had fulfilled the days, as they returned, the child Jesus tarried behind in Jerusalem; and Joseph and his mother knew not of it.

44. But they, supposing him to have been in the company, went a day's journey; and they sought him among their kinsfolk and acquaintance.

45. And when they found him not, they turned back again to Jerusalem, seeking him.

46. And it came to pass, that after three days they found him in the temple, sitting in the midst of the doctors, both hearing them, and asking them questions.

47. And all that heard him were astonished at his understanding and answers.

48. And when they saw him, they were amazed: and his mother said unto him, Son, why hast thou thus dealt with us? behold, thy father and I have sought thee sorrowing.

49. And he said unto them, How is it that ye sought me? wist ye not that I must be about my Father's business?

50. And they understood not the saying which he spake unto them.

51. And he went down with them, and came to Nazareth, and was subject unto them: but his mother kept all these sayings in her heart.

52. And Jesus increased in wisdom and stature, and in favour with God and man.

CHAPTER 3

1. Now in the fifteenth year of the reign of Tiberius Cæsar, Pontius Pilate being governor of Judæa, and Herod being tetrarch of Galilee, and his brother Philip tetrarch of Ituræa and of the region of Trachonitis, and Lysanias the tetrarch of Abilene,

2. Annas and Caiaphas being the high priests, the word of God came unto John the son of Zacharias in the wilderness.

3. And he came into all the country about Jordan, preaching the baptism of repentance for the remission of sins;

4. As it is written in the book of the words of Esaias the prophet, saying, The voice of one crying in the wilderness, Prepare ye the way of the Lord, make his paths straight.

5. Every valley shall be filled, and every mountain and hill shall be brought low; and the crooked shall be made straight, and the rough ways shall be made smooth;

6. And all flesh shall see the salvation of God.

7. Then said he to the multitude that came forth to be baptized of him, O generation of vipers, who hath warned you to flee from the wrath to come?

8. Bring forth therefore fruits worthy of repentance, and begin

Luke 2:40, 52 — "Jesus was a god before he came into the world and yet his knowledge was taken from him. He did not know his former greatness, neither do we know what greatness we had attained to before we came here" (Lorenzo Snow, *Office Journal of Lorenzo Snow*, 8 Oct. 1900, 181–82).

Luke 2:41–51 — It was a religious duty of all males to attend the Feast of Unleavened Bread, a feast that lasted seven days along with the twenty-four-hour Passover observance; women were also expected to attend unless otherwise lawfully detained. It took four days to journey from Nazareth to Jerusalem. Men and women traveled with their extended families in caravans as protection against marauders (see Victor W. Harris, ed., *We Believe in Christ*, 32–33).

Luke 2:44 — "A day's journey" didn't mean they had traveled an entire day (which would have been eighteen to thirty miles); custom was that the first day's journey was brief, usually only a few hours, or three to eight miles from where they had started (see James M. Freeman, *Manners and Customs of the Bible*, 409).

Luke 2:52 — We increase in favor with God by obeying His commandments. We increase in favor with man by serving.

Luke 3:1–6 — "John singlehandedly challenged the network of priestcraft and apostasy that existed among the Jewish heirarchy and was given the divine appointment 'to overthrow the kingdom of the Jews and to make straight the way of the Lord before the face of his people, to prepare them for the coming of the Lord' (D&C 84:28)" (Robert J. Matthews, *Behold the Messiah*, 46).

not to say within yourselves, We have Abraham to our father: for I say unto you, That God is able of these stones to raise up children unto Abraham.

9. And now also the axe is laid unto the root of the trees: every tree therefore which bringeth not forth good fruit is hewn down, and cast into the fire.

10. And the people asked him, saying, What shall we do then?

11. He answereth and saith unto them, He that hath two coats, let him impart to him that hath none; and he that hath meat, let him do likewise.

12. Then came also publicans to be baptized, and said unto him, Master, what shall we do?

13. And he said unto them, Exact no more than that which is appointed you.

14. And the soldiers likewise demanded of him, saying, And what shall we do? And he said unto them, Do violence to no man, neither accuse any falsely; and be content with your wages.

15. And as the people were in expectation, and all men mused in their hearts of John, whether he were the Christ, or not;

16. John answered, saying unto them all, I indeed baptize you with water; but one mightier than I cometh, the latchet of whose shoes I am not worthy to unloose: he shall baptize you with the Holy Ghost and with fire:

17. Whose fan is in his hand, and he will throughly purge his floor, and will gather the wheat into his garner; but the chaff he will burn with fire unquenchable.

18. And many other things in his exhortation preached he unto the people.

19. But Herod the tetrarch, being reproved by him for Herodias his brother Philip's wife, and for all the evils which Herod had done,

20. Added yet this above all, that he shut up John in prison.

21. Now when all the people were baptized, it came to pass, that Jesus also being baptized, and praying, the heaven was opened,

22. And the Holy Ghost descended in a bodily shape like a dove upon him, and a voice came from heaven, which said, Thou art my beloved Son; in thee I am well pleased.

23. And Jesus himself began to be about thirty years of age, being (as was supposed) the son of Joseph, which was the son of Heli,

24. Which was the son of Matthat, which was the son of Levi, which was the son of Melchi, which was the son of Janna, which was the son of Joseph,

25. Which was the son of Mattathias, which was the son of Amos, which was the son of Naum, which was the son of Esli, which was the son of Nagge,

26. Which was the son of Maath, which was the son of Mattathias, which was the son of Semei, which was the son of Joseph, which was the son of Juda,

27. Which was the son of Joanna, which was the son of Rhesa, which

Notes: _____

_____

_____

_____

_____

_____

_____

_____

_____

_____

_____

_____

_____

_____

_____

_____

_____

Luke 3:15–18—"John's voice was one of doctrine and of testimony. He proclaimed the divine Sonship of the Coming One, testified that He was to be the Holy Messiah, and invited all men to come unto Him and be saved" (Bruce R. McConkie, *The Mortal Messiah,* 1:390).

Luke 3:20—We know from the Joseph Smith Translation of the Bible that Jesus knew John had been imprisoned, and that He sent angels to minister to John during his imprisonment (see JST, Matt. 4:11).

was the son of Zorobabel, which was the son of Salathiel, which was the son of Neri,

28. Which was the son of Melchi, which was the son of Addi, which was the son of Cosam, which was the son of Elmodam, which was the son of Er,

29. Which was the son of Jose, which was the son of Eliezer, which was the son of Jorim, which was the son of Matthat, which was the son of Levi,

30. Which was the son of Simeon, which was the son of Juda, which was the son of Joseph, which was the son of Jonan, which was the son of Eliakim,

31. Which was the son of Melea, which was the son of Menan, which was the son of Mattatha, which was the son of Nathan, which was the son of David,

32. Which was the son of Jesse, which was the son of Obed, which was the son of Booz, which was the son of Salmon, which was the son of Naasson,

33. Which was the son of Aminadab, which was the son of Aram, which was the son of Esrom, which was the son of Phares, which was the son of Juda,

34. Which was the son of Jacob, which was the son of Isaac, which was the son of Abraham, which was the son of Thara, which was the son of Nachor,

35. Which was the son of Saruch, which was the son of Ragau, which was the son of Phalec, which was the son of Heber, which was the son of Sala,

36. Which was the son of Cainan, which was the son of Arphaxad, which was the son of Sem, which was the son of Noe, which was the son of Lamech,

37. Which was the son of Mathusala, which was the son of Enoch, which was the son of Jared, which was the son of Maleleel, which was the son of Cainan,

38. Which was the son of Enos, which was the son of Seth, which was the son of Adam, which was the son of God.

CHAPTER 4

1. And Jesus being full of the Holy Ghost returned from Jordan, and was led by the Spirit into the wilderness,

2. Being forty days tempted of the devil. And in those days he did eat nothing: and when they were ended, he afterward hungered.

3. And the devil said unto him, If thou be the Son of God, command this stone that it be made bread.

4. And Jesus answered him, saying, It is written, That man shall not live by bread alone, but by every word of God.

5. And the devil, taking him up into an high mountain, shewed unto him all the kingdoms of the world in a moment of time.

6. And the devil said unto him, All this power will I give thee, and the glory of them: for that is delivered unto me; and to whomsoever I will I give it.

7. If thou therefore wilt worship me, all shall be thine.

Temptation of Christ

Luke 4:1–13 — Jesus' example in overcoming temptation "provides some valuable insights and encouragements for all. Satan often makes his approach when the desire and need are both prominent. It will thus be difficult to resist unless there is a higher, spiritual morality dominating our lives. We must know as a point of fact and experiential logic that when temptation is resisted and we look back upon the victory, the sweetness of accomplishment will always far outweigh the depression of sin inherent in succumbing to the will of the evil one" (Kent P. Jackson and Robert L. Millet, eds., *Studies in Scripture, Vol. 5: The Gospels,* 184).

8. And Jesus answered and said unto him, Get thee behind me, Satan: for it is written, Thou shalt worship the Lord thy God, and him only shalt thou serve.

9. And he brought him to Jerusalem, and set him on a pinnacle of the temple, and said unto him, If thou be the Son of God, cast thyself down from hence:

10. For it is written, He shall give his angels charge over thee, to keep thee:

11. And in their hands they shall bear thee up, lest at any time thou dash thy foot against a stone.

12. And Jesus answering said unto him, It is said, Thou shalt not tempt the Lord thy God.

13. And when the devil had ended all the temptation, he departed from him for a season.

14. ¶ And Jesus returned in the power of the Spirit into Galilee: and there went out a fame of him through all the region round about.

15. And he taught in their synagogues, being glorified of all.

16. ¶ And he came to Nazareth, where he had been brought up: and, as his custom was, he went into the synagogue on the sabbath day, and stood up for to read.

17. And there was delivered unto him the book of the prophet Esaias. And when he had opened the book, he found the place where it was written,

18. The Spirit of the Lord is upon me, because he hath anointed me to preach the gospel to the poor; he hath sent me to heal the brokenhearted, to preach deliverance to the captives, and recovering of sight to the blind, to set at liberty them that are bruised,

19. To preach the acceptable year of the Lord.

20. And he closed the book, and he gave it again to the minister, and sat down. And the eyes of all them that were in the synagogue were fastened on him.

21. And he began to say unto them, This day is this scripture fulfilled in your ears.

22. And all bare him witness, and wondered at the gracious words which proceeded out of his mouth. And they said, Is not this Joseph's son?

23. And he said unto them, Ye will surely say unto me this proverb, Physician, heal thyself: whatsoever we have heard done in Capernaum, do also here in thy country.

24. And he said, Verily I say unto you, No prophet is accepted in his own country.

25. But I tell you of a truth, many widows were in Israel in the days of Elias, when the heaven was shut up three years and six months, when great famine was throughout all the land;

26. But unto none of them was Elias sent, save unto Sarepta, a city of Sidon, unto a woman that was a widow.

27. And many lepers were in Israel in the time of Eliseus the prophet; and none of them was cleansed, saving Naaman the Syrian.

Luke 4:8—During the Savior's forty-day fast in the wilderness, He was tempted by Satan, who tried to get Him to apply His divine power and agency in inappropriate ways. This verse is His response to Satan. The motto *Get thee behind me, Satan* provides a wonderful governing principle for our lives. It is a command, an order from one in charge of the situation. It is necessary for us to experience opposition in all things (see 2 Ne. 2:11) and to be tempted as a trial of our faith (see D&C 29:39). Our goal is to learn how to withstand and overcome temptation. How have you found it effective to take an active and commanding position against the tempter in order to stay on the right course?

Luke 4:17–21—"When the Savior came upon the earth he had two great missions; one was to work out the Messiahship, the atonement for the fall, and . . . the other was the work which he did among his brethren and sisters in the flesh by way of relieving their sufferings. . . . He left as a heritage to those two great things—work for the relief of the ills and sufferings of humanity, and the teaching of the spiritual truths which should bring us back into the presence of our Heavenly Father" (J. Reuben Clark, Jr., Conference Report, April 1937, 22).

28. And all they in the synagogue, when they heard these things, were filled with wrath,

29. And rose up, and thrust him out of the city, and led him unto the brow of the hill whereon their city was built, that they might cast him down headlong.

30. But he passing through the midst of them went his way,

31. And came down to Capernaum, a city of Galilee, and taught them on the sabbath days.

32. And they were astonished at his doctrine: for his word was with power.

33. ¶ And in the synagogue there was a man, which had a spirit of an unclean devil, and cried out with a loud voice,

34. Saying, Let us alone; what have we to do with thee, thou Jesus of Nazareth? art thou come to destroy us? I know thee who thou art; the Holy One of God.

35. And Jesus rebuked him, saying, Hold thy peace, and come out of him. And when the devil had thrown him in the midst, he came out of him, and hurt him not.

36. And they were all amazed, and spake among themselves, saying, What a word is this! for with authority and power he commandeth the unclean spirits, and they come out.

37. And the fame of him went out into every place of the country round about.

38. ¶ And he arose out of the synagogue, and entered into Simon's house. And Simon's wife's mother was taken with a great fever; and they besought him for her.

39. And he stood over her, and rebuked the fever; and it left her: and immediately she arose and ministered unto them.

40. ¶ Now when the sun was setting, all they that had any sick with divers diseases brought them unto him; and he laid his hands on every one of them, and healed them.

41. And devils also came out of many, crying out, and saying, Thou art Christ the Son of God. And he rebuking them suffered them not to speak: for they knew that he was Christ.

42. And when it was day, he departed and went into a desert place: and the people sought him, and came unto him, and stayed him, that he should not depart from them.

43. And he said unto them, I must preach the kingdom of God to other cities also: for therefore am I sent.

44. And he preached in the synagogues of Galilee.

CHAPTER 5

1. And it came to pass, that, as the people pressed upon him to hear the word of God, he stood by the lake of Gennesaret,

2. And saw two ships standing by the lake: but the fishermen were gone out of them, and were washing their nets.

3. And he entered into one of the ships, which was Simon's, and prayed him that he would thrust out a little from the land. And he sat down, and taught the people out of the ship.

4. Now when he had left speaking, he said unto Simon, Launch out into the deep, and let down your nets for a draught.

5. And Simon answering said unto

Luke 4:33–37 — According to Elder Bruce R. McConkie, it seems that people were more susceptible to being possessed by spirits during the time of the Savior than has been the case during other times and dispensations (see *The Mortal Messiah*, 2:37). This may be why we read of these accounts in the scriptures detailing the life and times of the Savior.

Notes: _____

_____

_____

_____

_____

_____

_____

_____

_____

_____

_____

_____

_____

_____

_____

_____

Luke 5:1–11 — "Real Christians must understand that the gospel of Jesus Christ is not just a gospel of belief; it is a plan of action. His gospel is a gospel of imperatives, and the very nature of its substance is a call to action" (Howard W. Hunter, *The Teachings of Howard W. Hunter*, 259).

him, Master, we have toiled all the night, and have taken nothing: nevertheless at thy word I will let down the net.

6. And when they had this done, they inclosed a great multitude of fishes: and their net brake.

7. And they beckoned unto their partners, which were in the other ship, that they should come and help them. And they came, and filled both the ships, so that they began to sink.

8. When Simon Peter saw it, he fell down at Jesus' knees, saying, Depart from me; for I am a sinful man, O Lord.

9. For he was astonished, and all that were with him, at the draught of the fishes which they had taken:

10. And so was also James, and John, the sons of Zebedee, which were partners with Simon. And Jesus said unto Simon, Fear not; from henceforth thou shalt catch men.

11. And when they had brought their ships to land, they forsook all, and followed him.

12. ¶ And it came to pass, when he was in a certain city, behold a man full of leprosy: who seeing Jesus fell on his face, and besought him, saying, Lord, if thou wilt, thou canst make me clean.

13. And he put forth his hand, and touched him, saying, I will: be thou clean. And immediately the leprosy departed from him.

14. And he charged him to tell no man: but go, and shew thyself to the priest, and offer for thy cleansing, according as Moses commanded, for a testimony unto them.

15. But so much the more went there a fame abroad of him: and great multitudes came together to hear, and to be healed by him of their infirmities.

16. ¶ And he withdrew himself into the wilderness, and prayed.

17. And it came to pass on a certain day, as he was teaching, that there were Pharisees and doctors of the law sitting by, which were come out of every town of Galilee, and Judæa, and Jerusalem: and the power of the Lord was present to heal them.

18. ¶ And, behold, men brought in a bed a man which was taken with a palsy: and they sought means to bring him in, and to lay him before him.

19. And when they could not find by what way they might bring him in because of the multitude, they went upon the housetop, and let him down through the tiling with his couch into the midst before Jesus.

20. And when he saw their faith, he said unto him, Man, thy sins are forgiven thee.

21. And the scribes and the Pharisees began to reason, saying, Who is this which speaketh blasphemies? Who can forgive sins, but God alone?

22. But when Jesus perceived their thoughts, he answering said unto them, What reason ye in your hearts?

23. Whether is easier, to say, Thy sins be forgiven thee; or to say, Rise up and walk?

24. But that ye may know that the Son of man hath power upon earth to forgive sins, (he said unto the sick of the palsy,) I say unto thee, Arise, and take up thy couch, and go into thine house.

25. And immediately he rose up before them, and took up that whereon he lay, and departed to his own house, glorifying God.

26. And they were all amazed, and they glorified God, and were filled

Luke 5:5 — "We know it is not when we are busy that we get into trouble. Herndon said: 'Satan selects his disciples when they are idle; Jesus selected his when they were busy at their work either mending their nets or casting them into the sea'" (John Longden, Conference Report, April 1966, 38–39).

The choice to follow Jesus

Luke 5:20 — "Forgiveness of sins comes only by compliance with that law of forgiveness which the Lord has ordained. That the paralytic here healed had complied with that law is evident; otherwise the Lord Jesus, whose law it is, would not have pronounced the heartening benediction" (Bruce R. McConkie, *Doctrinal New Testament Commentary*, 1:178).

with fear, saying, We have seen strange things to day.

27. ¶ And after these things he went forth, and saw a publican, named Levi, sitting at the receipt of custom: and he said unto him, Follow me.

28. And he left all, rose up, and followed him.

29. And Levi made him a great feast in his own house: and there was a great company of publicans and of others that sat down with them.

30. But their scribes and Pharisees murmured against his disciples, saying, Why do ye eat and drink with publicans and sinners?

31. And Jesus answering said unto them, They that are whole need not a physician; but they that are sick.

32. I came not to call the righteous, but sinners to repentance.

33. ¶ And they said unto him, Why do the disciples of John fast often, and make prayers, and likewise the disciples of the Pharisees; but thine eat and drink?

34. And he said unto them, Can ye make the children of the bridechamber fast, while the bridegroom is with them?

35. But the days will come, when the bridegroom shall be taken away from them, and then shall they fast in those days.

36. ¶ And he spake also a parable unto them; No man putteth a piece of a new garment upon an old; if otherwise, then both the new maketh a rent, and the piece that was taken out of the new agreeth not with the old.

37. And no man putteth new wine into old bottles; else the new wine will burst the bottles, and be spilled, and the bottles shall perish.

38. But new wine must be put into new bottles; and both are preserved.

39. No man also having drunk old wine straightway desireth new: for he saith, The old is better.

CHAPTER 6

1. And it came to pass on the second sabbath after the first, that he went through the corn fields; and his disciples plucked the ears of corn, and did eat, rubbing them in their hands.

2. And certain of the Pharisees said unto them, Why do ye that which is not lawful to do on the sabbath days?

3. And Jesus answering them said, Have ye not read so much as this, what David did, when himself was an hungred, and they which were with him;

4. How he went into the house of God, and did take and eat the shewbread, and gave also to them that were with him; which it is not lawful to eat but for the priests alone?

5. And he said unto them, That the Son of man is Lord also of the sabbath.

6. And it came to pass also on another sabbath, that he entered into the synagogue and taught: and there was a man whose right hand was withered.

7. And the scribes and Pharisees watched him, whether he would heal on the sabbath day; that they might find an accusation against him.

8. But he knew their thoughts, and said to the man which had the withered hand, Rise up, and stand forth in the midst. And he arose and stood forth.

9. Then said Jesus unto them, I will ask you one thing; Is it lawful on the

Notes: _____

_____

_____

_____

_____

_____

_____

_____

_____

_____

_____

_____

_____

_____

_____

_____

_____

_____

Luke 6:1–5—"The Sabbath is not a day for indolent lounging about the house or puttering around in the garden, but is a day for consistent attendance at meetings for the worship of the Lord, drinking at the fountain of knowledge and instruction, enjoying the family, and finding uplift in music and song" (Spencer W. Kimball, *Faith Precedes the Miracle*, 270).

sabbath days to do good, or to do evil? to save life, or to destroy it?

10. And looking round about upon them all, he said unto the man, Stretch forth thy hand. And he did so: and his hand was restored whole as the other.

11. And they were filled with madness; and communed one with another what they might do to Jesus.

12. And it came to pass in those days, that he went out into a mountain to pray, and continued all night in prayer to God.

13. ¶ And when it was day, he called unto him his disciples: and of them he chose twelve, whom also he named apostles;

14. Simon, (whom he also named Peter,) and Andrew his brother, James and John, Philip and Bartholomew,

15. Matthew and Thomas, James the son of Alphæus, and Simon called Zelotes,

16. And Judas the brother of James, and Judas Iscariot, which also was the traitor.

17. ¶ And he came down with them, and stood in the plain, and the company of his disciples, and a great multitude of people out of all Judæa and Jerusalem, and from the sea coast of Tyre and Sidon, which came to hear him, and to be healed of their diseases;

18. And they that were vexed with unclean spirits: and they were healed.

19. And the whole multitude sought to touch him: for there went virtue out of him, and healed them all.

20. ¶ And he lifted up his eyes on his disciples, and said, Blessed be ye poor: for yours is the kingdom of God.

21. Blessed are ye that hunger now: for ye shall be filled. Blessed are ye that weep now: for ye shall laugh.

22. Blessed are ye, when men shall hate you, and when they shall separate you from their company, and shall reproach you, and cast out your name as evil, for the Son of man's sake.

23. Rejoice ye in that day, and leap for joy: for, behold, your reward is great in heaven: for in the like manner did their fathers unto the prophets.

24. But woe unto you that are rich! for ye have received your consolation.

25. Woe unto you that are full! for ye shall hunger. Woe unto you that laugh now! for ye shall mourn and weep.

26. Woe unto you, when all men shall speak well of you! for so did their fathers to the false prophets.

27. ¶ But I say unto you which hear, Love your enemies, do good to them which hate you,

28. Bless them that curse you, and pray for them which despitefully use you.

29. And unto him that smiteth thee on the one cheek offer also the other; and him that taketh away thy cloke forbid not to take thy coat also.

30. Give to every man that asketh of thee; and of him that taketh away thy goods ask them not again.

Luke 6:20—The word *blessed* (from the Greek *makarios*) means "privileged to receive divine favor." Another translation of it could be "Oh, the happiness of." It signifies a state of true well-being. When it is the first word in an address, as it is in the beatitudes that begin here, it signifies a promise (see Kent P. Jackson and Robert L. Millet, eds., *Studies in Scripture, Vol. 5: The Gospels,* 236).

Elder James E. Talmage wrote, "In this day of counterfeits, adulterations, and base imitations, the devil is busier than he has ever been in the course of human history, in the manufacture of pleasures, both old and new; and these he offers for sale in most attractive fashion, falsely labeled, *Happiness*. In this soul-destroying craft he is without a peer; he has had centuries of experience and practice, and by his skill he controls the market. He has learned the tricks of the trade, and knows well how to catch the eye and arouse the desire of his customers. . . .

"Happiness includes all that is really desirable and of true worth. . . . Happiness leaves no bad after-taste, it is followed by no depressing reaction; it calls for no repentance, brings no regret, entails no remorse. . . . True happiness is lived over and over again in memory, always with a renewal of the original good" (*Jesus the Christ,* 230).

Luke 6:27–30—These verses provide one example of how the Savior was urging the people toward a higher law. Until He came, they were living by the lower law (a law that He had authored); now He taught how to take those lower laws and elevate themselves to a higher possibility.

Luke 6:29—The outer garment still worn by villagers in Palestine is a large cloak; it functions much as our overcoats do, providing warmth and shelter from the wind, rain, and other elements. Bedouins or peasants are often provided mats upon which to sleep, but they must provide their own cover; they use their cloak, which is tightly woven to provide heat and in some cases is even waterproof to repel moisture. It is against the law to take a man's cloak, because you are thereby denying him his warmth and protection. This context provides deeper understanding of this higher law the Savior gave (see Fred H. Wight, *Manners and Customs of Bible Lands,* 94–95).

31. And as ye would that men should do to you, do ye also to them likewise.

32. For if ye love them which love you, what thank have ye? for sinners also love those that love them.

33. And if ye do good to them which do good to you, what thank have ye? for sinners also do even the same.

34. And if ye lend to them of whom ye hope to receive, what thank have ye? for sinners also lend to sinners, to receive as much again.

35. But love ye your enemies, and do good, and lend, hoping for nothing again; and your reward shall be great, and ye shall be the children of the Highest: for he is kind unto the unthankful and to the evil.

36. Be ye therefore merciful, as your Father also is merciful.

37. Judge not, and ye shall not be judged: condemn not, and ye shall not be condemned: forgive, and ye shall be forgiven:

38. Give, and it shall be given unto you; good measure, pressed down, and shaken together, and running over, shall men give into your bosom. For with the same measure that ye mete withal it shall be measured to you again.

39. And he spake a parable unto them, Can the blind lead the blind? shall they not both fall into the ditch?

40. The disciple is not above his master: but every one that is perfect shall be as his master.

41. And why beholdest thou the mote that is in thy brother's eye, but perceivest not the beam that is in thine own eye?

42. Either how canst thou say to thy brother, Brother, let me pull out the mote that is in thine eye, when thou thyself beholdest not the beam that is in thine own eye? Thou hypocrite, cast out first the beam out of thine own eye, and then shalt thou see clearly to pull out the mote that is in thy brother's eye.

43. For a good tree bringeth not forth corrupt fruit; neither doth a corrupt tree bring forth good fruit.

44. For every tree is known by his own fruit. For of thorns men do not gather figs, nor of a bramble bush gather they grapes.

45. A good man out of the good treasure of his heart bringeth forth that which is good; and an evil man out of the evil treasure of his heart bringeth forth that which is evil: for of the abundance of the heart his mouth speaketh.

46. ¶ And why call ye me, Lord, Lord, and do not the things which I say?

47. Whosoever cometh to me, and heareth my sayings, and doeth them, I will shew you to whom he is like:

48. He is like a man which built an house, and digged deep, and laid the foundation on a rock: and when the flood arose, the stream beat vehemently upon that house, and could not shake it: for it was founded upon a rock.

49. But he that heareth, and doeth not, is like a man that without a foundation built an house upon the

The Savior delivering the Beatitudes

Notes: _____

_____

_____

_____

_____

_____

_____

_____

_____

_____

_____

_____

_____

_____

_____

_____

_____

_____

_____

_____

_____

earth; against which the stream did beat vehemently, and immediately it fell; and the ruin of that house was great.

CHAPTER 7

1. Now when he had ended all his sayings in the audience of the people, he entered into Capernaum.

2. And a certain centurion's servant, who was dear unto him, was sick, and ready to die.

3. And when he heard of Jesus, he sent unto him the elders of the Jews, beseeching him that he would come and heal his servant.

4. And when they came to Jesus, they besought him instantly, saying, That he was worthy for whom he should do this:

5. For he loveth our nation, and he hath built us a synagogue.

6. Then Jesus went with them. And when he was now not far from the house, the centurion sent friends to him, saying unto him, Lord, trouble not thyself: for I am not worthy that thou shouldest enter under my roof:

7. Wherefore neither thought I myself worthy to come unto thee: but say in a word, and my servant shall be healed.

8. For I also am a man set under authority, having under me soldiers, and I say unto one, Go, and he goeth; and to another, Come, and he cometh; and to my servant, Do this, and he doeth it.

9. When Jesus heard these things, he marvelled at him, and turned him about, and said unto the people that followed him, I say unto you, I have not found so great faith, no, not in Israel.

10. And they that were sent, returning to the house, found the servant whole that had been sick.

11. ¶ And it came to pass the day after, that he went into a city called Nain; and many of his disciples went with him, and much people.

12. Now when he came nigh to the gate of the city, behold, there was a dead man carried out, the only son of his mother, and she was a widow: and much people of the city was with her.

13. And when the Lord saw her, he had compassion on her, and said unto her, Weep not.

14. And he came and touched the bier: and they that bare him stood still. And he said, Young man, I say unto thee, Arise.

15. And he that was dead sat up, and began to speak. And he delivered him to his mother.

16. And there came a fear on all: and they glorified God, saying, That a great prophet is risen up among us; and, That God hath visited his people.

17. And this rumour of him went forth throughout all Judæa, and throughout all the region round about.

18. And the disciples of John shewed him of all these things.

19. ¶ And John calling unto him two of his disciples sent them to Jesus, saying, Art thou he that should come? or look we for another?

20. When the men were come unto him, they said, John Baptist hath sent us unto thee, saying, Art thou he that should come? or look we for another?

21. And in that same hour he cured many of their infirmities and plagues, and of evil spirits; and unto many that were blind he gave sight.

22. Then Jesus answering said unto them, Go your way, and tell John what things ye have seen and heard; how that the blind see, the lame walk, the lepers are cleansed, the

Christ raising the widow's son at Nain

deaf hear, the dead are raised, to the poor the gospel is preached.

23. And blessed is he, whosoever shall not be offended in me.

24. ¶ And when the messengers of John were departed, he began to speak unto the people concerning John, What went ye out into the wilderness for to see? A reed shaken with the wind?

25. But what went ye out for to see? A man clothed in soft raiment? Behold, they which are gorgeously apparelled, and live delicately, are in kings' courts.

26. But what went ye out for to see? A prophet? Yea, I say unto you, and much more than a prophet.

27. This is he, of whom it is written, Behold, I send my messenger before thy face, which shall prepare thy way before thee.

28. For I say unto you, Among those that are born of women there is not a greater prophet than John the Baptist: but he that is least in the kingdom of God is greater than he.

29. And all the people that heard him, and the publicans, justified God, being baptized with the baptism of John.

30. But the Pharisees and lawyers rejected the counsel of God against themselves, being not baptized of him.

31. ¶ And the Lord said, Whereunto then shall I liken the men of this generation? and to what are they like?

32. They are like unto children sitting in the marketplace, and calling one to another, and saying, We have piped unto you, and ye have not danced; we have mourned to you, and ye have not wept.

33. For John the Baptist came neither eating bread nor drinking wine; and ye say, He hath a devil.

34. The Son of man is come eating and drinking; and ye say, Behold a gluttonous man, and a winebibber, a friend of publicans and sinners!

35. But wisdom is justified of all her children.

36. ¶ And one of the Pharisees desired him that he would eat with him. And he went into the Pharisee's house, and sat down to meat.

37. And, behold, a woman in the city, which was a sinner, when she knew that Jesus sat at meat in the Pharisee's house, brought an alabaster box of ointment,

38. And stood at his feet behind him weeping, and began to wash his feet with tears, and did wipe them with the hairs of her head, and kissed his feet, and anointed them with the ointment.

39. Now when the Pharisee which had bidden him saw it, he spake within himself, saying, This man, if he were a prophet, would have known who and what manner of woman this is that toucheth him: for she is a sinner.

40. And Jesus answering said unto him, Simon, I have somewhat to say unto thee. And he saith, Master, say on.

41. There was a certain creditor which had two debtors: the one owed five hundred pence, and the other fifty.

42. And when they had nothing to pay, he frankly forgave them both. Tell me therefore, which of them will love him most?

43. Simon answered and said, I suppose that he, to whom he forgave most. And he said unto him, Thou hast rightly judged.

44. And he turned to the woman, and said unto Simon, Seest thou this woman? I entered into thine house, thou gavest me no water for my feet:

Notes: _____

_____

_____

_____

_____

_____

_____

_____

_____

_____

_____

_____

_____

_____

_____

_____

_____

_____

_____

Luke 7:36–50 — "To anoint the head of a guest with ordinary oil was to do him honor; to anoint his feet also was to show unusual and signal regard; but the anointing of head and feet with spikenard, and in such abundance, was an act of reverential homage rarely rendered even to kings. Mary's act was an expression of adoration; it was the fragrant outwelling of a heart overflowing with worship and affection" (James E. Talmage, *Jesus the Christ*, 475).

but she hath washed my feet with tears, and wiped them with the hairs of her head.

45. Thou gavest me no kiss: but this woman since the time I came in hath not ceased to kiss my feet.

46. My head with oil thou didst not anoint: but this woman hath anointed my feet with ointment.

47. Wherefore I say unto thee, Her sins, which are many, are forgiven; for she loved much: but to whom little is forgiven, the same loveth little.

48. And he said unto her, Thy sins are forgiven.

49. And they that sat at meat with him began to say within themselves, Who is this that forgiveth sins also?

50. And he said to the woman, Thy faith hath saved thee; go in peace.

CHAPTER 8

1. And it came to pass afterward, that he went throughout every city and village, preaching and shewing the glad tidings of the kingdom of God: and the twelve were with him,

2. And certain women, which had been healed of evil spirits and infirmities, Mary called Magdalene, out of whom went seven devils,

3. And Joanna the wife of Chuza Herod's steward, and Susanna, and many others, which ministered unto him of their substance.

4. ¶ And when much people were gathered together, and were come to him out of every city, he spake by a parable:

5. A sower went out to sow his seed: and as he sowed, some fell by the way side; and it was trodden down, and the fowls of the air devoured it.

6. And some fell upon a rock; and as soon as it was sprung up, it withered away, because it lacked moisture.

7. And some fell among thorns; and the thorns sprang up with it, and choked it.

8. And other fell on good ground, and sprang up, and bare fruit an hundredfold. And when he had said these things, he cried, He that hath ears to hear, let him hear.

9. And his disciples asked him, saying, What might this parable be?

10. And he said, Unto you it is given to know the mysteries of the kingdom of God: but to others in parables; that seeing they might not see, and hearing they might not understand.

11. Now the parable is this: The seed is the word of God.

12. Those by the way side are they that hear; then cometh the devil, and taketh away the word out of their hearts, lest they should believe and be saved.

13. They on the rock are they, which, when they hear, receive the word with joy; and these have no root, which for a while believe, and in time of temptation fall away.

14. And that which fell among thorns are they, which, when they have heard, go forth, and are choked with cares and riches and pleasures of this life, and bring no fruit to perfection.

15. But that on the good ground are they, which in an honest and good heart, having heard the word, keep it, and bring forth fruit with patience.

16. ¶ No man, when he hath lighted

Luke 8:1–3—"The first mention of Mary Magdalene by name presents her in association with other honorable women, among whom was the wife of the royal steward. They accompanied Jesus and the Twelve and 'ministered unto him of their substance.' These women of station were beneficiaries of the Lord's healing power, for each of them had been cured of infirmities, and specifically had been relieved of the combined physical and mental ailments incident to possession by evil spirits. Mary Magdalene, as we read, had been delivered from the affliction of seven devils; but the fact of even such grievous plague is without warrant for the imputation of unchastity.

"Mary Magdalene became one of the closest friends Christ had among women. Her devotion to Him as her Healer, and the One whom she adored as the Messiah, was as deep, as genuine, and as pure as her own soul. She stood by the cross while other women looked on from afar in the hour of His mortal agony. She was among the earliest at the tomb in the resurrection dawn. She conversed with angels, and was the first mortal to behold the resurrected Savior—the Lord whom she had loved with all the fervor of spiritual adoration. To say that this woman was once a fallen creature, her soul seared with the heat of unhallowed lust, is to perpetuate an infamy" (James E. Talmage, "Mary Magdalene," *Improvement Era*, July 1917).

a candle, covereth it with a vessel, or putteth it under a bed; but setteth it on a candlestick, that they which enter in may see the light.

17. For nothing is secret, that shall not be made manifest; neither any thing hid, that shall not be known and come abroad.

18. Take heed therefore how ye hear: for whosoever hath, to him shall be given; and whosoever hath not, from him shall be taken even that which he seemeth to have.

19. ¶ Then came to him his mother and his brethren, and could not come at him for the press.

20. And it was told him by certain which said, Thy mother and thy brethren stand without, desiring to see thee.

21. And he answered and said unto them, My mother and my brethren are these which hear the word of God, and do it.

22. ¶ Now it came to pass on a certain day, that he went into a ship with his disciples: and he said unto them, Let us go over unto the other side of the lake. And they launched forth.

23. But as they sailed he fell asleep: and there came down a storm of wind on the lake; and they were filled with water, and were in jeopardy.

24. And they came to him, and awoke him, saying, Master, master, we perish. Then he arose, and rebuked the wind and the raging of the water: and they ceased, and there was a calm.

25. And he said unto them, Where is your faith? And they being afraid wondered, saying one to another, What manner of man is this! for he commandeth even the winds and water, and they obey him.

26. ¶ And they arrived at the country of the Gadarenes, which is over against Galilee.

27. And when he went forth to land, there met him out of the city a certain man, which had devils long time, and ware no clothes, neither abode in any house, but in the tombs.

28. When he saw Jesus, he cried out, and fell down before him, and with a loud voice said, What have I to do with thee, Jesus, thou Son of God most high? I beseech thee, torment me not.

29. (For he had commanded the unclean spirit to come out of the man. For oftentimes it had caught him: and he was kept bound with chains and in fetters; and he brake the bands, and was driven of the devil into the wilderness.)

30. And Jesus asked him, saying, What is thy name? And he said, Legion: because many devils were entered into him.

31. And they besought him that he would not command them to go out into the deep.

32. And there was there an herd of many swine feeding on the mountain: and they besought him that he would suffer them to enter into them. And he suffered them.

33. Then went the devils out of the man, and entered into the swine: and the herd ran violently down a steep place into the lake, and were choked.

34. When they that fed them saw what was done, they fled, and went and told it in the city and in the country.

35. Then they went out to see what was done; and came to Jesus, and found the man, out of whom the devils were departed, sitting at the feet of Jesus, clothed, and in his right mind: and they were afraid.

36. They also which saw it told them

Casting out the devils

by what means he that was possessed of the devils was healed.

37. ¶ Then the whole multitude of the country of the Gadarenes round about besought him to depart from them; for they were taken with great fear: and he went up into the ship, and returned back again.

38. Now the man out of whom the devils were departed besought him that he might be with him: but Jesus sent him away, saying,

39. Return to thine own house, and shew how great things God hath done unto thee. And he went his way, and published throughout the whole city how great things Jesus had done unto him.

40. And it came to pass, that, when Jesus was returned, the people gladly received him: for they were all waiting for him.

41. ¶ And, behold, there came a man named Jairus, and he was a ruler of the synagogue: and he fell down at Jesus' feet, and besought him that he would come into his house:

42. For he had one only daughter, about twelve years of age, and she lay a dying. But as he went the people thronged him.

43. ¶ And a woman having an issue of blood twelve years, which had spent all her living upon physicians, neither could be healed of any,

44. Came behind him, and touched the border of his garment: and immediately her issue of blood stanched.

45. And Jesus said, Who touched me? When all denied, Peter and they that were with him said, Master, the multitude throng thee and press thee, and sayest thou, Who touched me?

46. And Jesus said, Somebody hath touched me: for I perceive that virtue is gone out of me.

47. And when the woman saw that she was not hid, she came trembling, and falling down before him, she declared unto him before all the people for what cause she had touched him and how she was healed immediately.

48. And he said unto her, Daughter, be of good comfort: thy faith hath made thee whole; go in peace.

49. ¶ While he yet spake, there cometh one from the ruler of the synagogue's house, saying to him, Thy daughter is dead; trouble not the Master.

50. But when Jesus heard it, he answered him, saying, Fear not: believe only, and she shall be made whole.

51. And when he came into the house, he suffered no man to go in, save Peter, and James, and John, and the father and the mother of the maiden.

52. And all wept, and bewailed her: but he said, Weep not; she is not dead, but sleepeth.

53. And they laughed him to scorn, knowing that she was dead.

54. And he put them all out, and took her by the hand, and called, saying, Maid, arise.

55. And her spirit came again, and she arose straightway: and he commanded to give her meat.

56. And her parents were astonished: but he charged them that they should tell no man what was done.

CHAPTER 9

1. Then he called his twelve disciples together, and gave them power and authority over all devils, and to cure diseases.

GADARENES

Gadarenes were inhabitants of the city of Gadara, very near one of the most dramatic episodes in the Savior's ministry.

The Gergesenes were inhabitants of the village of Gergesa, close to Gadara and near the eastern shore of the Sea of Galilee. It was in that vicinity that Christ encountered two individuals possessed of evil spirits. The Savior cast the evil spirits into a herd of swine, which subsequently ran into the sea and perished (see Matt. 8:28–32).

Thereafter the keepers of the swine went and told all to the inhabitants of the city, who came forth to Jesus and bade Him—no doubt, out of fear—to leave their coastal area (see Matt. 8:33–34). In the account in Mark, the locale is given as "the country of the Gadarenes" (Mark 5:1; see also Luke 8:26)—meaning inhabitants of the city of Gadara, also located in that vicinity.

Jesus is reported to have said to the man possessed of evil spirits (only one man, not two as in Matthew), "Go home to thy friends, and tell them how great things the Lord hath done for thee, and hath had compassion on thee" (Mark 5:19; see also Luke 8:39).

2. And he sent them to preach the kingdom of God, and to heal the sick.

3. And he said unto them, Take nothing for your journey, neither staves, nor scrip, neither bread, neither money; neither have two coats apiece.

4. And whatsoever house ye enter into, there abide, and thence depart.

5. And whosoever will not receive you, when ye go out of that city, shake off the very dust from your feet for a testimony against them.

6. And they departed, and went through the towns, preaching the gospel, and healing every where.

7. ¶ Now Herod the tetrarch heard of all that was done by him: and he was perplexed, because that it was said of some, that John was risen from the dead;

8. And of some, that Elias had appeared; and of others, that one of the old prophets was risen again.

9. And Herod said, John have I beheaded: but who is this, of whom I hear such things? And he desired to see him.

10. ¶ And the apostles, when they were returned, told him all that they had done. And he took them, and went aside privately into a desert place belonging to the city called Bethsaida.

11. And the people, when they knew it, followed him: and he received them, and spake unto them of the kingdom of God, and healed them that had need of healing.

12. And when the day began to wear away, then came the twelve, and said unto him, Send the multitude away, that they may go into the towns and country round about, and lodge, and get victuals: for we are here in a desert place.

13. But he said unto them, Give ye them to eat. And they said, We have no more but five loaves and two fishes; except we should go and buy meat for all this people.

14. For they were about five thousand men. And he said to his disciples, Make them sit down by fifties in a company.

15. And they did so, and made them all sit down.

16. Then he took the five loaves and the two fishes, and looking up to heaven, he blessed them, and brake, and gave to the disciples to set before the multitude.

17. And they did eat, and were all filled: and there was taken up of fragments that remained to them twelve baskets.

18. ¶ And it came to pass, as he was alone praying, his disciples were with him: and he asked them, saying, Whom say the people that I am?

19. They answering said, John the Baptist; but some say, Elias; and others say, that one of the old prophets is risen again.

20. He said unto them, But whom say ye that I am? Peter answering said, The Christ of God.

21. And he straitly charged them, and commanded them to tell no man that thing;

22. Saying, The Son of man must suffer many things, and be rejected of the elders and chief priests and scribes, and be slain, and be raised the third day.

23. ¶ And he said to them all, If any man will come after me, let him deny himself, and take up his cross daily, and follow me.

24. For whosoever will save his life

Notes: _____
_____
_____
_____
_____
_____
_____
_____
_____
_____
_____
_____
_____
_____
_____
_____
_____
_____
_____
_____
_____
_____
_____
_____
_____
_____
_____
_____
_____
_____
_____
_____
_____

shall lose it: but whosoever will lose his life for my sake, the same shall save it.

25. For what is a man advantaged, if he gain the whole world, and lose himself, or be cast away?

26. For whosoever shall be ashamed of me and of my words, of him shall the Son of man be ashamed, when he shall come in his own glory, and in his Father's, and of the holy angels.

27. But I tell you of a truth, there be some standing here, which shall not taste of death, till they see the kingdom of God.

28. ¶ And it came to pass about an eight days after these sayings, he took Peter and John and James, and went up into a mountain to pray.

29. And as he prayed, the fashion of his countenance was altered, and his raiment was white and glistering.

30. And, behold, there talked with him two men, which were Moses and Elias:

31. Who appeared in glory, and spake of his decease which he should accomplish at Jerusalem.

32. But Peter and they that were with him were heavy with sleep: and when they were awake, they saw his glory, and the two men that stood with him.

33. And it came to pass, as they departed from him, Peter said unto Jesus, Master, it is good for us to be here: and let us make three tabernacles; one for thee, and one for Moses, and one for Elias: not knowing what he said.

34. While he thus spake, there came a cloud, and overshadowed them: and they feared as they entered into the cloud.

35. And there came a voice out of the cloud, saying, This is my beloved Son: hear him.

36. And when the voice was past, Jesus was found alone. And they kept it close, and told no man in those days any of those things which they had seen.

37. ¶ And it came to pass, that on the next day, when they were come down from the hill, much people met him.

38. And, behold, a man of the company cried out, saying, Master, I beseech thee, look upon my son: for he is mine only child.

39. And, lo, a spirit taketh him, and he suddenly crieth out; and it teareth him that he foameth again, and bruising him hardly departeth from him.

40. And I besought thy disciples to cast him out; and they could not.

41. And Jesus answering said, O faithless and perverse generation, how long shall I be with you, and suffer you? Bring thy son hither.

42. And as he was yet a coming, the devil threw him down, and tare him. And Jesus rebuked the unclean spirit, and healed the child, and delivered him again to his father.

43. ¶ And they were all amazed at the mighty power of God. But while they wondered every one at all things which Jesus did, he said unto his disciples,

44. Let these sayings sink down into your ears: for the Son of man shall be delivered into the hands of men.

45. But they understood not this saying, and it was hid from them,

The transfiguration of Christ

that they perceived it not: and they feared to ask him of that saying.

46. ¶ Then there arose a reasoning among them, which of them should be greatest.

47. And Jesus, perceiving the thought of their heart, took a child, and set him by him,

48. And said unto them, Whosoever shall receive this child in my name receiveth me: and whosoever shall receive me receiveth him that sent me: for he that is least among you all, the same shall be great.

49. ¶ And John answered and said, Master, we saw one casting out devils in thy name; and we forbad him, because he followeth not with us.

50. And Jesus said unto him, Forbid him not: for he that is not against us is for us.

51. ¶ And it came to pass, when the time was come that he should be received up, he stedfastly set his face to go to Jerusalem,

52. And sent messengers before his face: and they went, and entered into a village of the Samaritans, to make ready for him.

53. And they did not receive him, because his face was as though he would go to Jerusalem.

54. And when his disciples James and John saw this, they said, Lord, wilt thou that we command fire to come down from heaven, and consume them, even as Elias did?

55. But he turned, and rebuked them, and said, Ye know not what manner of spirit ye are of.

56. For the Son of man is not come to destroy men's lives, but to save them. And they went to another village.

57. ¶ And it came to pass, that, as they went in the way, a certain man said unto him, Lord, I will follow thee whithersoever thou goest.

58. And Jesus said unto him, Foxes have holes, and birds of the air have nests; but the Son of man hath not where to lay his head.

59. And he said unto another, Follow me. But he said, Lord, suffer me first to go and bury my father.

60. Jesus said unto him, Let the dead bury their dead: but go thou and preach the kingdom of God.

61. And another also said, Lord, I will follow thee; but let me first go bid them farewell, which are at home at my house.

62. And Jesus said unto him, No man, having put his hand to the plough, and looking back, is fit for the kingdom of God.

CHAPTER 10

1. After these things the Lord appointed other seventy also, and sent them two and two before his face into every city and place, whither he himself would come.

2. Therefore said he unto them, The harvest truly is great, but the labourers are few: pray ye therefore the Lord of the harvest, that he would send forth labourers into his harvest.

3. Go your ways: behold, I send you forth as lambs among wolves.

Luke 9:51–56—"Seek to help save souls, not to destroy them: for verily you know, that 'there is more joy in heaven, over one sinner that repents, than there is over ninety and nine just persons that need no repentance'" (Joseph Smith, *History of the Church,* 2:230).

Luke 10:1–11—While there is no record of the organization of the first quorum of Seventy in the meridian dispensation, these verses make it clear that the Savior was organizing an additional quorum. This organization of a quorum of Seventy parallels the organization of the Twelve. Like the Twelve, Seventies hold the Melchizedek Priesthood and are special witnesses of the Savior to the world. They are "traveling ministers" (D&C 107:25) whose calling it is to "preach the gospel . . . in all the world" (D&C 107:97) (see Bruce R. McConkie, *Doctrinal New Testament Commentary,* 1:431, 433).

4. Carry neither purse, nor scrip, nor shoes: and salute no man by the way.

5. And into whatsoever house ye enter, first say, Peace be to this house.

6. And if the son of peace be there, your peace shall rest upon it: if not, it shall turn to you again.

7. And in the same house remain, eating and drinking such things as they give: for the labourer is worthy of his hire. Go not from house to house.

8. And into whatsoever city ye enter, and they receive you, eat such things as are set before you:

9. And heal the sick that are therein, and say unto them, The kingdom of God is come nigh unto you.

10. But into whatsoever city ye enter, and they receive you not, go your ways out into the streets of the same, and say,

11. Even the very dust of your city, which cleaveth on us, we do wipe off against you: notwithstanding be ye sure of this, that the kingdom of God is come nigh unto you.

12. But I say unto you, that it shall be more tolerable in that day for Sodom, than for that city.

13. Woe unto thee, Chorazin! woe unto thee, Bethsaida! for if the mighty works had been done in Tyre and Sidon, which have been done in you, they had a great while ago repented, sitting in sackcloth and ashes.

14. But it shall be more tolerable for Tyre and Sidon at the judgment, than for you.

15. And thou, Capernaum, which art exalted to heaven, shalt be thrust down to hell.

16. He that heareth you heareth me; and he that despiseth you despiseth me; and he that despiseth me despiseth him that sent me.

17. ¶ And the seventy returned again with joy, saying, Lord, even the devils are subject unto us through thy name.

18. And he said unto them, I beheld Satan as lightning fall from heaven.

19. Behold, I give unto you power to tread on serpents and scorpions, and over all the power of the enemy: and nothing shall by any means hurt you.

20. Notwithstanding in this rejoice not, that the spirits are subject unto you; but rather rejoice, because your names are written in heaven.

21. ¶ In that hour Jesus rejoiced in spirit, and said, I thank thee, O Father, Lord of heaven and earth, that thou hast hid these things from the wise and prudent, and hast revealed them unto babes: even so, Father; for so it seemed good in thy sight.

22. All things are delivered to me of my Father: and no man knoweth who the Son is, but the Father; and who the Father is, but the Son, and he to whom the Son will reveal him.

23. ¶ And he turned him unto his

Luke 10:17–19—Because of their faith, those who serve the Lord have power over all things, including devils and other evil things (see Bruce R. McConkie, *Doctrinal New Testament Commentary*, 1:465).

Luke 10:20—Elder Bruce R. McConkie explained that having our "names written in heaven" is another way of saying that the names of all those who are exalted are written in the Lamb's Book of Life (see *The Millennial Messiah*, 710).

Luke 10:21–22—Jesus Christ can properly be called by the name *Father* because:
• He is the Father of those who accept the gospel because it is His Atonement that made the gospel active on this earth.
• Because He created this earth, He is its Father
• He is the Father because He has been given authority by the Father to act in His name and represent Him on this earth.
• Definitions of the word *father* apply to the Savior: "one to whom respect is due," "an originator or source," "one who claims or accepts responsibility," and "one who cares as a father might."

Jesus can also properly be called the Son because:
• He is the firstborn of God in the spirit.
• He is the Only Begotten Son of the Father in the flesh.
• He submitted His will to that of the Father (see Daniel H. Ludlow, *A Companion to Your Study of the Book of Mormon*, 183–84).

disciples, and said privately, Blessed are the eyes which see the things that ye see:

24. For I tell you, that many prophets and kings have desired to see those things which ye see, and have not seen them; and to hear those things which ye hear, and have not heard them.

25. ¶ And, behold, a certain lawyer stood up, and tempted him, saying, Master, what shall I do to inherit eternal life?

26. He said unto him, What is written in the law? how readest thou?

27. And he answering said, Thou shalt love the Lord thy God with all thy heart, and with all thy soul, and with all thy strength, and with all thy mind; and thy neighbour as thyself.

28. And he said unto him, Thou hast answered right: this do, and thou shalt live.

29. But he, willing to justify himself, said unto Jesus, And who is my neighbour?

30. And Jesus answering said, A certain man went down from Jerusalem to Jericho, and fell among thieves, which stripped him of his raiment, and wounded him, and departed, leaving him half dead.

31. And by chance there came down a certain priest that way: and when he saw him, he passed by on the other side.

32. And likewise a Levite, when he was at the place, came and looked on him, and passed by on the other side.

33. But a certain Samaritan, as he journeyed, came where he was: and when he saw him, he had compassion on him,

34. And went to him, and bound up his wounds, pouring in oil and wine, and set him on his own beast, and brought him to an inn, and took care of him.

35. And on the morrow when he departed, he took out two pence, and gave them to the host, and said unto him, Take care of him; and whatsoever thou spendest more, when I come again, I will repay thee.

36. Which now of these three, thinkest thou, was neighbour unto him that fell among the thieves?

37. And he said, He that shewed mercy on him. Then said Jesus unto him, Go, and do thou likewise.

38. ¶ Now it came to pass, as they went, that he entered into a certain village: and a certain woman named Martha received him into her house.

39. And she had a sister called Mary, which also sat at Jesus' feet, and heard his word.

40. But Martha was cumbered about much serving, and came to him, and said, Lord, dost thou not care that my sister hath left me to serve alone? bid her therefore that she help me.

41. And Jesus answered and said unto her, Martha, Martha, thou art careful and troubled about many things:

42. But one thing is needful: and Mary hath chosen that good part, which shall not be taken away from her.

CHAPTER 11

1. And it came to pass, that, as he was praying in a certain place, when he ceased, one of his disciples said unto him, Lord, teach us to pray, as John also taught his disciples.

2. And he said unto them, When ye pray, say, Our Father which art in

Luke 10:30–37 — Elder B. H. Roberts taught, "The principal lesson of that parable is that you will not always find your neighbor among the priests, nor the Levites; you may sometimes find him among the Samaritans, whose name stands as a synonym for a despised people" (Conference Report, Apr. 1908, 105).

Referring to our responsibility, President Hugh B. Brown reminded us that "all whose lives we touch are our neighbors, whether they live across the street, over the fence, across the continent, or over the ocean" (Conference Report, Apr. 1963, 8).

Luke 10:38–42 — "There are times when we must 'be still and know that [there is a] God' (D&C 101:16). I speak of times when we sweep away the mundane things around us, cast away idle thoughts, and allow the intents of our hearts to center upon Him who is the discerner of the thoughts and intents of our hearts (see Hebrews 4:12). I speak of times when we assume a reverent posture and worship our Father in Heaven" (Carlos E. Asay, *Family Pecan Trees: Planting a Legacy of Faith at Home*, 205).

heaven, Hallowed be thy name. Thy kingdom come. Thy will be done, as in heaven, so in earth.

3. Give us day by day our daily bread.

4. And forgive us our sins; for we also forgive every one that is indebted to us. And lead us not into temptation; but deliver us from evil.

5. And he said unto them, Which of you shall have a friend, and shall go unto him at midnight, and say unto him, Friend, lend me three loaves;

6. For a friend of mine in his journey is come to me, and I have nothing to set before him?

7. And he from within shall answer and say, Trouble me not: the door is now shut, and my children are with me in bed; I cannot rise and give thee.

8. I say unto you, Though he will not rise and give him, because he is his friend, yet because of his importunity he will rise and give him as many as he needeth.

9. And I say unto you, Ask, and it shall be given you; seek, and ye shall find; knock, and it shall be opened unto you.

10. For every one that asketh receiveth; and he that seeketh findeth; and to him that knocketh it shall be opened.

11. If a son shall ask bread of any of you that is a father, will he give him a stone? or if he ask a fish, will he for a fish give him a serpent?

12. Or if he shall ask an egg, will he offer him a scorpion?

13. If ye then, being evil, know how to give good gifts unto your children: how much more shall your heavenly Father give the Holy Spirit to them that ask him?

14. ¶ And he was casting out a devil, and it was dumb. And it came to pass, when the devil was gone out, the dumb spake; and the people wondered.

15. But some of them said, He casteth out devils through Beelzebub the chief of the devils.

16. And others, tempting him, sought of him a sign from heaven.

17. But he, knowing their thoughts, said unto them, Every kingdom divided against itself is brought to desolation; and a house divided against a house falleth.

18. If Satan also be divided against himself, how shall his kingdom stand? because ye say that I cast out devils through Beelzebub.

19. And if I by Beelzebub cast out devils, by whom do your sons cast them out? therefore shall they be your judges.

20. But if I with the finger of God cast out devils, no doubt the kingdom of God is come upon you.

21. When a strong man armed keepeth his palace, his goods are in peace:

22. But when a stronger than he shall come upon him, and overcome him, he taketh from him all his armour wherein he trusted, and divideth his spoils.

23. He that is not with me is against me: and he that gathereth not with me scattereth.

24. When the unclean spirit is gone out of a man, he walketh through dry places, seeking rest; and finding

Luke 11:5–7 — The phrase *my children are with me in bed* likely referred to the fact that cushion-type mattresses were lined up side-by-side in the living room for sleeping. The father slept at one end of the line, and the mother slept at the other end of the line to keep the children from rolling off the cushions or out from under the blankets (see Abraham Mitrie Rihbani, *The Syrian Christ,* 216).

Notes: _____

_____

_____

_____

_____

_____

_____

_____

_____

_____

_____

_____

_____

_____

_____

_____

_____

none, he saith, I will return unto my house whence I came out.

25. And when he cometh, he findeth it swept and garnished.

26. Then goeth he, and taketh to him seven other spirits more wicked than himself; and they enter in, and dwell there: and the last state of that man is worse than the first.

27. ¶ And it came to pass, as he spake these things, a certain woman of the company lifted up her voice, and said unto him, Blessed is the womb that bare thee, and the paps which thou hast sucked.

28. But he said, Yea rather, blessed are they that hear the word of God, and keep it.

29. ¶ And when the people were gathered thick together, he began to say, This is an evil generation: they seek a sign; and there shall no sign be given it, but the sign of Jonas the prophet.

30. For as Jonas was a sign unto the Ninevites, so shall also the Son of man be to this generation.

31. The queen of the south shall rise up in the judgment with the men of this generation, and condemn them: for she came from the utmost parts of the earth to hear the wisdom of Solomon; and, behold, a greater than Solomon is here.

32. The men of Nineve shall rise up in the judgment with this generation, and shall condemn it: for they repented at the preaching of Jonas; and, behold, a greater than Jonas is here.

33. No man, when he hath lighted a candle, putteth it in a secret place, neither under a bushel, but on a candlestick, that they which come in may see the light.

34. The light of the body is the eye: therefore when thine eye is single, thy whole body also is full of light; but when thine eye is evil, thy body also is full of darkness.

35. Take heed therefore that the light which is in thee be not darkness.

36. If thy whole body therefore be full of light, having no part dark, the whole shall be full of light, as when the bright shining of a candle doth give thee light.

37. ¶ And as he spake, a certain Pharisee besought him to dine with him: and he went in, and sat down to meat.

38. And when the Pharisee saw it, he marvelled that he had not first washed before dinner.

39. And the Lord said unto him, Now do ye Pharisees make clean the outside of the cup and the platter; but your inward part is full of ravening and wickedness.

40. ¶ Ye fools, did not he that made that which is without make that which is within also?

41. But rather give alms of such things as ye have; and, behold, all things are clean unto you.

42. But woe unto you, Pharisees! for ye tithe mint and rue and all manner of herbs, and pass over judgment and the love of God: these ought ye to have done, and not to leave the other undone.

43. Woe unto you, Pharisees! for ye love the uppermost seats in the

Notes: _____

_____

_____

_____

_____

_____

_____

_____

_____

_____

_____

_____

_____

_____

_____

_____

Luke 11:41—The word *alms* comes from the Greek word meaning "righteousness" or "acts of religious devotion." *Almsgiving* means to donate to the poor, whether through the Church or another organized effort or whether through individual means. Almsgiving is a commandment. In many places in the scriptures it is clearly stated that the prayers of those who give alms are answered (see D&C 88:2; 112:1; 3 Ne. 13:1–4; Alma 34:28). But, as Elder Bruce R. McConkie wrote, the heavens are "sealed" against our prayers if we do not give alms to help our fellow beings (see *Mormon Doctrine,* 2nd ed., 30).

synagogues, and greetings in the markets.

44. Woe unto you, scribes and Pharisees, hypocrites! for ye are as graves which appear not, and the men that walk over them are not aware of them.

45. ¶ Then answered one of the lawyers, and said unto him, Master, thus saying thou reproachest us also.

46. And he said, Woe unto you also, ye lawyers! for ye lade men with burdens grievous to be borne, and ye yourselves touch not the burdens with one of your fingers.

47. Woe unto you! for ye build the sepulchres of the prophets, and your fathers killed them.

48. Truly ye bear witness that ye allow the deeds of your fathers: for they indeed killed them, and ye build their sepulchres.

49. Therefore also said the wisdom of God, I will send them prophets and apostles, and some of them they shall slay and persecute:

50. That the blood of all the prophets, which was shed from the foundation of the world, may be required of this generation;

51. From the blood of Abel unto the blood of Zacharias, which perished between the altar and the temple: verily I say unto you, It shall be required of this generation.

52. Woe unto you, lawyers! for ye have taken away the key of knowledge: ye entered not in yourselves, and them that were entering in ye hindered.

53. And as he said these things unto them, the scribes and the Pharisees began to urge him vehemently, and to provoke him to speak of many things:

54. Laying wait for him, and seeking to catch something out of his mouth, that they might accuse him.

CHAPTER 12

1. In the mean time, when there were gathered together an innumerable multitude of people, insomuch that they trode one upon another, he began to say unto his disciples first of all, Beware ye of the leaven of the Pharisees, which is hypocrisy.

2. For there is nothing covered, that shall not be revealed; neither hid, that shall not be known.

3. Therefore whatsoever ye have spoken in darkness shall be heard in the light; and that which ye have spoken in the ear in closets shall be proclaimed upon the housetops.

4. And I say unto you my friends, Be not afraid of them that kill the body, and after that have no more that they can do.

5. But I will forewarn you whom ye shall fear: Fear him, which after he hath killed hath power to cast into hell; yea, I say unto you, Fear him.

6. Are not five sparrows sold for two farthings, and not one of them is forgotten before God?

Luke 11:52–54—The Lord is here condemning those who have contaminated or even destroyed the scriptures—words that could have guided the Jews. Those who participate in such are led by the adversary. Elder Bruce R. McConkie stated, "The devil wages war against the scriptures. He hates them, perverts their plain meanings, and destroys them when he can. He entices those who heed his temptings to delete and discard, to change and corrupt, to alter and amend, thus taking away the key which will aid in making men 'wise unto salvation' (2 Tim. 3:15–17)" (Bruce R. McConkie, *Doctrinal New Testament Commentary,* 1:624).

Notes: _____

_____

_____

_____

_____

_____

_____

_____

_____

_____

_____

_____

_____

_____

_____

_____

_____

_____

_____

7. But even the very hairs of your head are all numbered. Fear not therefore: ye are of more value than many sparrows.

8. Also I say unto you, Whosoever shall confess me before men, him shall the Son of man also confess before the angels of God:

9. But he that denieth me before men shall be denied before the angels of God.

10. And whosoever shall speak a word against the Son of man, it shall be forgiven him: but unto him that blasphemeth against the Holy Ghost it shall not be forgiven.

11. And when they bring you unto the synagogues, and unto magistrates, and powers, take ye no thought how or what thing ye shall answer, or what ye shall say:

12. For the Holy Ghost shall teach you in the same hour what ye ought to say.

13. ¶ And one of the company said unto him, Master, speak to my brother, that he divide the inheritance with me.

14. And he said unto him, Man, who made me a judge or a divider over you?

15. And he said unto them, Take heed, and beware of covetousness: for a man's life consisteth not in the abundance of the things which he possesseth.

16. And he spake a parable unto them, saying, The ground of a certain rich man brought forth plentifully:

17. And he thought within himself, saying, What shall I do, because I have no room where to bestow my fruits?

18. And he said, This will I do: I will pull down my barns, and build greater; and there will I bestow all my fruits and my goods.

19. And I will say to my soul, Soul, thou hast much goods laid up for many years; take thine ease, eat, drink, and be merry.

20. But God said unto him, Thou fool, this night thy soul shall be required of thee: then whose shall those things be, which thou hast provided?

21. So is he that layeth up treasure for himself, and is not rich toward God.

22. ¶ And he said unto his disciples, Therefore I say unto you, Take no thought for your life, what ye shall eat; neither for the body, what ye shall put on.

23. The life is more than meat, and the body is more than raiment.

24. Consider the ravens: for they neither sow nor reap; which neither have storehouse nor barn; and God feedeth them: how much more are ye better than the fowls?

25. And which of you with taking thought can add to his stature one cubit?

26. If ye then be not able to do that thing which is least, why take ye thought for the rest?

27. Consider the lilies how they grow: they toil not, they spin not; and yet I say unto you, that Solomon in all his glory was not arrayed like one of these.

28. If then God so clothe the grass, which is to day in the field, and to morrow is cast into the oven; how much more will he clothe you, O ye of little faith?

Luke 12:13–21 — "Everyone wants to be successful. The question is: Successful at what? Successful at earning money, successful in marriage, successful in our own sight and in the eyes of our friends? None of these aspirations is necessarily wrong. But greed is an insidious trap that has the power to destroy those whose eager search for success becomes the driving force of their lives" (Gordon B. Hinckley, *Stand a Little Taller*, 334).

Luke 12:22–28 – The phrase "take no thought for" is generally translated from the Greek word *merimnesete,* which basically means to be extremely anxious over a particular thing. The Lord is telling his followers, and us, that is it foolish to be extremely anxious over things we cannot control (such as adding height to our statures, as in verse 25). In those things, we are to exercise faith and leave the matter to the Lord. We would be far better off focusing on the things of eternity that are impacted by matters over which we *do* have control and to focus on our obedience of the commandments and our treatment of our fellow man.

29. And seek not ye what ye shall eat, or what ye shall drink, neither be ye of doubtful mind.

30. For all these things do the nations of the world seek after: and your Father knoweth that ye have need of these things.

31. ¶ But rather seek ye the kingdom of God; and all these things shall be added unto you.

32. Fear not, little flock; for it is your Father's good pleasure to give you the kingdom.

33. Sell that ye have, and give alms; provide yourselves bags which wax not old, a treasure in the heavens that faileth not, where no thief approacheth, neither moth corrupteth.

34. For where your treasure is, there will your heart be also.

35. Let your loins be girded about, and your lights burning;

36. And ye yourselves like unto men that wait for their lord, when he will return from the wedding; that when he cometh and knocketh, they may open unto him immediately.

37. Blessed are those servants, whom the lord when he cometh shall find watching: verily I say unto you, that he shall gird himself, and make them to sit down to meat, and will come forth and serve them.

38. And if he shall come in the second watch, or come in the third watch, and find them so, blessed are those servants.

39. And this know, that if the goodman of the house had known what hour the thief would come, he would have watched, and not have suffered his house to be broken through.

40. Be ye therefore ready also: for the Son of man cometh at an hour when ye think not.

41. ¶ Then Peter said unto him, Lord, speakest thou this parable unto us, or even to all?

42. And the Lord said, Who then is that faithful and wise steward, whom his lord shall make ruler over his household, to give them their portion of meat in due season?

43. Blessed is that servant, whom his lord when he cometh shall find so doing.

44. Of a truth I say unto you, that he will make him ruler over all that he hath.

45. But and if that servant say in his heart, My lord delayeth his coming; and shall begin to beat the menservants and maidens, and to eat and drink, and to be drunken;

46. The lord of that servant will come in a day when he looketh not for him, and at an hour when he is not aware, and will cut him in sunder, and will appoint him his portion with the unbelievers.

47. And that servant, which knew his lord's will, and prepared not himself, neither did according to his will, shall be beaten with many stripes.

48. But he that knew not, and did commit things worthy of stripes, shall be beaten with few stripes. For unto whomsoever much is given, of him shall be much required: and to

Seeking the kingdom of God

Luke 12:48 — We are told that where much is given, much is required. President Gordon B. Hinckley wrote that "We have laid upon us as a people a greater charge, a greater responsibility than any other people ever had in the history of the world. We are responsible for the blessings of the gospel of Jesus Christ to all who have lived upon the earth, to all who now live upon the earth, and to all who will yet live upon the earth. No other people have had so great a responsibility as that" (*Stand a Little Taller*, 326).

whom men have committed much, of him they will ask the more.

49. ¶ I am come to send fire on the earth; and what will I if it be already kindled?

50. But I have a baptism to be baptized with; and how am I straitened till it be accomplished!

51. Suppose ye that I am come to give peace on earth? I tell you, Nay; but rather division:

52. For from henceforth there shall be five in one house divided, three against two, and two against three.

53. The father shall be divided against the son, and the son against the father; the mother against the daughter, and the daughter against the mother; the mother in law against her daughter in law, and the daughter in law against her mother in law.

54. ¶ And he said also to the people, When ye see a cloud rise out of the west, straightway ye say, There cometh a shower; and so it is.

55. And when ye see the south wind blow, ye say, There will be heat; and it cometh to pass.

56. Ye hypocrites, ye can discern the face of the sky and of the earth; but how is it that ye do not discern this time?

57. Yea, and why even of yourselves judge ye not what is right?

58. ¶ When thou goest with thine adversary to the magistrate, as thou art in the way, give diligence that thou mayest be delivered from him; lest he hale thee to the judge, and the judge deliver thee to the officer, and the officer cast thee into prison.

59. I tell thee, thou shalt not depart thence, till thou hast paid the very last mite.

CHAPTER 13

1. There were present at that season some that told him of the Galilæans, whose blood Pilate had mingled with their sacrifices.

2. And Jesus answering said unto them, Suppose ye that these Galilæans were sinners above all the Galilæans, because they suffered such things?

3. I tell you, Nay: but, except ye repent, ye shall all likewise perish.

4. Or those eighteen, upon whom the tower in Siloam fell, and slew them, think ye that they were sinners above all men that dwelt in Jerusalem?

5. I tell you,.Nay: but, except ye repent, ye shall all likewise perish.

6. ¶ He spake also this parable; A certain man had a fig tree planted in his vineyard; and he came and sought fruit thereon, and found none.

7. Then said he unto the dresser of his vineyard, Behold, these three years I come seeking fruit on this fig tree, and find none: cut it down; why cumbereth it the ground?

8. And he answering said unto him, Lord, let it alone this year also, till I shall dig about it, and dung it:

9. And if it bear fruit, well: and if not, then after that thou shalt cut it down.

10. And he was teaching in one of the synagogues on the sabbath.

11. ¶ And, behold, there was a woman which had a spirit of infirmity eighteen years, and was bowed together, and could in no wise lift up herself.

12. And when Jesus saw her, he called her to him, and said unto her,

Luke 13:1–5 — Joseph Smith wrote, "It is a false idea that the Saints will escape all the judgments, whilst the wicked suffer; for all flesh is subject to suffer, and the 'righteous shall hardly escape;' . . . many of the righteous shall fall prey to disease, to pestilence, etc., by reason of the weakness of the flesh, and yet be saved in the Kingdom of God" (*History of the Church,* 4:11).

"Imagine yourself as a living house. God comes in to rebuild that house. At first, perhaps, you can understand what He is doing. He is getting the drains right and stopping the leaks in the roof and so on: you knew that those jobs needed doing and so you are not surprised. But presently he starts knocking the house about in a way that hurts abominably and does not seem to make sense. What on earth is He up to? The explanation is that He is building quite a different house from the one you thought of — throwing out a new wing here, putting on an extra floor there, running up towers, making courtyards. You thought you were going to be made into a decent little cottage: but He is building a palace" (C. S. Lewis, *Mere Christianity,* 174).

Luke 13:6–9 — The parable of the barren fig tree is filled with symbolism that, once we understand, brings great meaning for our time: the husbandman is God; the fig tree is the Jewish remnant of Israel; the vineyard is the world; the fruit represents faith, righteousness, good works, and gifts of the Spirit. The dresser of the vineyard is the Savior; the three years refer to the Savior's mortal ministry; to "cut it down" means to destroy the Jewish nation as an organized kingdom; and to "dung it" means to preach the gospel, show signs and wonders, organize the Church, and offer every opportunity for conversion to the Jewish nation (see Bruce R. McConkie, *Doctrinal New Testament Commentary,* 1:477).

Woman, thou art loosed from thine infirmity.

13. And he laid his hands on her: and immediately she was made straight, and glorified God.

14. And the ruler of the synagogue answered with indignation, because that Jesus had healed on the sabbath day, and said unto the people, There are six days in which men ought to work: in them therefore come and be healed, and not on the sabbath day.

15. The Lord then answered him, and said, Thou hypocrite, doth not each one of you on the sabbath loose his ox or his ass from the stall, and lead him away to watering?

16. And ought not this woman, being a daughter of Abraham, whom Satan hath bound, lo, these eighteen years, be loosed from this bond on the sabbath day?

17. And when he had said these things, all his adversaries were ashamed: and all the people rejoiced for all the glorious things that were done by him.

18. ¶ Then said he, Unto what is the kingdom of God like? and whereunto shall I resemble it?

19. It is like a grain of mustard seed, which a man took, and cast into his garden; and it grew, and waxed a great tree; and the fowls of the air lodged in the branches of it.

20. And again he said, Whereunto shall I liken the kingdom of God?

21. It is like leaven, which a woman took and hid in three measures of meal, till the whole was leavened.

22. And he went through the cities and villages, teaching, and journeying toward Jerusalem.

23. Then said one unto him, Lord, are there few that be saved? And he said unto them,

24. ¶ Strive to enter in at the strait gate: for many, I say unto you, will seek to enter in, and shall not be able.

25. When once the master of the house is risen up, and hath shut to the door, and ye begin to stand without, and to knock at the door, saying, Lord, Lord, open unto us; and he shall answer and say unto you, I know you not whence ye are:

26. Then shall ye begin to say, We have eaten and drunk in thy presence, and thou hast taught in our streets.

27. But he shall say, I tell you, I know you not whence ye are; depart from me, all ye workers of iniquity.

28. There shall be weeping and gnashing of teeth, when ye shall see Abraham, and Isaac, and Jacob, and all the prophets, in the kingdom of God, and you yourselves thrust out.

29. And they shall come from the east, and from the west, and from the north, and from the south, and shall sit down in the kingdom of God.

30. And, behold, there are last which shall be first, and there are first which shall be last.

31. ¶ The same day there came certain of the Pharisees, saying unto him, Get thee out, and depart hence: for Herod will kill thee.

32. And he said unto them, Go ye, and tell that fox, Behold, I cast out devils, and I do cures to day and to

Luke 13:10–17 — Elder Bruce R. McConkie taught that Jesus deliberately sought out this woman and healed her on the Sabbath day to teach the fact that it is "lawful to do good and work righteousness on that holy day" (*Doctrinal New Testament Commentary*, 1:493).

Luke 13:22–30 — "Now, suppose that Christ had said unto them, 'Many will be saved, most of you, will be saved.' They would have taken that to mean that many of them, the most of them, practically all of them, would attain that place of bliss to which they referred as Abraham's bosom. If he had told them only few, they would have understood him to mean that the greater part would be consigned to hell with all its torments. He could not finish the sermon, he could not answer them directly because of their willful ignorance, because of their inability to understand him. . . .

"So, with masterful skill we find him here turning the occasion of this question to good account and preaching a very instructive sermon in connection therewith, but does he never answer the question? Does he let the inquiry go by the board; was it ever to remain unanswered? Not at all. You will find that he has answered that question very fully. Turn to the 76th section of the Doctrine and Covenants. . . .

"Now, those who are saved in the telestial glory are saved from the horrors of perdition; those who attain the terrestrial glory are saved from the lower state, in the telestial; and those who attain the celestial are saved from all lesser conditions and the lower glories of the telestial and the terrestrial. Those Jews, including even the twelve apostles, could not comprehend that condition of affairs and therefore the Christ did not answer the question directly but let it go with a very brief and incomplete answer" (James E. Talmage, Conference Report, Oct. 1917, 142–43).

morrow, and the third day I shall be perfected.

33. Nevertheless I must walk to day, and to morrow, and the day following: for it cannot be that a prophet perish out of Jerusalem.

34. O Jerusalem, Jerusalem, which killest the prophets, and stonest them that are sent unto thee; how often would I have gathered thy children together, as a hen doth gather her brood under her wings, and ye would not!

35. Behold, your house is left unto you desolate: and verily I say unto you, Ye shall not see me, until the time come when ye shall say, Blessed is he that cometh in the name of the Lord.

CHAPTER 14

1. And it came to pass, as he went into the house of one of the chief Pharisees to eat bread on the sabbath day, that they watched him.

2. And, behold, there was a certain man before him which had the dropsy.

3. And Jesus answering spake unto the lawyers and Pharisees, saying, Is it lawful to heal on the sabbath day?

4. And they held their peace. And he took him, and healed him, and let him go;

5. And answered them, saying, Which of you shall have an ass or an ox fallen into a pit, and will not straightway pull him out on the sabbath day?

6. And they could not answer him again to these things.

7. ¶ And he put forth a parable to those which were bidden, when he marked how they chose out the chief rooms; saying unto them,

8. When thou art bidden of any man to a wedding, sit not down in the highest room; lest a more honourable man than thou be bidden of him;

9. And he that bade thee and him come and say to thee, Give this man place; and thou begin with shame to take the lowest room.

10. But when thou art bidden, go and sit down in the lowest room; that when he that bade thee cometh, he may say unto thee, Friend, go up higher: then shalt thou have worship in the presence of them that sit at meat with thee.

11. For whosoever exalteth himself shall be abased; and he that humbleth himself shall be exalted.

12. ¶ Then said he also to him that bade him, When thou makest a dinner or a supper, call not thy friends, nor thy brethren, neither thy kinsmen, nor thy rich neighbours; lest they also bid thee again, and a recompence be made thee.

13. But when thou makest a feast, call the poor, the maimed, the lame, the blind:

14. And thou shalt be blessed; for they cannot recompense thee: for thou shalt be recompensed at the resurrection of the just.

15. ¶ And when one of them that sat at meat with him heard these things,

Luke 13:31–35—"Such a reply not only gave notice to the Pharisees that Jesus was not about to buy their supposed act of friendship, but also gave a message to them—and to Herod—that Jesus' death, when it did occur, would not be in Galilee but in Jerusalem, and he did not fear what they could do to him in Galilee" (Robert J. Matthews, *Behold the Messiah*, 59).

Luke 14:1–6—Jesus knew that His miracles testified of His divine mission. He also knew that the miracles He performed on the Sabbath were controversial and, as such, would be talked about and noticed and investigated by more people than any other of His miracles. As such, these Sabbath miracles likely went farther than any others to testify of the Savior's divinity (see Bruce R. McConkie, *Doctrinal New Testament Commentary*, 1:499).

Luke 14:7–11—The parable of the wedding guests actually summarizes the entire purpose of our mortal probation. Mortality is a test to determine whether we will humble ourselves and walk before God with an eye single to His glory, or whether we will spend our mortal probation in the pursuit of worldly things, such as power, wealth, and honors (see Bruce R. McConkie, *Doctrinal New Testament Commentary*, 1:500).

Luke 14:12–24—"The matters that engaged the time and attention of those who had been bidden, or as we would say, invited, to the feast, were not of themselves discreditable, far less sinful; but to arbitrarily allow personal affairs to annul an honorable engagement once accepted was to manifest discourtesy, disrespect and practical insult toward the provider of the feast" (James E. Talmage, *Jesus the Christ*, 420).

he said unto him, Blessed is he that shall eat bread in the kingdom of God.

16. Then said he unto him, A certain man made a great supper, and bade many:

17. And sent his servant at supper time to say to them that were bidden, Come; for all things are now ready.

18. And they all with one consent began to make excuse. The first said unto him, I have bought a piece of ground, and I must needs go and see it: I pray thee have me excused.

19. And another said, I have bought five yoke of oxen, and I go to prove them: I pray thee have me excused.

20. And another said, I have married a wife, and therefore I cannot come.

21. So that servant came, and shewed his lord these things. Then the master of the house being angry said to his servant, Go out quickly into the streets and lanes of the city, and bring in hither the poor, and the maimed, and the halt, and the blind.

22. And the servant said, Lord, it is done as thou hast commanded, and yet there is room.

23. And the lord said unto the servant, Go out into the highways and hedges, and compel them to come in, that my house may be filled.

24. For I say unto you, That none of those men which were bidden shall taste of my supper.

25. ¶ And there went great multitudes with him: and he turned, and said unto them,

26. If any man come to me, and hate not his father, and mother, and wife, and children, and brethren, and sisters, yea, and his own life also, he cannot be my disciple.

27. And whosoever doth not bear his cross, and come after me, cannot be my disciple.

28. For which of you, intending to build a tower, sitteth not down first, and counteth the cost, whether he have sufficient to finish it?

29. Lest haply, after he hath laid the foundation, and is not able to finish it, all that behold it begin to mock him,

30. Saying, This man began to build, and was not able to finish.

31. Or what king, going to make war against another king, sitteth not down first, and consulteth whether he be able with ten thousand to meet him that cometh against him with twenty thousand?

32. Or else, while the other is yet a great way off, he sendeth an ambassage, and desireth conditions of peace.

33. So likewise, whosoever he be of you that forsaketh not all that he hath, he cannot be my disciple.

34. ¶ Salt is good: but if the salt have lost his savour, wherewith shall it be seasoned?

35. It is neither fit for the land, nor yet for the dunghill; but men cast it out. He that hath ears to hear, let him hear.

Notes: _____

_____

_____

_____

_____

_____

_____

_____

_____

_____

_____

_____

_____

_____

_____

_____

Luke 14:25–33 — "Not only were our pioneer fathers and mothers required to sacrifice in order that they might prove themselves worthy to stand among the Saints of God who are to be gathered in these latter days, but we are required to make sacrifices also. We may not be required to forsake our homes and go into new lands; we may not be required to lay our loved ones away by the side of the road; we may not be driven out by friends and ridiculed and reviled, but the Lord nevertheless expects sacrifices at our hands. And I want to say to you that I think the Lord does not let such sacrifices go unrewarded" (LeGrand Richards, Conference Report, Oct. 1941, 126).

Luke 14:34 — The word *savor* refers to the physical senses of tasting and smelling; it also means "to have experience of" and "to delight in." Webster defines it as a verb meaning "to have a specified taste or quality; a special flavor or quality."

Elder Mark E. Petersen said that we lose our savor when we become casual in our obedience and as we cease to serve the Lord (see *Ensign*, Nov. 1976, 50).

CHAPTER 15

1. Then drew near unto him all the publicans and sinners for to hear him.

2. And the Pharisees and scribes murmured, saying, This man receiveth sinners, and eateth with them.

3. ¶ And he spake this parable unto them, saying,

4. What man of you, having an hundred sheep, if he lose one of them, doth not leave the ninety and nine in the wilderness, and go after that which is lost, until he find it?

5. And when he hath found it, he layeth it on his shoulders, rejoicing.

6. And when he cometh home, he calleth together his friends and neighbours, saying unto them, Rejoice with me; for I have found my sheep which was lost.

7. I say unto you, that likewise joy shall be in heaven over one sinner that repenteth, more than over ninety and nine just persons, which need no repentance.

8. ¶ Either what woman having ten pieces of silver, if she lose one piece, doth not light a candle, and sweep the house, and seek diligently till she find it?

9. And when she hath found it, she calleth her friends and her neighbours together, saying, Rejoice with me; for I have found the piece which I had lost.

10. Likewise, I say unto you, there is joy in the presence of the angels of God over one sinner that repenteth.

11. ¶ And he said, A certain man had two sons:

12. And the younger of them said to his father, Father, give me the portion of goods that falleth to me. And he divided unto them his living.

13. And not many days after the younger son gathered all together, and took his journey into a far country, and there wasted his substance with riotous living.

14. And when he had spent all, there arose a mighty famine in that land; and he began to be in want.

15. And he went and joined himself to a citizen of that country; and he sent him into his fields to feed swine.

16. And he would fain have filled his belly with the husks that the swine did eat: and no man gave unto him.

17. And when he came to himself, he said, How many hired servants of my father's have bread enough and to spare, and I perish with hunger!

18. I will arise and go to my father, and will say unto him, Father, I have sinned against heaven, and before thee,

19. And am no more worthy to be called thy son: make me as one of thy hired servants.

20. And he arose, and came to his father. But when he was yet a great way off, his father saw him, and had compassion, and ran, and fell on his neck, and kissed him.

21. And the son said unto him, Father, I have sinned against heaven, and in thy sight, and am no more worthy to be called thy son.

22. But the father said to his servants, Bring forth the best robe, and

Luke 15:8–10—Our responsibility is not only coins, but souls. We need to make sure that we watch out for those around us—that we take the time and exercise the care to go after those who are wandering or lost (see "Conditions of Becoming 'Lost and Found,'" *Church News,* Apr. 22, 1995).

Luke 15:11–32—"The parable of the prodigal son is loaded with elements atypical of first-century Palestine. . . . A first-century Jewish son would not have dared ask his father for his share of his inheritance while the father was still alive and in good health. And the typical father would hardly have capitulated so quickly. The son's request was equivalent to wishing the father's death, for there was no law or custom among the Jews or the Arabs that entitled a son to share the father's wealth while the father was still alive. . . . [A]side from this parable, scholars have been unable to find in all Middle Eastern literature, from ancient times to the present, a case of any son, older or younger, asking his inheritance from a father who was still in good health. The prodigal's request was even more surprising because he not only requested his inheritance but also the right to dispose of it as he pleased. . . .

"Jesus' Jewish audience must have been especially amazed and attentive as they then learned that the young son squandered his inheritance and was reduced to taking a job as a pig herder. His pride completely broken, the prodigal son resolved to return home. Then comes another surprise. If the story reflected true Oriental customs, a crowd would have gathered around the returning prodigal and subjected him to mocking, taunting songs, and perhaps even physical abuse. . . . The father ran down the road to greet his lost child. Yet 'an Oriental nobleman with flowing robes never runs anywhere.' To do so is humiliating. Great men are not seen running in public. . . . But instead of experiencing the ruthless hostility he deserved and anticipated, the son was overwhelmed with an unexpected, visible demonstration of love and forgiveness. . . . By such an unusual and unmerited response, Jesus adeptly illustrated God's amazing patience and love for even his ungrateful children" (Kenneth W. Godfrey, *The Land of the Gospels: The 1990 Sperry Symposium on the New Testament,* 58–60).

put it on him; and put a ring on his hand, and shoes on his feet:

23. And bring hither the fatted calf, and kill it; and let us eat, and be merry:

24. For this my son was dead, and is alive again; he was lost, and is found. And they began to be merry.

25. Now his elder son was in the field: and as he came and drew nigh to the house, he heard musick and dancing.

26. And he called one of the servants, and asked what these things meant.

27. And he said unto him, Thy brother is come; and thy father hath killed the fatted calf, because he hath received him safe and sound.

28. And he was angry, and would not go in: therefore came his father out, and intreated him.

29. And he answering said to his father, Lo, these many years do I serve thee, neither transgressed I at any time thy commandment: and yet thou never gavest me a kid, that I might make merry with my friends:

30. But as soon as this thy son was come, which hath devoured thy living with harlots, thou hast killed for him the fatted calf.

31. And he said unto him, Son, thou art ever with me, and all that I have is thine.

32. It was meet that we should make merry, and be glad: for this thy brother was dead, and is alive again; and was lost, and is found.

CHAPTER 16

1. And he said also unto his disciples, There was a certain rich man, which had a steward; and the same was accused unto him that he had wasted his goods.

2. And he called him, and said unto him, How is it that I hear this of thee? give an account of thy stewardship; for thou mayest be no longer steward.

3. Then the steward said within himself, What shall I do? for my lord taketh away from me the stewardship: I cannot dig; to beg I am ashamed.

4. I am resolved what to do, that, when I am put out of the stewardship, they may receive me into their houses.

5. So he called every one of his lord's debtors unto him, and said unto the first, How much owest thou unto my lord?

6. And he said, An hundred measures of oil. And he said unto him, Take thy bill, and sit down quickly, and write fifty.

7. Then said he to another, And how much owest thou? And he said, An hundred measures of wheat. And he said unto him, Take thy bill, and write fourscore.

8. And the lord commended the unjust steward, because he had done wisely: for the children of this world are in their generation wiser than the children of light.

9. And I say unto you, Make to yourselves friends of the mammon of unrighteousness; that, when ye fail, they may receive you into everlasting habitations.

10. He that is faithful in that which is least is faithful also in much: and he that is unjust in the least is unjust also in much.

11. If therefore ye have not been faithful in the unrighteous mammon, who will commit to your trust the true riches?

12. And if ye have not been faithful in that which is another man's, who shall give you that which is your own?

Notes: _____
_____
_____
_____
_____
_____
_____
_____
_____
_____
_____
_____
_____
_____
_____
_____
_____
_____

Luke 16:1–13—The parable of the unjust steward is a powerful reminder that we need to use our resources, including our property and money, to lay up treasures in heaven. "If you have not learned wisdom and prudence in the use of 'unrighteous mammon,' how can you be trusted with the more enduring riches?" (James E. Talmage, *Jesus the Christ*, 431).

13. ¶ No servant can serve two masters: for either he will hate the one, and love the other; or else he will hold to the one, and despise the other. Ye cannot serve God and mammon.

14. And the Pharisees also, who were covetous, heard all these things: and they derided him.

15. And he said unto them, Ye are they which justify yourselves before men; but God knoweth your hearts: for that which is highly esteemed among men is abomination in the sight of God.

16. The law and the prophets were until John: since that time the kingdom of God is preached, and every man presseth into it.

17. And it is easier for heaven and earth to pass, than one tittle of the law to fail.

18. Whosoever putteth away his wife, and marrieth another, committeth adultery: and whosoever marrieth her that is put away from her husband committeth adultery.

19. ¶ There was a certain rich man, which was clothed in purple and fine linen, and fared sumptuously every day:

20. And there was a certain beggar named Lazarus, which was laid at his gate, full of sores,

21. And desiring to be fed with the crumbs which fell from the rich man's table: moreover the dogs came and licked his sores.

22. And it came to pass, that the beggar died, and was carried by the angels into Abraham's bosom: the rich man also died, and was buried;

23. And in hell he lift up his eyes, being in torments, and seeth Abraham afar off, and Lazarus in his bosom.

24. And he cried and said, Father Abraham, have mercy on me, and send Lazarus, that he may dip the tip of his finger in water, and cool my tongue; for I am tormented in this flame.

25. But Abraham said, Son, remember that thou in thy lifetime receivedst thy good things, and likewise Lazarus evil things: but now he is comforted, and thou art tormented.

26. And beside all this, between us and you there is a great gulf fixed: so that they which would pass from hence to you cannot; neither can they pass to us, that would come from thence.

27. Then he said, I pray thee therefore, father, that thou wouldest send him to my father's house:

28. For I have five brethren; that he may testify unto them, lest they also come into this place of torment.

29. Abraham saith unto him, They have Moses and the prophets; let them hear them.

30. And he said, Nay, father Abraham: but if one went unto them from the dead, they will repent.

31. And he said unto him, If they hear not Moses and the prophets, neither will they be persuaded, though one rose from the dead.

CHAPTER 17

1. Then said he unto the disciples, It is impossible but that offences will

Luke 16:19–31 — Elder Robert E. Wells clarified in powerful terms the difference between Lazarus and the rich man: "Lazarus's festering body was probably thrown into a pauper's unmarked grave, while the rich man probably was given an elaborate funeral with pomp and ceremony befitting his status. He is now suffering in hell, but angels have borne Lazarus's immortal spirit up to paradise" (*The Mount and the Master*, 3).

"Can those persons who pursue a course of carelessness, neglect of duty, and disobedience, when they depart from this life, expect that their spirits will associate with the spirits of the righteous in the spirit world? I do not expect it, and when you depart from this state of existence, you will find it out for yourselves" (*Journal of Discourses*, 2:150).

come: but woe unto him, through whom they come!

2. It were better for him that a millstone were hanged about his neck, and he cast into the sea, than that he should offend one of these little ones.

3. ¶ Take heed to yourselves: If thy brother trespass against thee, rebuke him; and if he repent, forgive him.

4. And if he trespass against thee seven times in a day, and seven times in a day turn again to thee, saying, I repent; thou shalt forgive him.

5. And the apostles said unto the Lord, Increase our faith.

6. And the Lord said, If ye had faith as a grain of mustard seed, ye might say unto this sycamine tree, Be thou plucked up by the root, and be thou planted in the sea; and it should obey you.

7. But which of you, having a servant plowing or feeding cattle, will say unto him by and by, when he is come from the field, Go and sit down to meat?

8. And will not rather say unto him, Make ready wherewith I may sup, and gird thyself, and serve me, till I have eaten and drunken; and afterward thou shalt eat and drink?

9. Doth he thank that servant because he did the things that were commanded him? I trow not.

10. So likewise ye, when ye shall have done all those things which are commanded you, say, We are unprofitable servants: we have done that which was our duty to do.

11. ¶ And it came to pass, as he went to Jerusalem, that he passed through the midst of Samaria and Galilee.

12. And as he entered into a certain village, there met him ten men that were lepers, which stood afar off:

13. And they lifted up their voices, and said, Jesus, Master, have mercy on us.

14. And when he saw them, he said unto them, Go shew yourselves unto the priests. And it came to pass, that, as they went, they were cleansed.

15. And one of them, when he saw that he was healed, turned back, and with a loud voice glorified God,

16. And fell down on his face at his feet, giving him thanks: and he was a Samaritan.

17. And Jesus answering said, Were there not ten cleansed? but where are the nine?

18. There are not found that returned to give glory to God, save this stranger.

19. And he said unto him, Arise, go thy way: thy faith hath made thee whole.

20. ¶ And when he was demanded of the Pharisees, when the kingdom of God should come, he answered them and said, The kingdom of God cometh not with observation:

21. Neither shall they say, Lo here! or, lo there! for, behold, the kingdom of God is within you.

22. And he said unto the disciples, The days will come, when ye shall desire to see one of the days of the Son of man, and ye shall not see it.

23. And they shall say to you, See here; or, see there: go not after them, nor follow them.

24. For as the lightning, that lighteneth out of the one part under heaven, shineth unto the other part under heaven; so shall also the Son of man be in his day.

Luke 17:5—This was the supplication of the disciples to Jesus as He counseled them to forgive others unconditionally. If the disciples of the Lord needed an increase in faith, then how much more do we need faith in our lives! The Lord's next word of counsel to His disciples was to begin with the faith of a mustard seed, and then to behold miracles happening in their lives. If you were to approach the Lord in prayer and ask Him to increase your faith, what counsel do you believe He would give you in your circumstances?

Luke 17:7–10—"Why thank them for doing their duty?—for doing what the Lord commanded his people to do, and blesses them if they obey? Is it not a privilege to attend a stake or ward conference, to hear what is said by the servants of the Lord, to be reminded of our sacred duties, partake of the good Spirit that is always present at such times, and be strengthened and renewed, so as to be better able to play our part in the great work of our Divine Master?

"Ought the Saints to be *thanked* for receiving blessings from heaven? . . .

"We get far more out of our religion than we put into it" (Orson F. Whitney, *Improvement Era*, 29:316–17).

Luke 17:11–19—"Someone has said that an ungrateful man is like a hog under a tree eating apples and never looking up to see where they came from" (Ezra Taft Benson, *God, Family, Country: Our Three Great Loyalties*, 203).

Luke 17:21—The proper translation of this phrase is not "the kingdom of God is within you," but "the kingdom of God is *among* you." In scripture, the phrase *the kingdom of God* is usually used to indicate the Church that God has established on the earth. The improper translation might suggest an important perspective, however: perhaps it is just as important to have the Church *within us* as it is to merely be members of that Church. When the Church is within us, we should have those attitudes, qualities, talents, and virtues that qualify us for genuine Church membership (see Sterling W. Sill, *The Law of the Harvest*, 166).

25. But first must he suffer many things, and be rejected of this generation.

26. And as it was in the days of Noe, so shall it be also in the days of the Son of man.

27. They did eat, they drank, they married wives, they were given in marriage, until the day that Noe entered into the ark, and the flood came, and destroyed them all.

28. Likewise also as it was in the days of Lot; they did eat, they drank, they bought, they sold, they planted, they builded;

29. But the same day that Lot went out of Sodom it rained fire and brimstone from heaven, and destroyed them all.

30. Even thus shall it be in the day when the Son of man is revealed.

31. In that day, he which shall be upon the housetop, and his stuff in the house, let him not come down to take it away: and he that is in the field, let him likewise not return back.

32. Remember Lot's wife.

33. Whosoever shall seek to save his life shall lose it; and whosoever shall lose his life shall preserve it.

34. I tell you, in that night there shall be two men in one bed; the one shall be taken, and the other shall be left.

35. Two women shall be grinding together; the one shall be taken, and the other left.

36. Two men shall be in the field; the one shall be taken, and the other left.

37. And they answered and said unto him, Where, Lord? And he said unto them, Wheresoever the body is, thither will the eagles be gathered together.

CHAPTER 18

1. And he spake a parable unto them to this end, that men ought always to pray, and not to faint;

2. Saying, There was in a city a judge, which feared not God, neither regarded man:

3. And there was a widow in that city; and she came unto him, saying, Avenge me of mine adversary.

4. And he would not for a while: but afterward he said within himself, Though I fear not God, nor regard man;

5. Yet because this widow troubleth me, I will avenge her, lest by her continual coming she weary me.

6. And the Lord said, Hear what the unjust judge saith.

7. And shall not God avenge his own elect, which cry day and night unto him, though he bear long with them?

8. I tell you that he will avenge them speedily. Nevertheless when the Son of man cometh, shall he find faith on the earth?

9. And he spake this parable unto certain which trusted in themselves that they were righteous, and despised others:

10. Two men went up into the temple to pray; the one a Pharisee, and the other a publican.

11. The Pharisee stood and prayed thus with himself, God, I thank thee, that I am not as other men are, extortioners, unjust, adulterers, or even as this publican.

Parable of the unjust judge

Luke 18:1–8—"The Lord's purpose in giving the parable [of the unjust judge] is specifically stated: it was 'to this end, that men ought always to pray, and not to faint'" (James E. Talmage, *Jesus the Christ*, 404).

Luke 18:9–11—"Humility responds to God's will—to the fear of His judgments and to the needs of those around us. To the proud, the applause of the world rings in their ears; to the humble, the applause of heaven warms their hearts. Someone has said, 'Pride gets no pleasure out of having something, only out of having more of it than the next man'" (Ezra Taft Benson, *The Teachings of Ezra Taft Benson*, 436).

12. I fast twice in the week, I give tithes of all that I possess.

13. And the publican, standing afar off, would not lift up so much as his eyes unto heaven, but smote upon his breast, saying, God be merciful to me a sinner.

14. I tell you, this man went down to his house justified rather than the other: for every one that exalteth himself shall be abased; and he that humbleth himself shall be exalted.

15. And they brought unto him also infants, that he would touch them: but when his disciples saw it, they rebuked them.

16. But Jesus called them unto him, and said, Suffer little children to come unto me, and forbid them not: for of such is the kingdom of God.

17. Verily I say unto you, Whosoever shall not receive the kingdom of God as a little child shall in no wise enter therein.

18. And a certain ruler asked him, saying, Good Master, what shall I do to inherit eternal life?

19. And Jesus said unto him, Why callest thou me good? none is good, save one, that is, God.

20. Thou knowest the commandments, Do not commit adultery, Do not kill, Do not steal, Do not bear false witness, Honour thy father and thy mother.

21. And he said, All these have I kept from my youth up.

22. Now when Jesus heard these things, he said unto him, Yet lackest thou one thing: sell all that thou hast, and distribute unto the poor, and thou shalt have treasure in heaven: and come, follow me.

23. And when he heard this, he was very sorrowful: for he was very rich.

24. And when Jesus saw that he was very sorrowful, he said, How hardly shall they that have riches enter into the kingdom of God!

25. For it is easier for a camel to go through a needle's eye, than for a rich man to enter into the kingdom of God.

26. And they that heard it said, Who then can be saved?

27. And he said, The things which are impossible with men are possible with God.

28. Then Peter said, Lo, we have left all, and followed thee.

29. And he said unto them, Verily I say unto you, There is no man that hath left house, or parents, or brethren, or wife, or children, for the kingdom of God's sake,

30. Who shall not receive manifold more in this present time, and in the world to come life everlasting.

31. ¶ Then he took unto him the twelve, and said unto them, Behold, we go up to Jerusalem, and all things that are written by the prophets concerning the Son of man shall be accomplished.

32. For he shall be delivered unto the Gentiles, and shall be mocked, and spitefully entreated, and spitted on:

33. And they shall scourge him, and put him to death: and the third day he shall rise again.

34. And they understood none of these things: and this saying was hid

Luke 18:12—"The harder it is for an individual to comply with the requirements of the Lord in the payments of his tithing, the greater the benefit when he finally does pay it. . . . No man living upon the earth can pay donations for the poor, can pay for building meetinghouses and temples, academies, and universities, can take of his means and send his boys and girls to proclaim this gospel, without removing selfishness from his soul, no matter how selfish he was when he started in" (Heber J. Grant, *Gospel Standards,* 62).

Elder Jeffrey R. Holland gave five reasons why all of us, regardless of circumstance or situation, should pay tithing:

• To teach our children and grandchildren that the things they enjoy in the Church are financed through the tithes paid by faithful members

• To claim the blessings promised to those who pay tithing

• To declare that spiritual goods are more important to you than material goods

• To discharge our debt to Heavenly Father

• As a personal expression of love to a generous Father in Heaven (see *Ensign,* Nov. 2001, 33–35).

Luke 18:13—To "smite upon the breast" is one way of expressing deep grief among Eastern people, especially in mourning the dead. Generally, the breast is made bare by unbuttoning the top of the shirt, and the breast is often beat in cadence to the chanting of those who are joining in the mourning. The inclusion of this phrase in this parable is meaningful; it indicates that the publican was as sorrowful over his sins as he would have been over someone whose death he mourned (see James M. Freeman, *Manners and Customs of the Bible,* 420).

from them, neither knew they the things which were spoken.

35. ¶ And it came to pass, that as he was come nigh unto Jericho, a certain blind man sat by the way side begging:

36. And hearing the multitude pass by, he asked what it meant.

37. And they told him, that Jesus of Nazareth passeth by.

38. And he cried, saying, Jesus, thou Son of David, have mercy on me.

39. And they which went before rebuked him, that he should hold his peace: but he cried so much the more, Thou Son of David, have mercy on me.

40. And Jesus stood, and commanded him to be brought unto him: and when he was come near, he asked him,

41. Saying, What wilt thou that I shall do unto thee? And he said, Lord, that I may receive my sight.

42. And Jesus said unto him, Receive thy sight: thy faith hath saved thee.

43. And immediately he received his sight, and followed him, glorifying God: and all the people, when they saw it, gave praise unto God.

CHAPTER 19

1. And Jesus entered and passed through Jericho.

2. And, behold, there was a man named Zacchæus, which was the chief among the publicans, and he was rich.

3. And he sought to see Jesus who he was; and could not for the press, because he was little of stature.

4. And he ran before, and climbed up into a sycomore tree to see him: for he was to pass that way.

5. And when Jesus came to the place, he looked up, and saw him, and said unto him, Zacchæus, make haste, and come down; for to day I must abide at thy house.

6. And he made haste, and came down, and received him joyfully.

7. And when they saw it, they all murmured, saying, That he was gone to be guest with a man that is a sinner.

8. And Zacchæus stood, and said unto the Lord; Behold, Lord, the half of my goods I give to the poor; and if I have taken any thing from any man by false accusation, I restore him fourfold.

9. And Jesus said unto him, This day is salvation come to this house, forsomuch as he also is a son of Abraham.

10. For the Son of man is come to seek and to save that which was lost.

11. And as they heard these things, he added and spake a parable, because he was nigh to Jerusalem, and because they thought that the kingdom of God should immediately appear.

12. He said therefore, A certain nobleman went into a far country to receive for himself a kingdom, and to return.

13. And he called his ten servants, and delivered them ten pounds, and said unto them, Occupy till I come.

14. But his citizens hated him, and sent a message after him, saying, We will not have this man to reign over us.

15. And it came to pass, that when he was returned, having received the kingdom, then he commanded these servants to be called unto him, to whom he had given the money, that

Luke 19:2–10—President George Albert Smith reminded us, "It is customary for us, when instruction is given, to think that that instruction was meant for somebody else. . . . If we will . . . keep our ears open for the sound of those truths which are declared unto us, we will be likely to conform our lives to the Gospel, correct mistakes we have already made, and try to do better. If we conclude that the instruction is meant only for somebody else, we are liable to continue in the same old way to the end of our days, and discover when it is too late that the advice was for us as well as for the other person" (Conference Report, Apr. 1906, 52).

Luke 19:11–28—Elder Bruce R. McConkie explains the symbolism in the parable of the pounds:
- The nobleman—Christ
- The far off country—Heaven
- The kingdom to be given—All power
- The ten servants—Members of the Church who have been given all they need in order to be of service
- Citizens—Other people in the world who have not accepted the gospel

The principles and truths taught by this parable, which was given to a multitude, are the same as those taught in the parable of the talents, which the Savior gave to His Apostles (see Bruce R. McConkie, *Doctrinal New Testament Commentary*, 1:572).

he might know how much every man had gained by trading.

16. Then came the first, saying, Lord, thy pound hath gained ten pounds.

17. And he said unto him, Well, thou good servant: because thou hast been faithful in a very little, have thou authority over ten cities.

18. And the second came, saying, Lord, thy pound hath gained five pounds.

19. And he said likewise to him, Be thou also over five cities.

20. And another came, saying, Lord, behold, here is thy pound, which I have kept laid up in a napkin:

21. For I feared thee, because thou art an austere man: thou takest up that thou layedst not down, and reapest that thou didst not sow.

22. And he saith unto him, Out of thine own mouth will I judge thee, thou wicked servant. Thou knewest that I was an austere man, taking up that I laid not down, and reaping that I did not sow:

23. Wherefore then gavest not thou my money into the bank, that at my coming I might have required mine own with usury?

24. And he said unto them that stood by, Take from him the pound, and give it to him that hath ten pounds.

25. (And they said unto him, Lord, he hath ten pounds.)

26. For I say unto you, That unto every one which hath shall be given; and from him that hath not, even that he hath shall be taken away from him.

27. But those mine enemies, which would not that I should reign over them, bring hither, and slay them before me.

28. ¶ And when he had thus spoken, he went before, ascending up to Jerusalem.

29. And it came to pass, when he was come nigh to Bethphage and Bethany, at the mount called the mount of Olives, he sent two of his disciples,

30. Saying, Go ye into the village over against you; in the which at your entering ye shall find a colt tied, whereon yet never man sat: loose him, and bring him hither.

31. And if any man ask you, Why do ye loose him? thus shall ye say unto him, Because the Lord hath need of him.

32. And they that were sent went their way, and found even as he had said unto them.

33. And as they were loosing the colt, the owners thereof said unto them, Why loose ye the colt?

34. And they said, The Lord hath need of him.

35. And they brought him to Jesus: and they cast their garments upon the colt, and they set Jesus thereon.

36. And as he went, they spread their clothes in the way.

37. And when he was come nigh, even now at the descent of the mount of Olives, the whole multitude of the disciples began to rejoice and praise God with a loud voice for all the mighty works that they had seen;

38. Saying, Blessed be the King that cometh in the name of the Lord: peace in heaven, and glory in the highest.

39. And some of the Pharisees from among the multitude said unto him, Master, rebuke thy disciples.

40. And he answered and said unto them, I tell you that, if these should hold their peace, the stones would immediately cry out.

41. ¶ And when he was come near, he beheld the city, and wept over it,

42. Saying, If thou hadst known, even thou, at least in this thy day,

Notes: _____

the things which belong unto thy peace! but now they are hid from thine eyes.

43. For the days shall come upon thee, that thine enemies shall cast a trench about thee, and compass thee round, and keep thee in on every side,

44. And shall lay thee even with the ground, and thy children within thee; and they shall not leave in thee one stone upon another; because thou knewest not the time of thy visitation.

45. And he went into the temple, and began to cast out them that sold therein, and them that bought;

46. Saying unto them, It is written, My house is the house of prayer: but ye have made it a den of thieves.

47. And he taught daily in the temple. But the chief priests and the scribes and the chief of the people sought to destroy him,

48. And could not find what they might do: for all the people were very attentive to hear him.

CHAPTER 20

1. And it came to pass, that on one of those days, as he taught the people in the temple, and preached the gospel, the chief priests and the scribes came upon him with the elders,

2. And spake unto him, saying, Tell us, by what authority doest thou these things? or who is he that gave thee this authority?

3. And he answered and said unto them, I will also ask you one thing; and answer me:

4. The baptism of John, was it from heaven, or of men?

5. And they reasoned with themselves, saying, If we shall say, From heaven; he will say, Why then believed ye him not?

6. But and if we say, Of men; all the people will stone us: for they be persuaded that John was a prophet.

7. And they answered, that they could not tell whence it was.

8. And Jesus said unto them, Neither tell I you by what authority I do these things.

9. Then began he to speak to the people this parable; A certain man planted a vineyard, and let it forth to husbandmen, and went into a far country for a long time.

10. And at the season he sent a servant to the husbandmen, that they should give him of the fruit of the vineyard: but the husbandmen beat him, and sent him away empty.

11. And again he sent another servant: and they beat him also, and entreated him shamefully, and sent him away empty.

12. And again he sent a third: and they wounded him also, and cast him out.

13. Then said the lord of the vineyard, What shall I do? I will send my beloved son: it may be they will reverence him when they see him.

14. But when the husbandmen saw him, they reasoned among themselves, saying, This is the heir: come, let us kill him, that the inheritance may be ours.

15. So they cast him out of the vineyard, and killed him. What therefore shall the lord of the vineyard do unto them?

16. He shall come and destroy these husbandmen, and shall give the vineyard to others. And when they heard it, they said, God forbid.

17. And he beheld them, and said,

Luke 19:41–44 — In these verses, the Savior related what He saw by prophecy: that Jerusalem would be destroyed for rejecting Him. Fewer than four decades later, that prophecy was fulfilled in 70 A.D. when the Roman legions, under the direction of Titus, destroyed the city and its temple in a siege of unparalleled terror and devastation (see Bruce R. McConkie, *Doctrinal New Testament Commentary*, 1:580).

Luke 19:44 — "Now, as soon as part of the wall was battered down, and certain of the towers yielded to the impression of the battering-rams, those that opposed themselves fled away. . . . When those that came running before the rest told them that the western wall was entirely overthrown . . . they fell upon their faces, and greatly lamented their own mad conduct; and their nerves were so terribly loosed, that they could not flee away. . . .

"[A]s soon as the army had no more people to slay or plunder, because there remained none to be the objects of their fury, . . . César gave orders that they should now demolish the entire city and temple. . . . [The city and the wall were] so thoroughly laid even with the ground by those that dug it up to the foundation, that there was left nothing to make those that came thither believe it had ever been inhabited" (Flavius Josephus, *The Complete Works of Flavius Josephus*, 586–87, 589).

What is this then that is written, The stone which the builders rejected, the same is become the head of the corner?

18. Whosoever shall fall upon that stone shall be broken; but on whomsoever it shall fall, it will grind him to powder.

19. ¶ And the chief priests and the scribes the same hour sought to lay hands on him; and they feared the people: for they perceived that he had spoken this parable against them.

20. And they watched him, and sent forth spies, which should feign themselves just men, that they might take hold of his words, that so they might deliver him unto the power and authority of the governor.

21. And they asked him, saying, Master, we know that thou sayest and teachest rightly, neither acceptest thou the person of any, but teachest the way of God truly:

22. Is it lawful for us to give tribute unto Cæsar, or no?

23. But he perceived their craftiness, and said unto them, Why tempt ye me?

24. Shew me a penny. Whose image and superscription hath it? They answered and said, Cæsar's.

25. And he said unto them, Render therefore unto Cæsar the things which be Cæsar's, and unto God the things which be God's.

26. And they could not take hold of his words before the people: and they marvelled at his answer, and held their peace.

27. ¶ Then came to him certain of the Sadducees, which deny that there is any resurrection; and they asked him,

28. Saying, Master, Moses wrote unto us, If any man's brother die, having a wife, and he die without children, that his brother should take his wife, and raise up seed unto his brother.

29. There were therefore seven brethren: and the first took a wife, and died without children.

30. And the second took her to wife, and he died childless.

31. And the third took her; and in like manner the seven also: and they left no children, and died.

32. Last of all the woman died also.

33. Therefore in the resurrection whose wife of them is she? for seven had her to wife.

34. And Jesus answering said unto them, The children of this world marry, and are given in marriage:

35. But they which shall be accounted worthy to obtain that world, and the resurrection from the dead, neither marry, nor are given in marriage:

36. Neither can they die any more: for they are equal unto the angels; and are the children of God, being the children of the resurrection.

37. Now that the dead are raised, even Moses shewed at the bush, when he calleth the Lord the God of Abraham, and the God of Isaac, and the God of Jacob.

38. For he is not a God of the dead, but of the living: for all live unto him.

39. ¶ Then certain of the scribes answering said, Master, thou hast well said.

40. And after that they durst not ask him any question at all.

41. And he said unto them, How say they that Christ is David's son?

42. And David himself saith in the book of Psalms, The Lord said unto

The widow's mite

my Lord, Sit thou on my right hand,

43. Till I make thine enemies thy footstool.

44. David therefore calleth him Lord, how is he then his son?

45. ¶ Then in the audience of all the people he said unto his disciples,

46. Beware of the scribes, which desire to walk in long robes, and love greetings in the markets, and the highest seats in the synagogues, and the chief rooms at feasts;

47. Which devour widows' houses, and for a shew make long prayers: the same shall receive greater damnation.

CHAPTER 21

1. And he looked up, and saw the rich men casting their gifts into the treasury.

2. And he saw also a certain poor widow casting in thither two mites.

3. And he said, Of a truth I say unto you, that this poor widow hath cast in more than they all:

4. For all these have of their abundance cast in unto the offerings of God: but she of her penury hath cast in all the living that she had.

5. ¶ And as some spa ke of the temple, how it was adorned with goodly stones and gifts, he said,

6. As for these things which ye behold, the days will come, in the which there shall not be left one stone upon another, that shall not be thrown down.

7. And they asked him, saying, Master, but when shall these things be? and what sign will there be when these things shall come to pass?

8. And he said, Take heed that ye be not deceived: for many shall come in my name, saying, I am Christ; and the time draweth near: go ye not therefore after them.

9. But when ye shall hear of wars and commotions, be not terrified: for these things must first come to pass; but the end is not by and by.

10. Then said he unto them, Nation shall rise against nation, and kingdom against kingdom:

11. And great earthquakes shall be in divers places, and famines, and pestilences; and fearful sights and great signs shall there be from heaven.

12. But before all these, they shall lay their hands on you, and persecute you, delivering you up to the synagogues, and into prisons, being brought before kings and rulers for my name's sake.

13. And it shall turn to you for a testimony.

14. Settle it therefore in your hearts, not to meditate before what ye shall answer:

15. For I will give you a mouth and wisdom, which all your adversaries shall not be able to gainsay nor resist.

16. And ye shall be betrayed both by parents, and brethren, and kinsfolks, and friends; and some of you shall they cause to be put to death.

17. And ye shall be hated of all men for my name's sake.

18. But there shall not an hair of your head perish.

19. In your patience possess ye your souls.

Notes: _____
_____
_____
_____
_____
_____
_____
_____
_____
_____
_____
_____
_____
_____
_____
_____
_____
_____
_____
_____
_____
_____
_____
_____
_____
_____
_____
_____
_____
_____
_____

20. And when ye shall see Jerusalem compassed with armies, then know that the desolation thereof is nigh.

21. Then let them which are in Judæa flee to the mountains; and let them which are in the midst of it depart out; and let not them that are in the countries enter thereinto.

22. For these be the days of vengeance, that all things which are written may be fulfilled.

23. But woe unto them that are with child, and to them that give suck, in those days! for there shall be great distress in the land, and wrath upon this people.

24. And they shall fall by the edge of the sword, and shall be led away captive into all nations: and Jerusalem shall be trodden down of the Gentiles, until the times of the Gentiles be fulfilled.

25. ¶ And there shall be signs in the sun, and in the moon, and in the stars; and upon the earth distress of nations, with perplexity; the sea and the waves roaring;

26. Men's hearts failing them for fear, and for looking after those things which are coming on the earth: for the powers of heaven shall be shaken.

27. And then shall they see the Son of man coming in a cloud with power and great glory.

28. And when these things begin to come to pass, then look up, and lift up your heads; for your redemption draweth nigh.

29. And he spake to them a parable; Behold the fig tree, and all the trees;

30. When they now shoot forth, ye see and know of your own selves that summer is now nigh at hand.

31. So likewise ye, when ye see these things come to pass, know ye that the kingdom of God is nigh at hand.

32. Verily I say unto you, This generation shall not pass away, till all be fulfilled.

33. Heaven and earth shall pass away: but my words shall not pass away.

34. ¶ And take heed to yourselves, lest at any time your hearts be overcharged with surfeiting, and drunkenness, and cares of this life, and so that day come upon you unawares.

35. For as a snare shall it come on all them that dwell on the face of the whole earth.

36. Watch ye therefore, and pray always, that ye may be accounted worthy to escape all these things that shall come to pass, and to stand before the Son of man.

37. And in the day time he was teaching in the temple; and at night he went out, and abode in the mount that is called the mount of Olives.

38. And all the people came early in the morning to him in the temple, for to hear him.

Luke 21:24—The *time of the Gentiles* refers to the time when the gospel will be preached to the Gentiles instead of to the Jews. We are living in that time. The time of the Gentiles will end when missionary work is no longer done, and calamities and disasters begin in earnest, replacing the preaching of the gospel with their own testimony of the end.

Notes: _____

_____

_____

_____

_____

_____

_____

_____

_____

_____

_____

_____

_____

_____

_____

_____

_____

_____

_____

_____

CHAPTER 22

1. Now the feast of unleavened bread drew nigh, which is called the Passover.

2. And the chief priests and scribes sought how they might kill him; for they feared the people.

3. ¶ Then entered Satan into Judas surnamed Iscariot, being of the number of the twelve.

4. And he went his way, and communed with the chief priests and captains, how he might betray him unto them.

5. And they were glad, and covenanted to give him money.

6. And he promised, and sought opportunity to betray him unto them in the absence of the multitude.

7. ¶ Then came the day of unleavened bread, when the passover must be killed.

8. And he sent Peter and John, saying, Go and prepare us the passover, that we may eat.

9. And they said unto him, Where wilt thou that we prepare?

10. And he said unto them, Behold, when ye are entered into the city, there shall a man meet you, bearing a pitcher of water; follow him into the house where he entereth in.

11. And ye shall say unto the goodman of the house, The Master saith unto thee, Where is the guestchamber, where I shall eat the passover with my disciples?

12. And he shall shew you a large upper room furnished: there make ready.

13. And they went, and found as he had said unto them: and they made ready the passover.

14. And when the hour was come, he sat down, and the twelve apostles with him.

15. And he said unto them, With desire I have desired to eat this passover with you before I suffer:

16. For I say unto you, I will not any more eat thereof, until it be fulfilled in the kingdom of God.

17. ¶ And he took the cup, and gave thanks, and said, Take this, and divide it among yourselves:

18. For I say unto you, I will not drink of the fruit of the vine, until the kingdom of God shall come.

19. ¶ And he took bread, and gave thanks, and brake it, and gave unto them, saying, This is my body which is given for you: this do in remembrance of me.

20. Likewise also the cup after supper, saying, This cup is the new testament in my blood, which is shed for you.

21. ¶ But, behold, the hand of him that betrayeth me is with me on the table.

22. And truly the Son of man goeth, as it was determined: but woe unto that man by whom he is betrayed!

23. And they began to inquire among themselves, which of them it was that should do this thing.

24. ¶ And there was also a strife among them, which of them should be accounted the greatest.

25. And he said unto them, The

Luke 22:3—Elder Bruce R. McConkie pointed out that Satan may have very literally entered Judas, since Satan has only a spirit body; the followers of Satan, who lack physical bodies, have been known from many scriptural accounts to enter the physical bodies of those whom they possess. But regardless of whether these words are literal, it is obvious that Judas was completely subject to Satan (see Bruce R. McConkie, *Doctrinal New Testament Commentary*, 1:701–702).

Luke 22:3–6—President Gordon B. Hinckley quoted Channing Pollock, who said, "Judas, with his thirty pieces of silver, was a failure. Christ, on the cross, was the greatest figure of time and eternity" (*Brigham Young University Speeches of the Year*, Oct. 17, 1962, 6).

kings of the Gentiles exercise lordship over them; and they that exercise authority upon them are called benefactors.

26. But ye shall not be so: but he that is greatest among you, let him be as the younger; and he that is chief, as he that doth serve.

27. For whether is greater, he that sitteth at meat, or he that serveth? is not he that sitteth at meat? but I am among you as he that serveth.

28. Ye are they which have continued with me in my temptations.

29. And I appoint unto you a kingdom, as my Father hath appointed unto me;

30. That ye may eat and drink at my table in my kingdom, and sit on thrones judging the twelve tribes of Israel.

31. ¶ And the Lord said, Simon, Simon, behold, Satan hath desired to have you, that he may sift you as wheat:

32. But I have prayed for thee, that thy faith fail not: and when thou art converted, strengthen thy brethren.

33. And he said unto him, Lord, I am ready to go with thee, both into prison, and to death.

34. And he said, I tell thee, Peter, the cock shall not crow this day, before that thou shalt thrice deny that thou knowest me.

35. And he said unto them, When I sent you without purse, and scrip, and shoes, lacked ye any thing? And they said, Nothing.

36. Then said he unto them, But now, he that hath a purse, let him take it, and likewise his scrip: and he that hath no sword, let him sell his garment, and buy one.

37. For I say unto you, that this that is written must yet be accomplished in me, And he was reckoned among the transgressors: for the things concerning me have an end.

38. And they said, Lord, behold, here are two swords. And he said unto them, It is enough.

39. ¶ And he came out, and went, as he was wont, to the mount of Olives; and his disciples also followed him.

40. And when he was at the place, he said unto them, Pray that ye enter not into temptation.

41. And he was withdrawn from them about a stone's cast, and kneeled down, and prayed,

42. Saying, Father, if thou be willing, remove this cup from me: nevertheless not my will, but thine, be done.

43. And there appeared an angel unto him from heaven, strengthening him.

44. And being in an agony he prayed more earnestly: and his sweat was as it were great drops of blood falling down to the ground.

45. And when he rose up from prayer, and was come to his disciples, he found them sleeping for sorrow,

46. And said unto them, Why sleep ye? rise and pray, lest ye enter into temptation.

47. ¶ And while he yet spake, behold a multitude, and he that was

Luke 22:24–30 — The concept of who is the greatest is one that is futile; faithful service brings great personal satisfaction regardless of what type of service it is or what position is held. The service of a faithful home teacher is just as valued as the service of a General Authority (see Bruce R. McConkie, *Doctrinal New Testament Commentary,* 1:566).

Luke 22:32 — No one can endure on borrowed light. If you don't have a testimony sufficient to light the way, and that light is not within you, you will not be able to stand at the last day (see Harold B. Lee, *New Era,* Feb. 1971, 4).

Notes: _____

_____

_____

_____

_____

_____

_____

_____

_____

_____

_____

_____

_____

_____

_____

_____

_____

_____

called Judas, one of the twelve, went before them, and drew near unto Jesus to kiss him.

48. But Jesus said unto him, Judas, betrayest thou the Son of man with a kiss?

49. When they which were about him saw what would follow, they said unto him, Lord, shall we smite with the sword?

50. ¶ And one of them smote the servant of the high priest, and cut off his right ear.

51. And Jesus answered and said, Suffer ye thus far. And he touched his ear, and healed him.

52. Then Jesus said unto the chief priests, and captains of the temple, and the elders, which were come to him, Be ye come out, as against a thief, with swords and staves?

53. When I was daily with you in the temple, ye stretched forth no hands against me: but this is your hour, and the power of darkness.

54. ¶ Then took they him, and led him, and brought him into the high priest's house. And Peter followed afar off.

55. And when they had kindled a fire in the midst of the hall, and were set down together, Peter sat down among them.

56. But a certain maid beheld him as he sat by the fire, and earnestly looked upon him, and said, This man was also with him.

57. And he denied him, saying, Woman, I know him not.

58. And after a little while another saw him, and said, Thou art also of them. And Peter said, Man, I am not.

59. And about the space of one hour after another confidently affirmed, saying, Of a truth this fellow also was with him: for he is a Galilæan.

60. And Peter said, Man, I know not what thou sayest. And immediately, while he yet spake, the cock crew.

61. And the Lord turned, and looked upon Peter. And Peter remembered the word of the Lord, how he had said unto him, Before the cock crow, thou shalt deny me thrice.

62. And Peter went out, and wept bitterly.

63. ¶ And the men that held Jesus mocked him, and smote him.

64. And when they had blindfolded him, they struck him on the face, and asked him, saying, Prophesy, who is it that smote thee?

65. And many other things blasphemously spake they against him.

66. ¶ And as soon as it was day, the elders of the people and the chief priests and the scribes came together, and led him into their council, saying,

67. Art thou the Christ? tell us. And he said unto them, If I tell you, ye will not believe:

68. And if I also ask you, ye will not answer me, nor let me go.

69. Hereafter shall the Son of man sit on the right hand of the power of God.

70. Then said they all, Art thou then the Son of God? And he said unto them, Ye say that I am.

71. And they said, What need we any further witness? for we ourselves have heard of his own mouth.

CHAPTER 23

1. And the whole multitude of them arose, and led him unto Pilate.

2. And they began to accuse him,

Luke 22:64—The reference here to blindfolding is likely referring to a common ancient sport, one similar to what we know as "blind man's bluff." One man was blindfolded; others struck him, one at a time, and he was not allowed to take off the blindfold until he could correctly guess who was striking him. This was a perfect way to mock Jesus: if He really was a prophet, they reasoned, He ought to be able to name those who were striking Him even though He couldn't see them (see James M. Freeman, *Manners and Customs of the Bible*, 421).

saying, We found this fellow perverting the nation, and forbidding to give tribute to Cæsar, saying that he himself is Christ a King.

3. And Pilate asked him, saying, Art thou the King of the Jews? And he answered him and said, Thou sayest it.

4. Then said Pilate to the chief priests and to the people, I find no fault in this man.

5. And they were the more fierce, saying, He stirreth up the people, teaching throughout all Jewry, beginning from Galilee to this place.

6. When Pilate heard of Galilee, he asked whether the man were a Galilaean.

7. And as soon as he knew that he belonged unto Herod's jurisdiction, he sent him to Herod, who himself also was at Jerusalem at that time.

8. ¶ And when Herod saw Jesus, he was exceeding glad: for he was desirous to see him of a long season, because he had heard many things of him; and he hoped to have seen some miracle done by him.

9. Then he questioned with him in many words; but he answered him nothing.

10. And the chief priests and scribes stood and vehemently accused him.

11. And Herod with his men of war set him at nought, and mocked him, and arrayed him in a gorgeous robe, and sent him again to Pilate.

12. ¶ And the same day Pilate and Herod were made friends together: for before they were at enmity between themselves.

13. ¶ And Pilate, when he had called together the chief priests and the rulers and the people,

14. Said unto them, Ye have brought this man unto me, as one that perverteth the people: and, behold, I, having examined him before you, have found no fault in this man touching those things whereof ye accuse him:

15. No, nor yet Herod: for I sent you to him; and, lo, nothing worthy of death is done unto him.

16. I will therefore chastise him, and release him.

17. (For of necessity he must release one unto them at the feast.)

18. And they cried out all at once, saying, Away with this man, and release unto us Barabbas:

19. (Who for a certain sedition made in the city, and for murder, was cast into prison.)

20. Pilate therefore, willing to release Jesus, spake again to them.

21. But they cried, saying, Crucify him, crucify him.

22. And he said unto them the third time, Why, what evil hath he done? I have found no cause of death in him: I will therefore chastise him, and let him go.

23. And they were instant with loud voices, requiring that he might be crucified. And the voices of them and of the chief priests prevailed.

24. And Pilate gave sentence that it should be as they required.

25. And he released unto them him that for sedition and murder was cast into prison, whom they had desired; but he delivered Jesus to their will.

26. And as they led him away, they laid hold upon one Simon, a Cyrenian, coming out of the country, and on him they laid the cross, that he might bear it after Jesus.

27. ¶ And there followed him a great company of people, and of women, which also bewailed and lamented him.

28. But Jesus turning unto them said, Daughters of Jerusalem, weep not for me, but weep for yourselves, and for your children.

Luke 23:6–12 — Herod had once been afraid of Jesus, thinking Him to be the reincarnation of John the Baptist, whom Herod had ordered murdered. Now, with the Savior bound and in front of him, Herod became insulting and derisive as he questioned the Savior. But Jesus remained completely silent. As far as we know, Herod is the only person who saw the Savior face-to-face and spoke to Him, but never heard His voice (see Daniel H. Ludlow, *A Companion to Your Study of the New Testament: The Four Gospels*, 2:343).

Jesus brought to Pontius Pilate

29. For, behold, the days are coming, in the which they shall say, Blessed are the barren, and the wombs that never bare, and the paps which never gave suck.

30. Then shall they begin to say to the mountains, Fall on us; and to the hills, Cover us.

31. For if they do these things in a green tree, what shall be done in the dry?

32. And there were also two other, malefactors, led with him to be put to death.

33. And when they were come to the place, which is called Calvary, there they crucified him, and the malefactors, one on the right hand, and the other on the left.

34. ¶ Then said Jesus, Father, forgive them; for they know not what they do. And they parted his raiment, and cast lots.

35. And the people stood beholding. And the rulers also with them derided him, saying, He saved others; let him save himself, if he be Christ, the chosen of God.

36. And the soldiers also mocked him, coming to him, and offering him vinegar,

37. And saying, If thou be the king of the Jews, save thyself.

38. And a superscription also was written over him in letters of Greek, and Latin, and Hebrew, THIS IS THE KING OF THE JEWS.

39. ¶ And one of the malefactors which were hanged railed on him, saying, If thou be Christ, save thyself and us.

40. But the other answering rebuked him, saying, Dost not thou fear God, seeing thou art in the same condemnation?

41. And we indeed justly; for we receive the due reward of our deeds: but this man hath done nothing amiss.

42. And he said unto Jesus, Lord, remember me when thou comest into thy kingdom.

43. And Jesus said unto him, Verily I say unto thee, To day shalt thou be with me in paradise.

44. And it was about the sixth hour, and there was a darkness over all the earth until the ninth hour.

45. And the sun was darkened, and the veil of the temple was rent in the midst.

46. ¶ And when Jesus had cried with a loud voice, he said, Father, into thy hands I commend my spirit: and having said thus, he gave up the ghost.

47. Now when the centurion saw what was done, he glorified God, saying, Certainly this was a righteous man.

48. And all the people that came together to that sight, beholding the things which were done, smote their breasts, and returned.

49. And all his acquaintance, and the women that followed him from Galilee, stood afar off, beholding these things.

Luke 23:34—President Joseph F. Smith said of this utterance, "I say that no man could utter such words as these at such a time; it required the power and spirit, the love, mercy, charity and forgiveness of God himself. . . . If there was no other proof than this of the divine mission of Jesus Christ, this alone would convince me that Jesus was the Redeemer of the world."

The Crucifixion

50. ¶ And, behold, there was a man named Joseph, a counsellor; and he was a good man, and a just:

51. (The same had not consented to the counsel and deed of them;) he was of Arimathæa, a city of the Jews: who also himself waited for the kingdom of God.

52. This man went unto Pilate, and begged the body of Jesus.

53. And he took it down, and wrapped it in linen, and laid it in a sepulchre that was hewn in stone, wherein never man before was laid.

54. ¶ And that day was the preparation, and the sabbath drew on.

55. And the women also, which came with him from Galilee, followed after, and beheld the sepulchre, and how his body was laid.

56. And they returned, and prepared spices and ointments; and rested the sabbath day according to the commandment.

CHAPTER 24

1. Now upon the first day of the week, very early in the morning, they came unto the sepulchre, bringing the spices which they had prepared, and certain others with them.

2. And they found the stone rolled away from the sepulchre.

3. And they entered in, and found not the body of the Lord Jesus.

4. And it came to pass, as they were much perplexed thereabout, behold, two men stood by them in shining garments:

5. And as they were afraid, and bowed down their faces to the earth, they said unto them, Why seek ye the living among the dead?

6. He is not here, but is risen: remember how he spake unto you when he was yet in Galilee,

7. Saying, The Son of man must be delivered into the hands of sinful men, and be crucified, and the third day rise again.

8. And they remembered his words,

9. And returned from the sepulchre, and told all these things unto the eleven, and to all the rest.

10. It was Mary Magdalene, and Joanna, and Mary the mother of James, and other women that were with them, which told these things unto the apostles.

11. And their words seemed to them as idle tales, and they believed them not.

12. Then arose Peter, and ran unto the sepulchre; and stooping down, he beheld the linen clothes laid by themselves, and departed, wondering in himself at that which was come to pass.

13. ¶ And, behold, two of them went that same day to a village called Emmaus, which was from Jerusalem about threescore furlongs.

14. And they talked together of all these things which had happened.

15. And it came to pass, that, while they communed together and reasoned, Jesus himself drew near, and went with them.

16. But their eyes were holden that they should not know him.

17. And he said unto them, What manner of communications are these that ye have one to another, as ye walk, and are sad?

18. And the one of them, whose name was Cleopas, answering said unto him, Art thou only a stranger in Jerusalem, and hast not known

Luke 24:1—The women who came bringing spice to anoint the Lord's body included Mary, the mother of Jesus; Salome, the mother of James and John; Joanna, the wife of Herod's steward, Chuza; and other women who had kept vigil at the cross. Why were there women, but no men who came to attend the Savior? According to Elder Bruce R. McConkie, "We know that women in general are more spiritual than men, and certainly their instincts and desires to render compassionate service exceed those of their male counterparts" (*The Mortal Messiah*, 4:265–66).

Luke 24:7—"This specification of the third day must not be understood as meaning after three full days. The Jews began their counting of the daily hours with sunset; therefore the hour before sunset and the hour following belonged to different days. Jesus died and was interred during Friday afternoon. His body lay in the tomb, dead, during part of Friday (first day), throughout Saturday, or as we divide the days, from sunset Friday to sunset Saturday (second day), and part of Sunday (third day). We know not at what hour between Saturday sunset and Sunday dawn He rose" (James E. Talmage, *Jesus the Christ*, 647).

the things which are come to pass therein these days?

19. And he said unto them, What things? And they said unto him, Concerning Jesus of Nazareth, which was a prophet mighty in deed and word before God and all the people:

20. And how the chief priests and our rulers delivered him to be condemned to death, and have crucified him.

21. But we trusted that it had been he which should have redeemed Israel: and beside all this, to day is the third day since these things were done.

22. Yea, and certain women also of our company made us astonished, which were early at the sepulchre;

23. And when they found not his body, they came, saying, that they had also seen a vision of angels, which said that he was alive.

24. And certain of them which were with us went to the sepulchre, and found it even so as the women had said: but him they saw not.

25. Then he said unto them, O fools, and slow of heart to believe all that the prophets have spoken:

26. Ought not Christ to have suffered these things, and to enter into his glory?

27. And beginning at Moses and all the prophets, he expounded unto them in all the scriptures the things concerning himself.

28. And they drew nigh unto the village, whither they went: and he made as though he would have gone further.

29. But they constrained him, saying, Abide with us: for it is toward evening, and the day is far spent. And he went in to tarry with them.

30. And it came to pass, as he sat at meat with them, he took bread, and blessed it, and brake, and gave to them.

31. And their eyes were opened, and they knew him; and he vanished out of their sight.

32. And they said one to another, Did not our heart burn within us, while he talked with us by the way, and while he opened to us the scriptures?

33. And they rose up the same hour, and returned to Jerusalem, and found the eleven gathered together, and them that were with them,

34. Saying, The Lord is risen indeed, and hath appeared to Simon.

35. And they told what things were done in the way, and how he was known of them in breaking of bread.

36. ¶ And as they thus spake, Jesus himself stood in the midst of them, and saith unto them, Peace be unto you.

37. But they were terrified and affrighted, and supposed that they had seen a spirit.

38. And he said unto them, Why are ye troubled? and why do thoughts arise in your hearts?

39. Behold my hands and my feet, that it is I myself: handle me, and see; for a spirit hath not flesh and bones, as ye see me have.

40. And when he had thus spoken, he shewed them his hands and his feet.

41. And while they yet believed not for joy, and wondered, he said unto them, Have ye here any meat?

The Resurrection of Christ

Luke 24:33–34 — The reason the Savior had appeared to Peter alone was likely that he was the presiding officer of the First Presidency. There are other occasions we know of when the Savior dealt with Peter alone (see *Encyclopedia of Mormonism*, 512).

42. And they gave him a piece of a broiled fish, and of an honeycomb.

43. And he took it, and did eat before them.

44. And he said unto them, These are the words which I spake unto you, while I was yet with you, that all things must be fulfilled, which were written in the law of Moses, and in the prophets, and in the psalms, concerning me.

45. Then opened he their understanding, that they might understand the scriptures,

46. And said unto them, Thus it is written, and thus it behoved Christ to suffer, and to rise from the dead the third day:

47. And that repentance and remission of sins should be preached in his name among all nations, beginning at Jerusalem.

48. And ye are witnesses of these things.

49. ¶ And, behold, I send the promise of my Father upon you: but tarry ye in the city of Jerusalem, until ye be endued with power from on high.

50. ¶ And he led them out as far as to Bethany, and he lifted up his hands, and blessed them.

51. And it came to pass, while he blessed them, he was parted from them, and carried up into heaven.

52. And they worshipped him, and returned to Jerusalem with great joy:

53. And were continually in the temple, praising and blessing God. Amen.

THE GOSPEL ACCORDING TO

ST. JOHN

CHAPTER 1

1. In the beginning was the Word, and the Word was with God, and the Word was God.

2. The same was in the beginning with God.

3. All things were made by him; and without him was not any thing made that was made.

Luke 24:45—Who can better open our understanding to the scriptures than the Savior Himself, through the blessings of the Spirit? As you read and study the scriptures, think of yourself on the road to Emmaus, encountering the Lord and Redeemer, who loves you and unfolds to you the meaning of His sacred word.

Luke 24:45–48—The word *atonement* comes from the Hebrew word *kaphar,* which means "to cover" or "to forgive." There is a closely related word in Aramaic and Arabic, *kafat,* which means "to embrace." As recipients of the Savior's Atonement, we have been forgiven, our sins have been covered before our Heavenly Father, and we are held in the warm and loving embrace of Him who made it all possible (see Russell M. Nelson, *Ensign,* Nov. 1996, 34).

Luke 24:49—"In answer to a question as to whether the Holy Ghost was received by the apostles at or before Pentecost, a statement was published by the First Presidency of the Church on February 5, 1916 (see *Deseret News* of that date). . . . [Based on that statement, we know that] the promise was made, but the fulfillment came after, so that the Holy Ghost sent by Jesus from the Father did not come in person until the day of Pentecost, and the cloven tongues of fire were the sign of His coming" (James E. Talmage, *Jesus the Christ,* 668).

John 1:1–4—At the beginning of John's gospel, he laid down the framework for all creative enterprise in the universe, teaching us that it comes exclusively through the power and light of the Word of God, Jesus Christ. In general, the world considers Jesus to have been a great teacher and thinker. But He is infinitely more than that: He is the Creator of all things under the Father, and the Source of life and light for all mankind.

John 1:1—At first glance, *Word* may seem an odd word to describe the Savior. But when we consider a little more deeply, it makes much sense. Just as we use words to express ourselves, the Savior is the expression—or *Word*—of the Father to the world (see Russell M. Nelson, *Perfection Pending, and Other Favorite Discourses,* 148).

John 1:3—Jesus created not only this earth, but many other worlds as well. Both the Pearl of Great Price (see Moses 1) and the Book of Mormon (see Alma 11:39) testify to that truth (see Joseph Fielding Smith, *Church History and Modern Revelation,* 1:154).

4. In him was life; and the life was the light of men.

5. And the light shineth in darkness; and the darkness comprehended it not.

6. ¶ There was a man sent from God, whose name was John.

7. The same came for a witness, to bear witness of the Light, that all men through him might believe.

8. He was not that Light, but was sent to bear witness of that Light.

9. That was the true Light, which lighteth every man that cometh into the world.

10. He was in the world, and the world was made by him, and the world knew him not.

11. He came unto his own, and his own received him not.

12. But as many as received him, to them gave he power to become the sons of God, even to them that believe on his name:

13. Which were born, not of blood, nor of the will of the flesh, nor of the will of man, but of God.

14. And the Word was made flesh, and dwelt among us, (and we beheld his glory, the glory as of the only begotten of the Father,) full of grace and truth.

15. ¶ John bare witness of him, and cried, saying, This was he of whom I spake, He that cometh after me is preferred before me: for he was before me.

16. And of his fulness have all we received, and grace for grace.

17. For the law was given by Moses, but grace and truth came by Jesus Christ.

18. No man hath seen God at any time; the only begotten Son, which is in the bosom of the Father, he hath declared him.

19. ¶ And this is the record of John, when the Jews sent priests and Levites from Jerusalem to ask him, Who art thou?

20. And he confessed, and denied not; but confessed, I am not the Christ.

21. And they asked him, What then? Art thou Elias? And he saith, I am not. Art thou that prophet? And he answered, No.

22. Then said they unto him, Who art thou? that we may give an answer to them that sent us. What sayest thou of thyself?

23. He said, I am the voice of one crying in the wilderness, Make straight the way of the Lord, as said the prophet Esaias.

24. And they which were sent were of the Pharisees.

25. And they asked him, and said

John 1:4—"We believe that the spirit which enlightens the human family proceeds from the presence of the Almighty, that it spreads throughout all space, that it is the light and life of all things, and that every honest heart possesses it in proportion to his virtue, integrity, and his desire to know the truth and do good to his fellow men" (Lorenzo Snow, *The Teachings of Lorenzo Snow*, 107).

John 1:5—"He is the Light which shineth in darkness; not which *shone* formerly, but which *now* shineth. The Darkness is that condition of the world, which is unaffected by the light of divine revelation, because of ignorance, superstition, and enmity of men. In that condition the world does not comprehend the light of revelation. That kind of darkness remains apart, unyielding, unpenetrated, now as in the day when John wrote his Gospel" (Hyrum M. Smith and Janne M. Sjodahl, *Doctrine and Covenants Commentary*, 36–37).

John 1:12—"The Almighty is not alone in his eternal glory. Myriads of saved souls enjoy his society. Family relationships prevail there; spirit offspring are born there; our spirits were born there. Modern revelation affirms the fact that all the inhabitants of the world are the sons and daughters of God" (Marion G. Romney, *Learning for the Eternities*, 41).

John 1:16–17—"Those beings who receive of [Christ's] fullness are called sons of God, because they are perfected in all attributes and powers, and, being in communication with it, can, by its use, perform all things" (Parley P. Pratt, *Key to the Science of Theology/A Voice of Warning*, 47).

unto him, Why baptizest thou then, if thou be not that Christ, nor Elias, neither that prophet?

26. John answered them, saying, I baptize with water: but there standeth one among you, whom ye know not;

27. He it is, who coming after me is preferred before me, whose shoe's latchet I am not worthy to unloose.

28. These things were done in Bethabara beyond Jordan, where John was baptizing.

29. ¶ The next day John seeth Jesus coming unto him, and saith, Behold the Lamb of God, which taketh away the sin of the world.

30. This is he of whom I said, After me cometh a man which is preferred before me: for he was before me.

31. And I knew him not: but that he should be made manifest to Israel, therefore am I come baptizing with water.

32. And John bare record, saying, I saw the Spirit descending from heaven like a dove, and it abode upon him.

33. And I knew him not: but he that sent me to baptize with water, the same said unto me, Upon whom thou shalt see the Spirit descending, and remaining on him, the same is he which baptizeth with the Holy Ghost.

34. And I saw, and bare record that this is the Son of God.

35. ¶ Again the next day after John stood, and two of his disciples;

36. And looking upon Jesus as he walked, he saith, Behold the Lamb of God!

37. And the two disciples heard him speak, and they followed Jesus.

38. Then Jesus turned, and saw them following, and saith unto them, What seek ye? They said unto him, Rabbi, (which is to say, being interpreted, Master,) where dwellest thou?

39. He saith unto them, Come and see. They came and saw where he dwelt, and abode with him that day: for it was about the tenth hour.

40. One of the two which heard John speak, and followed him, was Andrew, Simon Peter's brother.

41. He first findeth his own brother Simon, and saith unto him, We have found the Messias, which is, being interpreted, the Christ.

42. And he brought him to Jesus. And when Jesus beheld him, he said, Thou art Simon the son of Jona: thou shalt be called Cephas, which is by interpretation, A stone.

43. ¶ The day following Jesus would go forth into Galilee, and findeth Philip, and saith unto him, Follow me.

44. Now Philip was of Bethsaida, the city of Andrew and Peter.

45. Philip findeth Nathanael, and saith unto him, We have found him, of whom Moses in the law, and the prophets, did write, Jesus of Nazareth, the son of Joseph.

46. And Nathanael said unto him, Can there any good thing come out of Nazareth? Philip saith unto him, Come and see.

47. Jesus saw Nathanael coming to him, and saith of him, Behold an Israelite indeed, in whom is no guile!

48. Nathanael saith unto him, Whence knowest thou me? Jesus

John 1:19–28—"At the dedication of the Kirtland Temple in April, 1836, several ancient prophets appeared and delivered their keys of authority to Joseph Smith and Oliver Cowdery. Among these worthies was Elias, who 'committed the dispensation of the gospel of Abraham, saying that in us and our seed all generations after us should be blessed.' . . . From this reference to 'the *dispensation* of the gospel of Abraham,' it has been concluded that Elias was a prophet who lived near the time of the patriarch, Abraham. . . . It is very evident that he was a personage of importance, for he held the 'keys' of authority in a mission of vital importance in carrying out on earth the plan of salvation. . . .

"This understanding of the mission and spirit of Elias has led many writers, ancient and modern, to speak of any person charged with preparatory work, one who goes before, as an Elias. Thus, John the Baptist was an Elias in his work as a forerunner of the Christ. Similarly, each personage, from Moroni to those appearing in the Kirtland Temple, who introduced the present, last dispensation of the gospel, may be spoken of as an Elias. Elias, then, is often used as a title, as the titles of bishop, prophet, or president are used, betokening a special position, mission, service, power, or authority" (John A. Widtsoe, *Evidences and Reconciliations,* 243–44).

John 1:29—Two goats were used as offerings on the Day of Atonement. One was sacrificed by the high priest. A second goat was symbolically chosen to bear the sins of all the people; this animal, the "scapegoat," was led out into the wilderness, where it was turned loose, taking with it the sins of the people. It became customary to lead the goat to a high mountain and push it over the edge of a cliff—certainly killing it—so it wouldn't return to the city and bring back the sins of the people. This practice was definitely symbolic of Christ and His sacrifice (see Fred H. Wight, *Manners and Customs of Bible Lands,* 168).

John 1:41—As used in the Old Testament, *Messiah,* or "Anointed One," was primarily a royal title, since the king was considered to be the anointed one (see Kent P. Jackson and Robert L. Millet, eds., *Studies in Scripture: Vol. 5: The Gospels,* 6).

John 1:42—Joseph Smith said that the meaning of *cephas* is "seer," and Elder Bruce R. McConkie said that this seership, bestowed on Peter, relates to the keys of the kingdom that were given to Peter on the Mount of Transfiguration (see Daniel H. Ludlow, ed., *Encyclopedia of Mormonism,* 3:1077).

answered and said unto him, Before that Philip called thee, when thou wast under the fig tree, I saw thee.

49. Nathanael answered and saith unto him, Rabbi, thou art the Son of God; thou art the King of Israel.

50. Jesus answered and said unto him, Because I said unto thee, I saw thee under the fig tree, believest thou? thou shalt see greater things than these.

51. And he saith unto him, Verily, verily, I say unto you, Hereafter ye shall see heaven open, and the angels of God ascending and descending upon the Son of man.

CHAPTER 2

1. And the third day there was a marriage in Cana of Galilee; and the mother of Jesus was there:

2. And both Jesus was called, and his disciples, to the marriage.

3. And when they wanted wine, the mother of Jesus saith unto him, They have no wine.

4. Jesus saith unto her, Woman, what have I to do with thee? mine hour is not yet come.

5. His mother saith unto the servants, Whatsoever he saith unto you, do it.

6. And there were set there six waterpots of stone, after the manner of the purifying of the Jews, containing two or three firkins apiece.

7. Jesus saith unto them, Fill the waterpots with water. And they filled them up to the brim.

8. And he saith unto them, Draw out now, and bear unto the governor of the feast. And they bare it.

9. When the ruler of the feast had tasted the water that was made wine, and knew not whence it was: (but the servants which drew the water knew;) the governor of the feast called the bridegroom,

10. And saith unto him, Every man at the beginning doth set forth good wine; and when men have well drunk, then that which is worse: but thou hast kept the good wine until now.

11. This beginning of miracles did Jesus in Cana of Galilee, and manifested forth his glory; and his disciples believed on him.

12. ¶ After this he went down to Capernaum, he, and his mother, and his brethren, and his disciples: and they continued there not many days.

13. ¶ And the Jews' passover was at hand, and Jesus went up to Jerusalem,

14. And found in the temple those that sold oxen and sheep and doves, and the changers of money sitting:

15. And when he had made a scourge of small cords, he drove them all out of the temple, and the sheep, and the oxen; and poured out the changers' money, and overthrew the tables;

16. And said unto them that sold doves, Take these things hence; make not my Father's house an house of merchandise.

17. And his disciples remembered that it was written, The zeal of thine house hath eaten me up.

18. ¶ Then answered the Jews and said unto him, What sign shewest thou unto us, seeing that thou doest these things?

19. Jesus answered and said unto them, Destroy this temple, and in three days I will raise it up.

John 2:1–12—"To deny the actuality of miracles on the ground that, because we cannot comprehend the means, the reported results are fictitious, is to arrogate to the human mind the attribute of omniscience, by implying that what man cannot comprehend cannot be, and that therefore he is able to comprehend all that is. The miracles of record in the Gospels are as fully supported by evidence as are many of the historical events which call forth neither protest nor demand for further proof. To the believer in the divinity of Christ, the miracles are sufficiently attested; to the unbeliever they appear but as myths and fables" (James E. Talmage, *Jesus the Christ,* 140).

John 2:3–5—The King James version of these verses appears as though Jesus is giving His mother a mild rebuke. His response to her as clarified by the Joseph Smith Translation makes much more sense: "What wilt thou have me to do for thee? that will I do" (JST, John 2:4). She then addressed the servants and instructed them to do whatever Jesus asked of them, something that illustrates the great confidence she had in her son (see Thomas M. Mumford, *CES New Testament Symposium,* 1984, 12).

John 2:4—"The noun of address, 'Woman,' as applied by a son to his mother may sound to our ears somewhat harsh, if not disrespectful; but its use was really an expression of opposite import. To every son the mother ought to be preeminently the woman of women; she is the one woman in the world to whom the son owes his earthy existence; and though the title 'Mother' belongs to every woman who has earned the honors of maternity, yet to no child is there more than one woman whom by natural right he can address by that title of respectful acknowledgement" (James E. Talmage, *Jesus the Christ,* 136).

John 2:16—This verse shows that Jesus was in perfect control of His temper when He cleansed the temple. To whip or throw down defenseless doves would have caused great harm to the birds. Instead of driving them with a whip, as He had the larger animals, He asked the owners to remove the doves—clearly demonstrating that even in a dramatic and heated situation, He was in complete control of His emotions (see Thomas M. Mumford, *CES New Testament Symposium,* 1984, 12).

20. Then said the Jews, Forty and six years was this temple in building, and wilt thou rear it up in three days?

21. But he spake of the temple of his body.

22. When therefore he was risen from the dead, his disciples remembered that he had said this unto them; and they believed the scripture, and the word which Jesus had said.

23. ¶ Now when he was in Jerusalem at the passover, in the feast day, many believed in his name, when they saw the miracles which he did.

24. But Jesus did not commit himself unto them, because he knew all men,

25. And needed not that any should testify of man: for he knew what was in man.

CHAPTER 3

1. There was a man of the Pharisees, named Nicodemus, a ruler of the Jews:

2. The same came to Jesus by night, and said unto him, Rabbi, we know that thou art a teacher come from God: for no man can do these miracles that thou doest, except God be with him.

3. Jesus answered and said unto him, Verily, verily, I say unto thee, Except a man be born again, he cannot see the kingdom of God.

4. Nicodemus saith unto him, How can a man be born when he is old? can he enter the second time into his mother's womb, and be born?

5. Jesus answered, Verily, verily, I say unto thee, Except a man be born of water and of the Spirit, he cannot enter into the kingdom of God.

6. That which is born of the flesh is flesh; and that which is born of the Spirit is spirit.

7. Marvel not that I said unto thee, Ye must be born again.

8. The wind bloweth where it listeth, and thou hearest the sound thereof, but canst not tell whence it cometh, and whither it goeth: so is every one that is born of the Spirit.

9. Nicodemus answered and said unto him, How can these things be?

10. Jesus answered and said unto him, Art thou a master of Israel, and knowest not these things?

11. Verily, verily, I say unto thee, We speak that we do know, and testify that we have seen; and ye receive not our witness.

12. If I have told you earthly things, and ye believe not, how shall ye believe, if I tell you of heavenly things?

13. And no man hath ascended up to heaven, but he that came down from heaven, even the Son of man which is in heaven.

14. ¶ And as Moses lifted up the

John 2:18–22 — Not until Jesus was actually resurrected did His disciples understand what that meant. Looking back, they remembered times such as this when the Savior taught this doctrine (see Bruce R. McConkie, *Doctrinal New Testament Commentary,* 1:139).

John 2:24 — The Joseph Smith Translation clarifies this to say that Jesus "knew all things."

John 3:1–12 — To gain exaltation in the celestial kingdom, we must be *born again.* Critical to that process is being baptized by immersion by one holding authority, and that we be given the gift of the Holy Ghost. But that is not all; we must give ourselves fully to the Lord, become completely converted, and enjoy the constant companionship of the Holy Ghost through our righteousness (see Bruce R. McConkie, *Mormon Doctrine,* 2nd ed., 100–101). As President James E. Faust commented, "The full benefit of forgiveness of sin through the Savior's Atonement begins with repentance and baptism and then expands upon receiving the Holy Ghost" (*Ensign,* May 2001, 55).

John 3:1–2 — Nicodemus, a highly educated man who was a ruler over the Jews as a member of the powerful Jewish Sanhedrin (ruling council), was clinging to apostate traditions when he sought answers from Jesus. Even though Nicodemus addressed Jesus as "a teacher come from God," he couldn't fully realize the powerful influence of the Savior even to this day and beyond (see Ann N. Madsen, *The Redeemer: Reflections on the Life and Teachings of Jesus the Christ,* 39).

John 3:13–15 — While the Israelites were wandering in the wilderness, the Lord told Moses to make a brass serpent and place it on a pole; if an Israelite were to be bitten by one of the fiery serpents that infested the area, all he had to do was look at the brass serpent, and he would live. This was a powerful symbol, or type, of the Savior, who would be "lifted up" on a cross — and who, through the power of His Atonement, would enable believers to avoid spiritual death if they would but believe and follow Him (see Gerald N. Lund, *Jesus Christ, Key to the Plan of Salvation,* 73).

serpent in the wilderness, even so must the Son of man be lifted up:

15. That whosoever believeth in him should not perish, but have eternal life.

16. ¶ For God so loved the world, that he gave his only begotten Son, that whosoever believeth in him should not perish, but have everlasting life.

17. For God sent not his Son into the world to condemn the world; but that the world through him might be saved.

18. ¶ He that believeth on him is not condemned: but he that believeth not is condemned already, because he hath not believed in the name of the only begotten Son of God.

19. And this is the condemnation, that light is come into the world, and men loved darkness rather than light, because their deeds were evil.

20. For every one that doeth evil hateth the light, neither cometh to the light, lest his deeds should be reproved.

21. But he that doeth truth cometh to the light, that his deeds may be made manifest, that they are wrought in God.

22. ¶ After these things came Jesus and his disciples into the land of Judæa; and there he tarried with them, and baptized.

23. ¶ And John also was baptizing in Ænon near to Salim, because there was much water there: and they came, and were baptized.

24. For John was not yet cast into prison.

25. ¶ Then there arose a question between some of John's disciples and the Jews about purifying.

26. And they came unto John, and said unto him, Rabbi, he that was with thee beyond Jordan, to whom thou barest witness, behold, the same baptizeth, and all men come to him.

27. John answered and said, A man can receive nothing, except it be given him from heaven.

28. Ye yourselves bear me witness, that I said, I am not the Christ, but that I am sent before him.

29. He that hath the bride is the bridegroom: but the friend of the bridegroom, which standeth and heareth him, rejoiceth greatly because of the bridegroom's voice: this my joy therefore is fulfilled.

30. He must increase, but I must decrease.

31. He that cometh from above is above all: he that is of the earth is earthly, and speaketh of the earth: he that cometh from heaven is above all.

32. And what he hath seen and heard, that he testifieth; and no man receiveth his testimony.

33. He that hath received his testi-

John 3:16 — The Pharisee Nicodemus was secretly visiting the Savior at night. During these visits, the Savior taught Nicodemus plain and simple truths about the gospel of the Atonement: our Heavenly Father loves us so much that He was willing to sacrifice His Son for our eternal welfare. How does this help you discover a feeling of gratitude that reinforces your love for Heavenly Father (see Matt. 22:36–40) and enhances your overwhelming desire to keep His commandments (see John 14:15)?

John 3:16–21 — "We should be full of gratitude to our Father, acknowledge Him as the Giver of all good; and we should plead with Him to help us appreciate His blessings even as they flow from His all-bountiful hands. We cannot say too much regarding the love of God to His children. . . . [His sending His Only Begotten Son is] the greatest manifestation of the love of God for His children" (Rulon S. Wells, Conference Report, Apr. 1909, Second Overflow Meeting, 34).

mony hath set to his seal that God is true.

34. For he whom God hath sent speaketh the words of God: for God giveth not the Spirit by measure unto him.

35. The Father loveth the Son, and hath given all things into his hand.

36. He that believeth on the Son hath everlasting life: and he that believeth not the Son shall not see life; but the wrath of God abideth on him.

CHAPTER 4

1. When therefore the Lord knew how the Pharisees had heard that Jesus made and baptized more disciples than John,

2. (Though Jesus himself baptized not, but his disciples,)

3. He left Judæa, and departed again into Galilee.

4. And he must needs go through Samaria.

5. Then cometh he to a city of Samaria, which is called Sychar, near to the parcel of ground that Jacob gave to his son Joseph.

6. Now Jacob's well was there. Jesus therefore, being wearied with his journey, sat thus on the well: and it was about the sixth hour.

7. There cometh a woman of Samaria to draw water: Jesus saith unto her, Give me to drink.

8. (For his disciples were gone away unto the city to buy meat.)

9. Then saith the woman of Samaria unto him, How is it that thou, being a Jew, askest drink of me, which am a woman of Samaria? for the Jews have no dealings with the Samaritans.

10. Jesus answered and said unto her, If thou knewest the gift of God, and who it is that saith to thee, Give me to drink; thou wouldest have asked of him, and he would have given thee living water.

11. The woman saith unto him, Sir, thou hast nothing to draw with, and the well is deep: from whence then hast thou that living water?

12. Art thou greater than our father Jacob, which gave us the well, and drank thereof himself, and his children, and his cattle?

13. Jesus answered and said unto her, Whosoever drinketh of this water shall thirst again:

14. But whosoever drinketh of the water that I shall give him shall never thirst; but the water that I shall give him shall be in him a well of water springing up into everlasting life.

15. The woman saith unto him, Sir, give me this water, that I thirst not, neither come hither to draw.

16. Jesus saith unto her, Go, call thy husband, and come hither.

17. The woman answered and said, I have no husband. Jesus said unto her, Thou hast well said, I have no husband:

18. For thou hast had five husbands; and he whom thou now hast

John 4:1–3 — The Joseph Smith Translation of these verses is instructive:

"When therefore the Pharisees had heard that Jesus made and baptized more disciples than John, they sought more diligently some means that they might put him to death; for many received John as a prophet, but they believed not on Jesus.

"Now the Lord knew this, though he himself baptized not so many as his disciples;

"For he suffered them for an example, preferring one another" (JST, John 4:2–4).

John 4:4–15 — In these verses we see how the Savior used simple situations from everyday life to teach the gospel. Elder Bruce R. McConkie wrote, "For the thirsty and choking traveler in a desert wilderness to find water, is to find life, to find an escape from agonizing death; similarly, the weary pilgrim traveling through the wilderness of mortality saves himself eternally by drinking from the wells of living water found in the gospel" (*Doctrinal New Testament Commentary,* 1:151).

John 4:16–24 — For members of The Church of Jesus Christ of Latter-day Saints, *worship* is defined as coming to the Father in spirit and truth in the name of Jesus Christ (see D&C 93:19). With that definition in mind, all of life can be worshipful (see Daniel H. Ludlow, ed., *Encyclopedia of Mormonism,* 4:1596).

is not thy husband: in that saidst thou truly.

19. The woman saith unto him, Sir, I perceive that thou art a prophet.

20. Our fathers worshipped in this mountain; and ye say, that in Jerusalem is the place where men ought to worship.

21. Jesus saith unto her, Woman, believe me, the hour cometh, when ye shall neither in this mountain, nor yet at Jerusalem, worship the Father.

22. Ye worship ye know not what: we know what we worship: for salvation is of the Jews.

23. But the hour cometh, and now is, when the true worshippers shall worship the Father in spirit and in truth: for the Father seeketh such to worship him.

24. God is a Spirit: and they that worship him must worship him in spirit and in truth.

25. The woman saith unto him, I know that Messias cometh, which is called Christ: when he is come, he will tell us all things.

26. Jesus saith unto her, I that speak unto thee am he.

27. ¶ And upon this came his disciples, and marvelled that he talked with the woman: yet no man said, What seekest thou? or, Why talkest thou with her?

28. The woman then left her waterpot, and went her way into the city, and saith to the men,

29. Come, see a man, which told me all things that ever I did: is not this the Christ?

30. Then they went out of the city, and came unto him.

31. ¶ In the mean while his disciples prayed him, saying, Master, eat.

32. But he said unto them, I have meat to eat that ye know not of.

33. Therefore said the disciples one to another, Hath any man brought him ought to eat?

34. Jesus saith unto them, My meat is to do the will of him that sent me, and to finish his work.

35. Say not ye, There are yet four months, and then cometh harvest? behold, I say unto you, Lift up your eyes, and look on the fields; for they are white already to harvest.

36. And he that reapeth receiveth wages, and gathereth fruit unto life eternal: that both he that soweth and he that reapeth may rejoice together.

37. And herein is that saying true, One soweth, and another reapeth.

38. I sent you to reap that whereon ye bestowed no labour: other men laboured, and ye are entered into their labours.

39. ¶ And many of the Samaritans of that city believed on him for the saying of the woman, which testified, He told me all that ever I did.

40. So when the Samaritans were come unto him, they besought him that he would tarry with them: and he abode there two days.

41. And many more believed because of his own word;

42. And said unto the woman, Now we believe, not because of thy saying: for we have heard him ourselves, and know that this is indeed the Christ, the Saviour of the world.

John 4:24—The proper translation of this verse is *God is Spirit,* not *God is a Spirit:* there are no indefinite articles (such as *a* or *an*) in the Greek language, from which the New Testament was translated. In this case, the word *a* was clearly added by a translator. As Stephen E. Robinson wrote, "Latter-day Saints sometimes give the mistaken impression that because they believe the Father has a body 'as tangible as man's,' they believe him to be corporeal in the limited human sense. But this is not the case. God is spirit, but he is also element; both aspects of existence are included and encompassed within his glorious being. That he is either one does not limit the fact that he is also the other—and infinitely more" (*Are Mormons Christians?*, 80–81).

John 4:25–30—This is one of several examples in scripture where Jesus acknowledges that He is the Messiah (see also Matt. 16:16 and John 1:41 as examples).

John 4:35—When it is ready to harvest, the heads of wheat take on a white color. Looking across the fields at harvest time, they appear to be white—hence the saying here and in various places in the Doctrine and Covenants that the field is "white already to harvest."

43. ¶ Now after two days he departed thence, and went into Galilee.

44. For Jesus himself testified, that a prophet hath no honour in his own country.

45. Then when he was come into Galilee, the Galilaeans received him, having seen all the things that he did at Jerusalem at the feast: for they also went unto the feast.

46. So Jesus came again into Cana of Galilee, where he made the water wine. And there was a certain nobleman, whose son was sick at Capernaum.

47. When he heard that Jesus was come out of Judæa into Galilee, he went unto him, and besought him that he would come down, and heal his son: for he was at the point of death.

48. Then said Jesus unto him, Except ye see signs and wonders, ye will not believe.

49. The nobleman saith unto him, Sir, come down ere my child die.

50. Jesus saith unto him, Go thy way; thy son liveth. And the man believed the word that Jesus had spoken unto him, and he went his way.

51. And as he was now going down, his servants met him, and told him, saying, Thy son liveth.

52. Then inquired he of them the hour when he began to amend. And they said unto him, Yesterday at the seventh hour the fever left him.

53. So the father knew that it was at the same hour, in the which Jesus said unto him, Thy son liveth: and himself believed, and his whole house.

54. This is again the second miracle that Jesus did, when he was come out of Judæa into Galilee.

CHAPTER 5

1. After this there was a feast of the Jews; and Jesus went up to Jerusalem.

2. Now there is at Jerusalem by the sheep market a pool, which is called in the Hebrew tongue Bethesda, having five porches.

3. In these lay a great multitude of impotent folk, of blind, halt, withered, waiting for the moving of the water.

4. For an angel went down at a certain season into the pool, and troubled the water: whosoever then first after the troubling of the water stepped in was made whole of whatsoever disease he had.

5. And a certain man was there, which had an infirmity thirty and eight years.

6. When Jesus saw him lie, and knew that he had been now a long time in that case, he saith unto him, Wilt thou be made whole?

7. The impotent man answered him, Sir, I have no man, when the water is troubled, to put me into the pool: but while I am coming, another steppeth down before me.

8. Jesus saith unto him, Rise, take up thy bed, and walk.

9. And immediately the man was made whole, and took up his bed, and walked: and on the same day was the sabbath.

10. ¶ The Jews therefore said unto him that was cured, It is the sabbath day: it is not lawful for thee to carry thy bed.

11. He answered them, He that

John 4:46–54 — Elder Bruce R. McConkie pointed out that healings performed by Jesus followed a specific pattern:

• They came in response to the faith of the people to whom He ministered.

• They should have convinced the Jews that Jesus was the Lord.

• They were acts of compassion that provided immense blessing and benefits to the diseased and suffering who were healed.

• They were in fulfillment of prophecies uttered in previous ages; see, for example, Mosiah 3:5 (see *Doctrinal New Testament Commentary,* 1:158–59).

John 5:1 — Many scholars think the feast mentioned in this verse is a Passover feast, and the footnote of the LDS edition of the scriptures indicates that as well. That actually becomes an important issue, because the number of Passover feasts is used to calculate the length of Jesus' ministry. The Synoptics mention only one Passover feast — the one when Jesus was crucified. The Gospel of John mentions three Passover feasts — see John 2:13, 6:4, and 13:1. If John is used as the source, then, Jesus' ministry lasted three years.

made me whole, the same said unto me, Take up thy bed, and walk.

12. Then asked they him, What man is that which said unto thee, Take up thy bed, and walk?

13. And he that was healed wist not who it was: for Jesus had conveyed himself away, a multitude being in that place.

14. Afterward Jesus findeth him in the temple, and said unto him, Behold, thou art made whole: sin no more, lest a worse thing come unto thee.

15. The man departed, and told the Jews that it was Jesus, which had made him whole.

16. And therefore did the Jews persecute Jesus, and sought to slay him, because he had done these things on the sabbath day.

17. ¶ But Jesus answered them, My Father worketh hitherto, and I work.

18. Therefore the Jews sought the more to kill him, because he not only had broken the sabbath, but said also that God was his Father, making himself equal with God.

19. Then answered Jesus and said unto them, Verily, verily, I say unto you, The Son can do nothing of himself, but what he seeth the Father do: for what things soever he doeth, these also doeth the Son likewise.

20. For the Father loveth the Son, and sheweth him all things that himself doeth: and he will shew him greater works than these, that ye may marvel.

21. For as the Father raiseth up the dead, and quickeneth them; even so the Son quickeneth whom he will.

22. For the Father judgeth no man, but hath committed all judgment unto the Son:

23. That all men should honour the Son, even as they honour the Father. He that honoureth not the Son honoureth not the Father which hath sent him.

24. Verily, verily, I say unto you, He that heareth my word, and believeth on him that sent me, hath everlasting life, and shall not come into condemnation; but is passed from death unto life.

25. Verily, verily, I say unto you, The hour is coming, and now is, when the dead shall hear the voice of the Son of God: and they that hear shall live.

26. For as the Father hath life in himself; so hath he given to the Son to have life in himself;

27. And hath given him authority to execute judgment also, because he is the Son of man.

28. Marvel not at this: for the hour is coming, in the which all that are in the graves shall hear his voice,

29. And shall come forth; they that have done good, unto the resurrection of life; and they that have done evil, unto the resurrection of damnation.

30. I can of mine own self do no-

John 5:17–24—In these verses, Jesus responds to those who persecuted Him for healing a man on the Sabbath and uses the opportunity to explain His relationship with His Father. As part of that explanation, He also gives some eternal truths about Himself as the Son:

• He worked by the power of the Father.
• He will be resurrected, a gift that will be given to all mankind.
• He will be honored along with the Father.
• He will judge all men.
• He will open the graves of all those who have died and will preach to the spirits who are in spirit prison (see Bruce R. McConkie, *The Promised Messiah*, 154).

John 5:25—President Joseph F. Smith, in his glorious vision of the spirit world, clarified that while the dead in spirit prison would hear the word of God, the Lord would not go in person among the wicked and the disobedient; instead, He would send "messengers, clothed with power and authority" to "go forth and carry the light of the gospel to them that were in darkness, even to all the spirits of men; and thus was the gospel preached to the dead" (D&C 138:29–30).

John 5:26—"As the Eternal Father's Only Begotten Son in the flesh, Christ possessed the inborn power to withstand death indefinitely, and this just as naturally as that He, being the offspring of a mortal mother, should derive the ability to die. Jesus Christ inherited through the operation of the natural law of heredity the physical, mental, and spiritual attributes of His parents—the Father immortal and glorified, the mother human. He could not be slain until His hour had come, the hour in which He would voluntarily give up His life, and permit His own decease as an act of will" (James E. Talmage, *The Vitality of Mormonism*, 57).

John 5:26–30—All men will be resurrected, but not all will be resurrected to the same degree of glory or at the same time. There will be two general resurrections. The first—which will begin at the Second Coming—is the resurrection of the just, or the righteous. The most righteous will come forth first, or in the morning of the first resurrection. The second—which will begin at the end of the Millennium—is the resurrection of the unjust or the resurrection of the damnation. At the very end of the second resurrection, the sons of perdition will come forth from their graves (see Daniel H. Ludlow, *A Companion to Your Study of the New Testament: The Four Gospels*, 232–233).

thing: as I hear, I judge: and my judgment is just; because I seek not mine own will, but the will of the Father which hath sent me.

31. If I bear witness of myself, my witness is not true.

32. ¶ There is another that beareth witness of me; and I know that the witness which he witnesseth of me is true.

33. Ye sent unto John, and he bare witness unto the truth.

34. But I receive not testimony from man: but these things I say, that ye might be saved.

35. He was a burning and a shining light: and ye were willing for a season to rejoice in his light.

36. ¶ But I have greater witness than that of John: for the works which the Father hath given me to finish, the same works that I do, bear witness of me, that the Father hath sent me.

37. And the Father himself, which hath sent me, hath borne witness of me. Ye have neither heard his voice at any time, nor seen his shape.

38. And ye have not his word abiding in you: for whom he hath sent, him ye believe not.

39. ¶ Search the scriptures; for in them ye think ye have eternal life: and they are they which testify of me.

40. And ye will not come to me, that ye might have life.

41. I receive not honour from men.

42. But I know you, that ye have not the love of God in you.

43. I am come in my Father's name, and ye receive me not: if another shall come in his own name, him ye will receive.

44. How can ye believe, which receive honour one of another, and seek not the honour that cometh from God only?

45. Do not think that I will accuse you to the Father: there is one that accuseth you, even Moses, in whom ye trust.

46. For had ye believed Moses, ye would have believed me: for he wrote of me.

47. But if ye believe not his writings, how shall ye believe my words?

CHAPTER 6

1. After these things Jesus went over the sea of Galilee, which is the sea of Tiberias.

2. And a great multitude followed him, because they saw his miracles which he did on them that were diseased.

3. And Jesus went up into a moun-

John 5:30—President Ezra Taft Benson wrote, "Men changed for Christ will be captained by Christ. . . . [M]en captained by Christ will be consumed in Christ. . . . Not only would they die for the Lord, but more important they want to live for Him" (*The Teachings of Ezra Taft Benson,* 329).

John 5:37–38—In these verses, the Savior explains that the Father has testified of the Savior's divine role.

John 5:39—Jesus was addressing Jewish leaders who had objected to Him healing a man on the Sabbath. He confirmed to them that they *thought* they had eternal life through the scriptures—but He made clear that they needed to search the scriptures, for they had not the love of God in their hearts, having rejected the Son of God. The counsel of the Lord to us is to search the scriptures and *know* that we have eternal life, for the scriptures confirm the reality and mission of the Redeemer. How have the scriptures given you confidence in the mission of Jesus as Redeemer?

John 5:39–47—President Gordon B. Hinckley advised that we read "the Gospel of John from its beginning to its end. Let the Lord speak for himself to you, and his words will come with a quiet conviction that will make the words of his critics meaningless" (*Be Thou an Example,* 83).

tain, and there he sat with his disciples.

4. And the passover, a feast of the Jews, was nigh.

5. ¶ When Jesus then lifted up his eyes, and saw a great company come unto him, he saith unto Philip, Whence shall we buy bread, that these may eat?

6. And this he said to prove him: for he himself knew what he would do.

7. Philip answered him, Two hundred pennyworth of bread is not sufficient for them, that every one of them may take a little.

8. One of his disciples, Andrew, Simon Peter's brother, saith unto him,

9. There is a lad here, which hath five barley loaves, and two small fishes: but what are they among so many?

10. And Jesus said, Make the men sit down. Now there was much grass in the place. So the men sat down, in number about five thousand.

11. And Jesus took the loaves; and when he had given thanks, he distributed to the disciples, and the disciples to them that were set down; and likewise of the fishes as much as they would.

12. When they were filled, he said unto his disciples, Gather up the fragments that remain, that nothing be lost.

13. Therefore they gathered them together, and filled twelve baskets with the fragments of the five barley loaves, which remained over and above unto them that had eaten.

14. Then those men, when they had seen the miracle that Jesus did, said, This is of a truth that prophet that should come into the world.

15. ¶ When Jesus therefore perceived that they would come and take him by force, to make him a king, he departed again into a mountain himself alone.

16. And when even was now come, his disciples went down unto the sea,

17. And entered into a ship, and went over the sea toward Capernaum. And it was now dark, and Jesus was not come to them.

18. And the sea arose by reason of a great wind that blew.

19. So when they had rowed about five and twenty or thirty furlongs, they see Jesus walking on the sea, and drawing nigh unto the ship: and they were afraid.

20. But he saith unto them, It is I; be not afraid.

21. Then they willingly received him into the ship: and immediately the ship was at the land whither they went.

22. ¶ The day following, when the people which stood on the other side of the sea saw that there was none other boat there, save that one whereinto his disciples were entered, and that Jesus went not with his disciples into the boat, but that his disciples were gone away alone;

23. (Howbeit there came other boats from Tiberias nigh unto the place where they did eat bread, after that the Lord had given thanks:)

24. When the people therefore saw that Jesus was not there, neither his disciples, they also took shipping, and came to Capernaum, seeking for Jesus.

25. And when they had found him on the other side of the sea, they said unto him, Rabbi, when camest thou hither?

26. Jesus answered them and said, Verily, verily, I say unto you, Ye seek me, not because ye saw the miracles, but because ye did eat of the loaves, and were filled.

27. Labour not for the meat which

Jesus feeding the multitude

perisheth, but for that meat which endureth unto everlasting life, which the Son of man shall give unto you: for him hath God the Father sealed.

28. Then said they unto him, What shall we do, that we might work the works of God?

29. Jesus answered and said unto them, This is the work of God, that ye believe on him whom he hath sent.

30. They said therefore unto him, What sign shewest thou then, that we may see, and believe thee? what dost thou work?

31. Our fathers did eat manna in the desert; as it is written, He gave them bread from heaven to eat.

32. Then Jesus said unto them, Verily, verily, I say unto you, Moses gave you not that bread from heaven; but my Father giveth you the true bread from heaven.

33. For the bread of God is he which cometh down from heaven, and giveth life unto the world.

34. Then said they unto him, Lord, evermore give us this bread.

35. And Jesus said unto them, I am the bread of life: he that cometh to me shall never hunger; and he that believeth on me shall never thirst.

36. But I said unto you, That ye also have seen me, and believe not.

37. All that the Father giveth me shall come to me; and him that cometh to me I will in no wise cast out.

38. For I came down from heaven, not to do mine own will, but the will of him that sent me.

39. And this is the Father's will which hath sent me, that of all which he hath given me I should lose nothing, but should raise it up again at the last day.

40. And this is the will of him that sent me, that every one which seeth the Son, and believeth on him, may have everlasting life: and I will raise him up at the last day.

41. The Jews then murmured at him, because he said, I am the bread which came down from heaven.

42. And they said, Is not this Jesus, the son of Joseph, whose father and mother we know? how is it then that he saith, I came down from heaven?

43. Jesus therefore answered and said unto them, Murmur not among yourselves.

44. No man can come to me, except the Father which hath sent me draw him: and I will raise him up at the last day.

45. It is written in the prophets, And they shall be all taught of God. Every man therefore that hath heard, and hath learned of the Father, cometh unto me.

46. Not that any man hath seen the Father, save he which is of God, he hath seen the Father.

47. Verily, verily, I say unto you, He that believeth on me hath everlasting life.

48. I am that bread of life.

49. Your fathers did eat manna in the wilderness, and are dead.

50. This is the bread which cometh down from heaven, that a man may eat thereof, and not die.

John 6:31–35 — The word *bread* is a metaphor for the Word of God. Just as manna from heaven provided life and survival for those who wandered in the wilderness, accepting Jesus as the Savior provides life and salvation for us (see Joseph Fielding McConkie and Donald W. Parry, *A Guide to Scriptural Symbols,* 118).

John 6:35 — Jesus spoke to some of the people who participated in the miracle of the loaves and fishes the previous day. The Savior wanted them to understand that the true bread of life comes through the blessings of the gospel of redemption. This scripture makes clear that the food of eternal life comes only through the Lord Jesus Christ. When we come unto Christ, He blesses us and strengthens us in all things. How does the sacrament remind you each week that the Savior is the "bread of life"? What does the word *life* mean in that expression?

John 6:41–51 — "The Church of Jesus Christ of Latter-day Saints appeals to the world to heed the fast ripening signs of the Lord's coming, to repent and be baptized, by which means alone is salvation through Christ attainable. Heed ye the merciful warning of the Lord, our Savior" (James E. Talmage, *The Vitality of Mormonism,* 360–361).

51. I am the living bread which came down from heaven: if any man eat of this bread, he shall live for ever: and the bread that I will give is my flesh, which I will give for the life of the world.

52. The Jews therefore strove among themselves, saying, How can this man give us his flesh to eat?

53. Then Jesus said unto them, Verily, verily, I say unto you, Except ye eat the flesh of the Son of man, and drink his blood, ye have no life in you.

54. Whoso eateth my flesh, and drinketh my blood, hath eternal life; and I will raise him up at the last day.

55. For my flesh is meat indeed, and my blood is drink indeed.

56. He that eateth my flesh, and drinketh my blood, dwelleth in me, and I in him.

57. As the living Father hath sent me, and I live by the Father: so he that eateth me, even he shall live by me.

58. This is that bread which came down from heaven: not as your fathers did eat manna, and are dead: he that eateth of this bread shall live for ever.

59. These things said he in the synagogue, as he taught in Capernaum.

60. Many therefore of his disciples, when they had heard this, said, This is an hard saying; who can hear it?

61. When Jesus knew in himself that his disciples murmured at it, he said unto them, Doth this offend you?

62. What and if ye shall see the Son of man ascend up where he was before?

63. It is the spirit that quickeneth; the flesh profiteth nothing: the words that I speak unto you, they are spirit, and they are life.

64. But there are some of you that believe not. For Jesus knew from the beginning who they were that believed not, and who should betray him.

65. And he said, Therefore said I unto you, that no man can come unto me, except it were given unto him of my Father.

66. ¶ From that time many of his disciples went back, and walked no more with him.

67. Then said Jesus unto the twelve, Will ye also go away?

68. Then Simon Peter answered him, Lord, to whom shall we go? thou hast the words of eternal life.

69. And we believe and are sure that thou art that Christ, the Son of the living God.

70. Jesus answered them, Have not I chosen you twelve, and one of you is a devil?

71. He spake of Judas Iscariot the son of Simon: for he it was that should betray him, being one of the twelve.

John 6:52–59 — "To eat the flesh and drink the blood of Christ was and is to believe in and accept Him as the literal Son of God and Savior of the world, and to obey His commandments. By these means only may the Spirit of God become an abiding part of man's individual being, even as the substance of the food he eats is assimilated with the tissues of his body" (James E. Talmage, *Jesus the Christ*, 317).

John 6:60–71 — The only way we can understand the things of God is to have our understanding quickened by the Spirit; the things of God can be understood only by those who are spiritually enlightened. When we try to use our own reason and intellect to understand those things, we fail. Some of the disciples at the time of Christ, like those described in these verses, relied on their own powers of reasoning and intellect instead of seeking the Spirit to understand the things taught by the Savior. As a result, they were weakened by unbelief and fell away.

CHAPTER 7

1. After these things Jesus walked in Galilee: for he would not walk in Jewry, because the Jews sought to kill him.

2. Now the Jews' feast of tabernacles was at hand.

3. His brethren therefore said unto him, Depart hence, and go into Judæa, that thy disciples also may see the works that thou doest.

4. For there is no man that doeth any thing in secret, and he himself seeketh to be known openly. If thou do these things, shew thyself to the world.

5. For neither did his brethren believe in him.

6. Then Jesus said unto them, My time is not yet come: but your time is alway ready.

7. The world cannot hate you; but me it hateth, because I testify of it, that the works thereof are evil.

8. Go ye up unto this feast: I go not up yet unto this feast; for my time is not yet full come.

9. When he had said these words unto them, he abode still in Galilee.

10. ¶ But when his brethren were gone up, then went he also up unto the feast, not openly, but as it were in secret.

11. Then the Jews sought him at the feast, and said, Where is he?

12. And there was much murmuring among the people concerning him: for some said, He is a good man: others said, Nay; but he deceiveth the people.

13. Howbeit no man spake openly of him for fear of the Jews.

14. ¶ Now about the midst of the feast Jesus went up into the temple, and taught.

15. And the Jews marvelled, saying, How knoweth this man letters, having never learned?

16. Jesus answered them, and said, My doctrine is not mine, but his that sent me.

17. If any man will do his will, he shall know of the doctrine, whether it be of God, or whether I speak of myself.

18. He that speaketh of himself seeketh his own glory: but he that seeketh his glory that sent him, the same is true, and no unrighteousness is in him.

19. Did not Moses give you the law, and yet none of you keepeth the law? Why go ye about to kill me?

20. The people answered and said, Thou hast a devil: who goeth about to kill thee?

21. Jesus answered and said unto them, I have done one work, and ye all marvel.

22. Moses therefore gave unto you circumcision; (not because it is of Moses, but of the fathers;) and ye on the sabbath day circumcise a man.

23. If a man on the sabbath day receive circumcision, that the law of Moses should not be broken; are ye angry at me, because I have made a man every whit whole on the sabbath day?

24. Judge not according to the appearance, but judge righteous judgment.

25. Then said some of them of Jerusalem, Is not this he, whom they seek to kill?

26. But, lo, he speaketh boldly, and

Notes: _____

_____

_____

_____

_____

_____

_____

_____

_____

_____

_____

_____

_____

_____

John 7:11–18 — Any person who wants to know the truth can receive a conviction of the truth. The Lord gives us the formula for doing just that in verse 17: to do the Father's will. It takes prayer, study, determination, and anxious seeking, but it also takes living the gospel. As President Gordon B. Hinckley wrote, "Many people in the world seem unable to believe that. What they do not realize is that the things of God are understood only by the Spirit of God. There must be effort. There must be humility. There must be prayer. But the results are certain and the testimony is true" (*Faith: The Essence of True Religion,* 5).

John 7:19–24 — "You and I, in our capacity as individuals, as members, outside of any official duty imposed upon us, should not sit in judgment upon one another. And yet we do it, and sometimes we say things about one another that we are not justified in saying. . . . We have no right, even if we are in official capacity, to form a one-sided judgment. There are two sides to every such question, if not more, always; and we should hear both. . . . Hear the other side before you begin to find fault, and pass judgment. Do not let us pass judgment upon our fellow creatures, our brothers and sisters, or even people in the world" (Charles W. Penrose, Conference Report, Oct. 1916, 22).

they say nothing unto him. Do the rulers know indeed that this is the very Christ?

27. Howbeit we know this man whence he is: but when Christ cometh, no man knoweth whence he is.

28. Then cried Jesus in the temple as he taught, saying, Ye both know me, and ye know whence I am: and I am not come of myself, but he that sent me is true, whom ye know not.

29. But I know him: for I am from him, and he hath sent me.

30. Then they sought to take him: but no man laid hands on him, because his hour was not yet come.

31. And many of the people believed on him, and said, When Christ cometh, will he do more miracles than these which this man hath done?

32. ¶ The Pharisees heard that the people murmured such things concerning him; and the Pharisees and the chief priests sent officers to take him.

33. Then said Jesus unto them, Yet a little while am I with you, and then I go unto him that sent me.

34. Ye shall seek me, and shall not find me: and where I am, thither ye cannot come.

35. Then said the Jews among themselves, Whither will he go, that we shall not find him? will he go unto the dispersed among the Gentiles, and teach the Gentiles?

36. What manner of saying is this that he said, Ye shall seek me, and shall not find me: and where I am, thither ye cannot come?

37. In the last day, that great day of the feast, Jesus stood and cried, saying, If any man thirst, let him come unto me, and drink.

38. He that believeth on me, as the scripture hath said, out of his belly shall flow rivers of living water.

39. (But this spake he of the Spirit, which they that believe on him should receive: for the Holy Ghost was not yet given; because that Jesus was not yet glorified.)

40. ¶ Many of the people therefore, when they heard this saying, said, Of a truth this is the Prophet.

41. Others said, This is the Christ. But some said, Shall Christ come out of Galilee?

42. Hath not the scripture said, That Christ cometh of the seed of David, and out of the town of Bethlehem, where David was?

43. So there was a division among the people because of him.

44. And some of them would have taken him; but no man laid hands on him.

45. ¶ Then came the officers to the chief priests and Pharisees; and they said unto them, Why have ye not brought him?

46. The officers answered, Never man spake like this man.

47. Then answered them the Pharisees, Are ye also deceived?

48. Have any of the rulers or of the Pharisees believed on him?

49. But this people who knoweth not the law are cursed.

50. Nicodemus saith unto them, (he that came to Jesus by night, being one of them,)

51. Doth our law judge any man,

John 7:37–39 — As taught by the Prophet Joseph Smith, "There is a difference between the Holy Ghost and the gift of the Holy Ghost" (*Teachings of the Prophet Joseph Smith,* 199). The Holy Ghost bears witness to investigators of the Church and convinces them of the truthfulness of the Book of Mormon and the gospel. But the actual gift of the Holy Ghost allows for greater light and testimony, a type of higher endowment that allows the Holy Ghost to purify and sanctify the recipient of that gift (see James E. Faust, *Ensign,* May 2001, 58).

before it hear him, and know what he doeth?

52. They answered and said unto him, Art thou also of Galilee? Search, and look: for out of Galilee ariseth no prophet.

53. And every man went unto his own house.

CHAPTER 8

1. Jesus went unto the mount of Olives.

2. And early in the morning he came again into the temple, and all the people came unto him; and he sat down, and taught them.

3. And the scribes and Pharisees brought unto him a woman taken in adultery; and when they had set her in the midst,

4. They say unto him, Master, this woman was taken in adultery, in the very act.

5. Now Moses in the law commanded us, that such should be stoned: but what sayest thou?

6. This they said, tempting him, that they might have to accuse him. But Jesus stooped down, and with his finger wrote on the ground, as though he heard them not.

7. So when they continued asking him, he lifted up himself, and said unto them, He that is without sin among you, let him first cast a stone at her.

8. And again he stooped down, and wrote on the ground.

9. And they which heard it, being convicted by their own conscience, went out one by one, beginning at the eldest, even unto the last: and Jesus was left alone, and the woman standing in the midst.

10. When Jesus had lifted up himself, and saw none but the woman, he said unto her, Woman, where are those thine accusers? hath no man condemned thee?

11. She said, No man, Lord. And Jesus said unto her, Neither do I condemn thee: go, and sin no more.

12. ¶ Then spake Jesus again unto them, saying, I am the light of the world: he that followeth me shall not walk in darkness, but shall have the light of life.

13. The Pharisees therefore said unto him, Thou bearest record of thyself; thy record is not true.

14. Jesus answered and said unto them, Though I bear record of myself, yet my record is true: for I know whence I came, and whither I go; but ye cannot tell whence I come, and whither I go.

15. Ye judge after the flesh; I judge no man.

16. And yet if I judge, my judgment is true: for I am not alone, but I and the Father that sent me.

17. It is also written in your law, that the testimony of two men is true.

18. I am one that bear witness of myself, and the Father that sent me beareth witness of me.

19. Then said they unto him, Where is thy Father? Jesus answered, Ye neither know me, nor my Father: if ye had known me, ye should have known my Father also.

20. These words spake Jesus in the

John 8:2–11 — "We do not know what Jesus wrote [on the ground], but we know that he regarded many of the Pharisees as adulterers themselves. When he said that any in that crowd who was 'without sin' could cast a stone, he didn't mean just any sin, he meant anyone there who was not as guilty of adultery as she was. We may only surmise what he wrote on the ground, but it is possible he spelled out particular persons, times, places, and partners wherein those Pharisees had performed the act" (Robert J. Matthews, *Behold the Messiah,* 197).

John 8:11 — "This was the method of the Master's laboratory. He might, on occasion, condemn with the righteous indignation of divinity. But He never tortured the human soul; He never planted doubt; His was always a healing ministration. To save, to exalt, not to harass or to destroy the spiritual life, was His mission" (J. Reuben Clark, Jr., *Improvement Era,* Mar. 1936, 133).

John 8:11 — "If you are ever called upon to chasten a person, never chasten beyond the balm you have within you to bind up" (Brigham Young, *Discourses of Brigham Young,* 278).

John 8:12–20 — From numerous prophecies of the Messiah, those who listened to Jesus knew that He had been promised to be "a light to the Gentiles" (Isa. 49:6), a light that would pierce the darkness of error and unbelief (see Isa. 60:1–3), and the light by which all men should travel through mortality (see 3 Ne. 15:9; 18:16, 24). When Jesus proclaimed that He was the light of the world, He was in essence bearing testimony that He was the Messiah (see Daniel H. Ludlow, *A Companion to Your Study of the New Testament,* 390–91).

treasury, as he taught in the temple: and no man laid hands on him; for his hour was not yet come.

21. Then said Jesus again unto them, I go my way, and ye shall seek me, and shall die in your sins: whither I go, ye cannot come.

22. Then said the Jews, Will he kill himself? because he saith, Whither I go, ye cannot come.

23. And he said unto them, Ye are from beneath; I am from above: ye are of this world; I am not of this world.

24. I said therefore unto you, that ye shall die in your sins: for if ye believe not that I am he, ye shall die in your sins.

25. Then said they unto him, Who art thou? And Jesus saith unto them, Even the same that I said unto you from the beginning.

26. I have many things to say and to judge of you: but he that sent me is true; and I speak to the world those things which I have heard of him.

27. They understood not that he spake to them of the Father.

28. Then said Jesus unto them, When ye have lifted up the Son of man, then shall ye know that I am he, and that I do nothing of myself; but as my Father hath taught me, I speak these things.

29. And he that sent me is with me: the Father hath not left me alone; for I do always those things that please him.

30. As he spake these words, many believed on him.

31. Then said Jesus to those Jews which believed on him, If ye continue in my word, then are ye my disciples indeed;

32. And ye shall know the truth, and the truth shall make you free.

33. ¶ They answered him, We be Abraham's seed, and were never in bondage to any man: how sayest thou, Ye shall be made free?

34. Jesus answered them, Verily, verily, I say unto you, Whosoever committeth sin is the servant of sin.

35. And the servant abideth not in the house for ever: but the Son abideth ever.

36. If the Son therefore shall make you free, ye shall be free indeed.

37. I know that ye are Abraham's seed; but ye seek to kill me, because my word hath no place in you.

38. I speak that which I have seen with my Father: and ye do that which ye have seen with your father.

39. They answered and said unto him, Abraham is our father. Jesus saith unto them, If ye were Abraham's children, ye would do the works of Abraham.

40. But now ye seek to kill me, a man that hath told you the truth, which I have heard of God: this did not Abraham.

41. Ye do the deeds of your father. Then said they to him, We be not born of fornication; we have one Father, even God.

42. Jesus said unto them, If God were your Father, ye would love me: for I proceeded forth and came

John 8:28–32—The Savior was explicit during His earthly ministry in bearing personal testimony of His true identity. Our moment of truth in the wake of such testimony is to seek the confirmation of the Spirit so that we might also stand as witnesses of the divinity of the Savior and His mission. Each time we express before others our heartfelt conviction of the truth of the gospel of Jesus Christ, we add a thread of strength and courage to the magnificent tapestry depicting the history of God's dealing with His children within the framework of the plan of salvation. What are your thoughts about how we can know the truth about the divine mission of the Savior and how this conviction can make us free?

John 8:34—"To hope for peace and love and gladness out of promiscuity is to hope for that which will never come. To wish for freedom out of immorality is to wish for something that cannot be" (Gordon B. Hinckley, *Stand a Little Taller,* 175).

John 8:37—"All who accept God's plan for his children on earth and who live it are the children of Abraham. Those who reject the gospel, whether children in the flesh, or others, forfeit the promises made to Abraham and are not children of Abraham" (John A. Widtsoe, *Evidences and Reconciliations,* 400).

John 8:37–50—Joseph Smith taught that the Holy Ghost "is more powerful in expanding the mind, enlightening the understanding, and storing the intellect with present knowledge, of a man who is of the literal seed of Abraham, than one that is a Gentile, though it may not have half as much visible effect upon the body; for as the Holy Ghost upon one of the literal seed of Abraham, it is calm and serene; and his whole soul and body are only exercised by the pure spirit of intelligence; while the effect of the Holy Ghost upon a Gentile, is to purge out the old blood, and make him actually of the seed of Abraham" (*History of the Church,* 3:380).

from God; neither came I of myself, but he sent me.

43. Why do ye not understand my speech? even because ye cannot hear my word.

44. Ye are of your father the devil, and the lusts of your father ye will do. He was a murderer from the beginning, and abode not in the truth, because there is no truth in him. When he speaketh a lie, he speaketh of his own: for he is a liar, and the father of it.

45. And because I tell you the truth, ye believe me not.

46. Which of you convinceth me of sin? And if I say the truth, why do ye not believe me?

47. He that is of God heareth God's words: ye therefore hear them not, because ye are not of God.

48. Then answered the Jews, and said unto him, Say we not well that thou art a Samaritan, and hast a devil?

49. Jesus answered, I have not a devil; but I honour my Father, and ye do dishonour me.

50. And I seek not mine own glory: there is one that seeketh and judgeth.

51. Verily, verily, I say unto you, If a man keep my saying, he shall never see death.

52. Then said the Jews unto him, Now we know that thou hast a devil. Abraham is dead, and the prophets; and thou sayest, If a man keep my saying, he shall never taste of death.

53. Art thou greater than our father Abraham, which is dead? and the prophets are dead: whom makest thou thyself?

54. Jesus answered, If I honour myself, my honour is nothing: it is my Father that honoureth me; of whom ye say, that he is your God:

55. Yet ye have not known him; but I know him: and if I should say, I know him not, I shall be a liar like unto you: but I know him, and keep his saying.

56. Your father Abraham rejoiced to see my day: and he saw it, and was glad.

57. Then said the Jews unto him, Thou art not yet fifty years old, and hast thou seen Abraham?

58. Jesus said unto them, Verily, verily, I say unto you, Before Abraham was, I am.

59. Then took they up stones to cast at him: but Jesus hid himself, and went out of the temple, going through the midst of them, and so passed by.

CHAPTER 9

1. And as Jesus passed by, he saw a man which was blind from his birth.

Notes: _____

2. And his disciples asked him, saying, Master, who did sin, this man, or his parents, that he was born blind?

3. Jesus answered, Neither hath this man sinned, nor his parents: but that the works of God should be made manifest in him.

4. I must work the works of him that sent me, while it is day: the night cometh, when no man can work.

5. As long as I am in the world, I am the light of the world.

6. When he had thus spoken, he spat on the ground, and made clay of the spittle, and he anointed the eyes of the blind man with the clay,

7. And said unto him, Go, wash in the pool of Siloam, (which is by interpretation, Sent.) He went his way therefore, and washed, and came seeing.

8. ¶ The neighbours therefore, and they which before had seen him that he was blind, said, Is not this he that sat and begged?

9. Some said, This is he: others said, He is like him: but he said, I am he.

10. Therefore said they unto him, How were thine eyes opened?

11. He answered and said, A man that is called Jesus made clay, and anointed mine eyes, and said unto me, Go to the pool of Siloam, and wash: and I went and washed, and I received sight.

12. Then said they unto him, Where is he? He said, I know not.

13. ¶ They brought to the Pharisees him that aforetime was blind.

14. And it was the sabbath day when Jesus made the clay, and opened his eyes.

15. Then again the Pharisees also asked him how he had received his sight. He said unto them, He put clay upon mine eyes, and I washed, and do see.

16. Therefore said some of the Pharisees, This man is not of God, because he keepeth not the sabbath day. Others said, How can a man that is a sinner do such miracles? And there was a division among them.

17. They say unto the blind man again, What sayest thou of him, that he hath opened thine eyes? He said, He is a prophet.

18. But the Jews did not believe concerning him, that he had been blind, and received his sight, until they called the parents of him that had received his sight.

19. And they asked them, saying, Is this your son, who ye say was born blind? how then doth he now see?

20. His parents answered them and said, We know that this is our son, and that he was born blind:

21. But by what means he now seeth, we know not; or who hath opened his eyes, we know not: he is of age; ask him: he shall speak for himself.

22. These words spake his parents, because they feared the Jews: for the Jews had agreed already, that if any man did confess that he was Christ, he should be put out of the synagogue.

23. Therefore said his parents, He is of age; ask him.

24. Then again called they the man that was blind, and said unto him, Give God the praise: we know that this man is a sinner.

25. He answered and said, Whether he be a sinner or no, I know not: one thing I know, that, whereas I was blind, now I see.

26. Then said they to him again,

Jesus healing the blind

What did he to thee? how opened he thine eyes?

27. He answered them, I have told you already, and ye did not hear: wherefore would ye hear it again? will ye also be his disciples?

28. Then they reviled him, and said, Thou art his disciple; but we are Moses' disciples.

29. We know that God spake unto Moses: as for this fellow, we know not from whence he is.

30. The man answered and said unto them, Why herein is a marvellous thing, that ye know not from whence he is, and yet he hath opened mine eyes.

31. Now we know that God heareth not sinners: but if any man be a worshipper of God, and doeth his will, him he heareth.

32. Since the world began was it not heard that any man opened the eyes of one that was born blind.

33. If this man were not of God, he could do nothing.

34. They answered and said unto him, Thou wast altogether born in sins, and dost thou teach us? And they cast him out.

35. Jesus heard that they had cast him out; and when he had found him, he said unto him, Dost thou believe on the Son of God?

36. He answered and said, Who is he, Lord, that I might believe on him?

37. And Jesus said unto him, Thou hast both seen him, and it is he that talketh with thee.

38. And he said, Lord, I believe. And he worshipped him.

39. ¶ And Jesus said, For judgment I am come into this world, that they which see not might see; and that they which see might be made blind.

40. And some of the Pharisees which were with him heard these words, and said unto him, Are we blind also?

41. Jesus said unto them, If ye were blind, ye should have no sin: but now ye say, We see; therefore your sin remaineth.

CHAPTER 10

1. Verily, verily, I say unto you, He that entereth not by the door into the sheepfold, but climbeth up some other way, the same is a thief and a robber.

2. But he that entereth in by the door is the shepherd of the sheep.

3. To him the porter openeth; and the sheep hear his voice: and he calleth his own sheep by name, and leadeth them out.

4. And when he putteth forth his own sheep, he goeth before them, and the sheep follow him: for they know his voice.

5. And a stranger will they not follow, but will flee from him: for they know not the voice of strangers.

6. This parable spake Jesus unto them: but they understood not what things they were which he spake unto them.

7. Then said Jesus unto them again, Verily, verily, I say unto you, I am the door of the sheep.

8. All that ever came before me are thieves and robbers: but the sheep did not hear them.

9. I am the door: by me if any man enter in, he shall be saved, and shall go in and out, and find pasture.

10. The thief cometh not, but for to steal, and to kill, and to destroy: I

Notes: _____

_____

_____

_____

_____

_____

_____

_____

_____

_____

_____

_____

_____

_____

_____

_____

_____

_____

John 10:1–16—In a poignant story, a young man asks a shepherd if one of his lambs, who was wearing a cast, had broken its leg. The shepherd confirms that the leg is broken, and then, in answer to the young man's query, says that he himself broke the leg. Seeing the shock on the young man's face, he continued, "This lamb kept straying from the flock—despite all I could do to prevent it. I knew its life was in jeopardy. I broke the leg so he would have to be carried. In a few weeks, the leg will be strong enough to walk, and the lamb will have gained a bond of love for me and will not stray again" (George Horton, in *We Believe in Christ*, 8–9).

John 10:1–16—"The cosmic Christ who creates and redeems worlds without number is the same gentle and good Shepherd who goes in search of one wandering lamb" (Robert L. Millet, *Alive in Christ: The Miracle of Spiritual Rebirth*, 35).

am come that they might have life, and that they might have it more abundantly.

11. I am the good shepherd: the good shepherd giveth his life for the sheep.

12. But he that is an hireling, and not the shepherd, whose own the sheep are not, seeth the wolf coming, and leaveth the sheep, and fleeth: and the wolf catcheth them, and scattereth the sheep.

13. The hireling fleeth, because he is an hireling, and careth not for the sheep.

14. I am the good shepherd, and know my sheep, and am known of mine.

15. As the Father knoweth me, even so know I the Father: and I lay down my life for the sheep.

16. And other sheep I have, which are not of this fold: them also I must bring, and they shall hear my voice; and there shall be one fold, and one shepherd.

17. Therefore doth my Father love me, because I lay down my life, that I might take it again.

18. No man taketh it from me, but I lay it down of myself. I have power to lay it down, and I have power to take it again. This commandment have I received of my Father.

19. ¶ There was a division therefore again among the Jews for these sayings.

20. And many of them said, He hath a devil, and is mad; why hear ye him?

21. Others said, These are not the words of him that hath a devil. Can a devil open the eyes of the blind?

22. ¶ And it was at Jerusalem the feast of the dedication, and it was winter.

23. And Jesus walked in the temple in Solomon's porch.

24. Then came the Jews round about him, and said unto him, How long dost thou make us to doubt? If thou be the Christ, tell us plainly.

25. Jesus answered them, I told you, and ye believed not: the works that I do in my Father's name, they bear witness of me.

26. But ye believe not, because ye are not of my sheep, as I said unto you.

27. My sheep hear my voice, and I know them, and they follow me:

28. And I give unto them eternal life; and they shall never perish, neither shall any man pluck them out of my hand.

29. My Father, which gave them me, is greater than all; and no man is able to pluck them out of my Father's hand.

30. I and my Father are one.

31. Then the Jews took up stones again to stone him.

32. Jesus answered them, Many good works have I shewed you from my Father; for which of those works do ye stone me?

33. The Jews answered him, saying,

John 10:12–13—There is a major difference between a shepherd and a hireling. A shepherd knows his sheep, and they know him; his love for his sheep is so great that he would lay down his life to protect them if necessary. Because of that great love, the sheep follow the shepherd; he leads, but does not have to drive, because the sheep know his voice and follow him. A hireling, on the other hand, is simply a paid employee who has little personally invested in the sheep—his interest is in his wage, not in his flock. He *does* need to drive, beg, cajole, and even physically strike the sheep in order to move them. They don't know his voice, so they respond only to his stick (see Stephen R. Covey, *The Redeemer: Reflections of the Life and Teachings of Jesus the Christ,* 109–110).

John 10:14–15—The relationship of a shepherd to his sheep helps us understand this passage with deeper meaning. A shepherd is always with his sheep, and so comes to know them intimately; shepherds often have a pet name for each one in the flock. Many don't even have to count their sheep at night, because the absence of even one is *felt* by the shepherd. One Lebanese shepherd indicated that were he blindfolded and allowed to feel the face of a sheep, he could immediately tell if the sheep belonged to him—a thought that gives great meaning to the Savior's pronouncement, "I am the good shepherd, and know my sheep" (see George M. Mackie, *Bible Manners and Customs,* 35).

John 10:16—"To my great joy I found that Jesus Christ, in his glorified resurrected body, had appeared to the remnant of Joseph on the continent of America, soon after his resurrection and ascension into heaven; and that he also administered, in person, to the ten lost tribes; and that through his personal ministry in these countries his gospel was revealed and written in countries and among nations entirely unknown to the Jewish apostles" (Parley P. Pratt, *Autobiography of Parley P. Pratt,* 38–39).'

John 10:22–23—The Feast of Dedication, instituted by Judas Maccabeus in 163 B.C., is celebrated more than two months after the Feast of Tabernacles and celebrates the rededication of the temple. Solomon's porch was a structure on the east side of the temple; according to Josephus, it was part of the original structure built by Solomon.

For a good work we stone thee not; but for blasphemy; and because that thou, being a man, makest thyself God.

34. Jesus answered them, Is it not written in your law, I said, Ye are gods?

35. If he called them gods, unto whom the word of God came, and the scripture cannot be broken;

36. Say ye of him, whom the Father hath sanctified, and sent into the world, Thou blasphemest; because I said, I am the Son of God?

37. If I do not the works of my Father, believe me not.

38. But if I do, though ye believe not me, believe the works: that ye may know, and believe, that the Father is in me, and I in him.

39. Therefore they sought again to take him: but he escaped out of their hand,

40. And went away again beyond Jordan into the place where John at first baptized; and there he abode.

41. And many resorted unto him, and said, John did no miracle: but all things that John spake of this man were true.

42. And many believed on him there.

CHAPTER 11

1. Now a certain man was sick, named Lazarus, of Bethany, the town of Mary and her sister Martha.

2. (It was that Mary which anointed the Lord with ointment, and wiped his feet with her hair, whose brother Lazarus was sick.)

3. Therefore his sisters sent unto him, saying, Lord, behold, he whom thou lovest is sick.

4. When Jesus heard that, he said, This sickness is not unto death, but for the glory of God, that the Son of God might be glorified thereby.

5. Now Jesus loved Martha, and her sister, and Lazarus.

6. When he had heard therefore that he was sick, he abode two days still in the same place where he was.

7. Then after that saith he to his disciples, Let us go into Judæa again.

8. His disciples say unto him, Master, the Jews of late sought to stone thee; and goest thou thither again?

9. Jesus answered, Are there not twelve hours in the day? If any man walk in the day, he stumbleth not, because he seeth the light of this world.

10. But if a man walk in the night, he stumbleth, because there is no light in him.

11. These things said he: and after that he saith unto them, Our friend Lazarus sleepeth; but I go, that I may awake him out of sleep.

12. Then said his disciples, Lord, if he sleep, he shall do well.

13. Howbeit Jesus spake of his death: but they thought that he had spoken of taking of rest in sleep.

14. Then said Jesus unto them plainly, Lazarus is dead.

15. And I am glad for your sakes that I was not there, to the intent ye may believe; nevertheless let us go unto him.

16. Then said Thomas, which is called Didymus, unto his fellow-

John 11:1–46—There were at least two other occasions on which Jesus raised someone from the dead before He raised Lazarus, but they were not nearly as dramatic or as public; in fact, in one case, he begged that those who saw the miracle keep it secret. In the first, He raised the daughter of Jairus within a matter of hours after her death (see Luke 8:41–42, 49–56); her body had not yet been prepared for burial. In the second, the widow's son in Nain was raised after most of the burial preparations had been made and as he was being carried to the burial place (see Luke 7:11–17).

The case of Lazarus was very different. While Martha and Mary had sent to Jesus to help heal their brother, Jesus did not come in time to prevent death. Jesus not only waited until Lazarus had died, been prepared for burial, and entombed, but He purposefully did not come until Lazarus had been buried for four days, at which time decomposition was under way. By so doing, the Savior was able to bear public testimony of His divinity in a way that could not be refuted. He was also able to powerfully teach the doctrine of the resurrection (see Daniel H. Ludlow, *A Companion to Your Study of the New Testament: The Four Gospels,* 404).

disciples, Let us also go, that we may die with him.

17. Then when Jesus came, he found that he had lain in the grave four days already.

18. Now Bethany was nigh unto Jerusalem, about fifteen furlongs off:

19. And many of the Jews came to Martha and Mary, to comfort them concerning their brother.

20. Then Martha, as soon as she heard that Jesus was coming, went and met him: but Mary sat still in the house.

21. Then said Martha unto Jesus, Lord, if thou hadst been here, my brother had not died.

22. But I know, that even now, whatsoever thou wilt ask of God, God will give it thee.

23. Jesus saith unto her, Thy brother shall rise again.

24. Martha saith unto him, I know that he shall rise again in the resurrection at the last day.

25. Jesus said unto her, I am the resurrection, and the life: he that believeth in me, though he were dead, yet shall he live:

26. And whosoever liveth and believeth in me shall never die. Believest thou this?

27. She saith unto him, Yea, Lord: I believe that thou art the Christ, the Son of God, which should come into the world.

28. And when she had so said, she went her way, and called Mary her sister secretly, saying, The Master is come, and calleth for thee.

29. As soon as she heard that, she arose quickly, and came unto him.

30. Now Jesus was not yet come into the town, but was in that place where Martha met him.

31. The Jews then which were with her in the house, and comforted her, when they saw Mary, that she rose up hastily and went out, followed her, saying, She goeth unto the grave to weep there.

32. Then when Mary was come where Jesus was, and saw him, she fell down at his feet, saying unto him, Lord, if thou hadst been here, my brother had not died.

33. When Jesus therefore saw her weeping, and the Jews also weeping which came with her, he groaned in the spirit, and was troubled,

34. And said, Where have ye laid him? They said unto him, Lord, come and see.

35. Jesus wept.

36. Then said the Jews, Behold how he loved him!

37. And some of them said, Could not this man, which opened the eyes of the blind, have caused that even this man should not have died?

38. Jesus therefore again groaning in himself cometh to the grave. It was a cave, and a stone lay upon it.

39. Jesus said, Take ye away the stone. Martha, the sister of him that was dead, saith unto him, Lord, by this time he stinketh: for he hath been dead four days.

40. Jesus saith unto her, Said I not unto thee, that, if thou wouldest believe, thou shouldest see the glory of God?

41. Then they took away the stone from the place where the dead was laid. And Jesus lifted up his eyes, and said, Father, I thank thee that thou hast heard me.

42. And I knew that thou hearest

John 11:17—Four days had special significance to the Jews. They believed that for three days after death, the deceased one's spirit hovered nearby, but that after the third day the spirit irretrievably departed so that decomposition could progress. Any raising of the dead that occurred prior to the end of three days could have met with the skepticism that the spirit had not really left the body, and therefore no miracle had occurred. But on the fourth day, experiencing the unmistakable stench of decomposition, even the skeptical Jews were forced to admit that a miracle had indeed occurred.

Jesus healing Lazarus

me always: but because of the people which stand by I said it, that they may believe that thou hast sent me.

43. And when he thus had spoken, he cried with a loud voice, Lazarus, come forth.

44. And he that was dead came forth, bound hand and foot with graveclothes: and his face was bound about with a napkin. Jesus saith unto them, Loose him, and let him go.

45. Then many of the Jews which came to Mary, and had seen the things which Jesus did, believed on him.

46. But some of them went their ways to the Pharisees, and told them what things Jesus had done.

47. ¶ Then gathered the chief priests and the Pharisees a council, and said, What do we? for this man doeth many miracles.

48. If we let him thus alone, all men will believe on him: and the Romans shall come and take away both our place and nation.

49. And one of them, named Caiaphas, being the high priest that same year, said unto them, Ye know nothing at all,

50. Nor consider that it is expedient for us, that one man should die for the people, and that the whole nation perish not.

51. And this spake he not of himself: but being high priest that year, he prophesied that Jesus should die for that nation;

52. And not for that nation only, but that also he should gather together in one the children of God that were scattered abroad.

53. Then from that day forth they took counsel together for to put him to death.

54. Jesus therefore walked no more openly among the Jews; but went thence unto a country near to the wilderness, into a city called Ephraim, and there continued with his disciples.

55. ¶ And the Jews' passover was nigh at hand: and many went out of the country up to Jerusalem before the passover, to purify themselves.

56. Then sought they for Jesus, and spake among themselves, as they stood in the temple, What think ye, that he will not come to the feast?

57. Now both the chief priests and the Pharisees had given a commandment, that, if any man knew where he were, he should shew it, that they might take him.

CHAPTER 12

1. Then Jesus six days before the passover came to Bethany, where Lazarus was which had been dead, whom he raised from the dead.

2. There they made him a supper; and Martha served: but Lazarus was one of them that sat at the table with him.

3. Then took Mary a pound of ointment of spikenard, very costly, and anointed the feet of Jesus, and wiped his feet with her hair: and the house was filled with the odour of the ointment.

4. Then saith one of his disciples, Judas Iscariot, Simon's son, which should betray him,

5. Why was not this ointment sold for three hundred pence, and given to the poor?

6. This he said, not that he cared for the poor; but because he was a

John 11:47–54 — Those who plotted the death of Christ were, in a very real way, a secret combination. Elder James E. Talmage described the "secret combinations of old, which the Lord hath said he hates, the members of which were pledged, and bound by oath and covenant, that they would stand by each other whether right or wrong, that they would cover up one another's crimes, that they would justify one another in theft and murder and in all things that were unclean" (Conference Report, Oct. 1920, 63).

John 11:55–57 — According to Elder Bruce R. McConkie, by this time in the Savior's ministry, public opinion had been worked up into a frenzy about Him, both good and bad. He wrote, "Every Sabbath in the synagogues his doings and sayings are discussed by friends and foes. Every marketplace is ablaze with gossip and rumor about him. On every street corner men congregate to exchange opinions and gain new views. The raising of Lazarus is discussed in every home; the name of Jesus is on every tongue" (*The Mortal Messiah,* 3:331–32).

thief, and had the bag, and bare what was put therein.

7. Then said Jesus, Let her alone: against the day of my burying hath she kept this.

8. For the poor always ye have with you; but me ye have not always.

9. Much people of the Jews therefore knew that he was there: and they came not for Jesus' sake only, but that they might see Lazarus also, whom he had raised from the dead.

10. ¶ But the chief priests consulted that they might put Lazarus also to death;

11. Because that by reason of him many of the Jews went away, and believed on Jesus.

12. On the next day much people that were come to the feast, when they heard that Jesus was coming to Jerusalem,

13. Took branches of palm trees, and went forth to meet him, and cried, Hosanna: Blessed is the King of Israel that cometh in the name of the Lord.

14. And Jesus, when he had found a young ass, sat thereon; as it is written,

15. Fear not, daughter of Sion: behold, thy King cometh, sitting on an ass's colt.

16. These things understood not his disciples at the first: but when Jesus was glorified, then remembered they that these things were written of him, and that they had done these things unto him.

17. The people therefore that was with him when he called Lazarus out of his grave, and raised him from the dead, bare record.

18. For this cause the people also met him, for that they heard that he had done this miracle.

19. The Pharisees therefore said among themselves, Perceive ye how ye prevail nothing? behold, the world is gone after him.

20. ¶ And there were certain Greeks among them that came up to worship at the feast:

21. The same came therefore to Philip, which was of Bethsaida of Galilee, and desired him, saying, Sir, we would see Jesus.

22. Philip cometh and telleth Andrew: and again Andrew and Philip tell Jesus.

23. ¶ And Jesus answered them, saying, The hour is come, that the Son of man should be glorified.

24. Verily, verily, I say unto you, Except a corn of wheat fall into the ground and die, it abideth alone: but if it die, it bringeth forth much fruit.

25. He that loveth his life shall lose it; and he that hateth his life in this world shall keep it unto life eternal.

26. If any man serve me, let him follow me; and where I am, there shall also my servant be: if any man serve me, him will my Father honour.

27. Now is my soul troubled; and what shall I say? Father, save me from this hour: but for this cause came I unto this hour.

28. Father, glorify thy name. Then came there a voice from heaven, saying, I have both glorified it, and will glorify it again.

29. The people therefore, that stood by, and heard it, said that it thundered: others said, An angel spake to him.

30. Jesus answered and said, This voice came not because of me, but for your sakes.

31. Now is the judgment of this

Jesus entering Jerusalem

John 12:20–26—Many at this time sought to see Jesus, believing that merely asking would bring Him to view. The same phenomenon occurs today: many who desire to see Him think that by merely asking they will have that unparalleled experience. President J. Reuben Clark emphasized that "he is not to be seen from the casual, curious, or doubting desire. To the millions of the humble and honest in heart who are discouraged, weary, grief-stricken, despairing, and who would see Jesus, and who, seeing him, would know him, we repeat the words spoken by Jesus to this generation: '. . . every soul who forsaketh his sins and cometh unto me, and calleth on my name, and obeyeth my voice, and keepeth my commandments, shall see my face and know that I am'" (*Behold the Lamb of God,* 233).

John 12:29—"So often today, men and women are living so far apart from things spiritual that when the Lord is speaking to their physical hearing, . . . they hear only a noise as did they at Jerusalem" (Harold B. Lee, *The Teachings of Harold B. Lee,* 423).

world: now shall the prince of this world be cast out.

32. And I, if I be lifted up from the earth, will draw all men unto me.

33. This he said, signifying what death he should die.

34. The people answered him, We have heard out of the law that Christ abideth for ever: and how sayest thou, The Son of man must be lifted up? who is this Son of man?

35. Then Jesus said unto them, Yet a little while is the light with you. Walk while ye have the light, lest darkness come upon you: for he that walketh in darkness knoweth not whither he goeth.

36. While ye have light, believe in the light, that ye may be the children of light. These things spake Jesus, and departed, and did hide himself from them.

37. But though he had done so many miracles before them, yet they believed not on him:

38. That the saying of Esaias the prophet might be fulfilled, which he spake, Lord, who hath believed our report? and to whom hath the arm of the Lord been revealed?

39. Therefore they could not believe, because that Esaias said again,

40. He hath blinded their eyes, and hardened their heart; that they should not see with their eyes, nor understand with their heart, and be converted, and I should heal them.

41. These things said Esaias, when he saw his glory, and spake of him.

42. ¶ Nevertheless among the chief rulers also many believed on him; but because of the Pharisees they did not confess him, lest they should be put out of the synagogue:

43. For they loved the praise of men more than the praise of God.

44. ¶ Jesus cried and said, He that believeth on me, believeth not on me, but on him that sent me.

45. And he that seeth me seeth him that sent me.

46. I am come a light into the world, that whosoever believeth on me should not abide in darkness.

47. And if any man hear my words, and believe not, I judge him not: for I came not to judge the world, but to save the world.

48. He that rejecteth me, and receiveth not my words, hath one that judgeth him: the word that I have spoken, the same shall judge him in the last day.

49. For I have not spoken of myself; but the Father which sent me, he gave me a commandment, what I should say, and what I should speak.

50. And I know that his commandment is life everlasting: whatsoever I speak therefore, even as the Father said unto me, so I speak.

CHAPTER 13

1. Now before the feast of the passover, when Jesus knew that his hour was come that he should depart out

John 12:37–43 — "Today some unbelievers among us spread seeds of heresy, claiming that Jesus could not cast out evil spirits and did not walk on water nor heal the sick nor miraculously feed five thousand nor calm storms nor raise the dead. These would have us believe that such claims are fantastic and that there is a natural explanation for each alleged miracle. Some have gone so far as to publish psychological explanations for His reported miracles. But Jesus' entire ministry was a mark of His divinity. He spoke as God, He acted as God, and He performed works that only God Himself can do. His works bear testimony to His divinity" (Ezra Taft Benson, *Come unto Christ,* 6).

John 12:44–50 — The Prophet Joseph Smith taught, "If John discovered that God the Father of Jesus Christ had a Father, you may suppose that He had a Father also. Where was there ever a son without a father? And where was there ever a father without first being a son? . . . Hence if Jesus had a Father, can we not believe that *He* had a Father also? . . . Jesus said that the Father wrought precisely in the same way as His Father had done before Him. As the Father had done before. He laid down His life, and took it up the same as His Father had done before. He did as He was sent, to lay down His life and take it up again" (*History of the Church,* 6:476–77).

of this world unto the Father, having loved his own which were in the world, he loved them unto the end.

2. And supper being ended, the devil having now put into the heart of Judas Iscariot, Simon's son, to betray him;

3. Jesus knowing that the Father had given all things into his hands, and that he was come from God, and went to God;

4. He riseth from supper, and laid aside his garments; and took a towel, and girded himself.

5. After that he poureth water into a bason, and began to wash the disciples' feet, and to wipe them with the towel wherewith he was girded.

6. Then cometh he to Simon Peter: and Peter saith unto him, Lord, dost thou wash my feet?

7. Jesus answered and said unto him, What I do thou knowest not now; but thou shalt know hereafter.

8. Peter saith unto him, Thou shalt never wash my feet. Jesus answered him, If I wash thee not, thou hast no part with me.

9. Simon Peter saith unto him, Lord, not my feet only, but also my hands and my head.

10. Jesus saith to him, He that is washed needeth not save to wash his feet, but is clean every whit: and ye are clean, but not all.

11. For he knew who should betray him; therefore said he, Ye are not all clean.

12. So after he had washed their feet, and had taken his garments, and was set down again, he said unto them, Know ye what I have done to you?

13. Ye call me Master and Lord: and ye say well; for so I am.

14. If I then, your Lord and Master, have washed your feet; ye also ought to wash one another's feet.

15. For I have given you an example, that ye should do as I have done to you.

16. Verily, verily, I say unto you, The servant is not greater than his lord; neither he that is sent greater than he that sent him.

17. If ye know these things, happy are ye if ye do them.

18. I speak not of you all: I know whom I have chosen: but that the scripture may be fulfilled, He that eateth bread with me hath lifted up his heel against me.

19. Now I tell you before it come, that, when it is come to pass, ye may believe that I am he.

20. Verily, verily, I say unto you, He that receiveth whomsoever I send receiveth me; and he that receiveth me receiveth him that sent me.

21. When Jesus had thus said, he was troubled in spirit, and testified, and said, Verily, verily, I say unto you, that one of you shall betray me.

22. Then the disciples looked one on another, doubting of whom he spake.

23. Now there was leaning on Jesus' bosom one of his disciples, whom Jesus loved.

24. Simon Peter therefore beckoned to him, that he should ask who it should be of whom he spake.

25. He then lying on Jesus' breast saith unto him, Lord, who is it?

John 13:5—The Prophet Joseph Smith wrote, "The house of the Lord must be prepared, . . . and in it we must attend to the ordinance of washing of feet. It was never intended for any but official members. It is calculated to unite our hearts, that we may be one in feeling and sentiment, and that our faith may be strong, so that Satan cannot overthrow us, nor have any power over us here" (*Commentary*, 1:709).

Notes: _____

_____

_____

_____

_____

_____

_____

_____

_____

John 13:15—When Jesus knew that His hour had come, He washed the feet of His disciples and gave them counsel, including this definitive statement on how they should conduct themselves once He was gone. We have our perfect example in the Lord Jesus Christ. Our goal should be to do as He has done as we build our Zion family. He will help us and provide a way (see D&C 84:88; 1 Ne. 3:7; Moro. 7:33). How has the pattern of the Savior been the key example you have followed in your family relationships and activities?

26. Jesus answered, He it is, to whom I shall give a sop, when I have dipped it. And when he had dipped the sop, he gave it to Judas Iscariot, the son of Simon.

27. And after the sop Satan entered into him. Then said Jesus unto him, That thou doest, do quickly.

28. Now no man at the table knew for what intent he spake this unto him.

29. For some of them thought, because Judas had the bag, that Jesus had said unto him, Buy those things that we have need of against the feast; or, that he should give something to the poor.

30. He then having received the sop went immediately out: and it was night.

31. ¶ Therefore, when he was gone out, Jesus said, Now is the Son of man glorified, and God is glorified in him.

32. If God be glorified in him, God shall also glorify him in himself, and shall straightway glorify him.

33. Little children, yet a little while I am with you. Ye shall seek me: and as I said unto the Jews, Whither I go, ye cannot come; so now I say to you.

34. A new commandment I give unto you, That ye love one another; as I have loved you, that ye also love one another.

35. By this shall all men know that ye are my disciples, if ye have love one to another.

36. ¶ Simon Peter said unto him, Lord, whither goest thou? Jesus answered him, Whither I go, thou canst not follow me now; but thou shalt follow me afterwards.

37. Peter said unto him, Lord, why cannot I follow thee now? I will lay down my life for thy sake.

38. Jesus answered him, Wilt thou lay down thy life for my sake? Verily, verily, I say unto thee, The cock shall not crow, till thou hast denied me thrice.

CHAPTER 14

1. Let not your heart be troubled: ye believe in God, believe also in me.

2. In my Father's house are many mansions: if it were not so, I would have told you. I go to prepare a place for you.

3. And if I go and prepare a place for you, I will come again, and receive you unto myself; that where I am, there ye may be also.

4. And whither I go ye know, and the way ye know.

5. Thomas saith unto him, Lord, we know not whither thou goest; and how can we know the way?

6. Jesus saith unto him, I am the way, the truth, and the life: no man cometh unto the Father, but by me.

7. If ye had known me, ye should have known my Father also: and from henceforth ye know him, and have seen him.

8. Philip saith unto him, Lord, shew us the Father, and it sufficeth us.

9. Jesus saith unto him, Have I been so long time with you, and yet hast thou not known me, Philip? he that hath seen me hath seen the Father;

John 13:26—*Sop* is a thin piece of bread that is dipped into food in a dish and that becomes saturated with the juices of the food. This verse is important because it indicates the position of Judas at the supper: Judas was obviously within reach of the Savior's hand, which indicates he was likely next to the Savior. We know that John lay on Jesus' right side, so Judas was very probably laying on His left. "If so, the Saviour must at times have laid his head on the traitor's breast; and thus the base treachery of Judas is seen in a most revolting aspect. While the Master was pillowing his head upon him he was meditating on the chances of securing the blood-money for which he had contracted to betray his Lord!" (James M. Freeman, *Manners and Customs of the Bible,* 434-35).

John 14:1–6—"I do not believe the Methodist doctrine of sending honest men and noble-minded men to hell, along with the murderer and the adulterer. . . . There are mansions for those who obey a celestial law, and there are other mansions for those who come short of the law every man in his own order" (Joseph Smith, *Teachings of the Prophet Joseph Smith,* 366).

"There are mansions in sufficient numbers to suit the different classes of mankind, and a variety will always exist to all eternity, requiring a classification and an arrangement into societies and communities in the many mansions which are in the Lord's house, and this will be so for ever and ever" (Brigham Young, *Journal of Discourses,* 11:275).

John 14:6—On the eve of His atoning sacrifice, Jesus taught His disciples about His divine commission. These words were the Savior's response when Thomas asked which way to go. The Savior Jesus Christ is the only way back to the presence of our Heavenly Father. Happiness and joy come through His infinite and eternal Atonement, the blessings of His gospel, the power of His priesthood with accompanying covenants and ordinances, and His teachings and doctrines. How would you respond if someone asked you the Thomas question: "What way should I go?"

and how sayest thou then, Shew us the Father?

10. Believest thou not that I am in the Father, and the Father in me? the words that I speak unto you I speak not of myself: but the Father that dwelleth in me, he doeth the works.

11. Believe me that I am in the Father, and the Father in me: or else believe me for the very works' sake.

12. Verily, verily, I say unto you, He that believeth on me, the works that I do shall he do also; and greater works than these shall he do; because I go unto my Father.

13. And whatsoever ye shall ask in my name, that will I do, that the Father may be glorified in the Son.

14. If ye shall ask any thing in my name, I will do it.

15. ¶ If ye love me, keep my commandments.

16. And I will pray the Father, and he shall give you another Comforter, that he may abide with you for ever;

17. Even the Spirit of truth; whom the world cannot receive, because it seeth him not, neither knoweth him: but ye know him; for he dwelleth with you, and shall be in you.

18. I will not leave you comfortless: I will come to you.

19. Yet a little while, and the world seeth me no more; but ye see me: because I live, ye shall live also.

20. At that day ye shall know that I am in my Father, and ye in me, and I in you.

21. He that hath my commandments, and keepeth them, he it is that loveth me: and he that loveth me shall be loved of my Father, and I will love him, and will manifest myself to him.

22. Judas saith unto him, not Iscariot, Lord, how is it that thou wilt manifest thyself unto us, and not unto the world?

23. Jesus answered and said unto him, If a man love me, he will keep my words: and my Father will love him, and we will come unto him, and make our abode with him.

24. He that loveth me not keepeth not my sayings: and the word which ye hear is not mine, but the Father's which sent me.

25. These things have I spoken unto you, being yet present with you.

26. But the Comforter, which is the Holy Ghost, whom the Father will send in my name, he shall teach you all things, and bring all things to your remembrance, whatsoever I have said unto you.

27. Peace I leave with you, my peace I give unto you: not as the world giveth, give I unto you. Let not your heart be troubled, neither let it be afraid.

28. Ye have heard how I said unto you, I go away, and come again unto you. If ye loved me, ye would rejoice, because I said, I go unto the

John 14:12 — "What is the meaning of that? It is that he will not only do the works that Christ did while He dwelt in the flesh, those works that Christ performed when He dwelt in morality, but that as He was going to the Father, they also would go to the Father; that when He went away from this earth, whatever He did then they would follow and do similar work, and as He was going to the Father, they also would go to the Father and be with the Father and the Son and the Holy Ghost and always be under their direction" (Charles W. Penrose, Conference Report, Oct. 1914, 39).

John 14:15 — The commandments of the Lord "are but the sweet music of the voice of our Father in heaven, in His mercy to us. They are but the advice and counsel of a loving parent, who is more concerned in our welfare than earthly parents can be" (George Albert Smith, Conference Report, Oct. 1911, 44).

"The real test is (and always has been), 'How much do we love Him?' We know how much He loves us" (Neal A. Maxwell, *Notwithstanding My Weakness*, 114).

John 14:16–27 — Jesus promised us that we can have three things here and now: (1) the gift and companionship of the Holy Ghost; (2) personal visitations from the Second Comforter, the Lord Himself; and (3) God the Father, who will reveal the mysteries (Daniel H. Ludlow, *A Companion to Your Study of the New Testament: The Four Gospels*, 2:418–419).

John 14:26 — As the time drew near for the Crucifixion, Jesus promised His Apostles that He would give them another Comforter, even the Holy Ghost. In the words of this verse, He shared with them the miraculous nature of the Comforter's blessing. The Spirit will console and encourage us in our times of need. The Spirit will lead us to do good, walk humbly, do justly, judge righteously — and will enlighten our souls (see D&C 11:12–13). We can have wonderful feelings through the Spirit, among them love, peace, joy, and faith (see Gal. 5:22–23).

Through obedience we show our love to the Savior; through His love He sends the Holy Ghost to teach us and remind us of His sayings. The Apostles were about to lose the immediate companionship of the Savior, but they would receive a marvelous blessing to remind them of all He had taught them. How does the Holy Ghost help you remember the truths of the gospel and put them into practice?

Father: for my Father is greater than I.

29. And now I have told you before it come to pass, that, when it is come to pass, ye might believe.

30. Hereafter I will not talk much with you: for the prince of this world cometh, and hath nothing in me.

31. But that the world may know that I love the Father; and as the Father gave me commandment, even so I do. Arise, let us go hence.

CHAPTER 15

1. I am the true vine, and my Father is the husbandman.

2. Every branch in me that beareth not fruit he taketh away: and every branch that beareth fruit, he purgeth it, that it may bring forth more fruit.

3. Now ye are clean through the word which I have spoken unto you.

4. Abide in me, and I in you. As the branch cannot bear fruit of itself, except it abide in the vine; no more can ye, except ye abide in me.

5. I am the vine, ye are the branches: He that abideth in me, and I in him, the same bringeth forth much fruit: for without me ye can do nothing.

6. If a man abide not in me, he is cast forth as a branch, and is withered; and men gather them, and cast them into the fire, and they are burned.

7. If ye abide in me, and my words abide in you, ye shall ask what ye will, and it shall be done unto you.

8. Herein is my Father glorified, that ye bear much fruit; so shall ye be my disciples.

9. As the Father hath loved me, so have I loved you: continue ye in my love.

10. If ye keep my commandments, ye shall abide in my love; even as I have kept my Father's commandments, and abide in his love.

11. These things have I spoken unto you, that my joy might remain in you, and that your joy might be full.

12. This is my commandment, That ye love one another, as I have loved you.

13. Greater love hath no man than this, that a man lay down his life for his friends.

14. Ye are my friends, if ye do whatsoever I command you.

15. Henceforth I call you not servants; for the servant knoweth not what his lord doeth: but I have called you friends; for all things that I have heard of my Father I have made known unto you.

16. Ye have not chosen me, but I have chosen you, and ordained

John 15:7—Elder Gene R. Cook wrote that there are some conditions if we expect to have our prayers answered. We must:
- Be believing (see Matt. 21:22; Enos 1:15)
- Abide in Christ (see John 15:4–6)
- Keep the commandments (see 1 Jn. 3:22)
- Ask according to the Lord's will (see 1 Jn. 5:14)
- Ask not "amiss" (see 2 Ne. 4:35)
- Ask for that which is right (see Mosiah 4:21)
- Believe in Christ, nothing doubting (see Morm. 9:21)
- Have the faith that we will receive (see Moro. 7:26)
- Ask for those things that are expedient for us (see D&C 88:64) (see *Receiving Answers to Our Prayers*, 40).

John 15:9–17—"As God has loved us, let us love one another, looking for the spark of divinity that burns in the hearts of all people, the seed of godhood that may grow and bear fruit as it is nourished in love. As the oak grows from the acorn and the butterfly from the caterpillar, so may we grow in our Father's love and in the love and empathy of one another" (Lloyd D. Newell, *The Divine Connection: Understanding Your Inherent Worth,* 184).

John 15:16—A prophet is not chosen based on his physical appearance, his station in life, his economic status, his educational degrees, or any other credentials we normally associate with "being chosen" in this life. What sets a prophet apart is that he is chosen by God (see A. Theodore Tuttle, *Ensign,* Jul. 1973, 18).

you, that ye should go and bring forth fruit, and that your fruit should remain: that whatsoever ye shall ask of the Father in my name, he may give it you.

17. These things I command you, that ye love one another.

18. If the world hate you, ye know that it hated me before it hated you.

19. If ye were of the world, the world would love his own: but because ye are not of the world, but I have chosen you out of the world, therefore the world hateth you.

20. Remember the word that I said unto you, The servant is not greater than his lord. If they have persecuted me, they will also persecute you; if they have kept my saying, they will keep yours also.

21. But all these things will they do unto you for my name's sake, because they know not him that sent me.

22. If I had not come and spoken unto them, they had not had sin: but now they have no cloke for their sin.

23. He that hateth me hateth my Father also.

24. If I had not done among them the works which none other man did, they had not had sin: but now have they both seen and hated both me and my Father.

25. But this cometh to pass, that the word might be fulfilled that is written in their law, They hated me without a cause.

26. But when the Comforter is come, whom I will send unto you from the Father, even the Spirit of truth, which proceedeth from the Father, he shall testify of me:

27. And ye also shall bear witness, because ye have been with me from the beginning.

CHAPTER 16

1. These things have I spoken unto you, that ye should not be offended.

2. They shall put you out of the synagogues: yea, the time cometh, that whosoever killeth you will think that he doeth God service.

3. And these things will they do unto you, because they have not known the Father, nor me.

4. But these things have I told you, that when the time shall come, ye may remember that I told you of them. And these things I said not unto you at the beginning, because I was with you.

5. But now I go my way to him that sent me; and none of you asketh me, Whither goest thou?

6. But because I have said these things unto you, sorrow hath filled your heart.

7. Nevertheless I tell you the truth; It is expedient for you that I go away: for if I go not away, the Comforter will not come unto you; but if I depart, I will send him unto you.

8. And when he is come, he will reprove the world of sin, and of righteousness, and of judgment:

9. Of sin, because they believe not on me;

10. Of righteousness, because I go to my Father, and ye see me no more;

John 15:18–27—"Before you joined this Church you stood on neutral ground. When the gospel was preached, good and evil were set before you. You could choose either or neither. There were two opposite masters inviting you to serve them. When you joined this Church you enlisted to serve God. When you did that, you left the neutral ground, and you never can get back on to it. Should you forsake the Master you enlisted to serve, it will be only by the instigation of the evil one, and you will follow his dictation and be his servant" (*The Teachings of Joseph Smith*, 42–43).

John 15:26–27—On the eve of His Crucifixion, Jesus taught His disciples about a grand gift they would soon receive from the Father. A central role of the Holy Ghost in our lives is to witness of the divinity of Christ and to edify us with the light of all truth (see D&C 50:17–22; Moro. 10:4–5). Paul taught, "Wherefore I give you to understand . . . that no man can say that Jesus is the Lord, but by the Holy Ghost" (1 Cor. 12:3).

The Holy Ghost proceeds from the Father through the agency of the Son. How does the Holy Ghost bless your own life as a witness of the reality of the Father and the Son?

John 16:7–15—"The gift of the Holy Spirit adapts itself to all these organs or attributes. It quickens all the intellectual faculties, increases, enlarges, expands and purifies all the natural passions and affections; and adapts them, by the gift of wisdom, to their lawful use. It inspires, develops, cultivates and matures all the fine-toned sympathies, joys, tastes, kindred feelings and affections of our nature. It develops beauty of person, form and features. It tends to health, vigor, animation and social feeling. It develops and invigorates all the faculties of the physical and intellectual man. It strengthens, invigorates, and gives tone to the nerves. In short, it is, as it were, marrow to the bone, joy to the heart, light to the eyes, music to the ears, and life to the whole being" (Parley P. Pratt, *Key to the Science of Theology/A Voice of Warning*, 101).

John 16:7—The Prophet Joseph Smith said, "No man can receive the Holy Ghost without receiving revelations. The Holy Ghost is a revelator" (*History of the Church,* 6:58).

11. Of judgment, because the prince of this world is judged.

12. I have yet many things to say unto you, but ye cannot bear them now.

13. Howbeit when he, the Spirit of truth, is come, he will guide you into all truth: for he shall not speak of himself; but whatsoever he shall hear, that shall he speak: and he will shew you things to come.

14. He shall glorify me: for he shall receive of mine, and shall shew it unto you.

15. All things that the Father hath are mine: therefore said I, that he shall take of mine, and shall shew it unto you.

16. A little while, and ye shall not see me: and again, a little while, and ye shall see me, because I go to the Father.

17. Then said some of his disciples among themselves, What is this that he saith unto us, A little while, and ye shall not see me: and again, a little while, and ye shall see me: and, Because I go to the Father?

18. They said therefore, What is this that he saith, A little while? we cannot tell what he saith.

19. Now Jesus knew that they were desirous to ask him, and said unto them, Do ye inquire among yourselves of that I said, A little while, and ye shall not see me: and again, a little while, and ye shall see me?

20. Verily, verily, I say unto you, That ye shall weep and lament, but the world shall rejoice: and ye shall be sorrowful, but your sorrow shall be turned into joy.

21. A woman when she is in travail hath sorrow, because her hour is come: but as soon as she is delivered of the child, she remembereth no more the anguish, for joy that a man is born into the world.

22. And ye now therefore have sorrow: but I will see you again, and your heart shall rejoice, and your joy no man taketh from you.

23. And in that day ye shall ask me nothing. Verily, verily, I say unto you, Whatsoever ye shall ask the Father in my name, he will give it you.

24. Hitherto have ye asked nothing in my name: ask, and ye shall receive, that your joy may be full.

25. These things have I spoken unto you in proverbs: but the time cometh, when I shall no more speak unto you in proverbs, but I shall shew you plainly of the Father.

26. At that day ye shall ask in my name: and I say not unto you, that I will pray the Father for you:

27. For the Father himself loveth you, because ye have loved me, and have believed that I came out from God.

28. I came forth from the Father, and am come into the world: again, I leave the world, and go to the Father.

29. His disciples said unto him, Lo, now speakest thou plainly, and speakest no proverb.

30. Now are we sure that thou knowest all things, and needest not that any man should ask thee: by this we believe that thou camest forth from God.

John 16:13–14—Once more, the Savior confirmed to His Apostles that the blessings of the Holy Ghost are of a universal and glorious nature, appropriate as a consoling force for the time when He would no longer be able to be among them. The Holy Ghost is the divine Agent of communication of truth from the Savior to His people. He is the divine Agent for disseminating to the honest at heart the light of Christ in the degree to which they are receptive of that light. In so doing, the Holy Ghost glorifies Christ by receiving all truth and then sharing it with the faithful and obedient. How can you also follow this pattern to glorify the Lord by receiving in gratitude His truths through the Holy Spirit and then sharing them with others?

John 16:16–33—In teaching of His death and resurrection, says Elder Bruce R. McConkie, the Savior could not have stated it in any better way. "For a brief moment he will go away to visit the spirits in prison. Because they live together in love, they shall weep at his death. But when he appears again—resurrected, glorified, perfected—their joy will be unbounded. Death is but the birth pang of life; as a man child is born through travail, so immortality is the child of death. Sorrow is for a moment; joy is eternal" (*The Mortal Messiah*, 4:101–102).

Notes: _____

_____

_____

_____

_____

_____

_____

_____

_____

_____

_____

_____

_____

_____

_____

_____

_____

31. Jesus answered them, Do ye now believe?

32. Behold, the hour cometh, yea, is now come, that ye shall be scattered, every man to his own, and shall leave me alone: and yet I am not alone, because the Father is with me.

33. These things I have spoken unto you, that in me ye might have peace. In the world ye shall have tribulation: but be of good cheer; I have overcome the world.

CHAPTER 17

1. These words spake Jesus, and lifted up his eyes to heaven, and said, Father, the hour is come; glorify thy Son, that thy Son also may glorify thee:

2. As thou hast given him power over all flesh, that he should give eternal life to as many as thou hast given him.

3. And this is life eternal, that they might know thee the only true God, and Jesus Christ, whom thou hast sent.

4. I have glorified thee on the earth: I have finished the work which thou gavest me to do.

5. And now, O Father, glorify thou me with thine own self with the glory which I had with thee before the world was.

6. I have manifested thy name unto the men which thou gavest me out of the world: thine they were, and thou gavest them me; and they have kept thy word.

7. Now they have known that all things whatsoever thou hast given me are of thee.

8. For I have given unto them the words which thou gavest me; and they have received them, and have known surely that I came out from thee, and they have believed that thou didst send me.

9. I pray for them: I pray not for the world, but for them which thou hast given me; for they are thine.

10. And all mine are thine, and thine are mine; and I am glorified in them.

11. And now I am no more in the world, but these are in the world, and I come to thee. Holy Father, keep through thine own name those whom thou hast given me, that they may be one, as we are.

12. While I was with them in the world, I kept them in thy name: those that thou gavest me I have kept, and none of them is lost, but the son of perdition; that the scripture might be fulfilled.

13. And now come I to thee; and

John 17:3—Having a relationship with God is what life is all about. When we know our Heavenly Father and our Savior, we will be humble because we will realize that we are the children of God and that we are totally dependent on Him for all things. Because we love our Heavenly Father, we will seek His will and will be forever grateful for all things.

these things I speak in the world, that they might have my joy fulfilled in themselves.

14. I have given them thy word; and the world hath hated them, because they are not of the world, even as I am not of the world.

15. I pray not that thou shouldest take them out of the world, but that thou shouldest keep them from the evil.

16. They are not of the world, even as I am not of the world.

17. Sanctify them through thy truth: thy word is truth.

18. As thou hast sent me into the world, even so have I also sent them into the world.

19. And for their sakes I sanctify myself, that they also might be sanctified through the truth.

20. Neither pray I for these alone, but for them also which shall believe on me through their word;

21. That they all may be one; as thou, Father, art in me, and I in thee, that they also may be one in us: that the world may believe that thou hast sent me.

22. And the glory which thou gavest me I have given them; that they may be one, even as we are one:

23. I in them, and thou in me, that they may be made perfect in one; and that the world may know that thou hast sent me, and hast loved them, as thou hast loved me.

24. Father, I will that they also, whom thou hast given me, be with me where I am; that they may behold my glory, which thou hast given me: for thou lovedst me before the foundation of the world.

25. O righteous Father, the world hath not known thee: but I have known thee, and these have known that thou hast sent me.

26. And I have declared unto them thy name, and will declare it: that the love wherewith thou hast loved me may be in them, and I in them.

CHAPTER 18

1. When Jesus had spoken these words, he went forth with his disciples over the brook Cedron, where was a garden, into the which he entered, and his disciples.

2. And Judas also, which betrayed him, knew the place: for Jesus ofttimes resorted thither with his disciples.

3. Judas then, having received a band of men and officers from the chief priests and Pharisees, cometh thither with lanterns and torches and weapons.

4. Jesus therefore, knowing all things that should come upon him, went forth, and said unto them, Whom seek ye?

5. They answered him, Jesus of Nazareth. Jesus saith unto them, I am he. And Judas also, which betrayed him, stood with them.

6. As soon then as he had said unto them, I am he, they went backward, and fell to the ground.

7. Then asked he them again, Whom seek ye? And they said, Jesus of Nazareth.

8. Jesus answered, I have told you that I am he: if therefore ye seek me, let these go their way:

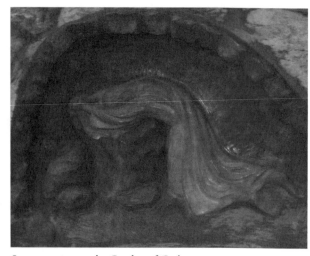

Stone carving at the Garden of Gethsemane

Notes: _____

_____

_____

_____

_____

_____

_____

_____

_____

_____

_____

_____

_____

_____

_____

_____

_____

_____

_____

_____

_____

9. That the saying might be fulfilled, which he spake, Of them which thou gavest me have I lost none.

10. Then Simon Peter having a sword drew it, and smote the high priest's servant, and cut off his right ear. The servant's name was Malchus.

11. Then said Jesus unto Peter, Put up thy sword into the sheath: the cup which my Father hath given me, shall I not drink it?

12. Then the band and the captain and officers of the Jews took Jesus, and bound him,

13. And led him away to Annas first; for he was father in law to Caiaphas, which was the high priest that same year.

14. Now Caiaphas was he, which gave counsel to the Jews, that it was expedient that one man should die for the people.

15. ¶ And Simon Peter followed Jesus, and so did another disciple: that disciple was known unto the high priest, and went in with Jesus into the palace of the high priest.

16. But Peter stood at the door without. Then went out that other disciple, which was known unto the high priest, and spake unto her that kept the door, and brought in Peter.

17. Then saith the damsel that kept the door unto Peter, Art not thou also one of this man's disciples? He saith, I am not.

18. And the servants and officers stood there, who had made a fire of coals; for it was cold: and they warmed themselves: and Peter stood with them, and warmed himself.

19. ¶ The high priest then asked Jesus of his disciples, and of his doctrine.

20. Jesus answered him, I spake openly to the world; I ever taught in the synagogue, and in the temple, whither the Jews always resort; and in secret have I said nothing.

21. Why askest thou me? ask them which heard me, what I have said unto them: behold, they know what I said.

22. And when he had thus spoken, one of the officers which stood by struck Jesus with the palm of his hand, saying, Answerest thou the high priest so?

23. Jesus answered him, If I have spoken evil, bear witness of the evil: but if well, why smitest thou me?

24. Now Annas had sent him bound unto Caiaphas the high priest.

25. And Simon Peter stood and warmed himself. They said therefore unto him, Art not thou also one of his disciples? He denied it, and said, I am not.

26. One of the servants of the high priest, being his kinsman whose ear Peter cut off, saith, Did not I see thee in the garden with him?

27. Peter then denied again: and immediately the cock crew.

28. ¶ Then led they Jesus from Caiaphas unto the hall of judgment: and it was early; and they themselves went not into the judgment hall, lest they should be defiled; but that they might eat the passover.

29. Pilate then went out unto them, and said, What accusation bring ye against this man?

30. They answered and said unto him, If he were not a malefactor, we would not have delivered him up unto thee.

31. Then said Pilate unto them, Take ye him, and judge him according to your law. The Jews therefore said unto him, It is not lawful for us to put any man to death:

32. That the saying of Jesus might be fulfilled, which he spake, signifying what death he should die.

33. Then Pilate entered into the judgment hall again, and called

The betrayal of Christ

Jesus, and said unto him, Art thou the King of the Jews?

34. Jesus answered him, Sayest thou this thing of thyself, or did others tell it thee of me?

35. Pilate answered, Am I a Jew? Thine own nation and the chief priests have delivered thee unto me: what hast thou done?

36. Jesus answered, My kingdom is not of this world: if my kingdom were of this world, then would my servants fight, that I should not be delivered to the Jews: but now is my kingdom not from hence.

37. Pilate therefore said unto him, Art thou a king then? Jesus answered, Thou sayest that I am a king. To this end was I born, and for this cause came I into the world, that I should bear witness unto the truth. Every one that is of the truth heareth my voice.

38. Pilate saith unto him, What is truth? And when he had said this, he went out again unto the Jews, and saith unto them, I find in him no fault at all.

39. But ye have a custom, that I should release unto you one at the passover: will ye therefore that I release unto you the King of the Jews?

40. Then cried they all again, saying, Not this man, but Barabbas. Now Barabbas was a robber.

CHAPTER 19

1. Then Pilate therefore took Jesus, and scourged him.

2. And the soldiers platted a crown of thorns, and put it on his head, and they put on him a purple robe,

3. And said, Hail, King of the Jews! and they smote him with their hands.

4. Pilate therefore went forth again, and saith unto them, Behold, I bring him forth to you, that ye may know that I find no fault in him.

5. Then came Jesus forth, wearing the crown of thorns, and the purple robe. And Pilate saith unto them, Behold the man!

6. When the chief priests therefore and officers saw him, they cried out, saying, Crucify him, crucify him. Pilate saith unto them, Take ye him, and crucify him: for I find no fault in him.

7. The Jews answered him, We have a law, and by our law he ought to die, because he made himself the Son of God.

8. ¶ When Pilate therefore heard that saying, he was the more afraid;

9. And went again into the judgment hall, and saith unto Jesus, Whence art thou? But Jesus gave him no answer.

10. Then saith Pilate unto him, Speakest thou not unto me? knowest thou not that I have power to crucify thee, and have power to release thee?

11. Jesus answered, Thou couldest have no power at all against me, except it were given thee from above: therefore he that delivered me unto thee hath the greater sin.

12. And from thenceforth Pilate sought to release him: but the Jews cried out, saying, If thou let this man go, thou art not Cæsar's friend: whosoever maketh himself a king speaketh against Cæsar.

13. ¶ When Pilate therefore heard

John 18:37—These were among the final words of the Savior during the proceedings against Him by the authorities. He bore solemn witness of His true identity. Never did He deny His mission, not even on the eve of His Crucifixion. The Savior's noble representation of the truth is a supreme example of His courage and His devotion to His commission from the Father. What opportunities have you had in your lifetime to stand firm in your testimony in the presence of disbelievers? What was the source of your courage and how did it make you feel to take a stand for the truth?

Notes: _____

_____

_____

_____

_____

_____

_____

_____

_____

_____

_____

_____

_____

_____

_____

_____

_____

_____

that saying, he brought Jesus forth, and sat down in the judgment seat in a place that is called the Pavement, but in the Hebrew, Gabbatha.

14. And it was the preparation of the passover, and about the sixth hour: and he saith unto the Jews, Behold your King!

15. But they cried out, Away with him, away with him, crucify him. Pilate saith unto them, Shall I crucify your King? The chief priest answered, We have no king but Cæsar.

16. Then delivered he him therefore unto them to be crucified. And they took Jesus, and led him away.

17. And he bearing his cross went forth into a place called the place of a skull, which is called in the Hebrew Golgotha:

18. Where they crucified him, and two other with him, on either side one, and Jesus in the midst.

19. ¶ And Pilate wrote a title, and put it on the cross. And the writing was, JESUS OF NAZARETH THE KING OF THE JEWS.

20. This title then read many of the Jews: for the place where Jesus was crucified was nigh to the city: and it was written in Hebrew, and Greek, and Latin.

21. Then said the chief priests of the Jews to Pilate, Write not, The King of the Jews; but that he said, I am King of the Jews.

22. Pilate answered, What I have written I have written.

23. ¶ Then the soldiers, when they had crucified Jesus, took his garments, and made four parts, to every soldier a part; and also his coat: now the coat was without seam, woven from the top throughout.

24. They said therefore among themselves, Let us not rend it, but cast lots for it, whose it shall be: that the scripture might be fulfilled, which saith, They parted my raiment among them, and for my vesture they did cast lots. These things therefore the soldiers did.

25. ¶ Now there stood by the cross of Jesus his mother, and his mother's sister, Mary the wife of Cleophas, and Mary Magdalene.

26. When Jesus therefore saw his mother, and the disciple standing by, whom he loved, he saith unto his mother, Woman, behold thy son!

27. Then saith he to the disciple, Behold thy mother! And from that hour that disciple took her unto his own home.

28. ¶ After this, Jesus knowing that all things were now accomplished, that the scripture might be fulfilled, saith, I thirst.

29. Now there was set a vessel full of vinegar: and they filled a spunge with vinegar, and put it upon hyssop, and put it to his mouth.

30. When Jesus therefore had received the vinegar, he said, It is finished: and he bowed his head, and gave up the ghost.

31. The Jews therefore, because it was the preparation, that the bodies should not remain upon the cross on the sabbath day, (for that sabbath day was an high day,) besought Pilate that their legs might be brok-

The Savior bearing the cross

en, and that they might be taken away.

32. Then came the soldiers, and brake the legs of the first, and of the other which was crucified with him.

33. But when they came to Jesus, and saw that he was dead already, they brake not his legs:

34. But one of the soldiers with a spear pierced his side, and forthwith came there out blood and water.

35. And he that saw it bare record, and his record is true: and he knoweth that he saith true, that ye might believe.

36. For these things were done, that the scripture should be fulfilled, A bone of him shall not be broken.

37. And again another scripture saith, They shall look on him whom they pierced.

38. ¶ And after this Joseph of Arimathæa, being a disciple of Jesus, but secretly for fear of the Jews, besought Pilate that he might take away the body of Jesus: and Pilate gave him leave. He came therefore, and took the body of Jesus.

39. And there came also Nicodemus, which at the first came to Jesus by night, and brought a mixture of myrrh and aloes, about an hundred pound weight.

40. Then took they the body of Jesus, and wound it in linen clothes with the spices, as the manner of the Jews is to bury.

41. Now in the place where he was crucified there was a garden; and in the garden a new sepulchre, wherein was never man yet laid.

42. There laid they Jesus therefore because of the Jews' preparation day; for the sepulchre was nigh at hand.

CHAPTER 20

1. The first day of the week cometh Mary Magdalene early, when it was yet dark, unto the sepulchre, and seeth the stone taken away from the sepulchre.

2. Then she runneth, and cometh to Simon Peter, and to the other disciple, whom Jesus loved, and saith unto them, They have taken away the Lord out of the sepulchre, and we know not where they have laid him.

3. Peter therefore went forth, and that other disciple, and came to the sepulchre.

4. So they ran both together: and the other disciple did outrun Peter, and came first to the sepulchre.

5. And he stooping down, and looking in, saw the linen clothes lying; yet went he not in.

6. Then cometh Simon Peter following him, and went into the sepulchre, and seeth the linen clothes lie,

7. And the napkin, that was about his head, not lying with the linen clothes, but wrapped together in a place by itself.

8. Then went in also that other disciple, which came first to the sepulchre, and he saw, and believed.

9. For as yet they knew not the scripture, that he must rise again from the dead.

10. Then the disciples went away again unto their own home.

John 19:31–37—"If the soldier's spear was thrust in to the left side of the Lord's body and actually penetrated the heart, the outrush of 'blood and water' observed by John is further evidence of a cardiac rupture; for it is known that in the rare instances of death resulting from a breaking of any part of the wall of the heart, blood accumulates within the pericardium, and there undergoes a change by which the corpuscles separate as a partially clotted mass from the almost colorless, watery serum. Similar accumulations of clotted corpuscles and serum occur within the pleura" (James E. Talmage, *Jesus the Christ,* 620).

Notes: _____

11. ¶ But Mary stood without at the sepulchre weeping: and as she wept, she stooped down, and looked into the sepulchre,

12. And seeth two angels in white sitting, the one at the head, and the other at the feet, where the body of Jesus had lain.

13. And they say unto her, Woman, why weepest thou? She saith unto them, Because they have taken away my Lord, and I know not where they have laid him.

14. And when she had thus said, she turned herself back, and saw Jesus standing, and knew not that it was Jesus.

15. Jesus saith unto her, Woman, why weepest thou? whom seekest thou? She, supposing him to be the gardener, saith unto him, Sir, if thou have borne him hence, tell me where thou hast laid him, and I will take him away.

16. Jesus saith unto her, Mary. She turned herself, and saith unto him, Rabboni; which is to say, Master.

17. Jesus saith unto her, Touch me not; for I am not yet ascended to my Father: but go to my brethren, and say unto them, I ascend unto my Father, and your Father; and to my God, and your God.

18. Mary Magdalene came and told the disciples that she had seen the Lord, and that he had spoken these things unto her.

19. ¶ Then the same day at evening, being the first day of the week, when the doors were shut where the disciples were assembled for fear of the Jews, came Jesus and stood in the midst, and saith unto them, Peace be unto you.

20. And when he had so said, he shewed unto them his hands and his side. Then were the disciples glad, when they saw the Lord.

21. Then said Jesus to them again, Peace be unto you: as my Father hath sent me, even so send I you.

22. And when he had said this, he breathed on them, and saith unto them, Receive ye the Holy Ghost:

23. Whose soever sins ye remit, they are remitted unto them; and whose soever sins ye retain, they are retained.

24. ¶ But Thomas, one of the twelve, called Didymus, was not with them when Jesus came.

25. The other disciples therefore said unto him, We have seen the Lord. But he said unto them, Except I shall see in his hands the print of the nails, and put my finger into the print of the nails, and thrust my hand into his side, I will not believe.

26. ¶ And after eight days again his disciples were within, and Thomas with them: then came Jesus, the doors being shut, and stood in the midst, and said, Peace be unto you.

27. Then saith he to Thomas, reach hither thy finger, and behold my hands; and reach hither thy hand, and thrust it into my side: and be not faithless, but believing.

28. And Thomas answered and said unto him, My Lord and my God.

29. Jesus saith unto him, Thomas, because thou hast seen me, thou hast believed: blessed are they that have not seen, and yet have believed.

John 20:22—In this verse, the Lord gave His disciples the gift of the Holy Ghost, which gave them the right to the constant companionship of the Holy Ghost based on their faithfulness. But they did not receive the Holy Ghost as long as the Savior was still with them (see John 7:39; 14:26; 15:26–27; 16:7–15; Acts 1:8). They did receive it in fulfillment of the Lord's promise on the day of Pentecost, a time when the Spirit was poured out abundantly and many were converted (see Acts 2:1–17) (see Bruce R. McConkie, *Mormon Doctrine,* 181).

John 20:24—We are told that when a man administers to a sick person, he also has the power to remit his sins. When asked how that occurs, President Joseph Fielding Smith said, "It is not the elder who remits or forgives the sick man's sins, but the Lord. If by the power of faith and through the administration by the elders the man is healed it is evidence that his sins have been forgiven. It is hardly reasonable to think that the Lord will forgive the sins of a man who is healed if he has not repented. Naturally he would repent of his sins if he seeks for the blessing by the elders" (*Answers to Gospel Questions,* 1:150).

30. ¶ And many other signs truly did Jesus in the presence of his disciples, which are not written in this book:

31. But these are written, that ye might believe that Jesus is the Christ, the Son of God; and that believing ye might have life through his name.

CHAPTER 21

1. After these things Jesus shewed himself again to the disciples at the sea of Tiberias; and on this wise shewed he himself.

2. There were together Simon Peter, and Thomas called Didymus, and Nathanael of Cana in Galilee, and the sons of Zebedee, and two other of his disciples.

3. Simon Peter saith unto them, I go a fishing. They say unto him, We also go with thee. They went forth, and entered into a ship immediately; and that night they caught nothing.

4. But when the morning was now come, Jesus stood on the shore: but the disciples knew not that it was Jesus.

5. Then Jesus saith unto them, Children, have ye any meat? They answered him, No.

6. And he said unto them, Cast the net on the right side of the ship, and ye shall find. They cast therefore, and now they were not able to draw it for the multitude of fishes.

7. Therefore that disciple whom Jesus loved saith unto Peter, It is the Lord. Now when Simon Peter heard that it was the Lord, he girt his fisher's coat unto him, (for he was naked,) and did cast himself into the sea.

8. And the other disciples came in a little ship; (for they were not far from land, but as it were two hundred cubits,) dragging the net with fishes.

9. As soon then as they were come to land, they saw a fire of coals there, and fish laid thereon, and bread.

10. Jesus saith unto them, Bring of the fish which ye have now caught.

11. Simon Peter went up, and drew the net to land full of great fishes, and hundred and fifty and three: and for all there were so many, yet was not the net broken.

12. Jesus saith unto them, Come and dine. And none of the disciples durst ask him, Who art thou? knowing that it was the Lord.

13. Jesus then cometh, and taketh bread, and giveth them, and fish likewise.

14. This is now the third time that Jesus shewed himself to his disciples, after that he was risen from the dead.

15. ¶ So when they had dined, Jesus saith to Simon Peter, Simon, son of Jonas, lovest thou me more than these? He saith unto him, Yea, Lord; thou knowest that I love thee. He saith unto him, Feed my lambs.

16. He saith to him again the second time, Simon, son of Jonas, lovest thou me? He saith unto him, Yea, Lord; thou knowest that I love thee. He saith unto him, Feed my sheep.

17. He saith unto him the third time, Simon, son of Jonas, lovest thou me? Peter was grieved because he said unto him the third time, Lovest thou me? And he said

John 20:31 — "Certainly no moral teacher, no prophet, however impressive, could break the bands of death or take our iniquities upon him and thus satisfy the demands of justice! . . . Passive acknowledgment of Jesus is not enough. . . . Hence such testifying and convincing is the purpose of all scripture" (Neal A. Maxwell, *Men and Women of Christ*, 36–37).

John 21:1–14 — "John's spirituality is evidenced by his being the first to perceive the identity of Jesus, but Peter's dominant characteristic is seen in his scramble to get to shore to see Jesus" (Robert J. Matthews, *Behold the Messiah*, 109).

Notes: _____

_____

_____

_____

_____

_____

_____

_____

_____

_____

_____

_____

_____

_____

_____

_____

_____

_____

_____

_____

_____

_____

_____

unto him, Lord, thou knowest all things; thou knowest that I love thee. Jesus saith unto him, Feed my sheep.

18. Verily, verily, I say unto thee, When thou wast young, thou girdedst thyself, and walkedst whither thou wouldest: but when thou shalt be old, thou shalt stretch forth thy hands, and another shall gird thee, and carry thee whither thou wouldest not.

19. This spake he, signifying by what death he should glorify God. And when he had spoken this, he saith unto him, Follow me.

20. Then Peter, turning about, seeth the disciple whom Jesus loved following; which also leaned on his breast at supper, and said, Lord, which is he that betrayeth thee?

21. Peter seeing him saith to Jesus, Lord, and what shall this man do?

22. Jesus saith unto him, If I will that he tarry till I come, what is that to thee? follow thou me.

23. Then went this saying abroad among the brethren, that that disciple should not die: yet Jesus said not unto him, He shall not die; but, If I will that he tarry till I come, what is that to thee?

24. This is the disciple which testifieth of these things, and wrote these things: and we know that his testimony is true.

25. And there are also many other things which Jesus did, the which, if they should be written every one, I suppose that even the world itself could not contain the books that should be written. Amen.

THE ACTS
OF THE APOSTLES

CHAPTER 1

1. The former treatise have I made, O Theophilus, of all that Jesus began both to do and teach,

2. Until the day in which he was taken up, after that he through the Holy Ghost had given commandments unto the apostles whom he had chosen:

3. To whom also he shewed himself

John 21:18–19—It was tradition in Rome to crucify people by first putting their necks in a yoke, then stretching their hands out and fastening them to the ends of the crossbar. At that point, they were carried through the city for all to see before being taken to the site of crucifixion. About thirty-four years after the prophecy in these verses was given, Peter was crucified; "he deemed it so *glorious* a thing to die for Christ that he begged to be crucified with his *head downwards,* not considering himself worthy to die in the same posture in which his Lord did" (Adam Clarke, *Clarke's Commentary: Matthew to Revelation,* 663).

John 21:20–24—John is one of those who were translated to fulfill a special ministry. Some, such as Moses and Elijah, needed to be translated so that they could later appear with physical bodies—had they been spirit only, they could not have laid their hands on the heads of Peter, James, and John on the Mount of Transfiguration. Those who are translated are not immediately taken into the presence of God; instead, they remain in the terrestrial order in a special place that has been prepared for those who are translated beings. They do not immediately enjoy the fullness as those who have been resurrected from the dead (see *Teachings of the Prophet Joseph Smith,* 170).

Acts 1:3—At the beginning of Acts—Luke's continuing saga of the life and ministry of the Savior and His disciples—we find confirmation that the resurrected Lord showed Himself to the Apostles and spent forty days with them, instructing them concerning heavenly things. It would have been a transcendent experience to spend forty days with the resurrected Son of God, learning more about the operation of the kingdom of God. The disciples in the New World had a similar experience for a period of time. Where can you go to be instructed in the higher truths of the gospel of salvation and exaltation? How does the temple experience relate to such instruction?

The kingdom of God on the earth is indeed The Church of Jesus Christ, whether it be among the former-day Saints or now in the latter days. The essence of this scripture is to show that the Lord instructed His Apostles on the establishment of His Church and kingdom here upon the earth. It is His Church and bears His name; therefore, it reflects His priesthood, His gospel, and His doctrine. We can have every confidence in following His anointed leaders, for they are led by our Savior Jesus Christ.

alive after his passion by many infallible proofs, being seen of them forty days, and speaking of the things pertaining to the kingdom of God:

4. And, being assembled together with them, commanded them that they should not depart from Jerusalem, but wait for the promise of the Father, which, saith he, ye have heard of me.

5. For John truly baptized with water; but ye shall be baptized with the Holy Ghost not many days hence.

6. When they therefore were come together, they asked of him, saying, Lord, wilt thou at this time restore again the kingdom to Israel?

7. And he said unto them, It is not for you to know the times or the seasons, which the Father hath put in his own power.

8. But ye shall receive power, after that the Holy Ghost is come upon you: and ye shall be witnesses unto me both in Jerusalem, and in all Judæa, and in Samaria, and unto the uttermost part of the earth.

9. And when he had spoken these things, while they beheld, he was taken up; and a cloud received him out of their sight.

10. And while they looked stedfastly toward heaven as he went up, behold, two men stood by them in white apparel;

11. Which also said, Ye men of Galilee, why stand ye gazing up into heaven? this same Jesus, which is taken up from you into heaven, shall so come in like manner as ye have seen him go into heaven.

12. Then returned they unto Jerusalem from the mount called Olivet, which is from Jerusalem a sabbath day's journey.

13. And when they were come in, they went up into an upper room, where abode both Peter, and James, and John, and Andrew, Philip, and Thomas, Bartholomew, and Matthew, James the son of Alphæus, and Simon Zelotes, and Judas the brother of James.

14. These all continued with one accord in prayer and supplication, with the women, and Mary the mother of Jesus, and with his brethren.

15. ¶ And in those days Peter stood up in the midst of the disciples, and said, (the number of names together were about an hundred and twenty,)

16. Men and brethren, this scripture must needs have been fulfilled, which the Holy Ghost by the mouth of David spake before concerning Judas, which was guide to them that took Jesus.

17. For he was numbered with us, and had obtained part of this ministry.

18. Now this man purchased a field with the reward of iniquity; and falling headlong, he burst asunder in the midst, and all his bowels gushed out.

19. And it was known unto all the dwellers at Jerusalem; insomuch as that field is called in their proper tongue, Aceldama, that is to say, The field of blood.

20. For it is written in the book of Psalms, Let his habitation be desolate, and let no man dwell therein: and his bishoprick let another take.

Acts 1:8—The Savior's commission to His disciples to "Go ye therefore, and teach all nations, baptizing them in the name of the Father, and of the Son, and of the Holy Ghost" (Matt. 28:19–20) included the elements of going forth, teaching, baptizing, cultivating obedience, and serving the people with God-like charity. To do these things with power and authenticity, the Apostles needed two things: (1) the Savior to be with them continually, as He promised them, and (2) the endowment of the Holy Ghost. His promise that they would receive the Holy Ghost, in the words of this verse, were the last recorded words of the Savior prior to His Ascension.

It is by the power of the Holy Ghost that we teach and preach the gospel (see 2 Ne. 33:1; D&C 42:14; 50:17–22). The Holy Ghost bears witness of the Father and the Son (see 2 Ne. 31:18; 3 Ne. 28:11).

21. Wherefore of these men which have companied with us all the time that the Lord Jesus went in and out among us,

22. Beginning from the baptism of John, unto that same day that he was taken up from us, must one be ordained to be a witness with us of his resurrection.

23. And they appointed two, Joseph called Barsabas, who was surnamed Justus, and Matthias.

24. And they prayed, and said, Thou, Lord, which knowest the hearts of all men, shew whether of these two thou hast chosen,

25. That he may take part of this ministry and apostleship, from which Judas by transgression fell, that he might go to his own place.

26. And they gave forth their lots; and the lot fell upon Matthias; and he was numbered with the eleven apostles.

CHAPTER 2

1. And when the day of Pentecost was fully come, they were all with one accord in one place.

2. And suddenly there came a sound from heaven as of a rushing mighty wind, and it filled all the house where they were sitting.

3. And there appeared unto them cloven tongues like as of fire, and it sat upon each of them.

4. And they were all filled with the Holy Ghost, and began to speak with other tongues, as the Spirit gave them utterance.

5. And there were dwelling at Jerusalem Jews, devout men, out of every nation under heaven.

6. Now when this was noised abroad, the multitude came together, and were confounded, because that every man heard them speak in his own language.

7. And they were all amazed and marvelled, saying one to another, Behold, are not all these which speak Galilæans?

8. And how hear we every man in our own tongue, wherein we were born?

9. Parthians, and Medes, and Elamites, and the dwellers in Mesopotamia, and in Judæa, and Cappadocia, in Pontus, and Asia,

10. Phrygia, and Pamphylia, in Egypt, and in the parts of Libya about Cyrene, and strangers of Rome, Jews and proselytes,

11. Cretes and Arabians, we do hear them speak in our tongues the wonderful works of God.

12. And they were all amazed, and were in doubt, saying one to another, What meaneth this?

13. Others mocking said, These men are full of new wine.

14. ¶ But Peter, standing up with the eleven, lifted up his voice, and said unto them, Ye men of Judæa, and all ye that dwell at Jerusalem, be this known unto you, and hearken to my words:

15. For these are not drunken, as ye suppose, seeing it is but the third hour of the day.

16. But this is that which was spoken by the prophet Joel;

17. And it shall come to pass in the last days, saith God, I will pour out of my Spirit upon all flesh: and your

Acts 2:2–4— The Feast of Pentecost—a name deriving from the Greek word for "fifty"—was held fifty days after the Feast of Passover. During that span of time, the harvest of corn was gathered in. The Old Testament account refers to "the feast of harvest, the firstfruits of thy labours, which thou hast sown in the field: and the feast of ingathering, which is in the end of the year, when thou hast gathered in thy labours out of the field" (Ex. 23:16). Originally, Pentecost was celebrated on a single day, but the time was extended in later generations. It was on the Day of Pentecost—the day of harvest—that the magnificent harvest of spiritual blessings occurred following the Atonement and Resurrection of the Savior. This harvest was conveyed through the promised bestowal of the Holy Ghost upon the successor leadership of the Church. The scriptures describe this milestone event in verses 2–4.

Notes: _____

_____

_____

_____

_____

_____

_____

_____

_____

_____

_____

_____

_____

_____

_____

_____

_____

_____

_____

sons and your daughters shall prophesy, and your young men shall see visions, and your old men shall dream dreams:

18. And on my servants and on my handmaidens I will pour out in those days of my Spirit; and they shall prophesy:

19. And I will shew wonders in heaven above, and signs in the earth beneath; blood, and fire, and vapour of smoke:

20. The sun shall be turned into darkness, and the moon into blood, before that great and notable day of the Lord come:

21. And it shall come to pass, that whosoever shall call on the name of the Lord shall be saved.

22. Ye men of Israel, hear these words; Jesus of Nazareth, a man approved of God among you by miracles and wonders and signs, which God did by him in the midst of you, as ye yourselves also know:

23. Him, being delivered by the determinate counsel and foreknowledge of God, ye have taken, and by wicked hands have crucified and slain:

24. Whom God hath raised up, having loosed the pains of death: because it was not possible that he should be holden of it.

25. For David speaketh concerning him, I foresaw the Lord always before my face, for he is on my right hand, that I should not be moved:

26. Therefore did my heart rejoice, and my tongue was glad; moreover also my flesh shall rest in hope:

27. Because thou wilt not leave my soul in hell, neither wilt thou suffer thine Holy One to see corruption.

28. Thou hast made known to me the ways of life; thou shalt make me full of joy with thy countenance.

29. Men and brethren, let me freely speak unto you of the patriarch David, that he is both dead and buried, and his sepulchre is with us unto this day.

30. Therefore being a prophet, and knowing that God had sworn with an oath to him, that of the fruit of his loins, according to the flesh, he would raise up Christ to sit on his throne;

31. He seeing this before spake of the resurrection of Christ, that his soul was not left in hell, neither his flesh did see corruption.

32. This Jesus hath God raised up, whereof we all are witnesses.

33. Therefore being by the right hand of God exalted, and having received of the Father the promise of the Holy Ghost, he hath shed forth this, which ye now see and hear.

34. For David is not ascended into the heavens: but he saith himself, The LORD said unto my Lord, Sit thou on my right hand,

35. Until I make thy foes thy footstool.

36. Therefore let all the house of Israel know assuredly, that God hath made that same Jesus, whom ye

Acts 2:44, 46; 4:32–37; 6:1–4—Elder James E. Talmage explains the unity and devotion of the earlier Saints at the time of Christ to be united by having all things in common:

"No condition recorded of the early apostolic ministry expresses more forcefully the unity and devotion of the Church in those days than does the fact of the members establishing a system of common ownership of property (Acts 2:44, 46; 4:32–37; 6:1–4). One result of this community of interest in temporal things was a marked unity in spiritual matters; they 'were of one heart and of one soul.' Lacking nothing, they lived in contentment and godliness. Over thirty centuries earlier the people of Enoch had rejoiced in a similar condition of oneness, and their attainments in spiritual excellence were so effective that 'the Lord came and dwelt with his people; . . . And the Lord called his people Zion, because they were of one heart and one mind, and dwelt in righteousness; and there was no poor among them' (Moses 7:16–18). The Nephite disciples grew in holiness, as 'they had all things common among them, every man dealing justly, one with another' (3 Ne. 26:19; see also 4 Ne. 1:2–3). A system of unity in material affairs has been revealed to the Church in this current dispensation (D&C 82:17, 18; 51:10–13, 18; 104:70–77), to the blessings of which the people may attain as they learn to replace selfish concern by altruism, and individual advantage by devotion to the general welfare" (*Jesus the Christ*, 667).

have crucified, both Lord and Christ.

37. ¶ Now when they heard this, they were pricked in their heart, and said unto Peter and to the rest of the apostles, Men and brethren, what shall we do?

38. Then Peter said unto them, Repent, and be baptized every one of you in the name of Jesus Christ for the remission of sins, and ye shall receive the gift of the Holy Ghost.

39. For the promise is unto you, and to your children, and to all that are afar off, even as many as the Lord our God shall call.

40. And with many other words did he testify and exhort, saying, Save yourselves from this untoward generation.

41. ¶ Then they that gladly received his word were baptized: and the same day there were added unto them about three thousand souls.

42. And they continued stedfastly in the apostles' doctrine and fellowship, and in breaking of bread, and in prayers.

43. And fear came upon every soul: and many wonders and signs were done by the apostles.

44. And all that believed were together, and had all things common;

45. And sold their possessions and goods, and parted them to all men, as every man had need.

46. And they, continuing daily with one accord in the temple, and breaking bread from house to house, did eat their meat with gladness and singleness of heart,

47. Praising God, and having favour with all the people. And the Lord added to the church daily such as should be saved.

CHAPTER 3

1. Now Peter and John went up together into the temple at the hour of prayer, being the ninth hour.

2. And a certain man lame from his mother's womb was carried, whom they laid daily at the gate of the temple which is called Beautiful, to ask alms of them that entered into the temple;

3. Who seeing Peter and John about to go into the temple asked an alms.

4. And Peter, fastening his eyes upon him with John, said, Look on us.

5. And he gave heed unto them, expecting to receive something of them.

6. Then Peter said, Silver and gold have I none; but such as I have give I thee: In the name of Jesus Christ of Nazareth rise up and walk.

7. And he took him by the right hand, and lifted him up: and immediately his feet and ankle bones received strength.

Acts 2:47— The multitudes assembled from many lands on that occasion were astonished to hear the truth expressed in their own native tongues. Peter stood with boldness and preached of Christ and His doctrine, inspiring the audience to ask what they should do. Peter responded with the classic missionary exhortation: "Repent, and be baptized every one of you in the name of Jesus Christ for the remission of sins, and ye shall receive the gift of the Holy Ghost. For the promise is unto you, and to your children, and to all that are afar off, even as many as the Lord our God shall call" (Acts 2:38–39). As a result of this extraordinary convocation, some 3,000 souls were added to the fold, with others following them: "And the Lord added to the church daily such as should be saved" (Acts 2:47).

Acts 3:6—Following the Crucifixion and Resurrection of the Lord, the Holy Spirit was poured out upon the multitude on the day of Pentecost as Peter, the chief Apostle, was preaching the truths of the gospel. Many were baptized and joined the fold of Christ at that time. Soon thereafter, Peter and John encountered an invalid near the temple who begged alms from them. Peter responded using the words given in this verse. The crippled man was healed instantly.

When inspired by the Holy Ghost, holders of the Melchizedek Priesthood can act according to the will of God to bless those with special needs. Just as Peter did, those who bear this holy priesthood can, under the direction of the Holy Ghost, perform miracles according to the operation of faith (see Ether 12:16). When the resurrected Lord visited His Saints in the New World, He discerned the faith of the people and compassionately healed all of their afflicted family members (see 3 Ne. 17:1–10). How does the gift of healing reflect the love of the Savior?

8. And he leaping up stood, and walked, and entered with them into the temple, walking, and leaping, and praising God.

9. And all the people saw him walking and praising God:

10. And they knew that it was he which sat for alms at the Beautiful gate of the temple: and they were filled with wonder and amazement at that which had happened unto him.

11. And as the lame man which was healed held Peter and John, all the people ran together unto them in the porch that is called Solomon's, greatly wondering.

12. ¶ And when Peter saw it, he answered unto the people, Ye men of Israel, why marvel ye at this? or why look ye so earnestly on us, as though by our own power or holiness we had made this man to walk?

13. The God of Abraham, and of Isaac, and of Jacob, the God of our fathers, hath glorified his Son Jesus; whom ye delivered up, and denied him in the presence of Pilate, when he was determined to let him go.

14. But ye denied the Holy One and the Just, and desired a murderer to be granted unto you;

15. And killed the Prince of life, whom God hath raised from the dead; whereof we are witnesses.

16. And his name through faith in his name hath made this man strong, whom ye see and know: yea, the faith which is by him hath given him this perfect soundness in the presence of you all.

17. And now, brethren, I wot that through ignorance ye did it, as did also your rulers.

18. But those things, which God before had shewed by the mouth of all his prophets, that Christ should suffer, he hath so fulfilled.

19. ¶ Repent ye therefore, and be converted, that your sins may be blotted out, when the times of refreshing shall come from the presence of the Lord;

20. And he shall send Jesus Christ, which before was preached unto you:

21. Whom the heaven must receive until the times of restitution of all things, which God hath spoken by the mouth of all his holy prophets since the world began.

22. For Moses truly said unto the fathers, A prophet shall the Lord your God raise up unto you of your brethren, like unto me; him shall ye hear in all things whatsoever he shall say unto you.

23. And it shall come to pass, that every soul, which will not hear that prophet, shall be destroyed from among the people.

24. Yea, and all the prophets from Samuel and those that follow after, as many as have spoken, have likewise foretold of these days.

25. Ye are the children of the prophets, and of the covenant which

Acts 3:19–21 — Peter and his associates had witnessed to miracle after miracle performed at the hands of the Master, including extraordinary healings. They had been schooled on the power of the priesthood invested and applied for the blessing of the faithful. It was now their moment to rise in majesty following the munificent tutelage of the Master Teacher and assume the leadership of the kingdom as His representatives on the earth. On their way to the temple, Peter and John passed near a man begging for his keep, having come into the world lame and crippled. When he saw the two Apostles, he beckoned to them for help. The well-known account found in Acts 3:4–8 never fails to kindle the flame of wonder at the power of faith and the benevolence of God.

The people who witnessed this miracle were astonished beyond measure. Peter took the occasion to render praise unto the Lord and bear witness of His divine calling. Whereas the crippled man had been liberated from his physical infirmities, Peter now called upon the people to be liberated from the shackles of their sins through the power of the Atonement. This doctrine he expressed in the famous words of verses 19–21 that anticipate the Restoration of the gospel in latter days, when the Redeemer would again return.

Acts 3:21 — The "times of restitution of all things" about which Peter spoke following the ascension of Christ, as spoken of in this verse, are *now*. The Restoration of the gospel has been accomplished in our day, involving, among other heavenly messengers, "Peter, and James, and John, whom I have sent to you, by whom I have ordained you and confirmed you to be apostles, and especial witnesses of my name, and bear the keys of your ministry and of the same things which I revealed unto them" (D&C 27:12). The same commission given by the Savior to His former Apostles has devolved, by modern-day revelation, upon us. Through the ultimate confirming witness of the Holy Ghost and the application of spiritual gifts bestowed upon the faithful, we can accomplish miracles by proclaiming the gospel with conviction and boldness and building up the kingdom of God in all of its glory.

God made with our fathers, saying unto Abraham, And in thy seed shall all the kindreds of the earth be blessed.

26. Unto you first God, having raised up his Son Jesus, sent him to bless you, in turning away every one of you from his iniquities.

CHAPTER 4

1. And as they spake unto the people, the priests, and the captain of the temple, and the Sadducees, came upon them,

2. Being grieved that they taught the people, and preached through Jesus the resurrection from the dead.

3. And they laid hands on them, and put them in hold unto the next day: for it was now eventide.

4. Howbeit many of them which heard the word believed; and the number of the men was about five thousand.

5. ¶ And it came to pass on the morrow, that their rulers, and elders, and scribes,

6. And Annas the high priest, and Caiaphas, and John, and Alexander, and as many as were of the kindred of the high priest, were gathered together at Jerusalem.

7. And when they had set them in the midst, they asked, By what power, or by what name, have ye done this?

8. Then Peter, filled with the Holy Ghost, said unto them, Ye rulers of the people, and elders of Israel,

9. If we this day be examined of the good deed done to the impotent man, by what means he is made whole;

10. Be it known unto you all, and to all the people of Israel, that by the name of Jesus Christ of Nazareth, whom ye crucified, whom God raised from the dead, even by him doth this man stand here before you whole.

11. This is the stone which was set at nought of you builders, which is become the head of the corner.

12. Neither is there salvation in any other: for there is none other name under heaven given among men, whereby we must be saved.

13. ¶ Now when they saw the boldness of Peter and John, and perceived that they were unlearned and ignorant men, they marvelled; and they took knowledge of them, that they had been with Jesus.

14. And beholding the man which was healed standing with them, they could say nothing against it.

15. But when they had commanded them to go aside out of the council, they conferred among themselves,

16. Saying, What shall we do to these men? for that indeed a notable miracle hath been done by them is manifest to all them that dwell in Jerusalem; and we cannot deny it.

17. But that it spread no further among the people, let us straitly threaten them, that they speak henceforth to no man in this name.

18. And they called them, and commanded them not to speak at all nor teach in the name of Jesus.

19. But Peter and John answered and said unto them, Whether it be

Acts 4:8–12—The Apostles set a glorious example of faith and courage as they sought to obey God and preach of the Lord Jesus Christ. When the priests and elders confronted Peter, demanding by what power or name he had healed the crippled man near the temple, it was the chief Apostle's turn to step forward fearlessly, as he did here. When the elders then commanded Peter and his colleagues to refrain from any ministry in the name of Christ, they steadfastly refused to comply and continued apace with their proselyting work (see Acts 4:33).

Notes: _____

_____

_____

_____

_____

_____

_____

_____

_____

_____

_____

_____

_____

_____

right in the sight of God to hearken unto you more than unto God, judge ye.

20. For we cannot but speak the things which we have seen and heard.

21. So when they had further threatened them, they let them go, finding nothing how they might punish them, because of the people: for all men glorified God for that which was done.

22. For the man was above forty years old, on whom this miracle of healing was shewed.

23. ¶ And being let go, they went to their own company, and reported all that the chief priests and elders had said unto them.

24. And when they heard that, they lifted up their voice to God with one accord, and said, Lord, thou art God, which hast made heaven, and earth, and the sea, and all that in them is:

25. Who by the mouth of thy servant David hast said, Why did the heathen rage, and the people imagine vain things?

26. The kings of the earth stood up, and the rulers were gathered together against the Lord, and against his Christ.

27. For of a truth against thy holy child Jesus, whom thou hast anointed, both Herod, and Pontius Pilate, with the Gentiles, and the people of Israel, were gathered together,

28. For to do whatsoever thy hand and thy counsel determined before to be done.

29. And now, Lord, behold their threatenings: and grant unto thy servants, that with all boldness they may speak thy word,

30. By stretching forth thine hand to heal; and that signs and wonders may be done by the name of thy holy child Jesus.

31. ¶ And when they had prayed, the place was shaken where they were assembled together; and they were all filled with the Holy Ghost, and they spake the word of God with boldness.

32. And the multitude of them that believed were of one heart and of one soul: neither said any of them that ought of the things which he possessed was his own; but they had all things common.

33. And with great power gave the apostles witness of the resurrection of the Lord Jesus: and great grace was upon them all.

34. Neither was there any among them that lacked: for as many as were possessors of lands or houses sold them, and brought the prices of the things that were sold,

35. And laid them down at the apostles' feet: and distribution was made unto every man according as he had need.

36. And Joses, who by the apostles was surnamed Barnabas, (which is, being interpreted, The son of consolation,) a Levite, and of the country of Cyprus,

37. Having land, sold it, and brought the money, and laid it at the apostles' feet.

Acts 4:33—Luke's account of the Acts of the Apostles (an extension of the Gospel of Luke) confirms the courage and valor of the Apostles in moving forward with their commission to take the gospel to the entire world. When the Jewish leaders commanded Peter and his colleagues to refrain from any ministry in the name of Christ, they steadfastly refused to comply and continued undeterred with their proselyting work. Not even imprisonment or death could dissuade them from honoring the call issued to them by the Savior, for the angel of the Lord liberated them and commanded them to continue preaching the gospel in the temple (see Acts 5:19–39).

How do we overcome any fear we might have of preaching the gospel using boldness and love? We overcome fear through the "great grace" of the Lord, which sustains courage and strengthens our witness of the truth of the gospel. How have you experienced the "great grace" of the Lord in helping you put your shoulder to the wheel and participate in missionary work?

CHAPTER 5

1. But a certain man named Ananias, with Sapphira his wife, sold a possession,

2. And kept back part of the price, his wife also being privy to it, and brought a certain part, and laid it at the apostles' feet.

3. But Peter said, Ananias, why hath Satan filled thine heart to lie to the Holy Ghost, and to keep back part of the price of the land?

4. Whiles it remained, was it not thine own? and after it was sold, was it not in thine own power? why hast thou conceived this thing in thine heart? thou hast not lied unto men, but unto God.

5. And Ananias hearing these words fell down, and gave up the ghost: and great fear came on all them that heard these things.

6. And the young men arose, wound him up, and carried him out, and buried him.

7. And it was about the space of three hours after, when his wife, not knowing what was done, came in.

8. And Peter answered unto her, Tell me whether ye sold the land for so much? And she said, Yea, for so much.

9. Then Peter said unto her, How is it that ye have agreed together to tempt the Spirit of the Lord? behold, the feet of them which have buried thy husband are at the door, and shall carry thee out.

10. Then fell she down straightway at his feet, and yielded up the ghost: and the young men came in, and found her dead, and, carrying her forth, buried her by her husband.

11. And great fear came upon all the church, and upon as many as heard these things.

12. ¶ And by the hands of the apostles were many signs and wonders wrought among the people; (and they were all with one accord in Solomon's porch.

13. And of the rest durst no man join himself to them: but the people magnified them.

14. And believers were the more added to the Lord, multitudes both of men and women.)

15. Insomuch that they brought forth the sick into the streets, and laid them on beds and couches, that at the least the shadow of Peter passing by might overshadow some of them.

16. There came also a multitude out of the cities round about unto Jerusalem, bringing sick folks, and them which were vexed with unclean spirits: and they were healed every one.

17. ¶ Then the high priest rose up, and all they that were with him, (which is the sect of the Sadducees,) and were filled with indignation,

18. And laid their hands on the apostles, and put them in the common prison.

19. But the angel of the Lord by night opened the prison doors, and brought them forth, and said,

20. Go, stand and speak in the temple to the people all the words of this life.

21. And when they heard that, they entered into the temple early in the morning, and taught. But the high priest came, and they that were with him, and called the council together, and all the senate of the children of Israel and sent to the prison to have them brought.

22. But when the officers came, and found them not in the prison, they returned, and told,

23. Saying, The prison truly found we shut with all safety, and the keepers standing without before the

Distribution of Alms and Death of Ananias

Acts 5:19–20—Not even imprisonment could dissuade Peter and his colleagues from honoring the call issued to them by the Savior, for the angel of the Lord liberated them and commanded them to continue preaching the gospel in the temple.

doors: but when we had opened, we found no man within.

24. Now when the high priest and the captain of the temple and the chief priests heard these things, they doubted of them whereunto this would grow.

25. Then came one and told them, saying, Behold, the men whom ye put in prison are standing in the temple, and teaching the people.

26. Then went the captain with the officers, and brought them without violence: for they feared the people, lest they should have been stoned.

27. And when they had brought them, they set them before the council: and the high priest asked them,

28. Saying, Did not we straitly command you that ye should not teach in this name? and, behold, ye have filled Jerusalem with your doctrine, and intend to bring this man's blood upon us.

29. ¶ Then Peter and the other apostles answered and said, We ought to obey God rather than men.

30. The God of our fathers raised up Jesus, whom ye slew and hanged on a tree.

31. Him hath God exalted with his right hand to be a Prince and a Saviour, for to give repentance to Israel, and forgiveness of sins.

32. And we are his witnesses of these things; and so is also the Holy Ghost, whom God hath given to them that obey him.

33. ¶ When they heard that, they were cut to the heart, and took counsel to slay them.

34. Then stood there up one in the council, a Pharisee, named Gamaliel, a doctor of the law, had in reputation among all the people, and commanded to put the apostles forth a little space;

35. And said unto them, Ye men of Israel, take heed to yourselves what ye intend to do as touching these men.

36. For before these days rose up Theudas, boasting himself to be somebody; to whom a number of men, about four hundred, joined themselves: who was slain; and all, as many as obeyed him, were scattered, and brought to nought.

37. After this man rose up Judas of Galilee in the days of the taxing, and drew away much people after him: he also perished; and all, even as many as obeyed him, were dispersed.

38. And now I say unto you, Refrain from these men, and let them alone: for if this counsel or this work be of men, it will come to nought:

39. But if it be of God, ye cannot overthrow it; lest haply ye be found even to fight against God.

40. And to him they agreed: and when they had called the apostles, and beaten them, they commanded that they should not speak in the name of Jesus, and let them go.

41. ¶ And they departed from the presence of the council, rejoicing that they were counted worthy to suffer shame for his name.

42. And daily in the temple, and in every house, they ceased not to teach and preach Jesus Christ.

Acts 5:29—We should always seek to obey God as Peter and the Apostles did. They were full of the Spirit and feared no man. The Lord will give us strength to do all things that He would have us do.

Acts 5:38–39— In response to threats from the authorities, Peter—the same one who had thrice denied the Savior on the eve of the Crucifixion—now unflinchingly and courageously declared: "We ought to obey God rather than men. The God of our fathers raised up Jesus, whom ye slew and hanged on a tree. Him hath God exalted with his right hand to be a Prince and a Saviour, for to give repentance to Israel, and forgiveness of sins. And we are his witnesses of these things; and so is also the Holy Ghost, whom God hath given to them that obey him" (Acts 5:29–32). At this point, it took the counsel of the Pharisee Gamaliel to dissuade his colleagues from executing the Apostles, saying, with more truth than he realized: "Let them alone: for if this counsel or this work be of men, it will come to naught: But if it be of God, ye cannot overthrow it" (Acts 5:38–39).

By following the Spirit as we open our mouths—boldly yet humbly—we can truly serve as willing and effective servants of the Lord in helping to build the kingdom of God. Just as the Apostles of old who followed the Savior's commission to carry the gospel to all peoples, we can venture forth—each member a missionary—to share the truths of the Restoration, for "it is necessary and expedient in me that you should open your mouths in proclaiming my gospel, the things of the kingdom, expounding the mysteries thereof out of the scriptures, according to that portion of Spirit and power which shall be given unto you, even as I will" (D&C 71:1).

CHAPTER 6

1. And in those days, when the number of the disciples was multiplied, there arose a murmuring of the Grecians against the Hebrews, because their widows were neglected in the daily ministration.

2. Then the twelve called the multitude of the disciples unto them, and said, It is not reason that we should leave the word of God, and serve tables.

3. Wherefore, brethren, look ye out among you seven men of honest report, full of the Holy Ghost and wisdom, whom we may appoint over this business.

4. But we will give ourselves continually to prayer, and to the ministry of the word.

5. ¶ And the saying pleased the whole multitude: and they chose Stephen, a man full of faith and of the Holy Ghost, and Philip, and Prochorus, and Nicanor, and Timon, and Parmenas, and Nicolas a proselyte of Antioch:

6. Whom they set before the apostles: and when they had prayed, they laid their hands on them.

7. And the word of God increased; and the number of the disciples multiplied in Jerusalem greatly; and a great company of the priests were obedient to the faith.

8. And Stephen, full of faith and power, did great wonders and miracles among the people.

9. ¶ Then there arose certain of the synagogue, which is called the synagogue of the Libertines, and Cyrenians, and Alexandrians, and of them of Cilicia and of Asia, disputing with Stephen.

10. And they were not able to resist the wisdom and the spirit by which he spake.

11. Then they suborned men, which said, We have heard him speak blasphemous words against Moses, and against God.

12. And they stirred up the people, and the elders, and the scribes, and came upon him, and caught him, and brought him to the council,

13. And set up false witnesses, which said, This man ceaseth not to speak blasphemous words against this holy place, and the law:

14. For we have heard him say, that this Jesus of Nazareth shall destroy this place, and shall change the customs which Moses delivered us.

15. And all that sat in the council, looking stedfastly on him, saw his face as it had been the face of an angel.

CHAPTER 7

1. Then said the high priest, Are these things so?

2. And he said, Men, brethren, and fathers, hearken; The God of glory appeared unto our father Abraham, when he was in Mesopotamia, before he dwelt in Charran,

3. And said unto him, Get thee out of thy country, and from thy kindred,

Acts 6:3— The business to which these seven were primarily assigned was ministering to the widows and their needs. However, every person is needed to build up the kingdom within his or her sphere of responsibility and influence.

Acts 6:3–4—The commission of the Savior to His Apostles was "Go ye therefore, and teach all nations, baptizing them in the name of the Father, and of the Son, and of the Holy Ghost" (Matt. 28:19). As the circle of adherents in the growing kingdom expanded, there was a concomitant expansion in the need to provide services to the flock, especially for groups such as the widows. As a result, the Apostles called for additional workers to assist in the cause: "Wherefore, brethren, look ye out among you seven men of honest report, full of the Holy Ghost and wisdom, whom we may appoint over this business" (Acts 6:3). The seven who were commissioned for the administration of services were these: Stephen ("a man full of faith and of the Holy Ghost"—Acts 6:5), Philip, Prochorus, Nicanor, Timon, Parmenas, and Nicolas. In this way, the first expansion in Church leadership was accomplished, allowing the Apostles to continue with their special calling for "the ministry of the word" (Acts 6:4).

and come into the land which I shall shew thee.

4. Then came he out of the land of the Chaldæans, and dwelt in Charran: and from thence, when his father was dead, he removed him into this land, wherein ye now dwell.

5. And he gave him none inheritance in it, no, not so much as to set his foot on: yet he promised that he would give it to him for a possession, and to his seed after him, when as yet he had no child.

6. And God spake on this wise, That his seed should sojourn in a strange land; and that they should bring them into bondage, and entreat them evil four hundred years.

7. And the nation to whom they shall be in bondage will I judge, said God: and after that shall they come forth, and serve me in this place.

8. And he gave him the covenant of circumcision: and so Abraham begat Isaac, and circumcised him the eighth day; and Isaac begat Jacob; and Jacob begat the twelve patriarchs.

9. And the patriarchs, moved with envy, sold Joseph into Egypt: but God was with him,

10. And delivered him out of all his afflictions, and gave him favour and wisdom in the sight of Pharaoh king of Egypt; and he made him governor over Egypt and all his house.

11. Now there came a dearth over all the land of Egypt and Chanaan, and great affliction: and our fathers found no sustenance.

12. But when Jacob heard that there was corn in Egypt, he sent out our fathers first.

13. And at the second time Joseph was made known to his brethren; and Joseph's kindred was made known unto Pharaoh.

14. Then sent Joseph, and called his father Jacob to him, and all his kindred, threescore and fifteen souls.

15. So Jacob went down into Egypt, and died, he, and our fathers,

16. And were carried over into Sychem, and laid in the sepulchre that Abraham bought for a sum of money of the sons of Emmor the father of Sychem.

17. But when the time of the promise drew nigh, which God had sworn to Abraham, the people grew and multiplied in Egypt,

18. Till another king arose, which knew not Joseph.

19. The same dealt subtilly with our kindred, and evil entreated our fathers, so that they cast out their young children, to the end they might not live.

20. In which time Moses was born, and was exceeding fair, and nourished up in his father's house three months:

21. And when he was cast out, Pharaoh's daughter took him up, and nourished him for her own son.

22. And Moses was learned in all the wisdom of the Egyptians, and was mighty in words and in deeds.

23. And when he was full forty years old, it came into his heart to visit his brethren the children of Israel.

24. And seeing one of them suffer wrong, he defended him, and avenged him that was oppressed, and smote the Egyptian:

25. For he supposed his brethren would have understood how that

Acts 6:15–8:39— The callous and sinister conspiracy among certain of the priests and elders to thwart the mission of the Savior was quickly extended to His followers in the faith. In the case of Stephen, one of the newly called group of seven administrators and assistants to the Twelve, the leaders of the synagogue advanced charges of blasphemy, which they supported through the testimony of false witnesses. As Stephen was brought before the council to answer to these charges of subverting the ways of Moses, a miraculous transformation in his appearance took place: "And all that sat in the council, looking steadfastly on him, saw his face as it had been the face of an angel" (Acts 6:15). It was in this transfigured state that Stephen delivered his inspired and powerful discourse on the history of God's dealings with the covenant people of Abraham, including the service of Moses in bringing about the deliverance from Egypt and prophesying of a future leader of the people: "A prophet shall the Lord your God raise up unto you of your brethren, like unto me; him shall ye hear" (Acts 7:37; compare Deut. 18:15).

Who was this prophet? It was Jesus Christ, declared Stephen to his detractors, "the Just One; of whom ye have been now the betrayers and murderers" (Acts 7:52). To this direct and bold accusation, the priests and elders responded by casting Stephen out of the city and stoning him to death (Acts 7:58). One of the participants in this egregious act was the young Saul of Tarsus.

Meanwhile, Philip, an associate of Stephen among the seven assistants, went down to Samaria, preaching Christ and performing mighty miracles (Acts 8:5–8). Soon thereafter, an angel of the Lord spoke to him and commanded him to go south from Jerusalem toward Gaza, where he encountered an emissary from the court of Queen Candace of Ethiopia. This eunuch was traveling in his chariot studying the section in the writings of Isaiah which reads in the King James version as follows: "He was oppressed, and he was afflicted, yet he opened not his mouth: he is brought as a lamb to the slaughter, and as a sheep before her shearers is dumb, so he openeth not his mouth. He was taken from prison and from judgment: and who shall declare his generation? for he was cut off out of the land of the living: for the transgression of my people was he stricken" (Isa. 53:7–8). When the eunuch inquired of Philip what this passage meant, Philip unfolded to him with great persuasion the ministry of the Savior. As a result, when they came to a body of water, the eunuch asked to be baptized (see Acts 8:37–39).

God by his hand would deliver them: but they understood not.

26. And the next day he shewed himself unto them as they strove, and would have set them at one again, saying, Sirs, ye are brethren; why do ye wrong one to another?

27. But he that did his neighbour wrong thrust him away, saying, Who made thee a ruler and a judge over us?

28. Wilt thou kill me, as thou diddest the Egyptian yesterday?

29. Then fled Moses at this saying, and was a stranger in the land of Madian, where he begat two sons.

30. And when forty years were expired, there appeared to him in the wilderness of mount Sina an angel of the Lord in a flame of fire in a bush.

31. When Moses saw it, he wondered at the sight: and as he drew near to behold it, the voice of the Lord came unto him,

32. Saying, I am the God of thy fathers, the God of Abraham, and the God of Isaac, and the God of Jacob. Then Moses trembled, and durst not behold.

33. Then said the Lord to him, Put off thy shoes from thy feet: for the place where thou standest is holy ground.

34. I have seen, I have seen the affliction of my people which is in Egypt, and I have heard their groaning, and am come down to deliver them. And now come, I will send thee into Egypt.

35. This Moses whom they refused, saying, Who made thee a ruler and a judge? the same did God send to be a ruler and a deliverer by the hand of the angel which appeared to him in the bush.

36. He brought them out, after that he had shewed wonders and signs in the land of Egypt, and in the Red sea, and in the wilderness forty years.

37. ¶ This is that Moses, which said unto the children of Israel, A prophet shall the Lord your God raise up unto you of your brethren, like unto me; him shall ye hear.

38. This is he, that was in the church in the wilderness with the angel which spake to him in the mount Sina, and with our fathers: who received the lively oracles to give unto us:

39. To whom our fathers would not obey, but thrust him from them, and in their hearts turned back again into Egypt,

40. Saying unto Aaron, Make us gods to go before us: for as for this Moses, which brought us out of the land of Egypt, we wot not what is become of him.

41. And they made a calf in those days, and offered sacrifice unto the idol, and rejoiced in the works of their own hands.

42. Then God turned, and gave them up to worship the host of heaven; as it is written in the book of the prophets, O ye house of Israel, have ye offered to me slain beasts and sacrifices by the space of forty years in the wilderness?

43. Yea, ye took up the tabernacle of Moloch, and the star of your god Remphan, figures which ye made to worship them: and I will carry you away beyond Babylon.

44. Our fathers had the tabernacle of witness in the wilderness, as he had appointed, speaking unto Moses, that he should make it according to the fashion that he had seen.

45. Which also our fathers that came after brought in with Jesus

Moses saving the children of Israel

into the possession of the Gentiles, whom God drave out before the face of our fathers, unto the days of David;

46. Who found favour before God, and desired to find a tabernacle for the God of Jacob.

47. But Solomon built him an house.

48. Howbeit the most High dwelleth not in temples made with hands; as saith the prophet,

49. Heaven is my throne, and earth is my footstool: what house will ye build me? saith the Lord: or what is the place of my rest?

50. Hath not my hand made all these things?

51. ¶ Ye stiffnecked and uncircumcised in heart and ears, ye do always resist the Holy Ghost: as your fathers did, so do ye.

52. Which of the prophets have not your fathers persecuted? and they have slain them which shewed before of the coming of the Just One; of whom ye have been now the betrayers and murderers:

53. Who have received the law by the disposition of angels, and have not kept it.

54. ¶ When they heard these things, they were cut to the heart, and they gnashed on him with their teeth.

55. But he, being full of the Holy Ghost, looked up stedfastly into heaven, and saw the glory of God, and Jesus standing on the right hand of God,

56. And said, Behold, I see the heavens opened, and the Son of man standing on the right hand of God.

57. Then they cried out with a loud voice, and stopped their ears, and ran upon him with one accord,

58. And cast him out of the city, and stoned him: and the witnesses laid down their clothes at a young man's feet, whose name was Saul.

59. And they stoned Stephen, calling upon God, and saying, Lord Jesus, receive my spirit.

60. And he kneeled down, and cried with a loud voice, Lord, lay not this sin to their charge. And when he had said this, he fell asleep.

CHAPTER 8

1. And Saul was consenting unto his death. And at that time there was a great persecution against the church which was at Jerusalem; and they were all scattered abroad

Acts 7:54–60 — It is our lot to be vigilant and watchful in standing on principle and guarding the truths of the gospel. Think of the courage and conviction of the Lord's Apostles in carrying on the work of the ministry with boldness and spiritual leadership following the Crucifixion, Resurrection, and Ascension of the Savior. Think of the fearless witness of Stephen — one of the seven newly called assistants to the Twelve — when he answered the council's charges of blasphemy and willingly gave his life to seal his testimony. These valiant heroes of truth were acting to secure and protect the work of building up the kingdom of God. They were continuing the work of so many prophets and leaders from earlier dispensations.

One example of stalwart vigilance from the Old Testament is Nehemiah, who contributed much toward the consolidation of covenant society by leading the movement to restore the protective walls of Jerusalem after the Babylonian conquest. An influential "cupbearer" at the court of King Artaxerxes of Persia (465–425 B.C.; see Neh. 1:11), Nehemiah was moved by the accounts of the sufferings of his compatriots at Jerusalem and launched a major campaign to come to their assistance for the purpose of restoring the security of the city. For twelve years, he labored as governor — against daunting odds and life-threatening plots by enemy forces — to complete the walls of the city: "They which builded on the wall, and they that bare burdens, with those that laded, every one with one of his hands wrought in the work, and with the other hand held a weapon" (Neh. 4:17). Thus Nehemiah, like his contemporary, Ezra, has left us a stirring example of restoration, rebuilding, fortifying, strengthening, renewing — all to the glory of God and the service of establishing His kingdom upon the earth.

Acts 7:60 — The righteousness of Stephen was exhibited by his willingness to forgive and not lay this sin upon them. Indeed, the attitude of mercy and forgiveness comes back to all who truly act in this manner (see Matt. 5:7; Luke 6:13). It should be our goal to show mercy and forgiveness, which is the ultimate display of charity.

throughout the regions of Judæa and Samaria, except the apostles.

2. And devout men carried Stephen to his burial, and made great lamentation over him.

3. As for Saul, he made havock of the church, entering into every house, and haling men and women committed them to prison.

4. Therefore they that were scattered abroad went every where preaching the word.

5. Then Philip went down to the city of Samaria, and preached Christ unto them.

6. And the people with one accord gave heed unto those things which Philip spake, hearing and seeing the miracles which he did.

7. For unclean spirits, crying with loud voice, came out of many that were possessed with them: and many taken with palsies, and that were lame, were healed.

8. And there was great joy in that city.

9. But there was a certain man, called Simon, which beforetime in the same city used sorcery, and bewitched the people of Samaria, giving out that himself was some great one:

10. To whom they all gave heed, from the least to the greatest, saying, This man is the great power of God.

11. And to him they had regard, because that of long time he had bewitched them with sorceries.

12. But when they believed Philip preaching the things concerning the kingdom of God, and the name of Jesus Christ, they were baptized, both men and women.

13. Then Simon himself believed also: and when he was baptized, he continued with Philip, and wondered, beholding the miracles and signs which were done.

14. Now when the apostles which were at Jerusalem heard that Samaria had received the word of God, they sent unto them Peter and John:

15. Who, when they were come down, prayed for them, that they might receive the Holy Ghost:

16. (For as yet he was fallen upon none of them: only they were baptized in the name of the Lord Jesus.)

17. Then laid they their hands on them, and they received the Holy Ghost.

18. And when Simon saw that through laying on of the apostles' hands the Holy Ghost was given, he offered them money,

19. Saying, Give me also this power, that on whomsoever I lay hands, he may receive the Holy Ghost.

20. But Peter said unto him, Thy money perish with thee, because thou hast thought that the gift of God may be purchased with money.

21. Thou hast neither part nor lot in this matter: for thy heart is not right in the sight of God.

22. Repent therefore of this thy wickedness, and pray God, if perhaps the thought of thine heart may be forgiven thee.

23. For I perceive that thou art in the gall of bitterness, and in the bond of iniquity.

The Jordan River

24. Then answered Simon, and said, Pray ye to the Lord for me, that none of these things which ye have spoken come upon me.

25. And they, when they had testified and preached the word of the Lord, returned to Jerusalem, and preached the gospel in many villages of the Samaritans.

26. And the angel of the Lord spake unto Philip, saying, Arise, and go toward the south unto the way that goeth down from Jerusalem unto Gaza, which is desert.

27. And he arose and went: and, behold, a man of Ethiopia, an eunuch of great authority under Candace queen of the Ethiopians, who had the charge of all her treasure, and had come to Jerusalem for to worship,

28. Was returning, and sitting in his chariot read Esaias the prophet.

29. Then the Spirit said unto Philip, Go near, and join thyself to this chariot.

30. And Philip ran thither to him, and heard him read the prophet Esaias, and said, Understandest thou what thou readest?

31. And he said, How can I, except some man should guide me? And he desired Philip that he would come up and sit with him.

32. The place of the scripture which he read was this, He was led as a sheep to the slaughter; and like a lamb dumb before his shearer, so opened he not his mouth:

33. In his humiliation his judgment was taken away: and who shall declare his generation? for his life is taken from the earth.

34. And the eunuch answered Philip, and said, I pray thee, of whom speaketh the prophet this? of himself, or of some other man?

35. Then Philip opened his mouth, and began at the same scripture, and preached unto him Jesus.

36. And as they went on their way, they came unto a certain water: and the eunuch said, See, here is water; what doth hinder me to be baptized?

37. And Philip said, If thou believest with all thine heart, thou mayest. And he answered and said, I believe that Jesus Christ is the Son of God.

38. And he commanded the chariot to stand still: and they went down both into the water, both Philip and the eunuch; and he baptized him.

39. And when they were come up out of the water, the Spirit of the Lord caught away Philip, that the eunuch saw him no more: and he went on his way rejoicing.

40. But Philip was found at Azotus: and passing through he preached in all the cities, till he came to Cæsarea.

CHAPTER 9

1. And Saul, yet breathing out threatenings and slaughter against the disciples of the Lord, went unto the high priest,

2. And desired of him letters to Damascus to the synagogues, that if he found any of this way, whether they were men or women, he might bring them bound unto Jerusalem.

3. And as he journeyed, he came near Damascus: and suddenly there shined round about him a light from heaven:

4. And he fell to the earth, and heard a voice saying unto him, Saul, Saul, why persecutest thou me?

Acts 9:1—Saul of Tarsus, who participated in the stoning of Stephen, is characterized in the scriptural account as one "breathing out threatenings and slaughter against the disciples of the Lord" (Acts 9:1). In his own words, he recalled: "And I persecuted this way unto the death, binding and delivering into prisons both men and women" (Acts 22:4). Before Agrippa, Saul confessed: "And many of the saints did I shut up in prison, having received authority from the chief priests; and when they were put to death, I gave my voice against them" (Acts 26:10). Saul was clearly no friend to the Saints of his day, using his influence, knowledge, and strategy in every way possible to contravene the work of the kingdom. But the Lord knew his soul and his potential—that he was destined to be a mighty tool for carrying the gospel message to many nations with authority and great spiritual power. Thus as he was journeying one day to Damascus to continue his campaign against the Christians, he experienced a most unexpected encounter (see Acts 26:13–16).

As a result, Saul went through a dramatic and miraculous conversion—emerging from the experience as Paul, an Apostle of the Lord who performed extraordinary missionary labors to build the kingdom of God.

In a similar manner, a century and half earlier on the distant American continent, Alma, son of the high priest Alma, experienced a dramatic intervention by an angel of the Lord sent to call him and his colleagues to repentance for their concerted efforts to destroy the Church of God (see Mosiah 27:11–16). From this life-changing event, the young Alma went forward with a commission to become one of the greatest of the Lord's prophets in effecting a mighty change for good in the hearts of the people.

5. And he said, Who art thou, Lord? And the Lord said, I am Jesus whom thou persecutest: it is hard for thee to kick against the pricks.

6. And he trembling and astonished said, Lord, what wilt thou have me to do? And the Lord said unto him, Arise, and go into the city, and it shall be told thee what thou must do.

7. And the men which journeyed with him stood speechless, hearing a voice, but seeing no man.

8. And Saul arose from the earth; and when his eyes were opened, he saw no man: but they led him by the hand, and brought him into Damascus.

9. And he was three days without sight, and neither did eat nor drink.

10. ¶ And there was a certain disciple at Damascus, named Ananias; and to him said the Lord in a vision, Ananias. And he said, Behold, I am here, Lord.

11. And the Lord said unto him, Arise, and go into the street which is called Straight, and inquire in the house of Judas for one called Saul, of Tarsus: for, behold, he prayeth,

12. And hath seen in a vision a man named Ananias coming in, and putting his hand on him, that he might receive his sight.

13. Then Ananias answered, Lord, I have heard by many of this man, how much evil he hath done to thy saints at Jerusalem:

14. And here he hath authority from the chief priests to bind all that call on thy name.

15. But the Lord said unto him, Go thy way: for he is a chosen vessel unto me, to bear my name before the Gentiles, and kings, and the children of Israel:

16. For I will shew him how great things he must suffer for my name's sake.

17. And Ananias went his way, and entered into the house; and putting his hands on him said, Brother Saul, the Lord, even Jesus, that appeared unto thee in the way as thou camest, hath sent me, that thou mightest receive thy sight, and be filled with the Holy Ghost.

18. And immediately there fell from his eyes as it had been scales: and he received sight forthwith, and arose, and was baptized.

19. And when he had received meat, he was strengthened. Then was Saul certain days with the disciples which were at Damascus.

20. And straightway he preached Christ in the synagogues, that he is the Son of God.

21. But all that heard him were amazed, and said; Is not this he that destroyed them which called on this name in Jerusalem, and came hither for that intent, that he might bring them bound unto the chief priests?

22. But Saul increased the more in strength, and confounded the Jews which dwelt at Damascus, proving that this is very Christ.

23. ¶ And after that many days were fulfilled, the Jews took counsel to kill him:

24. But their laying await was

Acts 9—Elder James E. Talmage describes the conversion of Saul and his work as he completed the marvelous transition from enemy of God to emissary of truth:

"The sudden change of heart by which an ardent persecutor of the saints was so transformed as to become a true disciple, is to the average mind a miracle. Saul of Tarsus was a devoted student and observer of the law, a strict Pharisee. We find no intimation that he ever met or saw Jesus during the Lord's life in the flesh; and his contact with the Christian movement appears to have been brought about through disputation with Stephen. In determining what he would call right and what wrong the young enthusiast was guided too much by mind and too little by heart. His learning, which should have been his servant, was instead his master. He was a leading spirit in the cruel persecution of the first converts to Christianity; yet none can doubt his belief that even in such he was rendering service to Jehovah (compare John 16:2). His unusual energy and superb ability were misdirected. As soon as he realized the error of his course, he turned about, without counting risk, cost, or the certainty of persecution and probable martyrdom. His repentance was as genuine as had been his persecuting zeal. All through his ministry he was tortured by the past (Acts 22:4, 19, 20; 1 Cor. 15:9; 2 Cor. 12:7; Gal. 1:13); yet he found a measure of relief in the knowledge that he had acted in good conscience (Acts 26:9–11). It was 'hard for him to kick against the pricks' (revised version 'goad,' Acts 9:5; 26:14) of tradition, training, and education; yet he hesitated not. He was a chosen instrument for the work of the Lord (Acts 9:15); and promptly he responded to the Master's will. Whatever error Saul of Tarsus had committed through youthful zeal, Paul the apostle gave his all—his time, talent, and life—to expiate" (*Jesus the Christ,* 667–68).

Acts 9:6—Paul had a revelation from the Lord and he responded with these clarion words, "Lord, what wilt thou have me do?" He had been called to repentance. The key to repentance and conversion is turning one's will over to the Lord. When we are truly converted, we have a desire to do good continually (see Mosiah 5:2), we strengthen our brothers and sisters (see Luke 22:32), we have a concern for the welfare of our brothers and sisters (see Enos 1:9, 11; Mosiah 28:3), and we truly seek to do the will of the Lord.

known of Saul. And they watched the gates day and night to kill him.

25. Then the disciples took him by night, and let him down by the wall in a basket.

26. And when Saul was come to Jerusalem, he assayed to join himself to the disciples: but they were all afraid of him, and believed not that he was a disciple.

27. But Barnabas took him, and brought him to the apostles, and declared unto them how he had seen the Lord in the way, and that he had spoken to him, and how he had preached boldly at Damascus in the name of Jesus.

28. And he was with them coming in and going out at Jerusalem.

29. And he spake boldly in the name of the Lord Jesus, and disputed against the Grecians: but they went about to slay him.

30. Which when the brethren knew, they brought him down to Cæsarea, and sent him forth to Tarsus.

31. Then had the churches rest throughout all Judæa and Galilee and Samaria, and were edified; and walking in the fear of the Lord, and in the comfort of the Holy Ghost, were multiplied.

32. ¶ And it came to pass, as Peter passed throughout all quarters, he came down also to the saints which dwelt at Lydda.

33. And there he found a certain man named Æneas, which had kept his bed eight years, and was sick of the palsy.

34. And Peter said unto him, Æneas, Jesus Christ maketh thee whole: arise, and make thy bed. And he arose immediately.

35. And all that dwelt at Lydda and Saron saw him, and turned to the Lord.

36. ¶ Now there was at Joppa a certain disciple named Tabitha, which by interpretation is called Dorcas: this woman was full of good works and almsdeeds which she did.

37. And it came to pass in those days, that she was sick, and died: whom when they had washed, they laid her in an upper chamber.

38. And forasmuch as Lydda was nigh to Joppa, and the disciples had heard that Peter was there, they sent unto him two men, desiring him that he would not delay to come to them.

39. Then Peter arose and went with them. When he was come, they brought him into the upper chamber: and all the widows stood by him weeping, and shewing the coats and garments which Dorcas made, while she was with them.

40. But Peter put them all forth, and kneeled down, and prayed; and turning him to the body said, Tabitha, arise. And she opened her eyes: and when she saw Peter, she sat up.

41. And he gave her his hand, and lifted her up, and when he had called the saints and widows, presented her alive.

42. And it was known throughout all Joppa; and many believed in the Lord.

43. And it came to pass, that he tarried many days in Joppa with one Simon a tanner.

CHAPTER 10

1. There was a certain man in Cæsarea called Cornelius, a centurion of the band called the Italian band,

2. A devout man, and one that feared God with all his house, which

Acts 10–14–The gospel of Jesus Christ was and is intended for all of God's children. We have been commanded to take the gospel to all the earth (see Mark 16:15; Morm. 9:22; D&C 39:15). The Lord has made it clear that we are to invite all to come unto Him: "And he doeth nothing save it be plain unto the children of men; and he inviteth them all to come unto him and partake of his goodness; and he denieth none that come unto him, black and white, bond and free, male and female; and he remembereth the heathen; and all are alike unto God, both Jew and Gentile" (2 Ne. 26:33). The Lord's servants have been blessed and are continually being blessed as they carry the message of Christ to all the world.

Since the beginning of time, the Lord has made known His gospel to His prophets through revelation. Continuous revelation is an eternal verity as it relates to the kingdom of God here upon the earth. We cannot operate the Lord's Church without His direction: "And I do this that I may prove unto many that I am the same yesterday, today, and forever; and that I speak forth my words according to mine own pleasure. And because that I have spoken one word ye need not suppose that I cannot speak another; for my work is not yet finished; neither shall it be until the end of man, neither from that time henceforth and forever" (2 Ne. 29:9). We see that the Lord will indeed reveal to mankind all that is necessary for our salvation and exaltation. The doctrine is clear: "We believe all that God has revealed, all that He does now reveal, and we believe that He will yet reveal many great and important things pertaining to the Kingdom of God" (A of F 1:9).

In addition, we know that the Holy Ghost reveals the truth to God's chosen servants and that the gifts of the Spirit are given to the faithful in rich abundance: "And I would exhort you, my beloved brethren, that ye remember that he is the same yesterday, today, and forever, and that all these gifts of which I have spoken, which are spiritual, never will be done away, even as long as the world shall stand, only according to the unbelief of the children of men" (Moro. 10:19). We learn that God's dealings with mankind are just and true and that He seeks our welfare above all else. Indeed, He is the same yesterday, today, and forever.

gave much alms to the people, and prayed to God alway.

3. He saw in a vision evidently about the ninth hour of the day an angel of God coming in to him, and saying unto him, Cornelius.

4. And when he looked on him, he was afraid, and said, What is it, Lord? And he said unto him, Thy prayers and thine alms are come up for a memorial before God.

5. And now send men to Joppa, and call for one Simon, whose surname is Peter:

6. He lodgeth with one Simon a tanner, whose house is by the sea side: he shall tell thee what thou oughtest to do.

7. And when the angel which spake unto Cornelius was departed, he called two of his household servants, and a devout soldier of them that waited on him continually;

8. And when he had declared all these things unto them, he sent them to Joppa.

9. ¶ On the morrow, as they went on their journey, and drew nigh unto the city, Peter went up upon the housetop to pray about the sixth hour:

10. And he became very hungry, and would have eaten: but while they made ready, he fell into a trance,

11. And saw heaven opened, and a certain vessel descending unto him, as it had been a great sheet knit at the four corners, and let down to the earth:

12. Wherein were all manner of fourfooted beasts of the earth, and wild beasts, and creeping things, and fowls of the air.

13. And there came a voice to him, Rise, Peter; kill, and eat.

14. But Peter said, Not so, Lord; for I have never eaten any thing that is common or unclean.

15. And the voice spake unto him again the second time, What God hath cleansed, that call not thou common.

16. This was done thrice: and the vessel was received up again into heaven.

17. Now while Peter doubted in himself what this vision which he had seen should mean, behold, the men which were sent from Cornelius had made inquiry for Simon's house, and stood before the gate,

18. And called, and asked whether Simon, which was surnamed Peter, were lodged there.

19. ¶ While Peter thought on the vision, the Spirit said unto him, Behold, three men seek thee.

20. Arise therefore, and get thee down, and go with them, doubting nothing: for I have sent them.

21. Then Peter went down to the men which were sent unto him from Cornelius; and said, Behold, I am he whom ye seek: what is the cause wherefore ye are come?

22. And they said, Cornelius the centurion, a just man, and one that feareth God, and of good report among all the nation of the Jews, was warned from God by an holy angel to send for thee into his house, and to hear words of thee.

23. Then called he them in, and lodged them. And on the morrow Peter went away with them, and certain brethren from Joppa accompanied him.

24. And the morrow after they entered into Cæsarea. And Cornelius waited for them, and had called together his kinsmen and near friends.

25. And as Peter was coming in, Cornelius met him, and fell down at his feet, and worshipped him.

26. But Peter took him up, saying, Stand up; I myself also am a man.

Acts 10 — Caesarea was an important Palestinian seaport community located about sixty miles northwest of Jerusalem on the main coastal road leading southward toward Egypt. The centurion Cornelius, of Gentile extraction, lived in Caesarea: "A devout man, and one that feared God with all his house, which gave much alms to the people, and prayed to God always" (Acts 10:2). An angel of the Lord appeared to Cornelius and bade him send to Joppa, a seaport to the north, to obtain counsel from Peter, who was staying there with Simon, the tanner. While the servants of Cornelius were underway, Peter received a manifestation from the Lord revealing to him that the time had come to preach the gospel of Jesus Christ to the Gentiles (see Acts 10:9–16). Thus Peter, moved upon by the Spirit, went with the servants of Cornelius and certain others from Joppa to Caesarea and met with the Gentile assemblage. The Apostle declared: "Of a truth I perceive that God is no respecter of persons: But in every nation he that feareth him, and worketh righteousness, is accepted with him" (Acts 10:34–35). As Peter proclaimed the gospel of Jesus Christ, the Holy Ghost fell on the audience of believers — an astounding extension of God's blessings to His non-Jewish flock (Acts 10:44) — and Peter commanded them to be baptized.

Subsequently, at Jerusalem, the disciples contended with Peter over this development, but he set their hearts at rest in recounting the events at Caesarea and the manifestation of the Holy Ghost: "Then remembered I the word of the Lord, how that he said, John indeed baptized with water; but ye shall be baptized with the Holy Ghost. Forasmuch then as God gave them the like gift as he did unto us, who believed on the Lord Jesus Christ; what was I, that I could withstand God? When they heard these things, they held their peace, and glorified God, saying, Then hath God also to the Gentiles granted repentance unto life" (Acts 11:16–18).

Paul and Barnabas, as well, extended their missionary labors to the Gentiles (see Acts 13:46–49).

27. And as he talked with him, he went in, and found many that were come together.

28. And he said unto them, Ye know how that it is an unlawful thing for a man that is a Jew to keep company, or come unto one of another nation; but God hath shewed me that I should not call any man common or unclean.

29. Therefore came I unto you without gainsaying, as soon as I was sent for: I ask therefore for what intent ye have sent for me?

30. And Cornelius said, Four days ago I was fasting until this hour; and at the ninth hour I prayed in my house, and, behold, a man stood before me in bright clothing,

31. And said, Cornelius, thy prayer is heard, and thine alms are had in remembrance in the sight of God.

32. Send therefore to Joppa, and call hither Simon, whose surname is Peter; he is lodged in the house of one Simon a tanner by the sea side: who, when he cometh, shall speak unto thee.

33. Immediately therefore I sent to thee; and thou hast well done that thou art come. Now therefore are we all here present before God, to hear all things that are commanded thee of God.

34. ¶ Then Peter opened his mouth, and said, Of a truth I perceive that God is no respecter of persons:

35. But in every nation he that feareth him, and worketh righteousness, is accepted with him.

36. The word which God sent unto the children of Israel, preaching peace by Jesus Christ: (he is Lord of all:)

37. That word, I say, ye know, which was published throughout all Judæa, and began from Galilee, after the baptism which John preached;

38. How God anointed Jesus of Nazareth with the Holy Ghost and with power: who went about doing good, and healing all that were oppressed of the devil; for God was with him.

39. And we are witnesses of all things which he did both in the land of the Jews, and in Jerusalem; whom they slew and hanged on a tree:

40. Him God raised up the third day, and shewed him openly;

41. Not to all the people, but unto witnesses chosen before of God, even to us, who did eat and drink with him after he rose from the dead.

42. And he commanded us to preach unto the people, and to testify that it is he which was ordained of God to be the Judge of quick and dead.

43. To him give all the prophets witness, that through his name whosoever believeth in him shall receive remission of sins.

44. ¶ While Peter yet spake these words, the Holy Ghost fell on all them which heard the word.

45. And they of the circumcision which believed were astonished, as many as came with Peter, because

Acts 10:34–35 — All mankind are the children of God and all are alike unto Him. Whoever will come unto Him through His Son Jesus Christ will be accepted by Him. All can become the sons and daughters of Christ (see Mosiah 5:7).

Notes: _____

_____

_____

_____

_____

_____

_____

_____

_____

_____

_____

_____

_____

_____

_____

_____

_____

_____

that on the Gentiles also was poured out the gift of the Holy Ghost.

46. For they heard them speak with tongues, and magnify God. Then answered Peter,

47. Can any man forbid water, that these should not be baptized, which have received the Holy Ghost as well as we?

48. And he commanded them to be baptized in the name of the Lord. Then prayed they him to tarry certain days.

CHAPTER 11

1. And the apostles and brethren that were in Judaea heard that the Gentiles had also received the word of God.

2. And when Peter was come up to Jerusalem, they that were of the circumcision contended with him,

3. Saying, Thou wentest in to men uncircumcised, and didst eat with them.

4. But Peter rehearsed the matter from the beginning, and expounded it by order unto them, saying,

5. I was in the city of Joppa praying: and in a trance I saw a vision, A certain vessel descend, as it had been a great sheet, let down from heaven by four corners; and it came even to me:

6. Upon the which when I had fastened mine eyes, I considered, and saw fourfooted beasts of the earth, and wild beasts, and creeping things, and fowls of the air.

7. And I heard a voice saying unto me, Arise, Peter; slay and eat.

8. But I said, Not so, Lord: for nothing common or unclean hath at any time entered into my mouth.

9. But the voice answered me again from heaven, What God hath cleansed, that call not thou common.

10. And this was done three times: and all were drawn up again into heaven.

11. And, behold, immediately there were three men already come unto the house where I was, sent from Cæsarea unto me.

12. And the spirit bade me go with them, nothing doubting. Moreover these six brethren accompanied me, and we entered into the man's house:

13. And he shewed us how he had seen an angel in his house, which stood and said unto him, Send men to Joppa, and call for Simon, whose surname is Peter;

14. Who shall tell thee words, whereby thou and all thy house shall be saved.

15. And as I began to speak, the Holy Ghost fell on them, as on us at the beginning.

16. Then remembered I the word of the Lord, how that he said, John indeed baptized with water; but ye shall be baptized with the Holy Ghost.

17. Forasmuch then as God gave them the like gift as he did unto us, who believed on the Lord Jesus Christ; what was I, that I could withstand God?

18. When they heard these things, they held their peace, and glorified God, saying, Then hath God also to the Gentiles granted repentance unto life.

19. ¶ Now they which were scattered abroad upon the persecution that arose about Stephen travelled

The Tower of David in Jerusalem

as far as Phenice, and Cyprus, and Antioch, preaching the word to none but unto the Jews only.

20. And some of them were men of Cyprus and Cyrene, which, when they were come to Antioch, spake unto the Grecians, preaching the Lord Jesus.

21. And the hand of the Lord was with them: and a great number believed, and turned unto the Lord.

22. ¶ Then tidings of these things came unto the ears of the church which was in Jerusalem: and they sent forth Barnabas, that he should go as far as Antioch.

23. Who, when he came, and had seen the grace of God, was glad, and exhorted them all, that with purpose of heart they would cleave unto the Lord.

24. For he was a good man, and full of the Holy Ghost and of faith: and much people was added unto the Lord.

25. Then departed Barnabas to Tarsus, for to seek Saul:

26. And when he had found him, he brought him unto Antioch. And it came to pass, that a whole year they assembled themselves with the church, and taught much people. And the disciples were called Christians first in Antioch.

27. ¶ And in these days came prophets from Jerusalem unto Antioch.

28. And there stood up one of them named Agabus, and signified by the spirit that there should be great dearth throughout all the world: which came to pass in the days of Claudius Cæsar.

29. Then the disciples, every man according to his ability, determined to send relief unto the brethren which dwelt in Judæa:

30. Which also they did, and sent it to the elders by the hands of Barnabas and Saul.

CHAPTER 12

1. Now about that time Herod the king stretched forth his hands to vex certain of the church.

2. And he killed James the brother of John with the sword.

3. And because he saw it pleased the Jews, he proceeded further to take Peter also. (Then were the days of unleavened bread.)

4. And when he had apprehended him, he put him in prison, and delivered him to four quaternions of soldiers to keep him; intending after Easter to bring him forth to the people.

5. Peter therefore was kept in prison: but prayer was made without ceasing of the church unto God for him.

6. And when Herod would have brought him forth, the same night Peter was sleeping between two soldiers, bound with two chains: and the keepers before the door kept the prison.

7. And, behold, the angel of the Lord came upon him, and a light shined in the prison: and he smote Peter on the side, and raised him up, saying, Arise up quickly. And his chains fell off from his hands.

8. And the angel said unto him, Gird thyself, and bind on thy sandals. And so he did. And he saith unto him, Cast thy garment about thee, and follow me.

9. And he went out, and followed

Acts 12:2, 23 — When Herod slew James, the brother of John, the Lord exacted judgment by ending the life of this evil king (see Acts 12:2, 23), thus permitting the ministry of the gospel to continue. Peter, who had been imprisoned by Herod pending execution, was liberated through the intervention of the angel of the Lord, much to the astonishment and delight of the disciples. Meanwhile, Paul and Barnabas were commissioned of the Holy Ghost to perform their missionary labors:

"As they [the disciples] ministered to the Lord, and fasted, the Holy Ghost said, Separate me Barnabas and Saul for the work whereunto I have called them.

"And when they had fasted and prayed, and laid their hands on them, they sent them away" (Acts 13:2–3).

Paul and Barnabas carried on their missions with honor and dignity in places such as Antioch. Elsewhere, they encountered much tribulation at the hands of envious and doubting authorities, Paul even being stoned for his pronouncements (see Acts 14:19) — though he was soon thereafter restored to health and continued to preach of Jesus throughout the region: "Confirming the souls of the disciples, and exhorting them to continue in the faith, and that we must through much tribulation enter into the kingdom of God. And when they had ordained them elders in every church, and had prayed with fasting, they commended them to the Lord, on whom they believed" (Acts 14:22–23). We see that the hand of the Lord was outstretched to prosper and bless the work of His chosen servants. In due time, Paul determined to revisit the cities where he had conducted his ministry among the Saints — "and see how they do" (Acts 15:36). With Silas, a new companion, he departed, "confirming the churches" (Acts 15:42).

him; and wist not that it was true which was done by the angel; but thought he saw a vision.

10. When they were past the first and the second ward, they came unto the iron gate that leadeth unto the city; which opened to them of his own accord: and they went out, and passed on through one street; and forthwith the angel departed from him.

11. And when Peter was come to himself, he said, Now I know of a surety, that the Lord hath sent his angel, and hath delivered me out of the hand of Herod, and from all the expectation of the people of the Jews.

12. And when he had considered the thing, he came to the house of Mary the mother of John, whose surname was Mark; where many were gathered together praying.

13. And as Peter knocked at the door of the gate, a damsel came to hearken, named Rhoda.

14. And when she knew Peter's voice, she opened not the gate for gladness, but ran in, and told how Peter stood before the gate.

15. And they said unto her, Thou art mad. But she constantly affirmed that it was even so. Then said they, It is his angel.

16. But Peter continued knocking: and when they had opened the door, and saw him, they were astonished.

17. But he, beckoning unto them with the hand to hold their peace, declared unto them how the Lord had brought him out of the prison. And he said, Go shew these things unto James, and to the brethren. And he departed, and went into another place.

18. Now as soon as it was day, there was no small stir among the soldiers, what was become of Peter.

19. And when Herod had sought for him, and found him not, he examined the keepers, and commanded that they should be put to death. And he went down from Judæa to Cæsarea, and there abode.

20. ¶ And Herod was highly displeased with them of Tyre and Sidon: but they came with one accord to him, and, having made Blastus the king's chamberlain their friend, desired peace; because their country was nourished by the king's country.

21. And upon a set day Herod, arrayed in royal apparel, sat upon his throne, and made an oration unto them.

22. And the people gave a shout, saying, It is the voice of a god, and not of a man.

23. And immediately the angel of the Lord smote him, because he gave not God the glory: and he was eaten of worms, and gave up the ghost.

24. ¶ But the word of God grew and multiplied.

25. And Barnabas and Saul returned from Jerusalem, when they had fulfilled their ministry, and took with them John, whose surname was Mark.

CHAPTER 13

1. Now there were in the church that was at Antioch certain prophets and teachers; as Barnabas, and Simeon that was called Niger, and Lucius of Cyrene, and Manaen, which had been brought up with Herod the tetrarch, and Saul.

2. As they ministered to the Lord, and fasted, the Holy Ghost said, Separate me Barnabas and Saul for the work whereunto I have called them.

3. And when they had fasted and

Notes: _____
_____
_____
_____
_____
_____
_____
_____
_____
_____
_____
_____
_____
_____
_____
_____
_____
_____
_____
_____
_____
_____
_____
_____
_____
_____
_____
_____
_____

prayed, and laid their hands on them, they sent them away.

4. ¶ So they, being sent forth by the Holy Ghost, departed unto Seleucia; and from thence they sailed to Cyprus.

5. And when they were at Salamis, they preached the word of God in the synagogues of the Jews: and they had also John to their minister.

6. And when they had gone through the isle unto Paphos, they found a certain sorcerer, a false prophet, a Jew, whose name was Bar-jesus:

7. Which was with the deputy of the country, Sergius Paulus, a prudent man; who called for Barnabas and Saul, and desired to hear the word of God.

8. But Elymas the sorcerer (for so is his name by interpretation) withstood them, seeking to turn away the deputy from the faith.

9. Then Saul, (who also is called Paul,) filled with the Holy Ghost, set his eyes on him,

10. And said, O full of all subtilty and all mischief, thou child of the devil, thou enemy of all righteousness, wilt thou not cease to pervert the right ways of the Lord?

11. And now, behold, the hand of the Lord is upon thee, and thou shalt be blind, not seeing the sun for a season. And immediately there fell on him a mist and a darkness; and he went about seeking some to lead him by the hand.

12. Then the deputy, when he saw what was done, believed, being astonished at the doctrine of the Lord.

13. Now when Paul and his company loosed from Paphos, they came to Perga in Pamphylia: and John departing from them returned to Jerusalem.

14. ¶ But when they departed from Perga, they came to Antioch in Pisidia, and went into the synagogue on the sabbath day, and sat down.

15. And after the reading of the law and the prophets the rulers of the synagogue sent unto them, saying, Ye men and brethren, if ye have any word of exhortation for the people, say on.

16. Then Paul stood up, and beckoning with his hand said, Men of Israel, and ye that fear God, give audience.

17. The God of this people of Israel chose our fathers, and exalted the people when they dwelt as strangers in the land of Egypt, and with an high arm brought he them out of it.

18. And about the time of forty years suffered he their manners in the wilderness.

19. And when he had destroyed seven nations in the land of Chanaan, he divided their land to them by lot.

20. And after that he gave unto them judges about the space of four hundred and fifty years, until Samuel the prophet.

21. And afterward they desired a king: and God gave unto them Saul the son of Cis, a man of the tribe of Benjamin, by the space of forty years.

22. And when he had removed him, he raised up unto them David to be their king; to whom also he gave testimony, and said, I have found David the son of Jesse, a man after mine own heart, which shall fulfil all my will.

23. Of this man's seed hath God according to his promise raised unto Israel a Saviour, Jesus:

Antioch

24. When John had first preached before his coming the baptism of repentance to all the people of Israel.

25. And as John fulfilled his course, he said, Whom think ye that I am? I am not he. But, behold, there cometh one after me, whose shoes of his feet I am not worthy to loose.

26. Men and brethren, children of the stock of Abraham, and whosoever among you feareth God, to you is the word of this salvation sent.

27. For they that dwell at Jerusalem, and their rulers, because they knew him not, nor yet the voices of the prophets which are read every sabbath day, they have fulfilled them in condemning him.

28. And though they found no cause of death in him, yet desired they Pilate that he should be slain.

29. And when they had fulfilled all that was written of him, they took him down from the tree, and laid him in a sepulchre.

30. But God raised him from the dead:

31. And he was seen many days of them which came up with him from Galilee to Jerusalem, who are his witnesses unto the people.

32. And we declare unto you glad tidings, how that the promise which was made unto the fathers,

33. God hath fulfilled the same unto us their children, in that he hath raised up Jesus again; as it is also written in the second psalm, Thou art my Son, this day have I begotten thee.

34. And as concerning that he raised him up from the dead, now no more to return to corruption, he said on this wise, I will give you the sure mercies of David.

35. Wherefore he saith also in another psalm, Thou shalt not suffer thine Holy One to see corruption.

36. For David, after he had served his own generation by the will of God, fell on sleep, and was laid unto his fathers, and saw corruption:

37. But he, whom God raised again, saw no corruption.

38. ¶ Be it known unto you therefore, men and brethren, that through this man is preached unto you the forgiveness of sins:

39. And by him all that believe are justified from all things, from which ye could not be justified by the law of Moses.

40. Beware therefore, lest that come upon you, which is spoken of in the prophets;

41. Behold, ye despisers, and wonder, and perish: for I work a work in your days, a work which ye shall in no wise believe, though a man declare it unto you.

42. And when the Jews were gone out of the synagogue, the Gentiles besought that these words might be preached to them the next sabbath.

43. Now when the congregation was broken up, many of the Jews and religious proselytes followed Paul and Barnabas: who, speaking to them, persuaded them to continue in the grace of God.

44. ¶ And the next sabbath day came almost the whole city together to hear the word of God.

45. But when the Jews saw the multitudes, they were filled with envy, and spake against those things which were spoken by Paul, contradicting and blaspheming.

46. Then Paul and Barnabas waxed bold, and said, It was necessary that

Notes: _____

the word of God should first have been spoken to you: but seeing ye put it from you, and judge yourselves unworthy of everlasting life, lo, we turn to the Gentiles.

47. For so hath the Lord commanded us, saying, I have set thee to be a light of the Gentiles, that thou shouldest be for salvation unto the ends of the earth.

48. And when the Gentiles heard this, they were glad, and glorified the word of the Lord: and as many as were ordained to eternal life believed.

49. And the word of the Lord was published throughout all the region.

50. But the Jews stirred up the devout and honourable women, and the chief men of the city, and raised persecution against Paul and Barnabas, and expelled them out of their coasts.

51. But they shook off the dust of their feet against them, and came unto Iconium.

52. And the disciples were filled with joy, and with the Holy Ghost.

CHAPTER 14

1. And it came to pass in Iconium, that they went both together into the synagogue of the Jews, and so spake, that a great multitude both of the Jews and also of the Greeks believed.

2. But the unbelieving Jews stirred up the Gentiles, and made their minds evil affected against the brethren.

3. Long time therefore abode they speaking boldly in the Lord, which gave testimony unto the word of his grace, and granted signs and wonders to be done by their hands.

4. But the multitude of the city was divided: and part held with the Jews, and part with the apostles.

5. And when there was an assault made both of the Gentiles, and also of the Jews with their rulers, to use them despitefully, and to stone them,

6. They were ware of it, and fled unto Lystra and Derbe, cities of Lycaonia, and unto the region that lieth round about:

7. And there they preached the gospel.

8. ¶ And there sat a certain man at Lystra, impotent in his feet, being a cripple from his mother's womb, who never had walked:

9. The same heard Paul speak: who stedfastly beholding him, and perceiving that he had faith to be healed,

10. Said with a loud voice, Stand upright on thy feet. And he leaped and walked.

11. And when the people saw what Paul had done, they lifted up their voices, saying in the speech of Lycaonia, The gods are come down to us in the likeness of men.

12. And they called Barnabas, Jupiter; and Paul, Mercurius, because he was the chief speaker.

13. Then the priest of Jupiter, which was before their city, brought oxen and garlands unto the gates, and would have done sacrifice with the people.

14. Which when the apostles, Barnabas and Paul, heard of, they rent their clothes, and ran in among the people, crying out,

Assault in Iconium

15. And saying, Sirs, why do ye these things? We also are men of like passions with you, and preach unto you that ye should turn from these vanities unto the living God, which made heaven, and earth, and the sea, and all things that are therein:

16. Who in times past suffered all nations to walk in their own ways.

17. Nevertheless he left not himself without witness, in that he did good, and gave us rain from heaven, and fruitful seasons, filling our hearts with food and gladness.

18. And with these sayings scarce restrained they the people, that they had not done sacrifice unto them.

19. ¶ And there came thither certain Jews from Antioch and Iconium, who persuaded the people, and, having stoned Paul, drew him out of the city, supposing he had been dead.

20. Howbeit, as the disciples stood round about him, he rose up, and came into the city: and the next day he departed with Barnabas to Derbe.

21. And when they had preached the gospel to that city, and had taught many, they returned again to Lystra, and to Iconium, and Antioch,

22. Confirming the souls of the disciples, and exhorting them to continue in the faith, and that we must through much tribulation enter into the kingdom of God.

23. And when they had ordained them elders in every church, and had prayed with fasting, they commended them to the Lord, on whom they believed.

24. And after they had passed throughout Pisidia, they came to Pamphylia.

25. And when they had preached the word in Perga, they went down into Attalia:

26. And thence sailed to Antioch, from whence they had been recommended to the grace of God for the work which they fulfilled.

27. And when they were come, and had gathered the church together, they rehearsed all that God had done with them, and how he had opened the door of faith unto the Gentiles.

28. And there they abode long time with the disciples.

CHAPTER 15

1. And certain men which came down from Judæa taught the brethren, and said, Except ye be circumcised after the manner of Moses, ye cannot be saved.

2. When therefore Paul and Barnabas had no small dissension and disputation with them, they determined that Paul and Barnabas, and certain other of them, should go up to Jerusalem unto the apostles and elders about this question.

3. And being brought on their way by the church, they passed through Phenice and Samaria, declaring the conversion of the Gentiles: and they caused great joy unto all the brethren.

4. And when they were come to Jerusalem, they were received of the church, and of the apostles and elders, and they declared all things that God had done with them.

5. But there rose up certain of the

Acts 15:7–11—A faction of the religious community in Antioch advocated the position that circumcision, in accordance with the Law of Moses, was essential to salvation. Paul and Barnabas were dispatched to Jerusalem to obtain counsel on this matter from the Brethren. Amidst considerable disputation, Peter, the chief Apostle, arose and made known his opinion (see Acts 15:7–11).

James answered by blending his testimony with that of Peter in confirming the wisdom of suspending the requirement for circumcision, asking the Gentile converts instead to hold to the faith and avoid any entanglement in sin, among other things (see Acts 15:20). This word was dispatched to Antioch, causing the new converts to rejoice "for the consolation" (Acts 15:31). In this, the Apostles did well, for the resurrected Savior Himself stated to the Saints in far-off America—His "other sheep" (John 10:16)—that the Law of Moses was fulfilled in Him and had an end: "And as many as have received me, to them have I given to become the sons of God; and even so will I to as many as shall believe on my name, for behold, by me redemption cometh, and in me is the law of Moses fulfilled. I am the light and the life of the world. I am Alpha and Omega, the beginning and the end" (3 Ne. 9:17–18). And further: "For behold, the covenant which I have made with my people is not all fulfilled; but the law which was given unto Moses hath an end in me" (3 Ne. 15:8; compare 3 Ne. 15:4; Ether 12:11; D&C 4:3).

sect of the Pharisees which believed, saying, That it was needful to circumcise them, and to command them to keep the law of Moses.

6. ¶ And the apostles and elders came together for to consider of this matter.

7. And when there had been much disputing, Peter rose up, and said unto them, Men and brethren, ye know how that a good while ago God made choice among us, that the Gentiles by my mouth should hear the word of the gospel, and believe.

8. And God, which knoweth the hearts, bare them witness, giving them the Holy Ghost, even as he did unto us;

9. And put no difference between us and them, purifying their hearts by faith.

10. Now therefore why tempt ye God, to put a yoke upon the neck of the disciples, which neither our fathers nor we were able to bear?

11. But we believe that through the grace of the Lord Jesus Christ we shall be saved, even as they.

12. ¶ Then all the multitude kept silence, and gave audience to Barnabas and Paul, declaring what miracles and wonders God had wrought among the Gentiles by them.

13. ¶ And after they had held their peace, James answered, saying, Men and brethren, hearken unto me:

14. Simeon hath declared how God at the first did visit the Gentiles, to take out of them a people for his name.

15. And to this agree the words of the prophets; as it is written,

16. After this I will return, and will build again the tabernacle of David, which is fallen down; and I will build again the ruins thereof, and I will set it up:

17. That the residue of men might seek after the Lord, and all the Gentiles, upon whom my name is called, saith the Lord, who doeth all these things.

18. Known unto God are all his works from the beginning of the world.

19. Wherefore my sentence is, that we trouble not them, which from among the Gentiles are turned to God:

20. But that we write unto them, that they abstain from pollutions of idols, and from fornication, and from things strangled, and from blood.

21. For Moses of old time hath in every city them that preach him, being read in the synagogues every sabbath day.

22. Then pleased it the apostles and elders, with the whole church, to send chosen men of their own company to Antioch with Paul and Barnabas; namely, Judas surnamed Barsabas, and Silas, chief men among the brethren:

23. And they wrote letters by them after this manner; The apostles and elders and brethren send greeting unto the brethren which are of the Gentiles in Antioch and Syria and Cilicia:

24. Forasmuch as we have heard, that certain which went out from us have troubled you with words, subverting your souls, saying, Ye must be circumcised, and keep the law: to whom we gave no such commandment:

25. It seemed good unto us, being

Acts 15–18 — Since the beginning of time, and throughout all dispensations, the message from God — whether in the canonized scriptures or through the counsel of living prophets — has been to proclaim the gospel, to teach and preach the plan of redemption through Jesus Christ the Savior and Redeemer of the world. This is especially true today, for this is the last time that the vineyard will be pruned: "And the Lord of the vineyard said unto them: Go to, and labor in the vineyard, with your might. For behold, this is the last time that I shall nourish my vineyard; for the end is nigh at hand, and the season speedily cometh; and if ye labor with your might with me ye shall have joy in the fruit which I shall lay up unto myself against the time which will soon come" (Jacob 5:71).

Joseph F. Smith received revelation reminding us that we were prepared from premortal times to come forth to labor in the vineyard: "Even before they were born, they, with many others, received their first lessons in the world of spirits and were prepared to come forth in the due time of the Lord to labor in his vineyard for the salvation of the souls of men" (D&C 138:56).

We preach here during our sojourn on the earth, and when we depart, we continue to preach the gospel in the spirit world, as the vision recounted by President Smith confirms (see D&C 138:57).

Yes, our joy and glory should be like that of Alma: "I know that which the Lord hath commanded me, and I glory in it. I do not glory of myself, but I glory in that which the Lord hath commanded me; yea, and this is my glory, that perhaps I may be an instrument in the hands of God to bring some soul to repentance; and this is my joy" (Alma 29:9). That is why Alma labored unceasingly, that he might help others to partake of the joy of which he did partake (see Alma 36:24). For that reason, full-time proselyting missionaries, when they return from their service to the Lord, are frequently heard to say, "It was the happiest two years of my life." "It was the best two years of my life." "I never realized I could feel so much joy for other people."

Love for others is at the core of all missionary endeavors. The sons of Mosiah displayed that kind of charitable concern on behalf of those whom they feared might be cast off (see Mosiah 28:3). It is evident that we have a duty that can generate for us a consuming joy when we seek to bless others by helping them come unto Christ.

assembled with one accord, to send chosen men unto you with our beloved Barnabas and Paul,

26. Men that have hazarded their lives for the name of our Lord Jesus Christ.

27. We have sent therefore Judas and Silas, who shall also tell you the same things by mouth.

28. For it seemed good to the Holy Ghost, and to us, to lay upon you no greater burden than these necessary things;

29. That ye abstain from meats offered to idols, and from blood, and from things strangled, and from fornication: from which if ye keep yourselves, ye shall do well. Fare ye well.

30. So when they were dismissed, they came to Antioch: and when they had gathered the multitude together, they delivered the epistle:

31. Which when they had read, they rejoiced for the consolation.

32. And Judas and Silas, being prophets also themselves, exhorted the brethren with many words, and confirmed them.

33. And after they had tarried there a space, they were let go in peace from the brethren unto the apostles.

34. Notwithstanding it pleased Silas to abide there still.

35. Paul also and Barnabas continued in Antioch, teaching and preaching the word of the Lord, with many others also.

36. ¶ And some days after Paul said unto Barnabas, Let us go again and visit our brethren in every city where we have preached the word of the Lord, and see how they do.

37. And Barnabas determined to take with them John, whose surname was Mark.

38. But Paul thought not good to take him with them, who departed from them from Pamphylia, and went not with them to the work.

39. And the contention was so sharp between them, that they departed asunder one from the other: and so Barnabas took Mark, and sailed unto Cyprus;

40. And Paul chose Silas, and departed, being recommended by the brethren unto the grace of God.

41. And he went through Syria and Cilicia, confirming the churches.

CHAPTER 16

1. Then came he to Derbe and Lystra: and, behold, a certain disciple was there, named Timotheus, the son of a certain woman, which was a Jewess, and believed; but his father was a Greek:

2. Which was well reported of by the brethren that were at Lystra and Iconium.

3. Him would Paul have to go forth with him; and took and circumcised him because of the Jews which were in those quarters: for they knew all that his father was a Greek.

4. And as they went through the cities, they delivered them the decrees for to keep, that were ordained of the apostles and elders which were at Jerusalem.

5. And so were the churches established in the faith, and increased in number daily.

6. Now when they had gone throughout Phrygia and the region of Galatia, and were forbidden of the

Acts 15:36—"The Saints need to share the gospel with their neighbors. It is my firm conviction, my brethren and sisters, that unless we stir ourselves more than we are doing, that when we go to the other side of the veil, we will meet there men and women who have been our neighbors, and associates, and lived among us, that will condemn us because we have been so inconsiderate of them in not telling them of the truth of the gospel of our Lord. When a man is sick, if he is our neighbor, we minister to him gladly; if there is a death in his family, we try to comfort him. But year in and year out we allow him to walk in paths that will destroy his opportunity for eternal life; we pass him by, as if he were a thing of naught" (George Albert Smith, *The Teachings of George Albert Smith,* 151–52).

Acts 16—As Paul and his associates labored in the vineyard of the Lord, they witnessed how the Lord dispensed the fruit of the gospel to the faithful Saints in abundance: "And so were the churches established in the faith, and increased in number daily" (Acts 16:5). The Holy Ghost directed them away from certain areas, but toward others, such as Macedonia (see Acts 16:6–10). In Philippi, a city in Macedonia, Paul brought Lydia and her family into the Church but came under condemnation from the authorities for casting a devil from a woman sorcerer (and thus curtailing the commercial revenues that her sponsors were bringing in). Paul and Silas were beaten and cast into prison, where they were able to convert the jailor, who asked them: "What must I do to be saved?" (Acts 16:30). Their response: "Believe on the Lord Jesus Christ, and thou shalt be saved, and thy house" (v. 31), whereupon the prisoners were authorized to go free and the jailor and his household were baptized into the Church. Paul and Silas then continued their missionary labors in Thessalonica, capital of Macedonia, where some believed their message and others reviled against them in envy. Thence they went to Berea where the people received them more willingly: "These were more noble than those in Thessalonica, in that they received the word with all readiness of mind, and searched the scriptures daily, whether those things were so" (Acts 17:11). Paul then journeyed to Athens, where he had his famous encounter with the local intelligentsia on Mars Hill.

Later, in Corinth, Paul had some success among the Jewish people—"and many of the Corinthians hearing believed, and were baptized" (Acts 18:8); however, most rejected him, so he turned chiefly to the Gentiles from that time on (see Acts 18:6), journeying to such additional places as Ephesus.

Holy Ghost to preach the word in Asia,

7. After they were come to Mysia, they assayed to go into Bithynia: but the Spirit suffered them not.

8. And they passing by Mysia came down to Troas.

9. And a vision appeared to Paul in the night; There stood a man of Macedonia, and prayed him, saying, Come over into Macedonia, and help us.

10. And after he had seen the vision, immediately we endeavored to go into Macedonia, assuredly gathering that the Lord had called us for to preach the gospel unto them.

11. Therefore loosing from Troas, we came with a straight course to Samothracia, and the next day to Neapolis;

12. And from thence to Philippi, which is the chief city of that part of Macedonia, and a colony: and we were in that city abiding certain days.

13. And on the sabbath we went out of the city by a river side, where prayer was wont to be made; and we sat down, and spake unto the women which resorted thither.

14. ¶ And a certain woman named Lydia, a seller of purple, of the city of Thyatira, which worshipped God, heard us: whose heart the Lord opened, that she attended unto the things which were spoken of Paul.

15. And when she was baptized, and her household, she besought us, saying, If ye have judged me to be faithful to the Lord, come into my house, and abide there. And she constrained us.

16. ¶ And it came to pass, as we went to prayer, a certain damsel possessed with a spirit of divination met us, which brought her masters much gain by soothsaying:

17. The same followed Paul and us, and cried, saying, These men are the servants of the most high God, which shew unto us the way of salvation.

18. And this did she many days. But Paul, being grieved, turned and said to the spirit, I command thee in the name of Jesus Christ to come out of her. And he came out the same hour.

19. ¶ And when her masters saw that the hope of their gains was gone, they caught Paul and Silas, and drew them into the marketplace unto the rulers,

20. And brought them to the magistrates, saying, These men, being Jews, do exceedingly trouble our city,

21. And teach customs, which are not lawful for us to receive, neither to observe, being Romans.

22. And the multitude rose up together against them: and the magistrates rent off their clothes, and commanded to beat them.

23. And when they had laid many stripes upon them, they cast them into prison, charging the jailor to keep them safely:

24. Who, having received such a charge, thrust them into the inner prison, and made their feet fast in the stocks.

25. ¶ And at midnight Paul and Silas prayed, and sang praises unto God: and the prisoners heard them.

26. And suddenly there was a great earthquake, so that the foundations of the prison were shaken: and immediately all the doors were opened, and every one's bands were loosed.

27. And the keeper of the prison awaking out of his sleep, and seeing the prison doors open, he drew out his sword, and would have killed himself, supposing that the prisoners had been fled.

28. But Paul cried with a loud voice,

Acts 16:6, 18:3— It is certain that Paul visited the Galatian churches on his second (see Acts 16:6) and third (see Acts 18:23) missionary journeys. While continuing his travels, probably across Macedonia, he received the troubling news that many of the Galatian Saints were abandoning the gospel plan and returning to the restrictive practices of their traditional Jewish religion. He therefore wrote his epistle to turn their hearts back to Jesus Christ. In this frank but loving call to repentance, Paul reminded the Galatians that the law of Moses was but a schoolmaster pointing to the Atonement and triumph of the Savior (see Gal. 3:24), and that the doctrine of faith superseded the preparatory gospel and led to a fulfillment of the promises given under the Abrahamic covenant: "And if ye be Christ's, then are ye Abraham's seed, and heirs according to the promise" (Gal. 3:29). Paul exhorted the people to cultivate the fruits of the Spirit (see Acts 5:22–24) and abide in Christ: "From henceforth let no man trouble me: for I bear in my body the marks of the Lord Jesus. Brethren, the grace of our Lord Jesus Christ be with your spirit" (Gal. 6:17–18). Through this magnificent apostolic chastening, we can savor the loving disposition of a servant of God led by the Spirit to bring wayward souls back to the mainstream of gospel living.

saying, Do thyself no harm: for we are all here.

29. Then he called for a light, and sprang in, and came trembling, and fell down before Paul and Silas,

30. And brought them out, and said, Sirs, what must I do to be saved?

31. And they said, Believe on the Lord Jesus Christ, and thou shalt be saved, and thy house.

32. And they spake unto him the word of the Lord, and to all that were in his house.

33. And he took them the same hour of the night, and washed their stripes; and was baptized, he and all his, straightway.

34. And when he had brought them into his house, he set meat before them, and rejoiced, believing in God with all his house.

35. And when it was day, the magistrates sent the serjeants, saying, Let those men go.

36. And the keeper of the prison told this saying to Paul, The magistrates have sent to let you go: now therefore depart, and go in peace.

37. But Paul said unto them, They have beaten us openly uncondemned, being Romans, and have cast us into prison; and now do they thrust us out privily? nay verily; but let them come themselves and fetch us out.

38. And the serjeants told these words unto the magistrates: and they feared, when they heard that they were Romans.

39. And they came and besought them, and brought them out, and desired them to depart out of the city.

40. And they went out of the prison, and entered into the house of Lydia and when they had seen the brethren, they comforted them, and departed.

CHAPTER 17

1. Now when they had passed through Amphipolis and Apollonia, they came to Thessalonica, where was a synagogue of the Jews:

2. And Paul, as his manner was, went in unto them, and three sabbath days reasoned with them out of the scriptures,

3. Opening and alleging, that Christ must needs have suffered, and risen again from the dead; and that this Jesus, whom I preach unto you, is Christ.

4. And some of them believed, and consorted with Paul and Silas; and of the devout Greeks a great multitude, and of the chief women not a few.

5. ¶ But the Jews which believed not, moved with envy, took unto them certain lewd fellows of the baser sort, and gathered a company, and set all the city on an uproar, and assaulted the house of Jason, and sought to bring them out to the people.

6. And when they found them not, they drew Jason and certain brethren unto the rulers of the city, crying, These that have turned the world upside down are come hither also;

7. Whom Jason hath received: and these all do contrary to the decrees of Cæsar, saying that there is another king, one Jesus.

8. And they troubled the people and the rulers of the city, when they heard these things.

9. And when they had taken security of Jason, and of the other, they let them go.

Acts 16–20— The gospel of Jesus Christ is anchored in eternal principles and is revisited and reinforced in every dispensation of time under the guidance of the Lord's anointed. To walk the pathways of gospel service with Paul is to experience a lofty review of these truths as presented by a master teacher and one of the Savior's most devoted servants. We are edified once again to see reconfirmed in the ministry of Paul the promise and bestowal of the Holy Ghost—the Lord's magnificent gift following conversion and baptism. We are inspired through Paul's exhortations to strengthen our own resolve to be effective and charitable guides to our fellow Saints. And we are reminded to be receptive of chastening from the Almighty, who acts always out of love and compassion for His children.

Notes: _____

_____

_____

_____

_____

_____

_____

_____

_____

_____

_____

_____

_____

_____

_____

_____

_____

_____

10. ¶ And the brethren immediately sent away Paul and Silas by night unto Berea: who coming thither went into the synagogue of the Jews.

11. These were more noble than those in Thessalonica, in that they received the word with all readiness of mind, and searched the scriptures daily, whether those things were so.

12. Therefore many of them believed; also of honourable women which were Greeks, and of men, not a few.

13. But when the Jews of Thessalonica had knowledge that the word of God was preached of Paul at Berea, they came thither also, and stirred up the people.

14. And then immediately the brethren sent away Paul to go as it were to the sea: but Silas and Timotheus abode there still.

15. And they that conducted Paul brought him unto Athens: and receiving a commandment unto Silas and Timotheus for to come to him with all speed, they departed.

16. ¶ Now while Paul waited for them at Athens, his spirit was stirred in him, when he saw the city wholly given to idolatry.

17. Therefore disputed he in the synagogue with the Jews, and with the devout persons, and in the market daily with them that met with him.

18. Then certain philosophers of the Epicureans, and of the Stoicks, encountered him. And some said, What will this babbler say? other some, He seemeth to be a setter forth of strange gods: because he preached unto them Jesus, and the resurrection.

19. And they took him, and brought him unto Areopagus, saying, May we know what this new doctrine, whereof thou speakest, is?

20. For thou bringest certain strange things to our ears: we would know therefore what these things mean.

21. (For all the Athenians and strangers which were there spent their time in nothing else, but either to tell, or to hear some new thing.)

22. ¶ Then Paul stood in the midst of Mars' hill, and said, Ye men of Athens, I perceive that in all things ye are too superstitious.

23. For as I passed by, and beheld your devotions, I found an altar with this inscription, TO THE UNKNOWN GOD. Whom therefore ye ignorantly worship, him declare I unto you.

24. God that made the world and all things therein, seeing that he is Lord of heaven and earth, dwelleth not in temples made with hands;

25. Neither is worshipped with men's hands, as though he needed any thing, seeing he giveth to all life, and breath, and all things;

26. And hath made of one blood all nations of men for to dwell on all the face of the earth, and hath determined the times before appointed, and the bounds of their habitation;

27. That they should seek the

Acts 17:23, 28–31 — When Paul journeyed to Athens, he perceived the idolatry that formed the fiber of that culture and spoke to the local philosophers on Mars Hill concerning the inscription he had seen, dedicated "To the Unknown God" (Acts 17:23). Paul contrasted that vague superstition to the clarity and verity of the gospel of Jesus Christ:

"For in him we live, and move, and have our being; as certain also of your own poets have said, For we are also his offspring.

"Forasmuch then as we are the offspring of God, we ought not to think that the Godhead is like unto gold, or silver, or stone, graven by art and man's device.

"And the times of this ignorance God winked at; but now commandeth all men every where to repent: Because he hath appointed a day, in the which he will judge the world in righteousness by that man whom he hath ordained; whereof he hath given assurance unto all men, in that he hath raised him from the dead" (Acts 17:28–31).

In response, the Athenians mocked Paul and, for the most part, rejected his gospel message. Some few, however, believed his witness and were touched by the truths he taught. Clearly, it is imperative that we stand up for truth and deliver our witness in the strength of the Lord. Not all will respond, but the honest at heart will be moved by the Spirit to come forward and join the flock.

Acts 17:24–26 — "Let every one get a knowledge for himself that this work is true. We do not want you to say that it is true until you know that it is; and if you know it, that knowledge is as good to you as though the Lord came down and told you" (Brigham Young, *Discourses of Brigham Young*, 429).

Lord, if haply they might feel after him, and find him, though he be not far from every one of us:

28. For in him we live, and move, and have our being; as certain also of your own poets have said, For we are also his offspring.

29. Forasmuch then as we are the offspring of God, we ought not to think that the Godhead is like unto gold, or silver, or stone, graven by art and man's device.

30. And the times of this ignorance God winked at; but now commandeth all men every where to repent:

31. Because he hath appointed a day, in the which he will judge the world in righteousness by that man whom he hath ordained; whereof he hath given assurance unto all men, in that he hath raised him from the dead.

32. ¶ And when they heard of the resurrection of the dead, some mocked: and others said, We will hear thee again of this matter.

33. So Paul departed from among them.

34. Howbeit certain men clave unto him, and believed: among the which was Dionysius the Areopagite, and a woman named Damaris, and others with them.

CHAPTER 18

1. After these things Paul departed from Athens, and came to Corinth;

2. And found a certain Jew named Aquila, born in Pontus, lately come from Italy, with his wife Priscilla; (because that Claudius had commanded all Jews to depart from Rome:) and came unto them.

3. And because he was of the same craft, he abode with them, and wrought: for by their occupation they were tentmakers.

4. And he reasoned in the synagogue every sabbath, and persuaded the Jews and the Greeks.

5. And when Silas and Timotheus were come from Macedonia, Paul was pressed in the spirit, and testified to the Jews that Jesus was Christ.

6. And when they opposed themselves, and blasphemed, he shook his raiment, and said unto them, Your blood be upon your own heads; I am clean: from henceforth I will go unto the Gentiles.

7. ¶ And he departed thence, and entered into a certain man's house, named Justus, one that worshipped God, whose house joined hard to the synagogue.

8. And Crispus, the chief ruler of the synagogue, believed on the Lord with all his house; and many of the Corinthians hearing believed, and were baptized.

Acts 17:28–29—Paul was expounding the truth of man's divine heritage before a group of philosophers and thinkers on Mars Hill in Athens. Knowing that we are the literal children of Heavenly Father should instill within us a feeling of great worth. We were created in the image of God. We have the capacity to become like Him. We are His children. When we truly believe this, we will not only feel differently about ourselves, but we will act differently—we will try to act like and be like the Lord. What role does this insight play as a source of continuing inspiration to stand firm against the immorality of our age and to stand solidly in tune with your covenant obligations?

Notes: _____

_____

_____

_____

_____

_____

_____

_____

_____

_____

_____

_____

_____

_____

_____

_____

_____

_____

9. Then spake the Lord to Paul in the night by a vision, Be not afraid, but speak, and hold not thy peace:

10. For I am with thee, and no man shall set on thee to hurt thee: for I have much people in this city.

11. And he continued there a year and six months, teaching the word of God among them.

12. ¶ And when Gallio was the deputy of Achaia, the Jews made insurrection with one accord against Paul, and brought him to the judgment seat,

13. Saying, This fellow persuadeth men to worship God contrary to the law.

14. And when Paul was now about to open his mouth, Gallio said unto the Jews, If it were a matter of wrong or wicked lewdness, O ye Jews, reason would that I should bear with you:

15. But if it be a question of words and names, and of your law, look ye to it; for I will be no judge of such matters.

16. And he drave them from the judgment seat.

17. Then all the Greeks took Sosthenes, the chief ruler of the synagogue, and beat him before the judgment seat. And Gallio cared for none of those things.

18. ¶ And Paul after this tarried there yet a good while, and then took his leave of the brethren, and sailed thence into Syria, and with him Priscilla and Aquila; having shorn his head in Cenchrea: for he had a vow.

19. And he came to Ephesus, and left them there: but he himself entered into the synagogue, and reasoned with the Jews.

20. When they desired him to tarry longer time with them, he consented not;

21. But bade them farewell, saying, I must by all means keep this feast that cometh in Jerusalem: but I will return again unto you, if God will. And he sailed from Ephesus.

22. And when he had landed at Cæsarea, and gone up, and saluted the church, he went down to Antioch.

23. And after he had spent some time there, he departed, and went over all the country of Galatia and Phrygia in order, strengthening all the disciples.

24. ¶ And a certain Jew named Apollos, born at Alexandria, an eloquent man, and mighty in the scriptures, came to Ephesus.

25. This man was instructed in the way of the Lord; and being fervent in the spirit, he spake and taught diligently the things of the Lord, knowing only the baptism of John.

26. And he began to speak boldly in the synagogue: whom when Aquila and Priscilla had heard, they took him unto them, and expounded unto him the way of God more perfectly.

27. And when he was disposed to pass into Achaia, the brethren wrote, exhorting the disciples to receive him: who, when he was come, helped them much which had believed through grace:

28. For he mightily convinced the Jews, and that publickly, shewing by the scriptures that Jesus was Christ.

CHAPTER 19

1. And it came to pass, that, while Apollos was at Corinth, Paul having

Acts 18–20—"Make up your minds to live by the Spirit. Make up your minds to live humbly and in such a way that you will always have the spirit of the Lord to be your friend, to make suggestions to you from time to time as shall be needed under the peculiar circumstances in which you may be placed. . . . I do desire, and it is something that you should desire, to have that humility, and that meekness, and that simplicity, to enjoy the spirit of revelation. It is your privilege, every one of you, to have enough of the spirit of revelation to know exactly what is proper for you to do. It is your privilege to know when men speak by the spirit of God and whether the counsel they give is proper or not" (Lorenzo Snow, *The Teachings of Lorenzo Snow*, 114).

passed through the upper coasts came to Ephesus: and finding certain disciples,

2. He said unto them, Have ye received the Holy Ghost since ye believed? And they said unto him, We have not so much as heard whether there be any Holy Ghost.

3. And he said unto them, Unto what then were ye baptized? And they said, Unto John's baptism.

4. Then said Paul, John verily baptized with the baptism of repentance, saying unto the people, that they should believe on him which should come after him, that is, on Christ Jesus.

5. When they heard this, they were baptized in the name of the Lord Jesus.

6. And when Paul had laid his hands upon them, the Holy Ghost came on them; and they spake with tongues, and prophesied.

7. And all the men were about twelve.

8. And he went into the synagogue, and spake boldly for the space of three months, disputing and persuading the things concerning the kingdom of God.

9. But when divers were hardened, and believed not, but spake evil of that way before the multitude, he departed from them, and separated the disciples, disputing daily in the school of one Tyrannus.

10. And this continued by the space of two years; so that all they which dwelt in Asia heard the word of the Lord Jesus, both Jews and Greeks.

11. And God wrought special miracles by the hands of Paul:

12. So that from his body were brought unto the sick handkerchiefs or aprons, and the diseases departed from them, and the evil spirits went out of them.

13. ¶ Then certain of the vagabond Jews, exorcists, took upon them to call over them which had evil spirits the name of the Lord Jesus, saying, We adjure you by Jesus whom Paul preacheth.

14. And there were seven sons of one Sceva, a Jew, and chief of the priests, which did so.

15. And the evil spirit answered and said, Jesus I know, and Paul I know; but who are ye?

16. And the man in whom the evil spirit was leaped on them, and overcame them, and prevailed against them, so that they fled out of that house naked and wounded.

17. And this was known to all the Jews and Greeks also dwelling at Ephesus; and fear fell on them all, and the name of the Lord Jesus was magnified.

18. And many that believed came, and confessed, and shewed their deeds.

19. Many of them also which used curious arts brought their books together, and burned them before all men: and they counted the price of them, and found it fifty thousand pieces of silver.

20. So mightily grew the word of God and prevailed.

21. ¶ After these things were ended, Paul purposed in the spirit, when he had passed through Macedonia and Achaia, to go to Jerusalem, saying, After I have been there, I must also see Rome.

22. So he sent into Macedonia two of them that ministered unto him, Timotheus and Erastus; but he himself stayed in Asia for a season.

Acts 19:2–6— As Paul returned to Ephesus, capital of the Roman province of Asia, on his third missionary journey, he inquired of the disciples there whether they had received the Holy Ghost since their conversion. Their response, and Paul's continuing dialogue with them, is contained in these verses. The influence of Paul the Apostle during his somewhat lengthy sojourn in that region, teaching the gospel to the people, was significant. As the scripture says: "And this continued by the space of two years; so that all they which dwelt in Asia heard the word of the Lord Jesus, both Jews and Greeks" (Acts 19:10). We read that "the name of the Lord Jesus was magnified" (Acts 19:17) and "mightily grew the word of God and prevailed" (Acts 19:20). Paul continued his ministry with devotion and power, even raising a young man from the dead (see Acts 20:9) and teaching faith, repentance, and selfless service in the name of Jesus Christ.

Notes: _____

23. And the same time there arose no small stir about that way.

24. For a certain man named Demetrius, a silversmith, which made silver shrines for Diana, brought no small gain unto the craftsmen;

25. Whom he called together with the workmen of like occupation, and said, Sirs, ye know that by this craft we have our wealth.

26. Moreover ye see and hear, that not alone at Ephesus, but almost throughout all Asia, this Paul hath persuaded and turned away much people, saying that they be no gods, which are made with hands:

27. So that not only this our craft is in danger to be set at nought; but also that the temple of the great goddess Diana should be despised, and her magnificence should be destroyed, whom all Asia and the world worshippeth.

28. And when they heard these sayings, they were full of wrath, and cried out, saying, Great is Diana of the Ephesians.

29. And the whole city was filled with confusion: and having caught Gaius and Aristarchus, men of Macedonia, Paul's companions in travel, they rushed with one accord into the theatre.

30. And when Paul would have entered in unto the people, the disciples suffered him not.

31. And certain of the chief of Asia, which were his friends, sent unto him, desiring him that he would not adventure himself into the theatre.

32. Some therefore cried one thing, and some another: for the assembly was confused; and the more part knew not wherefore they were come together.

33. And they drew Alexander out of the multitude, the Jews putting him forward. And Alexander beckoned with the hand, and would have made his defence unto the people.

34. But when they knew that he was a Jew, all with one voice about the space of two hours cried out, Great is Diana of the Ephesians.

35. And when the townclerk had appeased the people, he said, Ye men of Ephesus, what man is there that knoweth not how that the city of the Ephesians is a worshipper of the great goddess Diana, and of the image which fell down from Jupiter?

36. Seeing then that these things cannot be spoken against, ye ought to be quiet, and to do nothing rashly.

37. For ye have brought hither these men, which are neither robbers of churches, nor yet blasphemers of your goddess.

38. Wherefore if Demetrius, and the craftsmen which are with him, have a matter against any man, the law is open, and there are deputies: let them implead one another.

39. But if ye inquire any thing concerning other matters, it shall be determined in a lawful assembly.

40. For we are in danger to be called in question for this day's uproar, there being no cause whereby we may give an account of this concourse.

41. And when he had thus spoken, he dismissed the assembly.

CHAPTER 20

1. And after the uproar was ceased, Paul called unto him the disciples, and embraced them, and departed for to go into Macedonia.

PAUL

Paul is one of the Lord's greatest missionaries in any dispensation. From his intellectual and historical training as a Pharisee, including his studies under Gamaliel, he was intimately acquainted with the traditions and cultural nuances embraced by the Jewish leadership of his day. He could see through their window of view and understand their perspectives—thus, he was well prepared following his miraculous conversion to the Christian faith to address the concerns of his Jewish audience and frame the truths of the new covenant in such a way that they could understand them and believe them, if their hearts were willing to embrace Jesus Christ as the long-heralded Messiah.

Paul's record of intense persecution of the church prior to his rebirth (like that of Alma the Younger in the Book of Mormon) rendered his newfound devotion to the cause of the Savior even more passionate and vigorous. Having cultivated a multifaceted perspective on things spiritual, he emerged as a profoundly committed exponent of Christian views among the Gentile populations of his day.

As a teacher, Paul was unsurpassed in the articulation of supernal gospel truths in a way that has lost none of its ardor and intensity even today. He traveled endless miles in the cause of the Lord; he fostered friendship among countless numbers of Saints; he endured inexpressibly painful hardship and tribulation; he resolved differences with his companions; he continually practiced the art of communicating and cultivating understanding; he was inviolate in his witness of the divinity of the Savior; and he has left his legacy of love and devotion as the archetype of one who fulfilled an apostolic mission—for *Apostle* means, literally, "messenger."

According to tradition, he gave his life as a martyr for the cause of truth.

2. And when he had gone over those parts, and had given them much exhortation, he came into Greece,

3. And there abode three months. And when the Jews laid wait for him, as he was about to sail into Syria, he purposed to return through Macedonia.

4. And there accompanied him into Asia Sopater of Berea; and of the Thessalonians, Aristarchus and Secundus; and Gaius of Derbe, and Timotheus; and of Asia, Tychicus and Trophimus.

5. These going before tarried for us at Troas.

6. And we sailed away from Philippi after the days of unleavened bread, and came unto them to Troas in five days; where we abode seven days.

7. And upon the first day of the week, when the disciples came together to break bread, Paul preached unto them, ready to depart on the morrow; and continued his speech until midnight.

8. And there were many lights in the upper chamber, where they were gathered together.

9. And there sat in a window a certain young man named Eutychus, being fallen into a deep sleep: and as Paul was long preaching, he sunk down with sleep, and fell down from the third loft, and was taken up dead.

10. And Paul went down, and fell on him, and embracing him said, Trouble not yourselves; for his life is in him.

11. When he therefore was come up again, and had broken bread, and eaten, and talked a long while, even till break of day, so he departed.

12. And they brought the young man alive, and were not a little comforted.

13. ¶ And we went before to ship, and sailed unto Assos, there intending to take in Paul: for so had he appointed, minding himself to go afoot.

14. And when he met with us at Assos, we took him in, and came to Mitylene.

15. And we sailed thence, and came the next day over against Chios; and the next day we arrived at Samos, and tarried at Trogyllium; and the next day we came to Miletus.

16. For Paul had determined to sail by Ephesus, because he would not spend the time in Asia: for he hasted, if it were possible for him, to be at Jerusalem the day of Pentecost.

17. ¶ And from Miletus he sent to Ephesus, and called the elders of the church.

18. And when they were come to him, he said unto them, Ye know, from the first day that I came into Asia, after what manner I have been with you at all seasons,

19. Serving the Lord with all humility of mind, and with many tears, and temptations, which befell me by the lying in wait of the Jews:

20. And how I kept back nothing that was profitable unto you, but have shewed you, and have taught you publickly, and from house to house,

21. Testifying both to the Jews, and also to the Greeks, repentance toward God, and faith toward our Lord Jesus Christ.

22. And now, behold, I go bound in the spirit unto Jerusalem, not knowing the things that shall befall me there:

Acts 20:7—President George Q. Cannon taught, "'The Lord's Day' (Rev. 1:10) is the day on which He rose from the dead and on which His disciples at that period assembled to worship and break bread in His name. That was the 'first day of the week' (John 20:1; Acts 20:7), as they counted time. This custom was observed in the primitive Christian Church, and the Seventh Day was also observed by the Jewish disciples for a time. But Paul and other leading Elders of the Church set themselves against the observance of the rites and rules of the Mosaic law and proclaimed the liberty of the Gospel, the law having been fulfilled in Christ. He chided those who were sticklers for special days as required by the law but himself observed the Lord's Day—the first day of the week" (*Gospel Truth: Discourses and Writings of President George Q. Cannon*, ed. Jerreld L. Newquist, 391).

Notes: _____

_____

_____

_____

_____

_____

_____

_____

_____

_____

_____

_____

_____

_____

_____

_____

_____

_____

_____

23. Save that the Holy Ghost witnesseth in every city, saying that bonds and afflictions abide me.

24. But none of these things move me, neither count I my life dear unto myself, so that I might finish my course with joy, and the ministry, which I have received of the Lord Jesus, to testify the gospel of the grace of God.

25. And now, behold, I know that ye all, among whom I have gone preaching the kingdom of God, shall see my face no more.

26. Wherefore I take you to record this day, that I am pure from the blood of all men.

27. For I have not shunned to declare unto you all the counsel of God.

28. ¶ Take heed therefore unto yourselves, and to all the flock, over the which the Holy Ghost hath made you overseers, to feed the church of God, which he hath purchased with his own blood.

29. For I know this, that after my departing shall grievous wolves enter in among you, not sparing the flock.

30. Also of your own selves shall men arise, speaking perverse things, to draw away disciples after them.

31. Therefore watch, and remember, that by the space of three years I ceased not to warn every one night and day with tears.

32. And now, brethren, I commend you to God, and to the word of his grace, which is able to build you up, and to give you an inheritance among all them which are sanctified.

33. I have coveted no man's silver, or gold, or apparel.

34. Yea, ye yourselves know, that these hands have ministered unto my necessities, and to them that were with me.

35. I have shewed you all things, how that so labouring ye ought to support the weak, and to remember the words of the Lord Jesus, how he said, It is more blessed to give than to receive.

36. ¶ And when he had thus spoken, he kneeled down, and prayed with them all.

37. And they all wept sore, and fell on Paul's neck, and kissed him,

38. Sorrowing most of all for the words which he spake, that they should see his face no more. And they accompanied him unto the ship.

CHAPTER 21

1. And it came to pass, that after we were gotten from them, and had launched, we came with a straight course unto Coos, and the day following unto Rhodes, and from thence unto Patara:

2. And finding a ship sailing over unto Phenicia, we went aboard, and set forth.

3. Now when we had discovered Cyprus, we left it on the left hand, and sailed into Syria, and landed at Tyre: for there the ship was to unlade her burden.

4. And finding disciples, we tarried there seven days: who said to Paul through the Spirit, that he should not go up to Jerusalem.

5. And when we had accomplished those days, we departed and went

Acts 20:21–27— Paul was a consummate teacher and counselor, full of charity and imbued with the Spirit of the Lord, ever committed to speaking the truths of saving grace and obedience to the Lord's commandments—"Testifying both to the Jews, and also to the Greeks, repentance toward God, and faith toward our Lord Jesus Christ" (Acts 20:21). As such, Paul provides a sterling model for us to follow in learning how to fulfill our callings to teach the gospel with courage and forthrightness to our families, associates, and all students of truth. "For I have not shunned," he says, "to declare unto you all the counsel of God" (Acts 20:27).

Here is a sampling of the wisdom from the mouth or pen of the Apostle Paul—both words of warning as well as words of edification:

• On the coming apostasy: "Take heed therefore unto yourselves, and to all the flock, over the which the Holy Ghost hath made you overseers, to feed the church of God, which he hath purchased with his own blood. For I know this, that after my departing shall grievous wolves enter in among you, not sparing the flock" (Acts 20:28–29).

• On charitable service: "I have shewed you all things, how that so labouring ye ought to support the weak, and to remember the words of the Lord Jesus, how he said, It is more blessed to give than to receive" (Acts 20:35).

• On remembering our covenants: "And the scripture, foreseeing that God would justify the heathen through faith, preached before the gospel unto Abraham, saying, In thee shall all nations be blessed. So then they which be of faith are blessed with faithful Abraham" (Gal. 3:8–9).

• On the divine heritage of the seed of Abraham: "Wherefore the law was our schoolmaster to bring us unto Christ, that we might be justified by faith. But after that faith is come, we are no longer under a schoolmaster. For ye are all the children of God by faith in Christ Jesus. For as many of you as have been baptized into Christ have put on Christ. There is neither Jew nor Greek, there is neither bond nor free, there is neither male nor female: for ye are all one in Christ Jesus. And if ye be Christ's, then are ye Abraham's seed, and heirs according to the promise" (Gal. 3:24–29).

• On the need to live by the Spirit: "For all the law is fulfilled in one word, even in this; Thou shalt love thy neighbour as thyself. But if ye bite and devour one another, take heed that ye be not consumed one of another. This I say then, Walk in the Spirit, and ye shall not fulfil the lust of the flesh. . . . But the fruit of the Spirit is love, joy, peace, longsuffering, gentleness, goodness, faith, Meekness, temperance:

our way; and they all brought us on our way, with wives and children, till we were out of the city: and we kneeled down on the shore, and prayed.

6. And when we had taken our leave one of another, we took ship; and they returned home again.

7. And when we had finished our course from Tyre, we came to Ptolemais, and saluted the brethren, and abode with them one day.

8. And the next day we that were of Paul's company departed, and came unto Cæsarea: and we entered into the house of Philip the evangelist, which was one of the seven; and abode with him.

9. And the same man had four daughters, virgins, which did prophesy.

10. And as we tarried there many days, there came down from Judæa a certain prophet, named Agabus.

11. And when he was come unto us, he took Paul's girdle, and bound his own hands and feet, and said, Thus saith the Holy Ghost, So shall the Jews at Jerusalem bind the man that owneth this girdle, and shall deliver him into the hands of the Gentiles.

12. And when we heard these things, both we, and they of that place, besought him not to go up to Jerusalem.

13. Then Paul answered, What mean ye to weep and to break mine heart? for I am ready not to be bound only, but also to die at Jerusalem for the name of the Lord Jesus.

14. And when he would not be persuaded, we ceased, saying, The will of the Lord be done.

15. And after those days we took up our carriages, and went up to Jerusalem.

16. There went with us also certain of the disciples of Cæsarea, and brought with them one Mnason of Cyprus, an old disciple, with whom we should lodge.

17. And when we were come to Jerusalem, the brethren received us gladly.

18. And the day following Paul went in with us unto James; and all the elders were present.

19. And when he had saluted them, he declared particularly what things God had wrought among the Gentiles by his ministry.

20. And when they heard it, they glorified the Lord, and said unto him, Thou seest, brother, how many thousands of Jews there are which believe; and they are all zealous of the law:

21. And they are informed of thee, that thou teachest all the Jews which are among the Gentiles to forsake Moses, saying that they ought not to circumcise their children, neither to walk after the customs.

22. What is it therefore? the multitude must needs come together: for they will hear that thou art come.

23. Do therefore this that we say to thee: We have four men which have a vow on them;

24. Them take, and purify thyself with them, and be at charges with them, that they may shave their heads: and all may know that those things, whereof they were informed concerning thee, are nothing; but that thou thyself also walkest orderly, and keepest the law.

25. As touching the Gentiles which believe, we have written and concluded that they observe no such thing, save only that they keep themselves from things offered to

against such there is no law. . . . If we live in the Spirit, let us also walk in the Spirit" (Gal. 5:14–16, 22–23, 25).

• On the consequences of our behavior: "Be not deceived; God is not mocked: for whatsoever a man soweth, that shall he also reap. For he that soweth to his flesh shall of the flesh reap corruption; but he that soweth to the Spirit shall of the Spirit reap life everlasting. And let us not be weary in well doing: for in due season we shall reap, if we faint not. As we have therefore opportunity, let us do good unto all men, especially unto them who are of the household of faith" (Gal. 6:7–10).

Acts 21–28 — We may face all types of adversity as we bear witness of Jesus Christ and testify to the truthfulness of the gospel. Let us press forward with faith despite the apathy, indifference, worldliness, secular knowledge, nefarious ways, prideful attitudes and behaviors, lasciviousness, greed, and all manner of persecution we encounter in others. We are to share our testimonies regardless of the opposition and apparent hard-heartedness of others. Mormon described it this way to his son Moroni: "And now, my beloved son, notwithstanding their hardness, let us labor diligently; for if we should cease to labor, we should be brought under condemnation; for we have a labor to perform whilst in this tabernacle of clay, that we may conquer the enemy of all righteousness, and rest our souls in the kingdom of God" (Moro. 9:6). We can go forward, knowing that the Lord will bless us as we open our mouths (see D&C 33:8–11; 84:85–88; 100:5–6). The Holy Ghost empowers our testimony, for truth without testimony is hollow.

idols, and from blood, and from strangled, and from fornication.

26. Then Paul took the men, and the next day purifying himself with them entered into the temple, to signify the accomplishment of the days of purifcation, until that an offering should be offered for every one of them.

27. And when the seven days were almost ended, the Jews which were of Asia, when they saw him in the temple, stirred up all the people, and laid hands on him,

28. Crying out, Men of Israel, help: This is the man, that teacheth all men every where against the people, and the law, and this place: and further brought Greeks also into the temple, and hath polluted this holy place.

29. (For they had seen before with him in the city Trophimus an Ephesian, whom they supposed that Paul had brought into the temple.)

30. And all the city was moved, and the people ran together: and they took Paul, and drew him out of the temple: and forthwith the doors were shut.

31. And as they went about to kill him, tidings came unto the chief captain of the band, that all Jerusalem was in an uproar.

32. Who immediately took soldiers and centurions, and ran down unto them: and when they saw the chief captain and the soldiers, they left beating of Paul.

33. Then the chief captain came near, and took him, and commanded him to be bound with two chains; and demanded who he was, and what he had done.

34. And some cried one thing, some another, among the multitude: and when he could not know the certainty for the tumult, he commanded him to be carried into the castle.

35. And when he came upon the stairs, so it was, that he was borne of the soldiers for the violence of the people.

36. For the multitude of the people followed after, crying, Away with him.

37. And as Paul was to be led into the castle, he said unto the chief captain, May I speak unto thee? Who said, Canst thou speak Greek?

38. Art not thou that Egyptian, which before these days madest an uproar, and leddest out into the wilderness four thousand men that were murderers?

39. But Paul said, I am a man which am a Jew of Tarsus, a city in Cilicia, a citizen of no mean city: and, I beseech thee, suffer me to speak unto the people.

40. And when he had given him licence, Paul stood on the stairs, and beckoned with the hand unto the people. And when there was made a great silence, he spake unto them in the Hebrew tongue, saying,

CHAPTER 22

1. Men, brethren, and fathers, hear ye my defence which I make now unto you.

2. (And when they heard that he spake in the Hebrew tongue to them, they kept the more silence: and he saith,)

3. I am verily a man which am a Jew, born in Tarsus, a city in Cilicia, yet brought up in this city at the feet of Gamaliel, and taught according to the perfect manner of the

Acts 21–28 — The second half of the Acts of the Apostles (chapters 21–28) recounts the travails and courage of Paul while serving as a missionary for the Lord. En route back to Jerusalem at one point, he encounters adamant resistance from colleagues, who fear that he will face dire persecution if he returns. His courage, however, prevails: "What mean ye to weep and to break mine heart? for I am ready not to be bound only, but also to die at Jerusalem for the name of the Lord Jesus. And when he would not be persuaded, we ceased, saying, The will of the Lord be done" (Acts 21:13–14).

At Jerusalem he does, indeed, experience severe mistreatment and imprisonment from the Jewish leaders, who accuse him unjustly of undermining the law of Moses and degrading their traditional religious practices. It is their determination to see him executed. However, his case is heard before governmental authorities at ascending levels of power—from the chief captain of the military to Felix (procurator of Judaea), thence to Festus (successor procurator), next to King Agrippa at Caesarea, and thereafter with an eventual referral to Caesar at Rome. As a Roman citizen, Paul was accorded at least some sense of dignity in his lengthy process of defense and stood forth valiantly in declaring the truth about the gospel of Jesus Christ in spite of the most cruel persecution from his detractors.

We are to follow the Lord's commandment to labor as missionaries of the gospel: "Therefore, O ye that embark in the service of God, see that ye serve him with all your heart, might, mind and strength, that ye may stand blameless before God at the last day" (D&C 4:2). For we have been commanded: "Thou art called . . . to proclaim mine everlasting gospel unto the inhabitants thereof, in the midst of persecution and wickedness" (D&C 99:1).

In speaking of missionary labor that commenced in the early days of the Church, the Prophet Joseph Smith said that "the Standard of Truth has been erected; no unhallowed hand can stop the work from progressing; persecutions may rage, mobs may combine, armies may assemble, calumny may defame, but the truth of God will go forth boldly, nobly, and independent, till it has penetrated every continent, visited every clime, swept every country, and sounded in every ear, till the purposes of God shall be accomplished, and the Great Jehovah shall say the work is done" (*History of the Church*, 4:540).

law of the fathers, and was zealous toward God, as ye all are this day.

4. And I persecuted this way unto the death, binding and delivering into prisons both men and women.

5. As also the high priest doth bear me witness, and all the estate of the elders: from whom also I received letters unto the brethren, and went to Damascus, to bring them which were there bound unto Jerusalem, for to be punished.

6. And it came to pass, that, as I made my journey, and was come nigh unto Damascus about noon, suddenly there shone from heaven a great light round about me.

7. And I fell unto the ground, and heard a voice saying unto me, Saul, Saul, why persecutest thou me?

8. And I answered, Who art thou, Lord? And he said unto me, I am Jesus of Nazareth, whom thou persecutest.

9. And they that were with me saw indeed the light, and were afraid; but they heard not the voice of him that spake to me.

10. And I said, What shall I do, Lord? And the Lord said unto me, Arise, and go into Damascus; and there it shall be told thee of all things which are appointed for thee to do.

11. And when I could not see for the glory of that light, being led by the hand of them that were with me, I came into Damascus.

12. And one Ananias, a devout man according to the law, having a good report of all the Jews which dwelt there,

13. Came unto me, and stood, and said unto me, Brother Saul, receive thy sight. And the same hour I looked up upon him.

14. And he said, The God of our fathers hath chosen thee, that thou shouldest know his will, and see that Just One, and shouldest hear the voice of his mouth.

15. For thou shalt be his witness unto all men of what thou hast seen and heard.

16. And now why tarriest thou? arise, and be baptized, and wash away thy sins, calling on the name of the Lord.

17. And it came to pass, that, when I was come again to Jerusalem, even while I prayed in the temple, I was in a trance;

18. And saw him saying unto me, Make haste, and get thee quickly out of Jerusalem: for they will not receive thy testimony concerning me.

19. And I said, Lord, they know that I imprisoned and beat in every synagogue them that believed on thee:

20. And when the blood of thy martyr Stephen was shed, I also was standing by, and consenting unto his death, and kept the raiment of them that slew him.

21. And he said unto me, Depart: for I will send thee far hence unto the Gentiles.

22. And they gave him audience unto this word, and then lifted up their voices, and said, Away with such a fellow from the earth: for it is not fit that he should live.

23. And as they cried out, and cast off their clothes, and threw dust into the air,

24. The chief captain commanded him to be brought into the castle, and bade that he should be examined by scourging; that he

Acts 21:13–14— The statement by Paul's associates that "the will of the Lord be done" is truly the motto for all missionary work. In the face of all adversity, privation, and hardship, the Lord's errand moves forward: "And they shall go forth and none shall stay them, for I the Lord have commanded them" (D&C 5:1).

We are therefore to follow the example of devotion and sacrifice set by those who follow in the Lord's footsteps: "Verily I say unto you, all among them who know their hearts are honest, and are broken, and their spirits contrite, and are willing to observe their covenants by sacrifice—yea, every sacrifice which I, the Lord, shall command—they are accepted of me" (D&C 97:8).

One of the most celebrated farewells in the annals of missionary work during the Restoration period took place on September 14, 1839. On this day, amidst a severe malaria epidemic in the region, Brigham Young left his home in Montrose, Iowa, for his apostolic mission to Great Britain. "His health was very poor; he was unable to go thirty rods to the river without assistance. After he had crossed the ferry he got Brother Israel Barlow to carry him on his horse behind him to Heber C. Kimball's where he remained sick until the 18th. He left his wife sick with a babe only ten days old, and all his children sick, unable to wait upon each other" (*History of the Church*, 4:9). On the 18th, the two Apostles, both still sick, left the Kimball household in Nauvoo, all ailing except four-year-old Heber Parley. "'It seemed to me,' he [Brother Kimball] remarked afterwards in relating the circumstances, 'as though my very inmost parts would melt within me at the thought of leaving my family in such a condition, as it were, almost in the arms of death. I felt as though I could scarcely endure it.' 'Hold up!' said he to the teamster, who had just started, 'Brother Brigham, this is pretty tough, but let us rise and give them a cheer!' Brigham, with much difficulty, rose to his feet, and joined Elder Kimball in swinging his hat and shouting, 'Hurrah, hurrah, hurrah, for Israel!' The two sisters, hearing the cheer came to the door—Sister [Vilate] Kimball with much difficulty [Mary Ann Young having come to the Kimball household to help nurse her husband]—and waved a farewell; and the two apostles continued their journey, without purse, without scrip, for England" (*History of the Church*, 4:10).

Beneath the banner of such extraordinary devotion in the commission of service to the Lord, we can do no less than rise in courage to observe our covenants by sacrifice.

might know wherefore they cried so against him.

25. And as they bound him with thongs, Paul said unto the centurion that stood by, Is it lawful for you to scourge a man that is a Roman, and uncondemned?

26. When the centurion heard that, he went and told the chief captain, saying, Take heed what thou doest: for this man is a Roman.

27. Then the chief captain came, and said unto him, Tell me, art thou a Roman? He said, Yea.

28. And the chief captain answered, With a great sum obtained I this freedom. And Paul said, But I was free born.

29. Then straightway they departed from him which should have examined him: and the chief captain also was afraid, after he knew that he was a Roman, and because he had bound him.

30. On the morrow, because he would have known the certainty wherefore he was accused of the Jews, he loosed him from his bands, and commanded the chief priests and all their council to appear, and brought Paul down, and set him before them.

CHAPTER 23

1. And Paul, earnestly beholding the council, said, Men and brethren, I have lived in all good conscience before God until this day.

2. And the high priest Ananias commanded them that stood by him to smite him on the mouth.

3. Then said Paul unto him, God shall smite thee, thou whited wall: for sittest thou to judge me after the law, and commandest me to be smitten contrary to the law?

4. And they that stood by said, Revilest thou God's high priest?

5. Then said Paul, I wist not, brethren, that he was the high priest: for it is written, Thou shalt not speak evil of the ruler of thy people.

6. But when Paul perceived that the one part were Sadducees, and the other Pharisees, he cried out in the council, Men and brethren, I am a Pharisee, the son of a Pharisee: of the hope and resurrection of the dead I am called in question.

7. And when he had so said, there arose a dissension between the Pharisees and the Sadducees: and the multitude was divided.

8. For the Sadducees say that there is no resurrection, neither angel, nor spirit: but the Pharisees confess both.

9. And there arose a great cry: and the scribes that were of the Pharisees' part arose, and strove, saying, We find no evil in this man: but if a spirit or an angel hath spoken to him, let us not fight against God.

10. And when there arose a great dissension, the chief captain, fearing lest Paul should have been pulled in pieces of them, commanded the soldiers to go down, and to take him by force from among them, and to bring him into the castle.

11. And the night following the Lord stood by him, and said, Be of good cheer, Paul: for as thou hast testified of me in Jerusalem, so must thou bear witness also at Rome.

12. And when it was day, certain of the Jews banded together, and

Acts 22:3–10, 15— We should stand as witnesses at all times, and all places, and in all things (see Mosiah 18:8–9). We should bear our testimony of Jesus Christ and His kingdom whenever and wherever we can, by word and by deed.

While in military confinement, Paul was called on to face those who had pressed unjust and unholy accusations against him. He rose in majesty and recounted his extraordinary vision in which the resurrected Lord commanded him to cease persecuting the followers of Christ and called him into the service of the ministry (see Acts 22:3–10). Subsequently, as Paul explained, a devout man by the name of Ananias, one who had been called by the Lord to take the bewildered Paul under his care, confirmed the divine commission: "For thou shalt be his witness unto all men of what thou hast seen and heard" (Acts 22:15). Paul later recounted the same testimony before King Agrippa at Caesarea with such persuasive power that the king uttered the now famous words: "Almost thou persuadest me to be a Christian" (Acts 26:28). Paul's example of intrepid courage and unshakable testimony before vicious and unrelenting enemies is a model for us all to follow.

Acts 23:11— While in the hands of the chief captain of the military, having been falsely accused by Jewish leaders of sedition, blasphemy, and the attempt to overthrow the Jewish religious structure, Paul stood his ground and depended on the Lord to carry him through the crisis. In the midst of the bleakness of his confinement, Paul was again visited by the Lord: "And the night following the Lord stood by him, and said, Be of good cheer, Paul: for as thou hast testified of me in Jerusalem, so must thou bear witness also at Rome" (Acts 23:11).

Many have been unjustly accused in regard to preaching the gospel. Many, too, have been unjustly accused in everyday life. How do we rely on the Lord and deal with being unjustly accused?

We know that charity is one of the best ways to respond when being unjustly accused. We have the example of the exchange of correspondence between Moroni, head of the armies, and Pahoran, governor of Zarahemla, during a period of intense conflict between the Nephites and the Lamanites that included a serious internal insurrection (see Alma 60–61). As the miscommunication was resolved, Moroni "did take courage, and was filled with exceedingly great joy because of the faithfulness of Pahoran, that he was not also a traitor to the freedom and cause of his country" (Alma 62:1).

bound themselves under a curse, saying that they would neither eat nor drink till they had killed Paul.

13. And they were more than forty which had made this conspiracy.

14. And they came to the chief priests and elders, and said, We have bound ourselves under a great curse, that we will eat nothing until we have slain Paul.

15. Now therefore ye with the council signify to the chief captain that he bring him down unto you to morrow, as though ye would inquire something more perfectly concerning him: and we, or ever he come near, are ready to kill him.

16. And when Paul's sister's son heard of their lying in wait, he went and entered into the castle, and told Paul.

17. Then Paul called one of the centurions unto him, and said, Bring this young man unto the chief captain: for he hath a certain thing to tell him.

18. So he took him, and brought him to the chief captain, and said, Paul the prisoner called me unto him, and prayed me to bring this young man unto thee, who hath something to say unto thee.

19. Then the chief captain took him by the hand, and went with him aside privately, and asked him, What is that thou hast to tell me?

20. And he said, The Jews have agreed to desire thee that thou wouldest bring down Paul to morrow into the council, as though they would inquire somewhat of him more perfectly.

21. But do not thou yield unto them: for there lie in wait for him of them more than forty men, which have bound themselves with an oath, that they will neither eat nor drink till they have killed him: and now are they ready, looking for a promise from thee.

22. So the chief captain then let the young man depart, and charged him, See thou tell no man that thou hast shewed these things to me.

23. And he called unto him two centurions, saying, Make ready two hundred soldiers to go to Cæsarea, and horsemen threescore and ten, and spearmen two hundred, at the third hour of the night;

24. And provide them beasts, that they may set Paul on, and bring him safe unto Felix the governor.

25. And he wrote a letter after this manner:

26. Claudius Lysias unto the most excellent governor Felix sendeth greeting.

27. This man was taken of the Jews, and should have been killed of them: then came I with an army, and rescued him, having understood that he was a Roman.

28. And when I would have known the cause wherefore they accused him, I brought him forth into their council:

29. Whom I perceived to be accused of questions of their law, but to have nothing laid to his charge worthy of death or of bonds.

30. And when it was told me how that the Jews laid wait for the man, I sent straightway to thee, and gave commandment to his accusers also to say before thee what they had against him. Farewell.

31. Then the soldiers, as it was commanded them, took Paul, and brought him by night to Antipatris.

32. On the morrow they left the horsemen to go with him, and returned to the castle:

33. Who, when they came to Cæsarea, and delivered the epistle to the governor, presented Paul also before him.

34. And when the governor had read the letter, he asked of what

SADDUCEES

The Sadducees were a leading party among the Jews who held closely to the letter of the written Mosaic law rather than to the oral authority of traditional thought and practice. Unlike the Pharisees, they denied immortality and the Resurrection and, thus, found no place for angels or spirits in their theological position (see Acts 23:8). In all, the Sadducees are mentioned fourteen times in the New Testament, always in the context of their antagonism for and conspiracy against Jesus Christ and His Church.

The meaning of the name *Sadducees* is unclear. It may be related to the name *Zadok* (pronounced Zay'-dok), one of the leaders in the Aaronic/Levitical Priesthood order in the days of David and Solomon (see 2 Sam. 8:17; 1 Chron. 16:39) and a descendant in the line of priests stemming from Eleazar, son of Aaron (see 1 Chron. 6:4–8; 24:3). Zadok remained faithful to the cause of David and Solomon.

province he was. And when he understood that he was of Cilicia;
35. I will hear thee, said he, when thine accusers are also come. And he commanded him to be kept in Herod's judgment hall.

CHAPTER 24

1. And after five days Ananias the high priest descended with the elders, and with a certain orator named Tertullus, who informed the governor against Paul.
2. And when he was called forth, Tertullus began to accuse him, saying, Seeing that by thee we enjoy great quietness, and that very worthy deeds are done unto this nation by thy providence,
3. We accept it always, and in all places, most noble Felix, with all thankfulness.
4. Notwithstanding, that I be not further tedious unto thee, I pray thee that thou wouldest hear us of thy clemency a few words.
5. For we have found this man a pestilent fellow, and a mover of sedition among all the Jews throughout the world, and a ringleader of the sect of the Nazarenes:
6. Who also hath gone about to profane the temple: whom we took, and would have judged according to our law.
7. But the chief captain Lysias came upon us, and with great violence took him away out of our hands,
8. Commanding his accusers to come unto thee: by examining of whom thyself mayest take knowledge of all these things, whereof we accuse him.
9. And the Jews also assented, saying that these things were so.
10. Then Paul, after that the governor had beckoned unto him to speak, answered, Forasmuch as I know that thou hast been of many years a judge unto this nation, I do the more cheerfully answer for myself:
11. Because that thou mayest understand, that there are yet but twelve days since I went up to Jerusalem for to worship.
12. And they neither found me in the temple disputing with any man, neither raising up the people, neither in the synagogues, nor in the city:
13. Neither can they prove the things whereof they now accuse me.
14. But this I confess unto thee, that after the way which they call heresy, so worship I the God of my fathers, believing all things which are written in the law and in the prophets:
15. And have hope toward God, which they themselves also allow, that there shall be a resurrection of the dead, both of the just and unjust.
16. And herein do I exercise myself, to have always a conscience void of offence toward God, and toward men.
17. Now after many years I came to bring alms to my nation, and offerings.
18. Whereupon certain Jews from Asia found me purified in the temple, neither with multitude, nor with tumult.
19. Who ought to have been here before thee, and object, if they had ought against me.
20. Or else let these same here say, if they have found any evil doing in me, while I stood before the council,
21. Except it be for this one voice, that I cried standing among them, Touching the resurrection of the

Acts 24— Adversity and opposition are constants in our lives (see D&C 29:39; 2 Ne. 2:11). This is part of the test of mortality (see Abr. 3:25). We can transcend these challenges in the strength of the Lord (see Alma 20:4).

The experiences of Paul and his colleagues in the leadership of the newly established kingdom of God on the earth provide evidence that adversity and persecution follow the believers, just as the Savior had predicted: "Remember the word that I said unto you, The servant is not greater than his lord. If they have persecuted me, they will also persecute you" (John 15:20). And further: "These things have I spoken unto you, that ye should not be offended. They shall put you out of the synagogues: yea, the time cometh, that whosoever killeth you will think that he doeth God service. And these things will they do unto you, because they have not known the Father, nor me" (John 16:1–3).

Only in the strength of the Lord and through the guidance of the Spirit can we hope to overcome the daunting challenges placed in the pathway of light by the servants of darkness. The solution is given by the Lord: "Be faithful unto the end, and lo, I am with you. These words are not of man nor of men, but of me, even Jesus Christ, your Redeemer, by the will of the Father" (D&C 31:13; compare Matt. 28:20; John 13:33; D&C 33:9; 34:11; 100:12; 105:41; 108:8).

dead I am called in question by you this day.

22. And when Felix heard these things, having more perfect knowledge of that way, he deferred them, and said, When Lysias the chief captain shall come down, I will know the uttermost of your matter.

23. And he commanded a centurion to keep Paul, and to let him have liberty, and that he should forbid none of his acquaintance to minister or come unto him.

24. And after certain days, when Felix came with his wife Drusilla, which was a Jewess, he sent for Paul, and heard him concerning the faith in Christ.

25. And as he reasoned of righteousness, temperance, and judgment to come, Felix trembled, and answered, Go thy way for this time; when I have a convenient season, I will call for thee.

26. He hoped also that money should have been given him of Paul, that he might loose him: wherefore he sent for him the oftener, and communed with him.

27. But after two years Porcius Festus came into Felix' room: and Felix, willing to shew the Jews a pleasure, left Paul bound.

CHAPTER 25

1. Now when Festus was come into the province, after three days he ascended from Cæsarea to Jerusalem.

2. Then the high priest and the chief of the Jews informed him against Paul, and besought him,

3. And desired favour against him, that he would send for him to Jerusalem, laying wait in the way to kill him.

4. But Festus answered, that Paul should be kept at Cæsarea, and that he himself would depart shortly thither.

5. Let them therefore, said he, which among you are able, go down with me, and accuse this man, if there be any wickedness in him.

6. And when he had tarried among them more than ten days, he went down unto Cæsarea; and the next day sitting on the judgment seat commanded Paul to be brought.

7. And when he was come, the Jews which came down from Jerusalem stood round about, and laid many and grievous complaints against Paul, which they could not prove.

8. While he answered for himself, Neither against the law of the Jews, neither against the temple, nor yet against Cæsar, have I offended any thing at all.

9. But Festus, willing to do the Jews a pleasure, answered Paul, and said, Wilt thou go up to Jerusalem, and there be judged of these things before me?

10. Then said Paul, I stand at Cæsar's judgment seat, where I ought to be judged: to the Jews have I done no wrong, as thou very well knowest.

11. For if I be an offender, or have committed any thing worthy of death, I refuse not to die: but if there be none of these things whereof these accuse me, no man may deliver me unto them. I appeal unto Cæsar.

12. Then Festus, when he had conferred with the council, answered, Hast thou appealed unto Cæsar? unto Cæsar shalt thou go.

13. And after certain days king Agrippa and Bernice came unto Cæsarea to salute Festus.

14. And when they had been there many days, Festus declared Paul's cause unto the king, saying, There is a certain man left in bonds by Felix:

15. About whom, when I was at Jerusalem, the chief priests and the elders of the Jews informed me, desiring to have judgment against him.

FESTUS

Porcius Festus, succeeding Felix as procurator of Judea, brought Paul before the judgment seat at Caesarea, intending to arrange for his trial at Jerusalem. When Paul claimed the right of jurisdiction in Rome, Festus declared, "Hast thou appealed unto Cæsar? unto Cæsar shalt thou go" (Acts 25:12). Meanwhile, King Agrippa (Herod Agrippa II) and his sister Bernice arrived at Caesarea, and Paul was given a hearing before the king. After Paul had presented his case and borne witness to the truth, an exchange occurred in which Agrippa told Paul, "Almost thou persuadest me to be a Christian" (Acts 26:28).

After conferring with his associates, Agrippa—convinced of Paul's innocence—said to Festus, "This man might have been set at liberty, if he had not appealed unto Cæsar" (Acts 26:32). Thereafter, arrangements were made to send Paul to Rome. Festus remained in office for two years before passing away.

16. To whom I answered, It is not the manner of the Romans to deliver any man to die, before that he which is accused have the accusers face to face, and have licence to answer for himself concerning the crime laid against him.

17. Therefore, when they were come hither, without any delay on the morrow I sat on the judgment seat, and commanded the man to be brought forth.

18. Against whom when the accusers stood up, they brought none accusation of such things as I supposed:

19. But had certain questions against him of their own superstition, and of one Jesus, which was dead, whom Paul affirmed to be alive.

20. And because I doubted of such manner of questions, I asked him whether he would go to Jerusalem, and there be judged of these matters.

21. But when Paul had appealed to be reserved unto the hearing of Augustus, I commanded him to be kept till I might send him to Cæsar.

22. Then Agrippa said unto Festus, I would also hear the man myself. To morrow, said he, thou shalt hear him.

23. And on the morrow, when Agrippa was come, and Bernice, with great pomp, and was entered into the place of hearing, with the chief captains, and principal men of the city, at Festus' commandment Paul was brought forth.

24. And Festus said, King Agrippa, and all men which are here present with us, ye see this man, about whom all the multitude of the Jews have dealt with me, both at Jerusalem, and also here, crying that he ought not to live any longer.

25. But when I found that he had committed nothing worthy of death, and that he himself hath appealed to Augustus, I have determined to send him.

26. Of whom I have no certain thing to write unto my lord. Wherefore I have brought him forth before you, and specially before thee, O king Agrippa, that, after examination had, I might have somewhat to write.

27. For it seemeth to me unreasonable to send a prisoner, and not withal to signify the crimes laid against him.

CHAPTER 26

1. Then Agrippa said unto Paul, Thou art permitted to speak for thyself. Then Paul stretched forth the hand, and answered for himself:

2. I think myself happy, king Agrippa, because I shall answer for myself this day before thee touching all the things whereof I am accused of the Jews:

3. Especially because I know thee to be expert in all customs and questions which are among the Jews: wherefore I beseech thee to hear me patiently.

4. My manner of life from my youth, which was at the first among mine own nation at Jerusalem, know all the Jews;

5. Which knew me from the beginning, if they would testify, that after the most straitest sect of our religion I lived a Pharisee.

6. And now I stand and am judged for the hope of the promise made of God unto our fathers:

7. Unto which promise our twelve tribes, instantly serving God day and night, hope to come. For which hope's sake, king Agrippa, I am accused of the Jews.

AGRIPPA
(HEROD AGRIPPA II)

It was before this Agrippa (Herod Agrippa II, son of Herod Agrippa I, brother of Bernice and Drusilla, and great-grandson of Herod), that Paul, confined in Caesarea because of accusations made against him by the Jewish leaders, pled his innocence and delivered his celebrated speech about his conversion through a vision of the Savior while on the road to Damascus (see Acts 25:13–27; 26:1–32). So convincing was Paul that Agrippa declared at the end of the delivery the well-known words, "Almost thou persuadest me to be a Christian" (Acts 26:28).

8. Why should it be thought a thing incredible with you, that God should raise the dead?

9. I verily thought with myself, that I ought to do many things contrary to the name of Jesus of Nazareth.

10. Which thing I also did in Jerusalem: and many of the saints did I shut up in prison, having received authority from the chief priests; and when they were put to death, I gave my voice against them.

11. And I punished them oft in every synagogue, and compelled them to blaspheme; and being exceedingly mad against them, I persecuted them even unto strange cities.

12. Whereupon as I went to Damascus with authority and commission from the chief priests,

13. At midday, O king, I saw in the way a light from heaven, above the brightness of the sun, shining round about me and them which journeyed with me.

14. And when we were all fallen to the earth, I heard a voice speaking unto me, and saying in the Hebrew tongue, Saul, Saul, why persecutest thou me? it is hard for thee to kick against the pricks.

15. And I said, Who art thou, Lord? And he said, I am Jesus whom thou persecutest.

16. But rise, and stand upon thy feet: for I have appeared unto thee for this purpose, to make thee a minister and a witness both of these things which thou hast seen, and of those things in the which I will appear unto thee;

17. Delivering thee from the people, and from the Gentiles, unto whom now I send thee,

18. To open their eyes, and to turn them from darkness to light, and from the power of Satan unto God, that they may receive forgiveness of sins, and inheritance among them which are sanctified by faith that is in me.

19. Whereupon, O king Agrippa, I was not disobedient unto the heavenly vision:

20. But shewed first unto them of Damascus, and at Jerusalem, and throughout all the coasts of Judæa, and then to the Gentiles, that they should repent and turn to God, and do works meet for repentance.

21. For these causes the Jews caught me in the temple, and went about to kill me.

22. Having therefore obtained help of God, I continue unto this day, witnessing both to small and great, saying none other things than those which the prophets and Moses did say should come:

23. That Christ should suffer, and that he should be the first that should rise from the dead, and should shew light unto the people, and to the Gentiles.

24. And as he thus spake for himself, Festus said with a loud voice, Paul, thou art beside thyself; much learning doth make thee mad.

25. But he said, I am not mad, most noble Festus; but speak forth the words of truth and soberness.

26. For the king knoweth of these things, before whom also I speak freely: for I am persuaded that none of these things are hidden from him; for this thing was not done in a corner.

27. King Agrippa, believest thou the prophets? I know that thou believest.

Acts 26:22–23— Under the provisions and promise of the Abrahamic covenant, we are all enlisted in God's service with the obligation to carry the gospel of Jesus Christ to the four corners of the world. That task is often fraught with peril as well as inconvenience, danger as well as sacrifice, and persecution as well as a heavy investment of time and energy. But the rewards and joys are infinitely greater than the burdens. Paul's labors illustrate that missionary work proceeds despite persecution, that we are to stand valiantly upon principle when unjustly accused, and that we are to bear testimony of Jesus Christ and His gospel plan with courage and devotion—all with the promise that we can transcend the inevitable adversity and opposition in life in the strength of the Lord and through the guidance of His Spirit.

We can say with Paul: "Having therefore obtained help of God, I continue unto this day, witnessing both to small and great, saying none other things than those which the prophets and Moses did say should come: That Christ should suffer, and that he should be the first that should rise from the dead, and should shew light unto the people, and to the Gentiles" (Acts 26:22–23).

To this we can add our witness of the Restoration of the Church and kingdom of God in the latter days, including the coming forth of the Book of Mormon as another testament of Jesus Christ, and the availability of all the priesthood keys and ordinances leading to salvation, immortality, and eternal life. With so great a message, how can we shrink from the divine commission to be honorable in keeping our covenants and going forth, just as Paul, in our circles of friendship and assigned spheres of activity, to preach the gospel of Jesus Christ?

28. Then Agrippa said unto Paul, Almost thou persuadest me to be a Christian.

29. And Paul said, I would to God, that not only thou, but also all that hear me this day, were both almost, and altogether such as I am, except these bonds.

30. And when he had thus spoken, the king rose up, and the governor, and Bernice, and they that sat with them:

31. And when they were gone aside, they talked between themselves, saying, This man doeth nothing worthy of death or of bonds.

32. Then said Agrippa unto Festus, This man might have been set at liberty, if he had not appealed unto Cæsar.

CHAPTER 27

1. And when it was determined that we should sail into Italy, they delivered Paul and certain other prisoners unto one named Julius, a centurion of Augustus' band.

2. And entering into a ship of Adramyttium, we launched, meaning to sail by the coasts of Asia; one Aristarchus, a Macedonian of Thessalonica, being with us.

3. And the next day we touched at Sidon. And Julius courteously entreated Paul, and gave him liberty to go unto his friends to refresh himself.

4. And when we had launched from thence, we sailed under Cyprus, because the winds were contrary.

5. And when we had sailed over the sea of Cilicia and Pamphylia, we came to Myra, a city of Lycia.

6. And there the centurion found a ship of Alexandria sailing into Italy; and he put us therein.

7. And when we had sailed slowly many days, and scarce were come over against Cnidus, the wind not suffering us, we sailed under Crete, over against Salmone;

8. And, hardly passing it, came unto a place which is called The fair havens; nigh whereunto was the city of Lasea.

9. Now when much time was spent, and when sailing was now dangerous, because the fast was now already past, Paul admonished them,

10. And said unto them, Sirs, I perceive that this voyage will be with hurt and much damage, not only of the lading and ship, but also of our lives.

11. Nevertheless the centurion believed the master and the owner of the ship, more than those things which were spoken by Paul.

12. And because the haven was not commodious to winter in, the more part advised to depart thence also, if by any means they might attain to Phenice, and there to winter; which is an haven of Crete, and lieth toward the south west and north west.

13. And when the south wind blew softly, supposing that they had obtained their purpose, loosing thence, they sailed close by Crete.

14. But not long after there arose against it a tempestuous wind, called Euroclydon.

15. And when the ship was caught, and could not bear up into the wind, we let her drive.

16. And running under a certain island which is called Clauda, we had much work to come by the boat:

17. Which when they had taken up, they used helps, undergirding the ship; and, fearing lest they should fall into the quicksands, strake sail, and so were driven.

18. And we being exceedingly tossed with a tempest, the next day they lightened the ship;

JULIUS

Julius was a centurion who treated Paul with kindness on his journey to Rome (see Acts 27:1–3). A *centurion* was a Roman officer who was in command of a hundred men. Several centurions, including Julius, are mentioned in the New Testament, usually in a positive light.

19. And the third day we cast out with our own hands the tackling of the ship.

20. And when neither sun nor stars in many days appeared, and no small tempest lay on us, all hope that we should be saved was then taken away.

21. But after long abstinence Paul stood forth in the midst of them, and said, Sirs, ye should have hearkened unto me, and not have loosed from Crete, and to have gained this harm and loss.

22. And now I exhort you to be of good cheer: for there shall be no loss of any man's life among you, but of the ship.

23. For there stood by me this night the angel of God, whose I am, and whom I serve,

24. Saying, Fear not, Paul; thou must be brought before Cæsar: and, lo, God hath given thee all them that sail with thee.

25. Wherefore, sirs, be of good cheer: for I believe God, that it shall be even as it was told me.

26. Howbeit we must be cast upon a certain island.

27. But when the fourteenth night was come, as we were driven up and down in Adria, about midnight the shipmen deemed that they drew near to some country;

28. And sounded, and found it twenty fathoms: and when they had gone a little further, they sounded again, and found it fifteen fathoms.

29. Then fearing lest we should have fallen upon rocks, they cast four anchors out of the stern, and wished for the day.

30. And as the shipmen were about to flee out of the ship, when they had let down the boat into the sea, under colour as though they would have cast anchors out of the foreship,

31. Paul said to the centurion and to the soldiers, Except these abide in the ship, ye cannot be saved.

32. Then the soldiers cut off the ropes of the boat, and let her fall off.

33. And while the day was coming on, Paul besought them all to take meat, saying, This day is the fourteenth day that ye have tarried and continued fasting, having taken nothing.

34. Wherefore I pray you to take some meat: for this is for your health: for there shall not an hair fall from the head of any of you.

35. And when he had thus spoken, he took bread, and gave thanks to God in presence of them all: and when he had broken it, he began to eat.

36. Then were they all of good cheer, and they also took some meat.

37. And we were in all in the ship two hundred threescore and sixteen souls.

38. And when they had eaten enough, they lightened the ship, and cast out the wheat into the sea.

39. And when it was day, they knew not the land: but they discovered a certain creek with a shore, into the which they were minded, if it were possible, to thrust in the ship.

40. And when they had taken up the anchors, they committed themselves unto the sea, and loosed the rudder bands, and hoised up the mainsail to the wind, and made toward shore.

41. And falling into a place where two seas met, they ran the ship aground; and the forepart stuck fast, and remained unmoveable, but the hinder part was broken with the violence of the waves.

42. And the soldiers' counsel was to kill the prisoners, lest any of them should swim out, and escape.

43. But the centurion, willing to save Paul, kept them from their purpose; and commanded that they which could swim should cast themselves first into the sea, and get to land:

44. And the rest, some on boards,

Notes: _____

and some on broken pieces of the ship. And so it came to pass, that they escaped all safe to land.

CHAPTER 28

1. And when they were escaped, then they knew that the island was called Melita.

2. And the barbarous people shewed us no little kindness: for they kindled a fire, and received us every one, because of the present rain, and because of the cold.

3. And when Paul had gathered a bundle of sticks, and laid them on the fire, there came a viper out of the heat, and fastened on his hand.

4. And when the barbarians saw the venomous beast hang on his hand, they said among themselves, No doubt this man is a murderer, whom, though he hath escaped the sea, yet vengeance suffereth not to live.

5. And he shook off the beast into the fire, and felt no harm.

6. Howbeit they looked when he should have swollen, or fallen down dead suddenly: but after they had looked a great while, and saw no harm come to him, they changed their minds, and said that he was a god.

7. In the same quarters were possessions of the chief man of the island, whose name was Publius; who received us, and lodged us three days courteously.

8. And it came to pass, that the father of Publius lay sick of a fever and of a bloody flux: to whom Paul entered in, and prayed, and laid his hands on him, and healed him.

9. So when this was done, others also, which had diseases in the island, came, and were healed:

10. Who also honoured us with many honours; and when we departed, they laded us with such things as were necessary.

11. And after three months we departed in a ship of Alexandria, which had wintered in the isle, whose sign was Castor and Pollux.

12. And landing at Syracuse, we tarried there three days.

13. And from thence we fetched a compass, and came to Rhegium: and after one day the south wind blew, and we came the next day to Puteoli:

14. Where we found brethren, and were desired to tarry with them seven days: and so we went toward Rome.

15. And from thence, when the brethren heard of us, they came to meet us as far as Appii forum, and The three taverns: whom when Paul saw, he thanked God, and took courage.

16. And when we came to Rome, the centurion delivered the prisoners to the captain of the guard: but Paul was suffered to dwell by himself with a soldier that kept him.

17. And it came to pass, that after three days Paul called the chief of the Jews together: and when they were come together, he said unto them, Men and brethren, though I have committed nothing against the people, or customs of our fathers, yet was I delivered prisoner from Jerusalem into the hands of the Romans.

18. Who, when they had examined me, would have let me go, because there was no cause of death in me.

19. But when the Jews spake against it, I was constrained to appeal unto Cæsar; not that I had ought to accuse my nation of.

Notes: _____

_____

_____

_____

_____

_____

_____

_____

_____

_____

_____

_____

_____

_____

_____

_____

Acts 28:28–31 — Paul was involved in a tragic shipwreck while en route to Rome — an event that he had predicted by inspiration, warning the incredulous sailors and assuring them that there would be no loss of life if they went forward (see Acts 27:22). He survived the disaster to continue his labors in Rome, just as the Lord had promised him: "Be it known therefore unto you," he said to the Jews in Rome during his status of confinement at the behest of the authorities there, "that the salvation of God is sent unto the Gentiles, and that they will hear it. And when he had said these words, the Jews departed, and had great reasoning among themselves. And Paul dwelt two whole years in his own hired house, and received all that came in unto him, Preaching the kingdom of God, and teaching those things which concern the Lord Jesus Christ, with all confidence, no man forbidding him" (Acts 28:28–31).

20. For this cause therefore have I called for you, to see you, and to speak with you: because that for the hope of Israel I am bound with this chain.

21. And they said unto him, We neither received letters out of Judæa concerning thee, neither any of the brethren that came shewed or spake any harm of thee.

22. But we desire to hear of thee what thou thinkest: for as concerning this sect, we know that every where it is spoken against.

23. And when they had appointed him a day, there came many to him into his lodging; to whom he expounded and testified the kingdom of God, persuading them concerning Jesus, both out of the law of Moses, and out of the prophets, from morning till evening.

24. And some believed the things which were spoken, and some believed not.

25. And when they agreed not among themselves, they departed, after that Paul had spoken one word, Well spake the Holy Ghost by Esaias the prophet unto our fathers,

26. Saying, Go unto this people, and say, Hearing ye shall hear, and shall not understand; and seeing ye shall see, and not perceive:

27. For the heart of this people is waxed gross, and their ears are dull of hearing, and their eyes have they closed; lest they should see with their eyes, and hear with their ears, and understand with their heart, and should be converted, and I should heal them.

28. Be it known therefore unto you, that the salvation of God is sent unto the Gentiles, and that they will hear it.

29. And when he had said these words, the Jews departed, and had great reasoning among themselves.

30. And Paul dwelt two whole years in his own hired house, and received all that came in unto him,

31. Preaching the kingdom of God, and teaching those things which concern the Lord Jesus Christ, with all confidence, no man forbidding him.

THE EPISTLE OF PAUL THE APOSTLE TO

THE ROMANS

CHAPTER 1

1. Paul, a servant of Jesus Christ, called to be an apostle, separated unto the gospel of God,

Romans—Paul wrote his Epistle to the Romans in the time frame A.D. 55 to A.D. 57, toward the end of his stay in Corinth, as referred to in Acts 20:3. In part, the epistle was intended to prepare the Saints at Rome for a planned visit by Paul and, in part, to summarize and explicate certain key doctrines of truth that were being accepted and adopted by the new converts. Among these was the doctrine of justification through faith in Jesus Christ (see Rom. 3:10–25). At the basis of this doctrine is the fact that all people, by virtue of their mortal estate, fall short of perfection and absolute compliance with the laws of God: "As it is written, There is none righteous, no, not one: There is none that understandeth, there is none that seeketh after God. They are all gone out of the way, they are together become unprofitable; there is none that doeth good, no, not one. . . . Therefore by the deeds of the law there shall no flesh be justified in his sight: for by the law is the knowledge of sin" (Rom. 3:10–12, 20; compare Rom. 7:14–25). Against the bleakness of this awful verity shines forth the glory of the Atonement of the Lamb of God to bring about a reconciliation through grace: "For all have sinned, and come short of the glory of God; Being justified freely by his grace through the redemption that is in Christ Jesus: Whom God hath set forth to be a propitiation through faith in his blood, to declare his righteousness for the remission of sins that are past, through the forbearance of God" (Rom. 3:23–25).

Those who, through faith, accept the Lord and follow His counsel—and are thus justified before God—are counseled by Paul not to lapse into a state of self-satisfied boasting, for the gift comes of God, not of ourselves and not of our own doing in the absence of heavenly intervention: "Therefore we conclude that a man is justified by faith without the deeds of the law" (Rom. 3:28).

Many hundreds of years before the ministry of Paul, the prophet Lehi counseled Jacob and his other sons on this same doctrine, speaking in terms that cannot be misunderstood (see 2 Ne. 2:5–8).

2. (Which he had promised afore by his prophets in the holy scriptures,)

3. Concerning his Son Jesus Christ our Lord, which was made of the seed of David according to the flesh;

4. And declared to be the Son of God with power, according to the spirit of holiness, by the resurrection from the dead:

5. By whom we have received grace and apostleship, for obedience to the faith among all nations, for his name:

6. Among whom are ye also the called of Jesus Christ:

7. To all that be in Rome, beloved of God, called to be saints: Grace to you and peace from God our Father, and the Lord Jesus Christ.

8. First, I thank my God through Jesus Christ for you all, that your faith is spoken of throughout the whole world.

9. For God is my witness, whom I serve with my spirit in the gospel of his Son, that without ceasing I make mention of you always in my prayers;

10. Making request, if by any means now at length I might have a prosperous journey by the will of God to come unto you.

11. For I long to see you, that I may impart unto you some spiritual gift, to the end ye may be established;

12. That is, that I may be comforted together with you by the mutual faith both of you and me.

13. Now I would not have you ignorant, brethren, that oftentimes I purposed to come unto you, (but was let hitherto,) that I might have some fruit among you also, even as among other Gentiles.

14. I am debtor both to the Greeks, and to the Barbarians; both to the wise, and to the unwise.

15. So, as much as in me is, I am ready to preach the gospel to you that are at Rome also.

16. For I am not ashamed of the gospel of Christ: for it is the power of God unto salvation to every one that believeth; to the Jew first, and also to the Greek.

17. For therein is the righteousness of God revealed from faith to faith: as it is written, The just shall live by faith.

18. For the wrath of God is revealed from heaven against all ungodliness and unrighteousness of men, who hold the truth in unrighteousness;

19. Because that which may be known of God is manifest in them; for God hath shewed it unto them.

20. For the invisible things of him

Romans—We become "Saints" as we enter into the covenant of baptism and receive the Holy Ghost. We change because we are converted to Jesus Christ and His gospel. We take upon us the name of Jesus Christ, and because of this, we should think and act differently. We become a Saint as described by King Benjamin: "he yields to the enticings of the Holy Spirit, and putteth off the natural man and becometh a saint through the Atonement of Christ the Lord, and becometh as a child, submissive, meek, humble, patient, full of love, willing to submit to all things which the Lord seeth fit to inflict upon him, even as a child doth submit to his father" (Mosiah 3:19). This is a process of becoming, not an event. We become holy and without blemish, even unspotted from the world, as we apply the Atonement to our lives through faith unto repentance (see Alma 34:15–17). This requires great faith, the foundation of all righteousness, to make the mighty change and be born again. By so doing, we will be rewarded to become joint-heirs with Christ. We must press forward steadfastly as described by Nephi:

"And now, my beloved brethren, after ye have gotten into this strait and narrow path, I would ask if all is done? Behold, I say unto you, Nay; for ye have not come thus far save it were by the word of Christ with unshaken faith in him, relying wholly upon the merits of him who is mighty to save.

"Wherefore, ye must press forward with a steadfastness in Christ, having a perfect brightness of hope, and a love of God and of all men. Wherefore, if ye shall press forward, feasting upon the word of Christ, and endure to the end, behold, thus saith the Father: Ye shall have eternal life.

"And now, behold, my beloved brethren, this is the way; and there is none other way nor name given under heaven whereby man can be saved in the kingdom of God. And now, behold, this is the doctrine of Christ, and the only and true doctrine of the Father, and of the Son, and of the Holy Ghost, which is one God, without end. Amen" (2 Ne. 31:19–21).

from the creation of the world are clearly seen, being understood by the things that are made, even his eternal power and Godhead; so that they are without excuse:

21. Because that, when they knew God, they glorified him not as God, neither were thankful; but became vain in their imaginations, and their foolish heart was darkened.

22. Professing themselves to be wise, they became fools,

23. And changed the glory of the uncorruptible God into an image made like to corruptible man, and to birds, and fourfooted beasts, and creeping things.

24. Wherefore God also gave them up to uncleanness through the lusts of their own hearts, to dishonour their own bodies between themselves:

25. Who changed the truth of God into a lie, and worshipped and served the creature more than the Creator, who is blessed for ever. Amen.

26. For this cause God gave them up unto vile affections: for even their women did change the natural use into that which is against nature:

27. And likewise also the men, leaving the natural use of the woman, burned in their lust one toward another; men with men working that which is unseemly, and receiving in themselves that recompence of their error which was meet.

28. And even as they did not like to retain God in their knowledge, God gave them over to a reprobate mind, to do those things which are not convenient;

29. Being filled with all unrighteousness, fornication, wickedness, covetousness, maliciousness; full of envy, murder, debate, deceit, malignity; whisperers,

30. Backbiters, haters of God, despiteful, proud, boasters, inventors of evil things, disobedient to parents,

31. Without understanding, covenantbreakers, without natural affection, implacable, unmerciful:

32. Who knowing the judgment of God, that they which commit such things are worthy of death, not only do the same, but have pleasure in them that do them.

CHAPTER 2

1. Therefore thou art inexcusable, O man, whosoever thou art that judgest: for wherein thou judgest another, thou condemnest thyself; for thou that judgest doest the same things.

2. But we are sure that the judgment of God is according to truth against them which commit such things.

ROMANS

Life at the time of Christ was defined and regulated by the empire-building momentum of the Romans on one hand and by the traditional Jewish hegemony on the other. The blending of the two created the fabric of existence for the populations of the Holy Land as well as for those of the bordering Gentile provinces. In the same measure, it was the blending of the two that metastasized the cancerous growth of hatred against the cause of the Savior fomented by conspirators among the Jewish religious leadership—a hatred fulfilled in the Crucifixion carried out by the military men of the doubting but cooperative governor, Pontius Pilate. At the same time, and beyond, the Romans began to feel the Christian influence in their own homeland. During the decades following the Ascension, the Roman leadership served as a protecting influence for the growing Church until Nero began to institute a campaign of persecution against the Christians beginning in the mid 60s.

At one point in his apostolic career, when Paul was caught in the vortex of competing dangers from his most bitter enemies within the Jewish leadership, Paul was directed to turn his attention to the Romans (see Acts 23:11). He wrote his epistle to the Romans while not yet having set foot there; he was possibly in Corinth. His letter is a doctrinal masterpiece that defends his theological perspective on the Christian faith and practice.

Paul would soon visit Rome, not as an itinerant missionary, according to his desire, but as a prisoner of the state. After several years of enduring confinement and some concluding attempts to carry on his ministry, he would, as tradition claims, play the role of martyr among the Romans.

3. And thinkest thou this, O man, that judgest them which do such things, and doest the same, that thou shalt escape the judgment of God?

4. Or despisest thou the riches of his goodness and forbearance and longsuffering; not knowing that the goodness of God leadeth thee to repentance?

5. But after thy hardness and impenitent heart treasurest up unto thyself wrath against the day of wrath and revelation of the righteous judgment of God;

6. Who will render to every man according to his deeds:

7. To them who by patient continuance in well doing seek for glory and honour and immortality, eternal life:

8. But unto them that are contentious, and do not obey the truth, but obey unrighteousness, indignation and wrath,

9. Tribulation and anguish, upon every soul of man that doeth evil, of the Jew first, and also of the Gentile;

10. But glory, honour, and peace, to every man that worketh good, to the Jew first, and also to the Gentile:

11. For there is no respect of persons with God.

12. For as many as have sinned without law shall also perish without law: and as many as have sinned in the law shall be judged by the law;

13. (For not the hearers of the law are just before God, but the doers of the law shall be justified.

14. For when the Gentiles, which have not the law, do by nature the things contained in the law, these, having not the law, are a law unto themselves:

15. Which shew the work of the law written in their hearts, their conscience also bearing witness, and their thoughts the mean while accusing or else excusing one another;)

16. In the day when God shall judge the secrets of men by Jesus Christ according to my gospel.

17. Behold, thou art called a Jew, and restest in the law, and makest thy boast of God,

18. And knowest his will, and approvest the things that are more excellent, being instructed out of the law;

19. And art confident that thou thyself art a guide of the blind, a light of them which are in darkness,

20. An instructor of the foolish, a teacher of babes, which hast the form of knowledge and of the truth in the law.

21. Thou therefore which teachest another, teachest thou not thyself? thou that preachest a man should not steal, dost thou steal?

22. Thou that sayest a man should

Notes: _____
_____
_____
_____
_____
_____
_____
_____
_____
_____
_____
_____
_____
_____
_____
_____
_____
_____
_____
_____
_____
_____
_____
_____
_____
_____
_____
_____
_____
_____
_____
_____
_____
_____
_____

not commit adultery, dost thou commit adultery? thou that abhorrest idols, dost thou commit sacrilege?

23. Thou that makest thy boast of the law, through breaking the law dishonourest thou God?

24. For the name of God is blasphemed among the Gentiles through you, as it is written.

25. For circumcision verily profiteth, if thou keep the law: but if thou be a breaker of the law, thy circumcision is made uncircumcision.

26. Therefore if the uncircumcision keep the righteousness of the law, shall not his uncircumcision be counted for circumcision?

27. And shall not uncircumcision which is by nature, if it fulfil the law, judge thee, who by the letter and circumcision dost transgress the law?

28. For he is not a Jew, which is one outwardly; neither is that circumcision, which is outward in the flesh:

29. But he is a Jew, which is one inwardly; and circumcision is that of the heart, in the spirit, and not in the letter; whose praise is not of men, but of God.

CHAPTER 3

1. What advantage then hath the Jew? or what profit is there of circumcision?

2. Much every way: chiefly, because that unto them were committed the oracles of God.

3. For what if some did not believe? shall their unbelief make the faith of God without effect?

4. God forbid: yea, let God be true, but every man a liar; as it is written, That thou mightest be justified in thy sayings, and mightest overcome when thou art judged.

5. But if our unrighteousness commend the righteousness of God, what shall we say? Is God unrighteous who taketh vengeance? (I speak as a man)

6. God forbid: for then how shall God judge the world?

7. For if the truth of God hath more abounded through my lie unto his glory; why yet am I also judged as a sinner?

8. And not rather, (as we be slanderously reported, and as some affirm that we say,) Let us do evil, that good may come? whose damnation is just.

9. What then? are we better than they? No, in no wise: for we have before proved both Jews and Gentiles, that they are all under sin;

10. As it is written, There is none righteous, no, not one:

11. There is none that understandeth, there is none that seeketh after God.

12. They are all gone out of the way, they are together become unprofitable; there is none that doeth good, no, not one.

13. Their throat is an open sepulchre; with their tongues they have

---

CHRISTIANS

The words *Christian* or *Christians,* meaning those in Christ's fold, are used only three times in the New Testament: "And the disciples were called Christians first in Antioch" (Acts 11:26); "Then Agrippa said to Paul, Almost thou persuadest me to be a Christian" (Acts 26:28); "Yet if any man suffer as a Christian, let him not be ashamed; but let him glorify God on his behalf" (1 Pet. 4:16).

used deceit; the poison of asps is under their lips:

14. Whose mouth is full of cursing and bitterness:

15. Their feet are swift to shed blood:

16. Destruction and misery are in their ways:

17. And the way of peace have they not known:

18. There is no fear of God before their eyes.

19. Now we know that what things soever the law saith, it saith to them who are under the law: that every mouth may be stopped, and all the world may become guilty before God.

20. Therefore by the deeds of the law there shall no flesh be justified in his sight: for by the law is the knowledge of sin.

21. But now the righteousness of God without the law is manifested, being witnessed by the law and the prophets;

22. Even the righteousness of God which is by faith of Jesus Christ unto all and upon all them that believe: for there is no difference:

23. For all have sinned, and come short of the glory of God;

24. Being justified freely by his grace through the redemption that is in Christ Jesus:

25. Whom God hath set forth to be a propitiation through faith in his blood, to declare his righteousness for the remission of sins that are past, through the forbearance of God;

26. To declare, I say, at this time his righteousness: that he might be just, and the justifier of him which believeth in Jesus.

27. Where is boasting then? It is excluded. By what law? of works? Nay: but by the law of faith.

28. Therefore we conclude that a man is justified by faith without the deeds of the law.

29. Is he the God of the Jews only? is he not also of the Gentiles? Yes, of the Gentiles also:

30. Seeing it is one God, which shall justify the circumcision by faith, and uncircumcision through faith.

31. Do we then make void the law through faith? God forbid: yea, we establish the law.

CHAPTER 4

1. What shall we say then that Abraham our father, as pertaining to the flesh, hath found?

2. For if Abraham were justified by works, he hath whereof to glory; but not before God.

3. For what saith the scripture?

Abraham with Isaac

Abraham believed God, and it was counted unto him for righteousness.

4. Now to him that worketh is the reward not reckoned of grace, but of debt.

5. But to him that worketh not, but believeth on him that justifieth the ungodly, his faith is counted for righteousness.

6. Even as David also describeth the blessedness of the man, unto whom God imputeth righteousness without works,

7. Saying, Blessed are they whose iniquities are forgiven, and whose sins are covered.

8. Blessed is the man to whom the Lord will not impute sin.

9. Cometh this blessedness then upon the circumcision only, or upon the uncircumcision also? for we say that faith was reckoned to Abraham for righteousness.

10. How was it then reckoned? when he was in circumcision, or in uncircumcision? Not in circumcision, but in uncircumcision.

11. And he received the sign of circumcision, a seal of the righteousness of the faith which he had yet being uncircumcised: that he might be the father of all them that believe, though they be not circumcised; that righteousness might be imputed unto them also:

12. And the father of circumcision to them who are not of the circumcision only, but who also walk in the steps of that faith of our father Abraham, which he had being yet uncircumcised.

13. For the promise, that he should be the heir of the world, was not to Abraham, or to his seed, through the law, but through the righteousness of faith.

14. For if they which are of the law be heirs, faith is made void, and the promise made of none effect:

15. Because the law worketh wrath: for where no law is, there is no transgression.

16. Therefore it is of faith, that it might be by grace; to the end the promise might be sure to all the seed; not to that only which is of the law, but to that also which is of the faith of Abraham; who is the father of us all,

17. (As it is written, I have made thee a father of many nations,) before him whom he believed, even God, who quickeneth the dead, and calleth those things which be not as though they were.

18. Who against hope believed in hope, that he might become the father of many nations; according to that which was spoken, So shall thy seed be.

19. And being not weak in faith, he considered not his own body now dead, when he was about an hundred years old, neither yet the deadness of Sara's womb:

20. He staggered not at the promise of God through unbelief; but was strong in faith, giving glory to God;

21. And being fully persuaded that, what he had promised, he was able also to perform.

22. And therefore it was imputed to him for righteousness.

ABRAHAM

Abraham—father of Isaac, grandfather of Jacob, and great-grandfather of Joseph—was the exemplary patriarch whose descendants were commissioned to carry forth the cause of the Abrahamic covenant to spread the blessings of the gospel of salvation and the priesthood of God to the world (see Gen. 17:1–8; Abr. 2:9–11; 3 Ne. 20:25–27). That commission continues today under the ensign of the restored gospel.

According to the royal covenant, Israel was assured a homeland on earth with the blessings of the fulness of the gospel truth and an inheritance in the mansions of heaven with salvation and exaltation for the faithful and obedient. They were also promised a bounteous earthly progeny and, in keeping with the new and everlasting covenant of marriage, eternal increase in the hereafter. By divine decree, the obligation under this magnificent covenant was that Israel was to convey priesthood blessings to the entire world and spread the gospel of saving ordinances to the receptive children of God in all lands. In the context of this divine covenant, Abraham is among the most admired and celebrated of the Lord's chosen prophets, being mentioned frequently in all the standard works of the Church.

By invoking the memory of Abraham, the Savior and His followers were able to teach important lessons about gospel truths. Clearly the canopy of the Abrahamic lineage was perceived by the Jewish leaders as a primary source of their authority and power—a perception that the Savior consistently placed in juxtaposition with the authentic plan of salvation and exaltation, or the new covenant, that He was restoring through His ministry.

Following the Crucifixion, Peter incorporated references to Abraham in his discourse (see Acts 3:13). Prior to his martyrdom, Stephen repeatedly made reference to Abraham in bearing witness to the divinity of the Savior (see Acts 7:2, 8, 16, 17, 32). Paul referred to his audience as the "stock of Abraham" (Acts 13:26) and "the seed of Abraham" (Rom. 9:7; 2 Cor. 11:22) and to Abraham as "the father of us all" (Rom. 4:16).

23. Now it was not written for his sake alone, that it was imputed to him;

24. But for us also, to whom it shall be imputed, if we believe on him that raised up Jesus our Lord from the dead;

25. Who was delivered for our offences, and was raised again for our justification.

CHAPTER 5

1. Therefore being justified by faith, we have peace with God through our Lord Jesus Christ:

2. By whom also we have access by faith into this grace wherein we stand, and rejoice in hope of the glory of God.

3. And not only so, but we glory in tribulations also: knowing that tribulation worketh patience;

4. And patience, experience; and experience, hope:

5. And hope maketh not ashamed; because the love of God is shed abroad in our hearts by the Holy Ghost which is given unto us.

6. For when we were yet without strength, in due time Christ died for the ungodly.

7. For scarcely for a righteous man will one die: yet peradventure for a good man some would even dare to die.

8. But God commendeth his love toward us, in that, while we were yet sinners, Christ died for us.

9. Much more then, being now justified by his blood, we shall be saved from wrath through him.

10. For if, when we were enemies, we were reconciled to God by the death of his Son, much more, being reconciled, we shall be saved by his life.

11. And not only so, but we also joy in God through our Lord Jesus Christ, by whom we have now received the atonement.

12. Wherefore, as by one man sin entered into the world, and death by sin; and so death passed upon all men, for that all have sinned:

13. (For until the law sin was in the world: but sin is not imputed when there is no law.

14. Nevertheless death reigned from Adam to Moses, even over them that had not sinned after the similitude of Adam's transgression, who is the figure of him that was to come.

15. But not as the offence, so also is the free gift. For if through the offence of one many be dead, much more the grace of God, and the gift by grace, which is by one man, Jesus Christ, hath abounded unto many.

16. And not as it was by one that sinned, so is the gift: for the judgment was by one to condemnation, but the free gift is of many offences unto justification.

17. For if by one man's offence death reigned by one; much more they which receive abundance of grace and of the gift of righteousness shall reign in life by one, Jesus Christ.)

18. Therefore as by the offence of

Rom. 5:1–5—In these verses, Paul emphasizes the obligations that justification brings upon the believer to act in patience and love. It is for this reason—justification through the Atonement made effectual on the basis of faith—that Paul extols the magnificence of the gospel of Jesus Christ, saying: "For I am not ashamed of the gospel of Christ: for it is the power of God unto salvation to every one that believeth; to the Jew first, and also to the Greek. For therein is the righteousness of God revealed from faith to faith: as it is written, The just shall live by faith" (Rom. 1:16–17).

Elder Bruce R. McConkie taught, "As with all other doctrines of salvation, justification is available because of the atoning sacrifice of Christ, but it becomes operative in the life of an individual only on conditions of personal righteousness. As Paul taught, men are not justified by the works of the Mosaic law alone any more than men are saved by those works alone. The grace of God, manifest through the infinite and eternal Atonement wrought by his Son, makes justification a living reality for those who seek righteousness" (*Mormon Doctrine*, 408).

one judgment came upon all men to condemnation; even so by the righteousness of one the free gift came upon all men unto justification of life.

19. For as by one man's disobedience many were made sinners, so by the obedience of one shall many be made righteous.

20. Moreover the law entered, that the offence might abound. But where sin abounded, grace did much more abound:

21. That as sin hath reigned unto death, even so might grace reign through righteousness unto eternal life by Jesus Christ our Lord.

CHAPTER 6

1. What shall we say then? Shall we continue in sin, that grace may abound?

2. God forbid. How shall we, that are dead to sin, live any longer therein?

3. Know ye not, that so many of us as were baptized into Jesus Christ were baptized into his death?

4. Therefore we are buried with him by baptism into death: that like as Christ was raised up from the dead by the glory of the Father, even so we also should walk in newness of life.

5. For if we have been planted together in the likeness of his death, we shall be also in the likeness of his resurrection:

6. Knowing this, that our old man is crucified with him, that the body of sin might be destroyed, that henceforth we should not serve sin.

7. For he that is dead is freed from sin.

8. Now if we be dead with Christ, we believe that we shall also live with him:

9. Knowing that Christ being raised from the dead dieth no more; death hath no more dominion over him.

10. For in that he died, he died unto sin once: but in that he liveth, he liveth unto God.

11. Likewise reckon ye also yourselves to be dead indeed unto sin, but alive unto God through Jesus Christ our Lord.

12. Let not sin therefore reign in your mortal body, that ye should obey it in the lusts thereof.

13. Neither yield ye your members as instruments of unrighteousness unto sin: but yield yourselves unto God, as those that are alive from the dead, and your members as instruments of righteousness unto God.

14. For sin shall not have dominion over you: for ye are not under the law, but under grace.

15. What then? shall we sin, be-

Rom. 6:1–7—Paul here confirmed for the Roman Saints the transcendent symbolism of baptism as a representation of the death and Resurrection of the Lord, He willingly submersing Himself in the vault of death and then coming forth again as the curator of all life and the firstfruits of the Resurrection.

Notes: _____

cause we are not under the law, but under grace? God forbid.

16. Know ye not, that to whom ye yield yourselves servants to obey, his servants ye are to whom ye obey; whether of sin unto death, or of obedience unto righteousness?

17. But God be thanked, that ye were the servants of sin, but ye have obeyed from the heart that form of doctrine which was delivered you.

18. Being then made free from sin, ye became the servants of righteousness.

19. I speak after the manner of men because of the infirmity of your flesh: for as ye have yielded your members servants to uncleanness and to iniquity unto iniquity; even so now yield your members servants to righteousness unto holiness.

20. For when ye were the servants of sin, ye were free from righteousness.

21. What fruit had ye then in those things whereof ye are now ashamed? for the end of those things is death.

22. But now being made free from sin, and become servants to God, ye have your fruit unto holiness, and the end everlasting life.

23. For the wages of sin is death; but the gift of God is eternal life through Jesus Christ our Lord.

CHAPTER 7

1. Know ye not, brethren, (for I speak to them that know the law,) how that the law hath dominion over a man as long as he liveth?

2. For the woman which hath an husband is bound by the law to her husband so long as he liveth; but if the husband be dead, she is loosed from the law of her husband.

3. So then if, while her husband liveth, she be married to another man, she shall be called an adulteress: but if her husband be dead, she is free from that law; so that she is no adulteress, though she be married to another man.

4. Wherefore, my brethren, ye also are become dead to the law by the body of Christ; that ye should be married to another, even to him who is raised from the dead, that we should bring forth fruit unto God.

5. For when we were in the flesh, the motions of sins, which were by the law, did work in our members to bring forth fruit unto death.

6. But now we are delivered from the law, that being dead wherein we were held; that we should serve in newness of spirit, and not in the oldness of the letter.

7. What shall we say then? Is the law sin? God forbid. Nay, I had not known sin, but by the law: for I had not known lust, except the law had said, Thou shalt not covet.

8. But sin, taking occasion by the commandment, wrought in me all manner of concupiscence. For without the law sin was dead.

9. For I was alive without the law once: but when the commandment came, sin revived, and I died.

10. And the commandment, which was ordained to life, I found to be unto death.

11. For sin, taking occasion by the commandment, deceived me, and by it slew me.

12. Wherefore the law is holy, and the commandment holy, and just, and good.

13. Was then that which is good made death unto me? God forbid. But sin, that it might appear sin, working death in me by that which is good; that sin by the commandment might become exceeding sinful.

14. For we know that the law is spiritual: but I am carnal, sold under sin.

15. For that which I do I allow not: for what I would, that do I not; but what I hate, that do I.

16. If then I do that which I would not, I consent unto the law that it is good.

17. Now then it is no more I that do it, but sin that dwelleth in me.

18. For I know that in me (that is, in my flesh,) dwelleth no good thing: for to will is present with me; but how to perform that which is good I find not.

19. For the good that I would I do not: but the evil which I would not, that I do.

20. Now if I do that I would not, it is no more I that do it, but sin that dwelleth in me.

21. I find then a law, that, when I would do good, evil is present with me.

22. For I delight in the law of God after the inward man:

23. But I see another law in my members, warring against the law of my mind, and bringing me into captivity to the law of sin which is in my members.

24. O wretched man that I am! who shall deliver me from the body of this death?

25. I thank God through Jesus Christ our Lord. So then with the mind I myself serve the law of God; but with the flesh the law of sin.

CHAPTER 8

1. There is therefore now no condemnation to them which are in Christ Jesus, who walk not after the flesh, but after the Spirit.

2. For the law of the Spirit of life in Christ Jesus hath made me free from the law of sin and death.

3. For what the law could not do, in that it was weak through the flesh, God sending his own Son in the likeness of sinful flesh, and for sin, condemned sin in the flesh:

4. That the righteousness of the law might be fulfilled in us, who walk not after the flesh, but after the Spirit.

Notes: _____

_____

_____

_____

_____

_____

_____

_____

_____

_____

_____

_____

_____

_____

_____

_____

_____

_____

_____

_____

_____

_____

_____

_____

_____

_____

_____

_____

_____

_____

5. For they that are after the flesh do mind the things of the flesh; but they that are after the Spirit the things of the Spirit.

6. For to be carnally minded is death; but to be spiritually minded is life and peace.

7. Because the carnal mind is enmity against God: for it is not subject to the law of God, neither indeed can be.

8. So then they that are in the flesh cannot please God.

9. But ye are not in the flesh, but in the Spirit, if so be that the Spirit of God dwell in you. Now if any man have not the Spirit of Christ, he is none of his.

10. And if Christ be in you, the body is dead because of sin; but the Spirit is life because of righteousness.

11. But if the Spirit of him that raised up Jesus from the dead dwell in you, he that raised up Christ from the dead shall also quicken your mortal bodies by his Spirit that dwelleth in you.

12. Therefore, brethren, we are debtors, not to the flesh, to live after the flesh.

13. For if ye live after the flesh, ye shall die: but if ye through the Spirit do mortify the deeds of the body, ye shall live.

14. For as many as are led by the Spirit of God, they are the sons of God.

15. For ye have not received the spirit of bondage again to fear; but ye have received the Spirit of adoption, whereby we cry, Abba, Father.

16. The Spirit itself beareth witness with our spirit, that we are the children of God:

17. And if children, then heirs; heirs of God, and joint-heirs with Christ; if so be that we suffer with him, that we may be also glorified together.

18. For I reckon that the sufferings of this present time are not worthy to be compared with the glory which shall be revealed in us.

19. For the earnest expectation of the creature waiteth for the manifestation of the sons of God.

20. For the creature was made subject to vanity, not willingly, but by reason of him who hath subjected the same in hope,

21. Because the creature itself also shall be delivered from the bondage of corruption into the glorious liberty of the children of God.

22. For we know that the whole creation groaneth and travaileth in pain together until now.

23. And not only they, but ourselves also, which have the firstfruits of

Rom. 8:14–18, 23–24—The process of coming into the fold of Christ and participating in the Abrahamic covenant (either through lineage or through adoption—Rom. 8:23) brings with it extraordinary blessings, including becoming joint-heirs with Christ.

Rom. 8:16–17—As the divine spirit children of God the Eternal Father, we have the right of being heirs, provided we fulfill in obedience all things that the Lord requires of us. When we do all these things and partake of all the covenants and ordinances regarding exaltation, we can receive all that the Father has (see D&C 84:38).

the Spirit, even we ourselves groan within ourselves, waiting for the adoption, to wit, the redemption of our body.

24. For we are saved by hope: but hope that is seen is not hope: for what a man seeth, why doth he yet hope for?

25. But if we hope for that we see not, then do we with patience wait for it.

26. Likewise the Spirit also helpeth our infirmities: for we know not what we should pray for as we ought: but the Spirit itself maketh intercession for us with groanings which cannot be uttered.

27. And he that searcheth the hearts knoweth what is the mind of the Spirit, because he maketh intercession for the saints according to the will of God.

28. And we know that all things work together for good to them that love God, to them who are the called according to his purpose.

29. For whom he did foreknow, he also did predestinate to be conformed to the image of his Son, that he might be the firstborn among many brethren.

30. Moreover whom he did predestinate, them he also called: and whom he called, them he also justified: and whom he justified, them he also glorified.

31. What shall we then say to these things? If God be for us, who can be against us?

32. He that spared not his own Son, but delivered him up for us all, how shall he not with him also freely give us all things?

33. Who shall lay any thing to the charge of God's elect? It is God that justifieth.

34. Who is he that condemneth? It is Christ that died, yea rather, that is risen again, who is even at the right hand of God, who also maketh intercession for us.

35. Who shall separate us from the love of Christ? shall tribulation, or distress, or persecution, or famine, or nakedness, or peril, or sword?

36. As it is written, For thy sake we are killed all the day long; we are accounted as sheep for the slaughter.

37. Nay, in all these things we are more than conquerors through him that loved us.

38. For I am persuaded, that neither death, nor life, nor angels, nor principalities, nor powers, nor things present, nor things to come,

39. Nor height, nor depth, nor any other creature, shall be able to separate us from the love of God, which is in Christ Jesus our Lord.

Rom. 8:28 — As we read the epistles of Paul, we hear the word of God spoken to us. The word of God through Paul to the Romans embraces the doctrines of justification through faith in Jesus Christ, becoming joint-heirs with the Savior, and being perfected in righteousness by living a saintly and Christlike life. In this we are confirmed in our faith: "And we know that all things work together for good to them that love God, to them who are the called according to his purpose" (Rom. 8:28).

Rom. 8:28, 35–39 — According to Elder Bruce R. McConkie, "A joint-heir is one who inherits equally with all other heirs including the Chief Heir who is the Son. Each joint-heir has an equal and an undivided portion of the whole of everything. If one knows all things, so do all others. If one has all power, so do all those who inherit jointly with him. If the universe belongs to one, so it does equally to the total of all upon whom the joint inheritances are bestowed" (*Mormon Doctrine*, 395).

As joint-heirs of Christ, we can look forward in faith and hope — beyond the veil of tears and tribulation that all too often defines our mortal existence — to an eternal reward of glory in the hereafter with Father and Son.

CHAPTER 9

1. I say the truth in Christ, I lie not, my conscience also bearing me witness in the Holy Ghost,

2. That I have great heaviness and continual sorrow in my heart.

3. For I could wish that myself were accursed from Christ for my brethren, my kinsmen according to the flesh:

4. Who are Israelites; to whom pertaineth the adoption, and the glory, and the covenants, and the giving of the law, and the service of God, and the promises;

5. Whose are the fathers, and of whom as concerning the flesh Christ came, who is over all, God blessed for ever. Amen.

6. Not as though the word of God hath taken none effect. For they are not all Israel, which are of Israel:

7. Neither, because they are the seed of Abraham, are they all children: but, In Isaac shall thy seed be called.

8. That is, They which are the children of the flesh, these are not the children of God: but the children of the promise are counted for the seed.

9. For this is the word of promise, At this time will I come, and Sara shall have a son.

10. And not only this; but when Rebecca also had conceived by one, even by our father Isaac;

11. (For the children being not yet born, neither having done any good or evil, that the purpose of God according to election might stand, not of works, but of him that calleth;)

12. It was said unto her, The elder shall serve the younger.

13. As it is written, Jacob have I loved, but Esau have I hated.

14. What shall we say then? Is there unrighteousness with God? God forbid.

15. For he saith to Moses, I will have mercy on whom I will have mercy, and I will have compassion on whom I will have compassion.

16. So then it is not of him that willeth, nor of him that runneth, but of God that sheweth mercy.

17. For the scripture saith unto Pharaoh, Even for this same purpose have I raised thee up, that I might shew my power in thee, and that my name might be declared throughout all the earth.

18. Therefore hath he mercy on whom he will have mercy, and whom he will he hardeneth.

19. Thou wilt say then unto me, Why doth he yet find fault? For who hath resisted his will?

20. Nay but, O man, who art thou that repliest against God? Shall the thing formed say to him that formed it, Why hast thou made me thus?

21. Hath not the potter power over the clay, of the same lump to make one vessel unto honour, and another unto dishonour?

Jacob receiving Isaac's blessing

22. What if God, willing to shew his wrath, and to make his power known, endured with much longsuffering the vessels of wrath fitted to destruction:

23. And that he might make known the riches of his glory on the vessels of mercy, which he had afore prepared unto glory,

24. Even us, whom he hath called, not of the Jews only, but also of the Gentiles?

25. As he saith also in Osee, I will call them my people, which were not my people; and her beloved, which was not beloved.

26. And it shall come to pass, that in the place where it was said unto them, Ye are not my people; there shall they be called the children of the living God.

27. Esaias also crieth concerning Israel, Though the number of the children of Israel be as the sand of the sea, a remnant shall be saved:

28. For he will finish the work, and cut it short in righteousness: because a short work will the Lord make upon the earth.

29. And as Esaias said before, Except the Lord of Sabaoth had left us a seed, we had been as Sodoma, and been made like unto Gomorrha.

30. What shall we say then? That the Gentiles, which followed not after righteousness, have attained to righteousness, even the righteousness which is of faith.

31. But Israel, which followed after the law of righteousness, hath not attained to the law of righteousness.

32. Wherefore? Because they sought it not by faith, but as it were by the works of the law. For they stumbled at that stumblingstone;

33. As it is written, Behold, I lay in Sion a stumblingstone and rock of offence: and whosoever believeth on him shall not be ashamed.

CHAPTER 10

1. Brethren, my heart's desire and prayer to God for Israel is, that they might be saved.

2. For I bear them record that they have a zeal of God, but not according to knowledge.

3. For they being ignorant of God's righteousness, and going about to establish their own righteousness, have not submitted themselves unto the righteousness of God.

4. For Christ is the end of the law for righteousness to every one that believeth.

5. For Moses describeth the righteousness which is of the law, That the man which doeth those things shall live by them.

6. But the righteousness which is of faith speaketh on this wise, Say not in thine heart, Who shall ascend into heaven? (that is, to bring Christ down from above:)

7. Or, Who shall descend into the deep? (that is, to bring up Christ again from the dead.)

8. But what saith it? The word is nigh thee, even in thy mouth, and in

---

ISRAEL

During the time of his conflict with his twin brother, Esau, Jacob experienced an event in which he wrestled all night with a messenger from God who asked, "What is thy name? and he said, Jacob. And he said, Thy name shall be called no more Jacob, but Israel: for as a prince hast thou power with God and with men, and hast prevailed" (Gen. 32:27–28).

Thereafter, *Israel* was the name applied to Jacob and his posterity (see Gen. 49:28). In due course, after the kingdom was separated into two, the northern part came to be designated *Israel* and the southern part *Judah*.

In a general sense, the term *Israel* is applied to all those who are true believers in Christ, as Paul explained (see Rom. 10:1). Similarly, the Doctrine and Covenants uses the term *Israel* to denote all of those belonging to the covenant people of God, literally or through adoption, according to their obedience to gospel principles.

The names *Israel* or *Israelites* occur in the New Testament frequently (some seventy-seven times), often in connection with a phrase such as *people of Israel, house of Israel, children of Israel, land of Israel, God of Israel,* and *king of Israel.*

thy heart: that is, the word of faith, which we preach;

9. That if thou shalt confess with thy mouth the Lord Jesus, and shalt believe in thine heart that God hath raised him from the dead, thou shalt be saved.

10. For with the heart man believeth unto righteousness; and with the mouth confession is made unto salvation.

11. For the scripture saith, Whosoever believeth on him shall not be ashamed.

12. For there is no difference between the Jew and the Greek: for the same Lord over all is rich unto all that call upon him.

13. For whosoever shall call upon the name of the Lord shall be saved.

14. How then shall they call on him in whom they have not believed? and how shall they believe in him of whom they have not heard? and how shall they hear without a preacher?

15. And how shall they preach, except they be sent? as it is written, How beautiful are the feet of them that preach the gospel of peace, and bring glad tidings of good things!

16. But they have not all obeyed the gospel. For Esaias saith, Lord, who hath believed our report?

17. So then faith cometh by hearing, and hearing by the word of God.

18. But I say, Have they not heard? Yes verily, their sound went into all the earth, and their words unto the ends of the world.

19. But I say, Did not Israel know? First Moses saith, I will provoke you to jealousy by them that are no people, and by a foolish nation I will anger you.

20. But Esaias is very bold, and saith, I was found of them that sought me not; I was made manifest unto them that asked not after me.

21. But to Israel he saith, All day long I have stretched forth my hands unto a disobedient and gainsaying people.

CHAPTER 11

1. I say then, Hath God cast away his people? God forbid. For I also am an Israelite, of the seed of Abraham, of the tribe of Benjamin.

2. God hath not cast away his people which he foreknew. Wot ye not what the scripture saith of Elias? how he maketh intercession to God against Israel, saying,

3. Lord, they have killed thy prophets, and digged down thine altars; and I am left alone, and they seek my life.

4. But what saith the answer of God unto him? I have reserved to myself seven thousand men, who have not bowed the knee to the image of Baal.

Rom. 10:14–17 — We are privileged to sit at the feet of Paul the Apostle and bask in the light of truth, confirming our faith in the gospel of Jesus Christ according to the words of this devoted and magnanimous Apostle. As such, we participate in the faith-building process that Paul here recommended to the Roman Saints.

Rom. 10:17 — Paul gave this advice to the Roman Saints in his day on how to open the source of faith in their lives. How do we increase our faith through the word of the Lord? By listening to the living prophets (see D&C 21:4–5), searching the holy scriptures (see 2 Ne. 32:3), seeking the promptings of the Holy Spirit (see 2 Ne. 32:5), and applying the power of prayer in our lives (see James 1:5–6). How can you help those you love to make the word of the Lord an active part of their lives and thus increase their faith?

When our faith is exercised as the moving cause of all action, it gives us power to do all things. The most important thing we can do with our faith, as it relates to our individual exaltation, is to repent. Repentance is our part of the reconciliatory process acting on the goodness and grace of God in providing the Atonement of our Beloved Savior Jesus Christ. We can increase our faith as we hear the word of God through the words of those inspired by the Holy Ghost (see Rom. 10:14–17; D&C 68:3–7) and as we search the scriptures (see Rom. 10:17). Our faith will also increase as we fast and pray for this precious gift (see Hel. 3:35). Our faith, which moves us to repentance, is our link to the atoning sacrifice of our Savior. Paul reminds us that with faith we are doers of the word: "For not the hearers of the law are just before God, but the doers of the law shall be justified" (Rom. 2:13). The Holy Ghost can then put His seal upon this action, "For by the water ye keep the commandment; by the Spirit ye are justified, and by the blood ye are sanctified" (Moses 6:60).

5. Even so then at this present time also there is a remnant according to the election of grace.

6. And if by grace, then is it no more of works: otherwise grace is no more grace. But if it be of works, then is it no more grace: otherwise work is no more work.

7. What then? Israel hath not obtained that which he seeketh for; but the election hath obtained it, and the rest were blinded

8. (According as it is written, God hath given them the spirit of slumber, eyes that they should not see, and ears that they should not hear;) unto this day.

9. And David saith, Let their table be made a snare, and a trap, and a stumbling block, and a recompence unto them:

10. Let their eyes be darkened, that they may not see, and bow down their back alway.

11. I say then, Have they stumbled that they should fall? God forbid: but rather through their fall salvation is come unto the Gentiles, for to provoke them to jealousy.

12. Now if the fall of them be the riches of the world, and the diminishing of them the riches of the Gentiles; how much more their fulness?

13. For I speak to you Gentiles, inasmuch as I am the apostle of the Gentiles, I magnify mine office:

14. If by any means I may provoke to emulation them which are my flesh, and might save some of them.

15. For if the casting away of them be the reconciling of the world, what shall the receiving of them be, but life from the dead?

16. For if the firstfruit be holy, the lump is also holy: and if the root be holy, so are the branches.

17. And if some of the branches be broken off, and thou, being a wild olive tree, wert graffed in among them, and with them partakest of the root and fatness of the olive tree;

18. Boast not against the branches. But if thou boast, thou bearest not the root, but the root thee.

19. Thou wilt say then, The branches were broken off, that I might be graffed in.

20. Well; because of unbelief they were broken off, and thou standest by faith. Be not highminded, but fear:

21. For if God spared not the natural branches, take heed lest he also spare not thee.

22. Behold therefore the goodness and severity of God: on them which fell, severity; but toward thee, goodness, if thou continue in his goodness: otherwise thou also shalt be cut off.

23. And they also, if they abide not still in unbelief, shall be graffed in: for God is able to graff them in again.

24. For if thou wert cut out of the olive tree which is wild by nature, and wert graffed contrary to nature into a good olive tree: how much more shall these, which be the natural branches, be graffed into their own olive tree?

25. For I would not, brethren, that ye should be ignorant of this mystery, lest ye should be wise in your own conceits; that blindness in part is happened to Israel, until the fulness of the Gentiles be come in.

Notes: _____

_____

26. And so all Israel shall be saved: as it is written, There shall come out of Sion the Deliverer, and shall turn away ungodliness from Jacob:

27. For this is my covenant unto them, when I shall take away their sins.

28. As concerning the gospel, they are enemies for your sakes: but as touching the election, they are beloved for the fathers' sakes.

29. For the gifts and calling of God are without repentance.

30. For as ye in times past have not believed God, yet have now obtained mercy through their unbelief:

31. Even so have these also now not believed, that through your mercy they also may obtain mercy.

32. For God hath concluded them all in unbelief, that he might have mercy upon all.

33. O the depth of the riches both of the wisdom and knowledge of God! how unsearchable are his judgments, and his ways past finding out!

34. For who hath known the mind of the Lord? or who hath been his counsellor?

35. Or who hath first given to him, and it shall be recompensed unto him again?

36. For of him, and through him, and to him, are all things: to whom be glory for ever. Amen.

CHAPTER 12

1. I beseech you therefore, brethren, by the mercies of God, that ye present your bodies a living sacrifice, holy, acceptable unto God, which is your reasonable service.

2. And be not conformed to this world: but be ye transformed by the renewing of your mind, that ye may prove what is that good, and acceptable, and perfect, will of God.

3. For I say, through the grace given unto me, to every man that is among you, not to think of himself more highly than he ought to think; but to think soberly, according as God hath dealt to every man the measure of faith.

4. For as we have many members in one body, and all members have not the same office:

5. So we, being many, are one body in Christ, and every one members one of another.

6. Having then gifts differing according to the grace that is given to us, whether prophecy, let us prophesy according to the proportion of faith;

7. Or ministry, let us wait on our ministering: or he that teacheth, on teaching;

8. Or he that exhorteth, on exhorta-

Rom. 12–15—The task and test of mortality, following the reception of the lifesaving covenants and ordinances, is to live a saintly and Christlike life.

Paul concludes the doctrinal aspects of his epistle to the Romans with an exhortation to live a righteous life (see Rom. 12–15). A desirable and godlike quality of life reflects a commitment to do the following: apply the several gifts of the Spirit for the good of the community of Christ (see Rom. 12:6–8); "Abhor that which is evil; cleave to that which is good" (Rom. 12:9); cultivate brotherly love, industry, hope, patience, charity, forgiveness, and humility (see Rom. 12:9–20); "Be not overcome of evil, but overcome evil with good" (Rom. 12:21); sustain the anointed leaders of the Church (see Rom. 13:6); keep the commandments—sufficiently encapsulated in the enjoinder "Thou shalt love thy neighbour as thyself" (Rom. 13:9); "cast off the works of darkness" and "put on the armour of light" (Rom. 13:12); and avoid the unrighteous judgment of others (see Rom. 14:1–11), but rather fellowship the Saints in the spirit of love and harmony:

"Now the God of patience and consolation grant you to be likeminded one toward another according to Christ Jesus:

"That ye may with one mind and one mouth glorify God, even the Father of our Lord Jesus Christ.

"Wherefore receive ye one another, as Christ also received us to the glory of God" (Rom. 15:5–7).

Rom. 12:1–2—Our goal is to do all we can to conform our mind to the will of God. As we do this, our lives will be patterned after our Savior Jesus Christ—we will have charity, and when He appears, we will be like Him (see Moro. 7:48).

tion: he that giveth, let him do it with simplicity; he that ruleth, with diligence; he that sheweth mercy, with cheerfulness.

9. Let love be without dissimulation. Abhor that which is evil; cleave to that which is good.

10. Be kindly affectioned one to another with brotherly love; in honour preferring one another;

11. Not slothful in business; fervent in spirit; serving the Lord;

12. Rejoicing in hope; patient in tribulation; continuing instant in prayer;

13. Distributing to the necessity of saints; given to hospitality.

14. Bless them which persecute you: bless, and curse not.

15. Rejoice with them that do rejoice, and weep with them that weep.

16. Be of the same mind one toward another. Mind not high things, but condescend to men of low estate. Be not wise in your own conceits.

17. Recompense to no man evil for evil. Provide things honest in the sight of all men.

18. If it be possible, as much as lieth in you, live peaceably with all men.

19. Dearly beloved, avenge not yourselves, but rather give place unto wrath: for it is written, Vengeance is mine; I will repay, saith the Lord.

20. Therefore if thine enemy hunger, feed him; if he thirst, give him drink: for in so doing thou shalt heap coals of fire on his head.

21. Be not overcome of evil, but overcome evil with good.

CHAPTER 13

1. Let every soul be subject unto the higher powers. For there is no power but of God: the powers that be are ordained of God.

2. Whosoever therefore resisteth the power, resisteth the ordinance of God: and they that resist shall receive to themselves damnation.

3. For rulers are not a terror to good works, but to the evil. Wilt thou then not be afraid of the power? do that which is good, and thou shalt have praise of the same:

4. For he is the minister of God to thee for good. But if thou do that which is evil, be afraid; for he beareth not the sword in vain: for he is the minister of God, a revenger to execute wrath upon him that doeth evil.

5. Wherefore ye must needs be subject, not only for wrath, but also for conscience sake.

6. For for this cause pay ye tribute also: for they are God's ministers, attending continually upon this very thing.

Notes:

7. Render therefore to all their dues: tribute to whom tribute is due; custom to whom custom; fear to whom fear; honour to whom honour.

8. Owe no man any thing, but to love one another: for he that loveth another hath fulfilled the law.

9. For this, Thou shalt not commit adultery, Thou shalt not kill, Thou shalt not steal, Thou shalt not bear false witness, Thou shalt not covet; and if there be any other commandment, it is briefly comprehended in this saying, namely, Thou shalt love thy neighbour as thyself.

10. Love worketh no ill to his neighbour: therefore love is the fulfilling of the law.

11. And that, knowing the time, that now it is high time to awake out of sleep: for now is our salvation nearer than when we believed.

12. The night is far spent, the day is at hand: let us therefore cast off the works of darkness, and let us put on the armour of light.

13. Let us walk honestly, as in the day; not in rioting and drunkenness, not in chambering and wantonness, not in strife and envying.

14. But put ye on the Lord Jesus Christ, and make not provision for the flesh, to fulfil the lusts thereof.

CHAPTER 14

1. Him that is weak in the faith receive ye, but not to doubtful disputations.

2. For one believeth that he may eat all things: another, who is weak, eateth herbs.

3. Let not him that eateth despise him that eateth not; and let not him which eateth not judge him that eateth: for God hath received him.

4. Who art thou that judgest another man's servant? to his own master he standeth or falleth. Yea, he shall be holden up: for God is able to make him stand.

5. One man esteemeth one day above another: another esteemeth every day alike. Let every man be fully persuaded in his own mind.

6. He that regardeth the day, regardeth it unto the Lord; and he that regardeth not the day, to the Lord he doth not regard it. He that eateth, eateth to the Lord, for he giveth God thanks; and he that eateth not, to the Lord he eateth not, and giveth God thanks.

7. For none of us liveth to himself, and no man dieth to himself.

8. For whether we live, we live unto the Lord; and whether we die, we die unto the Lord: whether we live therefore, or die, we are the Lord's.

9. For to this end Christ both died, and rose, and revived, that he might

The Ten Commandments being received on the Mount

be Lord both of the dead and living.

10. But why dost thou judge thy brother? or why dost thou set at nought thy brother? for we shall all stand before the judgment seat of Christ.

11. For it is written, As I live, saith the Lord, every knee shall bow to me, and every tongue shall confess to God.

12. So then every one of us shall give account of himself to God.

13. Let us not therefore judge one another any more: but judge this rather, that no man put a stumblingblock or an occasion to fall in his brother's way.

14. I know, and am persuaded by the Lord Jesus, that there is nothing unclean of itself: but to him that esteemeth any thing to be unclean, to him it is unclean.

15. But if thy brother be grieved with thy meat, now walkest thou not charitably. Destroy not him with thy meat, for whom Christ died.

16. Let not then your good be evil spoken of:

17. For the kingdom of God is not meat and drink; but righteousness, and peace, and joy in the Holy Ghost.

18. For he that in these things serveth Christ is acceptable to God, and approved of men.

19. Let us therefore follow after the things which make for peace, and things wherewith one may edify another.

20. For meat destroy not the work of God. All things indeed are pure; but it is evil for that man who eateth with offence.

21. It is good neither to eat flesh, nor to drink wine, nor any thing whereby thy brother stumbleth, or is offended, or is made weak.

22. Hast thou faith? have it to thyself before God. Happy is he that condemneth not himself in that thing which he alloweth.

23. And he that doubteth is damned if he eat, because he eateth not of faith: for whatsoever is not of faith is sin.

CHAPTER 15

1. We then that are strong ought to bear the infirmities of the weak, and not to please ourselves.

2. Let every one of us please his neighbour for his good to edification.

3. For even Christ pleased not himself; but, as it is written, The reproaches of them that reproached thee fell on me.

4. For whatsoever things were written aforetime were written for our learning, that we through

Rom. 14:17—The Mosaic law as recorded in Leviticus listed many dietary restrictions. Here Paul tried to teach his audience that there is more to religion and spirituality than simply what one eats and drinks under the law of Moses. The Lord suggested the same thing (see Mark 7:18–19). How can we avoid going to extremes regarding the Word of Wisdom? How can we balance our obedience to the Word of Wisdom with our obedience to all of the commandments of the Lord?

patience and comfort of the scriptures might have hope.

5. Now the God of patience and consolation grant you to be likeminded one toward another according to Christ Jesus:

6. That ye may with one mind and one mouth glorify God, even the Father of our Lord Jesus Christ.

7. Wherefore receive ye one another, as Christ also received us to the glory of God.

8. Now I say that Jesus Christ was a minister of the circumcision for the truth of God, to confirm the promises made unto the fathers:

9. And that the Gentiles might glorify God for his mercy; as it is written, For this cause I will confess to thee among the Gentiles, and sing unto thy name.

10. And again he saith, Rejoice, ye Gentiles, with his people.

11. And again, Praise the Lord, all ye Gentiles; and laud him, all ye people.

12. And again, Esaias saith, There shall be a root of Jesse, and he that shall rise to reign over the Gentiles; in him shall the Gentiles trust.

13. Now the God of hope fill you with all joy and peace in believing, that ye may abound in hope, through the power of the Holy Ghost.

14. And I myself also am persuaded of you, my brethren, that ye also are full of goodness, filled with all knowledge, able also to admonish one another.

15. Nevertheless, brethren, I have written the more boldly unto you in some sort, as putting you in mind, because of the grace that is given to me of God,

16. That I should be the minister of Jesus Christ to the Gentiles, ministering the gospel of God, that the offering up of the Gentiles might be acceptable, being sanctified by the Holy Ghost.

17. I have therefore whereof I may glory through Jesus Christ in those things which pertain to God.

18. For I will not dare to speak of any of those things which Christ hath not wrought by me, to make the Gentiles obedient, by word and deed,

19. Through mighty signs and wonders, by the power of the Spirit of God; so that from Jerusalem, and round about unto Illyricum, I have fully preached the gospel of Christ.

20. Yea, so have I strived to preach the gospel, not where Christ was named, lest I should build upon another man's foundation:

21. But as it is written, To whom he was not spoken of, they shall see: and they that have not heard shall understand.

22. For which cause also I have been much hindered from coming to you.

23. But now having no more place in these parts, and having a great desire these many years to come unto you;

24. Whensoever I take my journey into Spain, I will come to you: for I trust to see you in my journey, and to be brought on my way thitherward by you, if first I be somewhat filled with your company.

GENTILES

The word *Gentiles* as used in the scriptures refers generally to those people who are not of the house of Israel. *Gentiles* can also refer to nations that do not yet have the gospel—even though there may be those of Israelite lineage among them (see Bible Dictionary, 679).

In the New Testament, the words *Gentile* or *Gentiles* are used 101 times, largely in the context of the unfolding of the gospel message beyond those of Israelite heritage to encompass the entire world, as the charge of the Savior commanded (see Matt. 28:19–20).

Examples of this process include the baptism of the Ethiopian eunuch by Philip (see Acts 8), the baptism of the centurion Cornelius by Peter (see Acts 10–11), and the expansive missionary outreach of Paul, who called himself "the apostle of the Gentiles" (Rom. 11:13).

25. But now I go unto Jerusalem to minister unto the saints.

26. For it hath pleased them of Macedonia and Achaia to make a certain contribution for the poor saints which are at Jerusalem.

27. It hath pleased them verily; and their debtors they are. For if the Gentiles have been made partakers of their spiritual things, their duty is also to minister unto them in carnal things.

28. When therefore I have performed this, and have sealed to them this fruit, I will come by you into Spain.

29. And I am sure that, when I come unto you, I shall come in the fulness of the blessing of the gospel of Christ.

30. Now I beseech you, brethren, for the Lord Jesus Christ's sake, and for the love of the Spirit, that ye strive together with me in your prayers to God for me;

31. That I may be delivered from them that do not believe in Judæa; and that my service which I have for Jerusalem may be accepted of the saints;

32. That I may come unto you with joy by the will of God, and may with you be refreshed.

33. Now the God of peace be with you all. Amen.

CHAPTER 16

1. I commend unto you Phebe our sister, which is a servant of the church which is at Cenchrea:

2. That ye receive her in the Lord, as becometh saints, and that ye assist her in whatsoever business she hath need of you: for she hath been a succourer of many, and of myself also.

3. Greet Priscilla and Aquila my helpers in Christ Jesus:

4. Who have for my life laid down their own necks: unto whom not only I give thanks, but also all the churches of the Gentiles.

5. Likewise greet the church that is in their house. Salute my wellbeloved Epænetus, who is the firstfruits of Achaia unto Christ.

6. Greet Mary, who bestowed much labour on us.

7. Salute Andronicus and Junia, my kinsmen, and my fellowprisoners, who are of note among the apostles, who also were in Christ before me.

8. Greet Amplias my beloved in the Lord.

9. Salute Urbane, our helper in Christ, and Stachys my beloved.

10. Salute Apelles approved in Christ. Salute them which are of Aristobulus' household.

11. Salute Herodion my kinsman. Greet them that be of the household of Narcissus, which are in the Lord.

12. Salute Tryphena and Tryphosa, who labour in the Lord. Salute the beloved Persis, which laboured much in the Lord.

13. Salute Rufus chosen in the Lord, and his mother and mine.

14. Salute Asyncritus, Phlegon, Hermas, Patrobas, Hermes, and the brethren which are with them.

15. Salute Philologus, and Julia, Nereus, and his sister, and Olympas, and all the saints which are with them.

16. Salute one another with an holy kiss. The churches of Christ salute you.

17. Now I beseech you, brethren, mark them which cause divisions

Notes: _____
_____
_____
_____
_____
_____
_____
_____
_____
_____
_____
_____
_____
_____
_____
_____
_____
_____
_____
_____
_____
_____
_____
_____
_____
_____
_____
_____
_____
_____
_____
_____

call upon the name of Jesus Christ our Lord, both theirs and ours:

3. Grace be unto you, and peace, from God our Father, and from the Lord Jesus Christ.

4. I thank my God always on your behalf, for the grace of God which is given you by Jesus Christ;

5. That in every thing ye are enriched by him, in all utterance, and in all knowledge;

6. Even as the testimony of Christ was confirmed in you:

7. So that ye come behind in no gift; waiting for the coming of our Lord Jesus Christ:

8. Who shall also confirm you unto the end, that ye may be blameless in the day of our Lord Jesus Christ.

9. God is faithful, by whom ye were called unto the fellowship of his Son Jesus Christ our Lord.

10. Now I beseech you, brethren, by the name of our Lord Jesus Christ, that ye all speak the same thing, and that there be no divisions among you; but that ye be perfectly joined together in the same mind and in the same judgment.

11. For it hath been declared unto me of you, my brethren, by them which are of the house of Chloe, that there are contentions among you.

12. Now this I say, that every one of you saith, I am of Paul; and I of Apollos; and I of Cephas; and I of Christ.

13. Is Christ divided? was Paul crucified for you? or were ye baptized in the name of Paul?

14. I thank God that I baptized none of you, but Crispus and Gaius;

15. Lest any should say that I had baptized in mine own name.

16. And I baptized also the household of Stephanas: besides, I know not whether I baptized any other.

17. For Christ sent me not to baptize, but to preach the gospel: not with wisdom of words, lest the cross of Christ should be made of none effect.

18. For the preaching of the cross is to them that perish foolishness; but unto us which are saved it is the power of God.

19. For it is written, I will destroy the wisdom of the wise, and will bring to nothing the understanding of the prudent.

20. Where is the wise? where is the scribe? where is the disputer of this world? hath not God made foolish the wisdom of this world?

21. For after that in the wisdom of God the world by wisdom knew not God, it pleased God by the foolishness of preaching to save them that believe.

22. For the Jews require a sign, and the Greeks seek after wisdom:

23. But we preach Christ crucified, unto the Jews a stumblingblock, and unto the Greeks foolishness;

24. But unto them which are call-

Notes: _____
_____
_____
_____
_____
_____
_____
_____
_____
_____
_____
_____
_____
_____
_____
_____
_____
_____
_____
_____
_____
_____
_____
_____
_____
_____
_____
_____

and offences contrary to the doctrine which ye have learned; and avoid them.

18. For they that are such serve not our Lord Jesus Christ, but their own belly; and by good words and fair speeches deceive the hearts of the simple.

19. For your obedience is come abroad unto all men. I am glad therefore on your behalf: but yet I would have you wise unto that which is good, and simple concerning evil.

20. And the God of peace shall bruise Satan under your feet shortly. The grace of our Lord Jesus Christ be with you. Amen.

21. Timotheus my workfellow, and Lucius, and Jason, and Sosipater, my kinsmen, salute you.

22. I Tertius, who wrote this epistle, salute you in the Lord.

23. Gaius mine host, and of the whole church, saluteth you. Erastus the chamberlain of the city saluteth you, and Quartus a brother.

24. The grace of our Lord Jesus Christ be with you all. Amen.

25. Now to him that is of power to stablish you according to my gospel, and the preaching of Jesus Christ, according to the revelation of the mystery, which was kept secret since the world began,

26. But now is made manifest, and by the scriptures of the prophets, according to the commandment of the everlasting God, made known to all nations for the obedience of faith:

27. To God only wise, be glory through Jesus Christ for ever. Amen.

THE FIRST EPISTLE OF PAUL THE APOSTLE TO

THE CORINTHIANS

CHAPTER 1

1. Paul, called to be an apostle of Jesus Christ through the will of God, and Sosthenes our brother,

2. Unto the church of God which is at Corinth, to them that are sanctified in Christ Jesus, called to be saints, with all that in every place

1 Cor. 1–6— Blessings of the Lord are poured out upon His children as they become unified in all things, live by the Spirit, and keep themselves clean from the sins of immorality. The Lord has counseled us to be one:

"Neither pray I for these alone, but for them also which shall believe on me through their word; That they all may be one; as thou, Father, art in me, and I in thee, that they also may be one in us: that the world may believe that thou hast sent me. And the glory which thou gavest me I have given them; that they may be one, even as we are one: I in them, and thou in me, that they may be made perfect in one; and that the world may know that thou hast sent me, and hast loved them, as thou hast loved me" (John 17:20–23).

Indeed the purpose of unity is being of one mind, one purpose, and one action—that the work of the Lord might go forward in blessing our brothers and sisters. In unity, we are not only strengthened and blessed with the Spirit to direct us in all things, but there will be no contention to separate us. The Lord has warned us, "I say unto you, be one; and if ye are not one ye are not mine" (D&C 38:27). When we are one with the Lord, we partake of His goodness. We live by the Spirit and seek to do as Christ would do. We seek to have the image of Christ in our countenance (see Alma 5:14). We strive to be like the people of Enoch (see Moses 7:16–21). Righteous living is a result of being one with the Lord, for we begin to possess charity, thus becoming like Him (see Moro. 7:48). There would be no contention or strife if we would begin to live like the people described in the Book of Mormon:

"And it came to pass that there was no contention in the land, because of the love of God which did dwell in the hearts of the people.

"And there were no envyings, nor strifes, nor tumults, nor whoredoms, nor lyings, nor murders, nor any manner of lasciviousness; and surely there could not be a happier people among all the people who had been created by the hand of God.

"There were no robbers, nor murderers, neither were there Lamanites, nor any manner of -ites; but they were in one, the children of Christ, and heirs to the kingdom of God" (4 Ne. 1:15–17).

And thus we would see the blessings of the love of God in our lives. We would not seek to encumber ourselves with the vanities of the world, but would anchor ourselves in heavenly things. We would enjoy the blessings of the Spirit and keep ourselves clean and pure before the Lord.

ed, both Jews and Greeks, Christ the power of God, and the wisdom of God.

25. Because the foolishness of God is wiser than men; and the weakness of God is stronger than men.

26. For ye see your calling, brethren, how that not many wise men after the flesh, not many mighty, not many noble, are called:

27. But God hath chosen the foolish things of the world to confound the wise; and God hath chosen the weak things of the world to confound the things which are mighty;

28. And base things of the world, and things which are despised, hath God chosen, yea, and things which are not, to bring to nought things that are:

29. That no flesh should glory in his presence.

30. But of him are ye in Christ Jesus, who of God is made unto us wisdom, and righteousness, and sanctification, and redemption:

31. That, according as it is written, He that glorieth, let him glory in the Lord.

CHAPTER 2

1. And I, brethren, when I came to you, came not with excellency of speech or of wisdom, declaring unto you the testimony of God.

2. For I determined not to know any thing among you, save Jesus Christ, and him crucified.

3. And I was with you in weakness, and in fear, and in much trembling.

4. And my speech and my preaching was not with enticing words of man's wisdom, but in demonstration of the Spirit and of power:

5. That your faith should not stand in the wisdom of men, but in the power of God.

6. Howbeit we speak wisdom among them that are perfect: yet not the wisdom of this world, nor of the princes of this world, that come to nought:

7. But we speak the wisdom of God in a mystery, even the hidden wisdom, which God ordained before the world unto our glory:

8. Which none of the princes of this world knew: for had they known it, they would not have crucified the Lord of glory.

9. But as it is written, Eye hath not seen, nor ear heard, neither have entered into the heart of man, the things which God hath prepared for them that love him.

10. But God hath revealed them unto us by his Spirit: for the Spirit searcheth all things, yea, the deep things of God.

11. For what man knoweth the things of a man, save the spirit of man which is in him? even so the

1 Cor. 1:10—The first of the two extant epistles of Paul to the Saints at Corinth—a major commercial seaport in southern Greece—was written (like 2 Corinthians, Galatians, and Romans) between A.D. 55 and 56. Paul begins his exhortations in 1 Corinthians with an impassioned plea to root out all contention and establish unity of purpose and spirit, as outlined in this verse.

1 Cor. 2:5—Continuing his exhortations, Paul tells the Corinthians to anchor their testimonies and faith in eternal principles, rather than worldly things. The key to wisdom is an enduring commitment to spiritual growth; by seeking after and cultivating the gifts and blessings of the Spirit, one transcends the learning of the world, which is transitory and ephemeral, and discerns the uplifting and transforming patterns of godliness (see 1 Cor. 2:14–16). Such wisdom is available to all who believe and obey. Thus even the weak can rise in majesty to confound the best wisdom the world can bring to bear (see 1 Cor. 1:27–28).

1 Cor. 2:9–10—These words of Paul to the Corinthian Saints echo the words of Isaiah (see Isa. 64:4). Paul gave the concluding dimension of Isaiah's theme by teaching that the Spirit reveals to us the glories that lie ahead. The key to wisdom is an enduring commitment to spiritual growth; by seeking after and cultivating the gifts and blessings of the Spirit, one transcends the transitory learning of the world and discerns the uplifting and transforming patterns of godliness leading to the blessings of eternity. How can you share with your family and other loved ones your vision of the magnificent blessings of eternal life that await the faithful? How has the Holy Ghost allowed you to view such grand future blessings so often obscured by the burdens of worldly care? (see 1 Cor. 1:27–31; 2:14–16).

things of God knoweth no man, but the Spirit of God.

12. Now we have received, not the spirit of the world, but the spirit which is of God; that we might know the things that are freely given to us of God.

13. Which things also we speak, not in the words which man's wisdom teacheth, but which the Holy Ghost teacheth; comparing spiritual things with spiritual.

14. But the natural man receiveth not the things of the Spirit of God: for they are foolishness unto him: neither can he know them, because they are spiritually discerned.

15. But he that is spiritual judgeth all things, yet he himself is judged of no man.

16. For who hath known the mind of the Lord, that he may instruct him? But we have the mind of Christ.

CHAPTER 3

1. And I, brethren, could not speak unto you as unto spiritual, but as unto carnal, even as unto babes in Christ.

2. I have fed you with milk, and not with meat: for hitherto ye were not able to bear it, neither yet now are ye able.

3. For ye are yet carnal: for whereas there is among you envying, and strife, and divisions, are ye not carnal, and walk as men?

4. For while one saith, I am of Paul; and another, I am of Apollos; are ye not carnal?

5. Who then is Paul, and who is Apollos, but ministers by whom ye believed, even as the Lord gave to every man?

6. I have planted, Apollos watered; but God gave the increase.

7. So then neither is he that planteth any thing, neither he that watereth; but God that giveth the increase.

8. Now he that planteth and he that watereth are one: and every man shall receive his own reward according to his own labour.

9. For we are labourers together with God: ye are God's husbandry, ye are God's building.

10. According to the grace of God which is given unto me, as a wise masterbuilder, I have laid the foundation, and another buildeth thereon. But let every man take heed how he buildeth thereupon.

11. For other foundation can no man lay than that is laid, which is Jesus Christ.

12. Now if any man build upon this foundation gold, silver, precious stones, wood, hay, stubble;

13. Every man's work shall be made manifest: for the day shall de-

1 Cor. 3:3–7—Paul cuts to the quick by pointing out evidence of the carnality still operating within the community of Saints at Corinth in these verses.

Though many have labored to lay the foundation of the Church and kingdom of God, it is incumbent upon all who continue the work to maintain singleness of purpose and harmony within the family of God according to the central, unifying power and influence of the Savior: "For other foundation can no man lay than that is laid, which is Jesus Christ" (1 Cor. 3:11). The fruit of unity in the body of Christ is the unfathomable reward of being heirs to all things heavenly: "Therefore let no man glory in men. For all things are yours; Whether Paul, or Apollos, or Cephas, or the world, or life, or death, or things present, or things to come; all are yours; And ye are Christ's; and Christ is God's" (1 Cor. 3:21–23).

1 Cor. 3:16–17—In this famous statement, Paul uses an effective metaphor to generate in his audience a renewed commitment to be morally clean and holy. Later on in his epistle, Paul reemphasizes this same principle with these words: "What? know ye not that your body is the temple of the Holy Ghost which is in you, which ye have of God, and ye are not your own? For ye are bought with a price: therefore glorify God in your body, and in your spirit, which are God's" (1 Cor. 6:19–20). Then in a subsequent detailed exposition (chapter 7), Paul extols self-discipline and temperance regarding issues of morality and answers questions about marriage among those who are called on missions.

Recognizing that we are the divine offspring of God should give us self-esteem. Knowing who we really are empowers us to realize that we must be clean and pure in order to enjoy the Spirit in our lives (see 1 Cor. 6:19; Mosiah 2:37; Hel. 4:24).

clare it, because it shall be revealed by fire; and the fire shall try every man's work of what sort it is.

14. If any man's work abide which he hath built thereupon, he shall receive a reward.

15. If any man's work shall be burned, he shall suffer loss: but he himself shall be saved; yet so as by fire.

16. Know ye not that ye are the temple of God, and that the Spirit of God dwelleth in you?

17. If any man defile the temple of God, him shall God destroy; for the temple of God is holy, which temple ye are.

18. Let no man deceive himself. If any man among you seemeth to be wise in this world, let him become a fool, that he may be wise.

19. For the wisdom of this world is foolishness with God. For it is written, He taketh the wise in their own craftiness.

20. And again, The Lord knoweth the thoughts of the wise, that they are vain.

21. Therefore let no man glory in men. For all things are yours;

22. Whether Paul, or Apollos, or Cephas, or the world, or life, or death, or things present, or things to come; all are yours;

23. And ye are Christ's; and Christ is God's.

CHAPTER 4

1. Let a man so account of us, as of the ministers of Christ, and stewards of the mysteries of God.

2. Moreover it is required in stewards, that a man be found faithful.

3. But with me it is a very small thing that I should be judged of you, or of man's judgment: yea, I judge not mine own self.

4. For I know nothing by myself; yet am I not hereby justified: but he that judgeth me is the Lord.

5. Therefore judge nothing before the time, until the Lord come, who both will bring to light the hidden things of darkness, and will make manifest the counsels of the hearts: and then shall every man have praise of God.

6. And these things, brethren, I have in a figure transferred to myself and to Apollos for your sakes; that ye might learn in us not to think of men above that which is written, that no one of you be puffed up for one against another.

7. For who maketh thee to differ from another? and what hast thou that thou didst not receive? now if thou didst receive it, why dost thou glory, as if thou hadst not received it?

8. Now ye are full, now ye are rich, ye have reigned as kings without us: and I would to God ye did reign, that we also might reign with you.

1 Cor. 3:16–17—In these well-known words of Paul to the Corinthians, he reminded his audience of their sacred station as sons and daughters of God, with the obligation of keeping themselves pure and untainted. When we understand the sacredness of our mortal tabernacle, we will be more diligent in keeping it healthy, strong, and pure. The blessings of the Spirit can be ours if we are pure and clean (see 1 Cor. 6:19–20). How can obedience to the Word of Wisdom help you qualify for magnificent blessings from God through the Spirit?

Notes: _____

_____

_____

_____

_____

_____

_____

_____

_____

_____

_____

_____

_____

_____

_____

_____

_____

9. For I think that God hath set forth us the apostles last, as it were appointed to death: for we are made a spectacle unto the world, and to angels, and to men.

10. We are fools for Christ's sake, but ye are wise in Christ; we are weak, but ye are strong; ye are honourable, but we are despised.

11. Even unto this present hour we both hunger, and thirst, and are naked, and are buffeted, and have no certain dwellingplace;

12. And labour, working with our own hands: being reviled, we bless; being persecuted, we suffer it:

13. Being defamed, we intreat: we are made as the filth of the world, and are the offscouring of all things unto this day.

14. I write not these things to shame you, but as my beloved sons I warn you.

15. For though ye have ten thousand instructors in Christ, yet have ye not many fathers: for in Christ Jesus I have begotten you through the gospel.

16. Wherefore I beseech you, be ye followers of me.

17. For this cause have I sent unto you Timotheus, who is my beloved son, and faithful in the Lord, who shall bring you into remembrance of my ways which be in Christ, as I teach every where in every church.

18. Now some are puffed up, as though I would not come to you.

19. But I will come to you shortly, if the Lord will, and will know, not the speech of them which are puffed up, but the power.

20. For the kingdom of God is not in word, but in power.

21. What will ye? shall I come unto you with a rod, or in love, and in the spirit of meekness?

CHAPTER 5

1. It is reported commonly that there is fornication among you, and such fornication as is not so much as named among the Gentiles, that one should have his father's wife.

2. And ye are puffed up, and have not rather mourned, that he that hath done this deed might be taken away from among you.

3. For I verily, as absent in body, but present in spirit, have judged already, as though I were present, concerning him that hath so done this deed,

4. In the name of our Lord Jesus Christ, when ye are gathered together, and my spirit, with the power of our Lord Jesus Christ,

5. To deliver such an one unto Satan for the destruction of the flesh, that the spirit may be saved in the day of the Lord Jesus.

6. Your glorying is not good. Know ye not that a little leaven leaveneth the whole lump?

7. Purge out therefore the old leaven, that ye may be a new lump, as ye are unleavened. For even

1 Corinthians—In his writings to the Corinthian Saints, the Apostle Paul provides a cogent reminder of the need to cultivate wisdom of the spiritual kind by placing one's trust in the Lord and the principles of salvation and exaltation, rather than in worldly things (see especially 1 Cor. 2:5, 9–12, 14–16, 27–28). At the same time, the Lord has counseled us to expand our understanding of the secular disciplines in order to be prepared as missionaries to communicate sacred truths to the world (see D&C 88:78–80).

The need to make heavenly wisdom dominant in our lives while at the same time cultivating a knowledge of earthly things in sufficient scope to communicate effectively with others is a principle of delicate balance and wise prudence. Years ago, as a graduate student at The Johns Hopkins University in Baltimore, I was searching through the library card index files one day and happened to come upon a number of entries under the authorship of James E. Talmage. It was a startling reminder of the range of knowledge that encompasses the human condition. Elder Talmage (1862–1933) did advanced work at Johns Hopkins in geology and related fields, going on later to serve as president of the University of Utah from 1894 to 1897. He was called as a member of the Quorum of the Twelve Apostles in 1911. While rising to preeminence in secular knowledge, he became a celebrated exponent of sacred knowledge as well, authoring such perennial classics as *Articles of Faith* (1899), *The House of the Lord* (1912), and *Jesus the Christ* (1915).

The example of Elder Talmage and his commitment to worthwhile teaching and learning of all kinds is a salient illustration of the Lord's commandment to be prepared in all things and seek a breadth of knowledge as a fundamental means of preparation in building up the kingdom of God on earth. While the quest for knowledge is to be broad and all-encompassing, the central goal for God's servants is to serve as well-prepared instruments in advancing the cause of the gospel and its saving principles.

Christ our passover is sacrificed for us:

8. Therefore let us keep the feast, not with old leaven, neither with the leaven of malice and wickedness; but with the unleavened bread of sincerity and truth.

9. I wrote unto you in an epistle not to company with fornicators:

10. Yet not altogether with the fornicators of this world, or with the covetous, or extortioners, or with idolaters; for then must ye needs go out of the world.

11. But now I have written unto you not to keep company, if any man that is called a brother be a fornicator, or covetous, or an idolater, or a railer, or a drunkard, or an extortioner; with such an one no not to eat.

12. For what have I to do to judge them also that are without? do not ye judge them that are within?

13. But them that are without God judgeth. Therefore put away from among yourselves that wicked person.

CHAPTER 6

1. Dare any of you, having a matter against another, go to law before the unjust, and not before the saints?

2. Do ye not know that the saints shall judge the world? and if the world shall be judged by you, are ye unworthy to judge the smallest matters?

3. Know ye not that we shall judge angels? how much more things that pertain to this life?

4. If then ye have judgments of things pertaining to this life, set them to judge who are least esteemed in the church.

5. I speak to your shame. Is it so, that there is not a wise man among you? no, not one that shall be able to judge between his brethren?

6. But brother goeth to law with brother, and that before the unbelievers.

7. Now therefore there is utterly a fault among you, because ye go to law one with another. Why do ye not rather take wrong? why do ye not rather suffer yourselves to be defrauded?

8. Nay, ye do wrong, and defraud, and that your brethren.

9. Know ye not that the unrighteous shall not inherit the kingdom of God? Be not deceived: neither fornicators, nor idolaters, nor adulterers, nor effeminate, nor abusers of themselves with mankind,

10. Nor thieves, nor covetous, nor drunkards, nor revilers, nor extortioners, shall inherit the kingdom of God.

11. And such were some of you: but ye are washed, but ye are sanctified, but ye are justified in the name

Notes: _____

of the Lord Jesus, and by the Spirit of our God.

12. All things are lawful unto me, but all things are not expedient: all things are lawful for me, but I will not be brought under the power of any.

13. Meats for the belly, and the belly for meats: but God shall destroy both it and them. Now the body is not for fornication, but for the Lord; and the Lord for the body.

14. And God hath both raised up the Lord, and will also raise up us by his own power.

15. Know ye not that your bodies are the members of Christ? shall I then take the members of Christ, and make them the members of an harlot? God forbid.

16. What? know ye not that he which is joined to an harlot is one body? for two, saith he, shall be one flesh.

17. But he that is joined unto the Lord is one spirit.

18. Flee fornication. Every sin that a man doeth is without the body; but he that committeth fornication sinneth against his own body.

19. What? know ye not that your body is the temple of the Holy Ghost which is in you, which ye have of God, and ye are not your own?

20. For ye are bought with a price: therefore glorify God in your body, and in your spirit, which are God's.

CHAPTER 7

1. Now concerning the things whereof ye wrote unto me: It is good for a man not to touch a woman.

2. Nevertheless, to avoid fornication, let every man have his own wife, and let every woman have her own husband.

3. Let the husband render unto the wife due benevolence: and likewise also the wife unto the husband.

4. The wife hath not power of her own body, but the husband: and likewise also the husband hath not power of his own body, but the wife.

5. Defraud ye not one the other, except it be with consent for a time, that ye may give yourselves to fasting and prayer; and come together again, that Satan tempt you not for your incontinency.

6. But I speak this by permission, and not of commandment.

7. For I would that all men were even as I myself. But every man hath his proper gift of God, one after this manner, and another after that.

8. I say therefore to the unmarried and widows, It is good for them if they abide even as I.

9. But if they cannot contain, let them marry: for it is better to marry than to burn.

1 Cor. 7:3—In answering questions about marriage, the Apostle Paul emphasized the mutual covenant of love and respect that should abound in the marital relationship. When our first concern is the well-being of our spouse, we show compassion and empathy; we are warmhearted and understanding, charitable in all things. The word *benevolent* derives from the Latin words *bene* ("well") and *volens* (a form of the verb *velle,* meaning "to wish"). If we are benevolent, then, our first wish is for the well-being of our spouse. How have you confirmed in your experience that "benevolence" is a rewarding and charitable way to govern relationships?

10. And unto the married I command, yet not I, but the Lord, Let not the wife depart from her husband:

11. But and if she depart, let her remain unmarried, or be reconciled to her husband: and let not the husband put away his wife.

12. But to the rest speak I, not the Lord: If any brother hath a wife that believeth not, and she be pleased to dwell with him, let him not put her away.

13. And the woman which hath an husband that believeth not, and if he be pleased to dwell with her, let her not leave him.

14. For the unbelieving husband is sanctified by the wife, and the unbelieving wife is sanctified by the husband: else were your children unclean; but now are they holy.

15. But if the unbelieving depart, let him depart. A brother or a sister is not under bondage in such cases: but God hath called us to peace.

16. For what knowest thou, O wife, whether thou shalt save thy husband? or how knowest thou, O man, whether thou shalt save thy wife?

17. But as God hath distributed to every man, as the Lord hath called every one, so let him walk. And so ordain I in all churches.

18. Is any man called being circumcised? let him not become uncircumcised. Is any called in uncircumcision? let him not be circumcised.

19. Circumcision is nothing, and uncircumcision is nothing, but the keeping of the commandments of God.

20. Let every man abide in the same calling wherein he was called.

21. Art thou called being a servant? care not for it: but if thou mayest be made free, use it rather.

22. For he that is called in the Lord, being a servant, is the Lord's freeman: likewise also he that is called, being free, is Christ's servant.

23. Ye are bought with a price; be not ye the servants of men.

24. Brethren, let every man, wherein he is called, therein abide with God.

25. Now concerning virgins I have no commandment of the Lord: yet I give my judgment, as one that hath obtained mercy of the Lord to be faithful.

26. I suppose therefore that this is good for the present distress, I say, that it is good for a man so to be.

27. Art thou bound unto a wife? seek not to be loosed. Art thou loosed from a wife? seek not a wife.

28. But and if thou marry, thou hast not sinned; and if a virgin marry, she hath not sinned. Nevertheless such shall have trouble in the flesh: but I spare you.

29. But this I say, brethren, the time is short: it remaineth, that both they that have wives be as though they had none;

30. And they that weep, as though they wept not; and they that rejoice, as though they rejoiced not; and they that buy, as though they possessed not;

31. And they that use this world, as not abusing it: for the fashion of this world passeth away.

CORINTHIANS

The Corinthians were inhabitants of Corinth, an important commercial city in the Roman province of Achaia in the southern part of Greece. Paul established a Christian community there (see Acts 18:1–18) and addressed his Corinthian epistles to the Saints with roots in that part of the realm. Among the noted Corinthian Saints were Aquila and Priscilla (see Acts 18:1–3).

AQUILA AND PRISCILLA

Aquila (meaning: eagle) and his wife Priscilla (meaning: ancient) are noteworthy examples of devout Saints who served as missionaries of the gospel and made their home available for Church meetings (see 1 Cor. 16:19).

The first mention of Aquila and Priscilla tells that they came to Corinth from Italy (see Acts 18:1–3). After a season, they moved to Ephesus, accompanied by Paul (see Acts 18:18), where the couple met Apollo, an articulate spokesperson from Alexandria visiting there to discourse on gospel themes (see Acts 18:26). Thanks to Aquila and Priscilla, Apollo, a Jew who was accepting of the ministry of John the Baptist, was able to grasp the full measure of the Savior's atoning mission and carry the message to others.

Subsequently, Aquila and Priscilla returned to Rome (see Rom. 16:3–5). Apparently, they later returned to Ephesus because Paul asks Timothy to greet them (see 2 Tim. 4:19).

32. But I would have you without carefulness. He that is unmarried careth for the things that belong to the Lord, how he may please the Lord:

33. But he that is married careth for the things that are of the world, how he may please his wife.

34. There is difference also between a wife and a virgin. The unmarried woman careth for the things of the Lord, that she may be holy both in body and in spirit: but she that is married careth for the things of the world, how she may please her husband.

35. And this I speak for your own profit; not that I may cast a snare upon you, but for that which is comely, and that ye may attend upon the Lord without distraction.

36. But if any man think that he behaveth himself uncomely toward his virgin, if she pass the flower of her age, and need so require, let him do what he will, he sinneth not: let them marry.

37. Nevertheless he that standeth stedfast in his heart, having no necessity, but hath power over his own will, and hath so decreed in his heart that he will keep his virgin, doeth well.

38. So then he that giveth her in marriage doeth well; but he that giveth her not in marriage doeth better.

39. The wife is bound by the law as long as her husband liveth; but if her husband be dead, she is at liberty to be married to whom she will; only in the Lord.

40. But she is happier if she so abide, after my judgment: and I think also that I have the Spirit of God.

CHAPTER 8

1. Now as touching things offered unto idols, we know that we all have knowledge. Knowledge puffeth up, but charity edifieth.

2. And if any man think that he knoweth any thing, he knoweth nothing yet as he ought to know.

3. But if any man love God, the same is known of him.

4. As concerning therefore the eating of those things that are offered in sacrifice unto idols, we know that an idol is nothing in the world, and that there is none other God but one.

5. For though there be that are called gods, whether in heaven or in earth, (as there be gods many, and lords many,)

6. But to us there is but one God, the Father, of whom are all things, and we in him; and one Lord Jesus Christ, by whom are all things, and we by him.

7. Howbeit there is not in every man that knowledge: for some with conscience of the idol unto this hour eat it as a thing offered unto an idol; and their conscience being weak is defiled.

8. But meat commendeth us not to God: for neither, if we eat, are we the better; neither, if we eat not, are we the worse.

9. But take heed lest by any means this liberty of yours become a

Modern-day view of ruins in Ephesus

stumblingblock to them that are weak.

10. For if any man see thee which hast knowledge sit at meat in the idol's temple, shall not the conscience of him which is weak be emboldened to eat those things which are offered to idols;

11. And through thy knowledge shall the weak brother perish, for whom Christ died?

12. But when ye sin so against the brethren, and wound their weak conscience, ye sin against Christ.

13. Wherefore, if meat make my brother to offend, I will eat no flesh while the world standeth, lest I make my brother to offend.

CHAPTER 9

1. Am I not an apostle? am I not free? have I not seen Jesus Christ our Lord? are not ye my work in the Lord?

2. If I be not an apostle unto others, yet doubtless I am to you: for the seal of mine apostleship are ye in the Lord.

3. Mine answer to them that do examine me is this,

4. Have we not power to eat and to drink?

5. Have we not power to lead about a sister, a wife, as well as other apostles, and as the brethren of the Lord, and Cephas?

6. Or I only and Barnabas, have not we power to forbear working?

7. Who goeth a warfare any time at his own charges? who planteth a vineyard, and eateth not of the fruit thereof? or who feedeth a flock, and eateth not of the milk of the flock?

8. Say I these things as a man? or saith not the law the same also?

9. For it is written in the law of Moses, Thou shalt not muzzle the mouth of the ox that treadeth out the corn. Doth God take care for oxen?

10. Or saith he it altogether for our sakes? For our sakes, no doubt, this is written: that he that ploweth should plow in hope; and that he that thresheth in hope should be partaker of his hope.

11. If we have sown unto you spiritual things, is it a great thing if we shall reap your carnal things?

12. If others be partakers of this power over you, are not we rather? Nevertheless we have not used this power; but suffer all things, lest we should hinder the gospel of Christ.

13. Do ye not know that they which minister about holy things live of the things of the temple? and they which wait at the altar are partakers with the altar?

14. Even so hath the Lord ordained that they which preach the gospel should live of the gospel.

15. But I have used none of these things: neither have I written these things, that it should be so done unto me: for it were better for me to die, than that any man should make my glorying void.

16. For though I preach the gospel, I have nothing to glory of: for

CEPHAS

Cephas (meaning: a stone) was the Aramaic name given by Jesus to Simon when he received his calling as a disciple (see John 1:42; see also 1 Cor. 9:5; 15:5; Gal. 2:9). *Petros* is the Greek term corresponding to Cephas.

In Doctrine and Covenants 76, concerning the degrees of glory, those who inherit the telestial kingdom are characterized as rejecting the Savior, though they might profess outward allegiance to some religious leader, such as Cephas, Moses, Paul, or some other cause (see D&C 76:99; see also 1 Cor. 1:12; 3:22).

BARNABUS

Barnabus (meaning: son of consolation) was a convert to the gospel of Jesus Christ who, like his close associates, showed great faith in setting aside worldly possessions for the cause of the kingdom of God (see Acts 4:33–37).

When Paul, following his miraculous conversion, was desirous to join with the disciples at Jerusalem, they were afraid and demurred, with only Barnabas having courage enough to step forward and welcome the former persecutor of the Saints (see Acts 9:27). It was Barnabas who the disciples sent soon thereafter to Antioch to counsel the Saints and converts there (see Acts 11:22–24). Thereafter, Barnabas sought after Paul to join with him, and they tarried a year in Antioch, where the disciples were first called *Christians* (see Acts 11:26).

As a companion with Paul, Barnabas served the Lord with devotion and courage. Barnabas and Paul separated in their journey when Paul declined to accept John Mark—nephew or cousin of Barnabas (see Col. 4:10)—into their circle, John Mark having earlier "departed from them from Pamphylia, and went not with them to the work" (Acts 15:38). Though Barnabas is not referred to in the New Testament as a member of the Twelve (in succession), he is identified by Paul as an Apostle (see Acts 14:4, 14; 1 Cor. 9:6).

necessity is laid upon me; yea, woe is unto me, if I preach not the gospel!

17. For if I do this thing willingly, I have a reward: but if against my will, a dispensation of the gospel is committed unto me.

18. What is my reward then? Verily that, when I preach the gospel, I may make the gospel of Christ without charge, that I abuse not my power in the gospel.

19. For though I be free from all men, yet have I made myself servant unto all, that I might gain the more.

20. And unto the Jews I became as a Jew, that I might gain the Jews; to them that are under the law, as under the law, that I might gain them that are under the law;

21. To them that are without law, as without law, (being not without law to God, but under the law to Christ,) that I might gain them that are without law.

22. To the weak became I as weak, that I might gain the weak: I am made all things to all men, that I might by all means save some.

23. And this I do for the gospel's sake, that I might be partaker thereof with you.

24. Know ye not that they which run in a race run all, but one receiveth the prize? So run, that ye may obtain.

25. And every man that striveth for the mastery is temperate in all things. Now they do it to obtain a corruptible crown; but we an incorruptible.

26. I therefore so run, not as uncertainly; so fight I, not as one that beateth the air:

27. But I keep under my body, and bring it into subjection: lest that by any means, when I have preached to others, I myself should be a castaway.

CHAPTER 10

1. Moreover, brethren, I would not that ye should be ignorant, how that all our fathers were under the cloud, and all passed through the sea;

2. And were all baptized unto Moses in the cloud and in the sea;

3. And did all eat the same spiritual meat;

4. And did all drink the same spiritual drink: for they drank of that spiritual Rock that followed them: and that Rock was Christ.

5. But with many of them God was not well pleased: for they were overthrown in the wilderness.

6. Now these things were our examples, to the intent we should not lust after evil things, as they also lusted.

7. Neither be ye idolaters, as were some of them; as it is written, The people sat down to eat and drink, and rose up to play.

8. Neither let us commit fornication, as some of them committed,

Notes: _____

_____

_____

_____

_____

_____

_____

_____

_____

_____

_____

_____

_____

_____

_____

_____

_____

_____

_____

_____

_____

_____

_____

_____

_____

_____

_____

_____

_____

_____

_____

_____

_____

and fell in one day three and twenty thousand.

9. Neither let us tempt Christ, as some of them also tempted, and were destroyed of serpents.

10. Neither murmur ye, as some of them also murmured, and were destroyed of the destroyer.

11. Now all these things happened unto them for ensamples: and they are written for our admonition, upon whom the ends of the world are come.

12. Wherefore let him that thinketh he standeth take heed lest he fall.

13. There hath no temptation taken you but such as is common to man: but God is faithful, who will not suffer you to be tempted above that ye are able; but will with the temptation also make a way to escape, that ye may be able to bear it.

14. Wherefore, my dearly beloved, flee from idolatry.

15. I speak as to wise men; judge ye what I say.

16. The cup of blessing which we bless, is it not the communion of the blood of Christ? The bread which we break, is it not the communion of the body of Christ?

17. For we being many are one bread, and one body: for we are all partakers of that one bread.

18. Behold Israel after the flesh: are not they which eat of the sacrifices partakers of the altar?

19. What say I then? that the idol is any thing, or that which is offered in sacrifice to idols is any thing?

20. But I say, that the things which the Gentiles sacrifice, they sacrifice to devils, and not to God: and I would not that ye should have fellowship with devils.

21. Ye cannot drink the cup of the Lord, and the cup of devils: ye cannot be partakers of the Lord's table, and of the table of devils.

22. Do we provoke the Lord to jealousy? are we stronger than he?

23. All things are lawful for me, but all things are not expedient: all things are lawful for me, but all things edify not.

24. Let no man seek his own, but every man another's wealth.

25. Whatsoever is sold in the shambles, that eat, asking no question for conscience sake:

26. For the earth is the Lord's, and the fulness thereof.

27. If any of them that believe not bid you to a feast, and ye be disposed to go; whatsoever is set before you, eat, asking no question for conscience sake.

28. But if any man say unto you, This is offered in sacrifice unto idols, eat not for his sake that shewed it, and for conscience sake: for the earth is the Lord's, and the fulness thereof:

29. Conscience, I say, not thine own, but of the other: for why is my

Notes: _____

liberty judged of another man's conscience?

30. For if I by grace be a partaker, why am I evil spoken of for that for which I give thanks?

31. Whether therefore ye eat, or drink, or whatsoever ye do, do all to the glory of God.

32. Give none offence, neither to the Jews, nor to the Gentiles, nor to the church of God:

33. Even as I please all men in all things, not seeking mine own profit, but the profit of many, that they may be saved.

CHAPTER 11

1. Be ye followers of me, even as I also am of Christ.

2. Now I praise you, brethren, that ye remember me in all things, and keep the ordinances, as I delivered them to you.

3. But I would have you know, that the head of every man is Christ; and the head of the woman is the man; and the head of Christ is God.

4. Every man praying or prophesying, having his head covered, dishonoureth his head.

5. But every woman that prayeth or prophesieth with her head uncovered dishonoureth her head: for that is even all one as if she were shaven.

6. For if the woman be not covered, let her also be shorn: but if it be a shame for a woman to be shorn or shaven, let her be covered.

7. For a man indeed ought not to cover his head, forasmuch as he is the image and glory of God: but the woman is the glory of the man.

8. For the man is not of the woman; but the woman of the man.

9. Neither was the man created for the woman; but the woman for the man.

10. For this cause ought the woman to have power on her head because of the angels.

11. Nevertheless neither is the man without the woman, neither the woman without the man, in the Lord.

12. For as the woman is of the man, even so is the man also by the woman; but all things of God.

13. Judge in yourselves: is it comely that a woman pray unto God uncovered?

14. Doth not even nature itself teach you, that, if a man have long hair, it is a shame unto him?

15. But if a woman have long hair, it is a glory to her: for her hair is given her for a covering.

16. But if any man seem to be contentious, we have no such custom, neither the churches of God.

17. Now in this that I declare unto you I praise you not, that ye come together not for the better, but for the worse.

18. For first of all, when ye come to-

1 Cor. 11–16—"The Savior compared the kingdom, in other words the Church, to ten virgins, five of whom were wise and five of whom were foolish; and so we must not get the understanding that because we are members of the Church it is all well with us, and our salvation is secure, that is, our exaltation is secure. It is not so.

"We must continue to the end; we must obey the commandments. We must keep the ordinances. We must receive covenants, sealings, the sealing power, and privileges which are obtained in the temple of the Lord, and then live in accordance with them. That we must do" (Joseph Fielding Smith, *Doctrines of Salvation,* 2:15).

1 Cor. 11—The Apostle Paul includes in his epistle to the Corinthians solemn advice concerning the sacred relationship that should exist between man and wife—and between them and the Lord. Paul's oft-cited statement in this regard is the following: "Nevertheless neither is the man without the woman, neither the woman without the man, in the Lord" (1 Cor. 11:11). In his discourse, Paul discusses a number of customs and practices that contribute to the preservation and cultivation of harmonious and righteous interdependence of husband and wife within the framework of covenant fidelity and honor. Then, as now, the importance of this holy relationship is key to progress along the pathway to perfection.

1 Cor. 11—"Partaking of the sacrament increases our spiritual strength. I feel that a comprehension of the sacredness of the sacrament of the Lord's Supper is important to the members of the Church. We partake of physical food—that is, we partake of bread and water, etc., to nourish the physical body. It is just as necessary that we partake of the emblems of the body and blood of our risen Lord to increase our spiritual strength. It is observed that men and women who go from year to year without partaking of the Lord's Supper gradually lose the Spirit of our Heavenly Father; they forfeit its companionship where they have had opportunity to participate in that blessing, but have failed to take advantage of it. The sacrament is of great importance. . . . It was regarded of such importance by our Father in Heaven that, through his Beloved Son, and the Apostles and prophets, as recorded in the scriptures, the Saints were admonished to partake of it regularly" (George Albert Smith, *The Teachings of George Albert Smith,* 95).

gether in the church, I hear that there be divisions among you; and I partly believe it.

19. For there must be also heresies among you, that they which are approved may be made manifest among you.

20. When ye come together therefore into one place, this is not to eat the Lord's supper.

21. For in eating every one taketh before other his own supper: and one is hungry, and another is drunken.

22. What? have ye not houses to eat and to drink in? or despise ye the church of God, and shame them that have not? What shall I say to you? shall I praise you in this? I praise you not.

23. For I have received of the Lord that which also I delivered unto you, That the Lord Jesus the same night in which he was betrayed took bread:

24. And when he had given thanks, he brake it, and said, Take, eat: this is my body, which is broken for you: this do in remembrance of me.

25. After the same manner also he took the cup, when he had supped, saying, This cup is the new testament in my blood: this do ye, as oft as ye drink it, in remembrance of me.

26. For as often as ye eat this bread, and drink this cup, ye do shew the Lord's death till he come.

27. Wherefore whosoever shall eat this bread, and drink this cup of the Lord, unworthily, shall be guilty of the body and blood of the Lord.

28. But let a man examine himself, and so let him eat of that bread, and drink of that cup.

29. For he that eateth and drinketh unworthily, eateth and drinketh damnation to himself, not discerning the Lord's body.

30. For this cause many are weak and sickly among you, and many sleep.

31. For if we would judge ourselves, we should not be judged.

32. But when we are judged, we are chastened of the Lord, that we should not be condemned with the world.

33. Wherefore, my brethren, when ye come together to eat, tarry one for another.

34. And if any man hunger, let him eat at home; that ye come not together unto condemnation. And the rest will I set in order when I come.

CHAPTER 12

1. Now concerning spiritual gifts, brethren, I would not have you ignorant.

2. Ye know that ye were Gentiles, carried away unto these dumb idols, even as ye were led.

3. Wherefore I give you to understand, that no man speaking by the Spirit of God calleth Jesus accursed: and that no man can say that Jesus is the Lord, but by the Holy Ghost.

4. Now there are diversities of gifts, but the same Spirit.

1 Cor. 11 — There is power given to us by the Lord as we keep the covenants and ordinances of the gospel of Jesus Christ. We honor our covenants and ordinances by keeping the commandments and we renew our commitments in partaking of the sacrament. The Lord "doth immediately bless" us (see Mosiah 2:24), in that we can always have His Spirit to guide, direct, and comfort us in our lives—as well as the appropriate gifts necessary to bless and serve our fellowmen. The key to having good relationships within the family, and particularly between husband and wife, is to live the doctrines of the gospel.

When we come to understand and appreciate any doctrine, principle, ordinance, or covenant, our attitude and behavior change. This is especially evident within the family unit. It is also observed in every walk of life in our interactions and relationships with our fellowmen. The Sermon on the Mount and at the Temple as recorded in Matthew 5–7 and 3 Nephi 12–14 literally comprise the celestial laws for living. The relationships and camaraderie we have here on earth will go with us into the eternities (see D&C 130:2). It is to this state of happiness and never-ending joy that we aspire as we look forward to eternal life with our Heavenly Father, Savior, and with our loved ones, knowing that all blessings are predicated upon our obedience (see Mosiah 2:41; D&C 130:20).

1 Cor. 11:24–28—Paul reminds the Corinthian Saints that the sacrament is an ordinance established personally by the Savior by way of commandment. He entreats his audience, and us, that they should partake of the sacrament worthily.

1 Cor. 12:3–Paul taught the Corinthians a central doctrine of the gospel—that revelation through the Holy Ghost is essential to salvation. The Revelator is the Holy Ghost. He will witness to us the divinity of Jesus Christ. What has been your experience in having your testimony confirmed through the influence of the Holy Ghost? How can you teach your loved ones concerning the sweetness and peace that come from this kind of revealed knowledge?

Paul's memorable confirmation of the doctrine of testimony through the Spirit reminds us that we should always say or speak our knowledge of the divinity of Christ and that we should allow the Holy Ghost to convey the truth of our inspired testimony to those who have hearts to listen. How is it a source of comfort to you to know that we need only bear witness in all sincerity, and the Holy Ghost will do the rest?

5. And there are differences of administrations, but the same Lord.

6. And there are diversities of operations, but it is the same God which worketh all in all.

7. But the manifestation of the Spirit is given to every man to profit withal.

8. For to one is given by the Spirit the word of wisdom; to another the word of knowledge by the same Spirit;

9. To another faith by the same Spirit; to another the gifts of healing by the same Spirit;

10. To another the working of miracles; to another prophecy; to another discerning of spirits; to another divers kinds of tongues; to another the interpretation of tongues:

11. But all these worketh that one and the selfsame Spirit, dividing to every man severally as he will.

12. For as the body is one, and hath many members, and all the members of that one body, being many, are one body: so also is Christ.

13. For by one Spirit are we all baptized into one body, whether we be Jews or Gentiles, whether we be bond or free; and have been all made to drink into one Spirit.

14. For the body is not one member, but many.

15. If the foot shall say, Because I am not the hand, I am not of the body; is it therefore not of the body?

16. And if the ear shall say, Because I am not the eye, I am not of the body; is it therefore not of the body?

17. If the whole body were an eye, where were the hearing? If the whole were hearing, where were the smelling?

18. But now hath God set the members every one of them in the body, as it hath pleased him.

19. And if they were all one member, where were the body?

20. But now are they many members, yet but one body.

21. And the eye cannot say unto the hand, I have no need of thee: nor again the head to the feet, I have no need of you.

22. Nay, much more those members of the body, which seem to be more feeble, are necessary:

23. And those members of the body, which we think to be less honourable, upon these we bestow more abundant honour; and our uncomely parts have more abundant comeliness.

24. For our comely parts have no need: but God hath tempered the body together, having given more abundant honour to that part which lacked:

25. That there should be no schism in the body; but that the members should have the same care one for another.

26. And whether one member suffer, all the members suffer with it; or one member be honoured, all the members rejoice with it.

27. Now ye are the body of Christ, and members in particular.

28. And God hath set some in the church, first apostles, secondarily prophets, thirdly teachers, after that miracles, then gifts of healings, helps, governments, diversities of tongues.

29. Are all apostles? are all pro-

1 Cor. 12—In the First Epistle to the Corinthians, Paul includes in chapter 12 a magnificent treatment of the gifts of the Spirit—one that has become (along with Moro. 10 and D&C 46) a staple in scriptural discourse on this important theme. The most fundamental gift of the Spirit, as Paul announces at the beginning of his explanation, is the gift of testimony granted by the Spirit: "Wherefore I give you to understand, that no man speaking by the Spirit of God calleth Jesus accursed: and that no man can say that Jesus is the Lord, but by the Holy Ghost" (1 Cor. 12:3). He then proceeds to outline the "diversities of gifts" as given by the same Spirit (v. 5–11), with the reminder that all of these various gifts, given severally to the members of the Church, contribute to the unity and oneness of the body of Christ, and that all members are important in contributing their respective roles and talents for the building up of the kingdom of God (v. 12–30).

Therefore, we should "covet earnestly the best gifts" (v. 31). Fundamental to the operation of all of the gifts of the Spirit is charity. Paul's succinct and elegant statement concerning charity (1 Cor. 13) is among the most celebrated and articulate of expressions on this divine quality. He concludes: "And now abideth faith, hope, charity, these three; but the greatest of these is charity" (1 Cor. 13:13; compare Moro. 7:43–48). In 1 Corinthians 14, Paul encourages the Saints to seek after the best spiritual gifts as a means of edification and unfolding the spiritual enlightenment of the community of God: "Even so ye, forasmuch as ye are zealous of spiritual gifts, seek that ye may excel to the edifying of the church" (1 Cor. 14:12).

1 Cor. 12:28–31—Paul taught the Corinthians concerning the operations of the Church, depending as it does on the blending together of the various gifts and talents of the membership. As you ponder the various people in your own ward and stake, how is a blending of the gifts of the Spirit being made manifest so as to profit everyone involved? Why is it often effective in the process of reactivating less-active members to ask them to participate in Church activities that use their special talents and gifts?

phets? are all teachers? are all workers of miracles?

30. Have all the gifts of healing? do all speak with tongues? do all interpret?

31. But covet earnestly the best gifts: and yet shew I unto you a more excellent way.

CHAPTER 13

1. Though I speak with the tongues of men and of angels, and have not charity, I am become as sounding brass, or a tinkling cymbal.

2. And though I have the gift of prophecy, and understand all mysteries, and all knowledge; and though I have all faith, so that I could remove mountains, and have not charity, I am nothing.

3. And though I bestow all my goods to feed the poor, and though I give my body to be burned, and have not charity, it profiteth me nothing.

4. Charity suffereth long, and is kind; charity envieth not; charity vaunteth not itself, is not puffed up,

5. Doth not behave itself unseemly, seeketh not her own, is not easily provoked, thinketh no evil;

6. Rejoiceth not in iniquity, but rejoiceth in the truth;

7. Beareth all things, believeth all things, hopeth all things, endureth all things.

8. Charity never faileth: but whether there be prophecies, they shall fail; whether there be tongues, they shall cease; whether there be knowledge, it shall vanish away.

9. For we know in part, and we prophesy in part.

10. But when that which is perfect is come, then that which is in part shall be done away.

11. When I was a child, I spake as a child, I understood as a child, I thought as a child: but when I became a man, I put away childish things.

12. For now we see through a glass, darkly; but then face to face: now I know in part; but then shall I know even as also I am known.

13. And now abideth faith, hope, charity, these three; but the greatest of these is charity.

CHAPTER 14

1. Follow after charity, and desire spiritual gifts, but rather that ye may prophesy.

2. For he that speaketh in an unknown tongue speaketh not unto men, but unto God: for no man understandeth him; howbeit in the spirit he speaketh mysteries.

3. But he that prophesieth speaketh unto men to edification, and exhortation, and comfort.

4. He that speaketh in an unknown tongue edifieth himself; but he that prophesieth edifieth the church.

1 Cor. 12—It is the blending together of the several gifts in the congregations of the Saints in the spirit of service that can remove from all of us the feelings of being out of place or lonely, for there are contributions that we can make that may be unique and indispensable. Paul said it this way: "Now therefore ye are no more strangers and foreigners, but fellowcitizens with the saints, and of the household of God . . . In whom ye also are builded together for an habitation of God through the Spirit" (Eph. 2:19, 22). And elsewhere, he said:

"And the eye cannot say unto the hand, I have no need of thee: nor again the head to the feet, I have no need of you.

"Nay, much more those members of the body, which seem to be more feeble, are necessary:

"And those members of the body, which we think to be less honourable, upon these we bestow more abundant honour; and our uncomely parts have more abundant comeliness.

"For our comely parts have no need: but God hath tempered the body together, having given more abundant honour to that part which lacked:

"That there should be no schism in the body; but that the members should have the same care one for another.

"And whether one member suffer, all the members suffer with it; or one member be honoured, all the members rejoice with it.

"Now ye are the body of Christ, and members in particular" (1 Cor. 12:21–27).

The plainest antidote to envy and jealousy is to focus on those gifts and talents we are given and to cultivate them for the building up of the kingdom. The Lord counsels: "And again, verily I say unto you, I would that ye should always remember, and always retain in your minds what those gifts are, that are given unto the church. For all have not every gift given unto them; for there are many gifts, and to every man is given a gift by the Spirit of God" (D&C 46:10–11). Since the Lord gives to everyone at least one of these spiritual gifts, we can gratefully cultivate our gift "for the benefit of the children of God" (v. 26) and "give thanks unto God in the Spirit for whatsoever blessing ye are blessed with" (v. 32). This being the case, there is no room in our hearts and minds for envy and jealousy, and we can instead "practice virtue and holiness" before the Lord continually (v. 33).

5. I would that ye all spake with tongues, but rather that ye prophesied: for greater is he that prophesieth than he that speaketh with tongues, except he interpret, that the church may receive edifying.

6. Now, brethren, if I come unto you speaking with tongues, what shall I profit you, except I shall speak to you either by revelation, or by knowledge, or by prophesying, or by doctrine?

7. And even things without life giving sound, whether pipe or harp, except they give a distinction in the sounds, how shall it be known what is piped or harped?

8. For if the trumpet give an uncertain sound, who shall prepare himself to the battle?

9. So likewise ye, except ye utter by the tongue words easy to be understood, how shall it be known what is spoken? for ye shall speak into the air.

10. There are, it may be, so many kinds of voices in the world, and none of them is without signification.

11. Therefore if I know not the meaning of the voice, I shall be unto him that speaketh a barbarian, and he that speaketh shall be a barbarian unto me.

12. Even so ye, forasmuch as ye are zealous of spiritual gifts, seek that ye may excel to the edifying of the church.

13. Wherefore let him that speaketh in an unknown tongue pray that he may interpret.

14. For if I pray in an unknown tongue, my spirit prayeth, but my understanding is unfruitful.

15. What is it then? I will pray with the spirit, and I will pray with the understanding also: I will sing with the spirit, and I will sing with the understanding also.

16. Else when thou shalt bless with the spirit, how shall he that occupieth the room of the unlearned say Amen at thy giving of thanks, seeing he understandeth not what thou sayest?

17. For thou verily givest thanks well, but the other is not edified.

18. I thank my God, I speak with tongues more than ye all:

19. Yet in the church I had rather speak five words with my understanding, that by my voice I might teach others also, than ten thousand words in an unknown tongue.

20. Brethren, be not children in understanding: howbeit in malice be ye children, but in understanding be men.

21. In the law it is written, With men of other tongues and other lips will I speak unto this people; and yet for all that will they not hear me, saith the Lord.

22. Wherefore tongues are for a sign, not to them that believe, but to them that believe not: but prophesying serveth not for them that believe not, but for them which believe.

23. If therefore the whole church be come together into one place, and all speak with tongues, and there come in those that are unlearned, or unbelievers, will they not say that ye are mad?

24. But if all prophesy, and there come in one that believeth not, or one unlearned, he is convinced of all, he is judged of all:

25. And thus are the secrets of his heart made manifest; and so falling down on his face he will worship God, and report that God is in you of a truth.

26. How is it then, brethren? when ye come together, everyone of you hath a psalm, hath a doctrine, hath a tongue, hath a revelation, hath an

Notes: _____

interpretation. Let all things be done unto edifying.

27. If any man speak in an unknown tongue, let it be by two, or at the most by three, and that by course; and let one interpret.

28. But if there be no interpreter, let him keep silence in the church; and let him speak to himself, and to God.

29. Let the prophets speak two or three, and let the other judge.

30. If any thing be revealed to another that sitteth by, let the first hold his peace.

31. For ye may all prophesy one by one, that all may learn, and all may be comforted.

32. And the spirits of the prophets are subject to the prophets.

33. For God is not the author of confusion, but of peace, as in all churches of the saints.

34. Let your women keep silence in the churches: for it is not permitted unto them to speak; but they are commanded to be under obedience, as also saith the law.

35. And if they will learn any thing, let them ask their husbands at home: for it is a shame for women to speak in the church.

36. What? came the word of God out from you? or came it unto you only?

37. If any man think himself to be a prophet, or spiritual, let him acknowledge that the things that I write unto you are the commandments of the Lord.

38. But if any man be ignorant, let him be ignorant.

39. Wherefore, brethren, covet to prophesy, and forbid not to speak with tongues.

40. Let all things be done decently and in order.

CHAPTER 15

1. Moreover, brethren, I declare unto you the gospel which I preached unto you, which also ye have received, and wherein ye stand;

2. By which also ye are saved, if ye keep in memory what I preached unto you, unless ye have believed in vain.

3. For I delivered unto you first of all that which I also received, how that Christ died for our sins according to the scriptures;

4. And that he was buried, and that he rose again the third day according to the scriptures:

5. And that he was seen of Cephas, then of the twelve:

6. After that, he was seen of above five hundred brethren at once; of whom the greater part remain unto this present, but some are fallen asleep.

7. After that, he was seen of James; then of all the apostles.

8. And last of all he was seen of me also, as of one born out of due time.

9. For I am the least of the apostles, that am not meet to be called an

1 Cor. 15:1–8—Evidence of the Resurrection of the Lord is summarized by Paul in these verses, including his own personal confirmation deriving from his encounter with the risen Lord on the road to Damascus: "And last of all he was seen of me also, as of one born out of due time" (v. 8). Paul's meekness and humility in bearing personal witness show forth his admirable qualities: "For I am the least of the apostles, that am not meet to be called an apostle, because I persecuted the church of God. But by the grace of God I am what I am: and his grace which was bestowed upon me was not in vain; but I laboured more abundantly than they all: yet not I, but the grace of God which was with me" (1 Cor. 15:9–10).

How to confirm and verify the resurrection then becomes Paul's agenda. The logic is irrefutable: "If in this life only we have hope in Christ, we are of all men most miserable" (1 Cor. 15:19). But such is not the case: "For as in Adam all die, even so in Christ shall all be made alive" (1 Cor. 15:22). In addition, there is the vicarious work for the dead, which depends wholly on the verity and reality of the resurrection: "Else what shall they do which are baptized for the dead, if the dead rise not at all? why are they then baptized for the dead?" (1 Cor. 15:29). This last statement is considered cryptic by all sectarian commentators who are not apprised of the blessings of temple work carried on in the Church and kingdom of God. Paul concludes his treatise on the resurrection by talking of the three degrees of glory to which resurrected beings can be assigned (1 Cor. 15:40–41—comparable, symbolically, to the relative glory of the sun, moon, and stars).

apostle, because I persecuted the church of God.

10. But by the grace of God I am what I am: and his grace which was bestowed upon me was not in vain; but I laboured more abundantly than they all: yet not I, but the grace of God which was with me.

11. Therefore whether it were I or they, so we preach, and so ye believed.

12. Now if Christ be preached that he rose from the dead, how say some among you that there is no resurrection of the dead?

13. But if there be no resurrection of the dead, then is Christ not risen:

14. And if Christ be not risen, then is our preaching vain, and your faith is also vain.

15. Yea, and we are found false witnesses of God; because we have testified of God that he raised up Christ: whom he raised not up, if so be that the dead rise not.

16. For if the dead rise not, then is not Christ raised:

17. And if Christ be not raised, your faith is vain; ye are yet in your sins.

18. Then they also which are fallen asleep in Christ are perished.

19. If in this life only we have hope in Christ, we are of all men most miserable.

20. But now is Christ risen from the dead, and become the firstfruits of them that slept.

21. For since by man came death, by man came also the resurrection of the dead.

22. For as in Adam all die, even so in Christ shall all be made alive.

23. But every man in his own order: Christ the firstfruits; afterward they that are Christ's at his coming.

24. Then cometh the end, when he shall have delivered up the kingdom to God, even the Father; when he shall have put down all rule and all authority and power.

25. For he must reign, till he hath put all enemies under his feet.

26. The last enemy that shall be destroyed is death.

27. For he hath put all things under his feet. But when he saith, all things are put under him, it is manifest that he is excepted, which did put all things under him.

28. And when all things shall be subdued unto him, then shall the Son also himself be subject unto him that put all things under him, that God may be all in all.

29. Else what shall they do which are baptized for the dead, if the dead rise not at all? why are they then baptized for the dead?

30. And why stand we in jeopardy every hour?

1 Cor. 15—No doctrine in the sacred canon of eternal principles captures the imagination with more compelling urgency than the resurrection. This word derives from the Latin term *resurgere,* meaning "to rise again." Mortals, without exception, understand the process whereby the miraculous human frame is gradually transformed through the passage of time into an increasingly frail and weathered state, tempered by the elements and reduced to a fraction of the original vigor and vitality. Some, from birth or through trauma, find this process of reduction suddenly imposed upon them or accelerated beyond measure. We know the process all too intimately: strength is diminished; wrinkles abound; infirmities arise.

Is it any wonder that the hope of the resurrection—bringing about the vanquishing of the process of human withering and aging and the eventual triumph over death—should engender in those who believe—or want to believe—an attitude of peaceful anticipation and a future-oriented vision of a glorious state of betterment that awaits all mortals? Faith in the truth of the resurrection brings a transformed view of things as they are and as they will be. Those who hope for the fruits of Christ's atoning sacrifice, with its promise of the resurrection, can see things in a different light. In the place of challenging handicaps, they see wholeness and liberation; in the place of degenerative illness, they see relief and vitality; in the place of separation from loved ones, they see union and conviviality.

Where can you find the vision of the resurrection at work in our daily lives? Consider this: Why is it that when you see an older couple walking together with hands clasped, the two partners are invariably smiling? That is the vision of the resurrection. These two, wizened perhaps and shuffling a bit, look at each other with refreshing love. The wrinkles, so visible to others, are invisible to them. Each sees the other as the fair and attractive person he or she first knew—and as the glorious and restored person he or she will accompany on celestial walks in the resurrected state, just as always.

Why is it that the temples of the Lord are havens of peace and security amidst a world of turmoil and ephemerality? Is it not because the perspective taught in the house of the Lord transcends the earthly vale of tears and lifts one's spirit to a state of wholeness and completion, a state of bringing all the elements together in an ultimate and permanent bonding through which process alone complete joy and happiness are possible? "The elements are eternal," says the scripture, "and the spirit and element,

31. I protest by your rejoicing which I have in Christ Jesus our Lord, I die daily.

32. If after the manner of men I have fought with beasts at Ephesus, what advantageth it me, if the dead rise not? let us eat and drink; for to morrow we die.

33. Be not deceived: evil communications corrupt good manners.

34. Awake to righteousness, and sin not; for some have not the knowledge of God: I speak this to your shame.

35. But some man will say, How are the dead raised up? and with what body do they come?

36. Thou fool, that which thou sowest is not quickened, except it die:

37. And that which thou sowest, thou sowest not that body that shall be, but bare grain, it may chance of wheat, or of some other grain:

38. But God giveth it a body as it hath pleased him, and to every seed his own body.

39. All flesh is not the same flesh: but there is one kind of flesh of men, another flesh of beasts, another of fishes, and another of birds.

40. There are also celestial bodies, and bodies terrestrial: but the glory of the celestial is one, and the glory of the terrestrial is another.

41. There is one glory of the sun, and another glory of the moon, and another glory of the stars: for one star differeth from another star in glory.

42. So also is the resurrection of the dead. It is sown in corruption; it is raised in incorruption:

43. It is sown in dishonour; it is raised in glory: it is sown in weakness; it is raised in power:

44. It is sown a natural body; it is raised a spiritual body. There is a natural body, and there is a spiritual body.

45. And so it is written, The first man Adam was made a living soul; the last Adam was made a quickening spirit.

46. Howbeit that was not first which is spiritual, but that which is natural; and afterward that which is spiritual.

47. The first man is of the earth, earthy: the second man is the Lord from heaven.

48. As is the earthy, such are they also that are earthy: and as is the heavenly, such are they also that are heavenly.

49. And as we have borne the image of the earthy, we shall also bear the image of the heavenly.

50. Now this I say, brethren, that flesh and blood cannot inherit the kingdom of God; neither doth corruption inherit incorruption.

51. Behold, I shew you a mystery; We shall not all sleep, but we shall all be changed,

52. In a moment, in the twinkling of an eye, at the last trump: for the trumpet shall sound, and the dead shall be raised incorruptible, and we shall be changed.

inseparably connected, receive a fulness of joy" (D&C 93:33; 138:17). That is the vision of the resurrection, made possible through the Atonement of the Savior.

On December 20, 1842, the Prophet Joseph Smith shared with his associates his view of the resurrection, imparted to him in a vision from the Almighty: "So plain was the vision, that I actually saw men, before they had ascended from the tomb, as though they were getting up slowly. They took each other by the hand and said to each other, 'My father, my son, my mother, my daughter, my brother, my sister.' And when the voice calls for the dead to arise, suppose I am laid by the side of my father, what would be the first joy of my heart? To meet my father, my mother, my brother, my sister; and when they are by my side, I embrace them and they me" (*History of the Church,* 5:362).

The Savior performed mighty miracles when He walked the earth—healing the infirm, causing the blind to see and the deaf to hear, even raising people from the grave. At times, we look back on those choice accounts and wish that He were here among us today to perform those same deeds of love: making our children whole, returning departed loved ones to our side, causing disease and malady to retreat behind the heavenly triumph of wellness and restoration. The truth of the matter is that the Savior *is* here today, and He will perform the desired miracles on our behalf—in His own due time. "Zion shall be redeemed in mine own due time" (D&C 136:18), said the Lord. That redemption also includes the resurrection, which will bring with it as many miracles as there are people to experience it. When we are operating within the Lord's time frame, then we are always on schedule, and with patience we will find that "His own due time" will be soon enough. Meanwhile, as we wait with faith, facing adversity and trial, we can take to heart that "all these things shall give thee experience, and shall be for thy good" (D&C 122:7).

And so it is that we go through life one day at a time—remembering the blessed promise of the resurrection, hoping in faith for a time when we will rise again and enter into the rest of God as whole and reclaimed beings at last, "which rest is the fullness of his glory" (D&C 84:24). That is the vision of the resurrection.

53. For this corruptible must put on incorruption, and this mortal must put on immortality.

54. So when this corruptible shall have put on incorruption, and this mortal shall have put on immortality, then shall be brought to pass the saying that is written, Death is swallowed up in victory.

55. O death, where is thy sting? O grave, where is thy victory?

56. The sting of death is sin; and the strength of sin is the law.

57. But thanks be to God, which giveth us the victory through our Lord Jesus Christ.

58. Therefore, my beloved brethren, be ye stedfast, unmoveable, always abounding in the work of the Lord, forasmuch as ye know that your labour is not in vain in the Lord.

CHAPTER 16

1. Now concerning the collection for the saints, as I have given order to the churches of Galatia, even so do ye.

2. Upon the first day of the week let every one of you lay by him in store, as God hath prospered him, that there be no gatherings when I come.

3. And when I come, whomsoever ye shall approve by your letters, them will I send to bring your liberality unto Jerusalem.

4. And if it be meet that I go also, they shall go with me.

5. Now I will come unto you, when I shall pass through Macedonia: for I do pass through Macedonia.

6. And it may be that I will abide, yea, and winter with you, that ye may bring me on my journey whithersoever I go.

7. For I will not see you now by the way; but I trust to tarry a while with you, if the Lord permit.

8. But I will tarry at Ephesus until Pentecost.

9. For a great door and effectual is opened unto me, and there are many adversaries.

10. Now if Timotheus come, see that he may be with you without fear: for he worketh the work of the Lord, as I also do.

11. Let no man therefore despise him: but conduct him forth in peace, that he may come unto me: for I look for him with the brethren.

12. As touching our brother Apollos, I greatly desired him to come unto you with the brethren: but his will was not at all to come at this time; but he will come when he shall have convenient time.

13. Watch ye, stand fast in the faith, quit you like men, be strong.

14. Let all your things be done with charity.

15. I beseech you, brethren, (ye know the house of Stephanas, that it is the firstfruits of Achaia, and that they have addicted themselves to the ministry of the saints,)

16. That ye submit yourselves unto such, and to every one that helpeth with us, and laboureth.

17. I am glad of the coming of Stephanas and Fortunatus and Achaicus: for that which was lacking on your part they have supplied.

18. For they have refreshed my

1 Cor. 15:55–58—Paul exhorts the Saints to remember the extraordinary and blessed outcome of the Savior's Atonement and Resurrection.

1 Corinthians— The First Epistle of Paul the Apostle to the Corinthians makes a compelling case for embracing three of the major themes of gospel life: seek unity and avoid contention, trust in the Spirit of the Lord rather than in man and worldly endeavors, and be morally clean. These universal themes are echoed in other scriptures as well. Alma the Elder taught the Saints who congregated at the Waters of Mormon the same doctrine: "And he commanded them that there should be no contention one with another, but that they should look forward with one eye, having one faith and one baptism, having their hearts knit together in unity and in love one towards another. And thus he commanded them to preach. And thus they became the children of God" (Mosiah 18:21–22). Like Paul, Isaiah reminded us to set our sights on heavenly wisdom:

"Seek ye the Lord while he may be found, call ye upon him while he is near:

"Let the wicked forsake his way, and the unrighteous man his thoughts: and let him return unto the Lord, and he will have mercy upon him; and to our God, for he will abundantly pardon.

"For my thoughts are not your thoughts, neither are your ways my ways, saith the Lord.

"For as the heavens are higher than the earth, so are my ways higher than your ways, and my thoughts than your thoughts" (Isa. 55:6–9; compare D&C 38:5).

And in our day, the Lord has renewed the vital commandment to be holy and morally clean: "And ye must practise virtue and holiness before me continually" (D&C 46:33; compare D&C 42:22–24).

The consequence of honoring and keeping these commandments is to be favored of the Lord and blessed with sacred spiritual wealth—wealth so overwhelming and glorious that only the spiritual senses can behold its magnificent scope and reality (1 Cor. 2:9–16; Isa. 64:4).

spirit and yours: therefore acknowledge ye them that are such.

19. The churches of Asia salute you. Aquila and Priscilla salute you much in the Lord, with the church that is in their house.

20. All the brethren greet you. Greet ye one another with an holy kiss.

21. The salutation of me Paul with mine own hand.

22. If any man love not the Lord Jesus Christ, let him be Anathema Maranatha.

23. The grace of our Lord Jesus Christ be with you.

24. My love be with you all in Christ Jesus. Amen.

THE SECOND EPISTLE OF PAUL THE APOSTLE TO

THE CORINTHIANS

CHAPTER 1

1. Paul, an apostle of Jesus Christ by the will of God, and Timothy our brother, unto the church of God which is at Corinth, with all the saints which are in all Achaia:

2. Grace be to you and peace from God our Father, and from the Lord Jesus Christ.

3. Blessed be God, even the Father of our Lord Jesus Christ, the Father of mercies, and the God of all comfort;

4. Who comforteth us in all our tribulation, that we may be able to comfort them which are in any trouble, by the comfort wherewith we ourselves are comforted of God.

5. For as the sufferings of Christ abound in us, so our consolation also aboundeth by Christ.

6. And whether we be afflicted, it is for your consolation and salvation, which is effectual in the enduring of the same sufferings which we also suffer: or whether we be comforted, it is for your consolation and salvation.

7. And our hope of you is stedfast, knowing, that as ye are partakers of the sufferings, so shall ye be also of the consolation.

8. For we would not, brethren, have you ignorant of our trouble which came to us in Asia, that we were pressed out of measure, above strength, insomuch that we despaired even of life:

1 Corinthians—It is a refreshing thing, amidst the cares and travails of daily life, to step into the circle of students being taught by the Apostle Paul and learn from him noble and edifying truths: the sacred relationship of husband and wife working interdependently beneath the canopy of heaven, the beauty and magnificence of the sacrament as a means to renew holy covenants, the breathtaking power of spiritual gifts as instruments of service in building the kingdom of God, and the hope and reality of the resurrection as the gateway to future degrees of glory. May we apply these doctrines and principles in our lives with devotion and thanksgiving, ever mindful of our obligations to obey all of God's commandments and follow in the footsteps of His Only Begotten Son.

2 Corinthians—In his Second Epistle to the Corinthians, Paul expounds on a variety of different topics and doctrines. In this epistle, we will emphasize the themes of trials and tribulations, forgiving others, the process of repentance—in particular, experiencing godly sorrow and learning how we must be reconciled to God through the Atonement of Jesus Christ. Opposition in all things is an eternal circumstances (see 2 Ne. 2:11). Likewise, temptation is necessary that we might exercise our moral agency: "And it must needs be that the devil should tempt the children of men, or they could not be agents unto themselves; for if they never should have bitter they could not know the sweet" (D&C 29:39). Forgiving and showing mercy to others is required of us as we come to acquire the attribute of charity in our lives. Surely we obtain mercy and forgiveness as we show mercy and forgiveness to others (see Matt. 5:7; Luke 6:37; 2 Cor. 2:10). True repentance requires godly sorrow, not sorrow for being caught or exposed, but a broken heart and contrite spirit of the soul. The Atonement of Christ and the process of repentance are essential in the process of becoming reconciled to God (see 2 Cor. 5:17–20; Rom. 5:8–12; Jacob 4:11). Through reconciliation we are restored to a state where we can become worthy of the presence of God.

9. But we had the sentence of death in ourselves, that we should not trust in ourselves, but in God which raiseth the dead:

10. Who delivered us from so great a death, and doth deliver: in whom we trust that he will yet deliver us;

11. Ye also helping together by prayer for us, that for the gift bestowed upon us by the means of many persons thanks may be given by many on our behalf.

12. For our rejoicing is this, the testimony of our conscience, that in simplicity and godly sincerity, not with fleshly wisdom, but by the grace of God, we have had our conversation in the world, and more abundantly to you-ward.

13. For we write none other things unto you, than what ye read or acknowledge; and I trust ye shall acknowledge even to the end;

14. As also ye have acknowledged us in part, that we are your rejoicing, even as ye also are ours in the day of the Lord Jesus.

15. And in this confidence I was minded to come unto you before, that ye might have a second benefit;

16. And to pass by you into Macedonia, and to come again out of Macedonia unto you, and of you to be brought on my way toward Judæa.

17. When I therefore was thus minded, did I use lightness? or the things that I purpose, do I purpose according to the flesh, that with me there should be yea yea, and nay nay?

18. But as God is true, our word toward you was not yea and nay.

19. For the Son of God, Jesus Christ, who was preached among you by us, even by me and Silvanus and Timotheus, was not yea and nay, but in him was yea.

20. For all the promises of God in him are yea, and in him Amen, unto the glory of God by us.

21. Now he which stablisheth us with you in Christ, and hath anointed us, is God;

22. Who hath also sealed us, and given the earnest of the Spirit in our hearts.

23. Moreover I call God for a record upon my soul, that to spare you I came not as yet unto Corinth.

24. Not for that we have dominion over your faith, but are helpers of your joy: for by faith ye stand.

CHAPTER 2

1. But I determined this with myself, that I would not come again to you in heaviness.

2. For if I make you sorry, who is he then that maketh me glad, but the same which is made sorry by me?

3. And I wrote this same unto you, lest, when I came, I should have sorrow from them of whom I ought to rejoice; having confidence in you all, that my joy is the joy of you all.

4. For out of much affliction and anguish of heart I wrote unto you with many tears; not that ye should be grieved, but that ye might know the love which I have more abundantly unto you.

5. But if any have caused grief, he hath not grieved me, but in part: that I may not overcharge you all.

6. Sufficient to such a man is this punishment, which was inflicted of many.

7. So that contrariwise ye ought rather to forgive him, and comfort him, lest perhaps such a one should

2 Cor. 1:3–7, 12 — Paul offers to the Saints at Corinth encouragement in the face of daunting opposition and adversity. Being no stranger to persecution and suffering himself (see 2 Cor. 11:23–33), he was in a position of considerable authority to speak on this subject, and in doing so, confirmed for his audience the doctrine of consolation (see 2 Cor. 1:3–7).

Paul then rejoices with the Saints concerning the grace of God, which has enabled them to cultivate righteous patterns of living and to support one another continually: "For our rejoicing is this, the testimony of our conscience, that in simplicity and godly sincerity, not with fleshly wisdom, but by the grace of God, we have had our conversation in the world, and more abundantly to you-ward" (2 Cor. 1:12). Though the burdens may seem heavy in this world, they are nevertheless light in the context of the bliss of the eternal rewards awaiting the faithful: "For our light affliction, which is but for a moment, worketh for us a far more exceeding and eternal weight of glory" (2 Cor. 4:17).

2 Cor. 1 — An anonymous author wrote this classic piece about overcoming adversity:

Cripple him, and you have a Sir Walter Scott. Lock him in a prison cell, and you have a John Bunyan. Bury him in the snows of Valley Forge, and you have a George Washington. Land him in poverty, and you have an Abraham Lincoln. Subject him to bitter religious strife, and you have a Disraeli. Strike him with infantile paralysis, and you have a Franklin D. Roosevelt, the only President of the United States to be elected to four terms of office. Burn him so severely in a schoolhouse fire that the doctors say he will never walk, and you have a Glenn Cunningham, who set a world record in 1934 for running the mile in 4 minutes, 6.7 seconds.

Deafen a genius composer who continues to compose some of the world's most beautiful music, and you have a Beethoven. Drag him more dead than alive out of a rice paddy in Vietnam, and you have a Rocky Blaier, that beautiful running back for the Pittsburgh Steelers. Have him or her born black in a society filled with racial discrimination, and you have a Booker T. Washington, Harriet Tubman, or Martin Luther King Jr. Have him born of parents who survived a Nazi concentration camp, paralyze him from the waist down at the age of four, and you have an Itzhak Perlman, the incomparable violinist. Call him "retarded" and write him off as "uneducable," and you have an Albert Einstein.

After losing both his legs in an airplane crash, let an RAF fighter pilot fly, and you have World War II ace Douglas Bader, who was captured by the

be swallowed up with overmuch sorrow.

8. Wherefore I beseech you that ye would confirm your love toward him.

9. For to this end also did I write, that I might know the proof of you, whether ye be obedient in all things.

10. To whom ye forgive any thing, I forgive also: for if I forgave any thing, to whom I forgave it, for your sakes forgave I it in the person of Christ;

11. Lest Satan should get an advantage of us: for we are not ignorant of his devices.

12. Furthermore, when I came to Troas to preach Christ's gospel, and a door was opened unto me of the Lord,

13. I had no rest in my spirit, because I found not Titus my brother: but taking my leave of them, I went from thence into Macedonia.

14. Now thanks be unto God, which always causeth us to triumph in Christ, and maketh manifest the savour of his knowledge by us in every place.

15. For we are unto God a sweet savour of Christ, in them that are saved, and in them that perish:

16. To the one we are the savour of death unto death; and to the other the savour of life unto life. And who is sufficient for these things?

17. For we are not as many, which corrupt the word of God: but as of sincerity, but as of God, in the sight of God speak we in Christ.

CHAPTER 3

1. Do we begin again to commend ourselves? or need we, as some others, epistles of commendation to you, or letters of commendation from you?

2. Ye are our epistle written in our hearts, known and read of all men:

3. Forasmuch as ye are manifestly declared to be the epistle of Christ ministered by us, written not with ink, but with the Spirit of the living God; not in tables of stone, but in fleshy tables of the heart.

4. And such trust have we through Christ to God-ward:

5. Not that we are sufficient of ourselves to think any thing as of ourselves; but our sufficiency is of God;

6. Who also hath made us able ministers of the new testament; not of the letter, but of the spirit: for the letter killeth, but the spirit giveth life.

7. But if the ministration of death, written and engraven in stones, was glorious, so that the children of Israel could not stedfastly behold the face of Moses for the glory of his countenance; which glory was to be done away:

8. How shall not the ministration of the spirit be rather glorious?

9. For if the ministration of condemnation be glory, much more doth the ministration of righteousness exceed in glory.

10. For even that which was made glorious had no glory in this respect, by reason of the glory that excelleth.

11. For if that which is done away was glorious, much more that which remaineth is glorious.

12. Seeing then that we have such hope, we use great plainness of speech:

13. And not as Moses, which put a vail over his face, that the children

Germans three times and escaped three times on two artificial limbs. Label him too stupid to learn, and you have a Thomas Edison. Label him a hopeless alcoholic, and you have a Bill Wilson, the founder of Alcoholics Anonymous. Tell her she is too old to start painting at 80, and you have a Grandma Moses. Blind him at age 44, and you have a John Milton, who 10 years later, wrote *Paradise Lost*. Call him dull and hopeless and flunk him in the sixth grade, and you have a Winston Churchill.

Tell a young boy who loved to draw and sketch that he had no talent, and you have a Walt Disney. Rate him mediocre in chemistry, and you have a Louis Pasteur. Take a crippled child whose only home was an orphanage, and you have a Louis E. West, who became the first chief executive of the Boy Scouts of America. Spit on him, humiliate him, betray his trust, say one thing and do another. Mistrust those whom he loves. Mock him. Make him carry a heavy wooden cross, and then crucify him— and he forgives you and calls you a friend.

2 Cor. 2:8–11 — Among the doctrines covered by Paul in 2 Corinthians is this commandment that the Saints should forgive others in a Christlike manner, lest Satan should gain power over them. In teaching this way, Paul was confirming the doctrine of the Savior: "For if ye forgive men their trespasses, your heavenly Father will also forgive you: But if ye forgive not men their trespasses, neither will your Father forgive your trespasses" (Matt. 6:14–15). And from modern-day revelation, we have further substantiation of this doctrine: "Wherefore, I say unto you, that ye ought to forgive one another; for he that forgiveth not his brother his trespasses standeth condemned before the Lord; for there remaineth in him the greater sin. I, the Lord, will forgive whom I will forgive, but of you it is required to forgive all men" (D&C 64:9–10).

The Prophet Joseph Smith taught, "Meekly persuade and urge everyone to forgive one another all their trespasses, offenses and sins, that they may work out their own salvation with fear and trembling. Brethren, bear and forbear one with another, for so the Lord does with us. Pray for your enemies in the Church and curse not your foes without: for vengeance is mine, saith the Lord, and I will repay. To every ordained member, and to all, we say, be merciful and you shall find mercy" (*History of the Church*, 2:229–30).

of Israel could not stedfastly look to the end of that which is abolished:

14. But their minds were blinded: for until this day remaineth the same vail untaken away in the reading of the old testament; which vail is done away in Christ.

15. But even unto this day, when Moses is read, the vail is upon their heart.

16. Nevertheless when it shall turn to the Lord, the vail shall be taken away.

17. Now the Lord is that Spirit: and where the Spirit of the Lord is, there is liberty.

18. But we all, with open face beholding as in a glass the glory of the Lord, are changed into the same image from glory to glory, even as by the Spirit of the Lord.

CHAPTER 4

1. Therefore seeing we have this ministry, as we have received mercy, we faint not;

2. But have renounced the hidden things of dishonesty, not walking in craftiness, nor handling the word of God deceitfully; but by manifestation of the truth commending ourselves to every man's conscience in the sight of God.

3. But if our gospel be hid, it is hid to them that are lost:

4. In whom the god of this world hath blinded the minds of them which believe not, lest the light of the glorious gospel of Christ, who is the image of God, should shine unto them.

5. For we preach not ourselves, but Christ Jesus the Lord; and ourselves your servants for Jesus' sake.

6. For God, who commanded the light to shine out of darkness, hath shined in our hearts, to give the light of the knowledge of the glory of God in the face of Jesus Christ.

7. But we have this treasure in earthen vessels, that the excellency of the power may be of God, and not of us.

8. We are troubled on every side, yet not distressed; we are perplexed, but not in despair;

9. Persecuted, but not forsaken; cast down, but not destroyed;

10. Always bearing about in the body the dying of the Lord Jesus, that the life also of Jesus might be made manifest in our body.

11. For we which live are alway delivered unto death for Jesus' sake, that the life also of Jesus might be made manifest in our mortal flesh.

12. So then death worketh in us, but life in you.

13. We having the same spirit of

2 Cor. 3— Many have experienced in life the feeling of being condemned by others unjustly or accused of unkind motives that they have never harbored. The Prophet Joseph Smith was repeatedly subjected to the most vile derision and persecution without cause or provocation. His response was consistent. He forgave. He fought for the right and defended the Church and its doctrines indefatigably in the face of the most outrageous lies and malicious attacks. He fought valiantly and forcefully, but he forgave, nonetheless.

Consider his behavior toward those who inflicted serious bodily harm upon him on March 24, 1832. At that time, he and his family were staying at the home of John Johnson in Hiram, Ohio. Suddenly, a mob of some two dozen drunken men tore Joseph from the side of his ailing son, eleven-month-old Joseph Murdock Smith (one of two adopted twins), dragged him from the house, stripped him of his clothes, beat him brutally, and tarred and feathered him. All during that night, friends and family removed the skin-searing tar from his body, taking up large areas of skin in the process. Sidney Rigdon had been dragged feet-first from his home, sustaining a concussion as his head thumped down the steps and along the frozen ground. He was beaten and left comatose in the snow. Young Joseph Murdock, already suffering with measles, contracted pneumonia from the exposure that night and died a few days later. On the morning of Sunday, March 25, the day after the brutal attack, Joseph delivered a sermon before the gathering of Saints. What was his theme? Forgiveness. A number of individuals were baptized that afternoon. Three of the mobsters present at the Prophet's sermon on forgiveness were converted and joined the Church (see *History of the Church*, 1:261–65).

It was a remarkable instance of unconditional forgiveness and a lasting memorial to the Prophet's understanding and embracing of the Lord's injunction to cultivate a forgiving heart and practice forgiveness every day: "Ye have heard that it hath been said, Thou shalt love thy neighbor, and hate thine enemy. But I say unto you, Love your enemies, bless them that curse you, do good to them that hate you, and pray for them which despitefully use you, and persecute you; That ye may be the children of your Father which is in heaven" (Matt. 5:43–45). It is clear that children of God should exemplify the epitome of unconditional forgiveness.

faith, according as it is written, I believed, and therefore have I spoken; we also believe, and therefore speak;

14. Knowing that he which raised up the Lord Jesus shall raise up us also by Jesus, and shall present us with you.

15. For all things are for your sakes, that the abundant grace might through the thanksgiving of many redound to the glory of God.

16. For which cause we faint not; but though our outward man perish, yet the inward man is renewed day by day.

17. For our light affliction, which is but for a moment, worketh for us a far more exceeding and eternal weight of glory;

18. While we look not at the things which are seen, but at the things which are not seen: for the things which are seen are temporal; but the things which are not seen are eternal.

CHAPTER 5

1. For we know that if our earthly house of this tabernacle were dissolved, we have a building of God, an house not made with hands, eternal in the heavens.

2. For in this we groan, earnestly desiring to be clothed upon with our house which is from heaven:

3. If so be that being clothed we shall not be found naked.

4. For we that are in this tabernacle do groan, being burdened: not for that we would be unclothed, but clothed upon, that mortality might be swallowed up of life.

5. Now he that hath wrought us for the selfsame thing is God, who also hath given unto us the earnest of the Spirit.

6. Therefore we are always confident, knowing that, whilst we are at home in the body, we are absent from the Lord:

7. (For we walk by faith, not by sight:)

8. We are confident, I say, and willing rather to be absent from the body, and to be present with the Lord.

9. Wherefore we labour, that, whether present or absent, we may be accepted of him.

10. For we must all appear before the judgment seat of Christ; that every one may receive the things done in his body, according to that he hath done, whether it be good or bad.

11. Knowing therefore the terror of the Lord, we persuade men; but we are made manifest unto God; and I trust also are made manifest in your consciences.

12. For we commend not ourselves again unto you, but give you occasion to glory on our behalf, that ye may have somewhat to answer them which glory in appearance, and not in heart.

13. For whether we be beside ourselves, it is to God: or whether we be sober, it is for your cause.

14. For the love of Christ constraineth us; because we thus judge, that if one died for all, then were all dead:

15. And that he died for all, that

2 Cor. 5—Becoming reconciled through repentance and the Atonement of Jesus Christ is the essence of spiritual regeneration. Reconciliation to the Father through the intercession of the Son is the essence of our hope in Christ. Paul taught this doctrine with clarity and eloquence in 2 Cor. 5:17–21.

The emissaries of the Lord—chief among whom was Paul in regard to conveying the gospel to the Gentiles—are most assuredly bearers of "the word of reconciliation," as he called it, for the message of the gospel is centered in the Atonement, which is based on divine intercession, love, and advocacy. "My grace is sufficient for thee, for my strength is made perfect in weakness" (2 Cor. 12:9) is how Paul—sensitive to his own weaknesses—quoted the consoling words of the Lord. Then Paul concludes his epistle with this apostolic blessing and admonition: "Finally, brethren, farewell. Be perfect, be of good comfort, be of one mind, live in peace; and the God of love and peace shall be with you" (2 Cor. 13:11).

In pleading with men to believe in Christ and be reconciled to God so as to gain a remission of their sins, Nephi wrote, "We talk of Christ, we rejoice in Christ, we preach of Christ, we prophesy of Christ, . . . [for] the right way is to believe in Christ, and deny him not; and Christ is the Holy One of Israel; wherefore ye must bow down before him, and worship him with all your might, mind, and strength, and your whole soul; and if ye do this ye shall in nowise be cast out" (2 Ne. 25:26, 29).

they which live should not henceforth live unto themselves, but unto him which died for them, and rose again.

16. Wherefore henceforth know we no man after the flesh: yea, though we have known Christ after the flesh, yet now henceforth know we him no more.

17. Therefore if any man be in Christ, he is a new creature: old things are passed away; behold, all things are become new.

18. And all things are of God, who hath reconciled us to himself by Jesus Christ, and hath given to us the ministry of reconciliation;

19. To wit, that God was in Christ, reconciling the world unto himself, not imputing their trespasses unto them; and hath committed unto us the word of reconciliation.

20. Now then we are ambassadors for Christ, as though God did beseech you by us: we pray you in Christ's stead, be ye reconciled to God.

21. For he hath made him to be sin for us, who knew no sin; that we might be made the righteousness of God in him.

CHAPTER 6

1. We then, as workers together with him, beseech you also that ye receive not the grace of God in vain.

2. (For he saith, I have heard thee in a time accepted, and in the day of salvation have I succoured thee: behold, now is the accepted time; behold, now is the day of salvation.)

3. Giving no offence in any thing, that the ministry be not blamed:

4. But in all things approving ourselves as the ministers of God, in much patience, in afflictions, in necessities, in distresses,

5. In stripes, in imprisonments, in tumults, in labours, in watchings, in fastings;

6. By pureness, by knowledge, by longsuffering, by kindness, by the Holy Ghost, by love unfeigned,

7. By the word of truth, by the power of God, by the armour of righteousness on the right hand and on the left,

8. By honour and dishonour, by evil report and good report: as deceivers, and yet true;

9. As unknown, and yet well known; as dying, and, behold, we live; as chastened, and not killed;

10. As sorrowful, yet alway rejoicing; as poor, yet making many rich; as having nothing, and yet possessing all things.

11. O ye Corinthians, our mouth is open unto you, our heart is enlarged.

12. Ye are not straitened in us, but ye are straitened in your own bowels.

13. Now for a recompence in the same, (I speak as unto my children,) be ye also enlarged.

2 Cor. 5:17–20—"Through the Lord's atoning sacrifice, reconciliation between God and man is possible (Jac. 4:11). In other words, man is ransomed from a state of sin and spiritual darkness and restored to one of harmony and unity with Deity" (Bruce R. McConkie, *Mormon Doctrine*, 620).

Notes: _____

_____

_____

_____

_____

_____

_____

_____

_____

_____

_____

_____

_____

_____

_____

_____

_____

14. Be ye not unequally yoked together with unbelievers: for what fellowship hath righteousness with unrighteousness? and what communion hath light with darkness?

15. And what concord hath Christ with Belial? or what part hath he that believeth with an infidel?

16. And what agreement hath the temple of God with idols? for ye are the temple of the living God; as God hath said, I will dwell in them, and walk in them; and I will be their God, and they shall be my people.

17. Wherefore come out from among them, and be ye separate, saith the Lord, and touch not the unclean thing; and I will receive you,

18. And will be a Father unto you, and ye shall be my sons and daughters, saith the Lord Almighty.

CHAPTER 7

1. Having therefore these promises, dearly beloved, let us cleanse ourselves from all filthiness of the flesh and spirit, perfecting holiness in the fear of God.

2. Receive us; we have wronged no man, we have corrupted no man, we have defrauded no man.

3. I speak not this to condemn you: for I have said before, that ye are in our hearts to die and live with you.

4. Great is my boldness of speech toward you, great is my glorying of you: I am filled with comfort, I am exceeding joyful in all our tribulation.

5. For, when we were come into Macedonia, our flesh had no rest, but we were troubled on every side; without were fightings, within were fears.

6. Nevertheless God, that comforteth those that are cast down, comforted us by the coming of Titus;

7. And not by his coming only, but by the consolation wherewith he was comforted in you, when he told us your earnest desire, your mourning, your fervent mind toward me; so that I rejoiced the more.

8. For though I made you sorry with a letter, I do not repent, though I did repent: for I perceive that the same epistle hath made you sorry, though it were but for a season.

9. Now I rejoice, not that ye were made sorry, but that ye sorrowed to repentance: for ye were made sorry after a godly manner, that ye might receive damage by us in nothing.

10. For godly sorrow worketh repentance to salvation not to be repented of: but the sorrow of the world worketh death.

11. For behold this selfsame thing, that ye sorrowed after a godly sort, what carefulness it wrought in you, yea, what clearing of yourselves, yea, what indignation, yea, what fear, yea, what vehement desire, yea, what zeal, yea, what revenge! In all things ye have approved yourselves to be clear in this matter.

2 Cor. 7—Godly sorrow works by the Spirit. Our hearts are broken and our spirits are contrite. We recognize our offense against God and against those whom we have wronged. We confess and forsake and seek to restore that which was taken or lost. This is why the phrase "godly sorrow worketh repentance to salvation" accurately defines true repentance (2 Cor. 7:10). Only through godly sorrow can we fully repent and be forgiven of our sins. The key to having godly sorrow lies in yielding our hearts to the Spirit and becoming a Saint. We then become innocent, like a child, because our guilt is swept away through faith on Jesus Christ and through our practicing the principle of repentance (see Enos 1:6–8). This is all made possible through the Atonement of the Savior.

The Apostle Paul, whose epistles rank among the most magnificent statements of doctrine in all of the scriptures, makes a compelling contrast at one point between lip service and the spiritual imprint of the touch of the Master upon the soul: "Ye are our epistle written in our hearts, known and read of all men: Forasmuch as ye are manifestly declared to be the epistle of Christ ministered by us, written not with ink, but with the Spirit of the living God; not in tables of stone, but in fleshy tables of the heart" (2 Cor. 3:3). This image recalls the similar words of Jeremiah, spoken many hundreds of years prior to the ministry of Paul, around the time Lehi left Jerusalem with his family: "But this shall be the covenant that I will make with the house of Israel; After those days, saith the Lord, I will put my law in their inward parts, and write it in their hearts; and will be their God, and they shall be my people" (Jer. 31:33). A key element in this new kind of covenant, written upon the heart, is penitence and sincere sorrow for sin. Paul's celebrated words capture the essence of the genuinely broken heart and contrite spirit (see 2 Cor. 7:9–11).

It is this godly sorrow for sin, with the resulting repentance and renewal of the spirit through the Atonement of Christ, that transforms individuals into liberated sons and daughters of God—those who find their "sufficiency" in God: "Not that we are sufficient of ourselves to think any thing as of ourselves; but our sufficiency is of God; Who also hath made us able ministers of the new testament; not of the letter, but of the spirit: for the letter killeth, but the spirit giveth life. . . . Now the Lord is that Spirit: and where the Spirit of the Lord is, there is liberty" (2 Cor. 3:5–6, 17).

12. Wherefore, though I wrote unto you, I did it not for his cause that had done the wrong, nor for his cause that suffered wrong, but that our care for you in the sight of God might appear unto you.

13. Therefore we were comforted in your comfort: yea, and exceedingly the more joyed we for the joy of Titus, because his spirit was refreshed by you all.

14. For if I have boasted any thing to him of you, I am not ashamed; but as we spake all things to you in truth, even so our boasting, which I made before Titus, is found a truth.

15. And his inward affection is more abundant toward you, whilst he remembereth the obedience of you all, how with fear and trembling ye received him.

16. I rejoice therefore that I have confidence in you in all things.

CHAPTER 8

1. Moreover, brethren, we do you to wit of the grace of God bestowed on the churches of Macedonia;

2. How that in a great trial of affliction the abundance of their joy and their deep poverty abounded unto the riches of their liberality.

3. For to their power, I bear record, yea, and beyond their power they were willing of themselves;

4. Praying us with much intreaty that we would receive the gift, and take upon us the fellowship of the ministering to the saints.

5. And this they did, not as we hoped, but first gave their own selves to the Lord, and unto us by the will of God.

6. Insomuch that we desired Titus, that as he had begun, so he would also finish in you the same grace also.

7. Therefore, as ye abound in every thing, in faith, and utterance, and knowledge, and in all diligence, and in your love to us, see that ye abound in this grace also.

8. I speak not by commandment, but by occasion of the forwardness of others, and to prove the sincerity of your love.

9. For ye know the grace of our Lord Jesus Christ, that, though he was rich, yet for your sakes he became poor, that ye through his poverty might be rich.

10. And herein I give my advice: for this is expedient for you, who have begun before, not only to do, but also to be forward a year ago.

11. Now therefore perform the doing of it; that as there was a readiness to will, so there may be a performance also out of that which ye have.

12. For if there be first a willing mind, it is accepted according to that a man hath, and not according to that he hath not.

13. For I mean not that other men be eased, and ye burdened:

14. But by an equality, that now at this time your abundance may be a supply for their want, that their abundance also may be a supply for your want: that there may be equality:

15. As it is written, He that had gathered much had nothing over; and he that had gathered little had no lack.

16. But thanks be to God, which put the same earnest care into the heart of Titus for you.

Notes: _____

17. For indeed he accepted the exhortation; but being more forward, of his own accord he went unto you.

18. And we have sent with him the brother, whose praise is in the gospel throughout all the churches;

19. And not that only, but who was also chosen of the churches to travel with us with this grace, which is administered by us to the glory of the same Lord, and declaration of your ready mind:

20. Avoiding this, that no man should blame us in this abundance which is administered by us:

21. Providing for honest things, not only in the sight of the Lord, but also in the sight of men.

22. And we have sent with them our brother, whom we have oftentimes proved diligent in many things, but now much more diligent, upon the great confidence which I have in you.

23. Whether any do inquire of Titus, he is my partner and fellowhelper concerning you: or our brethren be inquired of, they are the messengers of the churches, and the glory of Christ.

24. Wherefore shew ye to them, and before the churches, the proof of your love, and of our boasting on your behalf.

CHAPTER 9

1. For as touching the ministering to the saints, it is superfluous for me to write to you:

2. For I know the forwardness of your mind, for which I boast of you to them of Macedonia, that Achaia was ready a year ago; and your zeal hath provoked very many.

3. Yet have I sent the brethren, lest our boasting of you should be in vain in this behalf; that, as I said, ye may be ready:

4. Lest haply if they of Macedonia come with me, and find you unprepared, we (that we say not, ye) should be ashamed in this same confident boasting.

5. Therefore I thought it necessary to exhort the brethren, that they would go before unto you, and make up beforehand your bounty, whereof ye had notice before, that the same might be ready, as a matter of bounty, and not as of covetousness.

6. But this I say, He which soweth sparingly shall reap also sparingly; and he which soweth bountifully shall reap also bountifully.

7. Every man according as he purposeth in his heart, so let him give; not grudgingly, or of necessity: for God loveth a cheerful giver.

8. And God is able to make all grace abound toward you; that ye, always having all sufficiency in all things, may abound to every good work:

9. (As it is written, He hath dispersed abroad; he hath given to the poor: his righteousness remaineth for ever.

10. Now he that ministereth seed to the sower both minister bread for your food, and multiply your seed sown, and increase the fruits of your righteousness;)

11. Being enriched in every thing to all bountifulness, which causeth through us thanksgiving to God.

12. For the administration of this service not only supplieth the want of the saints, but is abundant also by many thanksgivings unto God;

13. Whiles by the experiment of this ministration they glorify God for your professed subjection unto the gospel of Christ, and for your liberal distribution unto them, and unto all men;

JEWS

The terms *Jew* or *Jews* occur frequently in the New Testament. In the most specific sense, *Jews* refers to people of the lineage of Judah, son of Jacob. The earliest use of the term *Jews* in the Old Testament occurs in 2 Kgs. 16:6, dating to about 740 B.C.

In a broader sense, the term can be applied to those who over the generations were citizens of Jerusalem, even though they were not of Jewish lineage (as in 2 Ne. 30:4). Thus, Lehi was part of the Jewish community in his day—although he was by lineage from the tribe of Joseph through Manasseh, son of Joseph (see Alma 10:3), while Ishmael and his posterity derived from the tribe of Ephraim, son of Joseph (see *Journal of Discourses*, 23:184–85).

The Doctrine and Covenants contains nineteen references to *Jews* and three to the word *Jew*—most of the references applying to the specific meaning of the term (the lineage of Judah). In one poignant reference, the Lord gives utterance to the state of mind of the Jews at the time of the Second Coming when they realize that the millennial Lord is indeed the same Jesus Christ whom their leaders had crucified (see D&C 45:51–53).

Interior of the Great Synagogue of Bukhara

14. And by their prayer for you, which long after you for the exceeding grace of God in you.

15. Thanks be unto God for his unspeakable gift.

CHAPTER 10

1. Now I Paul myself beseech you by the meekness and gentleness of Christ, who in presence am base among you, but being absent am bold toward you:

2. But I beseech you, that I may not be bold when I am present with that confidence, wherewith I think to be bold against some, which think of us as if we walked according to the flesh.

3. For though we walk in the flesh, we do not war after the flesh:

4. (For the weapons of our warfare are not carnal, but mighty through God to the pulling down of strong holds;)

5. Casting down imaginations, and every high thing that exalteth itself against the knowledge of God, and bringing into captivity every thought to the obedience of Christ;

6. And having in a readiness to revenge all disobedience, when your obedience is fulfilled.

7. Do ye look on things after the outward appearance? If any man trust to himself that he is Christ's, let him of himself think this again, that, as he is Christ's, even so are we Christ's.

8. For though I should boast somewhat more of our authority, which the Lord hath given us for edification, and not for your destruction, I should not be ashamed:

9. That I may not seem as if I would terrify you by letters.

10. For his letters, say they, are weighty and powerful; but his bodily presence is weak, and his speech contemptible.

11. Let such an one think this, that, such as we are in word by letters when we are absent, such will we be also in deed when we are present.

12. For we dare not make ourselves of the number, or compare ourselves with some that commend themselves: but they measuring themselves by themselves, and comparing themselves among themselves, are not wise.

13. But we will not boast of things without our measure, but according to the measure of the rule which God hath distributed to us, a measure to reach even unto you.

14. For we stretch not ourselves beyond our measure, as though we reached not unto you: for we are come as far as to you also in preaching the gospel of Christ:

15. Not boasting of things without our measure, that is, of other men's labours; but having hope, when your faith is increased, that we shall be enlarged by you according to our rule abundantly,

16. To preach the gospel in the regions beyond you, and not to boast in another man's line of things made ready to our hand.

17. But he that glorieth, let him glory in the Lord.

18. For not he that commendeth himself is approved, but whom the Lord commendeth.

Notes: _____
_____
_____
_____
_____
_____
_____
_____
_____
_____
_____
_____
_____
_____
_____
_____
_____
_____
_____
_____
_____
_____
_____
_____
_____
_____
_____
_____
_____
_____
_____

CHAPTER 11

1. Would to God ye could bear with me a little in my folly: and indeed bear with me.

2. For I am jealous over you with godly jealousy: for I have espoused you to one husband, that I may present you as a chaste virgin to Christ.

3. But I fear, lest by any means, as the serpent beguiled Eve through his subtilty, so your minds should be corrupted from the simplicity that is in Christ.

4. For if he that cometh preacheth another Jesus, whom we have not preached, or if ye receive another spirit, which ye have not received, or another gospel, which ye have not accepted, ye might well bear with him.

5. For I suppose I was not a whit behind the very chiefest apostles.

6. But though I be rude in speech, yet not in knowledge; but we have been throughly made manifest among you in all things.

7. Have I committed an offence in abasing myself that ye might be exalted, because I have preached to you the gospel of God freely?

8. I robbed other churches, taking wages of them, to do you service.

9. And when I was present with you, and wanted, I was chargeable to no man: for that which was lacking to me the brethren which came from Macedonia supplied: and in all things I have kept myself from being burdensome unto you, and so will I keep myself.

10. As the truth of Christ is in me, no man shall stop me of this boasting in the regions of Achaia.

11. Wherefore? because I love you not? God knoweth.

12. But what I do, that I will do, that I may cut off occasion from them which desire occasion; that wherein they glory, they may be found even as we.

13. For such are false apostles, deceitful workers, transforming themselves into the apostles of Christ.

14. And no marvel; for Satan himself is transformed into an angel of light.

15. Therefore it is no great thing if his ministers also be transformed as the ministers of righteousness; whose end shall be according to their works.

16. I say again, Let no man think me a fool; if otherwise, yet as a fool receive me, that I may boast myself a little.

17. That which I speak, I speak it not after the Lord, but as it were foolishly, in this confidence of boasting.

18. Seeing that many glory after the flesh, I will glory also.

19. For ye suffer fools gladly, seeing ye yourselves are wise.

20. For ye suffer, if a man bring you into bondage, if a man devour you, if a man take of you, if a man exalt himself, if a man smite you on the face.

21. I speak as concerning reproach, as though we had been weak. Howbeit whereinsoever any is bold, (I speak foolishly,) I am bold also.

22. Are they Hebrews? so am I. Are they Israelites? so am I. Are they the seed of Abraham? so am I.

23. Are they ministers of Christ?

GREEKS

The inhabitants of Greece are identified as descendants of Javan in the Old Testament (see Gen. 10:1–2). The book of Daniel refers to the land *Grecia* (see Dan. 8:21; 10:20; 11:2) and the book of Zechariah refers to the land of *Greece* (see Zech. 9:13).

The New Testament refers only once to Greece (see Acts 20:2) but three times to the *Grecians* (Hellenists, or Greek-speaking Jews)—see Acts 6:1, Acts 9:29–30, and Acts 11:20–21. Again, these Grecians were evidently Greek-speaking Jews of foreign descent now living in the Holy Land.

The words *Greek* or *Greeks* are used rather frequently in the New Testament and generally designate Hellenes (individuals of Greek descent). The gospel was preached in Greek as soon as the missionary program extended beyond Palestine. We know that Jesus spoke Aramaic, and the Gospels as we now have them were almost certainly originally written in Greek.

(I speak as a fool) I am more; in labours more abundant, in stripes above measure, in prisons more frequent, in deaths oft.

24. Of the Jews five times received I forty stripes save one.

25. Thrice was I beaten with rods, once was I stoned, thrice I suffered shipwreck, a night and a day I have been in the deep;

26. In journeyings often, in perils of waters, in perils of robbers, in perils by mine own countrymen, in perils by the heathen, in perils in the city, in perils in the wilderness, in perils in the sea, in perils among false brethren;

27. In weariness and painfulness, in watchings often, in hunger and thirst, in fastings often, in cold and nakedness.

28. Beside those things that are without, that which cometh upon me daily, the care of all the churches.

29. Who is weak, and I am not weak? who is offended, and I burn not?

30. If I must needs glory, I will glory of the things which concern mine infirmities.

31. The God and Father of our Lord Jesus Christ, which is blessed for evermore, knoweth that I lie not.

32. In Damascus the governor under Aretas the king kept the city of the Damascenes with a garrison, desirous to apprehend me:

33. And through a window in a basket was I let down by the wall, and escaped his hands.

CHAPTER 12

1. It is not expedient for me doubtless to glory. I will come to visions and revelations of the Lord.

2. I knew a man in Christ above fourteen years ago, (whether in the body, I cannot tell; or whether out of the body, I cannot tell: God knoweth;) such an one caught up to the third heaven.

3. And I knew such a man, (whether in the body, or out of the body, I cannot tell: God knoweth;)

4. How that he was caught up into paradise, and heard unspeakable words, which it is not lawful for a man to utter.

5. Of such an one will I glory: yet of myself I will not glory, but in mine infirmities.

6. For though I would desire to glory, I shall not be a fool; for I will say the truth: but now I forbear, lest any man should think of me above that which he seeth me to be, or that he heareth of me.

7. And lest I should be exalted above measure through the abundance of the revelations, there was given to me a thorn in the flesh, the messenger of Satan to buffet me, lest I should be exalted above measure.

8. For this thing I besought the Lord thrice, that it might depart from me.

9. And he said unto me, My grace is sufficient for thee: for my strength

Notes: _____

is made perfect in weakness. Most gladly therefore will I rather glory in my infirmities, that the power of Christ may rest upon me.

10. Therefore I take pleasure in infirmities, in reproaches, in necessities, in persecutions, in distresses for Christ's sake: for when I am weak, then am I strong.

11. I am become a fool in glorying; ye have compelled me: for I ought to have been commended of you: for in nothing am I behind the very chiefest apostles, though I be nothing.

12. Truly the signs of an apostle were wrought among you in all patience, in signs, and wonders, and mighty deeds.

13. For what is it wherein ye were inferior to other churches, except it be that I myself was not burdensome to you? forgive me this wrong.

14. Behold, the third time I am ready to come to you; and I will not be burdensome to you: for I seek not yours, but you: for the children ought not to lay up for the parents, but the parents for the children.

15. And I will very gladly spend and be spent for you; though the more abundantly I love you, the less I be loved.

16. But be it so, I did not burden you: nevertheless, being crafty, I caught you with guile.

17. Did I make a gain of you by any of them whom I sent unto you?

18. I desired Titus, and with him I sent a brother. Did Titus make a gain of you? walked we not in the same spirit? walked we not in the same steps?

19. Again, think ye that we excuse ourselves unto you? we speak before God in Christ: but we do all things, dearly beloved, for your edifying.

20. For I fear, lest, when I come, I shall not find you such as I would, and that I shall be found unto you such as ye would not: lest there be debates, envyings, wraths, strifes, backbitings, whisperings, swellings, tumults:

21. And lest, when I come again, my God will humble me among you, and that I shall bewail many which have sinned already, and have not repented of the uncleanness and fornication and lasciviousness which they have committed.

CHAPTER 13

1. This is the third time I am coming to you. In the mouth of two or three witnesses shall every word be established.

2. I told you before, and foretell you, as if I were present, the second time; and being absent now I write to them which heretofore have sinned, and to all other, that, if I come again, I will not spare:

3. Since ye seek a proof of Christ speaking in me, which to you-ward is not weak, but is mighty in you.

4. For though he was crucified through weakness, yet he liveth by the power of God. For we also are weak in him, but we shall live with him by the power of God toward you.

5. Examine yourselves, whether ye be in the faith; prove your own selves. Know ye not your own selves, how that Jesus Christ is in you, except ye be reprobates?

6. But I trust that ye shall know that we are not reprobates.

7. Now I pray to God that ye do no evil; not that we should appear approved, but that ye should do that

Notes: _____

_____

_____

_____

_____

_____

_____

_____

_____

_____

_____

_____

_____

_____

_____

_____

_____

_____

_____

_____

_____

_____

_____

_____

_____

_____

_____

which is honest, though we be as reprobates.

8. For we can do nothing against the truth, but for the truth.

9. For we are glad, when we are weak, and ye are strong: and this also we wish, even your perfection.

10. Therefore I write these things being absent, lest being present I should use sharpness, according to the power which the Lord hath given me to edification, and not to destruction.

11. Finally, brethren, farewell. Be perfect, be of good comfort, be of one mind, live in peace; and the God of love and peace shall be with you.

12. Greet one another with an holy kiss.

13. All the saints salute you.

14. The grace of the Lord Jesus Christ, and the love of God, and the communion of the Holy Ghost, be with you all. Amen.

THE EPISTLE OF PAUL THE APOSTLE TO

THE GALATIANS

CHAPTER 1

1. Paul, an apostle, (not of men, neither by man, but by Jesus Christ, and God the Father, who raised him from the dead;)

2. And all the brethren which are with me, unto the churches of Galatia:

3. Grace be to you and peace from God the Father, and from our Lord Jesus Christ,

4. Who gave himself for our sins, that he might deliver us from this present evil world, according to the will of God and our Father:

5. To whom be glory for ever and ever. Amen.

6. I marvel that ye are so soon removed from him that called you into the grace of Christ unto another gospel:

7. Which is not another; but there be some that trouble you, and would pervert the gospel of Christ.

8. But though we, or an angel from heaven, preach any other gospel unto you than that which we have preached unto you, let him be accursed.

9. As we said before, so say I now again, If any man preach any other

2 Corinthians—What a blessing it is to be able to open the pages of 2 Corinthians and savor the bread of life, served up by a master teacher in a banquet of timeless spiritual doctrine. We learn that we can overcome all trials and tribulations through the strength of the Lord. Is that not a relevant principle for our times as well as for the Corinthian Saints of old? We learn that forgiveness is the essence of the divine character of the Savior. Does that not still apply to each of us in modern times? We learn what it means to display godly sorrow for our sins, so that we can become reconciled to God through the intercession of the Only Begotten. What a timeless message that is!

gospel unto you than that ye have received, let him be accursed.

10. For do I now persuade men, or God? or do I seek to please men? for if I yet pleased men, I should not be the servant of Christ.

11. But I certify you, brethren, that the gospel which was preached of me is not after man.

12. For I neither received it of man, neither was I taught it, but by the revelation of Jesus Christ.

13. For ye have heard of my conversation in time past in the Jews' religion, how that beyond measure I persecuted the church of God, and wasted it:

14. And profited in the Jews' religion above many my equals in mine own nation, being more exceedingly zealous of the traditions of my fathers.

15. But when it pleased God, who separated me from my mother's womb, and called me by his grace,

16. To reveal his Son in me, that I might preach him among the heathen; immediately I conferred not with flesh and blood:

17. Neither went I up to Jerusalem to them which were apostles before me; but I went into Arabia, and returned again unto Damascus.

18. Then after three years I went up to Jerusalem to see Peter, and abode with him fifteen days.

19. But other of the apostles saw I none, save James the Lord's brother.

20. Now the things which I write unto you, behold, before God, I lie not.

21. Afterwards I came into the regions of Syria and Cilicia;

22. And was unknown by face unto the churches of Judæa which were in Christ:

23. But they had heard only, That he which persecuted us in times past now preacheth the faith which once he destroyed.

24. And they glorified God in me.

CHAPTER 2

1. Then fourteen years after I went up again to Jerusalem with Barnabas, and took Titus with me also.

2. And I went up by revelation, and communicated unto them that gospel which I preach among the Gentiles, but privately to them which were of reputation, lest by any means I should run, or had run, in vain.

3. But neither Titus, who was with me, being a Greek, was compelled to be circumcised:

4. And that because of false brethren unawares brought in, who came in privily to spy out our liberty which we have in Christ Jesus, that they might bring us into bondage:

5. To whom we gave place by subjection, no, not for an hour; that the truth of the gospel might continue with you.

6. But of these who seemed to be somewhat, (whatsoever they were, it maketh no matter to me: God accepteth no man's person:) for they

GALATIANS

The Galatians were residents of Galatia, the central region of Asia Minor. Paul visited Galatia on his second journey (see Acts 16:6) and also on his third journey (see Acts 18:23). The epistle of Paul to the Galatians emphasizes faith and spirituality as the core of the gospel, as contrasted with worship based on externalities.

PETER

Peter ("rock," the meaning of the Greek equivalent of his Aramaic name, *Cephas*), along with his brother Andrew, was the first of the Twelve Apostles called by the Lord during His mortal ministry (see Matt. 4:18–22). He was the leading Apostle belonging to the inner circle of three Apostles—Peter, James, and John—constituting, as it were, the First Presidency of the Church. All three were on the Mount of Transfiguration (see Matt. 17:1–13) and at Gethsemane (see Matt. 26:36–37). Peter's affirmation of the divine Sonship of Jesus (see Matt. 16:16) preceded the Savior's celebrated declaration (see Matt. 16:17–19).

It was through Peter's missionary work that the gospel was introduced among the Gentiles (see Acts 10–11). Peter's pronouncement to the people concerning the predicted "times of refreshing" and "times of restitution of all things" (see Acts 3:19, 21) coming through the future ministry of the Lord foreshadowed the Restoration in the latter days.

Peter is also identified as the exemplary gospel messenger when the Lord instructed Sidney Rigdon, Parley P. Pratt, and Leman Copley to go among the Shakers and proclaim the truths of the restored gospel (see D&C 49:11–14).

Moreover, it was through pondering the writings of Peter that President Joseph F. Smith was granted his grand vision of the work of salvation taking place in the spirit world (see D&C 138:5–6, 9–10, 28).

who seemed to be somewhat in conference added nothing to me:

7. But contrariwise, when they saw that the gospel of the uncircumcision was committed unto me, as the gospel of the circumcision was unto Peter;

8. (For he that wrought effectually in Peter to the apostleship of the circumcision, the same was mighty in me toward the Gentiles:)

9. And when James, Cephas, and John, who seemed to be pillars, perceived the grace that was given unto me, they gave to me and Barnabas the right hands of fellowship; that we should go unto the heathen, and they unto the circumcision.

10. Only they would that we should remember the poor; the same which I also was forward to do.

11. But when Peter was come to Antioch, I withstood him to the face, because he was to be blamed.

12. For before that certain came from James, he did eat with the Gentiles: but when they were come, he withdrew and separated himself, fearing them which were of the circumcision.

13. And the other Jews dissembled likewise with him; insomuch that Barnabas also was carried away with their dissimulation.

14. But when I saw that they walked not uprightly according to the truth of the gospel, I said unto Peter before them all, If thou, being a Jew, livest after the manner of Gentiles, and not as do the Jews, why compellest thou the Gentiles to live as do the Jews?

15. We who are Jews by nature, and not sinners of the Gentiles,

16. Knowing that a man is not justified by the works of the law, but by the faith of Jesus Christ, even we have believed in Jesus Christ, that we might be justified by the faith of Christ, and not by the works of the law: for by the works of the law shall no flesh be justified.

17. But if, while we seek to be justified by Christ, we ourselves also are found sinners, is therefore Christ the minister of sin? God forbid.

18. For if I build again the things which I destroyed, I make myself a transgressor.

19. For I through the law am dead to the law, that I might live unto God.

20. I am crucified with Christ: nevertheless I live; yet not I, but Christ liveth in me: and the life which I now live in the flesh I live by the faith of the Son of God, who loved me, and gave himself for me.

21. I do not frustrate the grace of God: for if righteousness come by the law, then Christ is dead in vain.

CHAPTER 3

1. O foolish Galatians, who hath bewitched you, that ye should not obey the truth, before whose eyes Jesus Christ hath been evidently set forth, crucified among you?

2. This only would I learn of you, Received ye the Spirit by the works of the law, or by the hearing of faith?

3. Are ye so foolish? having begun

Notes: _____
_____
_____
_____
_____
_____
_____
_____
_____
_____
_____
_____
_____
_____
_____
_____
_____
_____
_____
_____
_____
_____
_____
_____
_____
_____
_____
_____
_____
_____
_____
_____

in the Spirit, are ye now made perfect by the flesh?

4. Have ye suffered so many things in vain? if it be yet in vain.

5. He therefore that ministereth to you the Spirit, and worketh miracles among you, doeth he it by the works of the law, or by the hearing of faith?

6. Even as Abraham believed God, and it was accounted to him for righteousness.

7. Know ye therefore that they which are of faith, the same are the children of Abraham.

8. And the scripture, foreseeing that God would justify the heathen through faith, preached before the gospel unto Abraham, saying, In thee shall all nations be blessed.

9. So then they which be of faith are blessed with faithful Abraham.

10. For as many as are of the works of the law are under the curse: for it is written, Cursed is every one that continueth not in all things which are written in the book of the law to do them.

11. But that no man is justified by the law in the sight of God, it is evident: for, The just shall live by faith.

12. And the law is not of faith: but, The man that doeth them shall live in them.

13. Christ hath redeemed us from the curse of the law, being made a curse for us: for it is written, Cursed is every one that hangeth on a tree:

14. That the blessing of Abraham might come on the Gentiles through Jesus Christ; that we might receive the promise of the Spirit through faith.

15. Brethren, I speak after the manner of men; Though it be but a man's covenant, yet if it be confirmed, no man disannulleth, or addeth thereto.

16. Now to Abraham and his seed were the promises made. He saith not, And to seeds, as of many; but as of one, And to thy seed, which is Christ.

17. And this I say, that the covenant, that was confirmed before of God in Christ, the law, which was four hundred and thirty years after, cannot disannul, that it should make the promise of none effect.

18. For if the inheritance be of the law, it is no more of promise: but God gave it to Abraham by promise.

19. Wherefore then serveth the law? It was added because of transgressions, till the seed should come to whom the promise was made; and it was ordained by angels in the hand of a mediator.

20. Now a mediator is not a mediator of one, but God is one.

21. Is the law then against the promises of God? God forbid: for if there had been a law given which could have given life, verily righteousness should have been by the law.

22. But the scripture hath concluded all under sin, that the promise by faith of Jesus Christ might be given to them that believe.

23. But before faith came, we were kept under the law, shut up unto the faith which should afterwards be revealed.

24. Wherefore the law was our schoolmaster to bring us unto Christ,

Gal. 3:19—As we look back through the chronicles of God's dealings with His peoples over time, we are confirmed in our witness that His divine purposes are being fulfilled with precision. The Church is founded upon the gospel of Jesus Christ and is centered in Him, as are all things. The gospel was given to Moses, but due to the rebellious nature of the Israelites, they were also given a law of carnal commandments, which was a lesser law, a schoolmaster to point them toward Christ and prepare them to come unto Him. Thus the law of Moses was given to the Israelites. Moses gave the people many gospel truths, but due to their stiffneckedness and transgressions, they were still required to keep the performances of the law of Moses (see Gal. 3:19). We learn of this process from the clear teachings of the Nephites (see 2 Ne. 25:23–25). Then, when the Lord came, He fulfilled the law (see 3 Ne. 15:4–9).

Gal. 3:24—The entire purpose of the law of Moses was to help the people look forward to and come to know Jesus as the Messiah and Savior of the world. Likewise, all that the Lord has given us today through His word, ordinances, and covenants is to help us come to know our Heavenly Father and our Savior Jesus Christ and to keep the commandments.

that we might be justified by faith.

25. But after that faith is come, we are no longer under a schoolmaster.

26. For ye are all the children of God by faith in Christ Jesus.

27. For as many of you as have been baptized into Christ have put on Christ.

28. There is neither Jew nor Greek, there is neither bond nor free, there is neither male nor female: for ye are all one in Christ Jesus.

29. And if ye be Christ's, then are ye Abraham's seed, and heirs according to the promise.

CHAPTER 4

1. Now I say, That the heir, as long as he is a child, differeth nothing from a servant, though he be lord of all;

2. But is under tutors and governors until the time appointed of the father.

3. Even so we, when we were children, were in bondage under the elements of the world:

4. But when the fulness of the time was come, God sent forth his Son, made of a woman, made under the law,

5. To redeem them that were under the law, that we might receive the adoption of sons.

6. And because ye are sons, God hath sent forth the Spirit of his Son into your hearts, crying, Abba, Father.

7. Wherefore thou art no more a servant, but a son; and if a son, then an heir of God through Christ.

8. Howbeit then, when ye knew not God, ye did service unto them which by nature are no gods.

9. But now, after that ye have known God, or rather are known of God, how turn ye again to the weak and beggarly elements, whereunto ye desire again to be in bondage?

10. Ye observe days, and months, and times, and years.

11. I am afraid of you, lest I have bestowed upon you labour in vain.

12. Brethren, I beseech you, be as I am; for I am as ye are: ye have not injured me at all.

13. Ye know how through infirmity of the flesh I preached the gospel unto you at the first.

14. And my temptation which was in my flesh ye despised not, nor rejected; but received me as an angel of God, even as Christ Jesus.

15. Where is then the blessedness ye spake of? for I bear you record, that, if it had been possible, ye would have plucked out your own eyes, and have given them to me.

16. Am I therefore become your enemy, because I tell you the truth?

17. They zealously affect you, but not well; yea, they would exclude you, that ye might affect them.

18. But it is good to be zealously affected always in a good thing, and not only when I am present with you.

Moses teaching the new law

19. My little children, of whom I travail in birth again until Christ be formed in you,

20. I desire to be present with you now, and to change my voice; for I stand in doubt of you.

21. Tell me, ye that desire to be under the law, do ye not hear the law?

22. For it is written, that Abraham had two sons, the one by a bondmaid, the other by a freewoman.

23. But he who was of the bondwoman was born after the flesh; but he of the freewoman was by promise.

24. Which things are an allegory: for these are the two covenants; the one from the mount Sinai, which gendereth to bondage, which is Agar.

25. For this Agar is mount Sinai in Arabia, and answereth to Jerusalem which now is, and is in bondage with her children.

26. But Jerusalem which is above is free, which is the mother of us all.

27. For it is written, Rejoice, thou barren that bearest not; break forth and cry, thou that travailest not: for the desolate hath many more children than she which hath an husband.

28. Now we, brethren, as Isaac was, are the children of promise.

29. But as then he that was born after the flesh persecuted him that was born after the Spirit, even so it is now.

30. Nevertheless what saith the scripture? Cast out the bondwoman and her son: for the son of the bondwoman shall not be heir with the son of the freewoman.

31. So then, brethren, we are not children of the bondwoman, but of the free.

CHAPTER 5

1. Stand fast therefore in the liberty wherewith Christ hath made us free, and be not entangled again with the yoke of bondage.

2. Behold, I Paul say unto you, that if ye be circumcised, Christ shall profit you nothing.

3. For I testify again to every man that is circumcised, that he is a debtor to do the whole law.

4. Christ is become of no effect unto you, whosoever of you are justified by the law; ye are fallen from grace.

5. For we through the Spirit wait for the hope of righteousness by faith.

6. For in Jesus Christ neither circumcision availeth anything, nor uncircumcision; but faith which worketh by love.

7. Ye did run well; who did hinder you that ye should not obey the truth?

8. This persuasion cometh not of him that calleth you.

9. A little leaven leaveneth the whole lump.

10. I have confidence in you through the Lord, that ye will be none otherwise minded: but he that troubleth you shall bear his judgment, whosoever he be.

THE HOLY GHOST

The Holy Ghost is the third member of the Godhead. The presence of the Holy Ghost in the New Testament text is pervasive, the term *Holy Ghost* being used ninety times; the Holy Ghost is also referred to in the New Testament as the *Spirit of God,* the *Spirit of the Lord,* the *Holy Spirit,* the *Comforter,* and *Spirit* (capitalized, as in Galatians 4, among other passages, to indicate a member of the Godhead).

Some of the key manifestations of the Holy Ghost in the New Testament include:

• The divine conception of Jesus (see Matt. 1:18)

• The promise of Gabriel concerning the coming of John the Baptist (see Luke 1:15)

• The ministry of John the Baptist as a forerunner to Jesus (see Mark 1:8)

• The baptism of Jesus (see Matt. 3:16)

• The Savior being led by the Holy Ghost into the wilderness (see Luke 4:1)

• The Savior's promise of guidance to His disciples through the Holy Ghost (see Mark 13:11)

• The Savior on the power of prayer (see Luke 11:13)

• The resurrected Lord dispensing the Holy Ghost on His disciples (see John 20:19–20)

• The Holy Ghost on the Day of Pentecost (see Acts 2:1–4)

• The martyrdom of Stephen (see Acts 7:55)

• The conversion of Paul (see Acts 9:17)

• Paul concerning the Holy Ghost as the agent of divine love (see Rom. 5:5)

• Paul on the blessings of the Spirit (see 1 Cor. 2:9–11)

• Paul on personal revelation (see 1 Cor. 12:3)

• Paul on the Holy Spirit of Promise (see Eph. 1:13)

• Peter on the Holy Ghost as the inspiration for scripture (see 2 Pet. 1:20–21)

11. And I, brethren, if I yet preach circumcision, why do I yet suffer persecution? then is the offence of the cross ceased.

12. I would they were even cut off which trouble you.

13. For, brethren, ye have been called unto liberty; only use not liberty for an occasion to the flesh, but by love serve one another.

14. For all the law is fulfilled in one word, even in this; Thou shalt love thy neighbour as thyself.

15. But if ye bite and devour one another, take heed that ye be not consumed one of another.

16. This I say then, Walk in the Spirit, and ye shall not fulfil the lust of the flesh.

17. For the flesh lusteth against the Spirit, and the Spirit against the flesh: and these are contrary the one to the other: so that ye cannot do the things that ye would.

18. But if ye be led of the Spirit, ye are not under the law.

19. Now the works of the flesh are manifest, which are these; Adultery, fornication, uncleanness, lasciviousness,

20. Idolatry, witchcraft, hatred, variance, emulations, wrath, strife, seditions, heresies,

21. Envyings, murders, drunkenness, revellings, and such like: of the which I tell you before, as I have also told you in time past, that they which do such things shall not inherit the kingdom of God.

22. But the fruit of the Spirit is love, joy, peace, longsuffering, gentleness, goodness, faith,

23. Meekness, temperance: against such there is no law.

24. And they that are Christ's have crucified the flesh with the affections and lusts.

25. If we live in the Spirit, let us also walk in the Spirit.

26. Let us not be desirous of vain glory, provoking one another, envying one another.

CHAPTER 6

1. Brethren, if a man be overtaken in a fault, ye which are spiritual, restore such an one in the spirit of meekness; considering thyself, lest thou also be tempted.

2. Bear ye one another's burdens, and so fulfil the law of Christ.

3. For if a man think himself to be something, when he is nothing, he deceiveth himself.

4. But let every man prove his own work, and then shall he have rejoicing in himself alone, and not in another.

5. For every man shall bear his own burden.

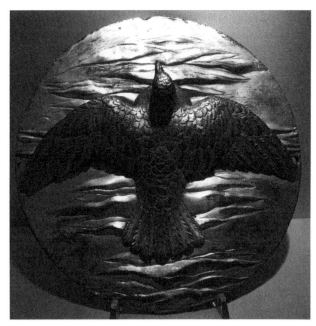

The Holy Spirit depicted in the form of a dove

6. Let him that is taught in the word communicate unto him that teacheth in all good things.

7. Be not deceived; God is not mocked: for whatsoever a man soweth, that shall he also reap.

8. For he that soweth to his flesh shall of the flesh reap corruption; but he that soweth to the Spirit shall of the Spirit reap life everlasting.

9. And let us not be weary in well doing: for in due season we shall reap, if we faint not.

10. As we have therefore opportunity, let us do good unto all men, especially unto them who are of the household of faith.

11. Ye see how large a letter I have written unto you with mine own hand.

12. As many as desire to make a fair shew in the flesh, they constrain you to be circumcised; only lest they should suffer persecution for the cross of Christ.

13. For neither they themselves who are circumcised keep the law; but desire to have you circumcised, that they may glory in your flesh.

14. But God forbid that I should glory, save in the cross of our Lord Jesus Christ, by whom the world is crucified unto me, and I unto the world.

15. For in Christ Jesus neither circumcision availeth any thing, nor uncircumcision, but a new creature.

16. And as many as walk according to this rule, peace be on them, and mercy, and upon the Israel of God.

17. From henceforth let no man trouble me: for I bear in my body the marks of the Lord Jesus.

18. Brethren, the grace of our Lord Jesus Christ be with your spirit. Amen.

THE EPISTLE OF PAUL THE APOSTLE TO

THE EPHESIANS

CHAPTER 1

1. Paul, an apostle of Jesus Christ by the will of God, to the saints which are at Ephesus, and to the faithful in Christ Jesus:

2. Grace be to you, and peace, from God our Father, and from the Lord Jesus Christ.

3. Blessed be the God and Father of our Lord Jesus Christ, who hath blessed us with all spiritual blessings in heavenly places in Christ:

4. According as he hath chosen us in him before the foundation of the world, that we should be holy and without blame before him in love:

Ephesians— Paul's epistle to the Ephesians was written in the time frame A.D. 60 to A.D. 62, similar to Philippians, Colossians, Philemon, and Hebrews. These epistles were written from Rome during Paul's confinement there at the behest of the Roman authorities. Ephesus (located near the western coast of modern-day Turkey) was the capital city of the Roman province of Asia and a major commercial center, connecting trade from east to west. Paul visited Ephesus toward the end of his second missionary journey (see Acts 18:19) and then returned during his third missionary journey, residing there for a period of some two years (see Acts 19). Missionary service in the city, which included some quarter million inhabitants in New Testament times, was productive, and a goodly circle of followers of Christ was established there. Paul was forced to leave the city under pressure from the silversmith industry, which provided silver shrines in honor of Artemis or Diana, whose temple—regarded as one of the seven wonders of the ancient world—was located within the city. The growing Christian circle—for which artifacts for idols were anathema—was compromising the silversmiths' trade, so they rose up against the Church and its expansion.

Paul's extraordinary epistle to the Ephesians is, among other things, a noteworthy exposition of the nature, organization, and future destiny of the Church and kingdom of God. Paul, naturally grounded in the details of the recent establishment of the Church under the personal and immediate leadership of the Redeemer and Lord, Jesus Christ, was also a man of keen retrospective vision (having intimate familiarity with covenant history and the canon of scripture leading back to Adam). He was also a person of forward-reaching spiritual vision concerning the unfolding of the kingdom of God, even unto the ends of the earth. As such, he was well versed in the prophetic view of the Restoration of the gospel in the latter days, as confirmed by his words to the Ephesians (see Eph. 1:9–12).

Paul invoked the blessings of the Lord upon the Saints at Ephesus, praying "That the God of our Lord Jesus Christ, the Father of glory, may give unto you the spirit of wisdom and revelation in the knowledge of him: The eyes of your understanding being enlightened; that ye may know what is the hope of his calling, and what the riches of the glory of his inheritance in the saints" (Eph. 1:17–18).

We should feel grateful to live in a day when all the blessings of the Lord are available to us and our progenitors who have gone before. We have a responsibility to strengthen others, proclaim the gospel, and redeem the dead.

5. Having predestinated us unto the adoption of children by Jesus Christ to himself, according to the good pleasure of his will,

6. To the praise of the glory of his grace, wherein he hath made us accepted in the beloved.

7. In whom we have redemption through his blood, the forgiveness of sins, according to the riches of his grace;

8. Wherein he hath abounded toward us in all wisdom and prudence;

9. Having made known unto us the mystery of his will, according to his good pleasure which he hath purposed in himself:

10. That in the dispensation of the fulness of times he might gather together in one all things in Christ, both which are in heaven, and which are on earth; even in him:

11. In whom also we have obtained an inheritance, being predestinated according to the purpose of him who worketh all things after the counsel of his own will:

12. That we should be to the praise of his glory, who first trusted in Christ.

13. In whom ye also trusted, after that ye heard the word of truth, the gospel of your salvation: in whom also after that ye believed, ye were sealed with that holy Spirit of promise,

14. Which is the earnest of our inheritance until the redemption of the purchased possession, unto the praise of his glory.

15. Wherefore I also, after I heard of your faith in the Lord Jesus, and love unto all the saints,

16. Cease not to give thanks for you, making mention of you in my prayers;

17. That the God of our Lord Jesus Christ, the Father of glory, may give unto you the spirit of wisdom and revelation in the knowledge of him:

18. The eyes of your understanding being enlightened; that ye may know what is the hope of his calling, and what the riches of the glory of his inheritance in the saints,

19. And what is the exceeding greatness of his power to us-ward who believe, according to the working of his mighty power,

20. Which he wrought in Christ, when he raised him from the dead, and set him at his own right hand in the heavenly places,

21. Far above all principality, and power, and might, and dominion, and every name that is named, not only in this world, but also in that which is to come:

22. And hath put all things under his feet, and gave him to be the head over all things to the church,

23. Which is his body, the fulness of him that filleth all in all.

Eph. 1 — The purpose of the dispensation of the fulness of times is to restore the fulness of the gospel, all the priesthood power, authority, and keys pertaining to the salvation, exaltation, and perfection of mankind, so that "he might gather together in one all things in Christ, both which are in heaven, and which are on earth; even in him" (Eph 1:10; see also D&C 27:13). This is indeed that restitution of all things spoken of by Peter (see Acts 3:21).

Everything pertaining to the plan of salvation and happiness will be brought together in and through the Lord Jesus Christ — all things that have been revealed and will yet be revealed between earth and heaven will be one under the direction and power of the Lord Jesus Christ as the chief cornerstone. He is our rock upon which we build both individually and as a church. He is our foundation (see Hel. 5:12). Our Savior has surely shown us the way, for He is the light and life of the world.

Through His holy prophets, He has revealed His teachings that can and will preserve the most sacred unit of the Church, even the family. The relationships between husband and wife are made clear. They must be one in purpose, cause, and action. The husband should love his wife even as Christ has loved the Church; hence the wife would cooperatively accept his leadership within the family in righteousness, even as we submit to the leadership of Christ in the Church and our lives.

As fathers and mothers lead with love and righteousness, their children will be more likely to obey and honor their parents. As families, we can prepare for the vicissitudes of life by putting on the armor of God, which can and will protect us from the adversary.

CHAPTER 2

1. And you hath he quickened, who were dead in trespasses and sins;

2. Wherein in time past ye walked according to the course of this world, according to the prince of the power of the air, the spirit that now worketh in the children of disobedience:

3. Among whom also we all had our conversation in times past in the lusts of our flesh, fulfilling the desires of the flesh and of the mind; and were by nature the children of wrath, even as others.

4. But God, who is rich in mercy, for his great love wherewith he loved us,

5. Even when we were dead in sins, hath quickened us together with Christ, (by grace ye are saved;)

6. And hath raised us up together, and made us sit together in heavenly places in Christ Jesus:

7. That in the ages to come he might shew the exceeding riches of his grace in his kindness toward us through Christ Jesus.

8. For by grace are ye saved through faith; and that not of yourselves: it is the gift of God:

9. Not of works, lest any man should boast.

10. For we are his workmanship, created in Christ Jesus unto good works, which God hath before ordained that we should walk in them.

11. Wherefore remember, that ye being in time past Gentiles in the flesh, who are called Uncircumcision by that which is called the Circumcision in the flesh made by hands;

12. That at that time ye were without Christ, being aliens from the commonwealth of Israel, and strangers from the covenants of promise, having no hope, and without God in the world:

13. But now in Christ Jesus ye who sometimes were far off are made nigh by the blood of Christ.

14. For he is our peace, who hath made both one, and hath broken down the middle wall of partition between us;

15. Having abolished in his flesh the enmity, even the law of commandments contained in ordinances; for to make in himself of twain one new man, so making peace;

16. And that he might reconcile both unto God in one body by the cross, having slain the enmity thereby:

17. And came and preached peace to you which were afar off, and to them that were nigh.

18. For through him we both have access by one Spirit unto the Father.

19. Now therefore ye are no more strangers and foreigners, but fellowcitizens with the saints, and of the household of God;

20. And are built upon the foundation of the apostles and prophets, Jesus Christ himself being the chief corner stone;

21. In whom all the building fitly framed together groweth unto an holy temple in the Lord:

22. In whom ye also are builded together for an habitation of God through the Spirit.

Eph. 2:19–22 — In the spirit of charity and friendship, Paul reaches out to the Gentile converts in the city of Ephesus and assures them of their full-fledged citizenship in the kingdom of God — just like the Jewish converts of Israelite lineage.

Eph. 2:20 — The image of a stone, symbolizing spiritual vitality and divine leadership, is used pervasively throughout the scriptures. The central icon in such metaphorical discourse is the Savior, whom Paul identified as "the chief corner stone" of God's program of salvation and exaltation (Eph. 2:19). The Psalmist declared: "I will praise thee: for thou hast heard me, and art become my salvation. The stone which the builders refused is become the head stone of the corner" (Ps. 118:21–22; compare Matt. 21:42; Mark 12:10; Luke 20:17; Acts 4:11; 1 Pet. 2:7).

Radiating from the central motif of the chief cornerstone of God's kingdom are connecting links to other "stones" that play essential roles in furthering the cause of Zion. Among these are the prophets, seers, and revelators whose office is anchored in the principle of continuous revelation through the Spirit of God. To Peter, the Lord declared: "And I say also unto thee, That thou art Peter, and upon this rock I will build my church; and the gates of hell shall not prevail against it. And I will give unto thee the keys of the kingdom of heaven: and whatsoever thou shalt bind on earth shall be bound in heaven: and whatsoever thou shalt loose on earth shall be loosed in heaven" (Matt. 16:18–19). The Lord was counseling His chief Apostle in the context of an interesting linguistic word play: The name *Peter* is related to the Greek word *petros,* meaning small rock, while at the same time the Greek word *petra* refers to bedrock, in the sense that Christ is "the stone of Israel" (D&C 50:44; see also John 1:42; 1 Cor. 3:11; 10:4; D&C 128:10).

Thus the Apostles and prophets are associate stones in the edifice of the kingdom of God, operating as they do through the foundational principle of divine revelation. Yet at the same time all of the members of the Church are in fact also "stones" in this monumental organization of God's kingdom. Peter admonished the people to come unto Christ, "as unto a living stone, disallowed indeed of men, but chosen of God, and precious, Ye also, as lively stones, are built up a spiritual house, an holy priesthood, to offer up spiritual sacrifices, acceptable to God by Jesus Christ. . . . But ye are a chosen generation, a royal priesthood, an holy nation, a peculiar people; that ye should shew forth the praises of him who hath called you out of darkness into his marvellous light" (1 Pet. 2:4–5, 9). (Continued)

CHAPTER 3

1. For this cause I Paul, the prisoner of Jesus Christ for you Gentiles,

2. If ye have heard of the dispensation of the grace of God which is given me to you-ward:

3. How that by revelation he made known unto me the mystery; (as I wrote afore in few words,

4. Whereby, when ye read, ye may understand my knowledge in the mystery of Christ)

5. Which in other ages was not made known unto the sons of men, as it is now revealed unto his holy apostles and prophets by the Spirit;

6. That the Gentiles should be fellowheirs, and of the same body, and partakers of his promise in Christ by the gospel:

7. Whereof I was made a minister, according to the gift of the grace of God given unto me by the effectual working of his power.

8. Unto me, who am less than the least of all saints, is this grace given, that I should preach among the Gentiles the unsearchable riches of Christ;

9. And to make all men see what is the fellowship of the mystery, which from the beginning of the world hath been hid in God, who created all things by Jesus Christ:

10. To the intent that now unto the principalities and powers in heavenly places might be known by the church the manifold wisdom of God,

11. According to the eternal purpose which he purposed in Christ Jesus our Lord:

12. In whom we have boldness and access with confidence by the faith of him.

13. Wherefore I desire that ye faint not at my tribulations for you, which is your glory.

14. For this cause I bow my knees unto the Father of our Lord Jesus Christ,

15. Of whom the whole family in heaven and earth is named,

16. That he would grant you, according to the riches of his glory, to be strengthened with might by his Spirit in the inner man;

17. That Christ may dwell in your hearts by faith; that ye, being rooted and grounded in love,

18. May be able to comprehend with all saints what is the breadth, and length, and depth, and height;

19. And to know the love of Christ, which passeth knowledge, that ye might be filled with all the fulness of God.

20. Now unto him that is able to do exceeding abundantly above all that we ask or think, according to the power that worketh in us,

21. Unto him be glory in the church by Christ Jesus throughout all ages, world without end. Amen.

CHAPTER 4

1. I therefore, the prisoner of the Lord, beseech you that ye walk worthy of the vocation wherewith ye are called,

2. With all lowliness and meekness, with longsuffering, forbearing one another in love;

As "lively stones" in the structure of God's kingdom, we are to reflect in our daily living the truths and saving principles of the gospel. We are not to have hearts of stone—Zechariah referred to such recalcitrant and hardened hearts as "an adamant stone" (Zech. 7:12)—but rather hearts that are softened and contrite, willing to do the will of the Father and honor the teachings of the "chief corner stone," even Jesus Christ. As "lively stones," we are to have hearts ready to be touched and transformed by the Master's hand, just as the sixteen stones gathered by the Brother of Jared were touched by the Lord and transformed into luminous objects that radiated light to guide the Jaredites' journey toward the promised land (see Ether 3:6).

Paul reminded us that we are ourselves in fact a temple structure: "Know ye not that ye are the temple of God, and that the Spirit of God dwelleth in you?" (1 Cor. 3:16). As the community of Christ, we, severally and unitedly, form the greater temple of God's kingdom—each supplying a stone—a "lively stone"—as an essential building unit for the spiritual construction, "in whom all the building fitly framed together groweth unto an holy temple in the Lord" (Eph. 2:21).

This growing and expanding kingdom can likewise be likened unto a stone, the stone that Daniel foresaw being "cut out of the mountain without hands" (Dan. 2:45) and rolling forth until it had become "a great mountain, and filled the whole earth" (Dan. 2:35; compare D&C 65:2; 109:72). We are part of that great stone, being as we are commissioned of God to fulfill the provisions and promises of the Abrahamic covenant to build and expand His kingdom without limits and to bless and edify the lives of all who will believe and come unto Christ with broken hearts and contrite spirits. In fact, the word *edify* itself means to build up a house, deriving as it does from a Greek term based on two smaller Greek words, *oikos* (house) and *demo* (to build). Thus we are to "edify" or build up a temple unto the Lord, which temple is the kingdom of God.

Eph. 3:14–19—Paul encapsulates the doctrine of adoption into the fold of Christ in this verse: "That the Gentiles should be fellowheirs, and of the same body, and partakers of his promise in Christ by the gospel" (Eph. 3:6). With Christ as the "chief corner stone" of the Church, all are welcome before Him as believers and followers of the principles of salvation and exaltation. Paul invokes this wonderful apostolic blessing upon the people.

3. Endeavouring to keep the unity of the Spirit in the bond of peace.

4. There is one body, and one Spirit, even as ye are called in one hope of your calling;

5. One Lord, one faith, one baptism,

6. One God and Father of all, who is above all, and through all, and in you all.

7. But unto every one of us is given grace according to the measure of the gift of Christ.

8. Wherefore he saith, When he ascended up on high, he led captivity captive, and gave gifts unto men.

9. (Now that he ascended, what is it but that he also descended first into the lower parts of the earth?

10. He that descended is the same also that ascended up far above all heavens, that he might fill all things.)

11. And he gave some, apostles; and some, prophets; and some, evangelists; and some, pastors and teachers;

12. For the perfecting of the saints, for the work of the ministry, for the edifying of the body of Christ:

13. Till we all come in the unity of the faith, and of the knowledge of the Son of God, unto a perfect man, unto the measure of the stature of the fulness of Christ:

14. That we henceforth be no more children, tossed to and fro, and carried about with every wind of doctrine, by the sleight of men, and cunning craftiness, whereby they lie in wait to deceive;

15. But speaking the truth in love, may grow up into him in all things, which is the head, even Christ:

16. From whom the whole body fitly joined together and compacted by that which every joint supplieth, according to the effectual working in the measure of every part, maketh increase of the body unto the edifying of itself in love.

17. This I say therefore, and testify in the Lord, that ye henceforth walk not as other Gentiles walk, in the vanity of their mind,

18. Having the understanding darkened, being alienated from the life of God through the ignorance that is in them, because of the blindness of their heart:

19. Who being past feeling have given themselves over unto lasciviousness, to work all uncleanness with greediness.

20. But ye have not so learned Christ;

21. If so be that ye have heard him, and have been taught by him, as the truth is in Jesus:

22. That ye put off concerning the former conversation the old man, which is corrupt according to the deceitful lusts;

23. And be renewed in the spirit of your mind;

Eph. 4:11–16— Expanding his discourse about the organization of the Church, Paul moves outward from the chief cornerstone of Christ to encompass all the offices and helps of the kingdom of God.

Every missionary of the Lord today is familiar with these words and freely uses them in bearing testimony about the grace and love of God in providing for us an organization designed to maximize the blessings to the Saints and open up for them a pathway to salvation, exaltation, and eternal life according to the designs of the Father and the Son.

Eph. 4:12— The message of the Spirit, through Paul the Apostle, is that the Lord, in His infinite wisdom, grace, and mercy, has given to us a divinely ordained and authorized organization "for the perfecting of the saints, for the work of the ministry, for the edifying of the body of Christ" (Eph. 4:12). That which was established by the Savior in the meridian of time has been restored in this, the dispensation of the fulness of times, with Christ Himself as the chief cornerstone, and key offices of the Melchizedek Priesthood—including the living Apostles and prophets—in presiding capacity over the unfolding of the work. Within the kingdom of God, the family is the central unit, to be sustained by an abundance of love always protected by the armor of God in its supernal commission to provide the seedbed for the raising up of the children of God. These are the lessons that Paul taught the Saints at Ephesus, and, by extension, all subsequent sons and daughters of God.

24. And that ye put on the new man, which after God is created in righteousness and true holiness.

25. Wherefore putting away lying, speak every man truth with his neighbour: for we are members one of another.

26. Be ye angry, and sin not: let not the sun go down upon your wrath:

27. Neither give place to the devil.

28. Let him that stole steal no more: but rather let him labour, working with his hands the thing which is good, that he may have to give to him that needeth.

29. Let no corrupt communication proceed out of your mouth, but that which is good to the use of edifying, that it may minister grace unto the hearers.

30. And grieve not the holy Spirit of God, whereby ye are sealed unto the day of redemption.

31. Let all bitterness, and wrath, and anger, and clamour, and evil speaking, be put away from you, with all malice:

32. And be ye kind one to another, tenderhearted, forgiving one another, even as God for Christ's sake hath forgiven you.

CHAPTER 5

1. Be ye therefore followers of God, as dear children;

2. And walk in love, as Christ also hath loved us, and hath given himself for us an offering and a sacrifice to God for a sweetsmelling savour.

3. But fornication, and all uncleanness, or covetousness, let it not be once named among you, as becometh saints;

4. Neither filthiness, nor foolish talking, nor jesting, which are not convenient: but rather giving of thanks.

5. For this ye know, that no whoremonger, nor unclean person, nor covetous man, who is an idolater, hath any inheritance in the kingdom of Christ and of God.

6. Let no man deceive you with vain words: for because of these things cometh the wrath of God upon the children of disobedience.

7. Be not ye therefore partakers with them.

8. For ye were sometimes darkness, but now are ye light in the Lord: walk as children of light:

9. (For the fruit of the Spirit is in all goodness and righteousness and truth;)

10. Proving what is acceptable unto the Lord.

11. And have no fellowship with the unfruitful works of darkness, but rather reprove them.

Notes: _____
_____
_____
_____
_____
_____
_____
_____
_____
_____
_____
_____
_____
_____
_____
_____
_____
_____
_____
_____
_____
_____
_____
_____
_____
_____
_____
_____
_____
_____
_____
_____

12. For it is a shame even to speak of those things which are done of them in secret.

13. But all things that are reproved are made manifest by the light: for whatsoever doth make manifest is light.

14. Wherefore he saith, Awake thou that sleepest, and arise from the dead, and Christ shall give thee light.

15. See then that ye walk circumspectly, not as fools, but as wise,

16. Redeeming the time, because the days are evil.

17. Wherefore be ye not unwise, but understanding what the will of the Lord is.

18. And be not drunk with wine, wherein is excess; but be filled with the Spirit;

19. Speaking to yourselves in psalms and hymns and spiritual songs, singing and making melody in your heart to the Lord;

20. Giving thanks always for all things unto God and the Father in the name of our Lord Jesus Christ;

21. Submitting yourselves one to another in the fear of God.

22. Wives, submit yourselves unto your own husbands, as unto the Lord.

23. For the husband is the head of the wife, even as Christ is the head of the church: and he is the saviour of the body.

24. Therefore as the church is subject unto Christ, so let the wives be to their own husbands in every thing.

25. Husbands, love your wives, even as Christ also loved the church, and gave himself for it;

26. That he might sanctify and cleanse it with the washing of water by the word,

27. That he might present it to himself a glorious church, not having spot, or wrinkle, or any such thing; but that it should be holy and without blemish.

28. So ought men to love their wives as their own bodies. He that loveth his wife loveth himself.

29. For no man ever yet hated his own flesh; but nourisheth and cherisheth it, even as the Lord the church:

30. For we are members of his body, of his flesh, and of his bones.

31. For this cause shall a man leave his father and mother, and shall be joined unto his wife, and they two shall be one flesh.

32. This is a great mystery: but I speak concerning Christ and the church.

33. Nevertheless let every one of you in particular so love his wife even as himself; and the wife see that she reverence her husband.

CHAPTER 6

1. Children, obey your parents in the Lord: for this is right.

2. Honour thy father and mother; (which is the first commandment with promise;)

3. That it may be well with thee, and thou mayest live long on the earth.

Eph. 5:22–25—The family is the basic unit of the Church. It is the Lord's plan to strengthen His children in and through the family unit (see D&C 68:25–28). A family can be united in all things if they have values based on the gospel of Jesus Christ. When they agree and build on these values, they will have unity in the family. In these verses, Paul's instructions to the Ephesian Saints includes warm and salient counsel for husbands and wives. Children are admonished to be obedient and to honor their parents—"which is the first commandment with promise" (Eph. 6:2), extending to them the assurance that things will go well with them and that they might live long in the land. Thus Paul reaches out to ensure the sanctity and well-being of the families within the Church and kingdom of God, just as our prophets and leaders do for us today (see *The Family: A Proclamation to the World,* 1995).

Eph. 5:25—Love begets love. Love is that ultimate concern that brings about righteous service. Everything the Lord has ever done for us has been motivated by His love for us (see 2 Ne. 26:24).

Love is the motivation behind every righteous act (see John 3:16; 2 Ne. 26:24). We as husbands and wives should do all in our power to love, serve, and help each other so as to enjoy the blessings of earth life and exaltation in the celestial kingdom. Let us love and serve each other.

Eph. 5:25, 27–28—Paul's counsel on loving relationships within marriage draws its power from a comparison with the love that Christ has for His Church (using Christ's symbolism of the bridegroom and bride relationship found in Matt. 9:15 and Matt. 25:1–10). Love is the ultimate concern that brings about righteous service. All the Lord has ever done for us has been motivated by His love for us (see 2 Ne. 26:24). Husbands are to love their wives even as Christ has loved the Church. Christ did everything for us, so likewise should husbands do everything for their wives. In reverencing their husbands, wives are involved in giving back—as each honors, respects, and treats the other with deference and kindness. Love translates into caring concern that serves others.

Eph. 5:25–28—Admiral Byrd was alone at Ross Barrier in the midst of a terrible Antarctic storm. The temperature was 72 degrees below zero. The stove in his makeshift shelter was faulty—and carbon monoxide threatened his life. He did, however, survive and lived to write his book, *Alone*. While keeping

4. And, ye fathers, provoke not your children to wrath: but bring them up in the nurture and admonition of the Lord.

5. Servants, be obedient to them that are your masters according to the flesh, with fear and trembling, in singleness of your heart, as unto Christ;

6. Not with eyeservice, as menpleasers; but as the servants of Christ, doing the will of God from the heart;

7. With good will doing service, as to the Lord, and not to men:

8. Knowing that whatsoever good thing any man doeth, the same shall he receive of the Lord, whether he be bond or free.

9. And, ye masters, do the same things unto them, forbearing threatening: knowing that your Master also is in heaven; neither is there respect of persons with him.

10. Finally, my brethren, be strong in the Lord, and in the power of his might.

11. Put on the whole armour of God, that ye may be able to stand against the wiles of the devil.

12. For we wrestle not against flesh and blood, but against principalities, against powers, against the rulers of the darkness of this world, against spiritual wickedness in high places.

13. Wherefore take unto you the whole armour of God, that ye may be able to withstand in the evil day, and having done all, to stand.

14. Stand therefore, having your loins girt about with truth, and having on the breastplate of righteousness;

15. And your feet shod with the preparation of the gospel of peace;

16. Above all, taking the shield of faith, wherewith ye shall be able to quench all the fiery darts of the wicked.

17. And take the helmet of salvation, and the sword of the Spirit, which is the word of God:

18. Praying always with all prayer and supplication in the Spirit, and watching thereunto with all perseverance and supplication for all saints;

19. And for me, that utterance may be given unto me, that I may open my mouth boldly, to make known the mystery of the gospel,

20. For which I am an ambassador in bonds: that therein I may speak boldly, as I ought to speak.

21. But that ye also may know my affairs, and how I do, Tychicus, a beloved brother and faithful minister in the Lord, shall make known to you all things:

22. Whom I have sent unto you for the same purpose, that ye might know our affairs, and that he might comfort your hearts.

23. Peace be to the brethren, and love with faith, from God the Father and the Lord Jesus Christ.

24. Grace be with all them that love our Lord Jesus Christ in sincerity. Amen.

his lonely vigil in that far part of our universe, he meditated much and penned these profound words:

"At the end only two things really matter to a man, regardless of who he is, and they are the affection and understanding of his family.

"Anything and everything else he creates are insubstantial; they are ships given over to the mercy of the winds and tides of prejudice. But the family is an everlasting anchorage, a quiet harbor where a man's ship can be left to swing in the moorings of pride and loyalty."

Eph. 6:13–18—Paul's concluding words in his epistle to the Ephesians is the admonition to "take unto you the whole armour of God" (Eph. 6:13) in order to remain valiant and well protected from the incursions of evil influences. These well-known verses outline a defense strategy of unlimited power, since they define our trust in the Lord as the source of our spiritual vitality.

Notes: _____

_____

_____

_____

_____

_____

_____

_____

_____

_____

_____

_____

_____

_____

_____

_____

_____

_____

_____

_____

_____

THE EPISTLE OF PAUL THE APOSTLE TO

THE PHILIPPIANS

CHAPTER 1

1. Paul and Timotheus, the servants of Jesus Christ, to all the saints in Christ Jesus which are at Philippi, with the bishops and deacons:

2. Grace be unto you, and peace, from God our Father, and from the Lord Jesus Christ.

3. I thank my God upon every remembrance of you,

4. Always in every prayer of mine for you all making request with joy,

5. For your fellowship in the gospel from the first day until now;

6. Being confident of this very thing, that he which hath begun a good work in you will perform it until the day of Jesus Christ:

7. Even as it is meet for me to think this of you all, because I have you in my heart; inasmuch as both in my bonds, and in the defence and confirmation of the gospel, ye all are partakers of my grace.

8. For God is my record, how greatly I long after you all in the bowels of Jesus Christ.

9. And this I pray, that your love may abound yet more and more in knowledge and in all judgment;

10. That ye may approve things that are excellent; that ye may be sincere and without offence till the day of Christ;

11. Being filled with the fruits of righteousness, which are by Jesus Christ, unto the glory and praise of God.

12. But I would ye should understand, brethren, that the things which happened unto me have fallen out rather unto the furtherance of the gospel;

13. So that my bonds in Christ are manifest in all the palace, and in all other places;

14. And many of the brethren in the Lord, waxing confident by my bonds, are much more bold to speak the word without fear.

15. Some indeed preach Christ even of envy and strife; and some also of good will:

16. The one preach Christ of contention, not sincerely, supposing to add affliction to my bonds:

17. But the other of love, knowing that I am set for the defence of the gospel.

18. What then? notwithstanding, every way, whether in pretence, or in truth, Christ is preached; and I therein do rejoice, yea, and will rejoice.

19. For I know that this shall turn to my salvation through your prayer, and the supply of the Spirit of Jesus Christ,

20. According to my earnest expec-

Philippians— Paul's epistles to the Philippians, the Colossians, and Philemon were written (like Ephesians and Hebrews) in the time frame A.D. 60 to A.D. 62. As previously noted, all of these epistles were written from Rome during Paul's confinement there under the direction of the Roman authorities. Philippi was a city in Macedonia (now part of northern Greece) that had been named in honor of the father of Alexander the Great. Paul had visited the city as part of his missionary service (see Acts 16:12–40; 20:6; Philip. 1:1; 1 Thes. 2:2). Colosse was a town in Phrygia (located in what is now Turkey) close to the commercial highway from Ephesus to the Euphrates. Philemon was a native of Colosse, and he was one of Paul's converts to the faith.

In these writings we see reflected the apostolic counsel to follow the Savior in all that we do. Here are some representative examples:

• On being unified in Christ (see Philip. 1:27–29; Philip. 2:2)

• On being steadfast in the Lord (see Philip. 4:1)

• On rejoicing in the Lord of Peace in the spirit of thanksgiving (see Philip. 4:4–7)

• On being worthy as "saints in light" (see Col. 1:10–12)

tation and my hope, that in nothing I shall be ashamed, but that with all boldness, as always, so now also Christ shall be magnified in my body, whether it be by life, or by death.

21. For to me to live is Christ, and to die is gain.

22. But if I live in the flesh, this is the fruit of my labour: yet what I shall choose I wot not.

23. For I am in a strait betwixt two, having a desire to depart, and to be with Christ; which is far better:

24. Nevertheless to abide in the flesh is more needful for you.

25. And having this confidence, I know that I shall abide and continue with you all for your furtherance and joy of faith;

26. That your rejoicing may be more abundant in Jesus Christ for me by my coming to you again.

27. Only let your conversation be as it becometh the gospel of Christ: that whether I come and see you, or else be absent, I may hear of your affairs, that ye stand fast in one spirit, with one mind striving together for the faith of the gospel;

28. And in nothing terrified by your adversaries: which is to them an evident token of perdition, but to you of salvation, and that of God.

29. For unto you it is given in the behalf of Christ, not only to believe on him, but also to suffer for his sake;

30. Having the same conflict which ye saw in me, and now hear to be in me.

CHAPTER 2

1. If there be therefore any consolation in Christ, if any comfort of love, if any fellowship of the Spirit, if any bowels and mercies,

2. Fulfil ye my joy, that ye be likeminded, having the same love, being of one accord, of one mind.

3. Let nothing be done through strife or vainglory; but in lowliness of mind let each esteem other better than themselves.

4. Look not every man on his own things, but every man also on the things of others.

5. Let this mind be in you, which was also in Christ Jesus:

6. Who, being in the form of God, thought it not robbery to be equal with God:

7. But made himself of no reputation, and took upon him the form of a servant, and was made in the likeness of men:

8. And being found in fashion as a man, he humbled himself, and became obedient unto death, even the death of the cross.

9. Wherefore God also hath highly exalted him, and given him a name which is above every name:

10. That at the name of Jesus every knee should bow, of things in heaven, and things in earth, and things under the earth;

Philip. 2–3— In Paul's writings we see confirmed the Apostle's unshakable faith in the atoning mission of the Savior as the only source for eternal salvation and exaltation. Paul writes:

• On the mission of the exalted Son, Creator, and Lord of all (see Philip. 2:5–11)

• On the Savior, Master of Life and spiritual transformation (see Philip. 3:20–21)

• On the Redeemer, Firstborn of God and eternal Head of the Kingdom (see Col. 1:13–20)

Notes: _____

_____

_____

_____

_____

_____

_____

_____

_____

_____

_____

_____

_____

_____

_____

_____

_____

_____

_____

_____

11. And that every tongue should confess that Jesus Christ is Lord, to the glory of God the Father.

12. Wherefore, my beloved, as ye have always obeyed, not as in my presence only, but now much more in my absence, work out your own salvation with fear and trembling.

13. For it is God which worketh in you both to will and to do of his good pleasure.

14. Do all things without murmurings and disputings:

15. That ye may be blameless and harmless, the sons of God, without rebuke, in the midst of a crooked and perverse nation, among whom ye shine as lights in the world;

16. Holding forth the word of life; that I may rejoice in the day of Christ, that I have not run in vain, neither laboured in vain.

17. Yea, and if I be offered upon the sacrifice and service of your faith, I joy, and rejoice with you all.

18. For the same cause also do ye joy, and rejoice with me.

19. But I trust in the Lord Jesus to send Timotheus shortly unto you, that I also may be of good comfort, when I know your state.

20. For I have no man likeminded, who will naturally care for your state.

21. For all seek their own, not the things which are Jesus Christ's.

22. But ye know the proof of him, that, as a son with the father, he hath served with me in the gospel.

23. Him therefore I hope to send presently, so soon as I shall see how it will go with me.

24. But I trust in the Lord that I also myself shall come shortly.

25. Yet I supposed it necessary to send to you Epaphroditus, my brother, and companion in labour, and fellowsoldier, but your messenger, and he that ministered to my wants.

26. For he longed after you all, and was full of heaviness, because that ye had heard that he had been sick.

27. For indeed he was sick nigh unto death: but God had mercy on him; and not on him only, but on me also, lest I should have sorrow upon sorrow.

28. I sent him therefore the more carefully, that, when ye see him again, ye may rejoice, and that I may be the less sorrowful.

29. Receive him therefore in the Lord with all gladness; and hold such in reputation:

30. Because for the work of Christ he was nigh unto death, not regarding his life, to supply your lack of service toward me.

CHAPTER 3

1. Finally, my brethren, rejoice in the Lord. To write the same things to you, to me indeed is not grievous, but for you it is safe.

2. Beware of dogs, beware of evil workers, beware of the concision.

3. For we are the circumcision, which worship God in the spirit, and rejoice in Christ Jesus, and have no confidence in the flesh.

4. Though I might also have confidence in the flesh. If any other man thinketh that he hath whereof he might trust in the flesh, I more:

5. Circumcised the eighth day, of the stock of Israel, of the tribe of Benjamin, an Hebrew of the Hebrews; as touching the law, a Pharisee;

6. Concerning zeal, persecuting the

Notes: _____
_____
_____
_____
_____
_____
_____
_____
_____
_____
_____
_____
_____
_____
_____
_____
_____
_____
_____
_____
_____
_____
_____
_____
_____
_____
_____
_____
_____
_____
_____
_____

church; touching the righteousness which is in the law, blameless.

7. But what things were gain to me, those I counted loss for Christ.

8. Yea doubtless, and I count all things but loss for the excellency of the knowledge of Christ Jesus my Lord: for whom I have suffered the loss of all things, and do count them but dung, that I may win Christ,

9. And be found in him, not having mine own righteousness, which is of the law, but that which is through the faith of Christ, the righteousness which is of God by faith:

10. That I may know him, and the power of his resurrection, and the fellowship of his sufferings, being made conformable unto his death;

11. If by any means I might attain unto the resurrection of the dead.

12. Not as though I had already attained, either were already perfect: but I follow after, if that I may apprehend that for which also I am apprehended of Christ Jesus.

13. Brethren, I count not myself to have apprehended: but this one thing I do, forgetting those things which are behind, and reaching forth unto those things which are before,

14. I press toward the mark for the prize of the high calling of God in Christ Jesus.

15. Let us therefore, as many as be perfect, be thus minded: and if in any thing ye be otherwise minded, God shall reveal even this unto you.

16. Nevertheless, whereto we have already attained, let us walk by the same rule, let us mind the same thing.

17. Brethren, be followers together of me, and mark them which walk so as ye have us for an ensample.

18. (For many walk, of whom I have told you often, and now tell you even weeping, that they are the enemies of the cross of Christ:

19. Whose end is destruction, whose God is their belly, and whose glory is in their shame, who mind earthly things.)

20. For our conversation is in heaven; from whence also we look for the Saviour, the Lord Jesus Christ:

21. Who shall change our vile body, that it may be fashioned like unto his glorious body, according to the working whereby he is able even to subdue all things unto himself.

CHAPTER 4

1. Therefore, my brethren dearly beloved and longed for, my joy and crown, so stand fast in the Lord, my dearly beloved.

2. I beseech Euodias, and beseech Syntyche, that they be of the same mind in the Lord.

3. And I intreat thee also, true yokefellow, help those women which laboured with me in the gospel, with Clement also, and with other my fellowlabourers, whose names are in the book of life.

4. Rejoice in the Lord alway: and again I say, Rejoice.

5. Let your moderation be known unto all men. The Lord is at hand.

Philippians and Colossians—Paul exhorts the Saints at Philippi and Colosse to honor their covenant obligations as Saints of the Most High by living a life reflecting the highest principles of the gospel. He preaches, among other things:

• On working out our salvation within the context of the Atonement (see Philip. 2:12–13)

• On cultivating Christian virtues (see Philip. 4:8–13)

• On walking after the pattern of Jesus Christ: "As ye have therefore received Christ Jesus the Lord, so walk ye in him" (Col. 2:6; see also verses 7–12)

• On setting our priorities on heavenly things (see Col. 3:2)

• On cultivating a life abounding in charity (see Col. 3:12–17; compare D&C 121:41–46)

• On preserving unity and love in the family (see Col. 3:18–21)

• On forgiving others (see Philem. 1:16–18)

A wise and virtuous woman

6. Be careful for nothing; but in every thing by prayer and supplication with thanksgiving let your requests be made known unto God.

7. And the peace of God, which passeth all understanding, shall keep your hearts and minds through Christ Jesus.

8. Finally, brethren, whatsoever things are true, whatsoever things are honest, whatsoever things are just, whatsoever things are pure, whatsoever things are lovely, whatsoever things are of good report; if there be any virtue, and if there be any praise, think on these things.

9. Those things, which ye have both learned, and received, and heard, and seen in me, do: and the God of peace shall be with you.

10. But I rejoiced in the Lord greatly, that now at the last your care of me hath flourished again; wherein ye were also careful, but ye lacked opportunity.

11. Not that I speak in respect of want: for I have learned, in whatsoever state I am, therewith to be content.

12. I know both how to be abased, and I know how to abound: every where and in all things I am instructed both to be full and to be hungry, both to abound and to suffer need.

13. I can do all things through Christ which strengtheneth me.

14. Notwithstanding ye have well done, that ye did communicate with my affliction.

15. Now ye Philippians know also, that in the beginning of the gospel, when I departed from Macedonia, no church communicated with me as concerning giving and receiving, but ye only.

16. For even in Thessalonica ye sent once and again unto my necessity.

17. Not because I desire a gift: but I desire fruit that may abound to your account.

18. But I have all, and abound: I am full, having received of Epaphroditus the things which were sent from you, an odour of a sweet smell, a sacrifice acceptable, wellpleasing to God.

19. But my God shall supply all your need according to his riches in glory by Christ Jesus.

20. Now unto God and our Father be glory for ever and ever. Amen.

21. Salute every saint in Christ Jesus. The brethren which are with me greet you.

22. All the saints salute you, chiefly they that are of Cæsar's household.

23. The grace of our Lord Jesus Christ be with you all. Amen.

Philip. 4:13—"None of us has attained perfection or the zenith of spiritual growth that is possible in mortality. Every person can and must make spiritual progress. The gospel of Jesus Christ is the divine plan for that spiritual growth eternally. It is more than a code of ethics. It is more than an ideal social order. It is more than positive thinking about self-improvement and determination. The gospel is the saving power of the Lord Jesus Christ with his priesthood and sustenance and with the Holy Spirit. With faith in the Lord Jesus Christ and obedience to his gospel, a step at a time improving as we go, pleading for strength, improving our attitudes and our ambitions, we will find ourselves successfully in the fold of the Good Shepherd. That will require discipline and training and exertion and strength. But as the Apostle Paul said, 'I can do all things through Christ which strengtheneth me' (Philip. 4:13)" (Howard W. Hunter, *That We Might Have Joy*, 184–85).

Notes: _____

_____

_____

_____

_____

_____

_____

_____

_____

_____

_____

_____

_____

_____

_____

_____

_____

_____

_____

_____

THE EPISTLE OF PAUL THE APOSTLE TO

THE COLOSSIANS

CHAPTER 1

1. Paul, an apostle of Jesus Christ by the will of God, and Timotheus our brother,

2. To the saints and faithful brethren in Christ which are at Colosse: Grace be unto you, and peace, from God our Father and the Lord Jesus Christ.

3. We give thanks to God and the Father of our Lord Jesus Christ, praying always for you,

4. Since we heard of your faith in Christ Jesus, and of the love which ye have to all the saints,

5. For the hope which is laid up for you in heaven, whereof ye heard before in the word of the truth of the gospel;

6. Which is come unto you, as it is in all the world; and bringeth forth fruit, as it doth also in you, since the day ye heard of it, and knew the grace of God in truth:

7. As ye also learned of Epaphras our dear fellowservant, who is for you a faithful minister of Christ;

8. Who also declared unto us your love in the Spirit.

9. For this cause we also, since the day we heard it, do not cease to pray for you, and to desire that ye might be filled with the knowledge of his will in all wisdom and spiritual understanding;

10. That ye might walk worthy of the Lord unto all pleasing, being fruitful in every good work, and increasing in the knowledge of God;

11. Strengthened with all might, according to his glorious power, unto all patience and longsuffering with joyfulness;

12. Giving thanks unto the Father, which hath made us meet to be partakers of the inheritance of the saints in light:

13. Who hath delivered us from the power of darkness, and hath translated us into the kingdom of his dear Son:

14. In whom we have redemption through his blood, even the forgiveness of sins:

15. Who is the image of the invisible God, the firstborn of every creature:

Colossians—"As Paul journeyed to Jerusalem to face bonds and chains for the testimony of Jesus, he charged the Ephesian elders, whose faces he would not again see in mortality, 'to feed the church of God, which he hath purchased with his own blood' (Acts 20:17–28). To both the Colossians and the Ephesians he wrote that the saints have 'redemption through his blood, even the forgiveness of sins' (Col. 1:14. See also Eph. 1:7)" (Bruce R. McConkie, *The Promised Messiah*, 254).

Col. 1:12–13, 16–17—Paul taught the Colossians about the role of Jesus as Creator and Redeemer. Gratitude for the mission and work of the Savior is essential if faith is to unfold and spiritual growth is to take place. How can you cultivate more gratitude for the Savior in your family circle and among your network of friends?

Col. 1:12–14—Gratitude should be felt and expressed for the goodness of God and the suffering of our Savior, that we might have deliverance from our sins if we but repent.

16. For by him were all things created, that are in heaven, and that are in earth, visible and invisible, whether they be thrones, or dominions, or principalities, or powers: all things were created by him, and for him:

17. And he is before all things, and by him all things consist.

18. And he is the head of the body, the church: who is the beginning, the firstborn from the dead; that in all things he might have the preeminence.

19. For it pleased the Father that in him should all fulness dwell;

20. And, having made peace through the blood of his cross, by him to reconcile all things unto himself; by him, I say, whether they be things in earth, or things in heaven.

21. And you, that were sometime alienated and enemies in your mind by wicked works, yet now hath he reconciled

22. In the body of his flesh through death, to present you holy and unblameable and unreproveable in his sight:

23. If ye continue in the faith grounded and settled, and be not moved away from the hope of the gospel, which ye have heard, and which was preached to every creature which is under heaven; whereof I Paul am made a minister;

24. Who now rejoice in my sufferings for you, and fill up that which is behind of the afflictions of Christ in my flesh for his body's sake, which is the church:

25. Whereof I am made a minister, according to the dispensation of God which is given to me for you, to fulfil the word of God;

26. Even the mystery which hath been hid from ages and from generations, but now is made manifest to his saints:

27. To whom God would make known what is the riches of the glory of this mystery among the Gentiles; which is Christ in you, the hope of glory:

28. Whom we preach, warning every man, and teaching every man in all wisdom; that we may present every man perfect in Christ Jesus:

29. Whereunto I also labour, striving according to his working, which worketh in me mightily.

CHAPTER 2

1. For I would that ye knew what great conflict I have for you, and for them at Laodicea, and for as many as have not seen my face in the flesh;

2. That their hearts might be comforted, being knit together in love, and unto all riches of the full assurance of understanding, to the acknowledgement of the mystery of God, and of the Father, and of Christ;

3. In whom are hid all the treasures of wisdom and knowledge.

Notes: _____
_____
_____
_____
_____
_____
_____
_____
_____
_____
_____
_____
_____
_____
_____
_____
_____
_____
_____
_____
_____
_____
_____
_____
_____
_____
_____
_____
_____
_____
_____
_____
_____

4. And this I say, lest any man should beguile you with enticing words.

5. For though I be absent in the flesh, yet am I with you in the spirit, joying and beholding your order, and the stedfastness of your faith in Christ.

6. As ye have therefore received Christ Jesus the Lord, so walk ye in him:

7. Rooted and built up in him, and stablished in the faith, as ye have been taught, abounding therein with thanksgiving.

8. Beware lest any man spoil you through philosophy and vain deceit, after the tradition of men, after the rudiments of the world, and not after Christ.

9. For in him dwelleth all the fulness of the Godhead bodily.

10. And ye are complete in him, which is the head of all principality and power:

11. In whom also ye are circumcised with the circumcision made without hands, in putting off the body of the sins of the flesh by the circumcision of Christ:

12. Buried with him in baptism, wherein also ye are risen with him through the faith of the operation of God, who hath raised him from the dead.

13. And you, being dead in your sins and the uncircumcision of your flesh, hath he quickened together with him, having forgiven you all trespasses;

14. Blotting out the handwriting of ordinances that was against us, which was contrary to us, and took it out of the way, nailing it to his cross;

15. And having spoiled principalities and powers, he made a shew of them openly, triumphing over them in it.

16. Let no man therefore judge you in meat, or in drink, or in respect of an holyday, or of the new moon, or of the sabbath days:

17. Which are a shadow of things to come; but the body is of Christ.

18. Let no man beguile you of your reward in a voluntary humility and worshipping of angels, intruding into those things which he hath not seen, vainly puffed up by his fleshly mind,

19. And not holding the Head, from which all the body by joints and bands having nourishment ministered, and knit together, increaseth with the increase of God.

20. Wherefore if ye be dead with Christ from the rudiments of the world, why, as though living in the world, are ye subject to ordinances,

21. (Touch not; taste not; handle not;

22. Which all are to perish with the using;) after the commandments and doctrines of men?

23. Which things have indeed a shew of wisdom in will worship, and humility, and neglecting of the body; not in any honour to the satisfying of the flesh.

Colossians— In his celebrated epistles, the Apostle Paul enjoined the Saints of his day to stand true to the principles of salvation by means of which they enjoyed a place of enduring peace and joy as the elect of God within the fold of the Church.

This brings to mind an experience from my own past. Several years after the completion of the Washington D.C. Temple, I invited two good nonmember friends and university colleagues to drive down with me to the visitors center at the temple for a tour. One was a young sociology professor and the other was a Catholic priest who taught courses in comparative religion. They listened and observed carefully.

Following the tour, my Catholic friend made a significant statement, which I recorded in my journal. He noted, in general, that many clergy have two religions, one that they "carry in their pocket" and one that they present in public. "Often there is a considerable gap between the two," he said, inferring that they might be more "religious" outwardly than inwardly. "With the Mormons, it is different," he observed. "The gap in their case seems to be rather small."

With this compliment, he was articulating his own perspective that members of the Church typically live by their convictions, and since they seem to accomplish much practical good, they must therefore, he believed, have a strong, genuine faith. He was right.

Such is indeed the case with Latter-day Saints who abide by the teachings of the Master and strive to make their lives consistently centered in spiritual paths—both outwardly as well as inwardly. They fulfill the harvest from the good seed about which Jesus spoke: "But that on the good ground are they, which in an honest and good heart, having heard the word, keep it, and bring forth fruit with patience" (Luke 8:15).

CHAPTER 3

1. If ye then be risen with Christ, seek those things which are above, where Christ sitteth on the right hand of God.

2. Set your affection on things above, not on things on the earth.

3. For ye are dead, and your life is hid with Christ in God.

4. When Christ, who is our life, shall appear, then shall ye also appear with him in glory.

5. Mortify therefore your members which are upon the earth; fornication, uncleanness, inordinate affection, evil concupiscence, and covetousness, which is idolatry:

6. For which things' sake the wrath of God cometh on the children of disobedience:

7. In the which ye also walked some time, when ye lived in them.

8. But now ye also put off all these; anger, wrath, malice, blasphemy, filthy communication out of your mouth.

9. Lie not one to another, seeing that ye have put off the old man with his deeds;

10. And have put on the new man, which is renewed in knowledge after the image of him that created him:

11. Where there is neither Greek nor Jew, circumcision nor uncircumcision, Barbarian, Scythian, bond nor free: but Christ is all, and in all.

12. Put on therefore, as the elect of God, holy and beloved, bowels of mercies, kindness, humbleness of mind, meekness, longsuffering;

13. Forbearing one another, and forgiving one another, if any man have a quarrel against any: even as Christ forgave you, so also do ye.

14. And above all these things put on charity, which is the bond of perfectness.

15. And let the peace of God rule in your hearts, to the which also ye are called in one body; and be ye thankful.

16. Let the word of Christ dwell in you richly in all wisdom; teaching and admonishing one another in psalms and hymns and spiritual songs, singing with grace in your hearts to the Lord.

17. And whatsoever ye do in word or deed, do all in the name of the Lord Jesus, giving thanks to God and the Father by him.

18. Wives, submit yourselves unto your own husbands, as it is fit in the Lord.

19. Husbands, love your wives, and be not bitter against them.

20. Children, obey your parents in

Col. 3—President John Taylor expounded on the doctrine of redemption through the Atonement of Jesus Christ:

"One great and very striking statement is here made by the Lord himself, to the effect that it behooved Christ to suffer, and the question at once presents itself before us, why did it behoove him? Or why was it necessary that he should suffer? For it would seem from his language, through his sufferings, death, Atonement, and resurrection, 'that repentance and remission of sins' could be preached among all nations, and that consequently if he had not atoned for the sins of the world, repentance and remission of sins could not have been preached to the nations. A very important principle is here enunciated, one in which the interests of the whole human family throughout all the world are involved. That principle is the offering up of the Son of God as a sacrifice, an Atonement, and a propitiation for our sins. . . .

"If it were not for the Atonement of Jesus Christ, the sacrifice he made, all the human family would have to lie in the grave throughout eternity without any hope. But God having provided, through the Atonement of the Lord Jesus Christ, the medium whereby we can be restored to the bosom and presence of the Father, to participate with him among the Gods in the eternal worlds—he having provided for that, has also provided for the resurrection. He proclaimed himself the resurrection and the life. Said he, 'I am the resurrection, and the life: he that believeth in me, though he were dead, yet shall he live' (John 11:25). By and by the tombs will be opened and the dead will hear the voice of the Son of God, and they shall come forth, they who have done good to the resurrection of the just, and they who have done evil to the resurrection of the unjust" (*The Gospel Kingdom: Selections from the Writings and Discourses of John Taylor,* 117–18).

Col. 3:12–14—In his epistle to the Colossians, Paul counseled them to "put on the new man, which is renewed in knowledge after the image of him that created him" (Col. 3:10). That image is reflected in the qualities of mercy, kindness, and the others listed in these verses. In your opinion, what does Paul mean by the word *bond* in the expression "bond of perfectness"? How does this relate to the latter-day scripture that counsels us to "search diligently, pray always, and be believing, and all things shall work together for your good, if ye walk uprightly and remember the covenant wherewith ye have covenanted one with another" (D&C 90:24)?

all things: for this is well pleasing unto the Lord.

21. Fathers, provoke not your children to anger, lest they be discouraged.

22. Servants, obey in all things your masters according to the flesh; not with eyeservice, as menpleasers; but in singleness of heart, fearing God:

23. And whatsoever ye do, do it heartily, as to the Lord, and not unto men;

24. Knowing that of the Lord ye shall receive the reward of the inheritance: for ye serve the Lord Christ.

25. But he that doeth wrong shall receive for the wrong which he hath done: and there is no respect of persons.

CHAPTER 4

1. Masters, give unto your servants that which is just and equal; knowing that ye also have a Master in heaven.

2. Continue in prayer, and watch in the same with thanksgiving;

3. Withal praying also for us, that God would open unto us a door of utterance, to speak the mystery of Christ, for which I am also in bonds:

4. That I may make it manifest, as I ought to speak.

5. Walk in wisdom toward them that are without, redeeming the time.

6. Let your speech be alway with grace, seasoned with salt, that ye may know how ye ought to answer every man.

7. All my state shall Tychicus declare unto you, who is a beloved brother, and a faithful minister and fellowservant in the Lord:

8. Whom I have sent unto you for the same purpose, that he might know your estate, and comfort your hearts;

9. With Onesimus, a faithful and beloved brother, who is one of you. They shall make known unto you all things which are done here.

10. Aristarchus my fellowprisoner saluteth you, and Marcus, sister's son to Barnabas, (touching whom ye received commandments: if he come unto you, receive him;)

11. And Jesus, which is called Justus, who are of the circumcision. These only are my fellowworkers unto the kingdom of God, which have been a comfort unto me.

12. Epaphras, who is one of you, a servant of Christ, saluteth you, always labouring fervently for you in prayers, that ye may stand perfect and complete in all the will of God.

13. For I bear him record, that he hath a great zeal for you, and them that are in Laodicea, and them in Hierapolis.

14. Luke, the beloved physician, and Demas, greet you.

15. Salute the brethren which are in Laodicea, and Nymphas, and the church which is in his house.

16. And when this epistle is read among you, cause that it be read also in the church of the Laodiceans; and

Col. 3:20— Parents are to lead and teach (see D&C 68:25–28). Children are to learn and obey. These roles need to be understood and appreciated so that all family members will be respectful of one another.

Stained glass portrayal of Christ in Gethsemane

that ye likewise read the epistle from Laodicea.

17. And say to Archippus, Take heed to the ministry which thou hast received in the Lord, that thou fulfil it.

18. The salutation by the hand of me Paul. Remember my bonds. Grace be with you. Amen.

THE FIRST EPISTLE OF PAUL THE APOSTLE TO

THE THESSALONIANS

CHAPTER 1

1. Paul, and Silvanus, and Timotheus, unto the church of the Thessalonians which is in God the Father and in the Lord Jesus Christ: Grace be unto you, and peace, from God our Father, and the Lord Jesus Christ.

2. We give thanks to God always for you all, making mention of you in our prayers;

3. Remembering without ceasing your work of faith, and labour of love, and patience of hope in our Lord Jesus Christ, in the sight of God and our Father;

4. Knowing, brethren beloved, your election of God.

5. For our gospel came not unto you in word only, but also in power, and in the Holy Ghost, and in much assurance; as ye know what manner of men we were among you for your sake.

6. And ye became followers of us, and of the Lord, having received the word in much affliction, with joy of the Holy Ghost:

7. So that ye were ensamples to all that believe in Macedonia and Achaia.

8. For from you sounded out the word of the Lord not only in Macedonia and Achaia, but also in every place your faith to God-ward is spread abroad; so that we need not to speak any thing.

9. For they themselves shew of us what manner of entering in we had

---

THESSALONIANS

The Thessalonians were residents of the Macedonian city of Thessalonica, founded in the fourth century B.C. and named in honor of Thessalonica, sister of Alexander the Great and wife of Cassander, a Greek military leader. Paul and his companion Silas taught the gospel here, assisted by Timothy (see Acts 16:1–3) and, for a time, possibly the physician and author Luke (see the "we" form of address that commenced with Acts 16:10–11). Their arrival in Thessalonica was perhaps around A.D. 50 (see Acts 17:1).

The message to the Thessalonians from Paul and his companions is to strengthen their faith, sanctify themselves and others, prepare for the Second Coming, look forward to the reward of heavenly glory, and pray for the gospel cause.

unto you, and how ye turned to God from idols to serve the living and true God;

10. And to wait for his Son from heaven, whom he raised from the dead, even Jesus, which delivered us from the wrath to come.

CHAPTER 2

1. For yourselves, brethren, know our entrance in unto you, that it was not in vain:

2. But even after that we had suffered before, and were shamefully entreated, as ye know, at Philippi, we were bold in our God to speak unto you the gospel of God with much contention.

3. For our exhortation was not of deceit, nor of uncleanness, nor in guile:

4. But as we were allowed of God to be put in trust with the gospel, even so we speak; not as pleasing men, but God, which trieth our hearts.

5. For neither at any time used we flattering words, as ye know, nor a cloke of covetousness; God is witness:

6. Nor of men sought we glory, neither of you, nor yet of others, when we might have been burdensome, as the apostles of Christ.

7. But we were gentle among you, even as a nurse cherisheth her children:

8. So being affectionately desirous of you, we were willing to have imparted unto you, not the gospel of God only, but also our own souls, because ye were dear unto us.

9. For ye remember, brethren, our labour and travail: for labouring night and day, because we would not be chargeable unto any of you, we preached unto you the gospel of God.

10. Ye are witnesses, and God also, how holily and justly and unblameably we behaved ourselves among you that believe:

11. As ye know how we exhorted and comforted and charged every one of you, as a father doth his children,

12. That ye would walk worthy of God, who hath called you unto his kingdom and glory.

13. For this cause also thank we God without ceasing, because, when ye received the word of God which ye heard of us, ye received it not as the word of men, but as it is in truth, the word of God, which effectually worketh also in you that believe.

14. For ye, brethren, became followers of the churches of God which in Judæa are in Christ Jesus: for ye also have suffered like things of your own countrymen, even as they have of the Jews:

15. Who both killed the Lord Jesus, and their own prophets, and have persecuted us; and they please not God, and are contrary to all men:

16. Forbidding us to speak to the Gentiles that they might be saved,

SILVANUS (SILAS)

Silvanus is another name for Silas, one of the chief leaders among the Christians at Jerusalem (see Acts 15:22). The purpose for the delegation to Antioch was to resolve a dispute among the Saints there concerning circumcision—that it was no longer required of those coming into the fold (see Acts 15:27).

Silas and Judas were characterized as being prophets (see Acts 15:32–34), and after Judas left Antioch, Silas was "pleased" to "abide there still."

Silas participated with Paul in missionary assignments (see Acts 15:40; 16:19–40; 17:1–15; 18:5). In addition, he was referred to as Silvanus—a faithful brother—in several different passages (see 1 Pet. 5:12; 1 Thes. 1:1–2; 2 Thes. 1:1).

to fill up their sins alway: for the wrath is come upon them to the uttermost.

17. But we, brethren, being taken from you for a short time in presence, not in heart, endeavoured the more abundantly to see your face with great desire.

18. Wherefore we would have come unto you, even I Paul, once and again; but Satan hindered us.

19. For what is our hope, or joy, or crown of rejoicing? Are not even ye in the presence of our Lord Jesus Christ at his coming?

20. For ye are our glory and joy.

CHAPTER 3

1. Wherefore when we could no longer forbear, we thought it good to be left at Athens alone;

2. And sent Timotheus, our brother, and minister of God, and our fellowlabourer in the gospel of Christ, to establish you, and to comfort you concerning your faith:

3. That no man should be moved by these afflictions: for yourselves know that we are appointed thereunto.

4. For verily, when we were with you, we told you before that we should suffer tribulation; even as it came to pass, and ye know.

5. For this cause, when I could no longer forbear, I sent to know your faith, lest by some means the tempter have tempted you, and our labour be in vain.

6. But now when Timotheus came from you unto us, and brought us good tidings of your faith and charity, and that ye have good remembrance of us always, desiring greatly to see us, as we also to see you:

7. Therefore, brethren, we were comforted over you in all our affliction and distress by your faith:

8. For now we live, if ye stand fast in the Lord.

9. For what thanks can we render to God again for you, for all the joy wherewith we joy for your sakes before our God;

10. Night and day praying exceedingly that we might see your face, and might perfect that which is lacking in your faith?

11. Now God himself and our Father, and our Lord Jesus Christ, direct our way unto you.

12. And the Lord make you to increase and abound in love one toward another, and toward all men, even as we do toward you:

13. To the end he may stablish your hearts unblameable in holiness before God, even our Father, at the coming of our Lord Jesus Christ with all his saints.

CHAPTER 4

1. Furthermore then we beseech you, brethren, and exhort you by the Lord Jesus, that as ye have received of us how ye ought to walk and to please God, so ye would abound more and more.

2. For ye know what command-

Notes: _____

_____

_____

_____

_____

_____

_____

_____

_____

_____

_____

_____

_____

_____

_____

_____

_____

_____

_____

_____

_____

_____

_____

_____

_____

_____

_____

_____

ments we gave you by the Lord Jesus.

3. For this is the will of God, even your sanctification, that ye should abstain from fornication:

4. That every one of you should know how to possess his vessel in sanctification and honour;

5. Not in the lust of concupiscence, even as the Gentiles which know not God:

6. That no man go beyond and defraud his brother in any matter: because that the Lord is the avenger of all such, as we also have forewarned you and testified.

7. For God hath not called us unto uncleanness, but unto holiness.

8. He therefore that despiseth, despiseth not man, but God, who hath also given unto us his holy Spirit.

9. But as touching brotherly love ye need not that I write unto you: for ye yourselves are taught of God to love one another.

10. And indeed ye do it toward all the brethren which are in all Macedonia: but we beseech you, brethren, that ye increase more and more;

11. And that ye study to be quiet, and to do your own business, and to work with your own hands, as we commanded you;

12. That ye may walk honestly toward them that are without, and that ye may have lack of nothing.

13. But I would not have you to be ignorant, brethren, concerning them which are asleep, that ye sorrow not, even as others which have no hope.

14. For if we believe that Jesus died and rose again, even so them also which sleep in Jesus will God bring with him.

15. For this we say unto you by the word of the Lord, that we which are alive and remain unto the coming of the Lord shall not prevent them which are asleep.

16. For the Lord himself shall descend from heaven with a shout, with the voice of the archangel, and with the trump of God: and the dead in Christ shall rise first:

17. Then we which are alive and remain shall be caught up together with them in the clouds, to meet the Lord in the air: and so shall we ever be with the Lord.

18. Wherefore comfort one another with these words.

TIMOTHY (TIMOTHEUS)

Timothy (with its Greek form, *Timotheus*) was a trusted young missionary companion of Paul. Paul accords Timothy—whom he identifies as "my workfellow" (Rom. 16:21), "my own son in the faith" (1 Tim. 1:20), "my beloved son, and faithful in the Lord" (1 Cor. 4:17), and "our fellowlabourer in the gospel of Christ" (1 Thes. 3:2)—with a magnificent expression of admiration (see 2 Tim. 1:1–8, 13).

Timothy served as Paul's emissary or companion in multiple projects (see Acts 17:14; 19:22; 20:4–5; Rom. 16:21; 1 Cor. 16:10; 2 Cor. 1:1, 19; Philip. 1:1; 2:19–23; Col. 1:1; 1 Thes. 1:1; 3:2; 2 Thes. 1:1; 1 Tim. 1:3; 2 Tim. 4:9, 21; Phil. 1:1). Timothy was at one point apparently imprisoned and then set free (Heb. 13:23).

Some of the most memorable passages of counsel in the post-Gospel writings of the New Testament emanated from the relationship between Paul and Timothy. Some examples include:

- Hold to the faith (see 1 Tim. 1:18–19)
- Work the cause of the Lord (see 1 Cor. 16:10–11)
- Be an example of the believers (see 1 Tim. 4:12–16)
- Avoid material things; follow after godliness (see 1 Tim. 2:1–3)
- Be strong in the grace of Christ (see 2 Tim. 2:1–3)
- Find wisdom through the scriptures (see 2 Tim. 3:14–17)

Perhaps the best summary statement from Paul about his love for Timothy is this one: "But ye know the proof of him, that, as a son with the father, he hath served me in the gospel" (Phil. 2:22).

CHAPTER 5

1. But of the times and the seasons, brethren, ye have no need that I write unto you.

2. For yourselves know perfectly that the day of the Lord so cometh as a thief in the night.

3. For when they shall say, Peace and safety; then sudden destruction cometh upon them, as travail upon a woman with child; and they shall not escape.

4. But ye, brethren, are not in darkness, that that day should overtake you as a thief.

5. Ye are all the children of light, and the children of the day: we are not of the night, nor of darkness.

6. Therefore let us not sleep, as do others; but let us watch and be sober.

7. For they that sleep sleep in the night; and they that be drunken are drunken in the night.

8. But let us, who are of the day, be sober, putting on the breastplate of faith and love; and for an helmet, the hope of salvation.

9. For God hath not appointed us to wrath, but to obtain salvation by our Lord Jesus Christ,

10. Who died for us, that, whether we wake or sleep, we should live together with him.

11. Wherefore comfort yourselves together, and edify one another, even as also ye do.

12. And we beseech you, brethren, to know them which labour among you, and are over you in the Lord, and admonish you;

13. And to esteem them very highly in love for their work's sake. And be at peace among yourselves.

14. Now we exhort you, brethren, warn them that are unruly, comfort the feebleminded, support the weak, be patient toward all men.

15. See that none render evil for evil unto any man; but ever follow that which is good, both among yourselves, and to all men.

16. Rejoice evermore.

17. Pray without ceasing.

18. In every thing give thanks: for this is the will of God in Christ Jesus concerning you.

19. Quench not the Spirit.

20. Despise not prophesyings.

21. Prove all things; hold fast that which is good.

22. Abstain from all appearance of evil.

23. And the very God of peace sanctify you wholly; and I pray God your whole spirit and soul and body be preserved blameless unto the coming of our Lord Jesus Christ.

Notes: _____

_____

_____

_____

_____

_____

_____

_____

_____

_____

_____

_____

_____

1 Thes. 5:16–21 — As he fulfilled his commission to preach the gospel, Paul was careful not to neglect the well-being and nurture of the convert Saints who came into the fold. While in Athens, for example, Paul sent two glorious epistles to the Thessalonians, exhorting them to be true to the faith and honor their covenants. Examples from these exhortations include the following:

• Rejoice evermore.

• Pray without ceasing.

• In every thing give thanks: for this is the will of God in Christ Jesus concerning you.

• Quench not the Spirit.

• Despise not prophesyings.

• Prove all things; hold fast to that which is good (see 1 Thes. 5:16–21).

And this famous line: "But ye, brethren, be not weary in well doing" (2 Thes. 3:13) — which anticipates the word of the Lord in the latter days: "Wherefore, be not weary in well-doing, for ye are laying the foundation of a great work. And out of small things proceedeth that which is great" (D&C 64:33).

24. Faithful is he that calleth you, who also will do it.

25. Brethren, pray for us.

26. Greet all the brethren with an holy kiss.

27. I charge you by the Lord that this epistle be read unto all the holy brethren.

28. The grace of our Lord Jesus Christ be with you. Amen.

THE SECOND EPISTLE OF PAUL THE APOSTLE TO

THE THESSALONIANS

CHAPTER 1

1. Paul, and Silvanus, and Timotheus, unto the church of the Thessalonians in God our Father and the Lord Jesus Christ:

2. Grace unto you, and peace, from God our Father and the Lord Jesus Christ.

3. We are bound to thank God always for you, brethren, as it is meet, because that your faith groweth exceedingly, and the charity of every one of you all toward each other aboundeth;

4. So that we ourselves glory in you in the churches of God for your patience and faith in all your persecutions and tribulations that ye endure:

5. Which is a manifest token of the righteous judgment of God, that ye may be counted worthy of the kingdom of God, for which ye also suffer:

6. Seeing it is a righteous thing with God to recompense tribulation to them that trouble you;

7. And to you who are troubled rest with us, when the Lord Jesus shall be revealed from heaven with his mighty angels,

8. In flaming fire taking vengeance on them that know not God, and that obey not the gospel of our Lord Jesus Christ:

9. Who shall be punished with everlasting destruction from the presence of the Lord, and from the glory of his power;

10. When he shall come to be glorified in his saints, and to be admired in all them that believe (because our testimony among you was believed) in that day.

11. Wherefore also we pray always

Notes: _____
_____
_____
_____
_____
_____
_____
_____
_____
_____
_____
_____
_____
_____
_____
_____
_____
_____
_____
_____
_____
_____
_____
_____
_____
_____
_____
_____
_____
_____
_____
_____
_____

for you, that our God would count you worthy of this calling, and fulfil all the good pleasure of his goodness, and the work of faith with power:

12. That the name of our Lord Jesus Christ may be glorified in you, and ye in him, according to the grace of our God and the Lord Jesus Christ.

CHAPTER 2

1. Now we beseech you, brethren, by the coming of our Lord Jesus Christ, and by our gathering together unto him,

2. That ye be not soon shaken in mind, or be troubled, neither by spirit, nor by word, nor by letter as from us, as that the day of Christ is at hand.

3. Let no man deceive you by any means: for that day shall not come, except there come a falling away first, and that man of sin be revealed, the son of perdition;

4. Who opposeth and exalteth himself above all that is called God, or that is worshipped; so that he as God sitteth in the temple of God, shewing himself that he is God.

5. Remember ye not, that, when I was yet with you, I told you these things?

6. And now ye know what withholdeth that he might be revealed in his time.

7. For the mystery of iniquity doth already work: only he who now letteth will let, until he be taken out of the way.

8. And then shall that Wicked be revealed, whom the Lord shall consume with the spirit of his mouth, and shall destroy with the brightness of his coming:

9. Even him, whose coming is after the working of Satan with all power and signs and lying wonders,

10. And with all deceivableness of unrighteousness in them that perish; because they received not the love of the truth, that they might be saved.

11. And for this cause God shall send them strong delusion, that they should believe a lie:

12. That they all might be damned who believed not the truth, but had pleasure in unrighteousness.

13. But we are bound to give thanks alway to God for you, brethren beloved of the Lord, because God hath from the beginning chosen you to salvation through sanctification of the Spirit and belief of the truth:

14. Whereunto he called you by our gospel, to the obtaining of the glory of our Lord Jesus Christ.

15. Therefore, brethren, stand fast, and hold the traditions which ye have been taught, whether by word, or our epistle.

16. Now our Lord Jesus Christ himself, and God, even our Father, which hath loved us, and hath

GOD (FATHER IN HEAVEN)

The encompassing influence and divine leadership of our Father in Heaven is pervasive throughout the events of the New Testament chronicle, as it is in all dimensions and aspects of the human experience from the beginning of time. Our Father in Heaven is the Supreme Lord and God of all Creation, the Eternal Source of light and truth, the benevolent and ever-loving Father of our spirits (see Heb. 12:9), the Author of the glorious gospel plan of happiness (see Abr. 3:23, 27), the Exemplar of the pattern for all holiness and perfection, the merciful Grantor of agency to His children, and the Benefactor of all mankind through the gift of His Only Begotten Son, whose atoning sacrifice empowers the process for achieving immortality and exaltation (see John 3:16). It is to our Father in Heaven that we pray, in the name of Jesus Christ.

Our Father in Heaven has granted unto Jesus Christ the sacred commission to be His agent in governing and directing the unfolding of the divine gospel plan for the benefit of all humankind (see John 17:3).

The sacred unity of purpose reflected among the three members of the Godhead makes the term *God* or *Lord* in the scriptures often interchangeable in regard to the Father and the Son. But there are distinctions among the individual beings of the Godhead (see D&C 130:22). As Joseph Smith confirmed, the Father has pre-eminence (see *Teachings of the Prophet Joseph Smith*, 190).

Paul declared, "But to us there is but one God, the Father, of whom are all things, and we in him; and one Lord Jesus Christ, by whom are all things, and we by him" (1 Cor. 8:6).

given us everlasting consolation and good hope through grace,

17. Comfort your hearts, and stablish you in every good word and work.

CHAPTER 3

1. Finally, brethren, pray for us, that the word of the Lord may have free course, and be glorified, even as it is with you:

2. And that we may be delivered from unreasonable and wicked men: for all men have not faith.

3. But the Lord is faithful, who shall stablish you, and keep you from evil.

4. And we have confidence in the Lord touching you, that ye both do and will do the things which we command you.

5. And the Lord direct your hearts into the love of God, and into the patient waiting for Christ.

6. Now we command you, brethren, in the name of our Lord Jesus Christ, that ye withdraw yourselves from every brother that walketh disorderly, and not after the tradition which he received of us.

7. For yourselves know how ye ought to follow us: for we behaved not ourselves disorderly among you;

8. Neither did we eat any man's bread for nought; but wrought with labour and travail night and day, that we might not be chargeable to any of you:

9. Not because we have not power, but to make ourselves an ensample unto you to follow us.

10. For even when we were with you, this we commanded you, that if any would not work, neither should he eat.

11. For we hear that there are some which walk among you disorderly, working not at all, but are busybodies.

12. Now them that are such we command and exhort by our Lord Jesus Christ, that with quietness they work, and eat their own bread.

13. But ye, brethren, be not weary in well doing.

14. And if any man obey not our word by this epistle, note that man, and have no company with him, that he may be ashamed.

15. Yet count him not as an enemy, but admonish him as a brother.

16. Now the Lord of peace himself give you peace always by all means. The Lord be with you all.

17. The salutation of Paul with mine own hand, which is the token in every epistle: so I write.

18. The grace of our Lord Jesus Christ be with you all. Amen.

The Christus

Notes:

THE FIRST EPISTLE OF PAUL THE APOSTLE TO

TIMOTHY

CHAPTER 1

1. Paul, an apostle of Jesus Christ by the commandment of God our Saviour, and Lord Jesus Christ, which is our hope;

2. Unto Timothy, my own son in the faith: Grace, mercy, and peace, from God our Father and Jesus Christ our Lord.

3. As I besought thee to abide still at Ephesus, when I went into Macedonia, that thou mightest charge some that they teach no other doctrine,

4. Neither give heed to fables and endless genealogies, which minister questions, rather than godly edifying which is in faith: so do.

5. Now the end of the commandment is charity out of a pure heart, and of a good conscience, and of faith unfeigned:

6. From which some having swerved have turned aside unto vain jangling;

7. Desiring to be teachers of the law; understanding neither what they say, nor whereof they affirm.

8. But we know that the law is good, if a man use it lawfully;

9. Knowing this, that the law is not made for a righteous man, but for the lawless and disobedient, for the ungodly and for sinners, for unholy and profane, for murderers of fathers and murderers of mothers, for manslayers,

10. For whoremongers, for them that defile themselves with mankind, for menstealers, for liars, for perjured persons, and if there be any other thing that is contrary to sound doctrine;

11. According to the glorious gospel of the blessed God, which was committed to my trust.

12. And I thank Christ Jesus our Lord, who hath enabled me, for that he counted me faithful, putting me into the ministry;

13. Who was before a blasphemer, and a persecutor, and injurious: but I obtained mercy, because I did it ignorantly in unbelief.

14. And the grace of our Lord was exceeding abundant with faith and love which is in Christ Jesus.

15. This is a faithful saying, and worthy of all acceptation, that Christ Jesus came into the world

1 and 2 Timothy—Paul's epistles to Titus and Timothy (1 and 2 Timothy) date from the period A.D. 64–65. They are the last of the extant writings of this choice Apostle of the Lord. The First Epistle to Timothy was written, following Paul's first imprisonment, as a means to counsel this trusted younger associate in his ministerial duties at Ephesus. The Second Epistle to Timothy dates from the period of Paul's second imprisonment, prior to his martyrdom. Titus and Timothy were among the most devoted associates of the Apostle Paul in his missionary and pastoral labors.

Paul's counsel to Timothy and Titus incorporates eternal principles of spiritual leadership in building the kingdom of God. We see that the essence of his message is expressed early on (see 1 Tim. 1:5). At the center of focus is the Savior: "For there is one God, and one mediator between God and men, the man Christ Jesus" (1 Tim. 2:5). The Church has a divine inner core, for it is indeed "the church of the living God, the pillar and ground of the truth. And without controversy great is the mystery of godliness: God was manifest in the flesh, justified in the Spirit, seen of angels, preached unto the Gentiles, believed on in the world, received up into glory" (1 Tim. 3:15–16). For that reason, meticulous care should be given to matters of governance, counseled Paul (see 1 Tim. 5:22). Such purity is aligned with the spiritual gifts of leadership, as Paul confirms (see 2 Tim. 1:6–10).

Through obedience to the principles of salvation, those who serve the Saints have divine assurances of God's intervening help (see 2 Tim. 2:19). Specifically, Paul admonishes Timothy to set his mind and heart on the word of God as the channel of divine counsel (see 2 Tim. 3:15–17). Above all, as Paul reminds Titus, one should depend on the Spirit for guidance in all spiritual matters: "Not by works of righteousness which we have done, but according to his mercy he saved us, by the washing of regeneration, and renewing of the Holy Ghost; Which he shed on us abundantly through Jesus Christ our Saviour; That being justified by his grace, we should be made heirs according to the hope of eternal life" (Titus 3:5–7).

to save sinners; of whom I am chief.

16. Howbeit for this cause I obtained mercy, that in me first Jesus Christ might shew forth all longsuffering, for a pattern to them which should hereafter believe on him to life everlasting.

17. Now unto the King eternal, immortal, invisible, the only wise God, be honour and glory for ever and ever. Amen.

18. This charge I commit unto thee, son Timothy, according to the prophecies which went before on thee, that thou by them mightest war a good warfare;

19. Holding faith, and a good conscience; which some having put away concerning faith have made shipwreck:

20. Of whom is Hymenæus and Alexander; whom I have delivered unto Satan, that they may learn not to blaspheme.

CHAPTER 2

1. I exhort therefore, that, first of all, supplications, prayers, intercessions, and giving of thanks, be made for all men;

2. For kings, and for all that are in authority; that we may lead a quiet and peaceable life in all godliness and honesty.

3. For this is good and acceptable in the sight of God our Saviour;

4. Who will have all men to be saved, and to come unto the knowledge of the truth.

5. For there is one God, and one mediator between God and men, the man Christ Jesus;

6. Who gave himself a ransom for all, to be testified in due time.

7. Whereunto I am ordained a preacher, and an apostle, (I speak the truth in Christ, and lie not;) a teacher of the Gentiles in faith and verity.

8. I will therefore that men pray every where, lifting up holy hands, without wrath and doubting.

9. In like manner also, that women adorn themselves in modest apparel, with shamefacedness and sobriety; not with broided hair, or gold, or pearls, or costly array;

10. But (which becometh women professing godliness) with good works.

11. Let the woman learn in silence with all subjection.

12. But I suffer not a woman to

1 Tim. 2:1–2—This is the only verse in the scriptures, including the entire King James Version of the Bible, in which the word *honesty* is used (although the word *honest* is used fairly frequently). We all desire peace, godliness, and honesty. Do we remember to pray for everyone, including those responsible for the government of the land, so we can have those blessings? How can you be an example in giving family and congregational prayers and of praying for others—including community, state, national, and international leaders—so that honesty and related virtues can prevail and peace can abound?

Notes: _____

_____

_____

_____

_____

_____

_____

_____

_____

_____

_____

_____

_____

_____

_____

_____

teach, nor to usurp authority over the man, but to be in silence.

13. For Adam was first formed, then Eve.

14. And Adam was not deceived, but the woman being deceived was in the transgression.

15. Notwithstanding she shall be saved in childbearing, if they continue in faith and charity and holiness with sobriety.

CHAPTER 3

1. This is a true saying, If a man desire the office of a bishop, he desireth a good work.

2. A bishop then must be blameless, the husband of one wife, vigilant, sober, of good behaviour, given to hospitality, apt to teach;

3. Not given to wine, no striker, not greedy of filthy lucre; but patient, not a brawler, not covetous;

4. One that ruleth well his own house, having his children in subjection with all gravity;

5. (For if a man know not how to rule his own house, how shall he take care of the church of God?)

6. Not a novice, lest being lifted up with pride he fall into the condemnation of the devil.

7. Moreover he must have a good report of them which are without; lest he fall into reproach and the snare of the devil.

8. Likewise must the deacons be grave, not doubletongued, not given to much wine, not greedy of filthy lucre;

9. Holding the mystery of the faith in a pure conscience.

10. And let these also first be proved; then let them use the office of a deacon, being found blameless.

11. Even so must their wives be grave, not slanderers, sober, faithful in all things.

12. Let the deacons be the husbands of one wife, ruling their children and their own houses well.

13. For they that have used the office of a deacon well purchase to themselves a good degree, and great boldness in the faith which is in Christ Jesus.

14. These things write I unto thee, hoping to come unto thee shortly:

15. But if I tarry long, that thou mayest know how thou oughtest to behave thyself in the house of God, which is the church of the living

---

BISHOP

The office of bishop is a key ecclesiastical calling in the priesthood of God. The word *bishop* derives from the Greek word *episkopos*, meaning "overseer" (see Acts 20:28). The assignment of the Apostles to be overseers, in the general sense, is confirmed in a verse about the fallen Judas (see Acts 1:20; see also D&C 114:1–2).

In the specific sense of the word, modern revelation makes clear that the bishop is an ordained office in the Aaronic Priesthood (see D&C 20:67) and that the bishop is the president of the priests quorum (see D&C 107:77–78).

For passages in the New Testament that describe the qualities a bishop should cultivate, see Titus 1:7–9 and 1 Tim. 3:1–7.

God, the pillar and ground of the truth.

16. And without controversy great is the mystery of godliness: God was manifest in the flesh, justified in the Spirit, seen of angels, preached unto the Gentiles, believed on in the world, received up into glory.

CHAPTER 4

1. Now the Spirit speaketh expressly, that in the latter times some shall depart from the faith, giving heed to seducing spirits, and doctrines of devils;

2. Speaking lies in hypocrisy; having their conscience seared with a hot iron;

3. Forbidding to marry, and commanding to abstain from meats, which God hath created to be received with thanksgiving of them which believe and know the truth.

4. For every creature of God is good, and nothing to be refused, if it be received with thanksgiving:

5. For it is sanctified by the word of God and prayer.

6. If thou put the brethren in remembrance of these things, thou shalt be a good minister of Jesus Christ, nourished up in the words of faith and of good doctrine, whereunto thou hast attained.

7. But refuse profane and old wives' fables, and exercise thyself rather unto godliness.

8. For bodily exercise profiteth little: but godliness is profitable unto all things, having promise of the life that now is, and of that which is to come.

9. This is a faithful saying and worthy of all acceptation.

10. For therefore we both labour and suffer reproach, because we trust in the living God, who is the Saviour of all men, specially of those that believe.

11. These things command and teach.

12. Let no man despise thy youth; but be thou an example of the believers, in word, in conversation, in charity, in spirit, in faith, in purity.

13. Till I come, give attendance to reading, to exhortation, to doctrine.

14. Neglect not the gift that is in thee, which was given thee by prophecy, with the laying on of the hands of the presbytery.

15. Meditate upon these things;

1 Tim. 4:5–6—We can become an instrument in the hands of God as we treasure up His words (see D&C 84:85) and seek to live by every word that proceeds from the mouth of God (see D&C 84:43–46).

1 Tim. 4:12—Being a good example requires the involvement of your entire being—your demeanor, your dress, your words, your countenance, and all that you radiate. The question might be asked, "What message are you sending today?"

1 Tim. 4:12–16—In his exhortations to Timothy, Paul places a crown of honor on the power of example. No matter what our role or our position, no matter what our age or our presence, we can invest our spirituality in the service of others with the assurance that the Lord will guide our footsteps for the good of the community of Saints. Above all, gentleness and meekness will engender good followership unto repentance and faith in the Lord: "And the servant of the Lord must not strive; but be gentle unto all men, apt to teach, patient, In meekness instructing those that oppose themselves; if God peradventure will give them repentance to the acknowledging of the truth" (2 Tim. 2:24–25).

give thyself wholly to them; that thy profiting may appear to all.

16. Take heed unto thyself, and unto the doctrine; continue in them: for in doing this thou shalt both save thyself, and them that hear thee.

CHAPTER 5

1. Rebuke not an elder, but intreat him as a father; and the younger men as brethren;

2. The elder women as mothers; the younger as sisters, with all purity.

3. Honour widows that are widows indeed.

4. But if any widow have children or nephews, let them learn first to shew piety at home, and to requite their parents: for that is good and acceptable before God.

5. Now she that is a widow indeed, and desolate, trusteth in God, and continueth in supplications and prayers night and day.

6. But she that liveth in pleasure is dead while she liveth.

7. And these things give in charge, that they may be blameless.

8. But if any provide not for his own, and specially for those of his own house, he hath denied the faith, and is worse than an infidel.

9. Let not a widow be taken into the number under threescore years old, having been the wife of one man,

10. Well reported of for good works; if she have brought up children, if she have lodged strangers, if she have washed the saints' feet, if she have relieved the afflicted, if she have diligently followed every good work.

11. But the younger widows refuse: for when they have begun to wax wanton against Christ, they will marry;

12. Having damnation, because they have cast off their first faith.

13. And withal they learn to be idle, wandering about from house to house; and not only idle, but tattlers also and busybodies, speaking things which they ought not.

14. I will therefore that the younger women marry, bear children, guide the house, give none occasion to the adversary to speak reproachfully.

15. For some are already turned aside after Satan.

16. If any man or woman that believeth have widows, let them relieve them, and let not the church be charged; that it may relieve them that are widows indeed.

17. Let the elders that rule well be counted worthy of double honour, especially they who labour in the word and doctrine.

18. For the scripture saith, Thou shalt not muzzle the ox that treadeth out the corn. And, The labourer is worthy of his reward.

19. Against an elder receive not an accusation, but before two or three witnesses.

20. Them that sin rebuke before all, that others also may fear.

Notes: _____

21. I charge thee before God, and the Lord Jesus Christ, and the elect angels, that thou observe these things without preferring one before another, doing nothing by partiality.

22. Lay hands suddenly on no man, neither be partaker of other men's sins: keep thyself pure.

23. Drink no longer water, but use a little wine for thy stomach's sake and thine often infirmities.

24. Some men's sins are open beforehand, going before to judgment; and some men they follow after.

25. Likewise also the good works of some are manifest beforehand; and they that are otherwise cannot be hid.

CHAPTER 6

1. Let as many servants as are under the yoke count their own masters worthy of all honour, that the name of God and his doctrine be not blasphemed.

2. And they that have believing masters, let them not despise them, because they are brethren; but rather do them service, because they are faithful and beloved, partakers of the benefit. These things teach and exhort.

3. If any man teach otherwise, and consent not to wholesome words, even the words of our Lord Jesus Christ, and to the doctrine which is according to godliness;

4. He is proud, knowing nothing, but doting about questions and strifes of words, whereof cometh envy, strife, railings, evil surmisings,

5. Perverse disputings of men of corrupt minds, and destitute of the truth, supposing that gain is godliness: from such withdraw thyself.

6. But godliness with contentment is great gain.

7. For we brought nothing into this world, and it is certain we can carry nothing out.

8. And having food and raiment let us be therewith content.

9. But they that will be rich fall into temptation and a snare, and into many foolish and hurtful lusts, which drown men in destruction and perdition.

10. For the love of money is the root of all evil: which while some coveted after, they have erred from the faith, and pierced themselves through with many sorrows.

11. But thou, O man of God, flee these things; and follow after righteousness, godliness, faith, love, patience, meekness.

12. Fight the good fight of faith, lay hold on eternal life, whereunto thou art also called, and hast professed a good profession before many witnesses.

13. I give thee charge in the sight of God, who quickeneth all things,

1 Tim. 6:10–11—When we love anything other than God, we will be of the world—and the love of money will envelope us in all manner of evil. When we love God, we will follow after righteousness in all things. We do this as we seek to build up the kingdom of God and His righteousness (see JST, Matt. 6:38).

1 Tim. 6:6–12— From their chief mentor and guide, Paul the Apostle, Timothy and Titus received inspiring counsel on how to use God-given agency wisely and how to instruct their followers to do the same. These verses are the famous passage on worldly wealth that Paul wrote to Timothy.

and before Christ Jesus, who before Pontius Pilate witnessed a good confession;

14. That thou keep this commandment without spot, unrebukeable, until the appearing of our Lord Jesus Christ:

15. Which in his times he shall shew, who is the blessed and only Potentate, the King of kings, and Lord of lords;

16. Who only hath immortality, dwelling in the light which no man can approach unto; whom no man hath seen, nor can see: to whom be honour and power everlasting. Amen.

17. Charge them that are rich in this world, that they be not highminded, nor trust in uncertain riches, but in the living God, who giveth us richly all things to enjoy;

18. That they do good, that they be rich in good works, ready to distribute, willing to communicate;

19. Laying up in store for themselves a good foundation against the time to come, that they may lay hold on eternal life.

20. O Timothy, keep that which is committed to thy trust, avoiding profane and vain babblings, and oppositions of science falsely so called:

21. Which some professing have erred concerning the faith. Grace be with thee. Amen.

THE SECOND EPISTLE OF PAUL THE APOSTLE TO

TIMOTHY

CHAPTER 1

1. Paul, an apostle of Jesus Christ by the will of God, according to the promise of life which is in Christ Jesus,

2. To Timothy, my dearly beloved son: Grace, mercy, and peace, from God the Father and Christ Jesus our Lord.

3. I thank God, whom I serve from my forefathers with pure conscience, that without ceasing I have remembrance of thee in my prayers night and day;

4. Greatly desiring to see thee, being mindful of thy tears, that I may be filled with joy;

5. When I call to remembrance the

Harvest

unfeigned faith that is in thee, which dwelt first in thy grandmother Lois, and thy mother Eunice; and I am persuaded that in thee also.

6. Wherefore I put thee in remembrance that thou stir up the gift of God, which is in thee by the putting on of my hands.

7. For God hath not given us the spirit of fear; but of power, and of love, and of a sound mind.

8. Be not thou therefore ashamed of the testimony of our Lord, nor of me his prisoner: but be thou partaker of the afflictions of the gospel according to the power of God;

9. Who hath saved us, and called us with an holy calling, not according to our works, but according to his own purpose and grace, which was given us in Christ Jesus before the world began,

10. But is now made manifest by the appearing of our Saviour Jesus Christ, who hath abolished death, and hath brought life and immortality to light through the gospel:

11. Whereunto I am appointed a preacher, and an apostle, and a teacher of the Gentiles.

12. For the which cause I also suffer these things: nevertheless I am not ashamed: for I know whom I have believed, and am persuaded that he is able to keep that which I have committed unto him against that day.

13. Hold fast the form of sound words, which thou hast heard of me, in faith and love which is in Christ Jesus.

14. That good thing which was committed unto thee keep by the Holy Ghost which dwelleth in us.

15. This thou knowest, that all they which are in Asia be turned away from me; of whom are Phygellus and Hermogenes.

16. The Lord give mercy unto the house of Onesiphorus; for he oft refreshed me, and was not ashamed of my chain:

17. But, when he was in Rome, he sought me out very diligently, and found me.

18. The Lord grant unto him that he may find mercy of the Lord in that day: and in how many things he ministered unto me at Ephesus, thou knowest very well.

CHAPTER 2

1. Thou therefore, my son, be strong in the grace that is in Christ Jesus.

2. And the things that thou hast heard of me among many witnesses, the same commit thou to faithful men, who shall be able to teach others also.

3. Thou therefore endure hardness, as a good soldier of Jesus Christ.

4. No man that warreth entangleth himself with the affairs of this life; that he may please him who hath chosen him to be a soldier.

5. And if a man also strive for masteries, yet is he not crowned, except he strive lawfully.

6. The husbandman that labour-

2 Tim. 2— Every faithful laborer in the kingdom is moved by a sacred ensign, and that is Christ Jesus, and Him crucified and raised up as the "author of eternal salvation unto all them that obey him" (Heb. 5:9). This is the ensign that is sustained and glorified throughout the holy scriptures in myriad variations around that central theme. From time to time, each person called on the errand of the Lord—and that includes all of us as Saints in the Church and kingdom of God—will be touched by this or that scriptural passage as a particularly keen reminder of the essence of the gospel of Jesus Christ.

Toward the end of his ministry as the Lord's great missionary to both Jew and Gentile, the Apostle Paul made a statement very similar to that of the Savior in His intercessory prayer. Paul wrote to his young associate, Timothy: "Therefore I endure all things for the elect's sakes, that they may also obtain the salvation which is in Christ Jesus with eternal glory" (2 Tim. 2:10). In doing so, Paul showed that he had adopted the theme of the Savior's all-encompassing design of sacrifice and redemption and applied it as a governing principle to his own ministry. We can do no less. Where the Savior said, "Here am I, send me" (Abr. 3:27), we are to say the same in response to the call to serve, just as Isaiah did, word for word (see Isa. 6:8).

We are called to prepare ourselves in order to strengthen our brethren and sisters and guide our families toward heavenly goals. Despite the challenges thrown up in our way by dissenting voices and worldly influences that would intrude and degrade, we can keep ourselves pure and remember what the Lord said: "And for their sakes I sanctify myself, that they also might be sanctified through the truth" (John 17:19). We can do no less, even though the sacrifice will test our very souls, as Peter confirmed: "But and if ye suffer for righteousness' sake, happy are ye: and be not afraid of their terror, neither be troubled" (1 Pet. 3:14; compare Isa. 45:4; D&C 84:48). By committing our whole being to the Lord and honoring our sacred covenants to render charitable service toward His children continually—doing it "for their sakes"—we can be blessed to view in our mind's eye the future moment in time when our journey will be done, when we will have given our best, and be able to say, with Paul: "I have fought a good fight, I have finished my course, I have kept the faith" (2 Tim. 4:7).

eth must be first partaker of the fruits.

7. Consider what I say; and the Lord give thee understanding in all things.

8. Remember that Jesus Christ of the seed of David was raised from the dead according to my gospel:

9. Wherein I suffer trouble, as an evil doer, even unto bonds; but the word of God is not bound.

10. Therefore I endure all things for the elect's sakes, that they may also obtain the salvation which is in Christ Jesus with eternal glory.

11. It is a faithful saying: For if we be dead with him, we shall also live with him:

12. If we suffer, we shall also reign with him: if we deny him, he also will deny us:

13. If we believe not, yet he abideth faithful: he cannot deny himself.

14. Of these things put them in remembrance, charging them before the Lord that they strive not about words to no profit, but to the subverting of the hearers.

15. Study to shew thyself approved unto God, a workman that needeth not to be ashamed, rightly dividing the word of truth.

16. But shun profane and vain babblings: for they will increase unto more ungodliness.

17. And their word will eat as doth a canker: of whom is Hymenæus and Philetus;

18. Who concerning the truth have erred, saying that the resurrection is past already; and overthrow the faith of some.

19. Nevertheless the foundation of God standeth sure, having this seal, The Lord knoweth them that are his. And, Let every one that nameth the name of Christ depart from iniquity.

20. But in a great house there are not only vessels of gold and of silver, but also of wood and of earth; and some to honour, and some to dishonour.

21. If a man therefore purge himself from these, he shall be a vessel unto honour, sanctified, and meet for the master's use, and prepared unto every good work.

22. Flee also youthful lusts: but follow righteousness, faith, charity, peace, with them that call on the Lord out of a pure heart.

23. But foolish and unlearned questions avoid, knowing that they do gender strifes.

24. And the servant of the Lord must not strive; but be gentle unto all men, apt to teach, patient,

25. In meekness instructing those that oppose themselves; if God peradventure will give them repentance to the acknowledging of the truth;

26. And that they may recover themselves out of the snare of the devil, who are taken captive by him at his will.

Notes: _____
_____
_____
_____
_____
_____
_____
_____
_____
_____
_____
_____
_____
_____
_____
_____
_____
_____
_____
_____
_____
_____
_____
_____
_____
_____
_____
_____
_____
_____
_____
_____
_____
_____
_____
_____
_____

CHAPTER 3

1. This know also, that in the last days perilous times shall come.

2. For men shall be lovers of their own selves, covetous, boasters, proud, blasphemers, disobedient to parents, unthankful, unholy,

3. Without natural affection, trucebreakers, false accusers, incontinent, fierce, despisers of those that are good,

4. Traitors, heady, highminded, lovers of pleasures more than lovers of God;

5. Having a form of godliness, but denying the power thereof: from such turn away.

6. For of this sort are they which creep into houses, and lead captive silly women laden with sins, led away with divers lusts,

7. Ever learning, and never able to come to the knowledge of the truth.

8. Now as Jannes and Jambres withstood Moses, so do these also resist the truth: men of corrupt minds, reprobate concerning the faith.

9. But they shall proceed no further: for their folly shall be manifest unto all men, as theirs also was.

10. But thou hast fully known my doctrine, manner of life, purpose, faith, longsuffering, charity, patience,

11. Persecutions, afflictions, which came unto me at Antioch, at Iconium, at Lystra; what persecutions I endured: but out of them all the Lord delivered me.

12. Yea, and all that will live godly in Christ Jesus shall suffer persecution.

13. But evil men and seducers shall wax worse and worse, deceiving, and being deceived.

14. But continue thou in the things which thou hast learned and hast been assured of, knowing of whom thou hast learned them;

15. And that from a child thou hast known the holy scriptures, which are able to make thee wise unto salvation through faith which is in Christ Jesus.

16. All scripture is given by inspiration of God, and is profitable for doctrine, for reproof, for correction, for instruction in righteousness:

17. That the man of God may be perfect, throughly furnished unto all good works.

2 Tim. 3:1–7—Paul counseled Timothy to teach through righteous conduct, separating himself from worldly entanglements: "Thou therefore, my son, be strong in the grace that is in Christ Jesus. And the things that thou hast heard of me among many witnesses, the same commit thou to faithful men, who shall be able to teach others also. Thou therefore endure hardness, as a good soldier of Jesus Christ. No man that warreth entangleth himself with the affairs of this life; that he may please him who hath chosen him to be a soldier" (2 Tim. 2:1–4). This is particularly pertinent advice, given Paul's dire prediction concerning the impending apostasy, which is contained in these verses (1–7).

In contrast to such devious patterns, Paul reminded Titus of the necessity of remaining pure and avoiding the pollutions of disbelief: "Unto the pure all things are pure: but unto them that are defiled and unbelieving is nothing pure; but even their mind and conscience is defiled" (Titus 1:15).

2 Tim. 3:11—Inspired by the example of Paul and all of God's servants past and present, we are never to forget that the Lord will deliver us from our persecutions. The Prophet Joseph Smith learned well, then taught us, that in and through persecutions we grow (see D&C 121:7–8; 122:5–8).

Timothy and his Grandmother

CHAPTER 4

1. I charge thee therefore before God, and the Lord Jesus Christ, who shall judge the quick and the dead at his appearing and his kingdom;

2. Preach the word; be instant in season, out of season; reprove, rebuke, exhort with all longsuffering and doctrine.

3. For the time will come when they will not endure sound doctrine; but after their own lusts shall they heap to themselves teachers, having itching ears;

4. And they shall turn away their ears from the truth, and shall be turned unto fables.

5. But watch thou in all things, endure afflictions, do the work of an evangelist, make full proof of thy ministry.

6. For I am now ready to be offered, and the time of my departure is at hand.

7. I have fought a good fight, I have finished my course, I have kept the faith:

8. Henceforth there is laid up for me a crown of righteousness, which the Lord, the righteous judge, shall give me at that day: and not to me only, but unto all them also that love his appearing.

9. Do thy diligence to come shortly unto me:

10. For Demas hath forsaken me, having loved this present world, and is departed unto Thessalonica; Crescens to Galatia, Titus unto Dalmatia.

11. Only Luke is with me. Take Mark, and bring him with thee: for he is profitable to me for the ministry.

12. And Tychicus have I sent to Ephesus.

13. The cloke that I left at Troas with Carpus, when thou comest, bring with thee, and the books, but especially the parchments.

14. Alexander the coppersmith did me much evil: the Lord reward him according to his works:

15. Of whom be thou ware also; for he hath greatly withstood our words.

16. At my first answer no man stood with me, but all men forsook me: I pray God that it may not be laid to their charge.

17. Notwithstanding the Lord stood with me, and strengthened me; that by me the preaching might be fully known, and that all the Gentiles might hear: and I was delivered out of the mouth of the lion.

18. And the Lord shall deliver me from every evil work, and will preserve me unto his heavenly kingdom: to whom be glory for ever and ever. Amen.

19. Salute Prisca and Aquila, and the household of Onesiphorus.

20. Erastus abode at Corinth: but Trophimus have I left at Miletum sick.

2 Tim. 4—The power of the gospel is to bring about a spiritual transformation in our hearts and minds, lifting us upward toward our divine potential as sons and daughters of God. The key for going through this "mighty change of heart," about which King Benjamin taught and concerning which Alma spoke so eloquently (Mosiah 5:2; Alma 5:14), is to apply gospel knowledge and true doctrine to our lives consistently. Paul confirmed this sacred strategy in his epistles and demonstrated its efficacy through his exemplary life. Moreover, those who experience the blessings of the Lord's Atonement in their lives have the obligation to share the gospel with others (as Paul and his colleagues did) by serving as honorable examples and by setting their priorities according to heavenly standards, denying themselves of all ungodliness (see Titus 2:12; Moro. 10:32). In doing so, we align our efforts with those of Paul and all other devoted servants of God and increase the chances of our being able to say, as did Paul at the end of his mortal journey: "For I am now ready to be offered, and the time of my departure is at hand. I have fought a good fight, I have finished my course, I have kept the faith" (2 Tim. 4:6–7; compare 2 Tim. 3:11–12).

21. Do thy diligence to come before winter. Eubulus greeteth thee, and Pudens, and Linus, and Claudia, and all the brethren.
22. The Lord Jesus Christ be with thy spirit. Grace be with you. Amen.

THE EPISTLE OF PAUL TO

TITUS

CHAPTER 1

1. Paul, a servant of God, and an apostle of Jesus Christ, according to the faith of God's elect, and the acknowledging of the truth which is after godliness;
2. In hope of eternal life, which God, that cannot lie, promised before the world began;
3. But hath in due times manifested his word through preaching, which is committed unto me according to the commandment of God our Saviour;
4. To Titus, mine own son after the common faith: Grace, mercy, and peace, from God the Father and the Lord Jesus Christ our Saviour.
5. For this cause left I thee in Crete, that thou shouldest set in order the things that are wanting, and ordain elders in every city, as I had appointed thee:
6. If any be blameless, the husband of one wife, having faithful children not accused of riot or unruly.
7. For a bishop must be blameless, as the steward of God; not selfwilled, not soon angry, not given to wine, no striker, not given to filthy lucre;
8. But a lover of hospitality, a lover of good men, sober, just, holy, temperate;
9. Holding fast the faithful word as he hath been taught, that he may be able by sound doctrine both to exhort and to convince the gainsayers.
10. For there are many unruly and vain talkers and deceivers, specially they of the circumcision:
11. Whose mouths must be stopped, who subvert whole houses, teaching

Titus—Gospel knowledge has to do with eternal truths given by God to man—the knowledge that can save. When we gain a clear understanding of the doctrines, principles, concepts, and covenants pertaining to the gospel and the kingdom of God, we have knowledge of the truth. We are enlightened. We increase in our intelligence, for we have acquired light and truth. This pure knowledge comes by the power of the Holy Ghost. "And by the power of the Holy Ghost ye may know the truth of all things" (Moro. 10:5). We should seek this knowledge that we might understand the things of God and the nature of God. Let us remember that gaining this knowledge is part of taking upon ourselves the divine nature of Jesus Christ (see 2 Pet.1:3–12). When we live according to these eternal truths, we will know God and Jesus Christ (see John 17:3).

When the Savior visited the Saints in ancient America following His resurrection, He provided His disciples with the consummate counsel for the unending process of self-perfection and covenant service: "Therefore, what manner of men ought ye to be? Verily I say unto you, even as I am" (3 Ne. 27:27). His example is the pinnacle of the "godly walk and conversation" (D&C 20:69) we are striving to acquire and practice, the ultimate righteousness.

Righteousness is that state of being in which one is blameless, full of faith, seeking the will of the Father with an eye single to His glory, full of good works, being exactly, immediately, and courageously obedient to the laws and commandments of the Lord. We seek to be righteous—that is our compass and our charge. Righteousness is the oil of our lamp. Righteousness is happiness (see 2 Ne. 2:13). The Prophet Joseph put into perspective the design of our existence, which brings the priority of righteousness to the forefront in obtaining happiness. He said, "Happiness is the object and design of our existence; and will be the end thereof, if we pursue the path that leads to it; and this path is virtue, uprightness, faithfulness, holiness, and keeping all the commandments of God" (*History of the Church*, 5:134–35).

things which they ought not, for filthy lucre's sake.

12. One of themselves, even a prophet of their own, said, The Cretians are alway liars, evil beasts, slow bellies.

13. This witness is true. Wherefore rebuke them sharply, that they may be sound in the faith;

14. Not giving heed to Jewish fables, and commandments of men, that turn from the truth.

15. Unto the pure all things are pure: but unto them that are defiled and unbelieving is nothing pure; but even their mind and conscience is defiled.

16. They profess that they know God; but in works they deny him, being abominable, and disobedient, and unto every good work reprobate.

CHAPTER 2

1. But speak thou the things which become sound doctrine:

2. That the aged men be sober, grave, temperate, sound in faith, in charity, in patience.

3. The aged women likewise, that they be in behaviour as becometh holiness, not false accusers, not given to much wine, teachers of good things;

4. That they may teach the young women to be sober, to love their husbands, to love their children,

5. To be discreet, chaste, keepers at home, good, obedient to their own husbands, that the word of God be not blasphemed.

6. Young men likewise exhort to be sober minded.

7. In all things shewing thyself a pattern of good works: in doctrine shewing uncorruptness, gravity, sincerity,

8. Sound speech, that cannot be condemned; that he that is of the contrary part may be ashamed, having no evil thing to say of you.

9. Exhort servants to be obedient unto their own masters, and to please them well in all things; not answering again;

10. Not purloining, but shewing all good fidelity; that they may adorn the doctrine of God our Saviour in all things.

11. For the grace of God that bringeth salvation hath appeared to all men,

12. Teaching us that, denying ungodliness and worldly lusts, we should live soberly, righteously, and godly, in this present world;

TITUS

Of Titus's and Paul's other companions, Paul said, "Whether any do enquire of Titus, he is my partner and fellowhelper concerning you: or our brethren be enquired of, they are the messengers of the churches, and the glory of Christ" (2 Cor. 8:23).

Titus, a Greek (see Gal. 2:3), probably converted by Paul himself, was an exceptional missionary and representative of the gospel of Jesus Christ. The affection and respect Paul had for Titus comes through in the opening passage of the epistle to Titus (see Titus 1:1–4).

Titus's ministry in support of the cause of Christ—whether in Corinth, Crete, or elsewhere—is set forth in these additional scriptures: 2 Cor. 7:6, 13–14; 2 Cor. 8:6, 16; 12:18; Gal. 2:1; and 2 Tim. 4:10.

13. Looking for that blessed hope, and the glorious appearing of the great God and our Saviour Jesus Christ;

14. Who gave himself for us, that he might redeem us from all iniquity, and purify unto himself a peculiar people, zealous of good works.

15. These things speak, and exhort, and rebuke with all authority. Let no man despise thee.

CHAPTER 3

1. Put them in mind to be subject to principalities and powers, to obey magistrates, to be ready to every good work,

2. To speak evil of no man, to be no brawlers, but gentle, shewing all meekness unto all men.

3. For we ourselves also were sometimes foolish, disobedient, deceived, serving divers lusts and pleasures, living in malice and envy, hateful, and hating one another.

4. But after that the kindness and love of God our Saviour toward man appeared,

5. Not by works of righteousness which we have done, but according to his mercy he saved us, by the washing of regeneration, and renewing of the Holy Ghost;

6. Which he shed on us abundantly through Jesus Christ our Saviour;

7. That being justified by his grace, we should be made heirs according to the hope of eternal life.

8. This is a faithful saying, and these things I will that thou affirm constantly, that they which have believed in God might be careful to maintain good works. These things are good and profitable unto men.

9. But avoid foolish questions, and genealogies, and contentions, and strivings about the law; for they are unprofitable and vain.

10. A man that is an heretick after the first and second admonition reject;

11. Knowing that he that is such is subverted, and sinneth, being condemned of himself.

12. When I shall send Artemas unto thee, or Tychicus, be diligent to come unto me to Nicopolis: for I have determined there to winter.

13. Bring Zenas the lawyer and Apollos on their journey diligently, that nothing be wanting unto them.

14. And let ours also learn to maintain good works for necessary uses, that they be not unfruitful.

15. All that are with me salute thee. Greet them that love us in the faith. Grace be with you all. Amen.

Notes: _____
_____
_____
_____
_____
_____
_____
_____
_____
_____
_____
_____
_____
_____
_____
_____
_____
_____
_____
_____
_____
_____
_____
_____
_____
_____
_____
_____
_____
_____

THE EPISTLE OF PAUL THE APOSTLE TO

PHILEMON

CHAPTER 1

1. Paul, a prisoner of Jesus Christ, and Timothy our brother, unto Philemon our dearly beloved, and fellowlabourer,

2. And to our beloved Apphia, and Archippus our fellowsoldier, and to the church in thy house:

3. Grace to you, and peace, from God our Father and the Lord Jesus Christ.

4. I thank my God, making mention of thee always in my prayers,

5. Hearing of thy love and faith, which thou hast toward the Lord Jesus, and toward all saints;

6. That the communication of thy faith may become effectual by the acknowledging of every good thing which is in you in Christ Jesus.

7. For we have great joy and consolation in thy love, because the bowels of the saints are refreshed by thee, brother.

8. Wherefore, though I might be much bold in Christ to enjoin thee that which is convenient,

9. Yet for love's sake I rather beseech thee, being such an one as Paul the aged, and now also a prisoner of Jesus Christ.

10. I beseech thee for my son Onesimus, whom I have begotten in my bonds:

11. Which in time past was to thee unprofitable, but now profitable to thee and to me:

12. Whom I have sent again: thou therefore receive him, that is, mine own bowels:

13. Whom I would have retained with me, that in thy stead he might have ministered unto me in the bonds of the gospel:

14. But without thy mind would I do nothing; that thy benefit should not be as it were of necessity, but willingly.

15. For perhaps he therefore departed for a season, that thou shouldest receive him for ever;

16. Not now as a servant, but above a servant, a brother beloved, specially to me, but how much more unto thee, both in the flesh, and in the Lord?

17. If thou count me therefore a partner, receive him as myself.

18. If he hath wronged thee, or oweth thee ought, put that on mine account;

19. I Paul have written it with mine own hand, I will repay it: albeit I do not say to thee how thou owest unto me even thine own self besides.

20. Yea, brother, let me have joy of thee in the Lord: refresh my bowels in the Lord.

21. Having confidence in thy obedience I wrote unto thee, knowing that thou wilt also do more than I say.

22. But withal prepare me also a lodging: for I trust that through your prayers I shall be given unto you.

23. There salute thee Epaphras, my fellowprisoner in Christ Jesus;

24. Marcus, Aristarchus, Demas, Lucas, my fellowlabourers.

25. The grace of our Lord Jesus Christ be with your spirit. Amen.

Philemon—Paul's timeless and universal counsel is a refreshing review of our gospel obligations to follow the Savior in all that we do, to remember that the name of Christ is the only name under which salvation and exaltation can be obtained, and to perform with full devotion our obligations and responsibilities as the Saints and the elect of God. Paul's injunction to "work out your own salvation with fear and trembling" (Philip. 2:12)—under the aegis and power of the Atonement—is reminiscent of what Amulek had taught nearly a century previous: "And now, my beloved brethren, I desire that ye should remember these things, and that ye should work out your salvation with fear before God, and that ye should no more deny the coming of Christ" (Alma 34:37; compare Morm. 9:27). Nephi, as well, had taught the primacy of the redemption of grace, which alone can assure salvation, after we have performed to our maximum ability the works of righteousness essential to please God: "For we labor diligently to write, to persuade our children, and also our brethren, to believe in Christ, and to be reconciled to God; for we know that it is by grace that we are saved, after all we can do" (2 Ne. 25:23). Through these and every other word of God we find the sustenance and strength needed for our transformation from the old to the new, from the proud and self-centered to the humble and receptive, and from drifting and lost to the secure and reclaimed of the Lord.

THE EPISTLE OF PAUL THE APOSTLE TO THE

HEBREWS

CHAPTER 1

1. God, who at sundry times and in divers manners spake in time past unto the fathers by the prophets,
2. Hath in these last days spoken unto us by his Son, whom he hath appointed heir of all things, by whom also he made the worlds;
3. Who being the brightness of his glory, and the express image of his person, and upholding all things by the word of his power, when he had by himself purged our sins, sat down on the right hand of the Majesty on high;
4. Being made so much better than the angels, as he hath by inheritance obtained a more excellent name than they.
5. For unto which of the angels said he at any time, Thou art my Son, this day have I begotten thee? And again, I will be to him a Father, and he shall be to me a Son?
6. And again, when he bringeth in the firstbegotten into the world, he saith, And let all the angels of God worship him.
7. And of the angels he saith, Who maketh his angels spirits, and his ministers a flame of fire.
8. But unto the Son he saith, Thy throne, O God, is for ever and ever: a sceptre of righteousness is the sceptre of thy kingdom.
9. Thou hast loved righteousness, and hated iniquity; therefore God, even thy God, hath anointed thee with the oil of gladness above thy fellows.
10. And, Thou, Lord, in the beginning hast laid the foundation of the earth; and the heavens are the works of thine hands:
11. They shall perish; but thou remainest; and they all shall wax old as doth a garment;
12. And as a vesture shalt thou fold

Hebrews—Jesus Christ is our only hope of salvation and eternal life. He was the Creator, the promised Messiah, the Only Begotten Son of God in the flesh, and the Anointed One who would atone for all mankind—who, through obedience to His commandments, can return to the presence of our Heavenly Father. Paul reminds us of our total dependence on our Savior Jesus Christ: "Looking unto Jesus the author and finisher of our faith; who for the joy that was set before him endured the cross, despising the shame, and is set down at the right hand of the throne of God" (Heb. 12:2). Through Jesus Christ, as the "author of eternal salvation unto all them that obey him" (Heb. 5:9), we can enter into God's rest. In bringing forth the new and higher covenant of salvation, the Lord restored the Melchizedek Priesthood (see Heb. 7:11). The law of Moses was fulfilled, and the gospel of Jesus Christ, with its new covenant, was established in the dispensation of the meridian of time. By exercising faith in Jesus Christ and entering into the higher law of grace and reconciliation, one could, by keeping the commandments, inherit the kingdom of God.

Heb. 1—"Christ is the Author of Salvation. This means that he made salvation available to all men in that he worked out the infinite and eternal atonement. Paul's statement that Christ is 'the author of eternal salvation unto all them that obey him' (Heb. 5:9), as the marginal reading shows, means that he is the 'cause' thereof; that is, salvation is possible because of his atoning sacrifice; without this sacrifice there would be no salvation. Paul's other statement that Christ is 'the author and finisher of our faith' (Heb. 12:2), also according to the marginal reading, means that he is the 'leader' in the cause of salvation" (Bruce R. McConkie, *Mormon Doctrine*, 66).

them up, and they shall be changed: but thou art the same, and thy years shall not fail.

13. But to which of the angels said he at any time, Sit on my right hand, until I make thine enemies thy footstool?

14. Are they not all ministering spirits, sent forth to minister for them who shall be heirs of salvation?

CHAPTER 2

1. Therefore we ought to give the more earnest heed to the things which we have heard, lest at any time we should let them slip.

2. For if the word spoken by angels was stedfast, and every transgression and disobedience received a just recompence of reward;

3. How shall we escape, if we neglect so great salvation; which at the first began to be spoken by the Lord, and was confirmed unto us by them that heard him;

4. God also bearing them witness, both with signs and wonders, and with divers miracles, and gifts of the Holy Ghost, according to his own will?

5. For unto the angels hath he not put in subjection the world to come, whereof we speak.

6. But one in a certain place testified, saying, What is man, that thou art mindful of him? or the son of man, that thou visitest him?

7. Thou madest him a little lower than the angels; thou crownedst him with glory and honour, and didst set him over the works of thy hands:

8. Thou hast put all things in subjection under his feet. For in that he put all in subjection under him, he left nothing that is not put under him. But now we see not yet all things put under him.

9. But we see Jesus, who was made a little lower than the angels for the suffering of death, crowned with glory and honour; that he by the grace of God should taste death for every man.

10. For it became him, for whom are all things, and by whom are all things, in bringing many sons unto glory, to make the captain of their salvation perfect through sufferings.

11. For both he that sanctifieth and they who are sanctified are all of one: for which cause he is not ashamed to call them brethren,

12. Saying, I will declare thy name unto my brethren, in the midst of the church will I sing praise unto thee.

13. And again, I will put my trust in him. And again, Behold I and the children which God hath given me.

14. Forasmuch then as the children are partakers of flesh and blood, he also himself likewise took part of the same; that through death he might destroy him that had the power of death, that is, the devil;

15. And deliver them who through

Heb. 1:1–3 — Sometime shortly after A.D. 60, at the end of his third mission, Paul wrote the epistle to the Hebrews—intended for the Jewish members of the Church—to confirm the doctrines and practices of the higher gospel law of Jesus Christ that had superseded the law of Moses. Many generations of tradition regarding the former ways of worship and religious practice were, for some, apparently, difficult to abandon. They had given themselves over to being "zealous of the law" (Acts 21:20) and needed redirection and refocusing on the truth that the work of Moses was a preparatory work pointing to the ministry and Atonement of the Savior. Paul provided in Hebrews an elegant and carefully crafted discourse on the mission of the Savior, incorporating numerous references from the Old Testament to substantiate the fact that the atoning sacrifice and the institution of the higher law was the fulfillment of centuries of prophetic anticipation.

The brief opening chapter of Hebrews is a superb and moving portrait of the Savior that begins:

"God, who at sundry times and in divers manners spake in time past unto the fathers by the prophets,

"Hath in these last days spoken unto us by his Son, whom he hath appointed heir of all things, by whom also he made the worlds;

"Who being the brightness of his glory, and the express image of his person, and upholding all things by the word of his power, when he had by himself purged our sins, sat down on the right hand of the Majesty on high" (Heb. 1:1–3).

The sublime language of this portrayal, which is extended and expanded in the subsequent chapters of Hebrews, stimulates readers to ask themselves the questions: "If I were asked to provide a characterization of the Savior from the depths of my heart, how would I render my feelings? How would I express my innermost convictions of the divinity and everlasting power of this magnificent Being?" Paul's language and treatment of this sacred subject provide a splendid model for us to follow.

Some analysts have thought the literary style of Hebrews to be somewhat different from that used in the other epistles of Paul; however, the Bible Dictionary says that the ideas are certainly Paul's (see 746). His authoritative leadership helped to stabilize the community of Saints in his day, uphold the doctrines and truths of the higher law, and testify through the Spirit of the truth of Christ's atoning mission—all in ways that still touch the hearts of believers and resound to the glory of God and the Son.

fear of death were all their lifetime subject to bondage.

16. For verily he took not on him the nature of angels; but he took on him the seed of Abraham.

17. Wherefore in all things it behoved him to be made like unto his brethren, that he might be a merciful and faithful high priest in things pertaining to God, to make reconciliation for the sins of the people.

18. For in that he himself hath suffered being tempted, he is able to succour them that are tempted.

CHAPTER 3

1. Wherefore, holy brethren, partakers of the heavenly calling, consider the Apostle and High Priest of our profession, Christ Jesus;

2. Who was faithful to him that appointed him, as also Moses was faithful in all his house.

3. For this man was counted worthy of more glory than Moses, inasmuch as he who hath builded the house hath more honour than the house.

4. For every house is builded by some man; but he that built all things is God.

5. And Moses verily was faithful in all his house, as a servant, for a testimony of those things which were to be spoken after;

6. But Christ as a son over his own house; whose house are we, if we hold fast the confidence and the rejoicing of the hope firm unto the end.

7. Wherefore (as the Holy Ghost saith, To day if ye will hear his voice,

8. Harden not your hearts, as in the provocation, in the day of temptation in the wilderness:

9. When your fathers tempted me, proved me, and saw my works forty years.

10. Wherefore I was grieved with that generation, and said, They do alway err in their heart; and they have not known my ways.

11. So I sware in my wrath, They shall not enter into my rest.)

12. Take heed, brethren, lest there be in any of you an evil heart of unbelief, in departing from the living God.

13. But exhort one another daily, while it is called To day; lest any of you be hardened through the deceitfulness of sin.

14. For we are made partakers of Christ, if we hold the beginning of our confidence stedfast unto the end;

15. While it is said, To day if ye will hear his voice, harden not your hearts, as in the provocation.

16. For some, when they had heard, did provoke: howbeit not all that came out of Egypt by Moses.

17. But with whom was he grieved forty years? was it not with them that had sinned, whose carcases fell in the wilderness?

Heb. 3— In chapter three of his epistle to the Hebrews, Paul invites his audience to consider the sacred office and calling of Jesus Christ (see Heb. 3:1–4). Paul then cites the words of the Lord to the ancient Israelites whereby He excluded the adults among them from entering into the promised land because they had "provoked" Him through disobedience (see Num. 14:21–23; compare Jacob 1:7–8; Alma 12:36), then applies this doctrine to his own audience: "For we are made partakers of Christ, if we hold the beginning of our confidence stedfast unto the end; While it is said, To day if ye will hear his voice, harden not your hearts, as in the provocation" (Heb. 3:14–15). Enjoining the Jewish Saints to exercise faith in the Savior, Paul goes on to confirm the divine calling of Jesus: "And no man taketh this honour unto himself, but he that is called of God, as was Aaron. So also Christ glorified not himself to be made an high priest; but he that said unto him, Thou art my Son, to day have I begotten thee. As he saith also in another place, Thou art a priest for ever after the order of Melchisedec" (Heb. 5:4–6). As such, Jesus became the author of salvation for mankind: "Though he were a Son, yet learned he obedience by the things which he suffered; And being made perfect, he became the author of eternal salvation unto all them that obey him" (Heb. 5:8–9).

As high priest after the order of Melchizedek, and author of eternal salvation, the Savior administers the unfolding majesty of the kingdom of God through the power and authority of the Melchizedek Priesthood, which transcends the office and function of the Levitical or Aaronic Priesthood: "And it is yet far more evident: for that after the similitude of Melchisedec there ariseth another priest, Who is made, not after the law of a carnal commandment, but after the power of an endless life. For he testifieth, Thou art a priest for ever after the order of Melchisedec. . . . For the law made nothing perfect, but the bringing in of a better hope did; by the which we draw nigh unto God" (Heb. 7:15–17, 19). It is through the power and authority of the higher priesthood that the new covenant of the gospel plan is put into effect (see Heb. 8).

18. And to whom sware he that they should not enter into his rest, but to them that believed not?

19. So we see that they could not enter in because of unbelief.

CHAPTER 4

1. Let us therefore fear, lest, a promise being left us of entering into his rest, any of you should seem to come short of it.

2. For unto us was the gospel preached, as well as unto them: but the word preached did not profit them, not being mixed with faith in them that heard it.

3. For we which have believed do enter into rest, as he said, As I have sworn in my wrath, if they shall enter into my rest: although the works were finished from the foundation of the world.

4. For he spake in a certain place of the seventh day on this wise, And God did rest the seventh day from all his works.

5. And in this place again, If they shall enter into my rest.

6. Seeing therefore it remaineth that some must enter therein, and they to whom it was first preached entered not in because of unbelief:

7. Again, he limiteth a certain day, saying in David, To day, after so long a time; as it is said, To day if ye will hear his voice, harden not your hearts.

8. For if Jesus had given them rest, then would he not afterward have spoken of another day.

9. There remaineth therefore a rest to the people of God.

10. For he that is entered into his rest, he also hath ceased from his own works, as God did from his.

11. Let us labour therefore to enter into that rest, lest any man fall after the same example of unbelief.

12. For the word of God is quick, and powerful, and sharper than any two-edged sword, piercing even to the dividing asunder of soul and spirit, and of the joints and marrow, and is a discerner of the thoughts and intents of the heart.

13. Neither is there any creature that is not manifest in his sight: but all things are naked and opened unto the eyes of him with whom we have to do.

14. Seeing then that we have a great high priest, that is passed into the heavens, Jesus the Son of God, let us hold fast our profession.

15. For we have not an high priest which cannot be touched with the feeling of our infirmities; but was in all points tempted like as we are, yet without sin.

16. Let us therefore come boldly unto the throne of grace, that we may obtain mercy, and find grace to help in time of need.

Heb. 3:1—Our Savior is referred to as being a High Priest forever after the order of Melchizedek. In this context, let us not forget the following scriptural explanation:

"There are, in the church, two priesthoods, namely, the Melchizedek and Aaronic, including the Levitical Priesthood.

"Why the first is called the Melchizedek Priesthood is because Melchizedek was such a great high priest.

"*Before his day it was called the Holy Priesthood, after the Order of the Son of God.*

"But out of respect or reverence to the name of the Supreme Being, to avoid the too frequent repetition of his name, they, the church, in ancient days, called that priesthood after Melchizedek, or the Melchizedek Priesthood.

"All other authorities or offices in the church are appendages to this priesthood" (D&C 107:1–5; emphasis added).

CHAPTER 5

1. For every high priest taken from among men is ordained for men in things pertaining to God, that he may offer both gifts and sacrifices for sins:

2. Who can have compassion on the ignorant, and on them that are out of the way; for that he himself also is compassed with infirmity.

3. And by reason hereof he ought, as for the people, so also for himself, to offer for sins.

4. And no man taketh this honour unto himself, but he that is called of God, as was Aaron.

5. So also Christ glorified not himself to be made an high priest; but he that said unto him, Thou art my Son, to day have I begotten thee.

6. As he saith also in another place, Thou art a priest for ever after the order of Melchisedec.

7. Who in the days of his flesh, when he had offered up prayers and supplications with strong crying and tears unto him that was able to save him from death, and was heard in that he feared;

8. Though he were a Son, yet learned he obedience by the things which he suffered;

9. And being made perfect, he became the author of eternal salvation unto all them that obey him;

10. Called of God an high priest after the order of Melchisedec.

11. Of whom we have many things to say, and hard to be uttered, seeing ye are dull of hearing.

12. For when for the time ye ought to be teachers, ye have need that one teach you again which be the first principles of the oracles of God; and are become such as have need of milk, and not of strong meat.

13. For every one that useth milk is unskilful in the word of righteousness: for he is a babe.

14. But strong meat belongeth to them that are of full age, even those who by reason of use have their senses exercised to discern both good and evil.

CHAPTER 6

1. Therefore leaving the principles of the doctrine of Christ, let us go on unto perfection; not laying again

Heb. 3—Let us remember that the purpose of our Savior is to assist us in doing all we can to bring about our immortality and eternal life. Our purpose is to center our lives on our Savior Jesus Christ and His gospel plan. As we live the gospel and receive the sacred ordinances of the temple, we come to know our Savior and can receive the blessings of exaltation. We hope and pray for all mankind to come unto Christ, that they may partake of His goodness and eventually return to our heavenly home in the celestial kingdom, blessed with the presence of both Father and Son.

Here are some ideas to help us understand and apply the principles and doctrines concerning how to know, accept, love, and follow Christ:

1. Know and accept that Jesus is the Christ—the Savior and Redeemer of the world.

• Search the scriptures, for they testify of Christ. The word of God testifies of Christ (see John 5:39). As we learn of Christ through His words, we will enjoy His peace (see D&C 19:23). The prophets and the scriptures speak of God and Christ (see Alma 30:44). The Book of Mormon is to convince the world that Jesus is the Christ (see title page of the Book of Mormon).

• Seek revelation from God. We can know that Jesus is the Christ by the power of revelation (see Matt. 16:17). The Holy Ghost will give us this knowledge (see 1 Cor. 12:3). Through our prayers, we can learn the truth of all things (see Moro. 10:5).

• Do the will of God and you will know of the truthfulness of the doctrine of Christ. When we live the doctrine of Christ, we will know the Author (see John 7:17).

• All things testify of God and Christ. The magnificent creation speaks of God (see Alma 30:44).

2. Love our Savior Jesus Christ.

• Remember the goodness of our Savior at all times. Everything the Lord has done for us, including the infinite Atonement, is because He loves us (see 2 Ne. 26:24). We should love Him because He first loved us (see 1 Jn. 4:19). Does this not fill our hearts with gratitude?

• Remember that He succors us in all things. The Savior suffered so He would be able to help us according to the flesh (see Alma 7:11–12). The Savior blesses us in all things. We truly are indebted to Him for our very lives (see Mosiah 2:21). Surely this should inspire us to keep the commandments (see

the foundation of repentance from dead works, and of faith toward God,

2. Of the doctrine of baptisms, and of laying on of hands, and of resurrection of the dead, and of eternal judgment.

3. And this will we do, if God permit.

4. For it is impossible for those who were once enlightened, and have tasted of the heavenly gift, and were made partakers of the Holy Ghost,

5. And have tasted the good word of God, and the powers of the world to come,

6. If they shall fall away, to renew them again unto repentance; seeing they crucify to themselves the Son of God afresh, and put him to an open shame.

7. For the earth which drinketh in the rain that cometh oft upon it, and bringeth forth herbs meet for them by whom it is dressed, receiveth blessing from God:

8. But that which beareth thorns and briers is rejected, and is nigh unto cursing; whose end is to be burned.

9. But, beloved, we are persuaded better things of you, and things that accompany salvation, though we thus speak.

10. For God is not unrighteous to forget your work and labour of love, which ye have shewed toward his name, in that ye have ministered to the saints, and do minister.

11. And we desire that every one of you do shew the same diligence to the full assurance of hope unto the end:

12. That ye be not slothful, but followers of them who through faith and patience inherit the promises.

13. For when God made promise to Abraham, because he could swear by no greater, he sware by himself,

14. Saying, Surely blessing I will bless thee, and multiplying I will multiply thee.

15. And so, after he had patiently endured, he obtained the promise.

16. For men verily swear by the greater: and an oath for confirmation is to them an end of all strife.

17. Wherein God, willing more abundantly to shew unto the heirs of promise the immutability of his counsel, confirmed it by an oath:

18. That by two immutable things, in which it was impossible for God to lie, we might have a strong consolation, who have fled for refuge to lay hold upon the hope set before us:

19. Which hope we have as an anchor of the soul, both sure and stedfast, and which entereth into that within the veil;

20. Whither the forerunner is for us entered, even Jesus, made an high priest for ever after the order of Melchisedec.

Mosiah 2:22), because when we love Him, we will keep His commandments (see John 14:15).

3. Follow our Savior Jesus Christ.
• In accepting the principles of the gospel of Jesus Christ, we "come unto Him." Through faith, repentance, baptism, and receiving the Holy Ghost, we take upon ourselves the name of Jesus Christ. We become His sons and daughters (see Mosiah 5:7). These are the first steps in following our Savior. As we endure to the end, we can be perfected and enter into our exaltation (see 3 Ne. 12:48; Moro. 10:32).
• We live by the word of God. We live by every word of our Lord and Savior (see D&C 84:43–46), and the Word will tell us all things that we should do (see 2 Ne. 32:3).
• We seek to build up the kingdom of God. As members of the Church, we seek to magnify our callings (see JST, Matt. 6:38) by bringing souls unto Christ (see Alma 29:9–10; Alma 36:24), strengthening our brothers and sisters (see D&C 108:7), and entering into our temple covenants for our eternal blessing and that of our forebears through vicarious service (see D&C 128:15).

CHAPTER 7

1. For this Melchisedec, king of Salem, priest of the most high God, who met Abraham returning from the slaughter of the kings, and blessed him;

2. To whom also Abraham gave a tenth part of all; first being by interpretation King of righteousness, and after that also King of Salem, which is, King of peace;

3. Without father, without mother, without descent, having neither beginning of days, nor end of life; but made like unto the Son of God; abideth a priest continually.

4. Now consider how great this man was, unto whom even the patriarch Abraham gave the tenth of the spoils.

5. And verily they that are of the sons of Levi, who receive the office of the priesthood, have a commandment to take tithes of the people according to the law, that is, of their brethren, though they come out of the loins of Abraham:

6. But he whose descent is not counted from them received tithes of Abraham, and blessed him that had the promises.

7. And without all contradiction the less is blessed of the better.

8. And here men that die receive tithes; but there he receiveth them, of whom it is witnessed that he liveth.

9. And as I may so say, Levi also, who receiveth tithes, payed tithes in Abraham.

10. For he was yet in the loins of his father, when Melchisedec met him.

11. If therefore perfection were by the Levitical priesthood, (for under it the people received the law,) what further need was there that another priest should rise after the order of Melchisedec, and not be called after the order of Aaron?

12. For the priesthood being changed, there is made of necessity a change also of the law.

13. For he of whom these things are spoken pertaineth to another tribe, of which no man gave attendance at the altar.

14. For it is evident that our Lord sprang out of Juda; of which tribe Moses spake nothing concerning priesthood.

15. And it is yet far more evident: for that after the similitude of Melchisedec there ariseth another priest,

16. Who is made, not after the law of a carnal commandment, but after the power of an endless life.

17. For he testifieth, Thou art a priest for ever after the order of Melchisedec.

18. For there is verily a disannulling of the commandment going before for the weakness and unprofitableness thereof.

19. For the law made nothing perfect, but the bringing in of a better hope did; by the which we draw nigh unto God.

20. And inasmuch as not without an oath he was made priest:

21. (For those priests were made without an oath; but this with an oath by him that said unto him, The Lord sware and will not repent,

Melchisedek holding up his hands and blessing Abraham

Thou art a priest for ever after the order of Melchisedec:)

22. By so much was Jesus made a surety of a better testament.

23. And they truly were many priests, because they were not suffered to continue by reason of death:

24. But this man, because he continueth ever, hath an unchangeable priesthood.

25. Wherefore he is able also to save them to the uttermost that come unto God by him, seeing he ever liveth to make intercession for them.

26. For such an high priest became us, who is holy, harmless, undefiled, separate from sinners, and made higher than the heavens;

27. Who needeth not daily, as those high priests, to offer up sacrifice, first for his own sins, and then for the people's: for this he did once, when he offered up himself.

28. For the law maketh men high priests which have infirmity; but the word of the oath, which was since the law, maketh the Son, who is consecrated for evermore.

CHAPTER 8

1. Now of the things which we have spoken this is the sum: We have such an high priest, who is set on the right hand of the throne of the Majesty in the heavens;

2. A minister of the sanctuary, and of the true tabernacle, which the Lord pitched, and not man.

3. For every high priest is ordained to offer gifts and sacrifices: wherefore it is of necessity that this man have somewhat also to offer.

4. For if he were on earth, he should not be a priest, seeing that there are priests that offer gifts according to the law:

5. Who serve unto the example and shadow of heavenly things, as Moses was admonished of God when he was about to make the tabernacle: for, See, saith he, that thou make all things according to the pattern shewed to thee in the mount.

6. But now hath he obtained a more excellent ministry, by how much also he is the mediator of a better covenant, which was established upon better promises.

7. For if that first covenant had been faultless, then should no place have been sought for the second.

8. For finding fault with them, he saith, Behold, the days come, saith the Lord, when I will make a new covenant with the house of Israel and with the house of Judah:

9. Not according to the covenant that I made with their fathers in the day when I took them by the hand

Notes: _____

_____

_____

_____

_____

_____

_____

_____

_____

_____

_____

_____

_____

_____

_____

_____

_____

_____

_____

_____

_____

Heb. 8:6–10 — Paul, with his superb command of the law and the prophets of the Old Testament, invokes for his audience the precise references to energize them around a spiritual commitment to Jesus Christ as "the mediator of a better covenant, which was established upon better promises" (Heb. 8:6). Citing Jeremiah, Paul characterizes the new covenant as follows:

"Behold, the days come, saith the Lord, when I will make a new covenant with the house of Israel and with the house of Judah:

"Not according to the covenant that I made with their fathers in the day when I took them by the hand to lead them out of the land of Egypt; because they continued not in my covenant, and I regarded them not, saith the Lord.

"For this is the covenant that I will make with the house of Israel after those days, saith the Lord; I will put my laws into their mind, and write them in their hearts: and I will be to them a God, and they shall be to me a people" (Heb. 8:8–10; compare Jer. 31:31–33).

to lead them out of the land of Egypt; because they continued not in my covenant, and I regarded them not, saith the Lord.

10. For this is the covenant that I will make with the house of Israel after those days, saith the Lord; I will put my laws into their mind, and write them in their hearts: and I will be to them a God, and they shall be to me a people:

11. And they shall not teach every man his neighbour, and every man his brother, saying, Know the Lord: for all shall know me, from the least to the greatest.

12. For I will be merciful to their unrighteousness, and their sins and their iniquities will I remember no more.

13. In that he saith, A new covenant, he hath made the first old. Now that which decayeth and waxeth old is ready to vanish away.

CHAPTER 9

1. Then verily the first covenant had also ordinances of divine service, and a worldly sanctuary.

2. For there was a tabernacle made; the first, wherein was the candlestick, and the table, and the shewbread; which is called the sanctuary.

3. And after the second veil, the tabernacle which is called the Holiest of all;

4. Which had the golden censer, and the ark of the covenant overlaid round about with gold, wherein was the golden pot that had manna, and Aaron's rod that budded, and the tables of the covenant;

5. And over it the cherubims of glory shadowing the mercyseat; of which we cannot now speak particularly.

6. Now when these things were thus ordained, the priests went always into the first tabernacle, accomplishing the service of God.

7. But into the second went the high priest alone once every year, not without blood, which he offered for himself, and for the errors of the people:

8. The Holy Ghost this signifying, that the way into the holiest of all was not yet made manifest, while as the first tabernacle was yet standing:

9. Which was a figure for the time then present, in which were offered both gifts and sacrifices, that could not make him that did the service perfect, as pertaining to the conscience;

10. Which stood only in meats and drinks, and divers washings, and carnal ordinances, imposed on them until the time of reformation.

11. But Christ being come an high priest of good things to come, by a greater and more perfect tabernacle, not made with hands, that is to say, not of this building;

12. Neither by the blood of goats and calves, but by his own blood he

Heb. 9—"To the Hebrews, whose practice it then was to shed the blood of animals in blood sacrifices, Paul taught that all Mosaic sacrifices were in fact similitudes of the coming sacrifice of the Messiah. He showed them that under both the old and the new covenants sins are purged only 'with blood,' and that 'without shedding of blood is no remission.' His witness was that 'the blood of Christ, who . . . offered himself without spot to God,' was the only thing that would purge men from 'dead works' and evil deeds and enable them 'to serve the living God' and gain salvation in his kingdom" (Bruce R. McConkie, *The Promised Messiah*, 254).

Heb. 9:11–22—Under the new covenant Paul taught the people (see Heb. 8:8–10), the ceremonial sacrifice of animals as under the Mosaic law—instituted to prefigure the Atonement of the Savior—is fulfilled through and superseded by the divine sacrifice of the Son of God:

"But Christ being come an high priest of good things to come, by a greater and more perfect tabernacle, not made with hands, that is to say, not of this building;

"Neither by the blood of goats and calves, but by his own blood he entered in once into the holy place, having obtained eternal redemption for us. . . .

"And for this cause he is the mediator of the new testament, that by means of death, for the redemption of the transgressions that were under the first testament, they which are called might receive the promise of eternal inheritance.

"For where a testament is, there must also of necessity be the death of the testator. . . .

"And almost all things are by the law purged with blood; and without shedding of blood is no remission" (Heb. 9:11–12, 15–16, 22).

entered in once into the holy place, having obtained eternal redemption for us.

13. For if the blood of bulls and of goats, and the ashes of an heifer sprinkling the unclean, sanctifieth to the purifying of the flesh:

14. How much more shall the blood of Christ, who through the eternal Spirit offered himself without spot to God, purge your conscience from dead works to serve the living God?

15. And for this cause he is the mediator of the new testament, that by means of death, for the redemption of the transgressions that were under the first testament, they which are called might receive the promise of eternal inheritance.

16. For where a testament is, there must also of necessity be the death of the testator.

17. For a testament is of force after men are dead: otherwise it is of no strength at all while the testator liveth.

18. Whereupon neither the first testament was dedicated without blood.

19. For when Moses had spoken every precept to all the people according to the law, he took the blood of calves and of goats, with water, and scarlet wool, and hyssop, and sprinkled both the book, and all the people,

20. Saying, This is the blood of the testament which God hath enjoined unto you.

21. Moreover he sprinkled with blood both the tabernacle, and all the vessels of the ministry.

22. And almost all things are by the law purged with blood; and without shedding of blood is no remission.

23. It was therefore necessary that the patterns of things in the heavens should be purified with these; but the heavenly things themselves with better sacrifices than these.

24. For Christ is not entered into the holy places made with hands, which are the figures of the true; but into heaven itself, now to appear in the presence of God for us:

25. Nor yet that he should offer himself often, as the high priest entereth into the holy place every year with blood of others;

26. For then must he often have suffered since the foundation of the world: but now once in the end of the world hath he appeared to put away sin by the sacrifice of himself.

27. And as it is appointed unto men once to die, but after this the judgment:

28. So Christ was once offered to bear the sins of many; and unto them that look for him shall he appear the second time without sin unto salvation.

I am the Resurrection and the Life

CHAPTER 10

1. For the law having a shadow of good things to come, and not the very image of the things, can never with those sacrifices which they offered year by year continually make the comers thereunto perfect.

2. For then would they not have ceased to be offered? because that the worshippers once purged should have had no more conscience of sins.

3. But in those sacrifices there is a remembrance again made of sins every year.

4. For it is not possible that the blood of bulls and of goats should take away sins.

5. Wherefore when he cometh into the world, he saith, Sacrifice and offering thou wouldest not, but a body hast thou prepared me:

6. In burnt offerings and sacrifices for sin thou hast had no pleasure.

7. Then said I, Lo, I come (in the volume of the book it is written of me,) to do thy will, O God.

8. Above when he said, Sacrifice and offering and burnt offerings and offering for sin thou wouldest not, neither hadst pleasure therein; which are offered by the law;

9. Then said he, Lo, I come to do thy will, O God. He taketh away the first, that he may establish the second.

10. By the which will we are sanctified through the offering of the body of Jesus Christ once for all.

11. And every priest standeth daily ministering and offering oftentimes the same sacrifices, which can never take away sins:

12. But this man, after he had offered one sacrifice for sins for ever, sat down on the right hand of God;

13. From henceforth expecting till his enemies be made his footstool.

14. For by one offering he hath perfected for ever them that are sanctified.

15. Whereof the Holy Ghost also is a witness to us: for after that he had said before,

16. This is the covenant that I will make with them after those days, saith the Lord, I will put my laws into their hearts, and in their minds will I write them;

17. And their sins and iniquities will I remember no more.

18. Now where remission of these is, there is no more offering for sin.

19. Having therefore, brethren, boldness to enter into the holiest by the blood of Jesus,

20. By a new and living way, which he hath consecrated for us, through the veil, that is to say, his flesh;

21. And having an high priest over the house of God;

22. Let us draw near with a true heart in full assurance of faith, having our hearts sprinkled from an evil conscience, and our bodies washed with pure water.

Notes: _____

_____

_____

_____

_____

_____

_____

_____

_____

_____

_____

_____

_____

_____

_____

_____

_____

_____

_____

Heb. 10:16–23 — Paul concluded the part of his epistle dealing with the new covenant with an admonition to honor and partake of that new covenant.

23. Let us hold fast the profession of our faith without wavering; (for he is faithful that promised;)

24. And let us consider one another to provoke unto love and to good works:

25. Not forsaking the assembling of ourselves together, as the manner of some is; but exhorting one another: and so much the more, as ye see the day approaching.

26. For if we sin wilfully after that we have received the knowledge of the truth, there remaineth no more sacrifice for sins,

27. But a certain fearful looking for of judgment and fiery indignation, which shall devour the adversaries.

28. He that despised Moses' law died without mercy under two or three witnesses:

29. Of how much sorer punishment, suppose ye, shall he be thought worthy, who hath trodden under foot the Son of God, and hath counted the blood of the covenant, wherewith he was sanctified, an unholy thing, and hath done despite unto the Spirit of grace?

30. For we know him that hath said, Vengeance belongeth unto me, I will recompense, saith the Lord. And again, The Lord shall judge his people.

31. It is a fearful thing to fall into the hands of the living God.

32. But call to remembrance the former days, in which, after ye were illuminated, ye endured a great fight of afflictions;

33. Partly, whilst ye were made a gazingstock both by reproaches and afflictions; and partly, whilst ye became companions of them that were so used.

34. For ye had compassion of me in my bonds, and took joyfully the spoiling of your goods, knowing in yourselves that ye have in heaven a better and an enduring substance.

35. Cast not away therefore your confidence, which hath great recompence of reward.

36. For ye have need of patience, that, after ye have done the will of God, ye might receive the promise.

37. For yet a little while, and he that shall come will come, and will not tarry.

38. Now the just shall live by faith: but if any man draw back, my soul shall have no pleasure in him.

39. But we are not of them who draw back unto perdition; but of them that believe to the saving of the soul.

CHAPTER 11

1. Now faith is the substance of things hoped for, the evidence of things not seen.

2. For by it the elders obtained a good report.

3. Through faith we understand that the worlds were framed by the word of God, so that things which

Heb. 11:1—By exercising faith in the Lord Jesus Christ, we have a belief and hope of things not seen that are true (see also Alma 32:21), we are moved to action (see James 2:18), and we have power to do all things according to the will of God (see Heb. 11; Ether 12).

are seen were not made of things which do appear.

4. By faith Abel offered unto God a more excellent sacrifice than Cain, by which he obtained witness that he was righteous, God testifying of his gifts: and by it he being dead yet speaketh.

5. By faith Enoch was translated that he should not see death; and was not found, because God had translated him: for before his translation he had this testimony, that he pleased God.

6. But without faith it is impossible to please him: for he that cometh to God must believe that he is, and that he is a rewarder of them that diligently seek him.

7. By faith Noah, being warned of God of things not seen as yet, moved with fear, prepared an ark to the saving of his house; by the which he condemned the world, and became heir of the righteousness which is by faith.

8. By faith Abraham, when he was called to go out into a place which he should after receive for an inheritance, obeyed; and he went out, not knowing whither he went.

9. By faith he sojourned in the land of promise, as in a strange country, dwelling in tabernacles with Isaac and Jacob, the heirs with him of the same promise:

10. For he looked for a city which hath foundations, whose builder and maker is God.

11. Through faith also Sara herself received strength to conceive seed, and was delivered of a child when she was past age, because she judged him faithful who had promised.

12. Therefore sprang there even of one, and him as good as dead, so many as the stars of the sky in multitude, and as the sand which is by the sea shore innumerable.

13. These all died in faith, not having received the promises, but having seen them afar off, and were persuaded of them, and embraced them, and confessed that they were strangers and pilgrims on the earth.

14. For they that say such things declare plainly that they seek a country.

15. And truly, if they had been mindful of that country from whence they came out, they might have had opportunity to have returned.

16. But now they desire a better country, that is, an heavenly: wherefore God is not ashamed to be called their God: for he hath prepared for them a city.

17. By faith Abraham, when he was tried, offered up Isaac: and he that had received the promises offered up his only begotten son,

18. Of whom it was said, That in Isaac shall thy seed be called:

19. Accounting that God was able to raise him up, even from the dead; from whence also he received him in a figure.

20. By faith Isaac blessed Jacob and Esau concerning things to come.

21. By faith Jacob, when he was a

Heb. 11—The epistle to the Hebrews is remarkable in its breadth of wisdom, grasp of preceding scripture, and compass of doctrine and principle. Almost every sentence and phrase is replete with insight and depth of understanding. The fabric of this composition is singularly marked by precision of detail and economy of expression—all measured and designed to bring about a logical acceptance of the mission and ministry of the Savior and a commitment to live by the precepts of His gospel plan. It is thus amazing that Paul, after having covered with masterful skill the doctrines of the divine Atonement, the function and operation of the Melchizedek Priesthood, and the gospel of the new covenant with the children of God, now gives to us in addition one of the most beautiful and edifying expositions of faith in all of the holy scriptures. "Now faith is the substance of things hoped for, the evidence of things not seen," he begins (Heb. 11:1), continuing with a comprehensive summary of events from Israelite history that illustrate and testify of the power of faith—the fundamental and defining principle of the gospel.

Heb. 11:6—As children of God, our desires are to please Him and do His will. Recognizing this fact makes having and exercising faith in God and the Lord Jesus Christ paramount in our lives. This sentence from Paul's superb treatise on faith captures the covenant power of the principle of faith: by acting in sincere faith, knowing that God lives and loves us, we receive the promised blessing of knowing that we are pleasing Him. As the children of God, our desire is to please Him and do His will. Recognizing this fact makes having and exercising faith in God and the Lord Jesus Christ paramount in our lives. What are your feelings about the connection between your faith and your confidence in having a pleasing relationship with God?

dying, blessed both the sons of Joseph; and worshipped, leaning upon the top of his staff.

22. By faith Joseph, when he died, made mention of the departing of the children of Israel; and gave commandment concerning his bones.

23. By faith Moses, when he was born, was hid three months of his parents, because they saw he was a proper child; and they were not afraid of the king's commandment.

24. By faith Moses, when he was come to years, refused to be called the son of Pharaoh's daughter;

25. Choosing rather to suffer affliction with the people of God, than to enjoy the pleasures of sin for a season;

26. Esteeming the reproach of Christ greater riches than the treasures in Egypt: for he had respect unto the recompence of the reward.

27. By faith he forsook Egypt, not fearing the wrath of the king: for he endured, as seeing him who is invisible.

28. Through faith he kept the passover, and the sprinkling of blood, lest he that destroyed the firstborn should touch them.

29. By faith they passed through the Red sea as by dry land: which the Egyptians assaying to do were drowned.

30. By faith the walls of Jericho fell down, after they were compassed about seven days.

31. By faith the harlot Rahab perished not with them that believed not, when she had received the spies with peace.

32. And what shall I more say? for the time would fail me to tell of Gedeon, and of Barak, and of Samson, and of Jephthae; of David also, and Samuel, and of the prophets:

33. Who through faith subdued kingdoms, wrought righteousness, obtained promises, stopped the mouths of lions,

34. Quenched the violence of fire, escaped the edge of the sword, out of weakness were made strong, waxed valiant in fight, turned to flight the armies of the aliens.

35. Women received their dead raised to life again: and others were tortured, not accepting deliverance; that they might obtain a better resurrection:

36. And others had trial of cruel mockings and scourgings, yea, moreover of bonds and imprisonment:

37. They were stoned, they were sawn asunder, were tempted, were slain with the sword: they wandered about in sheepskins and goatskins; being destitute, afflicted, tormented;

38. (Of whom the world was not worthy:) they wandered in deserts, and in mountains, and in dens and caves of the earth.

39. And these all, having obtained a good report through faith, received not the promise:

40. God having provided some better thing for us, that they without us should not be made perfect.

Notes: _____
_____
_____
_____
_____
_____
_____
_____
_____
_____
_____
_____
_____
_____
_____
_____
_____
_____
_____
_____
_____
_____
_____
_____
_____
_____
_____
_____
_____
_____
_____
_____
_____
_____

CHAPTER 12

1. Wherefore seeing we also are compassed about with so great a cloud of witnesses, let us lay aside every weight, and the sin which doth so easily beset us, and let us run with patience the race that is set before us,

2. Looking unto Jesus the author and finisher of our faith; who for the joy that was set before him endured the cross, despising the shame, and is set down at the right hand of the throne of God.

3. For consider him that endured such contradiction of sinners against himself, lest ye be wearied and faint in your minds.

4. Ye have not yet resisted unto blood, striving against sin.

5. And ye have forgotten the exhortation which speaketh unto you as unto children, My son, despise not thou the chastening of the Lord, nor faint when thou art rebuked of him:

6. For whom the Lord loveth he chasteneth, and scourgeth every son whom he receiveth.

7. If ye endure chastening, God dealeth with you as with sons; for what son is he whom the father chasteneth not?

8. But if ye be without chastisement, whereof all are partakers, then are ye bastards, and not sons.

9. Furthermore we have had fathers of our flesh which corrected us, and we gave them reverence: shall we not much rather be in subjection unto the Father of spirits, and live?

10. For they verily for a few days chastened us after their own pleasure; but he for our profit, that we might be partakers of his holiness.

11. Now no chastening for the present seemeth to be joyous, but grievous: nevertheless afterward it yieldeth the peaceable fruit of righteousness unto them which are exercised thereby.

12. Wherefore lift up the hands which hang down, and the feeble knees;

13. And make straight paths for your feet, lest that which is lame be turned out of the way; but let it rather be healed.

14. Follow peace with all men, and holiness, without which no man shall see the Lord:

15. Looking diligently lest any man fail of the grace of God; lest any root of bitterness springing up trouble you, and thereby many be defiled;

16. Lest there be any fornicator, or profane person, as Esau, who for one morsel of meat sold his birthright.

17. For ye know how that afterward, when he would have inherited the blessing, he was rejected: for he found no place of repentance, though he sought it carefully with tears.

Heb. 12:1–2 — Paul's concluding exhortations on faith contain this spiritual jewel. Paul then admonishes his audience that they should remember to:

• Endure in faith the inevitable process of chastening ("For whom the Lord loveth he chasteneth" — Heb. 12:6).

• Provide charitable service to the needy ("Wherefore lift up the hands which hang down, and the feeble knees" — Heb. 12:12).

• Take their place among "the general assembly and church of the firstborn" (Heb. 12:23).

• Go on to perfection in the Lord ("Make you perfect in every good work to do his will, working in you that which is wellpleasing in his sight, through Jesus Christ; to whom be glory for ever and ever" — Heb. 13:21).

18. For ye are not come unto the mount that might be touched, and that burned with fire, nor unto blackness, and darkness, and tempest,

19. And the sound of a trumpet, and the voice of words; which voice they that heard intreated that the word should not be spoken to them any more:

20. (For they could not endure that which was commanded, And if so much as a beast touch the mountain, it shall be stoned, or thrust through with a dart:

21. And so terrible was the sight, that Moses said, I exceedingly fear and quake:)

22. But ye are come unto mount Sion, and unto the city of the living God, the heavenly Jerusalem, and to an innumerable company of angels,

23. To the general assembly and church of the firstborn, which are written in heaven, and to God the Judge of all, and to the spirits of just men made perfect,

24. And to Jesus the mediator of the new covenant, and to the blood of sprinkling, that speaketh better things than that of Abel.

25. See that ye refuse not him that speaketh. For if they escaped not who refused him that spake on earth, much more shall not we escape, if we turn away from him that speaketh from heaven:

26. Whose voice then shook the earth: but now he hath promised, saying, Yet once more I shake not the earth only, but also heaven.

27. And this word, Yet once more, signifieth the removing of those things that are shaken, as of things that are made, that those things which cannot be shaken may remain.

28. Wherefore we receiving a kingdom which cannot be moved, let us have grace, whereby we may serve God acceptably with reverence and godly fear:

29. For our God is a consuming fire.

CHAPTER 13

1. Let brotherly love continue.

2. Be not forgetful to entertain strangers: for thereby some have entertained angels unawares.

3. Remember them that are in bonds, as bound with them; and them which suffer adversity, as being yourselves also in the body.

4. Marriage is honourable in all, and the bed undefiled: but whoremongers and adulterers God will judge.

5. Let your conversation be without covetousness; and be content with such things as ye have: for he hath said, I will never leave thee, nor forsake thee.

6. So that we may boldly say, The Lord is my helper, and I will not fear what man shall do unto me.

7. Remember them which have the rule over you, who have spoken unto you the word of God: whose faith follow, considering the end of their conversation.

Notes: _____

8. Jesus Christ the same yesterday, and to day, and for ever.

9. Be not carried about with divers and strange doctrines. For it is a good thing that the heart be established with grace; not with meats, which have not profited them that have been occupied therein.

10. We have an altar, whereof they have no right to eat which serve the tabernacle.

11. For the bodies of those beasts, whose blood is brought into the sanctuary by the high priest for sin, are burned without the camp.

12. Wherefore Jesus also, that he might sanctify the people with his own blood, suffered without the gate.

13. Let us go forth therefore unto him without the camp, bearing his reproach.

14. For here have we no continuing city, but we seek one to come.

15. By him therefore let us offer the sacrifice of praise to God continually, that is, the fruit of our lips giving thanks to his name.

16. But to do good and to communicate forget not: for with such sacrifices God is well pleased.

17. Obey them that have the rule over you, and submit yourselves: for they watch for your souls, as they that must give account, that they may do it with joy, and not with grief: for that is unprofitable for you.

18. Pray for us: for we trust we have a good conscience, in all things willing to live honestly.

19. But I beseech you the rather to do this, that I may be restored to you the sooner.

20. Now the God of peace, that brought again from the dead our Lord Jesus, that great shepherd of the sheep, through the blood of the everlasting covenant,

21. Make you perfect in every good work to do his will, working in you that which is wellpleasing in his sight, through Jesus Christ; to whom be glory for ever and ever. Amen.

22. And I beseech you, brethren, suffer the word of exhortation: for I have written a letter unto you in few words.

23. Know ye that our brother Timothy is set at liberty; with whom, if he come shortly, I will see you.

24. Salute all them that have the rule over you, and all the saints. They of Italy salute you.

25. Grace be with you all. Amen.

Heb. 13:8—When the resurrected Savior appeared to Saul of Tarsus as he journeyed on the road to Damascus (Acts 9), He enlisted a true warrior into the ranks of the spiritual leadership of the Church. As Paul the Apostle, this intrepid emissary carried the gospel to the Gentiles and confirmed and strengthened the Jewish Christians as well. The epistle to the Hebrews is a masterpiece of doctrinal wisdom, covering the key topics of the mission and Atonement of Jesus Christ as Savior and Redeemer, the purpose and operation of the Melchizedek Priesthood, the nature and supernal scope of the new covenant between the Father and His children, and the essential role of faith in the grand design of the gospel plan. Let us be grateful that these inspired words of Paul have been preserved to serve as a guide and beacon in our day, reinforcing and confirming the principles of truth again bestowed upon mankind through the latter-day Restoration, and witnessing that "Jesus Christ is the same yesterday, and to day, and for ever" (Heb. 13:8).

Christ as the Good Shepherd

THE GENERAL EPISTLE OF

JAMES

CHAPTER 1

1. James, a servant of God and of the Lord Jesus Christ, to the twelve tribes which are scattered abroad, greeting.
2. My brethren, count it all joy when ye fall into divers temptations;
3. Knowing this, that the trying of your faith worketh patience.
4. But let patience have her perfect work, that ye may be perfect and entire, wanting nothing.
5. If any of you lack wisdom, let him ask of God, that giveth to all men liberally, and upbraideth not; and it shall be given him.
6. But let him ask in faith, nothing wavering. For he that wavereth is like a wave of the sea driven with the wind and tossed.
7. For let not that man think that he shall receive any thing of the Lord.
8. A double minded man is unstable in all his ways.
9. Let the brother of low degree rejoice in that he is exalted:
10. But the rich, in that he is made low: because as the flower of the grass he shall pass away.
11. For the sun is no sooner risen with a burning heat, but it withereth the grass, and the flower thereof falleth, and the grace of the fashion of it perisheth: so also shall the rich man fade away in his ways.
12. Blessed is the man that endureth temptation: for when he is tried, he shall receive the crown of life, which the Lord hath promised to them that love him.
13. Let no man say when he is tempted, I am tempted of God: for God cannot be tempted with evil, neither tempteth he any man:
14. But every man is tempted, when he is drawn away of his own lust, and enticed.
15. Then when lust hath conceived, it bringeth forth sin: and sin, when it is finished, bringeth forth death.
16. Do not err, my beloved brethren.
17. Every good gift and every perfect gift is from above, and cometh down from the Father of lights, with whom is no variableness, neither shadow of turning.

James—The authorship of the general epistle of James is usually attributed to James, brother of the Savior (Gal. 1:19). This James (one of several in the New Testament) was an important Church leader in Jerusalem. His short epistle reflects the grace and conviction of a true believer and is written in an aphoristic style reminiscent of the Proverbs and much of Psalmic writing. A good example of such style is James's maxim about the importance of showing forth patience as servants of God (see James 1:3–4).

James 1:5–6—James gives wise counsel to those who seek the truth. This classic scripture about prayer was the one that energized the young Joseph Smith to inquire of the Lord in his quest for truth. Heavenly Father will give freely to His children as they ask, with no condemnation or scolding. He *wants* us to ask. We can pray in humility, with real intent, having faith, truly revealing our innermost thoughts, and knowing that He loves us and will help us. What wisdom do you currently lack about how to bless your loved ones? In what areas do you need divine attention and assistance? How can you best approach your merciful Father in Heaven for guidance?

James later warns his audience to not neglect the proper spiritual framework when they pray: "Ye ask, and receive not, because ye ask amiss, that ye may consume it upon your lusts" (James 4:3). His counsel is to ask in charity and purity: "Confess your faults one to another, and pray one for another, that ye may be healed. The effectual fervent prayer of a righteous man availeth much" (James 5:16).

James 1:12—James began his general epistle by encouraging people to pray for guidance and the strength to resist temptation. Those who repel the tempter and endure all things well on earth will be exalted with a crown of glory. How are you able to encourage your loved ones to keep in mind the rewards of being faithful? The superficial pleasures of life are eclipsed by the eternal joys that await those who pass the tests of life with honor.

18. Of his own will begat he us with the word of truth, that we should be a kind of firstfruits of his creatures.

19. Wherefore, my beloved brethren, let every man be swift to hear, slow to speak, slow to wrath:

20. For the wrath of man worketh not the righteousness of God.

21. Wherefore lay apart all filthiness and superfluity of naughtiness, and receive with meekness the engrafted word, which is able to save your souls.

22. But be ye doers of the word, and not hearers only, deceiving your own selves.

23. For if any be a hearer of the word, and not a doer, he is like unto a man beholding his natural face in a glass:

24. For he beholdeth himself, and goeth his way, and straightway forgetteth what manner of man he was.

25. But whoso looketh into the perfect law of liberty, and continueth therein, he being not a forgetful hearer, but a doer of the work, this man shall be blessed in his deed.

26. If any man among you seem to be religious, and bridleth not his tongue, but deceiveth his own heart, this man's religion is vain.

27. Pure religion and undefiled before God and the Father is this, To visit the fatherless and widows in their affliction, and to keep himself unspotted from the world.

CHAPTER 2

1. My brethren, have not the faith of our Lord Jesus Christ, the Lord of glory, with respect of persons.

2. For if there come unto your assembly a man with a gold ring, in goodly apparel, and there come in also a poor man in vile raiment;

3. And ye have respect to him that weareth the gay clothing, and say unto him, Sit thou here in a good place; and say to the poor, Stand thou there, or sit here under my footstool:

4. Are ye not then partial in yourselves, and are become judges of evil thoughts?

5. Hearken, my beloved brethren, Hath not God chosen the poor of this world rich in faith, and heirs of the kingdom which he hath promised to them that love him?

6. But ye have despised the poor. Do not rich men oppress you, and draw you before the judgment seats?

7. Do not they blaspheme that worthy name by the which ye are called?

8. If ye fulfil the royal law according to the scripture, Thou shalt love thy neighbour as thyself, ye do well:

James 1:19—Listen . . . don't judge. Be patient . . . don't react. Think . . . before you speak. Never yell or scream . . . unless the house is burning down or life is in danger. Remember . . . charity never faileth.

James 1:22–25, 27—James here preaches a most practical kind of religion—one that reflects compassion for one's fellows, translated into action and follow-through. For James, the measure of religion comes in the record of one's charitable deeds performed in righteousness, as reflected in this celebrated passage: "Pure religion and undefiled before God and the Father is this, To visit the fatherless and widows in their affliction, and to keep himself unspotted from the world" (James 1:27).

James—In his general epistle, James outlines a series of key doctrines leading to salvation and happiness, including prayer, patience, kindness, moderation in speech, and faith through good works. The virtue of patience is of primary importance in becoming like our Savior Jesus Christ. Patience is part of His divine nature. To emulate His example of patience is of great importance in enduring affliction, achieving spiritual success, and in dealing with people in productive and helpful ways. This does not mean that we are permissive, easily manipulated, or readily taken advantage of. Rather, patience truly signifies a level of maturity that ennobles one's character. Patience, like perseverance, is a governing virtue of success—success in all facets of life. This can be exhibited as we pray in faith and willingly accept the answer from Heavenly Father. The prayer of faith is heard and will be answered (see James 1:5–6).

As we gain strength from the Lord, we can become spiritually minded and even Spirit-directed in all things and thus gain self-mastery. We have the power, through the Spirit, to control our lives. This can be demonstrated as we begin to act as Christ would act and do as He would do. We would show our faith in Jesus Christ by our works. We would be doers of the word (see James 1:22).

9. But if ye have respect to persons, ye commit sin, and are convinced of the law as transgressors.

10. For whosoever shall keep the whole law, and yet offend in one point, he is guilty of all.

11. For he that said, Do not commit adultery, said also, Do not kill. Now if thou commit no adultery, yet if thou kill, thou art become a transgressor of the law.

12. So speak ye, and so do, as they that shall be judged by the law of liberty.

13. For he shall have judgment without mercy, that hath shewed no mercy; and mercy rejoiceth against judgment.

14. What doth it profit, my brethren, though a man say he hath faith, and have not works? can faith save him?

15. If a brother or sister be naked, and destitute of daily food,

16. And one of you say unto them, Depart in peace, be ye warmed and filled; notwithstanding ye give them not those things which are needful to the body; what doth it profit?

17. Even so faith, if it hath not works, is dead, being alone.

18. Yea, a man may say, Thou hast faith, and I have works: shew me thy faith without thy works, and I will shew thee my faith by my works.

19. Thou believest that there is one God; thou doest well: the devils also believe, and tremble.

20. But wilt thou know, O vain man, that faith without works is dead?

21. Was not Abraham our father justified by works, when he had offered Isaac his son upon the altar?

22. Seest thou how faith wrought with his works, and by works was faith made perfect?

23. And the scripture was fulfilled which saith, Abraham believed God, and it was imputed unto him for righteousness: and he was called the Friend of God.

24. Ye see then how that by works a man is justified, and not by faith only.

25. Likewise also was not Rahab the harlot justified by works, when she had received the messengers, and had sent them out another way?

26. For as the body without the spirit is dead, so faith without works is dead also.

CHAPTER 3

1. My brethren, be not many masters, knowing that we shall receive the greater condemnation.

2. For in many things we offend all. If any man offend not in word, the

James 2:18–22—As James here points out, good works can be taken as a measure of one's faith. What kinds of good works are singled out? Among others, ministering to the needs of the sick ("Is any sick among you? let him call for the elders of the church; and let them pray over him, anointing him with oil in the name of the Lord: And the prayer of faith shall save the sick, and the Lord shall raise him up; and if he have committed sins, they shall be forgiven him"—James 5:14–15), and bringing the gospel into the lives of God's children ("Brethren, if any of you do err from the truth, and one convert him; Let him know, that he which converteth the sinner from the error of his way shall save a soul from death, and shall hide a multitude of sins"—James 5:19–20).

President Spencer W. Kimball taught, "Faith is the power behind good works. The exercising of faith is a willingness to accept without total regular proof and to move forward and perform works. 'Faith without works is dead' (James 2:26), and a dead faith will not lead one to move forward to adjust a life or to serve valiantly. A real faith pushes one forward to constructive and beneficial acts as though he knew in absoluteness" (*Teachings of Spencer W. Kimball,* 71–72).

James 2:26—The celebrated counsel of James concerning the need to be an exemplar of righteous service is a reminder that faith is power unto action (see James 2:17–18). Good works and charitable service are at the heart of a covenant life. Faith is power leading to good works. As you observe others around you and note that many are demonstrating admirable works of service, what does that say about the strength of their faith? How do your own acts of service provide a measure of your own faith in the truths of the gospel?

James 2:22–26—Our works personify our faith. If one has little or no faith in Jesus Christ, there will be lack of good works. Let us remember that faith is the seedbed for good works and the precursor of all righteousness.

same is a perfect man, and able also to bridle the whole body.

3. Behold, we put bits in the horses' mouths, that they may obey us; and we turn about their whole body.

4. Behold also the ships, which though they be so great, and are driven of fierce winds, yet are they turned about with a very small helm, whithersoever the governor listeth.

5. Even so the tongue is a little member, and boasteth great things. Behold, how great a matter a little fire kindleth!

6. And the tongue is a fire, a world of iniquity: so is the tongue among our members, that it defileth the whole body, and setteth on fire the course of nature; and it is set on fire of hell.

7. For every kind of beasts, and of birds, and of serpents, and of things in the sea, is tamed, and hath been tamed of mankind:

8. But the tongue can no man tame; it is an unruly evil, full of deadly poison.

9. Therewith bless we God, even the Father; and therewith curse we men, which are made after the similitude of God.

10. Out of the same mouth proceedeth blessing and cursing. My brethren, these things ought not so to be.

11. Doth a fountain send forth at the same place sweet water and bitter?

12. Can the fig tree, my brethren, bear olive berries? either a vine, figs? so can no fountain both yield salt water and fresh.

13. Who is a wise man and endued with knowledge among you? let him shew out of a good conversation his works with meekness of wisdom.

14. But if ye have bitter envying and strife in your hearts, glory not, and lie not against the truth.

15. This wisdom descendeth not from above, but is earthly, sensual, devilish.

16. For where envying and strife is, there is confusion and every evil work.

17. But the wisdom that is from above is first pure, then peaceable, gentle, and easy to be intreated, full of mercy and good fruits, without partiality, and without hypocrisy.

18. And the fruit of righteousness is sown in peace of them that make peace.

CHAPTER 4

1. From whence come wars and fightings among you? come they not hence, even of your lusts that war in your members?

2. Ye lust, and have not: ye kill, and desire to have, and cannot obtain: ye fight and war, yet ye have not, because ye ask not.

3. Ye ask, and receive not, because ye ask amiss, that ye may consume it upon your lusts.

4. Ye adulterers and adulteresses,

James 3:4–5—Among the teachings included in James is this admonition to avoid contention and verbal abuse. Rather than kindle this kind of destructive fire, James encourages us to seek after the peaceable fire of the Spirit: "But the wisdom that is from above is first pure, then peaceable, gentle, and easy to be intreated, full of mercy and good fruits, without partiality, and without hypocrisy. And the fruit of righteousness is sown in peace of them that make peace" (James 3:17–18). Humility is the divine quality we should strive to cultivate: "But he giveth more grace. Wherefore he saith, God resisteth the proud, but giveth grace unto the humble. Submit yourselves therefore to God. Resist the devil, and he will flee from you. Draw nigh to God, and he will draw nigh to you. Cleanse your hands, ye sinners; and purify your hearts, ye double minded" (James 4:6–8).

President Ezra Taft Benson taught, "If a man does not control his temper, it is a sad admission that he is not in control of his thoughts. He then becomes a victim of his own passions and emotions, which leads him to actions that are totally unfit for civilized behavior, let alone behavior for a priesthood holder" (*Teachings of Ezra Taft Benson*, 446).

Notes: _____

know ye not that the friendship of the world is enmity with God? whosoever therefore will be a friend of the world is the enemy of God.

5. Do ye think that the scripture saith in vain, The spirit that dwelleth in us lusteth to envy?

6. But he giveth more grace. Wherefore he saith, God resisteth the proud, but giveth grace unto the humble.

7. Submit yourselves therefore to God. Resist the devil, and he will flee from you.

8. Draw nigh to God, and he will draw nigh to you. Cleanse your hands, ye sinners; and purify your hearts, ye double minded.

9. Be afflicted, and mourn, and weep: let your laughter be turned to mourning, and your joy to heaviness.

10. Humble yourselves in the sight of the Lord, and he shall lift you up.

11. Speak not evil one of another, brethren. He that speaketh evil of his brother, and judgeth his brother, speaketh evil of the law, and judgeth the law: but if thou judge the law, thou art not a doer of the law, but a judge.

12. There is one lawgiver, who is able to save and to destroy: who art thou that judgest another?

13. Go to now, ye that say, To day or to morrow we will go into such a city, and continue there a year, and buy and sell, and get gain:

14. Whereas ye know not what shall be on the morrow. For what is your life? It is even a vapour, that appeareth for a little time, and then vanisheth away.

15. For that ye ought to say, If the Lord will, we shall live, and do this, or that.

16. But now ye rejoice in your boastings: all such rejoicing is evil.

17. Therefore to him that knoweth to do good, and doeth it not, to him it is sin.

CHAPTER 5

1. Go to now, ye rich men, weep and howl for your miseries that shall come upon you.

2. Your riches are corrupted, and your garments are motheaten.

3. Your gold and silver is cankered; and the rust of them shall be a witness against you, and shall eat your flesh as it were fire. Ye have heaped treasure together for the last days.

4. Behold, the hire of the labourers who have reaped down your fields, which is of you kept back by fraud, crieth: and the cries of them which have reaped are entered into the ears of the Lord of sabaoth.

5. Ye have lived in pleasure on the earth, and been wanton; ye have nourished your hearts, as in a day of slaughter.

James 1 — James wrote in his general epistle to the twelve tribes: "But be ye doers of the word, and not hearers only, deceiving your own selves. . . . But whoso looketh into the perfect law of liberty, and continueth therein, he being not a forgetful hearer, but a doer of the work, this man shall be blessed in his deed" (James 1:22, 25). The Church and kingdom of God is the ideal and indispensable venue for learning and practicing this doctrine. Every Sunday, for instance, members of the Church have the singular opportunity to participate in the sacrament, a blessing and an opportunity of exceptional depth and reverence. As I watch those young men each week bear the vessels of the Lord with such humility and care, I am constantly reminded of the compassion of the Lord in allowing His young sons the sacred privilege of becoming His service representatives on earth, valiant future leaders in training. Alma taught that priesthood callings to the Saints were of very ancient date, being initiated in the premortal existence "according to the foreknowledge of God, on account of their exceeding faith and good works" (Alma 13:3). That being the case, we can view these stalwart, young Aaronic Priesthood brethren as fulfilling a destiny of the most extraordinary kind, being part of the elite corps of priesthood servants called "after the order of the Son, the Only Begotten of the Father" (Alma 13:9).

Alma explained that being called after the order of the Son imparts to the recipients a unique perspective, one that is forward-looking and future-centered (see Alma 13:16). What a marvelous blessing for these young men participating in the sacrament and other priesthood duties to be called after the order of Christ and thus have placed upon them this forward-viewing template of righteousness. Thus the priesthood that has been conferred upon them allows them, by its very nature (being named after the order of the Son), to look forward with hope and joy to a continual remission of their sins according to the laws of faith and repentance. Through this ordination, they can view through the eye of faith their ultimate state of becoming the literal sons of God, who will one day receive a reward of glory and immortality in keeping with Alma's admonition: "Having faith on the Lord; having a hope that ye shall receive eternal life; having the love of God always in your hearts, that ye may be lifted up at the last day and enter into his rest" (Alma 13:29).

By the same token, the Lord allows all of us — men, women, and children — to look forward with hope to the blessings of a future domicile in the mansions of heaven as part of the eternal family of God.

6. Ye have condemned and killed the just; and he doth not resist you.

7. Be patient therefore, brethren, unto the coming of the Lord. Behold, the husbandman waiteth for the precious fruit of the earth, and hath long patience for it, until he receive the early and latter rain.

8. Be ye also patient; stablish your hearts: for the coming of the Lord draweth nigh.

9. Grudge not one against another, brethren, lest ye be condemned: behold, the judge standeth before the door.

10. Take, my brethren, the prophets, who have spoken in the name of the Lord, for an example of suffering affliction, and of patience.

11. Behold, we count them happy which endure. Ye have heard of the patience of Job, and have seen the end of the Lord; that the Lord is very pitiful, and of tender mercy.

12. But above all things, my brethren, swear not, neither by heaven, neither by the earth, neither by any other oath: but let your yea be yea; and your nay, nay; lest ye fall into condemnation.

13. Is any among you afflicted? let him pray. Is any merry? let him sing psalms.

14. Is any sick among you? let him call for the elders of the church; and let them pray over him, anointing him with oil in the name of the Lord:

15. And the prayer of faith shall save the sick, and the Lord shall raise him up; and if he have committed sins, they shall be forgiven him.

16. Confess your faults one to another, and pray one for another, that ye may be healed. The effectual fervent prayer of a righteous man availeth much.

17. Elias was a man subject to like passions as we are, and he prayed earnestly that it might not rain: and it rained not on the earth by the space of three years and six months.

18. And he prayed again, and the heaven gave rain, and the earth brought forth her fruit.

19. Brethren, if any of you do err from the truth, and one convert him;

20. Let him know, that he which converteth the sinner from the error of his way shall save a soul from death, and shall hide a multitude of sins.

The pathway toward that supernal goal is illuminated with the light of faith in Jesus and marked with the milestones of service to family, community, and those seeking the truth. As James declared: "Yea, a man may say, Thou hast faith, and I have works: shew me thy faith without thy works, and I will shew thee my faith by my works" (James 2:18). In just that same way, the vision of any believer who practices a practical faith—faith unto good works—extends forward into the future of his or her spiritual possibilities, the ultimate goal of which is our reunion with our Father in Heaven and His Only Begotten Son.

James 5:11—James reminds us, in the spirit of grace and devotion, to endure affliction with patience, to pray to God in faith, to exercise temperance and self-control, and to continually show forth our faith to the Lord through the performance of worthy and charitable service. Above all, we are to endure to the end in valor and righteousness: "Behold, we count them happy which endure. Ye have heard of the patience of Job, and have seen the end of the Lord; that the Lord is very pitiful, and of tender mercy" (James 5:11). That we may endure in patience and honor is our goal under the guidance of the Spirit and through the blessings of perfecting grace.

THE FIRST EPISTLE GENERAL OF

PETER

CHAPTER 1

1. Peter, an apostle of Jesus Christ, to the strangers scattered throughout Pontus, Galatia, Cappadocia, Asia, and Bithynia,

2. Elect according to the foreknowledge of God the Father, through sanctification of the Spirit, unto obedience and sprinkling of the blood of Jesus Christ: Grace unto you, and peace, be multiplied.

3. Blessed be the God and Father of our Lord Jesus Christ, which according to his abundant mercy hath begotten us again unto a lively hope by the resurrection of Jesus Christ from the dead,

4. To an inheritance incorruptible, and undefiled, and that fadeth not away, reserved in heaven for you,

5. Who are kept by the power of God through faith unto salvation ready to be revealed in the last time.

6. Wherein ye greatly rejoice, though now for a season, if need be, ye are in heaviness through manifold temptations:

7. That the trial of your faith, being much more precious than of gold that perisheth, though it be tried with fire, might be found unto praise and honour and glory at the appearing of Jesus Christ:

8. Whom having not seen, ye love; in whom, though now ye see him not, yet believing, ye rejoice with joy unspeakable and full of glory:

9. Receiving the end of your faith, even the salvation of your souls.

10. Of which salvation the prophets have inquired and searched diligently, who prophesied of the grace that should come unto you:

11. Searching what, or what manner of time the Spirit of Christ which was in them did signify, when it testified beforehand the sufferings of Christ, and the glory that should follow.

12. Unto whom it was revealed, that not unto themselves, but unto us they did minister the things, which are now reported unto you by them that have preached the gospel unto you with the Holy Ghost sent down from heaven; which things the angels desire to look into.

13. Wherefore gird up the loins of your mind, be sober, and hope to

1 Pet. 1—The Apostle Peter wrote the first of his two extant epistles around A.D. 64, probably from Rome, in the wake of the persecutions of Christians under Nero's tenure. The first epistle is addressed (as also the second, presumably) to the Saints in "Pontus, Galatia, Cappadocia, Asia, and Bithynia" (1 Pet. 1:1), located in what is now Asia Minor. The agenda is to provide fortification and encouragement to those under intense pressure to deny the Lord and disavow their covenants. The message of Peter in his epistles is infused with a stirring spirit of courage and is composed of mighty threads of doctrine woven into a fabric of unsurpassed doctrinal power. According to the Prophet Joseph Smith, "Peter penned the most sublime language of any of the apostles" (*History of the Church,* 5:392).

Peter reminds the Saints of their noble heritage and encourages them to rise to their grand potential (see 1 Pet. 1:7–9).

Notes: _____

_____

_____

_____

_____

_____

_____

_____

_____

_____

_____

_____

_____

_____

_____

_____

_____

_____

_____

_____

the end for the grace that is to be brought unto you at the revelation of Jesus Christ;

14. As obedient children, not fashioning yourselves according to the former lusts in your ignorance:

15. But as he which hath called you is holy, so be ye holy in all manner of conversation;

16. Because it is written, Be ye holy; for I am holy.

17. And if ye call on the Father, who without respect of persons judgeth according to every man's work, pass the time of your sojourning here in fear:

18. Forasmuch as ye know that ye were not redeemed with corruptible things, as silver and gold, from your vain conversation received by tradition from your fathers;

19. But with the precious blood of Christ, as of a lamb without blemish and without spot:

20. Who verily was foreordained before the foundation of the world, but was manifest in these last times for you,

21. Who by him do believe in God, that raised him up from the dead, and gave him glory; that your faith and hope might be in God.

22. Seeing ye have purified your souls in obeying the truth through the Spirit unto unfeigned love of the brethren, see that ye love one another with a pure heart fervently:

23. Being born again, not of corruptible seed, but of incorruptible, by the word of God, which liveth and abideth for ever.

24. For all flesh is as grass, and all the glory of man as the flower of grass. The grass withereth, and the flower thereof falleth away:

25. But the word of the Lord endureth for ever. And this is the word which by the gospel is preached unto you.

CHAPTER 2

1. Wherefore laying aside all malice, and all guile, and hypocrisies, and envies, and all evil speakings,

2. As newborn babes, desire the sincere milk of the word, that ye may grow thereby:

3. If so be ye have tasted that the Lord is gracious.

4. To whom coming, as unto a living stone, disallowed indeed of men, but chosen of God, and precious,

5. Ye also, as lively stones, are built up a spiritual house, an holy priesthood, to offer up spiritual sacrifices, acceptable to God by Jesus Christ.

6. Wherefore also it is contained in

1 Pet. 2:3–7, 9–10, 17—Peter lifts the vision of the Saints to a realization of who they truly are with this proclamation: "But ye are a chosen generation, a royal priesthood, an holy nation, a peculiar people; that ye should shew forth the praises of him who hath called you out of darkness into his marvellous light: Which in time past were not a people, but are now the people of God: which had not obtained mercy, but now have obtained mercy" (1 Pet. 2:9–10).

No longer isolated and strangers, the Saints are an integral part of the kingdom of God, with a heavenly commission to stand for truth and right (see 1 Pet. 2:3–7).

As such, these Saints are to honor their allegiance to God and the Son while serving their fellows in charity and remaining productive citizens in the jurisdictions of their domicile: "Honour all men. Love the brotherhood. Fear God. Honour the king" (1 Pet. 2:17).

President Gordon B. Hinckley taught the following about being a chosen generation: "This is the greatest generation in the history of the world. How wonderful to be born at this time in the history of the earth. . . . 'A chosen generation.' You're not just here by chance. You are here under the design of God" (*Teachings of Gordon B. Hinckley,* 719–20).

1 Pet. 1:22–25—Peter, himself no stranger to suffering and persecution, was motivated by a fervent desire to strengthen his fellowcitizens in the household of God as they encountered the inevitable campaign of retribution and torment from their detractors. The highest model to be emulated, he confirmed, is the Savior (see 1 Pet. 1:7–9). In the midst of persecution, the Saints are to treat one another with a full measure of kindness and support, according to the word of truth (see 1 Pet. 1:22–25). As Christ, though perfect, suffered beyond all comprehension for all mankind, so must we endure in patience the burdens placed on us (see 1 Pet. 2:21–25).

the scripture, Behold, I lay in Sion a chief corner stone, elect, precious: and he that believeth on him shall not be confounded.

7. Unto you therefore which believe he is precious: but unto them which be disobedient, the stone which the builders disallowed, the same is made the head of the corner,

8. And a stone of stumbling, and a rock of offence, even to them which stumble at the word, being disobedient: whereunto also they were appointed.

9. But ye are a chosen generation, a royal priesthood, an holy nation, a peculiar people; that ye should shew forth the praises of him who hath called you out of darkness into his marvellous light:

10. Which in time past were not a people, but are now the people of God: which had not obtained mercy, but now have obtained mercy.

11. Dearly beloved, I beseech you as strangers and pilgrims, abstain from fleshly lusts, which war against the soul;

12. Having your conversation honest among the Gentiles: that, whereas they speak against you as evildoers, they may by your good works, which they shall behold, glorify God in the day of visitation.

13. Submit yourselves to every ordinance of man for the Lord's sake: whether it be to the king, as supreme;

14. Or unto governors, as unto them that are sent by him for the punishment of evildoers, and for the praise of them that do well.

15. For so is the will of God, that with well doing ye may put to silence the ignorance of foolish men:

16. As free, and not using your liberty for a cloke of maliciousness, but as the servants of God.

17. Honour all men. Love the brotherhood. Fear God. Honour the king.

18. Servants, be subject to your masters with all fear; not only to the good and gentle, but also to the froward.

19. For this is thankworthy, if a man for conscience toward God endure grief, suffering wrongfully.

20. For what glory is it, if, when ye be buffeted for your faults, ye shall take it patiently? but if, when ye do well, and suffer for it, ye take it patiently, this is acceptable with God.

1 Pet. 2:9—"We have one Lord, one faith, one baptism. In fulfillment of the words of Peter, we are 'a chosen generation, a royal priesthood, an holy nation, a peculiar people; that [we] should shew forth the praises of him who hath called [us] out of darkness into his marvellous light' (1 Pet. 2:9). . . .

"No matter where we are, no matter our circumstances, we all can be faithful Latter-day Saints. We can pray and worship the Lord in the privacy of our own closet. We can sing anthems of praise to the Almighty even when we are alone. We can study the scriptures. We can live the gospel. We can pay our tithes and offerings though the amount be ever so small. We can walk in faith. We can strive to live lives patterned after the life of our Master" (Gordon B. Hinckley, *Ensign,* Nov. 1998, 4–5).

We have been ransomed by the Lord. We are His people. We have a responsibility to teach by precept and example the Lord Jesus Christ. He has brought us into the light of His gospel; therefore, we should seek to bring others into the light of the Lord.

21. For even hereunto were ye called: because Christ also suffered for us, leaving us an example, that ye should follow his steps:

22. Who did no sin, neither was guile found in his mouth:

23. Who, when he was reviled, reviled not again; when he suffered, he threatened not; but committed himself to him that judgeth righteously:

24. Who his own self bare our sins in his own body on the tree, that we, being dead to sins, should live unto righteousness: by whose stripes ye were healed.

25. For ye were as sheep going astray; but are now returned unto the Shepherd and Bishop of your souls.

CHAPTER 3

1. Likewise, ye wives, be in subjection to your own husbands; that, if any obey not the word, they also may without the word be won by the conversation of the wives;

2. While they behold your chaste conversation coupled with fear.

3. Whose adorning let it not be that outward adorning of plaiting the hair, and of wearing of gold, or of putting on of apparel;

4. But let it be the hidden man of the heart, in that which is not corruptible, even the ornament of a meek and quiet spirit, which is in the sight of God of great price.

5. For after this manner in the old time the holy women also, who trusted in God, adorned themselves, being in subjection unto their own husbands:

6. Even as Sara obeyed Abraham, calling him lord: whose daughters ye are, as long as ye do well, and are not afraid with any amazement.

7. Likewise, ye husbands, dwell with them according to knowledge, giving honour unto the wife, as unto the weaker vessel, and as being heirs together of the grace of life; that your prayers be not hindered.

8. Finally, be ye all of one mind, having compassion one of another, love as brethren, be pitiful, be courteous:

9. Not rendering evil for evil, or railing for railing: but contrariwise blessing; knowing that ye are thereunto called, that ye should inherit a blessing.

10. For he that will love life, and see good days, let him refrain his tongue from evil, and his lips that they speak no guile:

1 Pet. 2:21–23— As we seek to become like Christ, let us remember to learn to grow even as He did through the things that He suffered (see Heb. 5:8–9).

Peter

11. Let him eschew evil, and do good; let him seek peace, and ensue it.

12. For the eyes of the Lord are over the righteous, and his ears are open unto their prayers: but the face of the Lord is against them that do evil.

13. And who is he that will harm you, if ye be followers of that which is good?

14. But and if ye suffer for righteousness' sake, happy are ye: and be not afraid of their terror, neither be troubled;

15. But sanctify the Lord God in your hearts: and be ready always to give an answer to every man that asketh you a reason of the hope that is in you with meekness and fear:

16. Having a good conscience; that, whereas they speak evil of you, as of evildoers, they may be ashamed that falsely accuse your good conversation in Christ.

17. For it is better, if the will of God be so, that ye suffer for well doing, than for evil doing.

18. For Christ also hath once suffered for sins, the just for the unjust, that he might bring us to God, being put to death in the flesh, but quickened by the Spirit:

19. By which also he went and preached unto the spirits in prison;

20. Which sometime were disobedient, when once the longsuffering of God waited in the days of Noah, while the ark was a preparing, wherein few, that is, eight souls were saved by water.

21. The like figure whereunto even baptism doth also now save us (not the putting away of the filth of the flesh, but the answer of a good conscience toward God,) by the resurrection of Jesus Christ:

22. Who is gone into heaven, and is on the right hand of God; angels and authorities and powers being made subject unto him.

CHAPTER 4

1. Forasmuch then as Christ hath suffered for us in the flesh, arm yourselves likewise with the same mind: for he that hath suffered in the flesh hath ceased from sin;

2. That he no longer should live the rest of his time in the flesh to the

1 Pet. 3:13–20 — Why should we fear men when so great blessings and rewards await those who faithfully honor their covenants with the Lord, for He extends His arm of mercy unto all, even the departed spirits in prison (see 1 Pet. 3:13–20). Thus in patience families should live in harmony and love (see 1 Pet. 3:7–8), feeding the flock of God (see 1 Pet. 5:2–3) and rejoicing in the Lord: "Inasmuch as ye are partakers of Christ's sufferings; that, when his glory shall be revealed, ye may be glad also with exceeding joy. If ye be reproached for the name of Christ, happy are ye; for the spirit of glory and of God resteth upon you" (1 Pet. 4:13–14).

1 Pet. 3:18–20 — These words of Peter confirm the Savior's ministry in the spirit world to provide all individuals with the opportunity to embrace the principles of the gospel of faith, repentance, and — through the coming work of the temples — vicarious ordinances for redemption. Concerning these words from Peter, President Joseph F. Smith pondered, and his eyes were opened to his great vision of the spirit world (see D&C 138). How has the knowledge of temple work served to strengthen your testimony of the mission of the Savior and the perfection of both the Father and the Son?

lusts of men, but to the will of God.

3. For the time past of our life may suffice us to have wrought the will of the Gentiles, when we walked in lasciviousness, lusts, excess of wine, revellings, banquetings, and abominable idolatries:

4. Wherein they think it strange that ye run not with them to the same excess of riot, speaking evil of you:

5. Who shall give account to him that is ready to judge the quick and the dead.

6. For for this cause was the gospel preached also to them that are dead, that they might be judged according to men in the flesh, but live according to God in the spirit.

7. But the end of all things is at hand: be ye therefore sober, and watch unto prayer.

8. And above all things have fervent charity among yourselves: for charity shall cover the multitude of sins.

9. Use hospitality one to another without grudging.

10. As every man hath received the gift, even so minister the same one to another, as good stewards of the manifold grace of God.

11. If any man speak, let him speak as the oracles of God; if any man minister, let him do it as of the ability which God giveth: that God in all things may be glorified through Jesus Christ, to whom be praise and dominion for ever and ever. Amen.

12. Beloved, think it not strange concerning the fiery trial which is to try you, as though some strange thing happened unto you:

13. But rejoice, inasmuch as ye are partakers of Christ's sufferings; that, when his glory shall be revealed, ye may be glad also with exceeding joy.

14. If ye be reproached for the name of Christ, happy are ye; for the spirit of glory and of God resteth upon you: on their part he is evil spoken of, but on your part he is glorified.

15. But let none of you suffer as a murderer, or as a thief, or as an evildoer, or as a busybody in other men's matters.

16. Yet if any man suffer as a Christian, let him not be ashamed; but let him glorify God on this behalf.

17. For the time is come that judgment must begin at the house of God: and if it first begin at us, what shall the end be of them that obey not the gospel of God?

18. And if the righteous scarcely be saved, where shall the ungodly and the sinner appear?

19. Wherefore let them that suffer according to the will of God commit the keeping of their souls to him in well doing, as unto a faithful Creator.

1 Peter—What are some of the wonderful examples Christ set for us? How do we incorporate those examples into our lives? How can we remember to do as Jesus would do?

Knowing is not enough. We are to cultivate the desire to follow Christ in all things. We are to develop a careful and specific plan to become as He is—not just be satisfied with an attitude of casually wanting to be better. Life is full of events that take our mind away from the Lord and our time away from things that matter most. True discipleship takes a concentrated effort . . . we must remember.

The word *remember* or a form of the word occurs frequently throughout the scriptures (occurring in more than 110 verses in the Book of Mormon and Doctrine and Covenants alone). We have made covenants with our Heavenly Father and promised to follow our Savior. It seems as though the power to do good and be good is tied to our ability to remember. The ability to keep sacred things in our minds is part of our covenants—to remember, to bear in mind, to keep in our mind, to recall and retain, and to think back upon these things, that we might remember the goodness of God and keep the commandments. To remember is more than just recalling the thought periodically. It means to always have the principles, doctrines, and covenants in our mind. In remembering, we should think, ponder, and meditate on the things of the Lord—and, in particular, our covenants. This is a key point in living the gospel. "For as he thinketh in his heart, so is he" (Prov. 23:7).

The process of thinking or mental exertion is the beginning point in gaining the vision, which leads to a desire to live the gospel, which in turn leads to actions that bring our visions and desires to fruition.

The catalyst for the transition from thoughts to desire is enhanced as we understand the gospel, appreciate the Lord's blessings, feel gratitude for His atoning sacrifice, and have an overwhelming desire to follow our Savior Jesus Christ. The question, at that point, is one of initiative and self-mastery: Now that we understand the principle, will we remember? Will we follow Jesus Christ in all things?

CHAPTER 5

1. The elders which are among you I exhort, who am also an elder, and a witness of the sufferings of Christ, and also a partaker of the glory that shall be revealed:

2. Feed the flock of God which is among you, taking the oversight thereof, not by constraint, but willingly; not for filthy lucre, but of a ready mind;

3. Neither as being lords over God's heritage, but being ensamples to the flock.

4. And when the chief Shepherd shall appear, ye shall receive a crown of glory that fadeth not away.

5. Likewise, ye younger, submit yourselves unto the elder. Yea, all of you be subject one to another, and be clothed with humility: for God resisteth the proud, and giveth grace to the humble.

6. Humble yourselves therefore under the mighty hand of God, that he may exalt you in due time:

7. Casting all your care upon him; for he careth for you.

8. Be sober, be vigilant; because your adversary the devil, as a roaring lion, walketh about, seeking whom he may devour:

9. Whom resist stedfast in the faith, knowing that the same afflictions are accomplished in your brethren that are in the world.

10. But the God of all grace, who hath called us unto his eternal glory by Christ Jesus, after that ye have suffered a while, make you perfect, stablish, strengthen, settle you.

11. To him be glory and dominion for ever and ever. Amen.

12. By Silvanus, a faithful brother unto you, as I suppose, I have written briefly, exhorting, and testifying that this is the true grace of God wherein ye stand.

13. The church that is at Babylon, elected together with you, saluteth you; and so doth Marcus my son.

14. Greet ye one another with a kiss of charity. Peace be with you all that are in Christ Jesus. Amen.

Notes:

THE SECOND EPISTLE GENERAL OF

PETER

CHAPTER 1

1. Simon Peter, a servant and an apostle of Jesus Christ, to them that have obtained like precious faith with us through the righteousness of God and our Saviour Jesus Christ:

2. Grace and peace be multiplied unto you through the knowledge of God, and of Jesus our Lord,

3. According as his divine power hath given unto us all things that pertain unto life and godliness, through the knowledge of him that hath called us to glory and virtue:

4. Whereby are given unto us exceeding great and precious promises: that by these ye might be partakers of the divine nature, having escaped the corruption that is in the world through lust.

5. And beside this, giving all diligence, add to your faith virtue; and to virtue knowledge;

6. And to knowledge temperance; and to temperance patience; and to patience godliness;

7. And to godliness brotherly kindness; and to brotherly kindness charity.

8. For if these things be in you, and abound, they make you that ye shall neither be barren nor unfruitful in the knowledge of our Lord Jesus Christ.

9. But he that lacketh these things is blind, and cannot see afar off, and hath forgotten that he was purged from his old sins.

10. Wherefore the rather, brethren, give diligence to make your calling and election sure: for if ye do these things, ye shall never fall:

11. For so an entrance shall be ministered unto you abundantly into the everlasting kingdom of our Lord and Saviour Jesus Christ.

12. Wherefore I will not be negligent to put you always in remembrance of these things, though ye know them, and be established in the present truth.

13. Yea, I think it meet, as long as I am in this tabernacle, to stir you up by putting you in remembrance;

14. Knowing that shortly I must put off this my tabernacle, even as our Lord Jesus Christ hath shewed me.

15. Moreover I will endeavour that ye may be able after my decease to

2 Pet. 1—We are a chosen people, a holy nation, a peculiar people with a responsibility to praise and extol the virtues and atoning sacrifice of the Lord Jesus Christ by letting our light shine to all mankind. Once we come to the knowledge of the Lord, we have a duty to follow Him in obedience by honoring His precepts and example. We should go forward in righteousness, living His teachings, regardless of the trials and tribulations that we face. The process of our development in becoming like the Lord—taking upon ourselves His divine nature—is described as adding to one's faith the qualities of virtue, knowledge, temperance, patience, brotherly kindness, godliness, and charity—accomplished with all humility and diligence (see 2 Pet. 1:3–12; D& C 4:6). We then can have our calling and election made sure (see 2 Pet. 1:10), so that when the Lord appears, we will be like Him (see Moro. 7:48). Once we come to the knowledge of the truth and live by the Spirit, we will have the ability to discern truth and error, being better able to resist false teachers and their false doctrines.

2 Pet. 1:3–11—The second epistle of Peter contains the celebrated passage in which the chief Apostle outlines the specific qualities of character that are associated with the divine nature of Christ, which we are commanded to acquire in our inward personalities through earnest and continual striving: "But let it be the hidden man of the heart, in that which is not corruptible, even the ornament of a meek and quiet spirit, which is in the sight of God of great price" (1 Pet. 3:4). Peter's oft-quoted passage about qualities of character is contained in verses 3–11.

These verses give us a list of how to develop in ourselves some of the divine nature of Christ:

Faith. The Prophet Joseph Smith, in the *Lectures on Faith,* describes the three degrees of faith. The first degree is the substance of things hoped for (see *Lectures on Faith* 1:7–8). Of the second degree, the Prophet Joseph said, "Faith is the moving cause of all action in intelligent beings" (*Lectures on Faith* 1:12). The third degree of faith is the principle and source of power (see *Lectures on Faith* 1:15). When all three degrees are applied, faith is exercised to its fullest. "Faith, then, is the first great governing principle which has power, dominion, and authority over all things; by it they exist, by it they are upheld, by it they are changed or by it they remain agreeable to the will of God" (*Lectures on Faith,* 1:24).

Virtue. Virtue has a double meaning. It refers to power (see Mark 5:30) as well as a moral goodness and uprightness in keeping the commandments. (Continued)

have these things always in remembrance.

16. For we have not followed cunningly devised fables, when we made known unto you the power and coming of our Lord Jesus Christ, but were eyewitnesses of his majesty.

17. For he received from God the Father honour and glory, when there came such a voice to him from the excellent glory, This is my beloved Son, in whom I am well pleased.

18. And this voice which came from heaven we heard, when we were with him in the holy mount.

19. We have also a more sure word of prophecy; whereunto ye do well that ye take heed, as unto a light that shineth in a dark place, until the day dawn, and the day star arise in your hearts:

20. Knowing this first, that no prophecy of the scripture is of any private interpretation.

21. For the prophecy came not in old time by the will of man: but holy men of God spake as they were moved by the Holy Ghost.

CHAPTER 2

1. But there were false prophets also among the people, even as there shall be false teachers among you, who privily shall bring in damnable heresies, even denying the Lord that bought them, and bring upon themselves swift destruction.

2. And many shall follow their pernicious ways; by reason of whom the way of truth shall be evil spoken of.

3. And through covetousness shall they with feigned words make merchandise of you: whose judgment now of a long time lingereth not, and their damnation slumbereth not.

4. For if God spared not the angels that sinned, but cast them down to hell, and delivered them into chains of darkness, to be reserved unto judgment;

5. And spared not the old world, but saved Noah the eighth person, a preacher of righteousness, bringing in the flood upon the world of the ungodly;

6. And turning the cities of Sodom and Gomorrha into ashes condemned them with an overthrow, making them an ensample unto those that after should live ungodly;

7. And delivered just Lot, vexed with the filthy conversation of the wicked:

8. (For that righteous man dwelling among them, in seeing and hearing,

Knowledge. Gospel knowledge has to do with eternal truths given by God to man—this is the pure knowledge that can save. This pure knowledge comes by the power of the Holy Ghost. "And by the power of the Holy Ghost ye may know the truth of all things" (Moro. 10:5).

Temperance (Self-control). The trial and test in life is making the body subject to the spirit and in following the principles of the gospel rather than responding only to appetite and emotion.

Patience. The virtue of patience is of primary importance in becoming like our Savior Jesus Christ. Everyone appreciates the patient person. Being patient does not mean that we are permissive, easily manipulated, or readily taken advantage of. Rather, patience truly signifies a level of maturity that ennobles one's character. Patience is an integral part of charity (Moro. 7:44–45).

Brotherly kindness. Kindness requires a character based on gospel principles. It becomes an outward expression of our love of God—a manifestation of a pure heart and genuine concern for others.

Godliness. Godliness implies those qualities associated with our Heavenly Father and our Savior Jesus Christ. We are devout in our worship of God and seek to be Christlike in our everyday behavior—we seek to do as He would do. Godliness has within it the qualities and virtues of God. This should be our goal—in everything we do and in everything we say.

Charity. Charity is the pure love of Christ. His pure love motivated His great sacrifice—the eternal, infinite, vicarious Atonement. When we possess that love, we act in our lives according to the principles of the Atonement.

Humility. Humility is a cardinal virtue of growth, the beginning virtue of exaltation. When we acknowledge and understand our relationship to and dependence on God, we begin to become humble. We will have a broken heart and a contrite spirit. Humility causes one to relate to God in gratitude and love.

Diligence. Diligence is the scriptural term for effort or work. Every blessing we receive is predicated on obedience to the principle on which it is based. In short, we must be diligent in all things (see D&C 75:29). Through diligence on our part and the grace of God we can enjoy the blessings of the Lord.

vexed his righteous soul from day to day with their unlawful deeds;)

9. The Lord knoweth how to deliver the godly out of temptations, and to reserve the unjust unto the day of judgment to be punished:

10. But chiefly them that walk after the flesh in the lust of uncleanness, and despise government. Presumptuous are they, selfwilled, they are not afraid to speak evil of dignities.

11. Whereas angels, which are greater in power and might, bring not railing accusation against them before the Lord.

12. But these, as natural brute beasts, made to be taken and destroyed, speak evil of the things that they understand not; and shall utterly perish in their own corruption;

13. And shall receive the reward of unrighteousness, as they that count it pleasure to riot in the day time. Spots they are and blemishes, sporting themselves with their own deceivings while they feast with you;

14. Having eyes full of adultery, and that cannot cease from sin; beguiling unstable souls: an heart they have exercised with covetous practices; cursed children:

15. Which have forsaken the right way, and are gone astray, following the way of Balaam the son of Bosor, who loved the wages of unrighteousness;

16. But was rebuked for his iniquity: the dumb ass speaking with man's voice forbad the madness of the prophet.

17. These are wells without water, clouds that are carried with a tempest; to whom the mist of darkness is reserved for ever.

18. For when they speak great swelling words of vanity, they allure through the lusts of the flesh, through much wantonness, those that were clean escaped from them who live in error.

19. While they promise them liberty, they themselves are the servants of corruption: for of whom a man is overcome, of the same is he brought in bondage.

20. For if after they have escaped the pollutions of the world through the knowledge of the Lord and Saviour Jesus Christ, they are again entangled therein, and overcome, the latter end is worse with them than the beginning.

21. For it had been better for them not to have known the way of righteousness, than, after they have known it, to turn from the holy commandment delivered unto them.

22. But it is happened unto them according to the true proverb, The dog is turned to his own vomit again; and the sow that was washed to her wallowing in the mire.

2 Pet. 1:19–21, 3:17–18—We should be aware that there are false teachers promulgating false doctrine all around us in various forms of delivery, such as constricted secular teaching, misguided sectarian preachers, and the polluted condition and values of some of the media groups, including certain aspects of the Internet. By being aware of this, we can take steps to fortify ourselves against the evils of the day.

Peter was fully apprised of the coming general Apostasy (see Matt. 24:24). Because of this, he was determined to provide a spiritual shield for his audience, which included, at the forefront, the holy scriptures: "We have also a more sure word of prophecy; whereunto ye do well that ye take heed, as unto a light that shineth in a dark place, until the day dawn, and the day star arise in your hearts: Knowing this first, that no prophecy of the scripture is of any private interpretation. For the prophecy came not in old time by the will of man: but holy men of God spake as they were moved by the Holy Ghost" (2 Pet. 1:19–21).

Through the power of the Holy Ghost, the Saints can deflect the encroachments of evil forces in the world and remain steadfast in the grace of the Lord: "Ye therefore, beloved, seeing ye know these things before, beware lest ye also, being led away with the error of the wicked, fall from your own stedfastness. But grow in grace, and in the knowledge of our Lord and Saviour Jesus Christ. To him be glory both now and for ever" (2 Pet. 3:17–18; compare 2 Pet. 2:1–4).

Jude, the brother of James, also contributed an epistle warning the members of the Church to resist the defectors among the Christian ranks who were allowing the incursion of pagan practices that could destroy the faith. He writes, "Beloved, when I gave all diligence to write unto you of the common salvation, it was needful for me to write unto you, and exhort you that ye should earnestly contend for the faith which was once delivered unto the saints" (Jude 1:3). Since this faith was under attack from evil forces, the Saints are reminded to be on guard: "Keep yourselves in the love of God, looking for the mercy of our Lord Jesus Christ unto eternal life" (Jude 1:21).

CHAPTER 3

1. This second epistle, beloved, I now write unto you; in both which I stir up your pure minds by way of remembrance:

2. That ye may be mindful of the words which were spoken before by the holy prophets, and of the commandment of us the apostles of the Lord and Saviour:

3. Knowing this first, that there shall come in the last days scoffers, walking after their own lusts,

4. And saying, Where is the promise of his coming? for since the fathers fell asleep, all things continue as they were from the beginning of the creation.

5. For this they willingly are ignorant of, that by the word of God the heavens were of old, and the earth standing out of the water and in the water:

6. Whereby the world that then was, being overflowed with water, perished:

7. But the heavens and the earth, which are now, by the same word are kept in store, reserved unto fire against the day of judgment and perdition of ungodly men.

8. But, beloved, be not ignorant of this one thing, that one day is with the Lord as a thousand years, and a thousand years as one day.

9. The Lord is not slack concerning his promise, as some men count slackness; but is longsuffering to us-ward, not willing that any should perish, but that all should come to repentance.

10. But the day of the Lord will come as a thief in the night; in the which the heavens shall pass away with a great noise, and the elements shall melt with fervent heat, the earth also and the works that are therein shall be burned up.

11. Seeing then that all these things shall be dissolved, what manner of persons ought ye to be in all holy conversation and godliness,

12. Looking for and hasting unto the coming of the day of God, wherein the heavens being on fire shall be dissolved, and the elements shall melt with fervent heat?

13. Nevertheless we, according to his promise, look for new heavens and a new earth, wherein dwelleth righteousness.

14. Wherefore, beloved, seeing that ye look for such things, be diligent that ye may be found of him in peace, without spot, and blameless.

15. And account that the longsuffering of our Lord is salvation; even as our beloved brother Paul also according to the wisdom given unto him hath written unto you;

16. As also in all his epistles, speaking in them of these things; in which are some things hard to be understood, which they that are unlearned

2 Pet. 3—"Unless we are on our guard we are in constant danger. This people who are under solemn covenants to keep the commandments of the Lord are threatened by the sins and worldly abominations of this generation, and many among us are liable to be led astray, unless we keep a careful vigil and hedge them about by every means at our command. We have been called out from the world into the kingdom of God, and while we are yet in the world, we are not of the world in the sense that we are under any necessity to partake of their evil customs, and fashions, their follies, false doctrines and theories, which are in conflict with the spirit of truth. . . .

"The man who receives the light of truth and then turns away, loses the light which he had, and if he continues in that course, eventually he will be bound by the chains of spiritual darkness. Darkness will take the place of truth, as the truth becomes gradually dimmed, until he has lost knowledge of spiritual things. He who walks in the light of truth receives more truth until he is glorified in divine truth—the truth that saves" (Joseph Fielding Smith, *Doctrines of Salvation*, 3:294).

and unstable wrest, as they do also the other scriptures, unto their own destruction.

17. Ye therefore, beloved, seeing ye know these things before, beware lest ye also, being led away with the error of the wicked, fall from your own stedfastness.

18. But grow in grace, and in the knowledge of our Lord and Saviour Jesus Christ. To him be glory both now and for ever. Amen.

THE FIRST EPISTLE GENERAL OF

JOHN

CHAPTER 1

1. That which was from the beginning, which we have heard, which we have seen with our eyes, which we have looked upon, and our hands have handled, of the Word of life;

2. (For the life was manifested, and we have seen it, and bear witness, and shew unto you that eternal life, which was with the Father, and was manifested unto us;)

3. That which we have seen and heard declare we unto you, that ye also may have fellowship with us: and truly our fellowship is with the Father, and with his Son Jesus Christ.

4. And these things write we unto you, that your joy may be full.

5. This then is the message which we have heard of him, and declare unto you, that God is light, and in him is no darkness at all.

6. If we say that we have fellowship with him, and walk in darkness, we lie, and do not the truth:

7. But if we walk in the light, as he is in the light, we have fellowship one with another, and the blood of Jesus Christ his Son cleanseth us from all sin.

8. If we say that we have no sin, we deceive ourselves, and the truth is not in us.

9. If we confess our sins, he is faith-

2 Pet. 3:17—We know the truth. Let us therefore be on guard continually to escape the temptations and snares of the devil, which at times seem innocuous, yet stealthily deploy the shackles that can lead us carefully down to hell (see 2 Ne. 28:21). No one is immune—it can happen to the very best. Let us press forward with a steadfastness in Christ.

As a chosen generation of faith and holiness, we are to follow the Savior's example in all we do and, eschewing all false doctrine and preachments, strive to partake of the divine nature of Christ. Faith, virtue, knowledge, temperance, patience, godliness, brotherly kindness, charity, accompanied by humility and diligence—these are the divine attributes that make up the heart of a just and faithful servant of the Lord, one prepared in all things to follow the will of God and rise triumphant as a loyal and devoted disciple of Christ.

1 John–3 John—John is not mentioned in the three epistles that bear his name; however, the style of these epistles is similar to that of the Gospel of John, and the epistles have therefore been attributed to him. It is assumed that the epistles postdate the writing of the Gospel. The first of the epistles is a memorable and moving statement about the love of God for all mankind and the need for us to love one another in that same spirit. "Beloved, let us love one another: for love is of God; and every one that loveth is born of God, and knoweth God. He that loveth not knoweth not God; for God is love" (1 Jn. 4:7–8). We are also warned about a general apostasy and encouraged to stay faithful to the Lord and His cause (see 1 Jn. 2:18–19; 2 Jn. 1:7–8).

ful and just to forgive us our sins, and to cleanse us from all unrighteousness.

10. If we say that we have not sinned, we make him a liar, and his word is not in us.

CHAPTER 2

1. My little children, these things write I unto you, that ye sin not. And if any man sin, we have an advocate with the Father, Jesus Christ the righteous:

2. And he is the propitiation for our sins: and not for ours only, but also for the sins of the whole world.

3. And hereby we do know that we know him, if we keep his commandments.

4. He that saith, I know him, and keepeth not his commandments, is a liar, and the truth is not in him.

5. But whoso keepeth his word, in him verily is the love of God perfected: hereby know we that we are in him.

6. He that saith he abideth in him ought himself also so to walk, even as he walked.

7. Brethren, I write no new commandment unto you, but an old commandment which ye had from the beginning. The old commandment is the word which ye have heard from the beginning.

8. Again, a new commandment I write unto you, which thing is true in him and in you: because the darkness is past, and the true light now shineth.

9. He that saith he is in the light, and hateth his brother, is in darkness even until now.

10. He that loveth his brother abideth in the light, and there is none occasion of stumbling in him.

11. But he that hateth his brother is in darkness, and walketh in darkness, and knoweth not whither he goeth, because that darkness hath blinded his eyes.

12. I write unto you, little children, because your sins are forgiven you for his name's sake.

13. I write unto you, fathers, because ye have known him that is from the beginning. I write unto you, young men, because ye have overcome the wicked one. I write unto you, little children, because ye have known the Father.

14. I have written unto you, fathers, because ye have known him that is from the beginning. I have written unto you, young men, because ye

2 John—Do we know our Heavenly Father? Life eternal is to know Heavenly Father and His Beloved Son. What can we do to know them better?

It is important to know the character of God so that we are not only willing to worship Him but eager to show reverence and obedience to His commands—that we might please Him in all that we do. It is imperative that we understand the following: Our Heavenly Father loves us. We are His children. He is all-powerful (see Ether 3:4). He is all-knowing (see 2 Ne. 9:20). He is in and through all things (see D&C 88:41). The Doctrine and Covenants teaches us: "By these things we know that there is a God in heaven, who is infinite and eternal, from everlasting to everlasting the same unchangeable God, the framer of heaven and earth, and all things which are in them" (D&C 20:17). Heavenly Father is not only unchangeable in His role and dealings with His children, but He is no respecter of persons (see Moro. 8:18; D&C 38:16). His work and His glory are the immortality and eternal life of all of His children (see Moses 1:39).

Having a relationship with God is what life is all about: "And this is life eternal, that they might know thee the only true God, and Jesus Christ, whom thou hast sent" (John 17:3). As we come to know our Heavenly Father and our Savior, we increase in humility, because we know that we are totally dependent on Him for all things. We will seek the will of God and be forever grateful for all things. We will come to know Heavenly Father as we seek Him in mighty prayer, and He will give according to our needs and faith (see D&C 67:10).

are strong, and the word of God abideth in you, and ye have overcome the wicked one.

15. Love not the world, neither the things that are in the world. If any man love the world, the love of the Father is not in him.

16. For all that is in the world, the lust of the flesh, and the lust of the eyes, and the pride of life, is not of the Father, but is of the world.

17. And the world passeth away, and the lust thereof: but he that doeth the will of God abideth for ever.

18. Little children, it is the last time: and as ye have heard that antichrist shall come, even now are there many antichrists; whereby we know that it is the last time.

19. They went out from us, but they were not of us; for if they had been of us, they would no doubt have continued with us: but they went out, that they might be made manifest that they were not all of us.

20. But ye have an unction from the Holy One, and ye know all things.

21. I have not written unto you because ye know not the truth, but because ye know it, and that no lie is of the truth.

22. Who is a liar but he that denieth that Jesus is the Christ? He is antichrist, that denieth the Father and the Son.

23. Whosoever denieth the Son, the same hath not the Father: [but] he that acknowledgeth the Son hath the Father also.

24. Let that therefore abide in you, which ye have heard from the beginning. If that which ye have heard from the beginning shall remain in you, ye also shall continue in the Son, and in the Father.

25. And this is the promise that he hath promised us, even eternal life.

26. These things have I written unto you concerning them that seduce you.

27. But the anointing which ye have received of him abideth in you, and ye need not that any man teach you: but as the same anointing teacheth you of all things, and is truth, and is no lie, and even as it hath taught you, ye shall abide in him.

28. And now, little children, abide in him; that, when he shall appear, we may have confidence, and not be ashamed before him at his coming.

29. If ye know that he is righteous, ye know that every one that doeth righteousness is born of him.

CHAPTER 3

1. Behold, what manner of love the Father hath bestowed upon us, that we should be called the sons of God: therefore the world knoweth us not, because it knew him not.

2. Beloved, now are we the sons of God, and it doth not yet appear what we shall be: but we know that, when he shall appear, we shall be

1 Jn. 1–5— John's epistles validate and expound on the Savior's commandment that we should love one another (see 1 Jn. 4:7; 1 Jn. 4:16–19; 1 Jn. 5:2; see also John 13:34; 15:12, 17). It is this spirit of love—manifested universally through the Father and the Son—that should resonate within us: "And he that keepeth his commandments dwelleth in him, and he in him. And hereby we know that he abideth in us, by the Spirit which he hath given us" (1 Jn. 3:24). By serving others in love, and helping them to come to the Lord in faith, we can experience the profound joy of the gospel: "I have no greater joy than to hear that my children walk in truth" (3 Jn. 1:4).

President Gordon B. Hinckley taught, "This must be the foundation of our instruction: love of God and love for and service to others—neighbors, family, and all with whom we have association. That which we teach must be constantly gauged against these two standards established by the Lord. If we shall do so, this work will continue to roll forward" (*Teachings of Gordon B. Hinckley,* 316–17).

Notes: _____

_____

_____

_____

_____

_____

_____

_____

_____

_____

_____

_____

_____

_____

_____

_____

_____

_____

_____

like him; for we shall see him as he is.

3. And every man that hath this hope in him purifieth himself, even as he is pure.

4. Whosoever committeth sin transgresseth also the law: for sin is the transgression of the law.

5. And ye know that he was manifested to take away our sins; and in him is no sin.

6. Whosoever abideth in him sinneth not: whosoever sinneth hath not seen him, neither known him.

7. Little children, let no man deceive you: he that doeth righteousness is righteous, even as he is righteous.

8. He that committeth sin is of the devil; for the devil sinneth from the beginning. For this purpose the Son of God was manifested, that he might destroy the works of the devil.

9. Whosoever is born of God doth not commit sin; for his seed remaineth in him: and he cannot sin, because he is born of God.

10. In this the children of God are manifest, and the children of the devil: whosoever doeth not righteousness is not of God, neither he that loveth not his brother.

11. For this is the message that ye heard from the beginning, that we should love one another.

12. Not as Cain, who was of that wicked one, and slew his brother. And wherefore slew he him? Because his own works were evil, and his brother's righteous.

13. Marvel not, my brethren, if the world hate you.

14. We know that we have passed from death unto life, because we love the brethren. He that loveth not his brother abideth in death.

15. Whosoever hateth his brother is a murderer: and ye know that no murderer hath eternal life abiding in him.

16. Hereby perceive we the love of God, because he laid down his life for us: and we ought to lay down our lives for the brethren.

17. But whoso hath this world's good, and seeth his brother have need, and shutteth up his bowels of compassion from him, how dwelleth the love of God in him?

18. My little children, let us not love in word, neither in tongue; but in deed and in truth.

19. And hereby we know that we are of the truth, and shall assure our hearts before him.

1 Jn. 3—"Love! The crowning glory of all the attributes of God! We may revel in this attribute. 'He that loveth not, knoweth not God; for God is Love' 'God is Love, and he that dwelleth in love dwelleth in God, and God in him.' 'Every one that loveth is born of God.' 'In this was manifested the Love of God towards us, because that God sent his only begotten Son into the world, that we might live through him. Herein is love, not that we loved God, but that he loved us, and sent his son to be the propitiation for our sins.' 'God so loved the world that he gave his only begotten Son, that whosoever believeth in him should not perish, but have everlasting life.' More perfect evidence than this of love, even God cannot give" (B. H. Roberts, *Seventy's Course in Theology,* 4:75).

Our Heavenly Father and our Savior Jesus Christ love us. We are the spirit children of God, the Eternal Father (see Acts 17:29). We become the children of Christ—since He spiritually begat us—as we accept His gospel (see Mosiah 5:7). The love of the Father is evident: "For God so loved the world, that he gave his only begotten Son, that whosoever believeth in him should not perish, but have everlasting life" (John 3:16). The Savior's love is likewise expressed (see 2 Ne. 26:24). Everything Heavenly Father and our Savior do is for the purpose of bringing to pass our immortality and eternal life (see Moses 1:39). Our gratitude for this great outpouring of love from our Heavenly Father and our Savior can be manifested in many ways: by keeping the commandments (see John 14:15), by doing good unto others (see Matt. 25:40), and by reverently worshipping Heavenly Father in the name of His Beloved Son, Jesus Christ. Our Heavenly Father and His Son have great joy over the soul who repents (see D&C 18:13). There is likewise great joy among our earthly fathers when we are obedient and committed to living the gospel: "I have no greater joy than to hear that my children walk in truth" (see 3 Jn. 1:4).

Love is indeed the motive of every righteous act. The directive is clear (see John 13:34–35). As we contemplate all the commandments and the counsel of the prophets, we see that these words are encapsulated in the two great commandments: "Thou shalt love the Lord thy God with all thy heart, and with all thy soul, and with all thy mind. This is the first and great commandment. And the second is like unto it, Thou shalt love thy neighbour as thyself. On these two commandments hang all the law and the prophets" (Matt. 22:37–40).

20. For if our heart condemn us, God is greater than our heart, and knoweth all things.

21. Beloved, if our heart condemn us not, then have we confidence toward God.

22. And whatsoever we ask, we receive of him, because we keep his commandments, and do those things that are pleasing in his sight.

23. And this is his commandment, That we should believe on the name of his Son Jesus Christ, and love one another, as he gave us commandment.

24. And he that keepeth his commandments dwelleth in him, and he in him. And hereby we know that he abideth in us, by the Spirit which he hath given us.

CHAPTER 4

1. Beloved, believe not every spirit, but try the spirits whether they are of God: because many false prophets are gone out into the world.

2. Hereby know ye the Spirit of God: Every spirit that confesseth that Jesus Christ is come in the flesh is of God:

3. And every spirit that confesseth not that Jesus Christ is come in the flesh is not of God: and this is that spirit of antichrist, whereof ye have heard that it should come; and even now already is it in the world.

4. Ye are of God, little children, and have overcome them: because greater is he that is in you, than he that is in the world.

5. They are of the world: therefore speak they of the world, and the world heareth them.

6. We are of God: he that knoweth God heareth us; he that is not of God heareth not us. Hereby know we the spirit of truth, and the spirit of error.

7. Beloved, let us love one another: for love is of God; and every one that loveth is born of God, and knoweth God.

8. He that loveth not knoweth not God; for God is love.

9. In this was manifested the love of God toward us, because that God sent his only begotten Son into the world, that we might live through him.

10. Herein is love, not that we loved God, but that he loved us, and sent his Son to be the propitiation for our sins.

11. Beloved, if God so loved us, we ought also to love one another.

12. No man hath seen God at any time. If we love one another, God

1 Jn. 4—John bears witness in his epistles that the Savior loves us, as confirmed by His willingness to do the will of the Father: "In this was manifested the love of God toward us, because that God sent his only begotten Son into the world, that we might live through him. Herein is love, not that we loved God, but that he loved us, and sent his Son to be the propitiation for our sins" (1 Jn. 4:9–10; compare 1 Jn. 2:1–3). And further: "Behold, what manner of love the Father hath bestowed upon us, that we should be called the sons of God: therefore the world knoweth us not, because it knew him not. Beloved, now are we the sons of God, and it doth not yet appear what we shall be: but we know that, when he shall appear, we shall be like him; for we shall see him as he is. And every man that hath this hope in him purifieth himself, even as he is pure" (1 Jn. 3:1–3).

1 Jn. 4:7–11—John shared sublime truths about the nature of God and how we can know God through love. The measure of the Father's love for us is His gift of the Lamb of God, given to bring to pass the "immortality and eternal life of man" (Moses 1:39). The measure of our love for God is how we love one another in following the pattern of divine love.

What are your thoughts about love being the key for knowing God? We are taught: "And this is life eternal, that they might know thee the only true God, and Jesus Christ, whom thou hast sent" (John 17:3). Could we interject John's witness by saying, "And this is life eternal, that they might *love, and thereby* know thee the only true God, and Jesus Christ, whom thou hast sent" (John 17:3)? How important, therefore, is love to our eternal salvation?

1 Jn. 4:11—We reflect the love of God for us as we love one another.

dwelleth in us, and his love is perfected in us.

13. Hereby know we that we dwell in him, and he in us, because he hath given us of his Spirit.

14. And we have seen and do testify that the Father sent the Son to be the Saviour of the world.

15. Whosoever shall confess that Jesus is the Son of God, God dwelleth in him, and he in God.

16. And we have known and believed the love that God hath to us. God is love; and he that dwelleth in love dwelleth in God, and God in him.

17. Herein is our love made perfect, that we may have boldness in the day of judgment: because as he is, so are we in this world.

18. There is no fear in love; but perfect love casteth out fear: because fear hath torment. He that feareth is not made perfect in love.

19. We love him, because he first loved us.

20. If a man say, I love God, and hateth his brother, he is a liar: for he that loveth not his brother whom he hath seen, how can he love God whom he hath not seen?

21. And this commandment have we from him, That he who loveth God love his brother also.

CHAPTER 5

1. Whosoever believeth that Jesus is the Christ is born of God: and every one that loveth him that begat loveth him also that is begotten of him.

2. By this we know that we love the children of God, when we love God, and keep his commandments.

3. For this is the love of God, that we keep his commandments: and his commandments are not grievous.

4. For whatsoever is born of God overcometh the world: and this is the victory that overcometh the world, even our faith.

5. Who is he that overcometh the world, but he that believeth that Jesus is the Son of God?

6. This is he that came by water and blood, even Jesus Christ; not by water only, but by water and blood. And it is the Spirit that beareth witness, because the Spirit is truth.

7. For there are three that bear record in heaven, the Father, the Word, and the Holy Ghost: and these three are one.

8. And there are three that bear witness in earth, the spirit, and the water, and the blood: and these three agree in one.

9. If we receive the witness of men, the witness of God is greater: for this is the witness of God which he hath testified of his Son.

1 Jn. 4—Knowing that the Savior loves you personally is the key to happiness. How can you know beyond any doubt that He—the Redeemer of all mankind—loves you? There are three ways that never fail: reading and pondering the scriptures, listening to the Spirit, and discerning love at work in the world.

I have often marveled at the accounts in the scriptures where the Savior—the Creator of all Creation under the leadership of our Father in Heaven—addressed individuals by name. To Moses on the mount the Lord said, "Behold, I am the Lord God Almighty, and Endless is my name . . . and I have a work for thee, Moses, my son" (Moses 1:3, 6). Clearly the relationship between the Savior and His children is meant to be personal and real. As the First Vision burst upon the world in 1820, the truth of this kind of relationship was confirmed once again (see JS—H 1:17). To be called by name by Deity is to know that a relationship with the divine is personal in nature. This same mutual friendship of the Shepherd and His sheep is repeated again and again in the scriptures (see D&C 6:20, 21; 11:23, 28; 4:9, 11).

It is a miracle to contemplate that the Savior loves us so much that He calls us by name and seeks to cultivate with each of us a personal relationship. It is a miracle that He includes us in the same pronouncement along with His own sacred name. And yet His name is our name, for we are to be known as His sheep, and we are to respond to His voice calling us. It is a measure of His generosity that He shares ownership of the Church with us, for it is both the Church of Jesus Christ, as well as The Church of Jesus Christ of Latter-day Saints. The scripture says, "And he numbereth his sheep, and they know him; and there shall be one fold and one shepherd; and he shall feed his sheep, and in him they shall find pasture" (1 Ne. 22:25). Nephi taught that we should apply the scriptures to ourselves (see 1 Ne. 19:23–24). With that authority, we can extend the personal love of the Savior to His chosen servants as recorded in the scriptures by knowing that this love is also applied to ourselves. "For God so loved the world, that he gave his only begotten Son, that whosoever believeth in him should not perish, but have everlasting life" (John 3:16).

The second way to know that the Savior loves us is to listen to the Spirit. When our personal prayers are answered in personal ways through the whisperings of the Spirit of the Lord, we can know in our hearts that He loves us and knows us personally. To Oliver Cowdery, the Lord said, "Verily, verily, I say unto you, if you desire a further witness, cast your mind upon the night that you cried unto me in your

10. He that believeth on the Son of God hath the witness in himself: he that believeth not God hath made him a liar; because he believeth not the record that God gave of his Son.

11. And this is the record, that God hath given to us eternal life, and this life is in his Son.

12. He that hath the Son hath life; and he that hath not the Son of God hath not life.

13. These things have I written unto you that believe on the name of the Son of God; that ye may know that ye have eternal life, and that ye may believe on the name of the Son of God.

14. And this is the confidence that we have in him, that, if we ask any thing according to his will, he heareth us:

15. And if we know that he hear us, whatsoever we ask, we know that we have the petitions that we desired of him.

16. If any man see his brother sin a sin which is not unto death, he shall ask, and he shall give him life for them that sin not unto death. There is a sin unto death: I do not say that he shall pray for it.

17. All unrighteousness is sin: and there is a sin not unto death.

18. We know that whosoever is born of God sinneth not; but he that is begotten of God keepeth himself, and that wicked one toucheth him not.

19. And we know that we are of God, and the whole world lieth in wickedness.

20. And we know that the Son of God is come, and hath given us an understanding, that we may know him that is true, and we are in him that is true, even in his Son Jesus Christ. This is the true God, and eternal life.

21. Little children, keep yourselves from idols. Amen.

THE SECOND EPISTLE OF

JOHN

CHAPTER 1

1. The elder unto the elect lady and her children, whom I love in the truth; and not I only, but also all they that have known the truth;

2. For the truth's sake, which dwelleth in us, and shall be with us for ever.

3. Grace be with you, mercy, and peace, from God the Father, and from the Lord Jesus Christ, the Son of the Father, in truth and love.

4. I rejoiced greatly that I found of

heart, that you might know concerning the truth of these things. Did I not speak peace to your mind concerning the matter? What greater witness can you have than from God? And now, behold, you have received a witness; for if I have told you things which no man knoweth have you not received a witness?" (D&C 6:22–24). Similarly, we can ask the Lord in faith, nothing doubting, and receive a personal witness of the truth of all things, including confirmation that we are loved by the Savior, our Redeemer. When we consider the kindness of the Savior in imparting truth and guidance to us individually through the avenue of a patriarchal blessing—truly a personal revelation from the Lord—we have further evidence through the Spirit of heavenly affection and love.

Finally, let us discern and appreciate the endless acts of charitable service being imparted all around us by the Lord's flock. One day I asked my wife the question, "How do you know the Savior loves you?" and she responded without hesitation: "Because there is so much love in the world imparted by God's children to one another." And so it is. We are "children of the prophets" and "children of the covenant," to use the Lord's expression (see 3 Ne. 20:25–26). As such, we partake of the divine nature through obedience and humility and thus have the innate potential of showing love to others. This love, displayed for all with eyes to see and hearts to feel, is evidence of the love of the Savior for us. It cannot be denied, for we are His children.

Amulek taught: "And thus he shall bring salvation to all those who shall believe on his name; this being the intent of this last sacrifice, to bring about the bowels of mercy, which overpowereth justice, and bringeth about means unto men that they may have faith unto repentance" (Alma 34:15). By reading and pondering the scriptures, listening to the whisperings of the Spirit, and discerning and participating in acts of charity in our everyday lives, we can know of the love of our Savior. We can increase our faith. We can respond in gratitude to the love and compassion shown by the Redeemer through His Atonement by our acts of love to further the cause of building up the kingdom of God.

thy children walking in truth, as we have received a commandment from the Father.

5. And now I beseech thee, lady, not as though I wrote a new commandment unto thee, but that which we had from the beginning, that we love one another.

6. And this is love, that we walk after his commandments. This is the commandment, That, as ye have heard from the beginning, ye should walk in it.

7. For many deceivers are entered into the world, who confess not that Jesus Christ is come in the flesh. This is a deceiver and an antichrist.

8. Look to yourselves, that we lose not those things which we have wrought, but that we receive a full reward.

9. Whosoever transgresseth, and abideth not in the doctrine of Christ, hath not God. He that abideth in the doctrine of Christ, he hath both the Father and the Son.

10. If there come any unto you, and bring not this doctrine, receive him not into your house, neither bid him God speed:

11. For he that biddeth him God speed is partaker of his evil deeds.

12. Having many things to write unto you, I would not write with paper and ink: but I trust to come unto you, and speak face to face, that our joy may be full.

13. The children of thy elect sister greet thee. Amen.

THE THIRD EPISTLE OF

JOHN

CHAPTER 1

1. The elder unto the wellbeloved Gaius, whom I love in the truth.

2. Beloved, I wish above all things that thou mayest prosper and be in health, even as thy soul prospereth.

3. For I rejoiced greatly, when the brethren came and testified of the truth that is in thee, even as thou walkest in the truth.

4. I have no greater joy than to hear that my children walk in truth.

5. Beloved, thou doest faithfully whatsoever thou doest to the brethren, and to strangers;

6. Which have borne witness of thy charity before the church: whom if thou bring forward on their journey after a godly sort, thou shalt do well:

7. Because that for his name's sake they went forth, taking nothing of the Gentiles.

8. We therefore ought to receive such, that we might be fellowhelpers to the truth.

9. I wrote unto the church: but Diotrephes, who loveth to have the

1 John–3 John—John's message is simple, pristine, and deeply moving as a testimony from one of the Lord's chosen Apostles, one who knew Him intimately throughout His ministry. It is the message of love. He confirms that Heavenly Father loves us, that the Savior Jesus Christ loves us, and that we should magnify our callings by loving one another in the same spirit. We have the sacred promise from heaven: "And this is the promise that he hath promised us, even eternal life" (1 Jn. 2:25). What we know, through the grace and infinite love of the Father, Son, and Holy Ghost, is the essence of life eternal: "And we know that the Son of God is come, and hath given us an understanding, that we may know him that is true, and we are in him that is true, even in his Son Jesus Christ. This is the true God, and eternal life" (1 Jn. 5:20). As beneficiaries of eternal life, through faith and obedience, we are to serve one another, not just in word, but in practical, everyday ways: "My little children, let us not love in word, neither in tongue; but in deed and in truth" (1 Jn. 3:18). Like John, who went on to even greater service in the kingdom of God in the days of the Restoration (see D&C 7; 27:12; 61:14; 77:1–15; 88:141; 3 Ne. 28:6), we can also move forward, in love, to assist in the great purposes of our Father in Heaven to bless the lives of His children everywhere.

preeminence among them, receiveth us not.

10. Wherefore, if I come, I will remember his deeds which he doeth, prating against us with malicious words: and not content therewith, neither doth he himself receive the brethren, and forbiddeth them that would, and casteth them out of the church.

11. Beloved, follow not that which is evil, but that which is good. He that doeth good is of God: but he that doeth evil hath not seen God.

12. Demetrius hath good report of all men, and of the truth itself: yea, and we also bear record; and ye know that our record is true.

13. I had many things to write, but I will not with ink and pen write unto thee:

14. But I trust I shall shortly see thee, and we shall speak face to face. Peace be to thee. Our friends salute thee. Greet the friends by name.

THE GENERAL EPISTLE OF

JUDE

CHAPTER 1

1. Jude, the servant of Jesus Christ, and brother of James, to them that are sanctified by God the Father, and preserved in Jesus Christ, and called:

2. Mercy unto you, and peace, and love, be multiplied.

3. Beloved, when I gave all diligence to write unto you of the common salvation, it was needful for me to write unto you, and exhort you that ye should earnestly contend for the faith which was once delivered unto the saints.

4. For there are certain men crept in unawares, who were before of old ordained to this condemnation, ungodly men, turning the grace of our God into lasciviousness, and denying the only Lord God, and our Lord Jesus Christ.

5. I will therefore put you in remembrance, though ye once knew this, how that the Lord, having saved the people out of the land of Egypt, afterward destroyed them that believed not.

6. And the angels which kept not

Fresco depicting eternal life

their first estate, but left their own habitation, he hath reserved in everlasting chains under darkness unto the judgment of the great day.

7. Even as Sodom and Gomorrha, and the cities about them in like manner, giving themselves over to fornication, and going after strange flesh, are set forth for an example, suffering the vengeance of eternal fire.

8. Likewise also these filthy dreamers defile the flesh, despise dominion, and speak evil of dignities.

9. Yet Michael the archangel, when contending with the devil he disputed about the body of Moses, durst not bring against him a railing accusation, but said, The Lord rebuke thee.

10. But these speak evil of those things which they know not: but what they know naturally, as brute beasts, in those things they corrupt themselves.

11. Woe unto them! for they have gone in the way of Cain, and ran greedily after the error of Balaam for reward, and perished in the gainsaying of Core.

12. These are spots in your feasts of charity, when they feast with you, feeding themselves without fear: clouds they are without water, carried about of winds; trees whose fruit withereth, without fruit, twice dead, plucked up by the roots;

13. Raging waves of the sea, foaming out their own shame; wandering stars, to whom is reserved the blackness of darkness for ever.

14. And Enoch also, the seventh from Adam, prophesied of these, saying, Behold, the Lord cometh with ten thousands of his saints,

15. To execute judgment upon all, and to convince all that are ungodly among them of all their ungodly deeds which they have ungodly committed, and of all their hard speeches which ungodly sinners have spoken against him.

16. These are murmurers, complainers, walking after their own lusts; and their mouth speaketh great swelling words, having men's persons in admiration because of advantage.

17. But, beloved, remember ye the words which were spoken before of the apostles of our Lord Jesus Christ;

18. How that they told you there should be mockers in the last time, who should walk after their own ungodly lusts.

19. These be they who separate themselves, sensual, having not the Spirit.

20. But ye, beloved, building up yourselves on your most holy faith, praying in the Holy Ghost,

21. Keep yourselves in the love of God, looking for the mercy of our Lord Jesus Christ unto eternal life.

22. And of some have compassion, making a difference:

23. And others save with fear, pull-

Notes: _____
_____
_____
_____
_____
_____
_____
_____
_____
_____
_____
_____
_____
_____
_____
_____
_____
_____
_____
_____
_____
_____
_____
_____
_____
_____
_____
_____
_____
_____
_____
_____
_____
_____

ing them out of the fire; hating even the garment spotted by the flesh.

24. Now unto him that is able to keep you from falling, and to present you faultless before the presence of his glory with exceeding joy,

25. To the only wise God our Saviour, be glory and majesty, dominion and power, both now and ever. Amen.

THE REVELATION
OF ST. JOHN THE DIVINE

CHAPTER 1

1. The Revelation of Jesus Christ, which God gave unto him, to shew unto his servants things which must shortly come to pass; and he sent and signified it by his angel unto his servant John:

2. Who bare record of the word of God, and of the testimony of Jesus Christ, and of all things that he saw.

3. Blessed is he that readeth, and they that hear the words of this prophecy, and keep those things which are written therein: for the time is at hand.

4. John to the seven churches which are in Asia: Grace be unto you, and peace, from him which is, and which was, and which is to come; and from the seven Spirits which are before his throne;

5. And from Jesus Christ, who is the faithful witness, and the first begotten of the dead, and the prince of the kings of the earth. Unto him that loved us, and washed us from our sins in his own blood,

6. And hath made us kings and priests unto God and his Father; to him be glory and dominion for ever and ever. Amen.

7. Behold, he cometh with clouds; and every eye shall see him, and they also which pierced him: and all kindreds of the earth shall wail because of him. Even so, Amen.

8. I am Alpha and Omega, the beginning and the ending, saith the Lord, which is, and which was, and which is to come, the Almighty.

9. I John, who also am your brother, and companion in tribulation, and

Revelation—Although the symbolism used in the book of Revelation is sometimes challenging to understand and apply to one's life, the predominant theme that pervades the book is crystal clear: the ultimate triumph of God's plan for the salvation, eternal life, and immortality of mankind. The Prophet Joseph Smith sought answers to many questions concerning the symbolism of this profound vision (see D&C 77). The message that is paramount in the portion of the book of Revelation included here is the continual testing and trial of mortals and their capacity—through the blessings of God—to overcome all things and enjoy the promised gift of eternal life. Perceiving our tests and trials from a higher perspective invariably leads to greater understanding and frequently to the discovery of ultimate solutions.

Opposition in all things is essential for our growth. Without opposition, we could not understand or appreciate joy in contrast to sorrow or righteousness in contrast to wickedness. Without opposition, everything would be "a compound in one" (see 2 Ne. 2:11)—devoid of vitality and bereft of the opportunity for eternal progression. It is requisite that Satan tempt us (see D&C 29:39). The Lord has not left us alone. He will strengthen and support us in all things through the power of His Atonement (see Alma 7:11).

Rev. 1:7—John was given the keys of writing the account of the history of God's dealings in the final phase of the earth's history. The same apocalyptic vision was granted to Nephi and to other prophets, but Nephi was commanded not to write them down, in deference to the commission given to John (see 1 Ne. 14:18–30). The message of John's witness is clear, for he presented a symbolic vision of the triumph of good over evil, the blessings promised to those who overcome through faith and obedience, and the surpassing glory and power of the infinite Atonement of Jesus Christ. By reading and pondering the words of the book of Revelation, we can renew our conviction that God's plan of salvation will prevail over all contravening forces, and that by honoring our covenants we can look forward to participating in the grand event of the Second Coming: "For behold, he cometh in the clouds with ten thousands of his saints in the kingdom, clothed with the glory of his Father. And every eye shall see him; and they who pierced him, and all kindreds of the earth shall wail because of him" (JST, Rev. 1:7).

in the kingdom and patience of Jesus Christ, was in the isle that is called Patmos, for the word of God, and for the testimony of Jesus Christ.

10. I was in the Spirit on the Lord's day, and heard behind me a great voice, as of a trumpet,

11. Saying, I am Alpha and Omega, the first and the last: and, What thou seest, write in a book, and send it unto the seven churches which are in Asia; unto Ephesus, and unto Smyrna, and unto Pergamos, and unto Thyatira, and unto Sardis, and unto Philadelphia, and unto Laodicea.

12. And I turned to see the voice that spake with me. And being turned, I saw seven golden candlesticks;

13. And in the midst of the seven candlesticks one like unto the Son of man, clothed with a garment down to the foot, and girt about the paps with a golden girdle.

14. His head and his hairs were white like wool, as white as snow; and his eyes were as a flame of fire;

15. And his feet like unto fine brass, as if they burned in a furnace; and his voice as the sound of many waters.

16. And he had in his right hand seven stars: and out of his mouth went a sharp twoedged sword: and his countenance was as the sun shineth in his strength.

17. And when I saw him, I fell at his feet as dead. And he laid his right hand upon me, saying unto me, Fear not; I am the first and the last:

18. I am he that liveth, and was dead; and, behold, I am alive for evermore, Amen; and have the keys of hell and of death.

19. Write the things which thou hast seen, and the things which are, and the things which shall be hereafter;

20. The mystery of the seven stars which thou sawest in my right hand, and the seven golden candlesticks. The seven stars are the angels of the seven churches: and the seven candlesticks which thou sawest are the seven churches.

CHAPTER 2

1. Unto the angel of the church of Ephesus write; These things saith he that holdeth the seven stars in his right hand, who walketh in the midst of the seven golden candlesticks;

2. I know thy works, and thy labour, and thy patience, and how thou canst not bear them which are evil: and thou hast tried them which say they are apostles, and are not, and hast found them liars:

Revelation—In general, Revelation can be divided into two main parts: chapters 1–3 dealing with the Lord's counsel to seven of the churches in what is called Asia (Asia Minor) and the remainder of the book dealing with future events, including the Restoration, Second Coming, and Millennium. The work was written down by John the Divine (or John the Beloved, as he was called) while in exile on the isle of Patmos. The Lord imparted to him the revelation from which he derived the record: "I was in the Spirit on the Lord's day, and heard behind me a great voice, as of a trumpet, Saying, I am Alpha and Omega, the first and the last: and, What thou seest, write in a book, and send it unto the seven churches which are in Asia; unto Ephesus, and unto Smyrna, and unto Pergamos, and unto Thyatira, and unto Sardis, and unto Philadelphia, and unto Laodicea" (Rev. 1:10–11).

The Book of Revelation is also known as the Apocalypse, deriving from a Greek word meaning to make known or uncover. Just as in the case of all of God's prophets, John makes known the visions of the Almighty imparted to him as a message to the Church and the world. Rich in symbolic imagery, this book of scripture engages the imagination of the readers, galvanizing them into an exercise of spiritual inquiry concerning the themes and principles of action imbedded in the narrative.

Rev. 1:16—Donald W. Parry, Jay A. Parry, and Tina M. Peterson explain the symbolism of the sword used throughout the scriptures to convey the essence of the word of God. They say the following concerning the phrase "mouth like a sharp sword" (Isa. 49:2): "This term refers to the power of the message brought by God's servant. It is an expression common in revelation (Heb. 4:12; Rev. 1:16; D&C 6:2, for example). Nephi spoke of the truth cutting people 'to the very center' (1 Ne. 16:2)" (*Understanding Isaiah*, 425).

Rev. 1:20—The units (branches/wards/stakes) of the church (candlesticks) convey the light of the Lord and the leaders/servants (angels) serve the people of the units. They hold up the light: "Therefore, hold up your light that it may shine unto the world. Behold I am the light which ye shall hold up—that which ye have seen me do. Behold ye see that I have prayed unto the Father, and ye all have witnessed" (3 Ne 18:24).

3. And hast borne, and hast patience, and for my name's sake hast laboured, and hast not fainted.

4. Nevertheless I have somewhat against thee, because thou hast left thy first love.

5. Remember therefore from whence thou art fallen, and repent, and do the first works; or else I will come unto thee quickly, and will remove thy candlestick out of his place, except thou repent.

6. But this thou hast, that thou hatest the deeds of the Nicolaitans, which I also hate.

7. He that hath an ear, let him hear what the Spirit saith unto the churches; To him that overcometh will I give to eat of the tree of life, which is in the midst of the paradise of God.

8. And unto the angel of the church in Smyrna write; These things saith the first and the last, which was dead, and is alive;

9. I know thy works, and tribulation, and poverty, (but thou art rich) and I know the blasphemy of them which say they are Jews, and are not, but are the synagogue of Satan.

10. Fear none of those things which thou shalt suffer: behold, the devil shall cast some of you into prison, that ye may be tried; and ye shall have tribulation ten days: be thou faithful unto death, and I will give thee a crown of life.

11. He that hath an ear, let him hear what the Spirit saith unto the churches; He that overcometh shall not be hurt of the second death.

12. And to the angel of the church in Pergamos write; These things saith he which hath the sharp sword with two edges;

13. I know thy works, and where thou dwellest, even where Satan's seat is: and thou holdest fast my name, and hast not denied my faith, even in those days wherein Antipas was my faithful martyr, who was slain among you, where Satan dwelleth.

14. But I have a few things against thee, because thou hast there them that hold the doctrine of Balaam, who taught Balac to cast a stumblingblock before the children of Israel, to eat things sacrificed unto idols, and to commit fornication.

15. So hast thou also them that hold the doctrine of the Nicolaitans, which thing I hate.

16. Repent; or else I will come unto thee quickly, and will fight against them with the sword of my mouth.

17. He that hath an ear, let him hear what the Spirit saith unto the churches; To him that overcometh will I give to eat of the hidden manna, and will give him a white stone, and in the stone a new name written, which no man knoweth saving he that receiveth it.

18. And unto the angel of the church in Thyatira write; These things saith the Son of God, who hath his eyes like unto a flame of fire, and his feet are like fine brass;

19. I know thy works, and charity, and service, and faith, and thy patience, and thy works; and the last to be more than the first.

Rev. 1–3—Why is it that the holy scriptures so frequently use symbols, metaphors, emblems, allegories, and parables to articulate the truths of the gospel? Is it not for the reason that these forms of expression tend to catch the imagination with more power, stimulate more effectively our engagement with the concepts and doctrines at hand, and effect a more complete transfer of truth from the prophetic source to the reader and listener? We should not be surprised that the visions imparted by the Lord to His servants are rich in visual imagery—imagery that invites us to "see" and "behold" (as in the sequence of supernal views granted unto Nephi—see 1 Nephi 11–14—or in the transcendent panoramas reported by Isaiah or in the visions described by John on the isle of Patmos).

The Lord, in His mercy and kindness, makes frequent use of images that relate to our everyday life: the sacramental emblems (bread of life, living water), baptism (related to the process of birth and bringing forth a new life), relationships and organizational issues (branches, the true vine), and the process of erecting and building things unto God (temple of God, mountain of the Lord's house). The Lord is a consummate storyteller, often using parables that draw us instinctively into situations where we can rehearse the drama of life and come to understand the blessings of keeping the commandments and applying the teachings of the gospel in practical ways.

We respond to pictures because our unconscious seems to make abundant use of internal imagery (shapes, forms, constructs) in solving problems and putting together creative structures that add value to our lives. It seems to be human nature for us to strive to complete incomplete pictures and shapes that live within us, waiting to emerge as whole entities. We seem to solve problems and fashion our productive lives out of the guiding imagery that is cultivated within our minds and hearts. We tend to think in scenes and depictions. We strive to build shapes and views that are complete and elegant, reflecting the harmony of the universe and the glory of the Creator. Could it be that the Lord intends to grant to all of us "greater views" such as those given to the people of King Benjamin (see Mosiah 5:3–4)? Through the blessings of the Spirit, we are able to view the big picture, behold the design of the heavens, perceive the pathway to salvation, and discern the guiding hand of the Lord in all things. These are the emblems of glory that give meaning to our lives and remind us of our divine parentage.

Certainly the Lord imparts to his prophets these "greater views" of the truth of all things—present,

20. Notwithstanding I have a few things against thee, because thou sufferest that woman Jezebel, which calleth herself a prophetess, to teach and to seduce my servants to commit fornication, and to eat things sacrificed unto idols.

21. And I gave her space to repent of her fornication; and she repented not.

22. Behold, I will cast her into a bed, and them that commit adultery with her into great tribulation, except they repent of their deeds.

23. And I will kill her children with death; and all the churches shall know that I am he which searcheth the reins and hearts: and I will give unto every one of you according to your works.

24. But unto you I say, and unto the rest in Thyatira, as many as have not this doctrine, and which have not known the depths of Satan, as they speak; I will put upon you none other burden.

25. But that which ye have already hold fast till I come.

26. And he that overcometh, and keepeth my works unto the end, to him will I give power over the nations:

27. And he shall rule them with a rod of iron; as the vessels of a potter shall they be broken to shivers: even as I received of my Father.

28. And I will give him the morning star.

29. He that hath an ear, let him hear what the Spirit saith unto the churches.

CHAPTER 3

1. And unto the angel of the church in Sardis write; These things saith he that hath the seven Spirits of God, and the seven stars; I know thy works, that thou hast a name that thou livest, and art dead.

2. Be watchful, and strengthen the things which remain, that are ready to die: for I have not found thy works perfect before God.

3. Remember therefore how thou hast received and heard, and hold fast, and repent. If therefore thou shalt not watch, I will come on thee as a thief, and thou shalt not know what hour I will come upon thee.

4. Thou hast a few names even in Sardis which have not defiled their garments; and they shall walk with me in white: for they are worthy.

5. He that overcometh, the same shall be clothed in white raiment; and I will not blot out his name out of the book of life, but I will confess his name before my Father, and before his angels.

6. He that hath an ear, let him hear what the Spirit saith unto the churches.

7. And to the angel of the church in

past, and future—which the prophets then pass on to us in the measure expedient for our salvation. Where John the Revelator speaks of candlesticks (the communities or congregations of the Saints), stars or angels (the servant leaders themselves), the emerging woman of glory (the church of God) and her delivered offspring (the priesthood governance power of the kingdom), or angels flying through the midst of heaven (the Restoration), we can rest assured that these images (see Rev. 1–3, 12, 14) are imparted to nourish and sustain our prayerful pondering of the doctrines of Christ in preparing ourselves for more faithful and devoted service to the cause. Let us be thankful the scriptures speak in symbols and imagery, for these emblems of glory are signs that our Father in Heaven is in charge of completing His design for our immortality and eternal life and granting us a glimpse of the blessings of eternity, which are to be perceived only through the Spirit of God opening up the inner eyes of the believers.

Rev. 2–3 — To rise above our mortal temptations and challenges—strengthened and supported by the Lord through His Spirit—qualifies us for the blessings of heaven. In Revelation, the word of the Lord is given to the seven branches, instructing them concerning their strengths and weaknesses and confirming the promised blessings when they overcome their temptations, trials, and tribulations and prevail through righteousness.

John is shown the circumstances (both good and bad) prevailing at seven of the churches of the kingdom and is given the promises of the Lord to the faithful. Among the righteous patterns of living recognized by the Lord in regard to various of the seven churches are patience, resisting wickedness and perversion, charitable service, overcoming adversity and tribulation, honoring the name of the Lord, keeping His word, faith, and purity.

On the other hand, the Lord is displeased with such lapses as a return to the former (preconversion) ways of life, seeking after earthly honors more than the things of God (as did Balaam of old—see Rev. 2:14), immorality (as in the case of the sect of the Nicolaitans—see Rev. 2:15), idolatry, lacking a firm commitment to righteousness (see Rev. 3:16), self-satisfaction, and pride. In such cases the Lord commands the people to repent of their evil ways and return to righteousness.

To those who are faithful, the Lord gives glorious promises. All of these promised blessings, though given to separate churches (congregations), apply universally (see Rev. 3:22).

Philadelphia write; These things saith he that is holy, he that is true, he that hath the key of David, he that openeth, and no man shutteth; and shutteth, and no man openeth;

8. I know thy works: behold, I have set before thee an open door, and no man can shut it: for thou hast a little strength, and hast kept my word, and hast not denied my name.

9. Behold, I will make them of the synagogue of Satan, which say they are Jews, and are not, but do lie; behold, I will make them to come and worship before thy feet, and to know that I have loved thee.

10. Because thou hast kept the word of my patience, I also will keep thee from the hour of temptation, which shall come upon all the world, to try them that dwell upon the earth.

11. Behold, I come quickly: hold that fast which thou hast, that no man take thy crown.

12. Him that overcometh will I make a pillar in the temple of my God, and he shall go no more out: and I will write upon him the name of my God, and the name of the city of my God, which is new Jerusalem, which cometh down out of heaven from my God: and I will write upon him my new name.

13. He that hath an ear, let him hear what the Spirit saith unto the churches.

14. And unto the angel of the church of the Laodiceans write; These things saith the Amen, the faithful and true witness, the beginning of the creation of God;

15. I know thy works, that thou art neither cold nor hot: I would thou wert cold or hot.

16. So then because thou art lukewarm, and neither cold nor hot, I will spue thee out of my mouth.

17. Because thou sayest, I am rich, and increased with goods, and have need of nothing; and knowest not that thou art wretched, and miserable, and poor, and blind, and naked:

18. I counsel thee to buy of me gold tried in the fire, that thou mayest be rich; and white raiment, that thou mayest be clothed, and that the shame of thy nakedness do not appear; and anoint thine eyes with eyesalve, that thou mayest see.

19. As many as I love, I rebuke and chasten: be zealous therefore, and repent.

20. Behold, I stand at the door, and knock: if any man hear my voice, and open the door, I will come in to him, and will sup with him, and he with me.

21. To him that overcometh will I grant to sit with me in my throne, even as I also overcame, and am set down with my Father in his throne.

22. He that hath an ear, let him hear what the Spirit saith unto the churches.

CHAPTER 4

1. After this I looked, and, behold, a door was opened in heaven: and the first voice which I heard was as it were of a trumpet talking with me; which said, Come up hither, and I

Rev. 4–7—Our Father in Heaven, omniscient and omnipotent, knows the future. We can only peer dimly into the future with hope and a measure of happiness as we rely on the Lord and His mercy and grace. We know that the plan of happiness cannot be frustrated by the devil. If we but keep the commandments, we have been promised everlasting life in the presence of Heavenly Father. Beginning in the premortal spirit world, Lucifer made war against the children of God, and that war continues here on earth and will continue until the ushering in of the millennial reign. At that moment, Satan will be bound and we will enjoy a measure of peace. When the millennial era ends, Satan will be loosed for a season, and the last great battle for the souls of all mankind will begin—the great battle between Israel and Gog and Magog (the leaders of the rebellious forces). The Lord will destroy those who fight against Israel (see Rev. 20:7–9; D&C 88:111–116). Then the end will come and all will be judged out of the books (see Rev. 20:12). The righteous will dwell with God. Pain and sorrow as we know it will pass away, and the righteous will inherit all things. This knowledge should motivate us to seek and serve God, keep the commandments, and bless our fellowmen.

will shew thee things which must be hereafter.

2. And immediately I was in the spirit: and, behold, a throne was set in heaven, and one sat on the throne.

3. And he that sat was to look upon like a jasper and a sardine stone: and there was a rainbow round about the throne, in sight like unto an emerald.

4. And round about the throne were four and twenty seats: and upon the seats I saw four and twenty elders sitting, clothed in white raiment; and they had on their heads crowns of gold.

5. And out of the throne proceeded lightnings and thunderings and voices: and there were seven lamps of fire burning before the throne, which are the seven Spirits of God.

6. And before the throne there was a sea of glass like unto crystal: and in the midst of the throne, and round about the throne, were four beasts full of eyes before and behind.

7. And the first beast was like a lion, and the second beast like a calf, and the third beast had a face as a man, and the fourth beast was like a flying eagle.

8. And the four beasts had each of them six wings about him; and they were full of eyes within: and they rest not day and night, saying, Holy, holy, holy, Lord God Almighty, which was, and is, and is to come.

9. And when those beasts give glory and honour and thanks to him that sat on the throne, who liveth for ever and ever,

10. The four and twenty elders fall down before him that sat on the throne, and worship him that liveth for ever and ever, and cast their crowns before the throne, saying,

11. Thou art worthy, O Lord, to receive glory and honour and power: for thou hast created all things, and for thy pleasure they are and were created.

CHAPTER 5

1. And I saw in the right hand of him that sat on the throne a book written within and on the backside, sealed with seven seals.

2. And I saw a strong angel proclaiming with a loud voice, Who is worthy to open the book, and to loose the seals thereof?

3. And no man in heaven, nor in earth, neither under the earth, was able to open the book, neither to look thereon.

4. And I wept much, because no man was found worthy to open and to read the book, neither to look thereon.

5. And one of the elders saith unto me, Weep not: behold, the Lion of the tribe of Juda, the Root of David, hath prevailed to open the book, and to loose the seven seals thereof.

6. And I beheld, and, lo, in the midst of the throne and of the four beasts, and in the midst of the elders, stood a Lamb as it had been slain, having

Rev. 4:11—The "pleasure" of the Lord consists of His joy and glory in bringing to pass the immortality and eternal life of the children of God (see Moses 1:39). What is the nature of your "pleasure" as you participate in building up the kingdom of God?

Rev. 4–5—Satan has been at war with the righteous since the war in heaven. The battle between good and evil continues today. He seeks to destroy the souls of the children of God, but his design will be frustrated through the inevitable triumph of God's plan of salvation.

John was granted the privilege and commission to view the magnificence of the celestial realm (see Rev. 4–5) in which all creation worshipped the Lord: "Saying with a loud voice, Worthy is the Lamb that was slain to receive power, and riches, and wisdom, and strength, and honour, and glory, and blessing. And every creature which is in heaven, and on the earth, and under the earth, and such as are in the sea, and all that are in them, heard I saying, Blessing, and honour, and glory, and power, be unto him that sitteth upon the throne, and unto the Lamb for ever and ever" (Rev. 5:12–13). The Lord Almighty is depicted as having all power over all the unfolding epochs of mortal history from the beginning to the end—as archived in the book with the seven seals: "We are to understand," explained the Prophet Joseph Smith, "that [the book] contains the revealed will, mysteries, and the works of God; the hidden things of his economy concerning this earth during the seven thousand years of its continuance, or its temporal existence" (D&C 77:6). John recorded what transpired as each of the seven seals was opened by the Lord, revealing the events relating to each succeeding period of a thousand years (see Rev. 6), leading to the period of the Restoration, associated with the sixth seal when the Saints who overcome all things through the Lord are enabled to serve Him forever in peace and light: "Therefore are they before the throne of God, and serve him day and night in his temple: and he that sitteth on the throne shall dwell among them. They shall hunger no more, neither thirst any more; neither shall the sun light on them, nor any heat. For the Lamb which is in the midst of the throne shall feed them, and shall lead them unto living fountains of waters: and God shall wipe away all tears from their eyes" (Rev. 7:15–17).

In contrast to this vista of rapture and bliss, we are also shown by John the raging evil of Satan and his hordes during the period of the seventh seal, prior to the Second Coming, as they amass in battle to destroy the agency of man and thwart the design

seven horns and seven eyes, which are the seven Spirits of God sent forth into all the earth.

7. And he came and took the book out of the right hand of him that sat upon the throne.

8. And when he had taken the book, the four beasts and four and twenty elders fell down before the Lamb, having every one of them harps, and golden vials full of odours, which are the prayers of saints.

9. And they sung a new song, saying, Thou art worthy to take the book, and to open the seals thereof: for thou wast slain, and hast redeemed us to God by thy blood out of every kindred, and tongue, and people, and nation;

10. And hast made us unto our God kings and priests: and we shall reign on the earth.

11. And I beheld, and I heard the voice of many angels round about the throne and the beasts and the elders: and the number of them was ten thousand times ten thousand, and thousands of thousands;

12. Saying with a loud voice, Worthy is the Lamb that was slain to receive power, and riches, and wisdom, and strength, and honour, and glory, and blessing.

13. And every creature which is in heaven, and on the earth, and under the earth, and such as are in the sea, and all that are in them, heard I saying, Blessing, and honour, and glory, and power, be unto him that sitteth upon the throne, and unto the Lamb for ever and ever.

14. And the four beasts said, Amen. And the four and twenty elders fell down and worshipped him that liveth for ever and ever.

CHAPTER 6

1. And I saw when the Lamb opened one of the seals, and I heard, as it were the noise of thunder, one of the four beasts saying, Come and see.

2. And I saw, and behold a white horse: and he that sat on him had a bow; and a crown was given unto him: and he went forth conquering, and to conquer.

3. And when he had opened the second seal, I heard the second beast say, Come and see.

4. And there went out another horse that was red: and power was given to him that sat thereon to take peace from the earth, and that they should kill one another: and there was given unto him a great sword.

5. And when he had opened the third seal, I heard the third beast say, Come and see. And I beheld, and lo a black horse; and he that sat on him had a pair of balances in his hand.

6. And I heard a voice in the midst of the four beasts say, A measure of wheat for a penny, and three measures of barley for a penny; and see thou hurt not the oil and the wine.

7. And when he had opened the fourth seal, I heard the voice of the fourth beast say, Come and see.

8. And I looked, and behold a pale horse: and his name that sat on him was Death, and Hell followed with him. And power was given unto them over the fourth part of the earth, to kill with sword, and with hunger, and with death, and with the beasts of the earth.

of God and the Lamb to bring to pass the immortality and eternal life of mankind (see Rev. 8–9, 11–13, 16–18). The fuming and insidious machinations of Satan in the last days are but an intensified reflection of his rebellion in the premortal realm, when a third of the hosts of heaven were cast down: "And the great dragon was cast out, that old serpent, called the Devil, and Satan, which deceiveth the whole world: he was cast out into the earth, and his angels were cast out with him" (Rev. 12:9). But as the chronicle of John unfolds, we are to see that evil will ultimately be trumped by the power and glory of God and the Son, and that Satan and his minions will again be cast out—this time forever. Thus the theme of Revelation—that God is ever in control of the design of "the salvation of man" (D&C 77:12)—shines through these pages to illuminate the panorama of the destined triumph of goodness and truth over hatred and evil.

President Wilford Woodruff taught: "This arch enemy of God and man, called the devil, . . . who dwells here on the earth, is a personage of great power; he has great influence and knowledge. He understands that if this kingdom, which he rebelled against in heaven, prevails on the earth, there will be no dominion here for him. He has great influence over the children of men; he labors continually to destroy the works of God in heaven, and he had to be cast out. He is here, mighty among the children of men. There is a vast number of fallen spirits, cast out with him, here on the earth. They do not die and disappear; they have not bodies only as they enter the tabernacles of men. . . . There never was a prophet in any age of the world but what the devil was continually at his elbow. This was the case with Jesus himself. The devil followed him continually trying to draw him from his purposes and to prevent him carrying out the great word of God. . . .

"This same character was with the disciples as well as with their master. He is with the Latter-day Saints; and he or his emissaries are with all men trying to lead them astray. He rules in the hearts of the inhabitants of the earth. They are governed and guided by him far more than by the power of God. This is strange, still it is true. See the wickedness in the world. See the abominations with which the earth is deluged, causing it to groan under the burden. Where does this evil come from? From the works of the devil. Everything that leads to good is from God, while everything that leads to evil is from the devil. Here are the two powers" (*The Discourses of Wilford Woodruff*, 237–39).

9. And when he had opened the fifth seal, I saw under the altar the souls of them that were slain for the word of God, and for the testimony which they held:

10. And they cried with a loud voice, saying, How long, O Lord, holy and true, dost thou not judge and avenge our blood on them that dwell on the earth?

11. And white robes were given unto every one of them; and it was said unto them, that they should rest yet for a little season, until their fellowservants also and their brethren, that should be killed as they were, should be fulfilled.

12. And I beheld when he had opened the sixth seal, and, lo, there was a great earthquake; and the sun became black as sackcloth of hair, and the moon became as blood;

13. And the stars of heaven fell unto the earth, even as a fig tree casteth her untimely figs, when she is shaken of a mighty wind.

14. And the heaven departed as a scroll when it is rolled together; and every mountain and island were moved out of their places.

15. And the kings of the earth, and the great men, and the rich men, and the chief captains, and the mighty men, and every bondman, and every free man, hid themselves in the dens and in the rocks of the mountains;

16. And said to the mountains and rocks, Fall on us, and hide us from the face of him that sitteth on the throne, and from the wrath of the Lamb:

17. For the great day of his wrath is come; and who shall be able to stand?

CHAPTER 7

1. And after these things I saw four angels standing on the four corners of the earth, holding the four winds of the earth, that the wind should not blow on the earth, nor on the sea, nor on any tree.

2. And I saw another angel ascending from the east, having the seal of the living God: and he cried with a loud voice to the four angels, to whom it was given to hurt the earth and the sea,

3. Saying, Hurt not the earth, neither the sea, nor the trees, till we have sealed the servants of our God in their foreheads.

4. And I heard the number of them which were sealed: and there were sealed an hundred and forty and four thousand of all the tribes of the children of Israel.

5. Of the tribe of Juda were sealed twelve thousand. Of the tribe of Reuben were sealed twelve thousand. Of the tribe of Gad were sealed twelve thousand.

6. Of the tribe of Aser were sealed twelve thou-

JOHN THE REVELATOR

John, son of Zebedee and brother of James, was one of the Savior's Twelve Apostles in the meridian of time (see Matt. 4:21–22; Luke 5:1–11). When Jesus ordained His Apostles, He conferred special names on some; John, his brother James, and Peter were all given the surname *Boanerges,* which means "the sons of thunder" (see Mark 3:14–17).

John was one of the three Apostles, along with Peter and James, who occupied a place of special leadership in the fold of the Savior. John also had a disposition of considerable energy and boldness (see Mark 10:37, 41–45; 13:5–5; Luke 9:54–56). He is designated in the Gospel of John (the anonymous author of which was most likely this same John) as a "disciple" (see John 13:23), at the Crucifixion (see John 19:26–27), and at the empty tomb (see John 20:2; 21:7, 20).

Unlike the synoptic Gospels of Matthew, Mark, and Luke—which present the narrative of Christ's life in similar fashion, as with "the same eye"—John presents a unique and profoundly moving unfolding of the thoughts and doctrines presented by the Savior at critical milestones in His ministry, always with the purpose of lifting one's perspective to the eternal level of understanding.

John was ultimately exiled to the isle of Patmos, where he recorded the magnificent words of the book of Revelation.

sand. Of the tribe of Nepthalim were sealed twelve thousand. Of the tribe of Manasses were sealed twelve thousand.

7. Of the tribe of Simeon were sealed twelve thousand. Of the tribe of Levi were sealed twelve thousand. Of the tribe of Issachar were sealed twelve thousand.

8. Of the tribe of Zabulon were sealed twelve thousand. Of the tribe of Joseph were sealed twelve thousand. Of the tribe of Benjamin were sealed twelve thousand.

9. After this I beheld, and, lo, a great multitude, which no man could number, of all nations, and kindreds, and people, and tongues, stood before the throne, and before the Lamb, clothed with white robes, and palms in their hands;

10. And cried with a loud voice, saying, Salvation to our God which sitteth upon the throne, and unto the Lamb.

11. And all the angels stood round about the throne, and about the elders and the four beasts, and fell before the throne on their faces, and worshipped God,

12. Saying, Amen: Blessing, and glory, and wisdom, and thanksgiving, and honour, and power, and might, be unto our God for ever and ever. Amen.

13. And one of the elders answered, saying unto me, What are these which are arrayed in white robes? and whence came they?

14. And I said unto him, Sir, thou knowest. And he said to me, These are they which came out of great tribulation, and have washed their robes, and made them white in the blood of the Lamb.

15. Therefore are they before the throne of God, and serve him day and night in his temple: and he that sitteth on the throne shall dwell among them.

16. They shall hunger no more, neither thirst any more; neither shall the sun light on them, nor any heat.

17. For the Lamb which is in the midst of the throne shall feed them, and shall lead them unto living fountains of waters: and God shall wipe away all tears from their eyes.

CHAPTER 8

1. And when he had opened the seventh seal, there was silence in heaven about the space of half an hour.

2. And I saw the seven angels which stood before God; and to them were given seven trumpets.

3. And another angel came and stood at the altar, having a golden censer; and there was given unto him much incense, that he should offer it with the prayers of all saints upon the golden altar which was before the throne.

4. And the smoke of the incense, which came with the prayers of the saints, ascended up before God out of the angel's hand.

5. And the angel took the censer, and filled it with fire of the altar, and cast it into the earth: and there were voices, and thunderings, and lightnings, and an earthquake.

6. And the seven angels which had the seven trumpets prepared themselves to sound.

7. The first angel sounded, and there followed hail and fire mingled with

The fifth angel, holding the key to the bottomless pit

blood, and they were cast upon the earth: and the third part of trees was burnt up, and all green grass was burnt up.

8. And the second angel sounded, and as it were a great mountain burning with fire was cast into the sea: and the third part of the sea became blood;

9. And the third part of the creatures which were in the sea, and had life, died; and the third part of the ships were destroyed.

10. And the third angel sounded, and there fell a great star from heaven, burning as it were a lamp, and it fell upon the third part of the rivers, and upon the fountains of waters;

11. And the name of the star is called Wormwood: and the third part of the waters became wormwood; and many men died of the waters, because they were made bitter.

12. And the fourth angel sounded, and the third part of the sun was smitten, and the third part of the moon, and the third part of the stars; so as the third part of them was darkened, and the day shone not for a third part of it, and the night likewise.

13. And I beheld, and heard an angel flying through the midst of heaven, saying with a loud voice, Woe, woe, woe, to the inhabiters of the earth by reason of the other voices of the trumpet of the three angels, which are yet to sound!

CHAPTER 9

1. And the fifth angel sounded, and I saw a star fall from heaven unto the earth: and to him was given the key of the bottomless pit.

2. And he opened the bottomless pit; and there arose a smoke out of the pit, as the smoke of a great furnace; and the sun and the air were darkened by reason of the smoke of the pit.

3. And there came out of the smoke locusts upon the earth: and unto them was given power, as the scorpions of the earth have power.

4. And it was commanded them that they should not hurt the grass of the earth, neither any green thing, neither any tree; but only those men which have not the seal of God in their foreheads.

5. And to them it was given that they should not kill them, but that they should be tormented five months: and their torment was as the torment of a scorpion, when he striketh a man.

6. And in those days shall men seek death, and shall not find it; and shall desire to die, and death shall flee from them.

7. And the shapes of the locusts were like unto horses prepared unto battle; and on their heads were as it were crowns like gold, and their faces were as the faces of men.

8. And they had hair as the hair of women, and their teeth were as the teeth of lions.

9. And they had breastplates, as it were breastplates of iron; and the sound of their wings was as the sound of chariots of many horses running to battle.

10. And they had tails like unto scorpions, and there were stings in their tails: and their power was to hurt men five months.

11. And they had a king over them, which is the angel of the bottomless pit, whose name in the Hebrew tongue is Abaddon, but in the Greek tongue hath his name Apollyon.

12. One woe is past; and, behold, there come two woes more hereafter.

13. And the sixth angel sounded, and I heard a voice from the four

Notes: _____

_____

_____

_____

_____

_____

_____

_____

_____

_____

_____

_____

_____

_____

_____

_____

_____

_____

_____

_____

_____

_____

_____

_____

_____

_____

_____

_____

_____

_____

_____

_____

horns of the golden altar which is before God,

14. Saying to the sixth angel which had the trumpet, Loose the four angels which are bound in the great river Euphrates.

15. And the four angels were loosed, which were prepared for an hour, and a day, and a month, and a year, for to slay the third part of men.

16. And the number of the army of the horsemen were two hundred thousand thousand: and I heard the number of them.

17. And thus I saw the horses in the vision, and them that sat on them, having breastplates of fire, and of jacinth, and brimstone: and the heads of the horses were as the heads of lions; and out of their mouths issued fire and smoke and brimstone.

18. By these three was the third part of men killed, by the fire, and by the smoke, and by the brimstone, which issued out of their mouths.

19. For their power is in their mouth, and in their tails: for their tails were like unto serpents, and had heads, and with them they do hurt.

20. And the rest of the men which were not killed by these plagues yet repented not of the works of their hands, that they should not worship devils, and idols of gold, and silver, and brass, and stone, and of wood: which neither can see, nor hear, nor walk:

21. Neither repented they of their murders, nor of their sorceries, nor of their fornication, nor of their thefts.

CHAPTER 10

1. And I saw another mighty angel come down from heaven, clothed with a cloud: and a rainbow was upon his head, and his face was as it were the sun, and his feet as pillars of fire:

2. And he had in his hand a little book open: and he set his right foot upon the sea, and his left foot on the earth,

3. And cried with a loud voice, as when a lion roareth: and when he had cried, seven thunders uttered their voices.

4. And when the seven thunders had uttered their voices, I was about to write: and I heard a voice from heaven saying unto me, Seal up those things which the seven thunders uttered, and write them not.

5. And the angel which I saw stand upon the sea and upon the earth lifted up his hand to heaven,

6. And sware by him that liveth for ever and ever, who created heaven, and the things that therein are, and the earth, and the things that therein are, and the sea, and the things which are therein, that there should be time no longer:

7. But in the days of the voice of the seventh angel, when he shall begin to sound, the mystery of God should be finished, as he hath declared to his servants the prophets.

8. And the voice which I heard from heaven spake unto me again, and said, Go and take the little book which is open in the hand of the angel which standeth upon the sea and upon the earth.

9. And I went unto the angel, and said unto him, Give me the little book. And he said unto me, Take it, and eat it up; and it shall make thy belly bitter, but it shall be in thy mouth sweet as honey.

10. And I took the little book out of the angel's hand, and ate it up; and it was in my mouth sweet as honey: and as soon as I had eaten it, my belly was bitter.

The four horsemen

11. And he said unto me, Thou must prophesy again before many peoples, and nations, and tongues, and kings.

CHAPTER 11

1. And there was given me a reed like unto a rod: and the angel stood, saying, Rise, and measure the temple of God, and the altar, and them that worship therein.

2. But the court which is without the temple leave out, and measure it not; for it is given unto the Gentiles: and the holy city shall they tread under foot forty and two months.

3. And I will give power unto my two witnesses, and they shall prophesy a thousand two hundred and threescore days, clothed in sackcloth.

4. These are the two olive trees, and the two candlesticks standing before the God of the earth.

5. And if any man will hurt them, fire proceedeth out of their mouth, and devoureth their enemies: and if any man will hurt them, he must in this manner be killed.

6. These have power to shut heaven, that it rain not in the days of their prophecy: and have power over waters to turn them to blood, and to smite the earth with all plagues, as often as they will.

7. And when they shall have finished their testimony, the beast that ascendeth out of the bottomless pit shall make war against them, and shall overcome them, and kill them.

8. And their dead bodies shall lie in the street of the great city, which spiritually is called Sodom and Egypt, where also our Lord was crucified.

9. And they of the people and kindreds and tongues and nations shall see their dead bodies three days and an half, and shall not suffer their dead bodies to be put in graves.

10. And they that dwell upon the earth shall rejoice over them, and make merry, and shall send gifts one to another; because these two prophets tormented them that dwelt on the earth.

11. And after three days and an half the Spirit of life from God entered into them, and they stood upon their feet; and great fear fell upon them which saw them.

12. And they heard a great voice from heaven saying unto them, Come up hither. And they ascended up to heaven in a cloud; and their enemies beheld them.

13. And the same hour was there a great earthquake, and the tenth part of the city fell, and in the earthquake were slain of men seven thousand: and the remnant were affrighted, and gave glory to the God of heaven.

14. The second woe is past; and, behold, the third woe cometh quickly.

15. And the seventh angel sounded; and there were great voices in heaven, saying, The kingdoms of this world are become the kingdoms of our Lord, and of his Christ; and he shall reign for ever and ever.

16. And the four and twenty elders, which sat before God on their seats, fell upon their faces, and worshipped God,

Notes: _____

_____

17. Saying, We give thee thanks, O Lord God Almighty, which art, and wast, and art to come; because thou hast taken to thee thy great power, and hast reigned.

18. And the nations were angry, and thy wrath is come, and the time of the dead, that they should be judged, and that thou shouldest give reward unto thy servants the prophets, and to the saints, and them that fear thy name, small and great; and shouldest destroy them which destroy the earth.

19. And the temple of God was opened in heaven, and there was seen in his temple the ark of his testament: and there were lightnings, and voices, and thunderings, and an earthquake, and great hail.

CHAPTER 12

1. And there appeared a great wonder in heaven; a woman clothed with the sun, and the moon under her feet, and upon her head a crown of twelve stars:

2. And she being with child cried, travailing in birth, and pained to be delivered.

3. And there appeared another wonder in heaven; and behold a great red dragon, having seven heads and ten horns, and seven crowns upon his heads.

4. And his tail drew the third part of the stars of heaven, and did cast them to the earth: and the dragon stood before the woman which was ready to be delivered, for to devour her child as soon as it was born.

5. And she brought forth a man child, who was to rule all nations with a rod of iron: and her child was caught up unto God, and to his throne.

6. And the woman fled into the wilderness, where she hath a place prepared of God, that they should feed her there a thousand two hundred and threescore days.

7. And there was war in heaven: Michael and his angels fought against the dragon; and the dragon fought and his angels,

8. And prevailed not; neither was their place found any more in heaven.

9. And the great dragon was cast out, that old serpent, called the Devil, and Satan, which deceiveth the whole world: he was cast out into the earth, and his angels were cast out with him.

10. And I heard a loud voice saying in heaven, Now is come salvation, and strength, and the kingdom of our God, and the power of his Christ: for the accuser of our brethren is cast down, which accused them before our God day and night.

11. And they overcame him by the blood of the Lamb, and by the word of their testimony; and they loved not their lives unto the death.

12. Therefore rejoice, ye heavens, and ye that dwell in them. Woe to the inhabiters of the earth and of the sea! for the devil is come down unto you, having great wrath, because he

Rev. 12 — It is to the Messiah and Redeemer that we owe the blessing of being able to overcome sin and darkness through the majesty of His Atonement. He is the same who prevailed against the rebellious spirits in heaven and caused them to be cast down — including the great dragon or Satan (see Rev. 12:3–9) — through the power of God's plan of salvation: "And they overcame him by the blood of the Lamb, and by the word of their testimony; and they loved not their lives unto the death. Therefore rejoice, ye heavens, and ye that dwell in them" (Rev. 12:11–12).

John was also privileged to see in his vision a womanly figure, clothed with sun, moon, and stars, who brought forth a man child "to rule all nations with a rod of iron" (Rev. 12:5; compare 12:1–2, 14–17) — a symbolic representation of the Church and kingdom of God empowered with the authority of priesthood governance to bless all mankind. "And the dragon prevailed not against Michael, neither the child, nor the woman which was the church of God, who had been delivered of her pains, and brought forth the kingdom of our God and his Christ" (JST, Rev. 12:7). Through the Atonement of Christ, the Church and kingdom are destined to prevail over the satanic forces of evil bent on destroying the work and glory of God. That is the pervasive theme of the book of Revelation.

Elder Bruce R. McConkie taught, "This life is a continuation of the war in heaven. In it Satan makes war with the saints, 'which keep the commandments of God, and have the testimony of Jesus' (Rev. 12:17). Those saints who overcome the world thereby triumph over Satan and gain the victory. Of King Mosiah, for instance, the Book of Mormon account records, after he had 'gone the way of all the earth,' that he had 'warred a good warfare, walking uprightly before God' (Alma 1:1)" (*Doctrinal New Testament Commentary,* 3:116).

Rev. 12:11 — We overcome adversity, deal with temptation, and are strengthened in our hour of need through the goodness, grace, and power of the Lord and the efficacy of His atoning sacrifice on our behalf. This is because we exercise our faith in Jesus Christ and bear testimony of Him. Even in death through martyrdom for the sake of Christ we would still emerge as having overcome all things and thus enjoy the presence of God.

knoweth that he hath but a short time.

13. And when the dragon saw that he was cast unto the earth, he persecuted the woman which brought forth the man child.

14. And to the woman were given two wings of a great eagle, that she might fly into the wilderness, into her place, where she is nourished for a time, and times, and half a time, from the face of the serpent.

15. And the serpent cast out of his mouth water as a flood after the woman, that he might cause her to be carried away of the flood.

16. And the earth helped the woman, and the earth opened her mouth, and swallowed up the flood which the dragon cast out of his mouth.

17. And the dragon was wroth with the woman, and went to make war with the remnant of her seed, which keep the commandments of God, and have the testimony of Jesus Christ.

CHAPTER 13

1. And I stood upon the sand of the sea, and saw a beast rise up out of the sea, having seven heads and ten horns, and upon his horns ten crowns, and upon his heads the name of blasphemy.

2. And the beast which I saw was like unto a leopard, and his feet were as the feet of a bear, and his mouth as the mouth of a lion: and the dragon gave him his power, and his seat, and great authority.

3. And I saw one of his heads as it were wounded to death; and his deadly wound was healed: and all the world wondered after the beast.

4. And they worshipped the dragon which gave power unto the beast: and they worshipped the beast, saying, Who is like unto the beast? who is able to make war with him?

5. And there was given unto him a mouth speaking great things and blasphemies; and power was given unto him to continue forty and two months.

6. And he opened his mouth in blasphemy against God, to blaspheme his name, and his tabernacle, and them that dwell in heaven.

7. And it was given unto him to make war with the saints, and to overcome them: and power was given him over all kindreds, and tongues, and nations.

8. And all that dwell upon the earth shall worship him, whose names are not written in the book of life of the Lamb slain from the foundation of the world.

9. If any man have an ear, let him hear.

10. He that leadeth into captivity shall go into captivity: he that killeth with the sword must be killed with the sword. Here is the patience and the faith of the saints.

11. And I beheld another beast coming up out of the earth; and he had two horns like a lamb, and he spake as a dragon.

12. And he exerciseth all the power of the first beast before him, and causeth the earth and them which dwell therein to worship the first beast, whose deadly wound was healed.

13. And he doeth great wonders, so that he maketh fire come down from

The seven-headed dragon

heaven on the earth in the sight of men,

14. And deceiveth them that dwell on the earth by the means of those miracles which he had power to do in the sight of the beast; saying to them that dwell on the earth, that they should make an image to the beast, which had the wound by a sword, and did live.

15. And he had power to give life unto the image of the beast, that the image of the beast should both speak, and cause that as many as would not worship the image of the beast should be killed.

16. And he causeth all, both small and great, rich and poor, free and bond, to receive a mark in their right hand, or in their foreheads:

17. And that no man might buy or sell, save he that had the mark, or the name of the beast, or the number of his name.

18. Here is wisdom. Let him that hath understanding count the number of the beast: for it is the number of a man; and his number is Six hundred threescore and six.

CHAPTER 14

1. And I looked, and, lo, a Lamb stood on the mount Sion, and with him an hundred forty and four thousand, having his Father's name written in their foreheads.

2. And I heard a voice from heaven, as the voice of many waters, and as the voice of a great thunder: and I heard the voice of harpers harping with their harps:

3. And they sung as it were a new song before the throne, and before the four beasts, and the elders: and no man could learn that song but the hundred and forty and four thousand, which were redeemed from the earth.

4. These are they which were not defiled with women; for they are virgins. These are they which follow the Lamb whithersoever he goeth. These were redeemed from among men, being the firstfruits unto God and to the Lamb.

5. And in their mouth was found no guile: for they are without fault before the throne of God.

6. And I saw another angel fly in the midst of heaven, having the everlasting gospel to preach unto them that dwell on the earth, and to every nation, and kindred, and tongue, and people,

7. Saying with a loud voice, Fear God, and give glory to him; for the hour of his judgment is come: and worship him that made heaven, and earth, and the sea, and the fountains of waters.

8. And there followed another angel, saying, Babylon is fallen, is fallen, that great city, because she made all nations drink of the wine of the wrath of her fornication.

9. And the third angel followed them, saying with a loud voice, If any man worship the beast and his image, and receive his mark in his forehead, or in his hand,

10. The same shall drink of the wine

Rev. 14—Wickedness and tribulation will be rampant prior to the Second Coming, which will usher in the millennial reign of our Savior Jesus Christ. At that point, Satan will be bound for a thousand years. At the end of the Millennium, Satan will be loosed for a little season before he and his hordes are banished forever.

John viewed the events associated with the Restoration of the gospel of Jesus Christ in the last days through angelic ministrations: "And I saw another angel fly in the midst of heaven, having the everlasting gospel to preach unto them that dwell on the earth, and to every nation, and kindred, and tongue, and people, Saying with a loud voice, Fear God, and give glory to him; for the hour of his judgment is come: and worship him that made heaven, and earth, and the sea, and the fountains of waters" (Rev. 14:6–7). Following the Restoration, and at the dawning of the millennial reign of the Savior, Satan will be bound: "And I saw an angel come down from heaven, having the key of the bottomless pit and a great chain in his hand. And he laid hold on the dragon, that old serpent, which is the Devil, and Satan, and bound him a thousand years, And cast him into the bottomless pit, and shut him up, and set a seal upon him, that he should deceive the nations no more, till the thousand years should be fulfilled: and after that he must be loosed a little season" (Rev. 20:1–3).

At the end of the thousand-year period, Satan will again be allowed to rage for a season and gather his armies of evil about the city of God: "And they went up on the breadth of the earth, and compassed the camp of the saints about, and the beloved city: and fire came down from God out of heaven, and devoured them. And the devil that deceived them was cast into the lake of fire and brimstone, where the beast and the false prophet are, and shall be tormented day and night for ever and ever" (Rev. 20:9–10). Until that day, the Saints of God are to toil in service to the cause of light and truth, keeping themselves unspotted and free of the stain of evil as they magnify their callings to build up the kingdom of God in the last days.

President Gordon B. Hinckley counseled, "Certainly there is no point in speculating concerning the day and the hour. Let us rather live each day so that if the Lord does come while we yet are upon the earth we shall be worthy of that change which will occur as in the twinkling of an eye and under which we shall be changed from mortal to immortal beings" (*Teachings of Gordon B. Hinckley*, 576).

of the wrath of God, which is poured out without mixture into the cup of his indignation; and he shall be tormented with fire and brimstone in the presence of the holy angels, and in the presence of the Lamb:

11. And the smoke of their torment ascendeth up for ever and ever: and they have no rest day nor night, who worship the beast and his image, and whosoever receiveth the mark of his name.

12. Here is the patience of the saints: here are they that keep the commandments of God, and the faith of Jesus.

13. And I heard a voice from heaven saying unto me, Write, Blessed are the dead which die in the Lord from henceforth: Yea, saith the Spirit, that they may rest from their labours; and their works do follow them.

14. And I looked, and behold a white cloud, and upon the cloud one sat like unto the Son of man, having on his head a golden crown, and in his hand a sharp sickle.

15. And another angel came out of the temple, crying with a loud voice to him that sat on the cloud, Thrust in thy sickle, and reap: for the time is come for thee to reap; for the harvest of the earth is ripe.

16. And he that sat on the cloud thrust in his sickle on the earth; and the earth was reaped.

17. And another angel came out of the temple which is in heaven, he also having a sharp sickle.

18. And another angel came out from the altar, which had power over fire; and cried with a loud cry to him that had the sharp sickle, saying, Thrust in thy sharp sickle, and gather the clusters of the vine of the earth; for her grapes are fully ripe.

19. And the angel thrust in his sickle into the earth, and gathered the vine of the earth, and cast it into the great winepress of the wrath of God.

20. And the winepress was trodden without the city, and blood came out of the winepress, even unto the horse bridles, by the space of a thousand and six hundred furlongs.

CHAPTER 15

1. And I saw another sign in heaven, great and marvellous, seven angels having the seven last plagues; for in them is filled up the wrath of God.

2. And I saw as it were a sea of glass mingled with fire: and them that had gotten the victory over the beast, and over his image, and over his mark, and over the number of his name, stand on the sea of glass, having the harps of God.

3. And they sing the song of Moses the servant of God, and the song of the Lamb, saying, Great and marvellous are thy works, Lord God Almighty; just and true are thy ways, thou King of saints.

4. Who shall not fear thee, O Lord, and glorify thy name? for thou only art holy: for all nations shall come and worship before thee; for thy judgments are made manifest.

5. And after that I looked, and, behold, the temple of the tabernacle of the testimony in heaven was opened:

6. And the seven angels came out of the temple, having the seven plagues, clothed in pure and white

The whore of Babylon

linen, and having their breasts girded with golden girdles.

7. And one of the four beasts gave unto the seven angels seven golden vials full of the wrath of God, who liveth for ever and ever.

8. And the temple was filled with smoke from the glory of God, and from his power; and no man was able to enter into the temple, till the seven plagues of the seven angels were fulfilled.

CHAPTER 16

1. And I heard a great voice out of the temple saying to the seven angels, Go your ways, and pour out the vials of the wrath of God upon the earth.

2. And the first went, and poured out his vial upon the earth; and there fell a noisome and grievous sore upon the men which had the mark of the beast, and upon them which worshipped his image.

3. And the second angel poured out his vial upon the sea; and it became as the blood of a dead man: and every living soul died in the sea.

4. And the third angel poured out his vial upon the rivers and fountains of waters; and they became blood.

5. And I heard the angel of the waters say, Thou art righteous, O Lord, which art, and wast, and shalt be, because thou hast judged thus.

6. For they have shed the blood of saints and prophets, and thou hast given them blood to drink; for they are worthy.

7. And I heard another out of the altar say, Even so, Lord God Almighty, true and righteous are thy judgments.

8. And the fourth angel poured out his vial upon the sun; and power was given unto him to scorch men with fire.

9. And men were scorched with great heat, and blasphemed the name of God, which hath power over these plagues: and they repented not to give him glory.

10. And the fifth angel poured out his vial upon the seat of the beast; and his kingdom was full of darkness; and they gnawed their tongues for pain,

11. And blasphemed the God of heaven because of their pains and their sores, and repented not of their deeds.

12. And the sixth angel poured out his vial upon the great river Euphrates; and the water thereof was dried up, that the way of the kings of the east might be prepared.

13. And I saw three unclean spirits like frogs come out of the mouth of the dragon, and out of the mouth of the beast, and out of the mouth of the false prophet.

14. For they are the spirits of devils, working miracles, which go forth unto the kings of the earth and of the whole world, to gather them to the battle of that great day of God Almighty.

15. Behold, I come as a thief. Blessed is he that watcheth, and keepeth his garments, lest he walk naked, and they see his shame.

16. And he gathered them together into a place called in the Hebrew tongue Armageddon.

17. And the seventh angel poured out his vial into the air; and there came a great voice out of the temple of heaven, from the throne, saying, It is done.

BABYLON

Babylon is an emblematic expression denoting a worldly culture antithetical to eternal principles and practices, one that will be destroyed according to the designs of the Almighty as His everlasting kingdom is unfolded:

"And after these things I saw another angel come down from heaven, having great power; and the earth was lightened with his glory.

"And he cried mightily with a strong voice, saying, Babylon the great is fallen, is fallen, and is become the habitation of devils, and the hold of every foul spirit, and a cage of every unclean and hateful bird" (Rev. 18:1–2; see also Rev. 14:8; 16:9; 17:5; 18:10, 21).

Babylon as a designation of worldliness is different from Babylonia, which was one of the great empires—along with Egypt and Assyria—that defined the broad geographical and cultural environment in which the people of Israel emerged as a chosen nation.

18. And there were voices, and thunders, and lightnings; and there was a great earthquake, such as was not since men were upon the earth, so mighty an earthquake, and so great.

19. And the great city was divided into three parts, and the cities of the nations fell: and great Babylon came in remembrance before God, to give unto her the cup of the wine of the fierceness of his wrath.

20. And every island fled away, and the mountains were not found.

21. And there fell upon men a great hail out of heaven, every stone about the weight of a talent: and men blasphemed God because of the plague of the hail; for the plague thereof was exceeding great.

CHAPTER 17

1. And there came one of the seven angels which had the seven vials, and talked with me, saying unto me, Come hither; I will shew unto thee the judgment of the great whore that sitteth upon many waters:

2. With whom the kings of the earth have committed fornication, and the inhabitants of the earth have been made drunk with the wine of her fornication.

3. So he carried me away in the spirit into the wilderness: and I saw a woman sit upon a scarlet coloured beast, full of names of blasphemy, having seven heads and ten horns.

4. And the woman was arrayed in purple and scarlet colour, and decked with gold and precious stones and pearls, having a golden cup in her hand full of abominations and filthiness of her fornication:

5. And upon her forehead was a name written, MYSTERY, BABYLON THE GREAT, THE MOTHER OF HARLOTS AND ABOMINATIONS OF THE EARTH.

6. And I saw the woman drunken with the blood of the saints, and with the blood of the martyrs of Jesus: and when I saw her, I wondered with great admiration.

7. And the angel said unto me, Wherefore didst thou marvel? I will tell thee the mystery of the woman, and of the beast that carrieth her, which hath the seven heads and ten horns.

8. The beast that thou sawest was, and is not; and shall ascend out of the bottomless pit, and go into perdition: and they that dwell on the earth shall wonder, whose names were not written in the book of life from the foundation of the world, when they behold the beast that was, and is not, and yet is.

9. And here is the mind which hath wisdom. The seven heads are seven mountains, on which the woman sitteth.

10. And there are seven kings: five are fallen, and one is, and the other is not yet come; and when he cometh, he must continue a short space.

11. And the beast that was, and is not, even he is the eighth, and is of the seven, and goeth into perdition.

12. And the ten horns which thou

Rev. 17–22—As we will be judged by the standards of the gospel of Jesus Christ, here are several points to ponder concerning our preparation for the Second Coming: How are we doing in that regard? Do our deeds reflect a life patterned after the Lord Jesus Christ? Are our works those of righteousness? Do we pass the test of Alma chapter 5? Are our thoughts pure? What are the desires of our hearts?

We should take the time to evaluate our lives. Let us all set some goals and make some plans on how we intend to keep the commandments, live a Christlike life, and serve our fellowmen. Let us commit ourselves to take seriously the thirteenth Article of Faith: "We believe in being honest, true, chaste, benevolent, virtuous, and in doing good to all men; indeed, we may say that we follow the admonition of Paul—We believe all things, we hope all things, we have endured many things, and hope to be able to endure all things. If there is anything virtuous, lovely, or of good report or praiseworthy, we seek after these things."

sawest are ten kings, which have received no kingdom as yet; but receive power as kings one hour with the beast.

13. These have one mind, and shall give their power and strength unto the beast.

14. These shall make war with the Lamb, and the Lamb shall overcome them: for he is Lord of lords, and King of kings: and they that are with him are called, and chosen, and faithful.

15. And he saith unto me, The waters which thou sawest, where the whore sitteth, are peoples, and multitudes, and nations, and tongues.

16. And the ten horns which thou sawest upon the beast, these shall hate the whore, and shall make her desolate and naked, and shall eat her flesh, and burn her with fire.

17. For God hath put in their hearts to fulfil his will, and to agree, and give their kingdom unto the beast, until the words of God shall be fulfilled.

18. And the woman which thou sawest is that great city, which reigneth over the kings of the earth.

CHAPTER 18

1. And after these things I saw another angel come down from heaven, having great power; and the earth was lightened with his glory.

2. And he cried mightily with a strong voice, saying, Babylon the great is fallen, is fallen, and is become the habitation of devils, and the hold of every foul spirit, and a cage of every unclean and hateful bird.

3. For all nations have drunk of the wine of the wrath of her fornication, and the kings of the earth have committed fornication with her, and the merchants of the earth are waxed rich through the abundance of her delicacies.

4. And I heard another voice from heaven, saying, Come out of her, my people, that ye be not partakers of her sins, and that ye receive not of her plagues.

5. For her sins have reached unto heaven, and God hath remembered her iniquities.

6. Reward her even as she rewarded you, and double unto her double according to her works: in the cup which she hath filled fill to her double.

7. How much she hath glorified herself, and lived deliciously, so much torment and sorrow give her: for she saith in her heart, I sit a queen, and am no widow, and shall see no sorrow.

8. Therefore shall her plagues come in one day, death, and mourning, and famine; and she shall be utterly burned with fire: for strong is the Lord God who judgeth her.

9. And the kings of the earth, who have committed fornication and lived deliciously with her, shall bewail her, and lament for her, when they shall see the smoke of her burning,

10. Standing afar off for the fear of her torment, saying, Alas, alas, that great city Babylon, that mighty city! for in one hour is thy judgment come.

Notes: _____

11. And the merchants of the earth shall weep and mourn over her; for no man buyeth their merchandise any more:

12. The merchandise of gold, and silver, and precious stones, and of pearls, and fine linen, and purple, and silk, and scarlet, and all thyine wood, and all manner vessels of ivory, and all manner vessels of most precious wood, and of brass, and iron, and marble,

13. And cinnamon, and odours, and ointments, and frankincense, and wine, and oil, and fine flour, and wheat, and beasts, and sheep, and horses, and chariots, and slaves, and souls of men.

14. And the fruits that thy soul lusted after are departed from thee, and all things which were dainty and goodly are departed from thee, and thou shalt find them no more at all.

15. The merchants of these things, which were made rich by her, shall stand afar off for the fear of her torment, weeping and wailing,

16. And saying, Alas, alas, that great city, that was clothed in fine linen, and purple, and scarlet, and decked with gold, and precious stones, and pearls!

17. For in one hour so great riches is come to nought. And every shipmaster, and all the company in ships, and sailors, and as many as trade by sea, stood afar off,

18. And cried when they saw the smoke of her burning, saying, What city is like unto this great city!

19. And they cast dust on their heads, and cried, weeping and wailing, saying, Alas, alas, that great city, wherein were made rich all that had ships in the sea by reason of her costliness! for in one hour is she made desolate.

20. Rejoice over her, thou heaven, and ye holy apostles and prophets; for God hath avenged you on her.

21. And a mighty angel took up a stone like a great millstone, and cast it into the sea, saying, Thus with violence shall that great city Babylon be thrown down, and shall be found no more at all.

22. And the voice of harpers, and musicians, and of pipers, and trumpeters, shall be heard no more at all in thee; and no craftsman, of whatsoever craft he be, shall be found any more in thee; and the sound of a millstone shall be heard no more at all in thee;

23. And the light of a candle shall shine no more at all in thee; and the voice of the bridegroom and of the bride shall be heard no more at all in thee: for thy merchants were the great men of the earth; for by thy sorceries were all nations deceived.

24. And in her was found the blood of prophets, and of saints, and of all that were slain upon the earth.

CHAPTER 19

1. And after these things I heard a great voice of much people in heaven, saying, Alleluia; Salvation, and glory, and honour, and power, unto the Lord our God:

2. For true and righteous are his judgments: for he hath judged the great whore, which did corrupt the earth with her fornication, and hath avenged the blood of his servants at her hand.

3. And again they said, Alleluia. And her smoke rose up for ever and ever.

4. And the four and twenty elders and the four beasts fell down and worshipped God that sat on the throne, saying, Amen; Alleluia.

LAMB OF GOD

The title *Lamb of God,* meaning the Only Begotten Son who gave His life in the atoning sacrifice, is mentioned twice in the New Testament—both in the words of John (see John 1:29–30, 35–37).

Of Christ, Peter said, "But with the precious blood of Christ, as of a lamb without blemish and without spot: Who was verily foreordained before the foundation of the world, but was manifest in these last times for you" (1 Pet. 1:19–20).

5. And a voice came out of the throne, saying, Praise our God, all ye his servants, and ye that fear him, both small and great.

6. And I heard as it were the voice of a great multitude, and as the voice of many waters, and as the voice of mighty thunderings, saying, Alleluia: for the Lord God omnipotent reigneth.

7. Let us be glad and rejoice, and give honour to him: for the marriage of the Lamb is come, and his wife hath made herself ready.

8. And to her was granted that she should be arrayed in fine linen, clean and white: for the fine linen is the righteousness of saints.

9. And he saith unto me, Write, Blessed are they which are called unto the marriage supper of the Lamb. And he saith unto me, These are the true sayings of God.

10. And I fell at his feet to worship him. And he said unto me, See thou do it not: I am thy fellowservant, and of thy brethren that have the testimony of Jesus: worship God: for the testimony of Jesus is the spirit of prophecy.

11. And I saw heaven opened, and behold a white horse; and he that sat upon him was called Faithful and True, and in righteousness he doth judge and make war.

12. His eyes were as a flame of fire, and on his head were many crowns; and he had a name written, that no man knew, but he himself.

13. And he was clothed with a vesture dipped in blood: and his name is called The Word of God.

14. And the armies which were in heaven followed him upon white horses, clothed in fine linen, white and clean.

15. And out of his mouth goeth a sharp sword, that with it he should smite the nations: and he shall rule them with a rod of iron: and he treadeth the winepress of the fierceness and wrath of Almighty God.

16. And he hath on his vesture and on his thigh a name written, KING OF KINGS, AND LORD OF LORDS.

17. And I saw an angel standing in the sun; and he cried with a loud voice, saying to all the fowls that fly in the midst of heaven, Come and gather yourselves together unto the supper of the great God;

18. That ye may eat the flesh of kings, and the flesh of captains, and the flesh of mighty men, and the flesh of horses, and of them that sit on them, and the flesh of all men, both free and bond, both small and great.

19. And I saw the beast, and the kings of the earth, and their armies, gathered together to make war against him that sat on the horse, and against his army.

The last judgment

20. And the beast was taken, and with him the false prophet that wrought miracles before him, with which he deceived them that had received the mark of the beast, and them that worshipped his image. These both were cast alive into a lake of fire burning with brimstone.

21. And the remnant were slain with the sword of him that sat upon the horse, which sword proceeded out of his mouth: and all the fowls were filled with their flesh.

CHAPTER 20

1. And I saw an angel come down from heaven, having the key of the bottomless pit and a great chain in his hand.

2. And he laid hold on the dragon, that old serpent, which is the Devil, and Satan, and bound him a thousand years,

3. And cast him into the bottomless pit, and shut him up, and set a seal upon him, that he should deceive the nations no more, till the thousand years should be fulfilled: and after that he must be loosed a little season.

4. And I saw thrones, and they sat upon them, and judgment was given unto them: and I saw the souls of them that were beheaded for the witness of Jesus, and for the word of God, and which had not worshipped the beast, neither his image, neither had received his mark upon their foreheads, or in their hands; and they lived and reigned with Christ a thousand years.

5. But the rest of the dead lived not again until the thousand years were finished. This is the first resurrection.

6. Blessed and holy is he that hath part in the first resurrection: on such the second death hath no power, but they shall be priests of God and of Christ, and shall reign with him a thousand years.

7. And when the thousand years are expired, Satan shall be loosed out of his prison,

8. And shall go out to deceive the nations which are in the four quarters of the earth, Gog and Magog, to gather them together to battle: the number of whom is as the sand of the sea.

9. And they went up on the breadth of the earth, and compassed the camp of the saints about, and the beloved city: and fire came down from God out of heaven, and devoured them.

10. And the devil that deceived them was cast into the lake of fire and brimstone, where the beast and the false prophet are, and shall be tormented day and night for ever and ever.

11. And I saw a great white throne, and him that sat on it, from whose face the earth and the heaven fled

Rev. 20—At the final and last judgment, we will be judged out of the books (see Rev. 20:12). If we prove ourselves worthy, becoming just men and women and obtaining a state of righteousness, we will dwell with God forever.

John's vision of the last days is consummated in the account of the final judgment: "And I saw the dead, small and great, stand before God; and the books were opened: and another book was opened, which is the book of life: and the dead were judged out of those things which were written in the books, according to their works" (Rev. 20:12). Those who were not written in the book of life were "cast into the lake of fire" (v. 15). The glorious blessings enjoyed by those found to be righteous surpass all understanding (see Rev. 21:3–7).

Rev. 20–22—The Lord's work is to "bring to pass the immortality and eternal life of man" (Moses 1:39). The vast design of God's plan of salvation is revealed in grandeur in the Revelation of John, serving as it does as a kind of epilogue and summation of all the declarations of God's holy prophets down through time. Our role within this heavenly design is clear: "Behold, this is your work, to keep my commandments, yea, with all your might, mind and strength" (D&C 11:20). How well we perform our labors in faith and obedience will determine the outcomes of our mortal experience. Our task is to overcome Satan, the enemy of all righteousness, and prepare for the coming of the millennial reign where the Lord will rule in glory and power and Satan will be bound. By virtue of the last and final judgment, each individual will come to know his or her ultimate resting place, either among those of a lesser glory or of outer darkness, or among those who will dwell in celestial precincts with the Father and the Son forever and ever. Through the strength of the Lord we can prevail and rise in majesty as the "children of the prophets" and the "children of the covenant" (3 Ne. 20:25–26), redeemed through the grace and mercy of the Lord to live with Him in everlasting peace and rest—"which rest is the fulness of his glory" (D&C 84:24).

away; and there was found no place for them.

12. And I saw the dead, small and great, stand before God; and the books were opened: and another book was opened, which is the book of life: and the dead were judged out of those things which were written in the books, according to their works.

13. And the sea gave up the dead which were in it; and death and hell delivered up the dead which were in them: and they were judged every man according to their works.

14. And death and hell were cast into the lake of fire. This is the second death.

15. And whosoever was not found written in the book of life was cast into the lake of fire.

CHAPTER 21

1. And I saw a new heaven and a new earth: for the first heaven and the first earth were passed away; and there was no more sea.

2. And I John saw the holy city, new Jerusalem, coming down from God out of heaven, prepared as a bride adorned for her husband.

3. And I heard a great voice out of heaven saying, Behold, the tabernacle of God is with men, and he will dwell with them, and they shall be his people, and God himself shall be with them, and be their God.

4. And God shall wipe away all tears from their eyes; and there shall be no more death, neither sorrow, nor crying, neither shall there be any more pain: for the former things are passed away.

5. And he that sat upon the throne said, Behold, I make all things new. And he said unto me, Write: for these words are true and faithful.

6. And he said unto me, It is done. I am Alpha and Omega, the beginning and the end. I will give unto him that is athirst of the fountain of the water of life freely.

7. He that overcometh shall inherit all things; and I will be his God, and he shall be my son.

8. But the fearful, and unbelieving, and the abominable, and murderers, and whoremongers, and sorcerers, and idolaters, and all liars, shall have their part in the lake which burneth with fire and brimstone: which is the second death.

9. And there came unto me one of the seven angels which had the seven vials full of the seven last plagues, and talked with me, saying, Come hither, I will shew thee the bride, the Lamb's wife.

10. And he carried me away in the spirit to a great and high mountain, and shewed me that great city, the

Rev. 21:7—"Man can inherit all God possesses. 'He that overcometh shall inherit all things' [Rev. 21:7]. What an expression is that? Who believes it? If a father were to say to his son, 'My son, be faithful, and follow my counsels, and when you become of age you shall inherit all that I possess,' it would mean something, would it not? If the father told the truth, that son would have something to encourage him to be faithful. Did Jesus want to deceive us when He made use of this expression? I will assure you that there is no deception in the language. He meant precisely what He said" (Lorenzo Snow, *The Teachings of Lorenzo Snow*, 6–7).

holy Jerusalem, descending out of heaven from God,

11. Having the glory of God: and her light was like unto a stone most precious, even like a jasper stone, clear as crystal;

12. And had a wall great and high, and had twelve gates, and at the gates twelve angels, and names written thereon, which are the names of the twelve tribes of the children of Israel:

13. On the east three gates; on the north three gates; on the south three gates; and on the west three gates.

14. And the wall of the city had twelve foundations, and in them the names of the twelve apostles of the Lamb.

15. And he that talked with me had a golden reed to measure the city, and the gates thereof, and the wall thereof.

16. And the city lieth foursquare, and the length is as large as the breadth: and he measured the city with the reed, twelve thousand furlongs. The length and the breadth and the height of it are equal.

17. And he measured the wall thereof, an hundred and forty and four cubits, according to the measure of a man, that is, of the angel.

18. And the building of the wall of it was of jasper: and the city was pure gold, like unto clear glass.

19. And the foundations of the wall of the city were garnished with all manner of precious stones. The first foundation was jasper; the second, sapphire; the third, a chalcedony; the fourth, an emerald;

20. The fifth, sardonyx; the sixth, sardius; the seventh, chrysolite; the eighth, beryl; the ninth, a topaz; the tenth, a chrysoprasus; the eleventh, a jacinth; the twelfth, an amethyst.

21. And the twelve gates were twelve pearls; every several gate was of one pearl: and the street of the city was pure gold, as it were transparent glass.

22. And I saw no temple therein: for the Lord God Almighty and the Lamb are the temple of it.

23. And the city had no need of the sun, neither of the moon, to shine in it: for the glory of God did lighten it, and the Lamb is the light thereof.

24. And the nations of them which are saved shall walk in the light of it: and the kings of the earth do bring their glory and honour into it.

25. And the gates of it shall not be shut at all by day: for there shall be no night there.

26. And they shall bring the glory and honour of the nations into it.

27. And there shall in no wise enter into it any thing that defileth, neither whatsoever worketh abomination, or maketh a lie: but they which are written in the Lamb's book of life.

CHAPTER 22

1. And he shewed me a pure river of water of life, clear as crystal, proceeding out of the throne of God and of the Lamb.

2. In the midst of the street of it, and on either side of the river, was there the tree of life, which bare twelve manner of fruits, and yielded her fruit every month: and the leaves of the tree were for the healing of the nations.

Rev. 22— The book of Revelation, written by John the Beloved at the Lord's command, is a compelling mixture of opposites juxtaposed in stark contradistinction: evil and good, death and life, destruction and renewal, tyranny and liberation, condemnation and sanctification—all unfolding before our eyes in a panoramic vision with one central theme: God is in control of the destiny of mankind to bring to pass the ultimate triumph of His plan of redemption and salvation. We are not shocked by contrast of this narrative with its intertwining shades of abysmal dark and celestial light because our mortal life experience reflects a parallel blending of opposites. In the midst of the most edifying and transporting spiritual events that we are blessed to experience, we are all too often surprised by the sudden and unexpected incursions of worldly debasement. Around each corner, it seems, the forces of evil lie in wait to deceive and detract—all the more so, since the time is short and Satan and his followers know that they must act in all haste to further their sinister designs before it is too late. Our lives are thus punctuated with temptations galore, the enticements of worldly entanglements, the constant beckoning of that which is carnal and degrading. Only through a definitive commitment to that which is holy and sacred can we hope to invite into our lives the overwhelming illumination of the Holy Spirit, which alone can open the way through the valley of mortal shadows toward the light of celestial glory. The revelations of the Lord through His prophets—including John's extraordinary chronicle—are the sure milestones along the way to perfection.

Many years ago, I had an experience that brought home to me the fact that "it must needs be, that there is an opposition in all things" (2 Ne. 2:11). It was at a time when there were relatively few operating temples in the world. A small group of Latter-day Saints, of which I was a participant, had visited an institution on the outskirts of Basel, Switzerland, where an art exposition on biblical themes was being shown. We found the display characterized (to quote from my journal) by "bright greens and yellows and hideous satanic characters and forms." The effect of these bizarre configurations combined with the strange asymmetrical structures of the edifice in which they were housed produced a most constricting and unsettling feeling in us, and several members of our group became physically ill and had to leave the site.

What happened next has become an enduring memory in my archive of cherished insights. The journal continues: "We ourselves didn't realize what an impression [the art exposition and gallery] had

3. And there shall be no more curse: but the throne of God and of the Lamb shall be in it; and his servants shall serve him:

4. And they shall see his face; and his name shall be in their foreheads.

5. And there shall be no night there; and they need no candle, neither light of the sun; for the Lord God giveth them light: and they shall reign for ever and ever.

6. And he said unto me, These sayings are faithful and true: and the Lord God of the holy prophets sent his angel to shew unto his servants the things which must shortly be done.

7. Behold, I come quickly: blessed is he that keepeth the sayings of the prophecy of this book.

8. And I John saw these things, and heard them. And when I had heard and seen, I fell down to worship before the feet of the angel which shewed me these things.

9. Then saith he unto me, See thou do it not: for I am thy fellowservant, and of thy brethren the prophets, and of them which keep the sayings of this book: worship God.

10. And he saith unto me, Seal not the sayings of the prophecy of this book: for the time is at hand.

11. He that is unjust, let him be unjust still: and he which is filthy, let him be filthy still: and he that is righteous, let him be righteous still: and he that is holy, let him be holy still.

12. And, behold, I come quickly; and my reward is with me, to give every man according as his work shall be.

13. I am Alpha and Omega, the beginning and the end, the first and the last.

14. Blessed are they that do his commandments, that they may have right to the tree of life, and may enter in through the gates into the city.

15. For without are dogs, and sorcerers, and whoremongers, and murderers, and idolaters, and whosoever loveth and maketh a lie.

16. I Jesus have sent mine angel to testify unto you these things in the churches. I am the root and the offspring of David, and the bright and morning star.

17. And the Spirit and the bride say, Come. And let him that heareth say, Come. And let him that is athirst come. And whosoever will, let him take the water of life freely.

18. For I testify unto every man that heareth the words of the prophecy of this book, If any man shall add unto these things, God shall add unto him the plagues that are written in this book:

19. And if any man shall take away from the words of the book of this prophecy, God shall take away his

made on us until we approached several hours later a small town just outside of Bern and saw through the trees the spire of an unusual edifice. The contrast between what we had experienced before and now the Swiss Temple was so great that it really opened our eyes. Truly this magnificent building nestled among the trees overlooking the white Alps on the horizon is a testimony of the order of heaven. What perfect symmetry and grace! We felt immediately a spirit of peace and serenity as we viewed the temple and read the inscription 'Holiness to the Lord.' How grateful we were to be members of His Church and possess the knowledge of His gospel!"

The peace and quiet within the walls of the temple is truly spiritually refreshing. The endowment of truth there dispensed quenches the thirst to learn the principles of the eternities: "But unto him that keepeth my commandments I will give the mysteries of my kingdom, and the same shall be in him a well of living water, springing up unto everlasting life" (D&C 63:23). At the end of the book of Revelation, John uses similar language in quoting the Savior: "I Jesus have sent mine angel to testify unto you these things in the churches. I am the root and the offspring of David, and the bright and morning star. And the Spirit and the bride say, Come. And let him that heareth say, Come. And let him that is athirst come. And whosoever will, let him take the water of life freely" (Rev. 22:16–17).

In light of this comforting doctrine, we can savor the precious experiences of life—such as the contrast we felt in Switzerland that day between the dark and the light—for they generate tranquility and joy: "And all thy children shall be taught of the Lord; and great shall be the peace of thy children" (3 Ne. 22:13).

part out of the book of life, and out of the holy city, and from the things which are written in this book.

20. He which testifieth these things saith, Surely I come quickly. Amen. Even so, come, Lord Jesus.

21. The grace of our Lord Jesus Christ be with you all. Amen.

Rev. 22—John ends his account of the revelation granted to him by outlining the promises that await the faithful and valiant of the Lord's children, promises that are beyond comprehension for their glory and the supernal joy they bring:

"And they shall see his face; and his name shall be in their foreheads.

"And there shall be no night there; and they need no candle, neither light of the sun; for the Lord God giveth them light: and they shall reign for ever and ever.

"And he said unto me, These sayings are faithful and true: and the Lord God of the holy prophets sent his angel to shew unto his servants the things which must shortly be done.

"Behold, I come quickly: blessed is he that keepeth the sayings of the prophecy of this book. . . . And, behold, I come quickly; and my reward is with me, to give every man according as his work shall be.

"I am Alpha and Omega, the beginning and the end, the first and the last.

"Blessed are they that do his commandments, that they may have right to the tree of life, and may enter in through the gates into the city. . . .

"And the Spirit and the bride say, Come. And let him that heareth say, Come. And let him that is athirst come. And whosoever will, let him take the water of life freely" (Rev. 22:4–7, 12–14, 17).

ART CREDITS

❦

Page 14: Christ in the Storm on the Sea of Galilee by Pieter Brueghel the Younger; for more information, visit www.commons.wikimedia.org.

Page 16: Christ Healing the Blind Man by Eustache Le Sueur; for more information, visit www.commons.wikimedia.org.

Page 26: Salome by Alonso González de Berruguete; for more information, visit www.commons.wikimedia.org.

Page 28: Das Wunder der Brotvermehrung, Wandgemälde in der Liebfrauenkirche Ravensburg; for more information, visit www.commons.wikimedia.org.

Page 55: Christ Leaving the Tomb, at the Oberammergau Passion Play, 1900; for more information, visit www.commons.wikimedia.org.

Page 56: Genter Altar, Altar des Mystischen Lammes, obere rechte Haupttafel, Szene: Thronender Johannes der Täufer by Jan van Eyck; for more information, visit www.commons.wikimedia.org.

Page 58: Relieftafel mit Szenen aus dem Leben Christi; for more information, visit www.commons.wikimedia.org.

Page 59: The Synaxis of the holy and the most praiseworthy Twelve Apostles; for more information, visit www.commons.wikimedia.org.

Page 61: Image of the Sower Parable; for more information, visit www.commons.wikimedia.org.

Page 63: Raising of Jairus' Daughter by Ilya Yefimovich Repin, for more information, visit www.commons.wikimedia.org.

Page 68: Jesus Feeds the Multitude by Julius Schnorr von Carolsfeld.

Page 70: Woodcut for "Die Bibel in Bildern" by Julius Schnorr von Carolsfeld; for more information, visit www.commons.wikimedia.org.

Page 81: Woodcut for "Die Bibel in Bildern" by Julius Schnorr von Carolsfeld; for more information, visit www.commons.wikimedia.org.

Page 88: Geburt Johannes des Täufers, Tondo by Jacopo Pontormo; for more information, visit www.commons.wikimedia.org.

Page 93: Temptation of Christ (mosaic in basilica di San Marco) Anonymous; for more information, visit www.commons.wikimedia.org.

Page 96: Woodcut for "Die Bibel in Bildern" by Julius Schnorr von Carolsfeld; for more information, visit www.commons.wikimedia.org.

Page 99: The Sermon of the Beatitudes, by James Tissot; for more information, visit www.commons.wikimedia.org.

Page 100: Woodcut for "Die Bibel in Bildern" by Julius Schnorr von Carolsfeld; for more information, visit www.commons.wikimedia.org.

Page 106: Great Feasts icon painted in the Greek Catholic Cathedral of Hajdúdorog, Hungary © Jojojoe; . Courtesy of wikimedia commons; for more information, visit www.commons.wikimedia.org.

Page 114: Sermon on the Mount by Alexander Bida; for more information, visit www.commons.wikimedia.org.

Page 128: Opfer der armen Witwe by Johannes Bockh photo Thomas Mirtsch © Mrilabs. Courtesy of wikimedia commons; for more information, visit www.commons.wikimedia.org.

Page 134: Christ in front of Pilate by Mihále Munkácsy; for more information, visit www.commons.wikimedia.org.

Page 135: Golgotha by Mihále Munkácsy; for more information, visit www.commons.wikimedia.org.

Page 137: Stained glass windows in the Mausoleum of the Roman Catholic Cathedral of Our Lady of the Angels, Los Angeles, California; originally created in the 1920s for Saint Vibiana Cathedral, Los Angeles

Resurrection of Christ; for more information, visit www.commons.wikimedia.org.

Page 149: Die wundersame Brotvermehrung, Kupferstich nach Tintoretto by Lucas Kilian after Tintoretto; for more information, visit www.commons.wikimedia.org.

Page 157: Sant' Apollinare Nuovo (Ravenna), Mosaic, Heilung der Blinden von Jericho; for more information, visit www.commons.wikimedia.org.

Page 161: The Raising of Lazarus by Sebastiano del Piombo; for more information, visit www.commons.wikimedia.org.

Page 163: Great Feasts icon painted in the Greek Catholic Cathedral of Hajdúdorog, Hungary © Jojojoe; . Courtesy of wikimedia commons; for more information, visit www.commons.wikimedia.org.